T0139957

Lecture Notes in Computer Science 13843

The series Lecture Notes in Computer Science (LNCS), including its subseries Lecture Notes in Artificial Intelligence (LNAI) and Lecture Notes in Bioinformatics (LNBI), has established itself as a medium for the publication of new developments in computer science and information technology research, teaching, and education.

LNCS enjoys close cooperation with the computer science R & D community, the series counts many renowned academics among its volume editors and paper authors, and collaborates with prestigious societies. Its mission is to serve this international community by providing an invaluable service, mainly focused on the publication of conference and workshop proceedings and postproceedings. LNCS commenced publication in 1973.

Lei Wang · Juergen Gall · Tat-Jun Chin ·
Imari Sato · Rama Chellappa
Editors

Computer Vision – ACCV 2022

16th Asian Conference on Computer Vision
Macao, China, December 4–8, 2022
Proceedings, Part III

 Springer

Editors
Lei Wang 🆔
University of Wollongong
Wollongong, NSW, Australia

Tat-Jun Chin 🆔
University of Adelaide
Adelaide, SA, Australia

Rama Chellappa 🆔
Johns Hopkins University
Baltimore, MD, USA

Juergen Gall 🆔
University of Bonn
Bonn, Germany

Imari Sato
National Institute of Informatics
Tokyo, Japan

ISSN 0302-9743   ISSN 1611-3349 (electronic)
Lecture Notes in Computer Science
ISBN 978-3-031-26312-5   ISBN 978-3-031-26313-2 (eBook)
https://doi.org/10.1007/978-3-031-26313-2

This Springer imprint is published by the registered company Springer Nature Switzerland AG
The registered company address is: Gewerbestrasse 11, 6330 Cham, Switzerland

Preface

The 16th Asian Conference on Computer Vision (ACCV) 2022 was held in a hybrid mode in Macau SAR, China during December 4–8, 2022. The conference featured novel research contributions from almost all sub-areas of computer vision.

For the main conference, 836 valid submissions entered the review stage after desk rejection. Sixty-three area chairs and 959 reviewers made great efforts to ensure that every submission received thorough and high-quality reviews. As in previous editions of ACCV, this conference adopted a double-blind review process. The identities of authors were not visible to the reviewers or area chairs; nor were the identities of the assigned reviewers and area chairs known to the authors. The program chairs did not submit papers to the conference.

After receiving the reviews, the authors had the option of submitting a rebuttal. Following that, the area chairs led the discussions and final recommendations were then made by the reviewers. Taking conflicts of interest into account, the area chairs formed 21 AC triplets to finalize the paper recommendations. With the confirmation of three area chairs for each paper, 277 papers were accepted. ACCV 2022 also included eight workshops, eight tutorials, and one grand challenge, covering various cutting-edge research topics related to computer vision. The proceedings of ACCV 2022 are open access at the Computer Vision Foundation website, by courtesy of Springer. The quality of the papers presented at ACCV 2022 demonstrates the research excellence of the international computer vision communities.

This conference is fortunate to receive support from many organizations and individuals. We would like to express our gratitude for the continued support of the Asian Federation of Computer Vision and our sponsors, the University of Macau, Springer, the Artificial Intelligence Journal, and OPPO. ACCV 2022 used the Conference Management Toolkit sponsored by Microsoft Research and received much help from its support team.

All the organizers, area chairs, reviewers, and authors made great contributions to ensure a successful ACCV 2022. For this, we owe them deep gratitude. Last but not least, we would like to thank the online and in-person attendees of ACCV 2022. Their presence showed strong commitment and appreciation towards this conference.

December 2022

Lei Wang
Juergen Gall
Tat-Jun Chin
Imari Sato
Rama Chellappa

Organization

General Chairs

Gérard Medioni   University of Southern California, USA
Shiguang Shan   Chinese Academy of Sciences, China
Bohyung Han   Seoul National University, South Korea
Hongdong Li   Australian National University, Australia

Program Chairs

Rama Chellappa   Johns Hopkins University, USA
Juergen Gall   University of Bonn, Germany
Imari Sato   National Institute of Informatics, Japan
Tat-Jun Chin   University of Adelaide, Australia
Lei Wang   University of Wollongong, Australia

Publication Chairs

Wenbin Li   Nanjing University, China
Wanqi Yang   Nanjing Normal University, China

Local Arrangements Chairs

Liming Zhang   University of Macau, China
Jianjia Zhang   Sun Yat-sen University, China

Web Chairs

Zongyuan Ge   Monash University, Australia
Deval Mehta   Monash University, Australia
Zhongyan Zhang   University of Wollongong, Australia

AC Meeting Chair

Chee Seng Chan   University of Malaya, Malaysia

Area Chairs

Aljosa Osep	Technical University of Munich, Germany
Angela Yao	National University of Singapore, Singapore
Anh T. Tran	VinAI Research, Vietnam
Anurag Mittal	Indian Institute of Technology Madras, India
Binh-Son Hua	VinAI Research, Vietnam
C. V. Jawahar	International Institute of Information Technology, Hyderabad, India
Dan Xu	The Hong Kong University of Science and Technology, China
Du Tran	Meta AI, USA
Frederic Jurie	University of Caen and Safran, France
Guangcan Liu	Southeast University, China
Guorong Li	University of Chinese Academy of Sciences, China
Guosheng Lin	Nanyang Technological University, Singapore
Gustavo Carneiro	University of Surrey, UK
Hyun Soo Park	University of Minnesota, USA
Hyunjung Shim	Korea Advanced Institute of Science and Technology, South Korea
Jiaying Liu	Peking University, China
Jun Zhou	Griffith University, Australia
Junseok Kwon	Chung-Ang University, South Korea
Kota Yamaguchi	CyberAgent, Japan
Li Liu	National University of Defense Technology, China
Liang Zheng	Australian National University, Australia
Mathieu Aubry	Ecole des Ponts ParisTech, France
Mehrtash Harandi	Monash University, Australia
Miaomiao Liu	Australian National University, Australia
Ming-Hsuan Yang	University of California at Merced, USA
Palaiahnakote Shivakumara	University of Malaya, Malaysia
Pau-Choo Chung	National Cheng Kung University, Taiwan

Qianqian Xu	Key Laboratory of Intelligent Information Processing, Institute of Computing Technology, Chinese Academy of Sciences, China
Qiuhong Ke	Monash University, Australia
Radu Timofte	University of Würzburg, Germany and ETH Zurich, Switzerland
Rajagopalan N. Ambasamudram	Indian Institute of Technology Madras, India
Risheng Liu	Dalian University of Technology, China
Ruiping Wang	Institute of Computing Technology, Chinese Academy of Sciences, China
Sajid Javed	Khalifa University of Science and Technology, Abu Dhabi, UAE
Seunghoon Hong	Korea Advanced Institute of Science and Technology, South Korea
Shang-Hong Lai	National Tsing Hua University, Taiwan
Shanshan Zhang	Nanjing University of Science and Technology, China
Sharon Xiaolei Huang	Pennsylvania State University, USA
Shin'ichi Satoh	National Institute of Informatics, Japan
Si Liu	Beihang University, China
Suha Kwak	Pohang University of Science and Technology, South Korea
Tae Hyun Kim	Hanyang Univeristy, South Korea
Takayuki Okatani	Tohoku University, Japan/RIKEN Center for Advanced Intelligence Project, Japan
Tatsuya Harada	University of Tokyo/RIKEN, Japan
Vicky Kalogeiton	Ecole Polytechnique, France
Vincent Lepetit	Ecole des Ponts ParisTech, France
Vineeth N. Balasubramanian	Indian Institute of Technology, Hyderabad, India
Wei Shen	Shanghai Jiao Tong University, China
Wei-Shi Zheng	Sun Yat-sen University, China
Xiang Bai	Huazhong University of Science and Technology, China
Xiaowei Zhou	Zhejiang University, China
Xin Yu	University of Technology Sydney, Australia
Yasutaka Furukawa	Simon Fraser University, Canada
Yasuyuki Matsushita	Osaka University, Japan
Yedid Hoshen	Hebrew University of Jerusalem, Israel
Ying Fu	Beijing Institute of Technology, China
Yong Jae Lee	University of Wisconsin-Madison, USA
Yu-Chiang Frank Wang	National Taiwan University, Taiwan
Yumin Suh	NEC Laboratories America, USA

Yung-Yu Chuang   National Taiwan University, Taiwan
Zhaoxiang Zhang   Chinese Academy of Sciences, China
Ziad Al-Halah   University of Texas at Austin, USA
Zuzana Kukelova   Czech Technical University, Czech Republic

Additional Reviewers

Abanob E. N. Soliman
Abdelbadie Belmouhcine
Adrian Barbu
Agnibh Dasgupta
Akihiro Sugimoto
Akkarit Sangpetch
Akrem Sellami
Aleksandr Kim
Alexander Andreopoulos
Alexander Fix
Alexander Kugele
Alexandre Morgand
Alexis Lechervy
Alina E. Marcu
Alper Yilmaz
Alvaro Parra
Amogh Subbakrishna
 Adishesha
Andrea Giachetti
Andrea Lagorio
Andreu Girbau Xalabarder
Andrey Kuehlkamp
Anh Nguyen
Anh T. Tran
Ankush Gupta
Anoop Cherian
Anton Mitrokhin
Antonio Agudo
Antonio Robles-Kelly
Ara Abigail Ambita
Ardhendu Behera
Arjan Kuijper
Arren Matthew C.
 Antioquia
Arjun Ashok
Atsushi Hashimoto

Atsushi Shimada
Attila Szabo
Aurelie Bugeau
Avatharam Ganivada
Ayan Kumar Bhunia
Azade Farshad
B. V. K. Vijaya Kumar
Bach Tran
Bailin Yang
Baojiang Zhong
Baoquan Zhang
Baoyao Yang
Basit O. Alawode
Beibei Lin
Benoit Guillard
Beomgu Kang
Bin He
Bin Li
Bin Liu
Bin Ren
Bin Yang
Bin-Cheng Yang
BingLiang Jiao
Bo Liu
Bohan Li
Boyao Zhou
Boyu Wang
Caoyun Fan
Carlo Tomasi
Carlos Torres
Carvalho Micael
Cees Snoek
Chang Kong
Changick Kim
Changkun Ye
Changsheng Lu

Chao Liu
Chao Shi
Chaowei Tan
Chaoyi Li
Chaoyu Dong
Chaoyu Zhao
Chen He
Chen Liu
Chen Yang
Chen Zhang
Cheng Deng
Cheng Guo
Cheng Yu
Cheng-Kun Yang
Chenglong Li
Chengmei Yang
Chengxin Liu
Chengyao Qian
Chen-Kuo Chiang
Chenxu Luo
Che-Rung Lee
Che-Tsung Lin
Chi Xu
Chi Nhan Duong
Chia-Ching Lin
Chien-Cheng Lee
Chien-Yi Wang
Chih-Chung Hsu
Chih-Wei Lin
Ching-Chun Huang
Chiou-Ting Hsu
Chippy M. Manu
Chong Wang
Chongyang Wang
Christian Siagian
Christine Allen-Blanchette

Christoph Schorn
Christos Matsoukas
Chuan Guo
Chuang Yang
Chuanyi Zhang
Chunfeng Song
Chunhui Zhang
Chun-Rong Huang
Ci Lin
Ci-Siang Lin
Cong Fang
Cui Wang
Cui Yuan
Cyrill Stachniss
Dahai Yu
Daiki Ikami
Daisuke Miyazaki
Dandan Zhu
Daniel Barath
Daniel Lichy
Daniel Reich
Danyang Tu
David Picard
Davide Silvestri
Defang Chen
Dehuan Zhang
Deunsol Jung
Difei Gao
Dim P. Papadopoulos
Ding-Jie Chen
Dong Gong
Dong Hao
Dong Wook Shu
Dongdong Chen
Donghun Lee
Donghyeon Kwon
Donghyun Yoo
Dongkeun Kim
Dongliang Luo
Dongseob Kim
Dongsuk Kim
Dongwan Kim
Dongwon Kim
DongWook Yang
Dongze Lian

Dubing Chen
Edoardo Remelli
Emanuele Trucco
Erhan Gundogdu
Erh-Chung Chen
Rickson R. Nascimento
Erkang Chen
Eunbyung Park
Eunpil Park
Eun-Sol Kim
Fabio Cuzzolin
Fan Yang
Fan Zhang
Fangyu Zhou
Fani Deligianni
Fatemeh Karimi Nejadasl
Fei Liu
Feiyue Ni
Feng Su
Feng Xue
Fengchao Xiong
Fengji Ma
Fernando Díaz-del-Rio
Florian Bernard
Florian Kleber
Florin-Alexandru
  Vasluianu
Fok Hing Chi Tivive
Frank Neumann
Fu-En Yang
Fumio Okura
Gang Chen
Gang Liu
Gao Haoyuan
Gaoshuai Wang
Gaoyun An
Gen Li
Georgy Ponimatkin
Gianfranco Doretto
Gil Levi
Guang Yang
Guangfa Wang
Guangfeng Lin
Guillaume Jeanneret
Guisik Kim

Gunhee Kim
Guodong Wang
Ha Young Kim
Hadi Mohaghegh
  Dolatabadi
Haibo Ye
Haili Ye
Haithem Boussaid
Haixia Wang
Han Chen
Han Zou
Hang Cheng
Hang Du
Hang Guo
Hanlin Gu
Hannah H. Kim
Hao He
Hao Huang
Hao Quan
Hao Ren
Hao Tang
Hao Zeng
Hao Zhao
Haoji Hu
Haopeng Li
Haoqing Wang
Haoran Wen
Haoshuo Huang
Haotian Liu
Haozhao Ma
Hari Chandana K.
Haripriya Harikumar
Hehe Fan
Helder Araujo
Henok Ghebrechristos
Heunseung Lim
Hezhi Cao
Hideo Saito
Hieu Le
Hiroaki Santo
Hirokatsu Kataoka
Hiroshi Omori
Hitika Tiwari
Hojung Lee
Hong Cheng

Hong Liu
Hu Zhang
Huadong Tang
Huajie Jiang
Huang Ziqi
Huangying Zhan
Hui Kong
Hui Nie
Huiyu Duan
Huyen Thi Thanh Tran
Hyung-Jeong Yang
Hyunjin Park
Hyunsoo Kim
HyunWook Park
I-Chao Shen
Idil Esen Zulfikar
Ikuhisa Mitsugami
Inseop Chung
Ioannis Pavlidis
Isinsu Katircioglu
Jaeil Kim
Jaeyoon Park
Jae-Young Sim
James Clark
James Elder
James Pritts
Jan Zdenek
Janghoon Choi
Jeany Son
Jenny Seidenschwarz
Jesse Scott
Jia Wan
Jiadai Sun
JiaHuan Ji
Jiajiong Cao
Jian Zhang
Jianbo Jiao
Jianhui Wu
Jianjia Wang
Jianjia Zhang
Jianqiao Wangni
JiaQi Wang
Jiaqin Lin
Jiarui Liu
Jiawei Wang

Jiaxin Gu
Jiaxin Wei
Jiaxin Zhang
Jiaying Zhang
Jiayu Yang
Jidong Tian
Jie Hong
Jie Lin
Jie Liu
Jie Song
Jie Yang
Jiebo Luo
Jiejie Xu
Jin Fang
Jin Gao
Jin Tian
Jinbin Bai
Jing Bai
Jing Huo
Jing Tian
Jing Wu
Jing Zhang
Jingchen Xu
Jingchun Cheng
Jingjing Fu
Jingshuai Liu
JingWei Huang
Jingzhou Chen
JinHan Cui
Jinjie Song
Jinqiao Wang
Jinsun Park
Jinwoo Kim
Jinyu Chen
Jipeng Qiang
Jiri Sedlar
Jiseob Kim
Jiuxiang Gu
Jiwei Xiao
Jiyang Zheng
Jiyoung Lee
John Paisley
Joonki Paik
Joonseok Lee
Julien Mille

Julio C. Zamora
Jun Sato
Jun Tan
Jun Tang
Jun Xiao
Jun Xu
Junbao Zhuo
Jun-Cheng Chen
Junfen Chen
Jungeun Kim
Junhwa Hur
Junli Tao
Junlin Han
Junsik Kim
Junting Dong
Junwei Zhou
Junyu Gao
Kai Han
Kai Huang
Kai Katsumata
Kai Zhao
Kailun Yang
Kai-Po Chang
Kaixiang Wang
Kamal Nasrollahi
Kamil Kowol
Kan Chang
Kang-Jun Liu
Kanchana Vaishnavi
  Gandikota
Kanoksak Wattanachote
Karan Sikka
Kaushik Roy
Ke Xian
Keiji Yanai
Kha Gia Quach
Kibok Lee
Kira Maag
Kirill Gavrilyuk
Kohei Suenaga
Koichi Ito
Komei Sugiura
Kong Dehui
Konstantinos Batsos
Kotaro Kikuchi

Kouzou Ohara
Kuan-Wen Chen
Kun He
Kun Hu
Kun Zhan
Kunhee Kim
Kwan-Yee K. Wong
Kyong Hwan Jin
Kyuhong Shim
Kyung Ho Park
Kyungmin Kim
Kyungsu Lee
Lam Phan
Lanlan Liu
Le Hui
Lei Ke
Lei Qi
Lei Yang
Lei Yu
Lei Zhu
Leila Mahmoodi
Li Jiao
Li Su
Lianyu Hu
Licheng Jiao
Lichi Zhang
Lihong Zheng
Lijun Zhao
Like Xin
Lin Gu
Lin Xuhong
Lincheng Li
Linghua Tang
Lingzhi Kong
Linlin Yang
Linsen Li
Litao Yu
Liu Liu
Liujie Hua
Li-Yun Wang
Loren Schwiebert
Lujia Jin
Lujun Li
Luping Zhou
Luting Wang

Mansi Sharma
Mantini Pranav
Mahmoud Zidan
  Khairallah
Manuel Günther
Marcella Astrid
Marco Piccirilli
Martin Kampel
Marwan Torki
Masaaki Iiyama
Masanori Suganuma
Masayuki Tanaka
Matan Jacoby
Md Alimoor Reza
Md. Zasim Uddin
Meghshyam Prasad
Mei-Chen Yeh
Meng Tang
Mengde Xu
Mengyang Pu
Mevan B. Ekanayake
Michael Bi Mi
Michael Wray
Michaël Clément
Michel Antunes
Michele Sasdelli
Mikhail Sizintsev
Min Peng
Min Zhang
Minchul Shin
Minesh Mathew
Ming Li
Ming Meng
Ming Yin
Ming-Ching Chang
Mingfei Cheng
Minghui Wang
Mingjun Hu
MingKun Yang
Mingxing Tan
Mingzhi Yuan
Min-Hung Chen
Minhyun Lee
Minjung Kim
Min-Kook Suh

Minkyo Seo
Minyi Zhao
Mo Zhou
Mohammad Amin A.
  Shabani
Moein Sorkhei
Mohit Agarwal
Monish K. Keswani
Muhammad Sarmad
Muhammad Kashif Ali
Myung-Woo Woo
Naeemullah Khan
Naman Solanki
Namyup Kim
Nan Gao
Nan Xue
Naoki Chiba
Naoto Inoue
Naresh P. Cuntoor
Nati Daniel
Neelanjan Bhowmik
Niaz Ahmad
Nicholas I. Kuo
Nicholas E. Rosa
Nicola Fioraio
Nicolas Dufour
Nicolas Papadakis
Ning Liu
Nishan Khatri
Ole Johannsen
P. Real Jurado
Parikshit V. Sakurikar
Patrick Peursum
Pavan Turaga
Peijie Chen
Peizhi Yan
Peng Wang
Pengfei Fang
Penghui Du
Pengpeng Liu
Phi Le Nguyen
Philippe Chiberre
Pierre Gleize
Pinaki Nath Chowdhury
Ping Hu

Ping Li
Ping Zhao
Pingping Zhang
Pradyumna Narayana
Pritish Sahu
Qi Li
Qi Wang
Qi Zhang
Qian Li
Qian Wang
Qiang Fu
Qiang Wu
Qiangxi Zhu
Qianying Liu
Qiaosi Yi
Qier Meng
Qin Liu
Qing Liu
Qing Wang
Qingheng Zhang
Qingjie Liu
Qinglin Liu
Qingsen Yan
Qingwei Tang
Qingyao Wu
Qingzheng Wang
Qizao Wang
Quang Hieu Pham
Rabab Abdelfattah
Rabab Ward
Radu Tudor Ionescu
Rahul Mitra
Raül Pérez i Gonzalo
Raymond A. Yeh
Ren Li
Renán Rojas-Gómez
Renjie Wan
Renuka Sharma
Reyer Zwiggelaar
Robin Chan
Robin Courant
Rohit Saluja
Rongkai Ma
Ronny Hänsch
Rui Liu

Rui Wang
Rui Zhu
Ruibing Hou
Ruikui Wang
Ruiqi Zhao
Ruixing Wang
Ryo Furukawa
Ryusuke Sagawa
Saimunur Rahman
Samet Akcay
Samitha Herath
Sanath Narayan
Sandesh Kamath
Sanghoon Jeon
Sanghyun Son
Satoshi Suzuki
Saumik Bhattacharya
Sauradip Nag
Scott Wehrwein
Sebastien Lefevre
Sehyun Hwang
Seiya Ito
Selen Pehlivan
Sena Kiciroglu
Seok Bong Yoo
Seokjun Park
Seongwoong Cho
Seoungyoon Kang
Seth Nixon
Seunghwan Lee
Seung-Ik Lee
Seungyong Lee
Shaifali Parashar
Shan Cao
Shan Zhang
Shangfei Wang
Shaojian Qiu
Shaoru Wang
Shao-Yuan Lo
Shengjin Wang
Shengqi Huang
Shenjian Gong
Shi Qiu
Shiguang Liu
Shih-Yao Lin

Shin-Jye Lee
Shishi Qiao
Shivam Chandhok
Shohei Nobuhara
Shreya Ghosh
Shuai Yuan
Shuang Yang
Shuangping Huang
Shuigeng Zhou
Shuiwang Li
Shunli Zhang
Shuo Gu
Shuoxin Lin
Shuzhi Yu
Sida Peng
Siddhartha Chandra
Simon S. Woo
Siwei Wang
Sixiang Chen
Siyu Xia
Sohyun Lee
Song Guo
Soochahn Lee
Soumava Kumar Roy
Srinjay Soumitra Sarkar
Stanislav Pidhorskyi
Stefan Gumhold
Stefan Matcovici
Stefano Berretti
Stylianos Moschoglou
Sudhir Yarram
Sudong Cai
Suho Yang
Sumitra S. Malagi
Sungeun Hong
Sunggu Lee
Sunghyun Cho
Sunghyun Myung
Sungmin Cho
Sungyeon Kim
Suzhen Wang
Sven Sickert
Syed Zulqarnain Gilani
Tackgeun You
Taehun Kim

Takao Yamanaka
Takashi Shibata
Takayoshi Yamashita
Takeshi Endo
Takeshi Ikenaga
Tanvir Alam
Tao Hong
Tarun Kalluri
Tat-Jen Cham
Tatsuya Yatagawa
Teck Yian Lim
Tejas Indulal Dhamecha
Tengfei Shi
Thanh-Dat Truong
Thomas Probst
Thuan Hoang Nguyen
Tian Ye
Tianlei Jin
Tianwei Cao
Tianyi Shi
Tianyu Song
Tianyu Wang
Tien-Ju Yang
Tingting Fang
Tobias Baumgartner
Toby P. Breckon
Torsten Sattler
Trung Tuan Dao
Trung Le
Tsung-Hsuan Wu
Tuan-Anh Vu
Utkarsh Ojha
Utku Ozbulak
Vaasudev Narayanan
Venkata Siva Kumar
   Margapuri
Vandit J. Gajjar
Vi Thi Tuong Vo
Victor Fragoso
Vikas Desai
Vincent Lepetit
Vinh Tran
Viresh Ranjan
Wai-Kin Adams Kong
Wallace Michel Pinto Lira

Walter Liao
Wang Yan
Wang Yong
Wataru Shimoda
Wei Feng
Wei Mao
Wei Xu
Weibo Liu
Weichen Xu
Weide Liu
Weidong Chen
Weihong Deng
Wei-Jong Yang
Weikai Chen
Weishi Zhang
Weiwei Fang
Weixin Lu
Weixin Luo
Weiyao Wang
Wenbin Wang
Wenguan Wang
Wenhan Luo
Wenju Wang
Wenlei Liu
Wenqing Chen
Wenwen Yu
Wenxing Bao
Wenyu Liu
Wenzhao Zheng
Whie Jung
Williem Williem
Won Hwa Kim
Woohwan Jung
Wu Yirui
Wu Yufeng
Wu Yunjie
Wugen Zhou
Wujie Sun
Wuman Luo
Xi Wang
Xianfang Sun
Xiang Chen
Xiang Li
Xiangbo Shu
Xiangcheng Liu

Xiangyu Wang
Xiao Wang
Xiao Yan
Xiaobing Wang
Xiaodong Wang
Xiaofeng Wang
Xiaofeng Yang
Xiaogang Xu
Xiaogen Zhou
Xiaohan Yu
Xiaoheng Jiang
Xiaohua Huang
Xiaoke Shen
Xiaolong Liu
Xiaoqin Zhang
Xiaoqing Liu
Xiaosong Wang
Xiaowen Ma
Xiaoyi Zhang
Xiaoyu Wu
Xieyuanli Chen
Xin Chen
Xin Jin
Xin Wang
Xin Zhao
Xindong Zhang
Xingjian He
Xingqun Qi
Xinjie Li
Xinqi Fan
Xinwei He
Xinyan Liu
Xinyu He
Xinyue Zhang
Xiyuan Hu
Xu Cao
Xu Jia
Xu Yang
Xuan Luo
Xubo Yang
Xudong Lin
Xudong Xie
Xuefeng Liang
Xuehui Wang
Xuequan Lu

Xuesong Yang
Xueyan Zou
XuHu Lin
Xun Zhou
Xupeng Wang
Yali Zhang
Ya-Li Li
Yalin Zheng
Yan Di
Yan Luo
Yan Xu
Yang Cao
Yang Hu
Yang Song
Yang Zhang
Yang Zhao
Yangyang Shu
Yani A. Ioannou
Yaniv Nemcovsky
Yanjun Zhu
Yanling Hao
Yanling Tian
Yao Guo
Yao Lu
Yao Zhou
Yaping Zhao
Yasser Benigmim
Yasunori Ishii
Yasushi Yagi
Yawei Li
Ye Ding
Ye Zhu
Yeongnam Chae
Yeying Jin
Yi Cao
Yi Liu
Yi Rong
Yi Tang
Yi Wei
Yi Xu
Yichun Shi
Yifan Zhang
Yikai Wang
Yikang Ding
Yiming Liu

Yiming Qian
Yin Li
Yinghuan Shi
Yingjian Li
Yingkun Xu
Yingshu Chen
Yingwei Pan
Yiping Tang
Yiqing Shen
Yisheng Zhu
Yitian Li
Yizhou Yu
Yoichi Sato
Yong A.
Yongcai Wang
Yongheng Ren
Yonghuai Liu
Yongjun Zhang
Yongkang Luo
Yongkang Wong
Yongpei Zhu
Yongqiang Zhang
Yongrui Ma
Yoshimitsu Aoki
Yoshinori Konishi
Young Jun Heo
Young Min Shin
Youngmoon Lee
Youpeng Zhao
Yu Ding
Yu Feng
Yu Zhang
Yuanbin Wang
Yuang Wang
Yuanhong Chen
Yuanyuan Qiao
Yucong Shen
Yuda Song
Yue Huang
Yufan Liu
Yuguang Yan
Yuhan Xie
Yu-Hsuan Chen
Yu-Hui Wen
Yujiao Shi

Yujin Ren
Yuki Tatsunami
Yukuan Jia
Yukun Su
Yu-Lun Liu
Yun Liu
Yunan Liu
Yunce Zhao
Yun-Chun Chen
Yunhao Li
Yunlong Liu
Yunlong Meng
Yunlu Chen
Yunqian He
Yunzhong Hou
Yuqiu Kong
Yusuke Hosoya
Yusuke Matsui
Yusuke Morishita
Yusuke Sugano
Yuta Kudo
Yu-Ting Wu
Yutong Dai
Yuxi Hu
Yuxi Yang
Yuxuan Li
Yuxuan Zhang
Yuzhen Lin
Yuzhi Zhao
Yvain Queau
Zanwei Zhou
Zebin Guo
Ze-Feng Gao
Zejia Fan
Zekun Yang
Zelin Peng
Zelong Zeng
Zenglin Xu
Zewei Wu
Zhan Li
Zhan Shi
Zhe Li
Zhe Liu
Zhe Zhang
Zhedong Zheng

Zhenbo Xu
Zheng Gu
Zhenhua Tang
Zhenkun Wang
Zhenyu Weng
Zhi Zeng
Zhiguo Cao
Zhijie Rao
Zhijie Wang
Zhijun Zhang
Zhimin Gao
Zhipeng Yu
Zhiqiang Hu
Zhisong Liu
Zhiwei Hong
Zhiwei Xu

Zhiwu Lu
Zhixiang Wang
Zhixin Li
Zhiyong Dai
Zhiyong Huang
Zhiyuan Zhang
Zhonghua Wu
Zhongyan Zhang
Zhongzheng Yuan
Zhu Hu
Zhu Meng
Zhujun Li
Zhulun Yang
Zhuojun Zou
Ziang Cheng
Zichuan Liu

Zihan Ding
Zihao Zhang
Zijiang Song
Zijin Yin
Ziqiang Zheng
Zitian Wang
Ziwei Yao
Zixun Zhang
Ziyang Luo
Ziyi Bai
Ziyi Wang
Zongheng Tang
Zongsheng Cao
Zongwei Wu
Zoran Duric

Contents – Part III

RGBD and Depth Image Processing

Low-Level Vision, Image Processing

Modular Degradation Simulation and Restoration for Under-Display Camera

Yang Zhou, Yuda Song, and Xin Du$^{(\boxtimes)}$

Zhejiang University, Hangzhou, China
{yang_zhou,syd,duxin}@zju.edu.cn

Abstract. Under-display camera (UDC) provides an elegant solution for full-screen smartphones. However, UDC captured images suffer from severe degradation since sensors lie under the display. Although this issue can be tackled by image restoration networks, these networks require large-scale image pairs for training. To this end, we propose a modular network dubbed MPGNet trained using the generative adversarial network (GAN) framework for simulating UDC imaging. Specifically, we note that the UDC imaging degradation process contains brightness attenuation, blurring, and noise corruption. Thus we model each degradation with a characteristic-related modular network, and all modular networks are cascaded to form the generator. Together with a pixel-wise discriminator and supervised loss, we can train the generator to simulate the UDC imaging degradation process. Furthermore, we present a Transformer-style network named DWFormer for UDC image restoration. For practical purposes, we use depth-wise convolution instead of the multi-head self-attention to aggregate local spatial information. Moreover, we propose a novel channel attention module to aggregate global information, which is critical for brightness recovery. We conduct evaluations on the UDC benchmark, and our method surpasses the previous state-of-the-art models by 1.23 dB on the P-OLED track and 0.71 dB on the T-OLED track, respectively. Code is available at Github.

1 Introduction

Driven by the strong demand for full-screen mobile phones, the under-display camera (UDC) increasingly draws researchers' attention. UDC technology can deliver a higher screen-to-body ratio without disrupting the screen's integrity and introducing additional mechanics. However, UDC provides a better user experience at the expense of image quality. Since the sensor is mounted behind the display, the UDC images inevitably suffer severe degradation. Such image degradation is mainly caused by low light transmittance, undesirable light diffraction, and high-level noise, resulting in dark, blurred, and noisy images.

Y. Zhou and Y. Song—Equal contribution.

Supplementary Information The online version contains supplementary material available at https://doi.org/10.1007/978-3-031-26313-2_1.

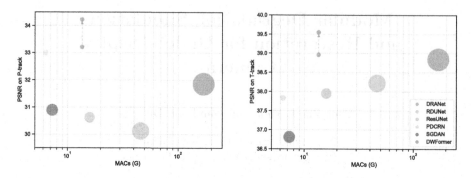

Fig. 1. Comparison of DWFormer with other UDC image restoration methods. The size of the dots indicates the Params of the method, and MACs are shown with the logarithmic axis. The arrows indicate that we use the generated data to improve the restoration model's performance further.

Following the prior work [1], the UDC imaging degradation process can be formulated as:

$$y = (\gamma \cdot x) \otimes k + n, \tag{1}$$

where $\cdot$ and $\otimes$ are multiplication and convolution operations, respectively, γ is the luminance scaling factor under the current gain setting and display type, k donates the point spread function (PSF) [2], and n is the zero-mean signal-dependent noise. Considering the attenuation of light transmission is wavelength-related [3], the luminance scaling factor γ should be different for each channel. Also, the PSF is spatially varying due to the different angles of the incident light [4]. And the signal-dependent noise n consists of shot and read noise [5] which can be modeled by heteroscedastic Gaussian distribution [6].

In recent years, many learning-based methods [7–10] have been introduced to improve the quality of UDC images and made significant advancements as they can learn strong priors from large-scale datasets. However, such methods require large amounts of data, and collecting aligned image pairs is labor-intensive. Facing insufficient data, generating realistic datasets can be a promising solution.

This paper proposes a modular pipeline generative network named MPGNet to simulate the UDC imaging degradation process and then use it to generate realistic image pairs. Unlike other end-to-end generation methods [11–13], we replace each degradation process with a subnetwork to preserve the physical properties of the imaging process. Specifically, we treat the image degradation process as three sequential steps, *i.e.*, brightness attenuation, non-uniform blurring, and noise corruption. And all modular subnetworks form the UDC imaging pipeline network. Besides the supervised learning, we employ GAN framework [14] to enhance the realism of generated images.

Based on the large amount of data generated by MPGNet, we can obtain a restoration model with well-generalized performance. However, designing a network suitable for the UDC image restoration task is not trivial. Recently, Transformers have attracted researchers' interest in the computer vision since

ViT's [15] success on the high-level vision tasks. Thus we hope to build an efficient and effective UDC image restoration network based on the vision Transformer. Considering that MetaFormer [16] reveals the general architecture of the
transformers is more critical than the multi-head self-attention, we use depth-
wise convolution and channel attention module to aggregate global information.
Finally, we build a U-Net-like restoration network dubbed DWFormer for UDC
image restoration.

We conduct evaluations on the UDC benchmark to verify the effectiveness of
our MPGNet and DWFormer. Figure 1 compares DWFormer with other UDC
image restoration methods. Without synthetic datasets generated by MPGNet,
DWFormer still achieves 33.21 dB on the P-OLED track and 38.96 dB on the
T-OLED track, which surpasses the previous state-of-the-art models by 0.22 dB
and 0.12 dB, respectively. Furthermore, if we use both generated and real data
to train our DWFormer, it achieves 34.22 dB on the P-OLED track and 39.55 dB
on the T-OLED track, 1.01 dB and 0.59 dB higher than the DWFormer trained
with only real data. These results indicate that MPGNet can precisely model
the UDC imaging process, and DWFormer can restore UDC images effectively.
We hope our work can promote the application of UDC on full-screen phones.

2   Related Works

2.1   UDC Imaging

Several previous works [1,4,17,18] have constructed the optical system of under-
display camera (UDC) imaging and analyzed its degradation components as well
as the causes. While these works provided good insights into the UDC imaging
system, their modeling approaches simplify the actual degradation process. Thus
the derived degradation images differ significantly from the real ones. Therefore,
how to generate realistic degradation images is still a problem to be solved, and
this is one of the focuses of our work. We found that some work has been done
to study the degradation module individually.

Blur Modeling. The blurring process can be modeled as a blurring kernel
performing a convolution operation on a sharp image [19,20]. Many methods [21–
23] estimate the blur kernel by assuming the characteristics of the blur kernel,
and other methods [1,4] models blur by a point spread function (PSF). However,
the blur in UDC imaging is blind and spatially varying, increasing the difficulty
of accurately estimating the blur kernel. Unlike previous works, we try to model
the blur directly using a convolutional neural network.

Noise Modeling. The noise is usually modeled as Poissonian-Gaussian noise [24]
or heteroscedastic Gaussian [25]. While the heteroscedastic Gaussian noise model
can provide a proper approximation of the realistic noise [26] to some extent, several studies [27,28] have demonstrated that the real-world cases appear to be much
more complicated. To this end, GCBD [11] proposed a generation-based method
to generate realistic blind noise. C2N [29] adopted a new generator architecture to represent the signal-dependent and spatially correlated noise distribution.

Compared to C2N, our proposed generator has a receptive field limited by the demosaicing method [30] and considers quantization noise.

2.2 Generative Adversarial Network (GAN)

GAN [14] was proposed to estimate the generative model via simultaneous optimization of the generator and discriminator. And many researchers have leveraged GANs for image-to-image translation [31–35], whose goal is to translate an input image from one domain to another domain. However, GAN may suffer from gradient vanishing or exploding during training, and several works [36–38] have proposed proper loss functions to stabilize training. We build our GAN framework using supervised loss and adversarial loss, thus stabilizing training and achieving promising results.

2.3 Image Restoration Architecture

A popular solution for recovering degraded images is to use CNN-based U-Net-like networks to capture hierarchical information for various image restoration tasks, including image denoising [26,39], deblurring [40,41] and low-light enhancement [42,43]. Recently, Transformer achieved great advancements in high-level vision problem [15,16,44] and has also been introduced for image restoration [45, 46]. IPT [45] uses standard Transformer to build a general backbone for various restoration problems. However, IPT is quite huge and requires large-scale datasets. And Uformer [46] proposed a U-Net-like architecture based on the Swin Transformer [44] for noise and blur removal. Motivated by MetaFormer [16], we use depth-wise convolution instead of multi-head self-attention to aggregate spatial information. The most similar work to ours is NAFNet [47], which also uses depth-wise convolution and channel attention module to build a MetaFormer-like network. However, we choose FrozenBN [48] instead of LN as the normalization layer. We also propose a novel channel attention module dubbed ACA, which increases the computational cost slightly compared to the SE modules [49] but can aggregate global information more effectively.

3   Method

3.1   Overall Network Architecture

Our method consists of a new generative network called MPGNet for modeling the UDC imaging degradation process and a U-Net-like network called DWFormer for UDC image restoration.

For MPGNet, we adopt GAN framework [14] to improve the realism of generated images. As shown in Fig. 2, our generate network architecture consists of a degradation generator and a pixel-wise discriminator. The degradation generator MPGNet comprises three parts, *i.e.*, brightness attenuation module, blurring module, and noise module. The three parts correspond to channel scaling, diffraction blurring, and Poisson-Gaussian noise corruption in the Statistical

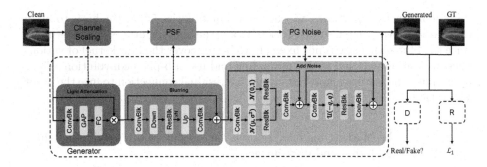

Fig. 2. Generator network architecture of our proposed MPGNet. We replace each degradation process with a characteristic-related subnetwork to simulate the UDC imaging pipeline and use a GAN-based training scheme for more realistic results.

Generation Method (SGM) [1]. Since the generation process can be considered an image-to-image translation task, we employ a pixel-wise U-Net-like discriminator [50] for better performance. DWFormer is a U-Net-like network, as shown in Fig. 3, built with our proposed DWFormer Block (DWB). The DWB evolves from the standard Transformer, and we replace the multi-head self-attention with a depth-wise convolution and channel attention module.

3.2   MPGNet

Brightness Attenuation. The brightness attenuation occurs due to organic light-emitting diode (OLED) displays [51] absorbing part of the light. Since the attenuation is wavelength-related [3], the attenuation coefficients to be estimated should be channel-dependent. Besides, brightness is a global statistic and therefore requires global information to be aggregated. To this end, we use several convolution blocks H_{FE} to extract features, a global average pooling H_{GAP} to aggregate information, and a multi-layer perceptron (MLP) to encode attenuation coefficients [52]. We multiply attenuation coefficients of size $1 \times 1 \times C$ with the clean image to obtain the dark image:

$$
\begin{aligned}
F_{BF} &= H_{FE}(x_{clean}), \\
F_G &= H_{GAP}(F_{BF}), \\
x_{dark} &= x_{clean} \cdot \sigma(H_D(\delta(H_U(F_G))))
\end{aligned}
\tag{2}
$$

where δ is ReLU and σ is Sigmoid function, H_D and H_U are the channel reduction and channel upsampling operators, respectively [49].

Blurring. The blurring in UDC imaging is caused by light diffraction as the size of the openings in the pixel layout is on the order of the wavelength of visible light. Although the blur kernel of diffraction could be accurately estimated by computing the Fourier transform of the wavefront function [53], it is too complicated, especially when light enters from all directions and forms spatially varying

PSFs. For practical purposes, we choose residual blocks [54] as the basis to build the characteristic-related subnetwork to model the blurring process. Furthermore, since the blur kernel size is not fixed [4], to better cover the blur kernel of various sizes, we use convolution to downsampling and use sub-pixel convolution [55] to upsampling the feature maps. Finally, we use residual connection to fuse the input and output:

$$x_{blur} = H_B(x_{dark}) + x_{dark}, \tag{3}$$

where H_B is the blurring module, x_{dark} is the output of the previous module, and x_{blur} is the blurred and dark image.

Noise. The noise consists of read and shot noise [5], which are usually formulated as heteroscedastic Gaussian distribution [6]. However, noise in the real world is more complicated and spatially correlated, making the heteroscedastic Gaussian distribution model inaccurate. Inspired by C2N [56], we generate realistic noise by combining signal-independent and signal-dependent noise. First, we use a residual block H_{R_1} to transform the noise $n_{s_1} \in \mathbb{R}^{h \times w \times d}$ (d=32 is the feature dimension) sampled from the standard normal distribution $\mathcal{N}(0,1)$ to noise n_i with a more complicated distribution:

$$n_i = H_{R_1}(n_{s_1}). \tag{4}$$

Second, the mean and variance of signal-dependent noise should be highly related to the image signal. We use a convolutional block to encode the pixel-wise mean $\mu \in \mathbb{R}^{h \times w \times d}$ and variance $\sigma \in \mathbb{R}^{h \times w \times d}$ from x_{blur}. Since the sampling is not differentiable, we use the reparameterization trick to transform the noise. Specifically, we sample the noise $n_{s_2} \in \mathbb{R}^{h \times w \times d}$ from $\mathcal{N}(0,1)$, and transform it to noise $n_d \sim \mathcal{N}(\mu, \sigma^2)$ via

$$n_d = H_{R_2}(n_{s_2} \cdot \sigma + \mu), \tag{5}$$

where H_{R_2} is also a residual block to transform the distribution of signal-dependent noise to a more complicated distribution. Considering that the noise is spatially correlated, we use residual blocks with two pixel-wise convolutions and one 3×3 convolution for both noises. After mapping these noises from the initial noise to noise with the target distribution, we take 1×1 convolution H_M to reduce the dimension to the color space and add them to output x_{blur} of the blurring module:

$$x_{noisy} = x_{blur} + H_M(n_i + n_d). \tag{6}$$

Moreover, recent work [57] shows that the quantification noise significantly impact on low-light imaging. And following the ISP pipeline, the quantization noise should be signal-dependent and added after other noise. Thus we use a convolutional block to encode the pixel-wise quantization noise interval $q \in \mathbb{R}^{h \times w \times d}$ from x_{noisy}. Also, we use a residual block H_{R_3} to transform the quantization noise $n_{s_3} \in \mathbb{R}^{h \times w \times d}$ sampled from the uniform distribution $\mathcal{U}(-q, q)$ to more realistic noise n_q:

$$n_q = H_{R_3}(n_{s_3}). \tag{7}$$

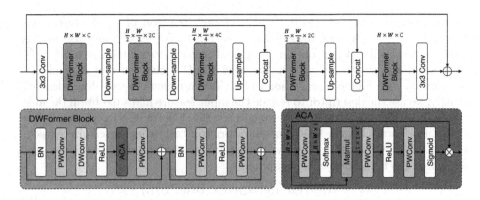

Fig. 3. Restoration network architecture of our proposed DWFormer.

After transforming n_q to the color space by a pixel-wise convolution, we add the quantization noise to the previous noisy image x_{noisy} by a residual connection:

$$x_{final} = H_{N_q} + x_{noisy}, \tag{8}$$

where H_{N_q} is the quantization noise module, and x_{final} is the final degraded image.

3.3 DWFormer

Overall Pipeline. The overall structure of the proposed DWFormer is a U-Net-like hierarchical network with skip connections. Specifically, given a degraded image $x \in \mathbb{R}^{h \times w \times 3}$, DWFormer firstly applied a 3×3 convolution to extract image features $F_0 \in \mathbb{R}^{h \times w \times c}$. Then, the feature map F_0 passes through all stages, and each stage contains a stack of proposed DWBs and a downsampling layer or upsampling layer. We use convolution operation to downsampling and sub-pixel convolution to upsampling, respectively. Finally, we also use a 3×3 convolution to get the residual image $r \in \mathbb{R}^{h \times w \times 3}$ and the restored image is obtained by $\hat{x} = y + r$.

DWFormer Block. Transformer [58] conducts global self-attention, which leads to quadratic complexity with respect to the number of tokens and has much less inductive bias than CNNs, which may be helpful for low-level tasks. Thus, we modify it to be more suitable for the UDC image restoration task. Specifically, considering local information is more favorable for noise and blur removal, we use a depth-wise convolution H_D to achieve spatial aggregation and thus significantly reduce the computational cost. Further, since brightness correction requires global information for each color channel, we propose an augmented channel attention (ACA) module H_{ACA} to capture global information and place it after the depth-wise convolution. Unlike SENet [49], which uses global average pooling to get the global feature descriptor, our proposed ACA starts with a pixel-wise convolution followed by reshape and softmax operations to obtain the weights $W_p \in \mathbb{R}^{1 \times 1 \times HW}$ of each position of the feature maps $F_{in} \in \mathbb{R}^{H \times W \times C}$. Then we also reshape the F_{in} to $\mathbb{R}^{1 \times HW \times C}$ and use matrix multiplication with W_p to obtain the global feature descriptor $F_C \in \mathbb{R}^{1 \times 1 \times C}$. Also, we use a pixel-wise convolution with ReLU activation and a pixel-wise convolution with Sigmoid activation to fully capture channel-wise dependencies. Finally, we use the descriptor to rescale the input feature maps to obtain the augmented feature maps. Besides, we found that BatchNorm (BN) performs better than LayerNorm (LN) in UDC image restoration task when batch size exceeds 16 on a single GPU. Therefore, we choose BN as the normalization layer, and the whole DWFormer block is computed as:

$$
\begin{aligned}
\hat{z}^l &= H_{P_2}(H_{ACA}(\delta(H_D(H_{P_1}(\mathrm{BN}(z^l)))))) + z^l, \\
z^{l+1} &= \mathrm{MLP}(\mathrm{BN}(\hat{z}^l)) + \hat{z}^l,
\end{aligned}
\tag{9}
$$

where δ is ReLU and z^l and z^{l+1} denote the input feature maps and output feature maps of DWB respectively. Note that we use the FrozenBN [48] to avoid the inconsistency in training and testing, *i.e.*, we first train with minibatch statistics in the early training period and use fixed population statistics in the later training period.

3.4   Training

Our degradation generator network G is designed to generate a realistic degraded image $\hat{y} \in \mathbb{R}^{h \times w \times 3}$ from its clean version $x \in \mathbb{R}^{h \times w \times 3}$ and our discriminator network D is designed to distinguish each pixel's real probability. Similar to other GAN applications [31,59], the two networks G and D can be simultaneously optimized in an adversarial way [14] with the least-squares loss function [38]:

$$
\begin{aligned}
\min_G \max_D \mathcal{L}_{adv}(G, D) &= \mathbb{E}_{y \sim p_{real}(y)}[log D(y)] \\
&+ \mathbb{E}_{x \sim p_{real}(x)}[1 - log D(G(x))],
\end{aligned}
\tag{10}
$$

where y is the real degraded image and x is the corresponding clean image. Here we concat the degraded images with clean images as inputs to D. And since there have been real paired data [31,60], we can also use supervised algorithms to optimize our model. However, the noise is a distribution-unknown random variable, and if we directly adopted $\mathcal{L}_1$ loss on generated and real degraded images, the noise will be eliminated while constructing the image alignment. To this end, we feed generated degraded images $G(x)$ and real degraded images y into a pre-trained restoration model R to obtain their restored versions and then perform $\mathcal{L}_1$ loss between them [61].

$$
\mathcal{L}_{sup} = ||R(G(x)) - R(y)||_1.
\tag{11}
$$

We use a hyperparameter λ to balance the supervised loss and adversarial loss, and the final loss is:

$$
\mathcal{L} = \mathcal{L}_{adv} + \lambda \mathcal{L}_{sup}.
\tag{12}
$$

For convenience, we set the λ to 10 for both the T-OLED and P-OLED tracks. For DWFormer, we just use $\mathcal{L}_1$ to train it.

3.5   Implementation Details

We train MPGNet for the UDC image generation task and DWFormer for the UDC image restoration task. Thus the training settings are different. MPGNet is trained with Adam [62] optimizer ($\beta_1 = 0.5$, and $\beta_2 = 0.999$) for 6×10^4 iterations. We update the generator once and the discriminator three times in each iteration. The initial learning rates are set to 1×10^{-4} and 1×10^{-3} for generator and discriminator, respectively. We employ the cosine annealing strategy [63] to steadily decrease the learning rate from an initial value to 1×10^{-6} and 1×10^{-5} during training. The batch size is set to 8, and we randomly perform horizontal and vertical flips for data augmentation. And DWFormer has five stages, and the number of DWB in each layer is $\{8, 8, 8, 6, 6\}$, respectively. The model is also trained with Adam optimize ($\beta_1 = 0.9$, and $\beta_2 = 0.999$) for 2×10^5 iterations. The initial learning rate is set to 1×10^{-4} and the cosine annealing strategy is adopted to steadily decrease the learning rate to 1×10^{-6}. The batch size is 64, and we achieve data augmentation by randomly performing flips and rotations.

4   Experiment

4.1   Dataset

The real image pairs used in the experiments are the P-OLED and T-OLED datasets [1] provided by UDC 2020 Image Restoration Challenge. Both datasets have 300 clean-degraded image pairs of size 1024×2048. Also, we leverage the high-resolution DIV2K dataset [64] captured under real environments to generate realistic degraded images. The DIV2K dataset provides 900 clean images. Similar to prior work [1], we optionally rotate and resize the clean images and generate clean-degraded image pairs with the resolution of 1024×2048. The real and generated image pairs are cropped into patches of size 256×256 and are randomly sampled to gather training mini-batches.

4.2   Comparison of Generators

To holistically evaluate the quality of MPGNet-generated images, we employ several tactics. First, we present several qualitative examples for perceptual studies in Fig. 4. The results demonstrate that the SGM-generated [1] degraded images cannot accurately estimate the blur and noise distribution. In contrast, the MPGNet-generated results are closer to the ground truths and preserve the degradation's diversity.

Second, we use different generated datasets to train the restoration models and evaluate them on the UDC benchmark. Figure 5 shows that the model trained with the SGM-generated dataset yields still blurry and brightness-unaligned results, while the model trained with the MPGNet-generated dataset produces results closer to the ground truth. Also, Table 1 illustrates that our method outperforms SGM by 3.31 dB on the P-OLED track and 2.49 dB on the T-OLED track by only using the synthetic dataset. We can further improve the

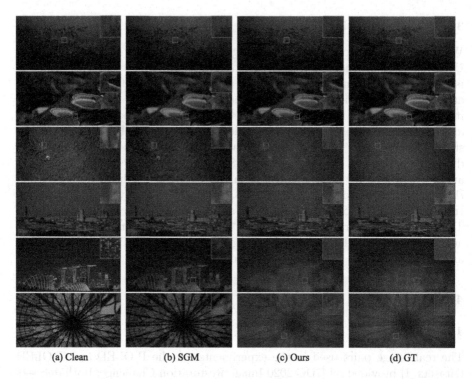

(a) Clean   (b) SGM   (c) Ours   (d) GT

Fig. 4. Visual comparison of the generated degraded image samples on the UDC dataset. (a) A clean image. (b–e) Generated degraded image of SGM and Ours, respectively. (f) The ground truth degraded image. The top half of the figure is on the T-OLED track, and the bottom half of the figure is on the P-OLED track. We amplify the images on the P-OLED track for comparison.

restoration model's performance by using both generated and real datasets for training, implying that our generated data can complement the real data and thus enhance the model's generalization.

Intuitively, using a single model as a generator is more common. Thus we replace the entire generation model with an end-to-end U-Net [64], which has a competitive number of parameters and computation cost to MPGNet. However, the U-Net performs poorly. We believe this is mainly because a single network tends to confuse multiple degradation processes, leading to model convergence to a poor local optimum. We assign the degradation process to multiple characteristic-related sub-networks, which dramatically avoids this local optimum, showing that physical constraints work. Also, from the results, we find that SGM performs worse than U-Net, which may be due to the inaccurate parameters from the manual statistics. We argue that our MPGNet provides a solution to avoid it.

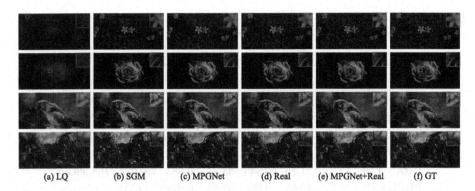

(a) LQ   (b) SGM   (c) MPGNet   (d) Real   (e) MPGNet+Real   (f) GT

Fig. 5. Comparison between restoration results on the UDC dataset. (a) The degraded image. (b–c) The clean images are restored using the models trained by the different datasets. (f) The ground-truth. The top two are from the T-OLED track, and the bottom two are from the P-OLED track.

Table 1. Performance comparison between other methods and our MPGNet.

Methods	P-OLED		T-OLED	
	PSNR	SSIM	PSNR	SSIM
Real	33.21	0.960	38.96	0.984
SGM	$28.61_{\downarrow 4.60}$	$0.911_{\downarrow 0.049}$	$34.82_{\downarrow 4.14}$	$0.950_{\downarrow 0.034}$
SGM + Real	$32.56_{\downarrow 0.65}$	$0.957_{\downarrow 0.003}$	$38.42_{\downarrow 0.54}$	$0.980_{\downarrow 0.004}$
U-Net	$30.41_{\downarrow 2.80}$	$0.912_{\downarrow 0.048}$	$36.20_{\downarrow 2.76}$	$0.958_{\downarrow 0.026}$
MPGNet	$31.95_{\downarrow 1.26}$	$0.941_{\downarrow 0.019}$	$37.33_{\downarrow 1.63}$	$0.970_{\downarrow 0.014}$
MPGNet + Real	$34.22_{\uparrow 1.01}$	$0.964_{\uparrow 0.004}$	$39.55_{\uparrow 0.59}$	$0.986_{\uparrow 0.002}$

4.3   Comparison of Restoration Models

We compare the performance of the proposed DWFormer with other learning-based approaches on the UDC benchmark, and the quantitative comparisons in terms of PSNR and SSIM metrics are summarized in Table 2. The results show that our method achieves state-of-the-art results for both the P-OLED track and T-OLED track. In particular, our DWFormer achieves 0.22 and 0.12 dB PSNR improvements over the previous best methods PDCRN [7] and DRANet [9] on the P-OLED and T-OLED tracks, respectively. Using both generated and real data to train our model, DWFormer can improve 1.01 dB on the P-OLED track and 0.59 dB on the T-OLED track over the previous one.

Table 2. Restore qualitative evaluation on the UDC benchmark. Note that [†] means that the models are trained with both generated and real datasets.

Methods	P-OLED		T-OLED		Overhead	
	PSNR	SSIM	PSNR	SSIM	Params	MACs
ResNet [1]	27.42	0.918	36.26	0.970	1.37M	40.71G
UNet [1]	29.45	0.934	36.71	0.971	8.94M	17.09G
SGDAN [65]	30.89	0.947	36.81	0.971	21.1M	7.25G
ResUNet [66]	30.62	0.945	37.95	0.979	16.50M	15.79G
DRANet [9]	31.86	0.949	38.84	0.983	79.01M	168.98G
PDCRN [7]	32.99	0.958	37.83	0.978	3.65M	6.31G
RDUNet [66]	30.12	0.941	38.22	0.980	47.93M	46.01G
DWFormer (Ours)	33.21	0.960	38.96	0.984	1.21M	13.46G
PDCRN[†]	34.02	0.962	38.75	0.982	3.65M	6.31G
RDUNet[†]	32.45	0.952	39.05	0.984	47.93M	46.01G
DWFormer[†] (Ours)	34.22	0.964	39.55	0.986	1.21M	13.46G

4.4   Ablation Studies

We first study the impact of each module in MPGNet on performance. Specifically, we replace brightness correction, blurring, and noise modules with corresponding modules in SGM. Further, we remove each noise component, *i.e.*, quantization noise n_q, signal-dependent noise n_d and signal-independent noise n_i to explore their effects. We use these modified networks to generate datasets that are used to train restoration models. And we evaluate the restoration models on the UDC benchmark as shown in Table 3.

As we can see, the blurring module has the most significant impact on the model performance, indicating that diffraction caused by hardware structure is the most critical degradation factor in the UDC imaging process. And ablation studies of noise and brightness modules show that different materials' main degradation components differ. Surprisingly, quantization noise plays such a significant role in the noise module. It may be due to the brightness attenuation during the imaging process and the low number of image bits. Also, such a phenomenon indicates that the actual noise module of the UDC images is quite complex and challenging to simulate using only Poisson-Gaussian distribution.

To verify the effectiveness of the DWFormer modules, we performed ablation studies for the normalization, depth-wise convolution, and attention mechanism module, and Table 3 shows the results. We notice that the removal of ACA causes a significant performance drop, implying that global information is indispensable. And our ACA is much better than SE with negligible additional computation cost. Also, the performance decreased if we used Swin Transformer's block, indicating that the locality properties provided by depth-wise convolution work for the UDC restoration task. Besides, BatchNorm surpasses LayerNorm. It is worth

Table 3. Different modules' effects on the MPGNet's performance. The performance is evaluated on the generated datasets using our DWFormer.

Methods	P-OLED		T-OLED	
	PSNR	SSIM	PSNR	SSIM
MPGNet	31.95	0.941	37.33	0.970
MPGNet w/SGM-Light	$30.81_{\downarrow 1.14}$	$0.930_{\downarrow 0.011}$	$36.96_{\downarrow 0.37}$	$0.965_{\downarrow 0.005}$
MPGNet w/SGM-Blur	$30.10_{\downarrow 1.85}$	$0.915_{\downarrow 0.026}$	$35.87_{\downarrow 1.46}$	$0.959_{\downarrow 0.011}$
MPGNet w/SGM-Noise	$31.16_{\downarrow 0.79}$	$0.934_{\downarrow 0.007}$	$36.30_{\downarrow 1.03}$	$0.962_{\downarrow 0.008}$
MPGNet w/o n_q	$31.36_{\downarrow 0.59}$	$0.935_{\downarrow 0.006}$	$36.87_{\downarrow 0.46}$	$0.964_{\downarrow 0.006}$
MPGNet w/o n_d	$31.26_{\downarrow 0.69}$	$0.935_{\downarrow 0.006}$	$36.55_{\downarrow 0.78}$	$0.963_{\downarrow 0.007}$
MPGNet w/o n_i	$31.64_{\downarrow 0.31}$	$0.937_{\downarrow 0.004}$	$37.04_{\downarrow 0.29}$	$0.967_{\downarrow 0.003}$

Table 4. Different modules' effects on the DWFormer's performance.

Methods	P-OLED		T-OLED		MACs
	PSNR	SSIM	PSNR	SSIM	
DWFormer	33.21	0.960	38.96	0.984	13.46G
ACA → None	$32.62_{\downarrow 0.59}$	$0.951_{\downarrow 0.009}$	$38.45_{\downarrow 0.51}$	$0.980_{\downarrow 0.004}$	13.42G
ACA → SE	$33.00_{\downarrow 0.21}$	$0.958_{\downarrow 0.002}$	$38.72_{\downarrow 0.24}$	$0.982_{\downarrow 0.002}$	13.43G
DWB → Swin	$33.07_{\downarrow 0.14}$	$0.959_{\downarrow 0.001}$	$38.84_{\downarrow 0.12}$	$0.982_{\downarrow 0.002}$	16.22G
BN → LN	$33.11_{\downarrow 0.10}$	$0.957_{\downarrow 0.003}$	$38.90_{\downarrow 0.06}$	$0.982_{\downarrow 0.002}$	13.46G

noting that BatchNorm can be fused into a convolutional layer when inferring, which makes the network run faster than the network with LayerNorm (Table 4).

Moreover, we explore the effect of $\mathcal{L}_{sup}$ and $\mathcal{L}_{adv}$ and use them for training MPGNet. Figure 6 shows the generated results. $\mathcal{L}_{sup}$ alone leads to reasonable but noiseless results. $\mathcal{L}_{adv}$ alone gives much blurrier results. It is because the $\mathcal{L}_{sup}$ loss will still eliminate the noise while constructing the image alignment though we have attempted to alleviate it, and the weak constraint of GAN causes the content restoration to be more difficult.

We further use these generated datasets to train our DWFormer and evaluate them on the UDC benchmark for quantitative assessment, and the results are shown in Table 5. Note that $\mathcal{L}_1$ means that we directly compute the $\mathcal{L}_1$ loss on the generated image. In contrast, $\mathcal{L}_{sup}$ means we take the generated images through a restoration network and then calculate the loss. The $\mathcal{L}_1$ is worse than the $\mathcal{L}_{sup}$, implying that the latter can preserve the random noise to some extent. Note that if we do not feed clean images as extra inputs to D, MPGNet fails to generate valid degraded images and falls into a mode collapse.

Here, we use both $\mathcal{L}_{sup}$ and $\mathcal{L}_{adv}$ to boost the model performance. And We further evaluate it with different ratios (changing the value of λ). It is found that the optimal ratio is highly correlated with the data itself, and different

| Input | GT | L_sup | L_adv | L_sup+L_adv |

Fig. 6. Different losses lead to different generation results. Each column shows the results of training at different losses.

Table 5. Different loss terms for training MPGNets. The performance is evaluated on the generated datasets using our DWFormer.

Methods	P-OLED		T-OLED	
	PSNR	SSIM	PSNR	SSIM
$\mathcal{L}_1$	31.13	0.908	35.98	0.951
$\mathcal{L}_{sup}$	31.23	0.911	36.08	0.966
$\mathcal{L}_{adv}$	31.55	0.945	36.02	0.957
$\mathcal{L}_{adv} + \mathcal{L}_{sup}$	33.22	0.960	38.80	0.981
$\mathcal{L}_{adv} + 10\mathcal{L}_{sup}$	33.21	0.960	38.96	0.984
$\mathcal{L}_{adv} + 100\mathcal{L}_{sup}$	33.03	0.956	38.98	0.984

datasets hold different optimal ratios. Experiments show that $\mathcal{L}_{adv}$ plays a more significant role on the P-OLED track because the dataset is severely degraded. And the degradation is diminished on the T-OLED track, so the weight of $\mathcal{L}_1$ needs to be increased to ensure content consistency.

5   Conclusion

In this paper, we start from the degradation pipeline of the UDC imaging and replace each degradation process with a subnetwork, which forms our MPGNet. Further, the GAN framework is adopted to generate more realistic degraded images. Based on the analysis of UDC image degradation, we propose a novel block modified from Transformer and use it to build a U-Net-like image restoration network named DWFormer. Experiments show that our MPGNet generates more realistic degraded images than previous work, and DWFormer achieves superior performance. Finally, We use both generated and real datasets to train DWFormer, and further boost its performance, showing our generated data can be complementary to real data.

References

1. Zhou, Y., Ren, D., Emerton, N., Lim, S., Large, T.: Image restoration for under-display camera. In: Proceedings of the IEEE/CVF Conference on Computer Vision and Pattern Recognition, pp. 9179–9188 (2021)
2. Heath, M.T.: Scientific Computing: An Introductory Survey, Revised 2nd edn. SIAM (2018)
3. Nayar, S.K., Narasimhan, S.G.: Vision in bad weather. In: Proceedings of the Seventh IEEE International Conference on Computer Vision, vol. 2, pp. 820–827. IEEE (1999)
4. Kwon, K., et al.: Controllable image restoration for under-display camera in smartphones. In: Proceedings of the IEEE/CVF Conference on Computer Vision and Pattern Recognition, pp. 2073–2082 (2021)
5. Hasinoff, S.W.: Photon, poisson noise (2014)
6. Kersting, K., Plagemann, C., Pfaff, P., Burgard, W.: Most likely heteroscedastic Gaussian process regression. In: Proceedings of the 24th International Conference on Machine Learning, pp. 393–400 (2007)
7. Panikkasseril Sethumadhavan, H., Puthussery, D., Kuriakose, M., Charangatt Victor, J.: Transform domain pyramidal dilated convolution networks for restoration of under display camera images. In: Bartoli, A., Fusiello, A. (eds.) ECCV 2020. LNCS, vol. 12539, pp. 364–378. Springer, Cham (2020). https://doi.org/10.1007/978-3-030-68238-5_28
8. Sundar, V., Hegde, S., Kothandaraman, D., Mitra, K.: Deep atrous guided filter for image restoration in under display cameras. In: Bartoli, A., Fusiello, A. (eds.) ECCV 2020. LNCS, vol. 12539, pp. 379–397. Springer, Cham (2020). https://doi.org/10.1007/978-3-030-68238-5_29
9. Nie, S., et al.: A dual residual network with channel attention for image restoration. In: Bartoli, A., Fusiello, A. (eds.) ECCV 2020. LNCS, vol. 12539, pp. 352–363. Springer, Cham (2020). https://doi.org/10.1007/978-3-030-68238-5_27
10. Feng, R., Li, C., Chen, H., Li, S., Loy, C.C., Gu, J.: Removing diffraction image artifacts in under-display camera via dynamic skip connection network. In: Proceedings of the IEEE/CVF Conference on Computer Vision and Pattern Recognition, pp. 662–671 (2021)
11. Chen, J., Chen, J., Chao, H., Yang, M.: Image blind denoising with generative adversarial network based noise modeling. In: Proceedings of the IEEE Conference on Computer Vision and Pattern Recognition, pp. 3155–3164 (2018)
12. Chang, K.-C., et al.: Learning camera-aware noise models. In: Vedaldi, A., Bischof, H., Brox, T., Frahm, J.-M. (eds.) ECCV 2020. LNCS, vol. 12369, pp. 343–358. Springer, Cham (2020). https://doi.org/10.1007/978-3-030-58586-0_21
13. Kim, D.W., Ryun Chung, J., Jung, S.W.: GRDN: grouped residual dense network for real image denoising and GAN-based real-world noise modeling. In: Proceedings of the IEEE/CVF Conference on Computer Vision and Pattern Recognition Workshops (2019)
14. Goodfellow, I., et al.: Generative adversarial nets. In: Advances in Neural Information Processing Systems, vol. 27 (2014)
15. Dosovitskiy, A., et al.: An image is worth 16 × 16 words: transformers for image recognition at scale. arXiv preprint arXiv:2010.11929 (2020)
16. Yu, W., et al.: MetaFormer is actually what you need for vision. arXiv preprint arXiv:2111.11418 (2021)

17. Kwon, H.J., Yang, C.M., Kim, M.C., Kim, C.W., Ahn, J.Y., Kim, P.R.: Modeling of luminance transition curve of transparent plastics on transparent OLED displays. Electron. Imaging **2016**, 1–4 (2016)
18. Qin, Z., Yeh, Y.-W., Tsai, Y.H., Cheng, W.-Y., Huang, Y.-P., Shieh, H.P.D.: See-through image blurring of transparent OLED display: diffraction analysis and OLED pixel optimization. In: SID International Symposium: Digest of Technology Papers, vol. 47, pp. 393–396 (2016)
19. Whyte, O., Sivic, J., Zisserman, A., Ponce, J.: Non-uniform deblurring for shaken images. Int. J. Comput. Vis. **98**, 168–186 (2012)
20. Gupta, A., Joshi, N., Lawrence Zitnick, C., Cohen, M., Curless, B.: Single image deblurring using motion density functions. In: Daniilidis, K., Maragos, P., Paragios, N. (eds.) ECCV 2010. LNCS, vol. 6311, pp. 171–184. Springer, Heidelberg (2010). https://doi.org/10.1007/978-3-642-15549-9_13
21. Sun, J., Cao, W., Xu, Z., Ponce, J.: Learning a convolutional neural network for non-uniform motion blur removal. In: Proceedings of the IEEE Conference on Computer Vision and Pattern Recognition, pp. 769–777 (2015)
22. Xu, L., Ren, J.S., Liu, C., Jia, J.: Deep convolutional neural network for image deconvolution. In: Advances in Neural Information Processing Systems, vol. 27 (2014)
23. Chakrabarti, A.: A neural approach to blind motion deblurring. In: Leibe, B., Matas, J., Sebe, N., Welling, M. (eds.) ECCV 2016. LNCS, vol. 9907, pp. 221–235. Springer, Cham (2016). https://doi.org/10.1007/978-3-319-46487-9_14
24. Foi, A., Trimeche, M., Katkovnik, V., Egiazarian, K.: Practical Poissonian-Gaussian noise modeling and fitting for single-image raw-data. IEEE Trans. Image Process. **17**, 1737–1754 (2008)
25. Hasinoff, S.W., Durand, F., Freeman, W.T.: Noise-optimal capture for high dynamic range photography. In: 2010 IEEE Computer Society Conference on Computer Vision and Pattern Recognition, pp. 553–560. IEEE (2010)
26. Guo, S., Yan, Z., Zhang, K., Zuo, W., Zhang, L.: Toward convolutional blind denoising of real photographs. In: Proceedings of the IEEE/CVF Conference on Computer Vision and Pattern Recognition, pp. 1712–1722 (2019)
27. Wei, K., Fu, Y., Yang, J., Huang, H.: A physics-based noise formation model for extreme low-light raw denoising. In: Proceedings of the IEEE/CVF Conference on Computer Vision and Pattern Recognition, pp. 2758–2767 (2020)
28. Zhang, Y., Qin, H., Wang, X., Li, H.: Rethinking noise synthesis and modeling in raw denoising. In: Proceedings of the IEEE/CVF International Conference on Computer Vision, pp. 4593–4601 (2021)
29. Hong, Z., Fan, X., Jiang, T., Feng, J.: End-to-end unpaired image denoising with conditional adversarial networks. In: Proceedings of the AAAI Conference on Artificial Intelligence, vol. 34, pp. 4140–4149 (2020)
30. Zhang, K., Zuo, W., Chen, Y., Meng, D., Zhang, L.: Beyond a Gaussian denoiser: residual learning of deep CNN for image denoising. IEEE Trans. Image Process. **26**, 3142–3155 (2017)
31. Isola, P., Zhu, J.Y., Zhou, T., Efros, A.A.: Image-to-image translation with conditional adversarial networks. In: Proceedings of the IEEE Conference on Computer Vision and Pattern Recognition, pp. 1125–1134 (2017)
32. Dong, H., Yu, S., Wu, C., Guo, Y.: Semantic image synthesis via adversarial learning. In: Proceedings of the IEEE International Conference on Computer Vision, pp. 5706–5714 (2017)

33. Kaneko, T., Hiramatsu, K., Kashino, K.: Generative attribute controller with conditional filtered generative adversarial networks. In: Proceedings of the IEEE Conference on Computer Vision and Pattern Recognition, pp. 6089–6098 (2017)

34. Ledig, C., et al.: Photo-realistic single image super-resolution using a generative adversarial network. In: Proceedings of the IEEE Conference on Computer Vision and Pattern Recognition, pp. 4681–4690 (2017)

35. Pathak, D., Krahenbuhl, P., Donahue, J., Darrell, T., Efros, A.A.: Context encoders: feature learning by inpainting. In: Proceedings of the IEEE Conference on Computer Vision and Pattern Recognition, pp. 2536–2544 (2016)

36. Gulrajani, I., Ahmed, F., Arjovsky, M., Dumoulin, V., Courville, A.C.: Improved training of Wasserstein GANs. In: Advances in Neural Information Processing Systems, vol. 30 (2017)

37. Lim, J.H., Ye, J.C.: Geometric GAN. arXiv preprint arXiv:1705.02894 (2017)

38. Mao, X., Li, Q., Xie, H., Lau, R.Y., Wang, Z., Paul Smolley, S.: Least squares generative adversarial networks. In: Proceedings of the IEEE International Conference on Computer Vision, pp. 2794–2802 (2017)

39. Yue, Z., Zhao, Q., Zhang, L., Meng, D.: Dual adversarial network: toward real-world noise removal and noise generation. In: Vedaldi, A., Bischof, H., Brox, T., Frahm, J.-M. (eds.) ECCV 2020. LNCS, vol. 12355, pp. 41–58. Springer, Cham (2020). https://doi.org/10.1007/978-3-030-58607-2_3

40. Kupyn, O., Budzan, V., Mykhailych, M., Mishkin, D., Matas, J.: DeblurGAN: blind motion deblurring using conditional adversarial networks. In: Proceedings of the IEEE Conference on Computer Vision and Pattern Recognition, pp. 8183–8192 (2018)

41. Kupyn, O., Martyniuk, T., Wu, J., Wang, Z.: DeblurGAN-v2: deblurring (orders-of-magnitude) faster and better. In: Proceedings of the IEEE/CVF International Conference on Computer Vision, pp. 8878–8887 (2019)

42. Chen, C., Chen, Q., Xu, J., Koltun, V.: Learning to see in the dark. In: Proceedings of the IEEE Conference on Computer Vision and Pattern Recognition, pp. 3291–3300 (2018)

43. Xia, Z., Gharbi, M., Perazzi, F., Sunkavalli, K., Chakrabarti, A.: Deep denoising of flash and no-flash pairs for photography in low-light environments. In: Proceedings of the IEEE/CVF Conference on Computer Vision and Pattern Recognition, pp. 2063–2072 (2021)

44. Liu, Z., et al.: Swin transformer: hierarchical vision transformer using shifted windows. In: Proceedings of the IEEE/CVF International Conference on Computer Vision, pp. 10012–10022 (2021)

45. Chen, H., et al.: Pre-trained image processing transformer. In: Proceedings of the IEEE/CVF Conference on Computer Vision and Pattern Recognition, pp. 12299–12310 (2021)

46. Wang, Z., Cun, X., Bao, J., Liu, J.: UFormer: a general U-shaped transformer for image restoration. arXiv preprint arXiv:2106.03106 (2021)

47. Chen, L., Chu, X., Zhang, X., Sun, J.: Simple baselines for image restoration. arXiv preprint arXiv:2204.04676 (2022)

48. Wu, Y., Johnson, J.: Rethinking "batch" in batchnorm. arXiv preprint arXiv:2105.07576 (2021)

49. Hu, J., Shen, L., Sun, G.: Squeeze-and-excitation networks. In: Proceedings of the IEEE Conference on Computer Vision and Pattern Recognition, pp. 7132–7141 (2018)

50. Schonfeld, E., Schiele, B., Khoreva, A.: A U-net based discriminator for generative adversarial networks. In: Proceedings of the IEEE/CVF Conference on Computer Vision and Pattern Recognition, pp. 8207–8216 (2020)
51. Li, D., Zhang, H., Wang, Y.: Four-coordinate organoboron compounds for organic light-emitting diodes (OLEDs). Chem. Soc. Rev. **42**, 8416–8433 (2013)
52. Fu, Q., Di, X., Zhang, Y.: Learning an adaptive model for extreme low-light raw image processing. arXiv preprint arXiv:2004.10447 (2020)
53. Voelz, D.G.: Computational Fourier Optics: a MATLAB Tutorial. SPIE Press Bellingham (2011)
54. He, K., Zhang, X., Ren, S., Sun, J.: Deep residual learning for image recognition. In: Proceedings of the IEEE Conference on Computer Vision and Pattern Recognition, pp. 770–778 (2016)
55. Shi, W., et al.: Real-time single image and video super-resolution using an efficient sub-pixel convolutional neural network. In: Proceedings of the IEEE Conference on Computer Vision and Pattern Recognition, pp. 1874–1883 (2016)
56. Jang, G., Lee, W., Son, S., Lee, K.M.: C2N: practical generative noise modeling for real-world denoising. In: Proceedings of the IEEE/CVF International Conference on Computer Vision, pp. 2350–2359 (2021)
57. Monakhova, K., Richter, S.R., Waller, L., Koltun, V.: Dancing under the stars: video denoising in starlight. arXiv preprint arXiv:2204.04210 (2022)
58. Vaswani, A., et al.: Attention is all you need. In: Advances in Neural Information Processing Systems, vol. 30 (2017)
59. Wang, T.C., Liu, M.Y., Zhu, J.Y., Tao, A., Kautz, J., Catanzaro, B.: High-resolution image synthesis and semantic manipulation with conditional GANs. In: Proceedings of the IEEE Conference on Computer Vision and Pattern Recognition, pp. 8798–8807 (2018)
60. Zhu, J.Y., Park, T., Isola, P., Efros, A.A.: Unpaired image-to-image translation using cycle-consistent adversarial networks. In: Proceedings of the IEEE International Conference on Computer Vision, pp. 2223–2232 (2017)
61. Cai, Y., Hu, X., Wang, H., Zhang, Y., Pfister, H., Wei, D.: Learning to generate realistic noisy images via pixel-level noise-aware adversarial training. In: Advances in Neural Information Processing Systems, vol. 34 (2021)
62. Kingma, D.P., Ba, J.: Adam: a method for stochastic optimization. arXiv preprint arXiv:1412.6980 (2014)
63. Loshchilov, I., Hutter, F.: SGDR: stochastic gradient descent with warm restarts. arXiv preprint arXiv:1608.03983 (2016)
64. Agustsson, E., Timofte, R.: NTIRE 2017 challenge on single image super-resolution: dataset and study. In: Proceedings of the IEEE Conference on Computer Vision and Pattern Recognition Workshops, pp. 126–135 (2017)
65. Zhou, Y., et al.: UDC 2020 challenge on image restoration of under-display camera: methods and results. In: Bartoli, A., Fusiello, A. (eds.) ECCV 2020. LNCS, vol. 12539, pp. 337–351. Springer, Cham (2020). https://doi.org/10.1007/978-3-030-68238-5_26
66. Yang, Q., Liu, Y., Tang, J., Ku, T.: Residual and dense UNet for under-display camera restoration. In: Bartoli, A., Fusiello, A. (eds.) ECCV 2020. LNCS, vol. 12539, pp. 398–408. Springer, Cham (2020). https://doi.org/10.1007/978-3-030-68238-5_30

UHD Underwater Image Enhancement via Frequency-Spatial Domain Aware Network

Yiwen Wei, Zhuoran Zheng, and Xiuyi Jia[✉]

School of Computer Science and Engineering, Nanjing University of Science
and Technology, Nanjing, China
jiaxy@njust.edu.cn

Abstract. Currently, carrying ultra high definition (UHD) imaging equipment to record rich environmental conditions in deep water has become a hot issue in underwater exploration. However, due to the poor light transmission in deep water spaces and the large number of impurity particles, UHD underwater imaging is often plagued by low contrast and blur. To overcome these challenges, we propose an efficient two-path model (UHD-SFNet) that recovers the color and the texture of an underwater blurred image in the frequency and the spatial domains. Specifically, the method consists of two branches: in the first branch, we use a bilateral enhancement pipeline that extracts the frequency domain information of a degraded image to reconstruct clear textures. In the pipeline, we embed 1D convolutional layers in the MLP-based framework to capture the local characteristics of the token sequence. In the second branch, we develop U-RSGNet to capture the color features of the image after Gaussian blurring to generate a feature map rich in color information. Finally, the extracted texture features are fused with the color features to produce a clear underwater image. In addition, to construct paired high-quality underwater image enhancement dataset, we propose UHD-CycleGAN with the help of domain adaptation to produce more realistic UHD synthetic images. Experimental results show that our algorithm outperforms existing methods significantly in underwater image enhancement on a single GPU with 24G RAM. Codes are available at https://github.com/wyw0112/UHD-SFNet.

1 Introduction

Over the past few years, underwater image enhancement has received increasing attention as a fundamental task to improve advanced marine applications and services. Especially with the popularity of ultra high definition (UHD) imaging devices, there is an increasing demand for clear UHD underwater images for marine applications and services. Unfortunately, light in deep water is affected by wavelength-dependent absorption and scattering [1–4], resulting in problems such as low contrast and color cast in underwater images. In addition, underwater microorganisms and impurities can further enhance light scattering,

L. Wang et al. (Eds.): ACCV 2022, LNCS 13843, pp. 21–36, 2023.
https://doi.org/10.1007/978-3-031-26313-2_2

Fig. 1. The figure shows the difference in the normalized Fourier coefficients and the high frequency information between a pair of clear and blurred images. Where (a) is the clear image, (b) and (c) are the real and imaginary parts of (a) in the frequency domain after conversion to a grayscale map, respectively, (d) is the high-frequency part of (a), (e) is the blurred image, and (f)–(h) as above.

which can seriously interfere with the subsequent analysis of the computer vision. Therefore, it is difficult but very important to design efficient underwater image enhancement methods.

Traditional methods [3,5–7] implement the task of underwater image enhancement with the help of statistical properties of the image and physical assumptions. However, these methods solve the color cast of images mainly by using manual priors, which make it difficult to correct low contrast and missing texture information in dynamic scenes. Recently, deep learning methods have been widely used to enhance underwater images, including standard convolution methods [8,9], methods with physical priors [10], and GAN-based methods [11–13]. Although these methods accomplish state-of-the-art results, their modeling pattern is to stack a large number of convolution kernels on the spatial domain to reconstruct the missing details, the masking of impurities, and the bluish (greenish) tones, ignoring the role of information in the frequency domain.

In order to use the spatial properties in the frequency domain to better learn feature patterns that are difficult to learn in the spatial domain, another research line [14–16] try to enhance images in the frequency domain, such as underwater image enhancement [16], and image deblurring [14]. These methods usually use Fourier transform or wavelet transform to obtain the frequency domain coefficients of the degraded image, and later use methods such as thresholding, filtering or deep learning to bridge the gap between the degraded image and the clear image. However, most of these methods ignore the role played by the real and imaginary parts of the frequency domain coefficients (complex tensor). The common practice of these methods is to assign a weight to a set of complex numbers, or discretize an image to obtain high-frequency and low-frequency features and process them separately. However, using fixed weights will result in the model being not able to reconcile the different semantic information of the images well, so we use a dynamic aggregation token method to process the real and imaginary parts of the frequency domain features. The viewpoint can be supported by Wave-MLP [17], which obtains a sizable performance benefit by splitting the real and imaginary parts of the estimated Fourier coefficients and refining them separately. Although PRWNet [16] deals with high-frequency and low-frequency features after wavelet transform respectively, the recovery of the frequency-domain characteristics of the image requires long-distance dependent features of the image. So it needs to stack a lot of convolutions to recover vibrant color and textures, which results in its inability to process UHD images on a single 24G RAM GPU. Since the framework of MLP is easy to establish long-distance dependence on the image, in the paper, we use the MLP-based model to extract features on the frequency domain to recover the blurred texture information. Furthermore, as shown in Fig. 1, we demonstrate the difference in the normalized Fourier coefficients and the high frequency information between a pair of clear and blurred images.

To solve the above problems, we propose UHD-CycleGAN to generate more realistic underwater blurred images on a single GPU with 24G RAM, and develop UHD-SFNet to generate high quality underwater enhanced images. To better recover the image texture information, our frequency domain perception sub-network based on MLP extracts the frequency domain information of an image by embedding the spatial induction bias in the bilateral technique. It is worth noting that by using a parallel twin channel, the real and imaginary parts of the estimated Fourier coefficients are refined separately to produce a high-quality bilateral grid. For the spatial domain branch, we use U-RSGNet to reconstruct the color information of the blurred underwater image by ingesting a gated residual to enhance the channel domain properties.

The contributions of this paper are summarized as follows:

- We propose a new network framework that can enhance UHD underwater images by extracting information in the spatial and the frequency domains. The framework complements the frequency and the spatial domain information of the image to better recover the color and texture information of the image, and the framework can process UHD underwater images on a single 24G RAM GPU.
- In the frequency domain branch, we embed the 1D convolution in the MLP-based method to capture the local features inside the image patches as a complement to the global frequency domain information that can recover the sharp edges of the image. In the spatial domain branch, we introduce the gated residual to enhance the properties of the channel domain to restore the natural color.
- We propose the novel UHD-CycleGAN to generate the U-Water100 dataset using 100 high-quality underwater clear images of different sizes. A large number of experimental results demonstrate the SOTA results achieved by our underwater image enhancement method.

2   Related Work

2.1   Underwater Image Enhancement

The early research methods were mainly physical model-free and physical model-based methods. The physical model-free methods aim to modify the image pixel values to improve the contrast of underwater blurred images. Iqbal et al. [18] stretched the dynamic pixel range of RGB color space and HSV color space to improve the contrast and saturation of underwater images. Ghani and Isa [19,20] made improvement for the problem that Iqbal et al. [18] method causes over-enhancement or under-enhancement. Ancuti et al. [21] recovered clear images by mixing contrast-enhanced images and color-corrected images in a multiscale fusion strategy. Fu et al. [22] proposed a new retinex-based enhancement method to enhance a single underwater image.

The physical model-based methods treat underwater image enhancement as an uncertain inverse problem where handcrafted priors are used to estimate the potential parameters of the image formation model. Chiang et al. [5] and Drews-Jr et al. [6] implemented underwater image enhancement by modifying the dark channel prior (DCP) proposed by He et al. [23]. Li et al. [7] proposed a hybrid method including color correction and underwater image deblurring to improve the visual quality of degraded underwater images. Akkaynak et al. [3] proposed a modified underwater image formation equation which is a physically more accurate model.

With the continuous development of deep learning and the accumulation of large datasets, data-driven methods have become increasingly popular in recent years. These methods mainly use convolutional operations to extract image features instead of using various manually extracted prior features. Due to the lack of underwater image enhancement datasets, early work used generative adversarial networks (GAN) to generate datasets or perform unpaired learning. Li et al. [24] first applied GAN to the generation of underwater blurred images. Jamadandi et al. [12] used wavelet transform to reconstruct the signal better. Uplavikar et al. [13] enabled the model to better discriminate between different types of underwater blur by introducing a classifier. Li et al. [9] constructed an underwater image enhancement benchmark (UIEB) and proposed a convolutional neural network trained on this benchmark. Li et al. [10] proposed an underwater image enhancement network with multicolor spatial embedding guided by medium transport, combining the advantages of physical models to deal with off-color and low-contrast problems. Huo et al. [16] enabled the network to progressively refine the underwater images in the spatial and the frequency domains by using a wavelet boosting learning strategy.

2.2   UHD Image Processing

Gabiger-Rose et al. [25] used a simultaneous field-programmable gate array implementation of bilateral filters to make more efficient use of dedicated resources. Jie et al. [26] proposed the Laplace Pyramid Translation Network

(LPTN) to avoid direct processing of high resolution images by feature extraction and fusion of multiple low resolution images. Lin et al. [27] used a base network to compute a low-resolution result and a second network to refine selected patches at high resolution to perform image keying in real time. Wang et al. [28] used a light weight two-head weight predictor with two outputs to perform fast image enhancement.

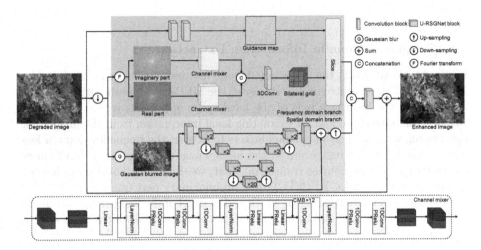

Fig. 2. In the purple region, the frequency domain coefficients are divided into the real and imaginary parts. The real and imaginary parts are processed separately in a pair of channel mixers to extract the frequency domain information of the image. Afterwards, the generated pairs of frequency domain feature maps are concatenated together and filtered using 3D convolution kernel to produce a bilateral grid. Next, the bilateral grid is queried using the guidance map to reconstruct the texture of the clear image. In the light green region, the spatial domain branch uses an encoder-decoder structure with gated residuals to process the blurred image to extract the color information of the image. Finally, the extracted frequency domain information and spatial domain information are fused to produce a clear image. (Color figure online)

3   Proposed Method

As shown in Fig. 2, in order to efficiently reconstruct the texture and color of a degraded image, we develop a two-path network dealing with the spatial and the frequency features. Specifically, we first use bilinear interpolation to downsample an underwater blurred image of arbitrary size to improve the speed of the model in extracting features in the frequency and the spatial domains. Next, in the spatial domain branch, we use Gaussian blur for the low-resolution input image (focusing on reconstructing the color information [29]), and then extract the spatial domain information of the image with the help of U-RSGNet. In the frequency domain branch, we use the fast Fourier transform to obtain the Fourier coefficients of an image. In particular, we extract features from the real and imaginary parts of the obtained Fourier coefficients using a pair of channel mixers to construct a high-quality bilateral grid. Then we slice [30] the obtained bilateral grid with the guidance map to obtain a frequency domain feature map rich in texture information. Finally, the output feature maps in the spatial and the frequency domains are fused with the input image to obtain a clear and colorful image.

3.1   Frequency Domain Information Extraction

Inspired by Wave-MLP, the frequency domain features can easily be modelled by MLPs to obtain accurate results. However, the MLP-based methods do not take into account the inductive bias of the local space of patches within the image, which is undoubtedly a loss for extracting local information from the image. For this reason, we use a pair of channel mixers to extract the frequency domain features of the degraded image. First, the input image I is converted into Fourier coefficients F by fast Fourier transform. Next, we divide the Fourier coefficients F into a real part $real \in \mathbb{R}^{(C \times H \times W)}$ and an imaginary part $imag \in \mathbb{R}^{(C \times H \times W)}$, where H, W and C are the length, width and channel of the image respectively. In addition, we divide $real$ and $imag$ into patches of length and width P and stretch them into 1D sequences of token embeddings $T_{real} \in \mathbb{R}^{(((H/P) \times (W/P)) \times (C \times P \times P))}$ and $T_{imag} \in \mathbb{R}^{(((H/P) \times (W/P)) \times (C \times P \times P))}$. Then, they are processed using channel mixers to obtain a real part feature F_r and an imaginary part feature F_i, respectively. The Channel Mixer Block (CMB) consists of several LayerNorm layers, linear layers, 1D convolutional layers, and PReLU activation function layers. The details are as follows:

$$T = CN_3(I + P(CN_2(P(CN_1(N(I)))))), \tag{1}$$

$$T^{'} = CN_4(T + P(L_2(P(L_1(N(T)))))), \tag{2}$$

where I is the input feature map, N is the layer normalization, CN is the 1D convolutional layer, L is the fully connected layer, and P is the PReLU activation function. The overall channel mixer first processes the input image by using a linear layer, and then feeds the feature maps into twelve CMBs to extract the image frequency domain information. The output feature map of the last CMB is processed by using a layer normalization, two 1D convolutions and PReLU activation functions to refine the high frequency features to obtain the final output.

We concatenate the real part features F_r and the imaginary part features F_i. Then we compress the frequency domain features into a four-dimensional affine bilateral grid after filtering by a 3D convolution kernel. The coordinates of the grid are in three dimensions. The reshaped frequency domain features can be viewed as a $16 \times 16 \times 16$ bilateral grid B, where each grid cell contains 3 digits. We process the original resolution image using convolution blocks to generate a guidance map G with bootstrap functionality. We use the slicing operation [30] to generate a high-quality feature map F_f by querying the bilateral grid through the guidance map.

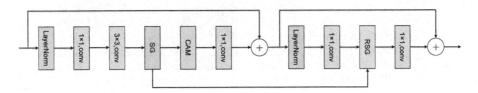

Fig. 3. The proposed structure of the U-RSGNet block in which the gated residual is ingested to enhance the channel domain characteristics.

3.2 Spatial Domain Information Extraction

To further utilize the rich color information in the spatial domain to recover colorful images, we introduce the spatial domain branch. This branch utilizes U-RSGNet to progressively enhance the channel information (color information) of the input features. The branch is a U-shaped structure consisting of a contracting path and an expansive path. The branch has five layers, in the first four layers each path is composed of two U-RSGNet blocks, and in the last layer twenty U-RSGNet blocks are used to mix the channel information of the lowest resolution feature map. In order to shrink or expand the feature map, a 2D convolution or sub-pixel convolution is inserted after each processing stage of the path. The structure of the U-RSGNet block is shown in Fig. 3. Because gated linear unit [31] can effectively improve the ability of the model to handle the long-distance dependence, we incorporate gated linear units in the network. The structure of the gated linear unit is as follows:

$$Gate(X) = f(X) \otimes \sigma(g(X)), \tag{3}$$

where X is the feature map, f and g denote linear transformations, $\otimes$ denotes element multiplication, and σ denotes the nonlinear activation function. Although the gating method with GELU activation function can enhance the modeling capability of the model, this will undoubtedly lead to higher model complexity. This runs counter to our philosophy of designing a lightweight model. To alleviate this problem, we use SimpleGate (SG) [32] as the basic feature enhancement unit to replace the traditional gating strategy. The details are as follows:

$$T_1, T_2 = Chunk(X), \tag{4}$$

$$O = T_1 \otimes T_2, \tag{5}$$

where the $Chunk$ operation is to cut $X \in \mathbb{R}^{(C \times H \times W)}$ directly in the channel dimension into feature sub-images $T_1 \in \mathbb{R}^{((C/2) \times H \times W)}$ and $T_2 \in \mathbb{R}^{((C/2) \times H \times W)}$.

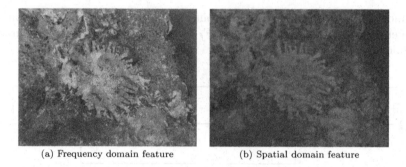

(a) Frequency domain feature   (b) Spatial domain feature

Fig. 4. (a) is the normalized output feature map of the frequency domain branch, and (b) is the normalized output feature map of the spatial domain branch.

T_1 and T_2 have the same size in each dimension. To further improve the U-RSGNet's ability to model the channel information to reconstruct the color of a blurred image, we propose the Residual Simple Gate (RSG) as follows:

$$RSG(X,Y) = SG(Y + \beta * SG(X)), \tag{6}$$

where $X \in \mathbb{R}^{(C \times H \times W)}$ and $Y \in \mathbb{R}^{((C/2) \times H \times W)}$ are the input feature map of the simple gate and the output feature map of the previous layer of the residual simple gate, respectively, $*$ is the channelwise product operation, and $\beta \in \mathbb{R}^{((C/2) \times 1 \times 1)}$ is the learnable channel attention vector. To further enhance the global attention capability of the model to obtain richer color information, our channel attention module (CAM) performs a global average pooling operation on the feature map to turn it into a channel attention vector $A \in \mathbb{R}^{(C \times 1 \times 1)}$, and then transposes A to $A^T \in \mathbb{R}^{(1 \times 1 \times C)}$, where C is the number of channels. Then, A^T is processed through a linear layer to enhance the global attention capability of the model. Finally, the transposed A^T is multiplied in the channel dimension with the input feature map to obtain the feature map rich in global information. The details are as follows:

$$CAM(X) = X * L(pooling(X)), \tag{7}$$

where X is the input feature map, L is the fully connected layer, and *pooling* is the global average pooling.

The whole process can be described as an input image I is Gaussian blurred to obtain a color image I_g, and then the color image is input to U-RSGNet to obtain a color-enhanced feature map F_c.

3.3   Spatial-Frequency Feature Fusion

To efficiently obtain a clear and colorful enhanced image, we use a standard feature fusion strategy at the end of the algorithm. Specifically, we concatenate the frequency domain feature map F_f and the spatial domain feature map F_c

in the channel dimension and process them with a standard convolution block (containing 3×3 and 1×1 convolutions with PReLU activation functions behind) to obtain a 3-channel feature map F_o. Finally, the final feature map F_o is summed with the original input image I with weights to obtain an enhanced image with sharp edges and rich color.

As seen in Fig. 4(a), the output feature map of the frequency domain branch has sharper edges. In contrast, the recovery of an image's color requires the network to have the ability to accurately extract channel features, which is capable of capturing the image's long-distance dependent features. Therefore, we develop U-RSGNet to enhance the color characteristics of degraded images. In detail, we add gated residuals to enhance the characteristics of the channel domain to improve the color reconstruction capability of the model. As seen in Fig. 4(b), the spatial domain branch focuses more on the color features of the image.

4   Experimental Results

In this section, we evaluate the proposed method by conducting experiments on synthetic datasets and real-world images. All results are compared with six state-of-the-art underwater image enhancement methods and one generic image enhancement method. These include two traditional methods (Ancuti et al. [21], Berman et al. [33]), a GAN-based method (FUnIE-GAN [11]), and four CNN-based methods (WaterNet [9], Ucolor [10], PRWNet [16], and NAFNet [32]). In addition, we perform ablation studies to show the effectiveness of each module of our network.

4.1   Training Data

To train and evaluate the proposed network as well as the comparison methods, we propose UHD-CycleGAN for migrating the style of underwater clear images to the style of blurred images on a single GPU. To generate high-quality UHD underwater images without noise, our generator first downsamples the images and feeds them into a convolutional network with an encoding-decoding structure (this structure can effectively mitigate the noise interference [34]). To avoid checkerboard artifacts caused by transposed convolution, we use bilinear interpolation for upsampling and downsampling, and add a 1×1 convolution with PReLU activation function to fill the gaps after the upsampling and downsampling operations. Specifically, we use all the blurred images of UIEBD as one style (including challenging images without corresponding reference) and clear images from U-Water100 and clear images from UIEBD as another style. We then migrate their styles to each other. Then a discriminator is used to determine whether the conversion is realistic or not. Notably, we also convert the converted images to the original style by a reverse generator and calculate their L1 loss from the original images to further promote more realistic conversion. We migrate the styles of 100 selected underwater clear images to the styles of underwater real blurred images in the UIEB dataset [9] to generate the

U-Water100 dataset. Our training dataset consists of a total of 890 underwater images. Among them, 800 are from UIEBD [9], and 90 are from U-Water100 that we produce. Accordingly, we use 90 images from UIEBD (T90) and 10 images from U-Water100 as the test set.

4.2   Implementation Details

The models are implemented in PyTorch and the networks are trained using the Adam optimizer. In this case, we use images of size 512×512 as input to train networks, with the batch size of 6. The initial learning rates for UHD-CycleGAN and UHD-SFNet are set to 0.00002 and 0.001, respectively. We train the UHD-SFNet for 400 epochs and UHD-CycleGAN for 10 epochs respectively. For WaterNet [9] and Ucolor [10], we fine-tune the networks using the same training data as ours based on the official models provided by the authors. For PRWNet [16] and NAFNet [32], we train their networks using the same dataset and the same experimental setup as ours. Notably, to allow the network to train and test UHD images on a single 24G RAM GPU, we downsample the inputs of Ucolor [10], PRWNet [16], and NAFNet [32] to 512×512 resolution and upsample them to the original resolution at the end.

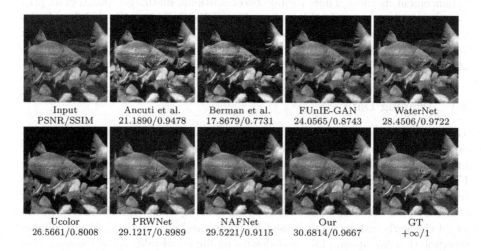

Fig. 5. Results of underwater image enhancement on the U-Water100 test dataset. Compared to other state-of-the-art methods, our method obtains better visual quality and recovers more image details.

4.3   Evaluation and Results

Quantitative Evaluation. Our proposed method is evaluated on two datasets, namely UIEB and U-Water100 datasets. All CNN-based methods are fine-tuned or trained on UIEBD and U-Water100. We use PSNR and SSIM as evaluation

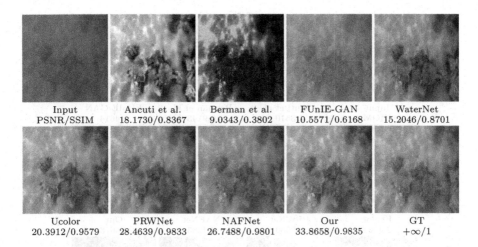

Input PSNR/SSIM	Ancuti et al. 18.1730/0.8367	Berman et al. 9.0343/0.3802	FUnIE-GAN 10.5571/0.6168	WaterNet 15.2046/0.8701
Ucolor 20.3912/0.9579	PRWNet 28.4639/0.9833	NAFNet 26.7488/0.9801	Our 33.8658/0.9835	GT +∞/1

Fig. 6. Results of underwater image enhancement on the T90 dataset. Compared to other state-of-the-art methods, our method obtains better visual quality and recovers more image details.

metrics for full-reference images. For the reference-free real-world images, we use UIQM [35] as the evaluation metric. For all the three metrics, the higher score means better image quality. As can be seen in Table 1, we achieve the best results for both SSIM and PSNR metrics, but we only achieve the second best results for UIQM. However, due to the limited applicability of UIQM, it can only be used as a reference.

Qualitative Evaluation. Figures 5 and 6 show the results of the proposed method and the comparison methods on one UHD image from the U-Water100 and one image from the UIEB dataset, respectively. Figure 7 shows the results of the proposed method and the comparison methods on two challenging and unreferenced images from the UIEB dataset. It can be seen that the conventional methods [21,33] tend to over-enhance the results and lead to color distortion. The GAN-based method [11] has weak color recovery capability and is prone to generate pseudo-streaks. The recent deep learning models [10,16,32] still have some ambiguity and color distortion in the results due to the lack of modeling capability. And the deep learning models [16,32] stack a lot of convolutions in order to have higher performance resulting in the inability to process UHD images on a single 24G RAM GPU directly. Our algorithm is able to directly process UHD images and better recover the color and edges of the image. The enhanced underwater images produced by our algorithm in Fig. 5–6 are close to the ground truth clear images. The images generated by our algorithm in Fig. 7 have more realistic color and sharp edges.

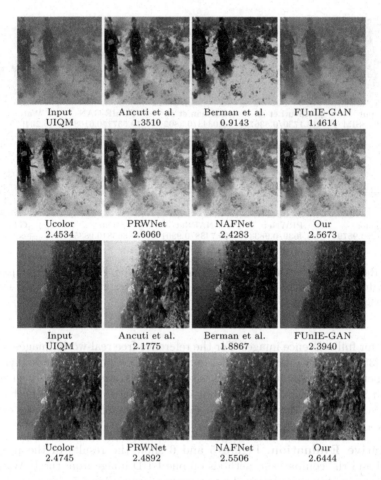

Fig. 7. Results of underwater image enhancement on the T60 dataset. Compared to other state-of-the-art methods, our method obtains better visual quality and recovers more image details.

4.4 Ablation Study

To demonstrate the effectiveness of each module introduced in the proposed network, we perform an ablation study including the following six experiments.

The Effectiveness of the Network of the Frequency Domain Branch. We keep the structure of the network of the spatial domain branch unchanged and replace the network of the frequency domain branch with the network of the spatial domain branch. The images are processed with the new two-branch network to obtain the final outputs.

The Effectiveness of the Network of the Spatial Domain Branch. We keep the structure of the network of the frequency domain branch unchanged

Table 1. Quantitative evaluation of the T60 dataset on UIQM metrics and quantitative evaluation of the T90 and U-Water100 datasets on PSNR and SSIM metrics.

	U-Water100		T90		T60
	PSNR	SSIM	PSNR	SSIM	UIQM
Input	21.8028	0.8955	17.5543	0.8191	1.6961
Ancuti et al. [21]	20.6852	0.8779	23.1564	0.9180	2.0978
Berman et al. [33]	16.1752	0.7197	15.5902	0.7205	1.5523
FUnIE-GAN [11]	20.4901	0.7891	17.9076	0.8057	2.3789
WaterNet [9]	22.3721	0.8859	19.5718	0.9057	2.1338
Ucolor [10]	23.7193	0.8578	20.3287	0.8538	2.2145
PRWNet [16]	23.5255	0.8390	23.8358	0.9293	**2.4209**
NAFNet [32]	24.2579	0.8615	24.3782	0.9288	2.2959
UHD-SFNet	**25.0462**	**0.9158**	**25.2020**	**0.9426**	2.4037

Table 2. The ablation studies of the network of the frequency domain branch, the network of the spatial domain branch, 1D convolution, residual simple gate, spatial domain information and frequency domain information are denoted as A, B, C, D, E and F, respectively.

	U-Water100		T90	
	PSNR	SSIM	PSNR	SSIM
A	20.4543	0.8741	23.6186	0.8890
B	22.9176	0.8749	19.8691	0.8997
C	24.7120	0.9085	22.0638	0.8482
D	24.4870	0.8957	24.2489	0.9210
E	16.2886	0.8599	18.9768	0.8771
F	24.5104	0.9089	24.1519	0.9229
Our	**25.0462**	**0.9158**	**25.2020**	**0.9426**

and replace the network of the spatial domain branch with the network of the frequency domain branch. The images are processed with the new two-branch network to obtain the final outputs.

The Effectiveness of the 1D Convolution. To ensure that the parameters and computational complexity of the model are similar to our method, we replace the 1D convolution in the channel mixer with the linear layer and compare it with our proposed method.

The Effectiveness of the Residual Simple Gate. We replace the residual simple gate with the simple gate in the network and compare it with our proposed method.

The Effectiveness of the Spatial Domain Information. The inputs to both branches of the network are images in the frequency domain. In this case, the input of the spatial domain branch is replaced by the real and imaginary parts of the frequency domain of the image with the same resolution as the inputs of the spatial domain branch.

The Effectiveness of the Frequency Domain Information. The inputs to both branches of the network are images in the spatial domain. In this case, the inputs of both the real and imaginary parts of the frequency domain branch are replaced by the images in the spatial domain with the same resolution as the inputs of the frequency domain branch.

Table 2 shows the results of our method compared with these six baselines on the U-Water100 and UIEB datasets. As can be seen in Table 2, the network of the spatial domain branch can achieve better metrics to some extent by relying on the color features of the images, but its edge recovery capability is still insufficient. Using only the network of the frequency domain branch does not produce satisfactory results, but its better ability to extract high-frequency information can be complemented by the ability to recover color from the network of the spatial-domain branch to produce enhanced images with rich color and sharp edges. Because 1D convolution can enhance the ability of the network to extract high-frequency features, it is used to compensate for the loss of local features caused by processing channel features with only linear layers. RSG can further improve the color recovery capability of the network by enhancing the channel domain features. Using the frequency domain information and the spatial domain information to complement each other can further refine the image edges and color to obtain a clearer and more colorful image.

5   Conclusion

In this paper, we propose a new framework for UHD underwater image enhancement in the spatial and the frequency domains. Our algorithm learns the features of the real and imaginary parts of the Fourier coefficients of the image to reconstruct the details of the image with the help of the channel mixer. In addition, we use the U-RSGNet with the RSG to recover the color information of the images. Quantitative and qualitative results show that our proposed network compares well with state-of-the-art underwater enhancement methods in terms of accuracy and produces visually pleasing results on real-world underwater images.

Acknowledgements. This work was supported by National Key Reserach and Development Program of China (2019YFB1706900), National Natural Science Foundation of China (62176123), Fundamental Research Funds for the Central Universities (30920021131) and Postgraduate Research & Practice Innovation Program of Jiangsu Province (KYCX22_0461).

References

1. McGlamery, B.: A computer model for underwater camera systems. In: Ocean Optics VI, vol. 208, pp. 221–231 (1980)
2. Jaffe, J.S.: Computer modeling and the design of optimal underwater imaging systems. JOE **15**(2), 101–111 (1990)
3. Akkaynak, D., Treibitz, T.: A revised underwater image formation model. In: CVPR, pp. 6723–6732 (2018)
4. Akkaynak, D., Treibitz, T., Shlesinger, T., Loya, Y., Tamir, R., Iluz, D.: What is the space of attenuation coefficients in underwater computer vision? In: CVPR, pp. 4931–4940 (2017)
5. Chiang, J.Y., Chen, Y.C.: Underwater image enhancement by wavelength compensation and dehazing. TIP **21**(4), 1756–1769 (2011)
6. Drews, P.L., Nascimento, E.R., Botelho, S.S., Campos, M.F.M.: Underwater depth estimation and image restoration based on single images. CG&A **36**(2), 24–35 (2016)
7. Li, C., Guo, J., Guo, C., Cong, R., Gong, J.: A hybrid method for underwater image correction. PRL **94**, 62–67 (2017)
8. Li, C., Anwar, S., Porikli, F.: Underwater scene prior inspired deep underwater image and video enhancement. PR **98**, 107038 (2020)
9. Li, C., et al.: An underwater image enhancement benchmark dataset and beyond. TIP **29**, 4376–4389 (2019)
10. Li, C., Anwar, S., Hou, J., Cong, R., Guo, C., Ren, W.: Underwater image enhancement via medium transmission-guided multi-color space embedding. TIP **30**, 4985–5000 (2021)
11. Islam, M.J., Xia, Y., Sattar, J.: Fast underwater image enhancement for improved visual perception. RA-L **5**(2), 3227–3234 (2020)
12. Jamadandi, A., Mudenagudi, U.: Exemplar-based underwater image enhancement augmented by wavelet corrected transforms. In: CVPRW, pp. 11–17 (2019)
13. Uplavikar, P.M., Wu, Z., Wang, Z.: All-in-one underwater image enhancement using domain-adversarial learning. In: CVPRW, pp. 1–8 (2019)
14. Mao, X., Liu, Y., Shen, W., Li, Q., Wang, Y.: Deep residual fourier transformation for single image deblurring. arXiv preprint arXiv:2111.11745 (2021)
15. Qin, F., et al.: Blind image restoration with defocus blur by estimating point spread function in frequency domain. In: ICAIP, pp. 62–67 (2021)
16. Huo, F., Li, B., Zhu, X.: Efficient wavelet boost learning-based multi-stage progressive refinement network for underwater image enhancement. In: ICCV, pp. 1944–1952 (2021)
17. Tang, Y., et al.: An image patch is a wave: phase-aware vision MLP. In: CVPR, pp. 10935–10944 (2022)
18. Iqbal, K., Odetayo, M., James, A., Salam, R.A., Talib, A.Z.H.: Enhancing the low quality images using unsupervised colour correction method. In: SMC, pp. 1703–1709 (2010)
19. Ghani, A.S.A., Isa, N.A.M.: Underwater image quality enhancement through integrated color model with rayleigh distribution. Appl. Soft Comput. **27**, 219–230 (2015)
20. Ghani, A.S.A., Isa, N.A.M.: Enhancement of low quality underwater image through integrated global and local contrast correction. Appl. Soft Comput. **37**, 332–344 (2015)

21. Ancuti, C., Ancuti, C.O., Haber, T., Bekaert, P.: Enhancing underwater images and videos by fusion. In: CVPR, pp. 81–88 (2012)
22. Fu, X., Zhuang, P., Huang, Y., Liao, Y., Zhang, X.P., Ding, X.: A retinex-based enhancing approach for single underwater image. In: ICIP, pp. 4572–4576 (2014)
23. He, K., Sun, J., Tang, X.: Single image haze removal using dark channel prior. TPAMI **33**(12), 2341–2353 (2010)
24. Li, J., Skinner, K.A., Eustice, R.M., Johnson-Roberson, M.: WaterGAN: unsupervised generative network to enable real-time color correction of monocular underwater images. RA-L **3**(1), 387–394 (2017)
25. Gabiger-Rose, A., Kube, M., Weigel, R., Rose, R.: An FPGA-based fully synchronized design of a bilateral filter for real-time image denoising. TIE **61**(8), 4093–4104 (2013)
26. Liang, J., Zeng, H., Zhang, L.: High-resolution photorealistic image translation in real-time: a laplacian pyramid translation network. In: CVPR, pp. 9392–9400 (2021)
27. Lin, S., Ryabtsev, A., Sengupta, S., Curless, B.L., Seitz, S.M., Kemelmacher-Shlizerman, I.: Real-time high-resolution background matting. In: CVPR, pp. 8762–8771 (2021)
28. Wang, T., et al.: Real-time image enhancer via learnable spatial-aware 3D lookup tables. In: ICCV, pp. 2471–2480 (2021)
29. Zheng, Z., Ren, W., Cao, X., Wang, T., Jia, X.: Ultra-high-definition image HDR reconstruction via collaborative bilateral learning. In: ICCV, pp. 4449–4458 (2021)
30. Gharbi, M., Chen, J., Barron, J.T., Hasinoff, S.W., Durand, F.: Deep bilateral learning for real-time image enhancement. TOG **36**(4), 1–12 (2017)
31. Dauphin, Y.N., Fan, A., Auli, M., Grangier, D.: Language modeling with gated convolutional networks. In: ICML, pp. 933–941 (2017)
32. Chen, L., Chu, X., Zhang, X., Sun, J.: Simple baselines for image restoration. arXiv preprint arXiv:2204.04676 (2022)
33. Berman, D., Treibitz, T., Avidan, S.: Diving into haze-lines: color restoration of underwater images. In: BMVC (2017)
34. Li, S., Liu, X., Jiang, R., Zhou, F., Chen, Y.: Dilated residual encode-decode networks for image denoising. JEI **27**(6), 063005 (2018)
35. Panetta, K., Gao, C., Agaian, S.: Human-visual-system-inspired underwater image quality measures. JOE **41**(3), 541–551 (2015)

Towards Real-Time High-Definition Image Snow Removal: Efficient Pyramid Network with Asymmetrical Encoder-Decoder Architecture

Tian Ye[1], Sixiang Chen[1], Yun Liu[2], Yi Ye[1], JinBin Bai[3], and Erkang Chen[1]([✉])

[1] School of Ocean Information Engineering, Jimei University, Xiamen, China
{201921114031,201921114013,201921114003,ekchen}@jmu.edu.cn
[2] College of Artificial Intelligence, Southwest University, Chonqing, China
yunliu@swu.edu.cn
[3] Department of Computer Science and Technology, Nanjing University,
Nanjing, China
jinbin.bai@smail.nju.edu.cn

Abstract. In winter scenes, the degradation of images taken under snow can be pretty complex, where the spatial distribution of snowy degradation varies from image to image. Recent methods adopt deep neural networks to recover clean scenes from snowy images directly. However, due to the paradox caused by the variation of complex snowy degradation, achieving reliable High-Definition image desnowing performance in real time is a considerable challenge. We develop a novel Efficient Pyramid Network with asymmetrical encoder-decoder architecture for real-time HD image desnowing. The general idea of our proposed network is to utilize the multi-scale feature flow fully and implicitly to mine clean cues from features. Compared with previous state-of-the-art desnowing methods, our approach achieves a better complexity-performance trade-off and effectively handles the processing difficulties of HD and Ultra-HD images.

The extensive experiments on three large-scale image desnowing datasets demonstrate that our method surpasses all state-of-the-art approaches by a large margin both quantitatively and qualitatively, boosting the PSNR metric from 31.76 dB to 34.10 dB on the CSD test dataset and from 28.29 dB to 30.87 dB on the SRRS test dataset. The source code is available at https://github.com/Owen718/Towards-Real-time-High-Definition-Image-Snow-Removal-Efficient-Pyramid-Network.

Keywords: Desnowing · Real-time · Asymmetrical encoder-decoder architecture

T. Ye, S. Chen and Y. Liu—Equal contribution.
This work was supported by Natural Science Foundation of Chongqing, China (Grant No. cstc2020jcyj-msxmX0324), the project of science and technology research program of Chongqing Education Commission of China (Grant No. KJQN202200206), Natural Science Foundation of Fujian Province (Grant No. 2021J01867), the Education Department of Fujian Province (Grant No. JAT190301) and Foundation of Jimei University (Grant No. ZP2020034).

L. Wang et al. (Eds.): ACCV 2022, LNCS 13843, pp. 37–51, 2023.
https://doi.org/10.1007/978-3-031-26313-2_3

1 Introduction

In nasty weather scenes, snow is an essential factor that causes noticeable visual quality degradation. Degraded images captured under snow scenes significantly affect the performance of high-level computer vision tasks [8,9,12,14–16].

Snowy images suffer more complex degradation by various factors than common weather degradation,i.e., haze and rain. According to previous works, snow scenes usually contain the snowflake, snow streak, and veiling effect. The formation of snow can be modeled as:

$$\mathbf{I}(x) = \mathbf{K}(x)\mathbf{T}(x) + \mathbf{A}(x)(1 - \mathbf{T}(x)), \tag{1}$$

where $\mathbf{K}(x) = \mathbf{J}(x)(1-\mathbf{Z}(x)\mathbf{R}(x))+\mathbf{C}(x)\mathbf{Z}(x)\mathbf{R}(x)$, $\mathbf{I}(x)$ denotes the snow image, $\mathbf{K}(x)$ denotes the veiling-free snowy image,, $\mathbf{A}(x)$ is the atmospheric light, and $\mathbf{J}(x)$ is the scene radiance. $\mathbf{T}(\mathbf{x})$ is the transmission map. $\mathbf{C}(x)$ and $\mathbf{Z}(x)$ are the chromatic aberration map for snow images and the snow mask, respectively. $\mathbf{R}(x)$ is the binary mask, presenting the snow location information.

As described in Eq. 1, the chromatic aberration degradation of snow and the veiling effect of haze are mixed in an entangled way. Existing snow removal methods can be categorized into two classes: model-based methods and model-free methods. For model-based methods [3,11,20], JSTASR [3] tries to recover a clean one from a snow image in an uncoupled way. Utilizing the veiling effect recovery branch to recover the veiling effect-free image, and the snow removal branch to recover the snow-free image. However, the divide and conquer strategy ignores the influence of inner entanglement degradation in snow scenes, and complicated networks by hand-craft design results in unsatisfactory model complexity and inference efficiency. For model-free methods [4,10,17], HDCW-Net [4] proposed the hierarchical decomposition paradigm, which leverages frequency domain operations to extract clean features for a better understanding of the various diversity of snow particles. But the dual-tree complex wavelet limits the inference performance of HDCW-Net, and it still has scope for improvement in its performance.

Single image snow removal methods have made remarkable progress recently. Yet, there are few studies on the efficient single image snow removal network, which attract us to explore the following exciting topic:

*How to design an **efficient** network to **effectively** perform single image desnowing?*

Most previous learning-based methods [3,4,17] hardly achieve real-time inference efficiency with HD resolution, even running on the expensive advanced graphics processing unit. We present a detailed run-time comparison in the experiment section to verify this point. Most methods can not perform real-time processing ability to handle High-Definition degraded images. In this manuscript, we propose an efficient manner to perform **HD(1280 × 720)** resolution image snow removal in real time, which is faster and more deployment-friendly than previous methods. Moreover, our method is the first desnowing network that can handle $UHD(4096 \times 2160)$ image processing problem.

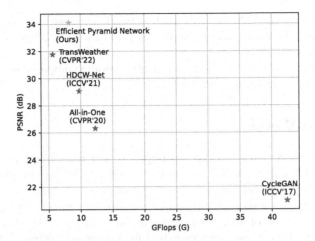

Fig. 1. Trade-off between performance vs: number of operations on CSD (2000) [4] testing dataset. Multi-adds are calculated on 256×256 image. The results show the superiority of our model among existing methods

Previous desnowing networks [3,4] usually only have 2 to 3 scale-level, which limits the desnowing performance and inferencing efficiency. Different from the previous mainstream designs of desnowing CNN architecture, the proposed network owns five scale levels, which means the smallest feature resolution of the feature flow in our pyramid network is only $\frac{1}{32}$ of input snow image. Sufficient multi-scale information brings impressive representation ability. Furthermore, the efficient and excellent basic block is also a significant factor for network performance and actual efficiency. Thus we propose a Channel Information Mining Block (**CIMB**) as our basic block to mine clean cues from channel-expanded features, which is inspired by NAFNet [2]. Besides that, we propose a novel External Attention Module (EAM) to introduce reliable information from original degraded images to optimize feature flows in the pyramid architecture. The proposed EAM can adaptively learn more useful sample-wise features and emphasize the most informative region on the feature map for image desnowing.

Motivated by the proposed efficient and effective components, our method achieves excellent desnowing performance. Compared with the previous best method transweather [17], the proposed method has better quantitative results (**31.76 dB/0.93 vs. 34.10 dB/0.95**) on CSD [4] dataset. And as shown in Fig. 1, compared with previous state-of-the-art desnowing methods, our method achieves a better complexity-performance trade-off.

The main contributions of this paper are summarized as follows:

- a) We propose a Channel Information Mining Block (CIMB) to explore clean cues efficiently. Furthermore, the External Attention Module (EAM) is proposed to introduce external instructive information to optimize features. Our ablation study demonstrates the effectiveness of CIMB and EAM.

- b) We propose the Efficient Pyramid Network with asymmetrical encoder-decoder architecture, which achieves real-time High-Definition image desnowing.
- c) Our method achieves the best quantitative results compared with the state-of-the single image desnowing approaches.

2   Related Works

Traditional methods usually make assumptions and use typical priors to handle the ill-posed nature of the desnowing problem. One of the limitations of these prior-based methods is that these methods can not hold well for natural scenes containing various snowy degradation and hazy effect. Recently, due to the impressive success of deep learning in computer vision tasks, many learning-based approaches have also been proposed for image desnowing [3,4,10,11]. In these methods, the key idea is to directly learn an effective mapping between the snow image and the corresponding clean image using a solid CNN architecture. However, these methods usually involve complex architecture and large-kernel size of essential convolution components and consume long inferencing times, which cannot cover the deployment demand for real-time snow image processing, especially for High-Definition (HD) and Ultra-High-Definition (UHD) images.

The first desnowing network is named DesnowNet [11], which focuses on removing translucent and snow particles in sequence based on a multi-stage CNN architecture. Li *et al.* propose an all-in-one framework to handle multiple degradations, including snow, rain, and haze. JSTASR [3] propose a novel snowy scene imaging model and develop a size-aware snow removal network that can handle the veiling effect and various snow particles. HDCW-Net [4] performs single image snow removal by utilizing the dual-tree wavelet transform and designing a multi-scale architecture to handle the various degradation of snow particles. Most previous methods are model-based, which limits the representation ability of CNNs. Moreover, the wavelet-based method is not deployment-friendly for applications.

3   Proposed Method

This section will first introduce the Channel Information Mining Block (CIMB) and External Attention Module. Then, we present the proposed pyramid architecture. Worth noting that profit from the asymmetrical encoder-decoder design and efficient encoder blocks, the proposed method is faster and more effective than previous CNN methods.

3.1   Channel Information Mining Block

Previous classical basic block in desnowing networks [3,4,11] usually utilize large kernel-size convolution and frequency-domain operations. In contrast with the

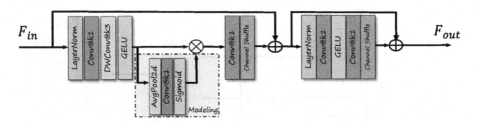

Fig. 2. The proposed Channel Information Mining Block (**CIMB**). The *DWConv* denotes the depth-wise convolution operation, and the kernel size of the convolution is denoted by @k∗. The design of our CIMB is motivated by NAFNet [2].

previous design, the proposed Channel Information Mining Block (CIMB) focus on how to effectively mine clean cues from incoming features with minimum computational cost.

As shown in Fig. 2, let's denote the input feature as F_{in}^c and output feature as F_{out}^c. The computational process of CIMB can be presented by:

$$F_{out} = CIMB(F_{in}). \tag{2}$$

Our design is simple and easy to implement in a widely-used deep learning framework. We utilize Layer Normalization to stabilize the training of the network and use the convolution with the kernel size of 1×1 to expand the channel of feature maps from c to αc, where the α is the channel-expand factor, is set as 2 in our all experiments. The channel-expanding way is crucial to motivate state-of-the-art performance because we found that high-dimension information mining is significantly suitable for single image desnowing. We further utilize channel information modeling to model the distribution of snow degradation and explore clean cues in the channel dimension. The channel-expanding design is motivated by NAFNet [2], which is an impressive image restoration work. Nevertheless, it ignores achieving efficient information interaction across different channels. We deeply realize the lack of effective channel interaction and introduce channel shuffle operation to achieve efficient and effective channel information interaction. Our ablation study demonstrates that the clever combination of channel-expanding and channel-shuffle achieves better performance with little computational cost by channel-shuffle.

3.2 External Attention Module

In the past few years, more and more attention mechanisms [7,18,18] have been proposed to improve the representation ability of the convolution neural network. However, most attention module [6,7,13,18] only focus on exploring useful information from incoming features, which ignores capturing and utilizing implicit instruction information from original input images. Moreover, information loss in multi-scale architecture cannot be avoided; thus, we utilize down-sampled snow

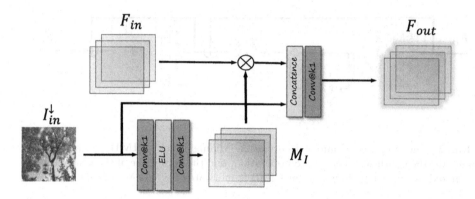

Fig. 3. The proposed External Attention Module (**EAM**). The kernel size of the convolution is denoted by @$k*$. The tensor size of the external attention map M_I is the same as the incoming feature F_{in} and generated feature F_{out}.

degraded images to introduce original information, relieving the information loss by multi-scale feature flow design.

As shown in Fig. 3, the External Attention Module is a plug-and-play architectural unit that can be directly used in CNNs for image restoration tasks. Specifically, we perform a series of operations on the down-sampled $I_{in}^{\downarrow}$ to generate the external attention map $\mathcal{M}_I^{H \times W \times C}$:

$$\text{Conv} \circ \text{ELU} \circ \text{Conv with } 1 \times 1 : I_{in}^{\downarrow} \rightarrow \mathcal{M}_I^{H \times W \times C}, \tag{3}$$

where the $I_{in}^{\downarrow}$ is the down-sampled original image, whose spatial size is the same as the incoming feature map F_{in}. Then we multiply the $\mathcal{M}_I^{H \times W \times C}$ with the F_{in}:

$$F_{att}^{H \times W \times C} = \mathcal{M}_I^{H \times W \times C} \cdot F_{in}^{H \times W \times C}, \tag{4}$$

where the $F_{att}^{H \times W \times C}$ is the scaled feature map. And we further utilize $I_{in}^{\downarrow}$ and channel-wise compression to introduce the original information:

$$\text{Concatence: } I_{in}^{\downarrow} + F_{att}^{H \times W \times C} \rightarrow F_{fusion}^{H \times W \times (C+3)}. \tag{5}$$

And a convolution with a kernel size of 3×3 is used to compress the dimension of F_{fusion} and get the final output feature F_{out}:

$$\text{Conv:} F_{fusion}^{H \times W \times (C+3)} \rightarrow F_{out}^{H \times W \times C}. \tag{6}$$

The benefits of our EAM are twofold: i) Fully utilize original degradation information to instruct the feature rebuilding explicitly. ii) Relief the information loss by repeat down-up sampling in multi-scale architecture. Please refer to our experiments section for the ablation study about the External Attention Module, which demonstrates the effectiveness of our proposed EAM.

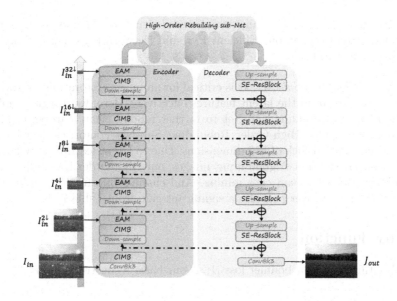

Fig. 4. Overview of the proposed Efficient Pyramid Network.

3.3 Efficient Pyramid Network with Asymmetrical Encoder-Decoder Architecture

Efficient Pyramid Network. U-Net style architectures can bring sufficient multi-scale information compared with single-scale-level architectures. However, the fully symmetrical architecture of U-Net style architectures results in redundant computational costs. Unlike previous mainstream designs [2,19] in the image restoration area, we develop an efficient pyramid architecture to explore clean cues from features of 5 scale levels, which is a more efficient way to handle the complex degradation, aka, snowy particles, and uneven hazy effect.

As shown in Fig. 4, our efficient pyramid network consists of three parts: encoder, decoder, and High-Order Rebuilding Sub-Net. Every scale-level encoder block only has a CIMB and an EAM in the encoder stage. For the decoder, we utilize ResBlock with SE attention [7] as our basic decoder block. Our decoder is fast and light. In the following sections, we further present the straight idea about Asymmetrical E-D design and High-Order Rebuilding Sub-Net.

Asymmetrical Encoder-Decoder Architecture. The symmetrical encoder-decoder architecture has been proven work well in many CNNs [2,4,19]. Most methods tend to add more conv-based blocks in every scale level with a symmetrical design to improve the model performance further. However, directly utilizing symmetrical architecture is not the best choice for our aims for the following reasons. First, we aim to process **HD** *(*1280 × 720*)* snowy images in real time, so we have to make trade-offs between performance and model complexity. Second, we found that a heavy encoder with a light decoder has a better representation ability to explore clean cues than a symmetrical structure. Thanks to the asymmetrical ED architecture, our Efficient Pyramid Network performs well on HD snow images in real time.

High-Order Rebuilding Sub-Net. It is critical for an image restoration network to exploit clean cues from the latent features effectively. Here, we design an effective High-Order Rebuilding Sub-Net to further rebuild clean features in high-dimension space. Our High-Order Rebuilding Sub-Net comprises 20 Channel Information Mining Block of 512 dimensions. Due to latent features only having $\frac{1}{32}\times$ resolution size than original input images, our High-Order Rebuilding Sub-Net quickly performs clean cues mining. And channel information exploration ability in the latent layer provides a significant gain from Table 7.

4   Loss Function

We only utilize the Charbonnier loss [1] as our basic reconstruction loss:

$$\mathcal{L}_{\text{char}} = \frac{1}{N} \sum_{i=1}^{N} \sqrt{\left\| J_{out}^{i} - J_{gt}^{i} \right\|^2 + \epsilon^2}, \tag{7}$$

with constant ϵ empirically set to $1e^{-3}$ for all experiments. And J_{gt}^{i} denotes the ground-truth of J_{out}^{i} correspondingly.

5   Experiments

5.1   Datasets and Evaluation Criteria

We choose the widely used PSNR and SSIM as experimental metrics to measure the performance of our network. We train and test the proposed network on three large datasets: CSD [4], SRRS [3] and Snow100k [3], following the benchmark-setting of latest desnowing methods [4] for authoritative evaluation. Moreover, we re-train the latest bad weather removal method TransWeather (CVPR'22) [17] to make a better comparison and analysis. Worth noting that we reproduce the TransWeather-based for a fair comparison, provided by the official repository of TransWeather [17].

5.2   Implementation Details

We augment the training dataset by randomly rotating by 90,180,270° and horizontal flip. The training patches with the size 256×256 are extracted as input paired data of our network. We utilize the AdamW optimizer with an initial learning rate of 4×10^{-4} and adopt the CyclicLR to adjust the learning rate progressively, where on the mode of triangular, the value of gamma is 1.0, base momentum is 0.9, the max learning rate is 6×10^{-4} and base learning rate is the same as the initial learning rate. We utilize the Pytorch framework to implement

Table 1. Quantitative comparisons of our method with the state-of-the-art desnowing methods on CSD, SRRS and Snow 100K desnowing datasets (PSNR(dB)/SSIM). The best results are shown in **bold**, and second best results are underlined.

Method	CSD(2000)		SRRS (2000)		Snow 100K (2000)		#Param	#GMacs
	PSNR	SSIM	PSNR	SSIM	PSNR	SSIM		
(TIP'18)Desnow-Net [11]	20.13	0.81	20.38	0.84	30.50	0.94	26.15 M	1717.04G
(ICCV'17)CycleGAN [5]	20.98	0.80	20.21	0.74	26.81	0.89	7.84M	42.38G
(CVPR'20)All-in-One [10]	26.31	0.87	24.98	0.88	26.07	0.88	44 M	12.26G
(ECCV'20)JSTASR [3]	27.96	0.88	25.82	0.89	23.12	0.86	65M	-
(ICCV'21)HDCW-Net [4]	29.06	0.91	27.78	0.92	31.54	0.95	6.99M	9.78G
(CVPR'22)TransWeather [17]	31.76	0.93	28.29	0.92	31.82	0.93	21.9M	5.64G
Ours	**34.10**	**0.95**	**30.87**	**0.94**	**33.62**	**0.96**	66.54M	8.17G

our network with 4 RTX 3080 GPU with a total batch size of 60. For channel settings, we set the channel as $[16, 32, 64, 128, 256, 512]$ in each scale-level stage respectively.

5.3 Performance Comparison

In this section, we compare our Efficient Pyramid Network method with the state-of-the-art image desnowing methods of [3,4,11], classical image translation method of [5] and the bad weather removal methods of [10,17].

Visual Comparison with SOTA Methods. We compare our method with the state-of-the-art image desnowing methods on the quality of restored images, presented in Fig. 5 and 6. Our approach generates the most natural desnowing images compared to other methods. The proposed method effectively restores the degraded area of the snow streaks or snow particles in both synthetic and authentic snow images.

Quantitative Results Comparison. In Table 1, we summarize the performance of our Efficient Pyramid Network and SOTA methods on CSD [4], SRRS [3] and Snow 100K [11]. Our method achieves the best performance with 34.10dB PSNR and 0.95 SSIM on the test dataset of CSD. Moreover, it achieves the best performance with 30.87dB PSNR, 33.62 dB PSNR, and 0.94 SSIM, 0.96 SSIM on SRRS and Snow100k test datasets.

Run-Time Discussion. In Table 2, 3, 4, we present detailed run-time and model-complexity comparison with different processing resolution settings. Worth noting that TransWeather [17] can not handle **UHD**(4096 × 2160) degraded images, as shown in Table 3, although it is minorly faster than ours when the input image is HD or smaller size. As shown in Table 2, our Efficient Pyramid Network achieves real-time performance when processing HD resolution images.

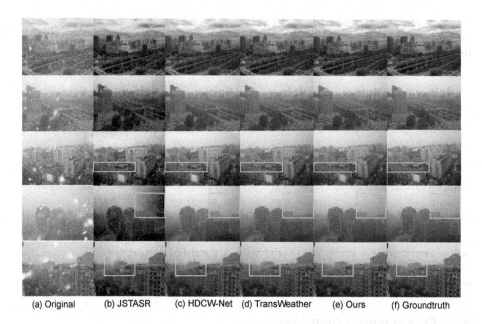

(a) Original   (b) JSTASR   (c) HDCW-Net   (d) TransWeather   (e) Ours   (f) Groundtruth

Fig. 5. Visual comparisons on results of various methods (b–e) and our proposed network (e) on synthetic winter photos. Please zoom in for a better illustration.

(a) Original   (b) JSTASR   (c) HDCW-Net   (d) TransWeather   (e) Ours

Fig. 6. Visual comparisons on results of various methods (b–d) and our method (e) on real winter photos. Please zoom in for a better illustration.

Table 2. Comparison of Inference time, GMACs (fixed-point multiply accumulate operations performed persecond) and Parameters when input HD (1280 × 720) **images.** Our method achieves the best runtime-performance trade-off compared to the state-of-the-art approaches. The time reported in the table corresponds to the time taken by each model to feed-forward an image of dimension 1280 × 720 during the inference stage. We perform all inference testing on an A100 GPU for a fair comparison. Notably, we utilize the *torch.cuda.synchronize()* API function to get accurate feed forward run-time.

Method	Inf. Time(in s)	GMACs(G)	Params(M)
TransWeather [17]	0.0300	79.66	21.9
Ours	0.0384	113.72	65.56

Table 3. Comparison of Inference time, GMACs (fixed-point multiply accumulate operations performed persecond) and Parameters when input UHD (4096 × 2160) **images.** We perform all inference testing on an A100 GPU for a fair comparison.

Method	Inf. Time(in s)	GMACs(G)	Params(M)
TransWeather [17]	Out of Memory	-	21.9
Ours	0.23	1097.03	65.56

Table 4. Comparison of Inference time, FPS and Parameters when input small (512 × 672) **images.** Following the testing platform of HDCW-Net [4], we perform all inference testing on a RTX 1080ti GPU for a fair comparison.

Method	Inf. Time(in s)	FPS	Params(M)
JSTASR [3]	0.87	1.14	65
HDCW-Net [4]	0.14	7.14	6.99
Ours	0.0584	17.11	65.56

Fig. 7. Synthetic snow images (left) and corresponding desnowing results (right) by the proposed method with the high-level vision task results and confidences supported by Google Vision API.

Model Complexity and Parameter Discussion. For real-time deployment of CNNs, computational complexity is an important aspect to consider. To check the computational complexity, we tabulate the GMAC in Table 1 for previous state-of-the-art methods and our proposed method when the input image is 256×256. We note that our network has less computational complexity when compared to previous methods. Notably, Desnow-Net is highly computationally complex than ours, even though it has less number of parameters.

5.4 Quantifiable Performance for High-Level Vision Tasks

As shown in Fig. 7, we offer subjective but quantifiable results for a concrete demonstration, in which the vision task results and corresponding confidences are both supported by Google Vision API. Our comparison illustrates that these snowy degradations could impede the actual performance of high-level vision tasks. And our method could significantly boost the performance of high-level vision tasks.

5.5 Ablation Study

For a reliable ablation study, we utilize the latest desnowing dataset,*i.e.*, CSD [4] dataset as the benchmark for training and testing in all ablation study experiments.

Table 5. Configurations of the proposed Channel Information Mining Block.

Metric	wo LN	GELU→ReLU	wo Channel Shuffle	Ours
CSD(2000) PSNR/SSIM	33.79/0.93	33.76/0.94	32.61/0.93	34.10 /0.95

Configurations of the Channel Information Mining Block. In Table 5, we present the quantitative results of different configuration settings for CIMB. Specifically, we remove the Layer Normalization (**wo LN**), replace the GELU with ReLU (**GELU → ReLU**) and remove the channel shuffle operation (**wo Channel Shuffle**). From the results of Table 5, We found that LayerNorm is essential to stabilizing the training process, GELU and LN can provide a certain improvement on PSNR and SSIM, which is in line with NAFNet [2]. For the channel shuffle, we observe that it attracts an obvious gain compared with LN or GELU. Therefore, we believe that the channel interaction by channel shuffle operation benefits information mining in high-dimension space.

Table 6. Verification for the proposed External Attention Module.

Metric	wo Concat $I_{in}^{\downarrow}$	$I_{in}^{\downarrow} \to F_{in}$	ELU → ReLU	Ours
CSD(2000) PSNR/SSIM	32.16/0.93	32.89/0.94	33.96/0.94	34.10/0.95

Verification of Key Designs for the Proposed External Attention Module. In Table 6, we present our verification about designs of the External Attention Module. (a) **wo Concat** $I_{in}^{\downarrow}$. To verify the effectiveness of introducing down-sampled original images, we remove the setting of image-feature fusion by concatence. (b) $I_{in}^{\downarrow} \rightarrow F_{in}$. To verify the key idea that generates an external attention map from the original degraded image to optimize current scale features, we replace the I_{in} with incoming F_{in}. (c) **ELU $\rightarrow$ ReLU.** We replace the *ELU* with *ReLU* to explore the influence of the non-linear function on network performance. we remove the image-feature fusion by concatence. We believe that the clean external cues from the degraded image are key to improving performance instead of a simple attention mechanism. In addition, we demonstrate the effectiveness of external information from the results. Compared with the feature, the original degradation information can instruct the feature rebuilding and alleviate the information loss. We also notice ELU and ReLU non-linear activation almost have no impact on performance.

Table 7. Ablation study of the High-Order Rebuilding Sub-Net.

Block Num.	0	6	12	Ours
CSD(2000) PSNR/SSIM	29.76/0.93	32.41/0.93	33.69/0.94	34.10/0.95
Params.(M)	12.81	28.64	44.46	65.56

Ablation Study of the High-Order Rebuilding Sub-Net. In Table 7, we explore the influence of the depth of High-Oder Rebuilding Sub-Net. We found that deeper architecture has better performance on image desnowing. Due to 5 level down-sampling design, simply stacking more blocks cannot result in an unacceptable computational burden.

Table 8. Ablation study of the Efficient Pyramid Network.

Metric	CIMB $\rightarrow$ SE-ResBlock	wo EAM	wo HOR Sub-Net	Ours
CSD(2000) PSNR/SSIM	32.94/0.94	31.79/0.93	29.76/0.93	34.10/0.95

Ablation Study of the Efficient Pyramid Network. To verify the effectiveness of each proposed component, we present comparison results in Table 8. (a) **CIMB $\rightarrow$ SE-ResBlock.** We replace the proposed CIMB with SE-ResBlock [7]. (b) **wo EAM.** We remove the proposed External Attention Module from our complete neural network. (d) **wo HOR Sub-set.** We remove the HOR Sub-net, and only reserve our encoder and decoder. Each proposed component is necessary for our Efficient Pyramid Network. We observe that the proposed basic block CIMB has superiority compared to SE-ResBlock [7], which is based on the spatial and channel modeling, and the interaction between channels in high-dimension space. Besides, we also demonstrate the necessity of EAM and HOR Sub-Net. Our framework achieves SOTA performance in real time.

Effectiveness of Scale Levels of Efficient Pyramid Network. We also carry out the discussion on the number of the semantic level and presented the results in Table 9. We explore different levels in our framework and demonstrate that using five semantic levels is best for our design. Specifically, too many scale levels can cause the feature size in the latent layer to be too small, so it will lose much information. On the other hand, too few scale levels will limit the speed of model inference due to resolution.

Table 9. Ablation study of Scale levels of Efficient Pyramid Network.

Metric	$\frac{1}{16}$x	$\frac{1}{64}$x	Ours
PSNR/SSIM	33.11/0.94	32.08/0.93	34.10/0.95

6 Limitations

Compared with previous lightweight desnowing methods, for instance, HDCW-Net (only 6.99M params.). The proposed Efficient Pyramid Network has better desnowing performance, but the much bigger parameters of our network will result in difficulty when deployed in edge devices.

7 Conclusion

In this work, we propose an Efficient Pyramid Network to handle High-Definition snow images in real time. Our extensive experiment and ablation study demonstrate the effectiveness of our proposed method and proposed blocks.

Although our method is simple, it is superior to all the previous state-of-art desnowing methods with a considerable margin on three widely-used large-scale snow datasets. We hope to further promote our method to other low-level vision tasks such as deraining and dehazing.

References

1. Charbonnier, P., Blanc-Feraud, L., Aubert, G., Barlaud, M.: Two deterministic half-quadratic regularization algorithms for computed imaging. In: Proceedings of 1st International Conference on Image Processing, vol. 2, pp. 168–172. IEEE (1994)
2. Chen, L., Chu, X., Zhang, X., Sun, J.: Simple baselines for image restoration. arXiv preprint arXiv:2204.04676 (2022)
3. Chen, W.-T., Fang, H.-Y., Ding, J.-J., Tsai, C.-C., Kuo, S.-Y.: JSTASR: joint size and transparency-aware snow removal algorithm based on modified partial convolution and veiling effect removal. In: Vedaldi, A., Bischof, H., Brox, T., Frahm, J.-M. (eds.) ECCV 2020. LNCS, vol. 12366, pp. 754–770. Springer, Cham (2020). https://doi.org/10.1007/978-3-030-58589-1_45

4. Chen, W.T., et al.: All snow removed: single image desnowing algorithm using hierarchical dual-tree complex wavelet representation and contradict channel loss. In: Proceedings of the IEEE/CVF International Conference on Computer Vision, pp. 4196–4205 (2021)
5. Engin, D., Genç, A., Kemal Ekenel, H.: Cycle-dehaze: enhanced cyclegan for single image dehazing. In: Proceedings of the IEEE Conference on Computer Vision and Pattern Recognition Workshops, pp. 825–833 (2018)
6. Hou, Q., Zhou, D., Feng, J.: Coordinate attention for efficient mobile network design. In: Proceedings of the IEEE/CVF Conference on Computer Vision and Pattern Recognition, pp. 13713–13722 (2021)
7. Hu, J., Shen, L., Sun, G.: Squeeze-and-excitation networks. In: Proceedings of the IEEE Conference on Computer Vision and Pattern Recognition, pp. 7132–7141 (2018)
8. Huang, X., Ge, Z., Jie, Z., Yoshie, O.: NMS by representative region: towards crowded pedestrian detection by proposal pairing. In: Proceedings of the IEEE/CVF Conference on Computer Vision and Pattern Recognition, pp. 10750–10759 (2020)
9. Lan, M., Zhang, Y., Zhang, L., Du, B.: Global context based automatic road segmentation via dilated convolutional neural network. Inf. Sci. **535**, 156–171 (2020)
10. Li, R., Tan, R.T., Cheong, L.F.: All in one bad weather removal using architectural search. In: Proceedings of the IEEE/CVF Conference on Computer Vision and Pattern Recognition, pp. 3175–3185 (2020)
11. Liu, Y.F., Jaw, D.W., Huang, S.C., Hwang, J.N.: Desnownet: context-aware deep network for snow removal. IEEE Trans. Image Process. **27**(6), 3064–3073 (2018)
12. Ouyang, W., Wang, X.: Joint deep learning for pedestrian detection. In: Proceedings of the IEEE International Conference on Computer Vision, pp. 2056–2063 (2013)
13. Qin, X., Wang, Z., Bai, Y., Xie, X., Jia, H.: FFA-Net: feature fusion attention network for single image dehazing. In: Proceedings of the AAAI Conference on Artificial Intelligence, vol. 34, pp. 11908–11915 (2020)
14. Redmon, J., Divvala, S., Girshick, R., Farhadi, A.: You only look once: unified, real-time object detection. In: Proceedings of the IEEE Conference on Computer Vision and Pattern Recognition, pp. 779–788 (2016)
15. Shafiee, M.J., Chywl, B., Li, F., Wong, A.: Fast yolo: a fast you only look once system for real-time embedded object detection in video. arXiv preprint arXiv:1709.05943 (2017)
16. Szegedy, C., Toshev, A., Erhan, D.: Deep neural networks for object detection. In: Advances in Neural Information Processing Systems, vol. 26 (2013)
17. Valanarasu, J.M.J., Yasarla, R., Patel, V.M.: Transweather: transformer-based restoration of images degraded by adverse weather conditions. arXiv preprint arXiv:2111.14813 (2021)
18. Woo, S., Park, J., Lee, J.Y., Kweon, I.S.: CBAM: convolutional block attention module. In: Proceedings of the European Conference on Computer Vision (ECCV), pp. 3–19 (2018)
19. Wu, H., et al.: Contrastive learning for compact single image dehazing. In: Proceedings of the IEEE/CVF Conference on Computer Vision and Pattern Recognition, pp. 10551–10560 (2021)
20. Zheng, X., Liao, Y., Guo, W., Fu, X., Ding, X.: Single-image-based rain and snow removal using multi-guided filter. In: Lee, M., Hirose, A., Hou, Z.-G., Kil, R.M. (eds.) ICONIP 2013. LNCS, vol. 8228, pp. 258–265. Springer, Heidelberg (2013). https://doi.org/10.1007/978-3-642-42051-1_33

Uncertainty-Based Thin Cloud Removal Network via Conditional Variational Autoencoders

Haidong Ding, Yue Zi, and Fengying Xie$^{(\boxtimes)}$

School of Astronautics, Beihang University, Beijing 100191, China
{dinghaidong,ziyue91,xfy_73}@buaa.edu.cn

Abstract. Existing thin cloud removal methods treat this image restoration task as a point estimation problem, and produce a single cloud-free image following a deterministic pipeline. In this paper, we propose a novel thin cloud removal network via Conditional Variational Autoencoders (CVAE) to generate multiple reasonable cloud-free images for each input cloud image. We analyze the image degradation process with a probabilistic graphical model and design the network in an encoder-decoder fashion. Since the diversity in sampling from the latent space, the proposed method can avoid the shortcoming caused by the inaccuracy of a single estimation. With the uncertainty analysis, we can generate a more accurate clear image based on these multiple predictions. Furthermore, we create a new benchmark dataset with cloud and clear image pairs from real-world scenes, overcoming the problem of poor generalization performance caused by training on synthetic datasets. Quantitative and qualitative experiments show that the proposed method significantly outperforms state-of-the-art methods on real-world cloud images. The source code and dataset are available at https://github.com/haidong-Ding/Cloud-Removal.

1 Introduction

Remote sensing images often suffer from absorption and scattering effects caused by thin clouds, resulting in degraded images. These low-quality images limit their utilization on subsequent high-level computer vision tasks, *e.g.*, object detection [1–3] and segmentation [4–6]. Therefore, it is significant to develop an effective method for single remote sensing image de-clouding.

Existing methods can generally be divided into two categories: prior-based approaches and data-driven approaches. Prior-based cloud removal models [7–9] are mainly built upon the atmospheric scattering model with various physical assumptions imposed on image statistics. These prior-based methods are more explanatory but can not perform well when the statistical prior does not hold in real-world images.

Supplementary Information The online version contains supplementary material available at https://doi.org/10.1007/978-3-031-26313-2_4.

To alleviate these limitations, data-driven methods adopt the deep learning approach to train the network in supervised learning paradigm. Several methods [10–12] directly learn how to generate clear images from their cloud counterparts in an end-to-end manner. Such algorithms are based on learning from large amounts of data and can produce decent results. However, the end-to-end training fashion usually regards de-clouding as a black box problem, making it poorly interpretable. To avoid this issue, other methods [13–15] combine the imaging model with Convolutional Neural Networks (CNNs). They mainly focus on building a neural network to replace part of the physical model in the conventional methods.

Although many excellent works have shown outstanding results, there are still many difficulties and misconceptions about the thin cloud removal task. Therefore, it is necessary to examine this problem in a broader context, two of which are highlighted below.

1) *The role of synthetic datasets.* It is hard to obtain image pairs with and without thin clouds in real-world scenes, so most algorithms [13,16,17] are trained on synthetic datasets. The differences between the synthetic and the real-world images make the network learn the law of data synthesis rather than the essence of image degradation during the optimization process. In addition, the synthetic dataset is based on the physical model of image degradation, so it is worth considering whether to rely on this physical model when designing the algorithm. As a result, this type of method can show excellent performance on synthetic data while performing poorly in real-world scenes. It demonstrates that the use of synthetic datasets inhibits the generalization performance of the model to a certain extent.

2) *The diversity of solutions.* A single cloud image loses some essential information of scene radiance, and recovering a completely clear image from it is equivalent to using little information to recover the whole scene structure, which makes this problem highly ill-posed. Therefore, this low-level computer vision problem is inherently uncertain. The exact value of each pixel in the clear image cannot be obtained by using only the degraded image without other auxiliary information. To our best knowledge, none of the existing methods take this into consideration. All of them established a one-to-one mapping from cloud image to cloud-free image. Therefore, considering uncertainty has great potential to improve the performance of cloud removal algorithms.

To address the aforementioned challenges, we propose a probabilistic model via CVAE for remote sensing image thin cloud removal. Based on the above analysis of uncertainty, we tackle this problem from the perspective of multi-solution. Each time the output from the proposed method is a sample of possible solutions. Our method is not based on an explicit prior model to avoid the insufficient understanding of the image degradation mechanism. Meanwhile, we do not use synthetic datasets so that the underlying de-clouding principles can be learned directly from real-world cloud images. The diverse output can ultimately enhance the generalization ability of the proposed thin cloud removal network.

Our contributions can be summarized as follows:

- Aiming at the uncertainty of thin cloud removal, we propose a probabilistic model based on CVAE for remote sensing image de-clouding, which solves this multi-solution problem from a probabilistic perspective. The network outputs multiple interpretable results, which fits the property of indefinite solutions to the problem.
- We propose an encoder network based on Vision Transformer (ViT) and a multi-scale feature fusion decoder network to achieve a one-to-many mapping from cloud image to clear image.
- We create a new benchmark dataset for single image thin cloud removal. The cloud and clear image pairs are from different moments of the same real scene to overcome the low generalization performance of the model due to training on synthetic datasets.

2   Related Work

2.1   Prior-Based Methods

Most conventional methods are based on the physical prior, estimate some important quantities (*e.g.*, the transmission map) in the model, and then recover a clear image from its cloud counterpart. Chavez [18] proposed an additive model to describe the generation principle of cloud images under the assumption that the distance between the sensor and the ground is fixed. He *et al.* [9] proposed a dark channel prior based on statistical laws, showing that the pixel value of one or more color channels tends to zero in the non-sky area of the image, which is used to estimate the transmission map. Fattal *et al.* [19] proposed a color-lines prior to estimate the transmission map based on the distribution of images in the RGB color space. Berman *et al.* [20] assumed that the color of a clear image can be approximated by hundreds of distinct colors, and proposed a dehazing algorithm based on this novel non-local prior. Xu *et al.* [21] proposed a method based on signal transmission and airspace hybrid analysis, combined with atmospheric scattering theory to remove clouds.

These prior knowledge-based methods show superior statistical properties in specific scenarios but fail easily in real-world images where physical assumptions do not hold.

2.2   Data-Driven Methods

In recent years, thanks to the establishment of large-scale datasets and the development of deep learning techniques, many data-driven supervised cloud removal methods have been proposed to overcome the shortcomings of traditional methods. Mao *et al.* [22] proposed a deep encoder-decoder framework and added skip connections to improve the efficiency of image restoration. Praveer Singh *et al.* [23] proposed an adversarial training-based network named Cloud-GAN to directly learn the mapping relationship between cloud and clear images.

Qin *et al.* [16] proposed a multi-scale deblurring convolutional neural network with the residual structure to remove the thin cloud. Li *et al.* [11] designed an end-to-end residual symmetric connection network for thin cloud removal. Xu *et al.* [10] introduced a generative adversarial network based on the attention mechanism to guide the network to invest more efforts in denser cloud regions.

Inspired by traditional methods, some researchers combine deep learning technology with imaging physical models. Cai *et al.* [14] showed that medium transmission estimation can be reformulated as a learnable end-to-end system. Ren *et al.* [24] used deep learning to learn the transmission map and solve atmospheric scattering model. Zheng *et al.* [17] combined the existing atmospheric scattering model with UNet to remove thin clouds. According to the additive model of cloud images, Zi *et al.* [13] utilized deep neural networks combined with the imaging model to achieve thin cloud removal.

Although these data-driven methods have made immense progress in thin cloud removal performance, all of them achieve a one-to-one mapping with respect to the input. They only found a reasonable one out of all the solutions to this multi-solution problem. Unlike existing methods, we treat single image cloud removal as an indeterminate solution problem. We combine cloud removal with uncertainty analysis to better solve this ill-posed problem.

3   Uncertainty Cloud Removal Framework

3.1   Analysis of Image Degradation Process

Several researchers [18, 25, 26] have proposed that the satellite image degradation process can be described as an additive model (1):

$$S = G + C. \tag{1}$$

or a non-linear model (2):

$$S = (1 - C) \cdot G + C. \tag{2}$$

where S, G, and C represent cloud images acquired by satellite sensors, clear ground scene images, and thin cloud thickness maps, respectively.

However, designing a network based on the explicit model raises two questions: whether the model fully conforms to the degradation process and whether the unknown variables can be estimated accurately. Both of these factors can affect the outcome of recovery and even lead to failure.

To tackle these problems, firstly, we do not rely on the atmosphere scattering model of satellite images. We note that these model-based algorithms have a common idea: estimate the unknown variables from the observed images and then combine the imaging model to restore clear images. In our method, we redefine the unobservable variables as degeneration factors, which results in low-quality images. The image degradation system is determined by the cloud image, clear image, and degradation factors. Instead of giving the relationship between these three variables, we leverage the powerful representation ability of the neural network to express implicitly.

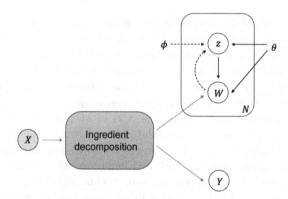

Fig. 1. The probabilistic graphical model for the degradation process of cloud images. The solid black line represents the generative model, and the dashed black line represents the variational approximation. θ and ϕ are the parameters of the model.

We analyze image degradation employing a probabilistic graphical model, as shown in Fig. 1. The observable variable X is the cloud image obtained by the satellite sensor, which can be decomposed into degeneration factors W and ground scene information Y. The ground scene Y is more complex and changeable, which results in describing its generation mechanism with a probability graph model is a challenging task. So it is more feasible to infer degeneration factors W from cloud images.

Since the essential intrinsic relationship between these three variables is unknown, variable W cannot be obtained explicitly. To get this crucial variable, we assume that the latent variable z determines its generation. Because the cloud image contains the information of degeneration factors, we estimate z through X and then generate W from a sampling of z.

Due to the diversity of the sampling process, multiple estimations can be generated. This diversity mitigates the problems caused by inaccurate estimations and makes the algorithm more robust.

The overall model framework is based on the CVAE, the inference network estimates the variational distribution, and the generative network achieves final cloud-free results.

The variational lower bound of the model is as follows (detailed derivation is available in supplementary material):

$$\log p_\theta(Y|X) = -D_{KL}(q_\phi(z|X)||p_\theta(z|X)) + \mathbb{E}_{q_\phi(z|X)}[\log p_\theta(Y|X,z)]. \quad (3)$$

where the proposal distribution $q_\phi(z|X)$ is introduced to approximate the posterior $p_\theta(z|X)$; the latent variable z drawn from $q_\phi(z|X)$. θ and ϕ represent the parameter set of distribution. Our CVAE framework is composed of a encoder network $q_\phi(z|X)$ and a generative encoder network $p_\theta(Y|X,z)$. The Kullback-Leibler (KL) Divergence $D_{KL}(q_\phi(z|X)||p_\theta(z|X))$ work as a regularization loss to narrow the gap between the posterior $p_\theta(z|X)$ and the proposal distribution

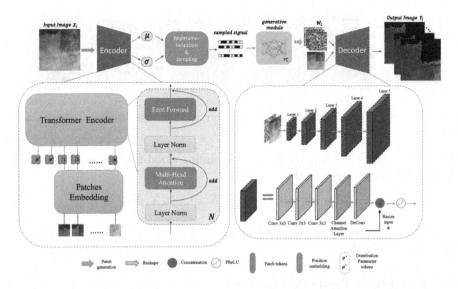

Fig. 2. An overview of the proposed cloud removal network. (1) The encoder network based on ViT learns the distribution of degradation factors W from cloud image X. (2) The decoder samples in the latent space with the reparameterization trick. Then the generative module utilizes the sampled signal to yield the image manifold of W. (3) Then, the combination of X and W is fed into the decoder network, which consists of five convolutional blocks of different scales. Each block contains convolution operation, channel attention, and deconvolution operation.

$q_\phi(z|X)$. To simplify the network and reduce computation, we assume that the posterior follows the standard normal distribution $\mathcal{N}(\mathbf{0}, \mathbf{I})$.

3.2 Transformer-Based Encoder

The encoder works as the recognition model to infer the proposal distribution $q_\phi(z|X)$. To allow the network can be trained using the gradient descent algorithm, z is drawn with the reparameterization trick, which is written as (4):

$$z = \mu + \sigma \cdot \varepsilon. \tag{4}$$

where $\varepsilon \sim \mathcal{N}(\mathbf{0}, \mathbf{I})$. This trick allows error backpropagation through the Gaussian latent variables, which is essential in the training process.

In designing the network architecture, we exploit the self-attention mechanism to learn the mapping between degeneration factors and standard normal distribution. Different from the original ViT [27], we design a more lightweight model, reducing the number of stacked layers of the transformer encoder, the embedding dimension, and the number of heads of the multi-head attention mechanism. Let $\mathcal{D} = \{X_i, Y_i^{ref}\}_{i=1}^N$ be the training dataset, where X_i denotes

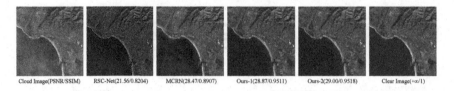

Cloud Image(PSNR/SSIM)   RSC-Net(21.56/0.8204)   MCRN(28.47/0.8907)   Ours-1(28.87/0.9511)   Ours-2(29.00/0.9518)   Clear Image(+∞/1)

Fig. 3. Results of the proposed algorithm. Our method can achieve a one-to-many mapping.

the cloud image, Y_i^{ref} denotes the corresponding cloud-free image. The goal of the encoder network is as follows:

$$\phi^* = \arg\min_{\phi} D_{KL}(q(z|X;\phi)||p(z|X;\theta)). \tag{5}$$

The whole pipeline of the encoder network during training and testing is illustrated in Fig. 2.

3.3 Multi-scale Prediction Decoder

With the latent variables z obtained by the inference network and the original input cloud image, we develop a decoder network to reconstruct the cloud-free image. In the decoder, the variable z is first passed through a generative module $p_\theta(W|z)$ (See Fig. 2), which contains a MLP with two hidden layers and generates the image manifold of degeneration factors W_i. The latent variables z allow for modeling multiple modes, making the decoder network suitable for modeling one-to-many mapping. As shown in Fig. 3, the clear images recovered from different sampling results are different in PSNR and SSIM scores.

We downsample the input cloud image X to the same size as W_i. After that, we concatenate these two variables and feed them to the first layer of the decoder network. The decoder network consists of five convolutional layers. Each layer focuses on extracting features and learning the underlying principles of de-clouding at different scales. The input to each layer is composed of the original cloud image as conditional variable and feature maps from the previous layer. We utilize the channel attention mechanism [28] to invest more learning attention on valuable matters.

The decoder network combines the latent variables z_i obtained by a single sampling and the original cloud image to produce a clear image. It can be written with the formula as $Y_i = f_D(X, z_i)$, where $f_D(\cdot)$ is the decoder network. We sample multiple variables z_i to produce multiple clear images corresponding to the original cloud image. We take the expectation of these multiple clear images as the final clear image. This procedure can be written as:

$$Y = \frac{1}{M}\sum_{i=1}^{M} Y_i. \tag{6}$$

where we set $M = 10$ and the goal is to maximize the posterior probability:

$$\theta^* = \arg\max_{\theta} \log p_\theta(Y|X, z). \tag{7}$$

3.4   Loss Function

The loss of the overall CVAE framework consists of two parts: the inference network and the decoder network. Combining (5) and (7), it can be formulated as follow:

$$\mathcal{L}_{CVAE} = D_{KL}(q_\phi(z|X)||p_\theta(z|X)) + \frac{1}{M}\sum_{m=1}^{M} -\log p_\theta(Y|X, z^{(m)}). \qquad (8)$$

where M is the number of samples. The first term in the loss function is the KL divergence. We assume that $q_\phi(z|X)$ obeys a normal distribution with parameters μ, $\sigma^2 I$, and $p_\theta(z|X)$ obeys the standard normal distribution, then this loss can directly calculate the closed-form solution:

$$D_{KL}(q(z|X;\phi)||p(z|X;\theta)) = \frac{1}{2}(tr(\sigma^2 I) + \mu^T\mu - d - \log(|\sigma^2 I|)). \qquad (9)$$

where the $tr(\cdot)$, $|\cdot|$ represent the trace and determinant of the matrix, respectively, d is the dimensions of the distribution.

The second term is the reconstruction loss. In supervised training, the declouding performance can be quantified by counting the differences between the encoder network output Y with its corresponding reference clear image Y^{ref} under some proper loss L, e.g. the L_1 norm and Mean Square Error (MSE). In our method, we choose SmoothL1Loss as the criterion to optimize the parameters and the reconstruction loss can be expressed as:

$$\mathcal{L}_{rec} = \frac{1}{CP}\sum_{c=1}^{C}\sum_{p=1}^{P} F_s((Y_c(p) - Y_c^{ref}(p)); \beta). \qquad (10)$$

where

$$F_s(e; \beta) = \begin{cases} 0.5e^2/\beta & if \ |e| < \beta, \\ |e| - \beta/2 & otherwise. \end{cases} \qquad (11)$$

C represents the channel number and P denotes the total number of pixels.

In addition, to guide the network to focus on details, we introduce an edge loss function to preserve the edges of the output image. The edge loss is defined as:

$$\mathcal{L}_{edge} = \left\|\nabla^2 Y - \nabla^2 Y^{ref}\right\|. \qquad (12)$$

where ∇^2 is the Laplace operator for image edge detection.

Based on the above consideration, the total loss function for the proposed CVAE cloud removal network is as follows:

$$\mathcal{L} = \lambda_1 D_{KL} + \lambda_2\mathcal{L}_{rec} + \lambda_3\mathcal{L}_{edge}. \qquad (13)$$

where λ_1, λ_2, and λ_3 represent the weight parameters.

4 Experiments

To demonstrate the superiority of the proposed algorithm, we compare it with several state-of-the-art methods including the prior-based method (DCP [9]), the data-driven methods (RSC-Net [11], SPA-GAN [29], MSAR-DefogNet [12], PCFAN [30], Pix2Pix [31]), and the methods combining deep learning with physical models (MCRN [32], Qin *et al.* [16], Zheng *et al.* [17]). For fair comparisons, we train these networks on the same dataset with the same learning rate and the number of training epochs. We use full-reference image quality evaluation metrics PSNR and SSIM [33] and no-reference evaluation metrics NIQE [34] and BRISQUE [35] for quantitative evaluation.

4.1 Dataset

To overcome the limitation of synthetic datasets for thin cloud removal, we collect a real scene image dataset called T-CLOUD. Both training and test sets are from Landsat 8 RGB images. Our dataset contains 2939 doublets of cloud images and their clear counterpart separated by one satellite re-entry period (16 days). We select the image pairs which has similar lighting conditions and crop them into 256 x 256 patches. We split the dataset with a ratio of 8:2, with 2351 images in the training set and 588 images in the test set.

There are three main characteristics in the proposed dataset: (1) T-CLOUD is a large-scale natural benchmark for remote sensing image thin cloud removal while the previous datasets are only composed of synthetic data; (2) T-CLOUD includes many different ground scenarios such as cities, mountains, and coasts; (3) The proposed dataset is much more challenging because the cloud is non-homogeneous and the texture details of the image are more complex.

Note that these cloud and cloud-free image pairs are captured by the same satellite sensor at different times, the illumination noises are unavoidable due to the change of ambient light. Although we try to select images with the same lighting conditions as possible, achieving outstanding results on this dataset is still a challenging task.

4.2 Implementation Details

The proposed algorithm is implemented with the PyTorch framework. The hardware facilities of the computing platform include an Intel Gold 6252 CPU and an NVIDIA A100 GPU. To optimize the proposed network, we use the Adam optimizer [36] with parameters $\beta_1 = 0.5$, $\beta_2 = 0.999$. The batch size and training epochs are set to 1 and 300, respectively. The initial learning rate is set to 0.0001, which decreases by 10 times after training for half the number of epochs. We set the size of the interference factor image manifold to 16 x 16. The values of the parameters λ_1, λ_2, and λ_3 are empirically set to 0.01, 1.0 and 0.18, respectively.

Table 1. Quantitative Evaluations on the real-world dataset. Where bold texts and underlined texts indicate the best and second-best performance, respectively. ↑: The larger the better. ↓: The smaller the better.

Method	PSNR↑	SSIM↑	NIQE↓	BRISQUE↓
DCP	19.94	0.6646	3.300	53.60
Qin *et al.*	26.35	0.8035	3.306	**47.39**
RSC-Net	23.98	0.7596	3.407	50.24
SPA-GAN	15.36	0.5280	2.860	56.90
Zheng *et al.*	23.71	0.7630	2.969	51.01
MSAR-DefogNet	<u>28.84</u>	0.8432	2.786	51.07
PCFAN	28.27	0.8342	2.800	50.69
MCRN	26.60	0.8091	2.888	50.73
Pix2Pix	28.77	<u>0.8476</u>	**2.677**	50.77
Ours	**30.14**	**0.8600**	<u>2.762</u>	<u>49.61</u>

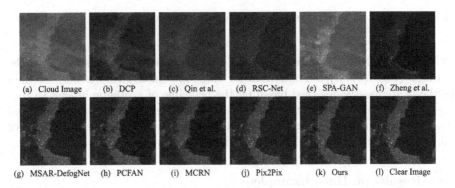

(a) Cloud Image   (b) DCP   (c) Qin et al.   (d) RSC-Net   (e) SPA-GAN   (f) Zheng et al.

(g) MSAR-DefogNet   (h) PCFAN   (i) MCRN   (j) Pix2Pix   (k) Ours   (l) Clear Image

Fig. 4. Thin cloud removal results of the real-world cloud image. Zoom in for a better view. More examples can be found in supplementary material.

4.3 Results on Real Dataset

Table 1 shows the quantitative results in terms of PSNR, SSIM, NIQE, and BRISQUE on our dataset. It can be seen that our method achieves the best performance on both the full-reference metrics PSNR and SSIM. Also in the no-reference metrics, excellent results have been achieved.

For evaluating the visual effect of each method, we compare the qualitative results (see Fig. 4). It can be observed that DCP tends to over-enhance the cloud image and is unable to remove the dense cloud. The CNN-based methods achieve competitive results, however, some of them are still poor in visual quality. For example, restoration results of Qin *et al.* and RSC-Net miss a lot of detailed information. SPA-GAN fails to remove the cloud. The method of Zheng *et al.* has some obvious grid artifacts. The de-clouding results by MSAR-DefogNet,

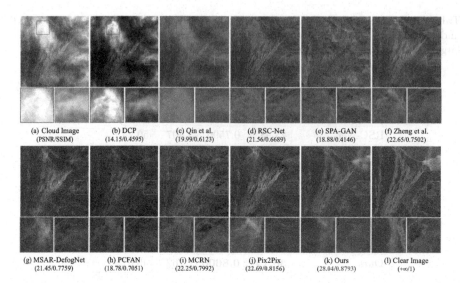

| (a) Cloud Image (PSNR/SSIM) | (b) DCP (14.15/0.4595) | (c) Qin et al. (19.99/0.6123) | (d) RSC-Net (21.56/0.6689) | (e) SPA-GAN (18.88/0.4146) | (f) Zheng et al. (22.65/0.7502) |

| (g) MSAR-DefogNet (21.45/0.7759) | (h) PCFAN (18.78/0.7051) | (i) MCRN (22.25/0.7992) | (j) Pix2Pix (22.69/0.8156) | (k) Ours (28.04/0.8793) | (l) Clear Image (+∞/1) |

Fig. 5. Thin cloud removal results of the hard examples. Zoom in for a better view.

PCFAN, MCRN, and Pix2Pix have different degrees of color distortion in the sea area (Fig. 4(g)–4(j)). The reason for these low-quality results may be their methods are mostly designed based on the principle of synthetic images so that the underlying cloud removal laws cannot be well learned on real-world cloud images. In contrast, the result of our method shown in Fig. 4(k) has high color fidelity and is more effective in texture detail preservation.

4.4 Results on Hard Examples

One of the most distinctive characteristics of clouds is that they are heterogeneous. We further select some images with thick clouds and evaluate our method on this non-homogeneous dataset. The uneven cloud images are very common in remote sensing images. Therefore, comparing the performance of different methods on these challenging data can verify their effectiveness in practical applications.

The visual results are illustrated in Fig. 6. The result produced by RSC-Net suffers from severe color distortion. The GAN-based method SPA-GAN fails to keep the semantic information consistent. Zheng *et al.*, MSAR-DefogNet, PCFAN, MCRN, and Pix2Pix yield unnatural results with varying degrees of color distortion. Recovering details under thick clouds is highly uncertain due to the heavy loss of scenario information. Our method keeps the semantic information as consistent as possible through probability estimation. It can be observed that our algorithm can effectively mitigate color distortion compared to other methods. The quantitative results also demonstrate that our method has overwhelming advantages. It is much higher than other methods in terms of PSNR

Table 2. Quantitative Evaluations on the clear images.

	DCP	Qin et al.	RSC-Net	SPA-GAN	Zheng et al.	MSAR-DefogNet	PCFAN	MCRN	Pix2-Pix	Ours
PSNR↑	21.46	22.87	25.99	15.77	28.21	27.78	25.43	26.14	28.01	**28.76**
SSIM↑	0.8585	0.7018	0.9079	0.6237	0.9268	0.9174	0.8948	0.8999	0.9224	**0.9448**

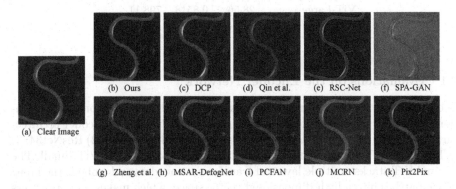

(a) Clear Image

(b) Ours   (c) DCP   (d) Qin et al.   (e) RSC-Net   (f) SPA-GAN

(g) Zheng et al. (h) MSAR-DefogNet (i) PCFAN   (j) MCRN   (k) Pix2Pix

Fig. 6. The visual comparison of image fidelity on the clear image. Zoom in for a better view.

and SSIM. Our PSNR is higher than the Pix2Pix with 5.35dB showing that the CVAE framework is more robust in such scenarios.

4.5   Results on Clear Dataset

To further verify the fidelity of our algorithm, we additionally compare the results of various de-clouding methods on a clear image dataset. The visual comparisons are shown in Fig. 5. It can be observed that several methods (DCP, Qin et al., MSAR-DefogNet, PCFAN) tend to over-darken or over-enhance the clear image and are inconsistent in the color space. The checkerboard artifacts can be observed in Zheng et al. and SPA-GAN changes the original scene radiance information. Our result does not produce color distortion and is very close to the original clear image, which is necessary for practical applications because not all image patches obtained by satellite sensors are occluded by clouds. Table 2 shows the quantitative results. The PSNR and SSIM values also indicate that our algorithm surpasses other methods in terms of image fidelity.

5   Ablation Study

To further demonstrate the effectiveness of the proposed algorithm, we conduct ablation experiments to verify whether the network structure is effective. The ablation experiments are divided into the following parts: 1) the structure of the encoder network; and 2) the choice of the reconstruction loss function.

Table 3. Ablation studies on the structure of encoder network.

Encoder-Network	PSNR↑	SSIM↑	Size(Mb)
ResNet34	28.42	0.8512	<u>111.95</u>
VGG-19	28.37	0.8495	567.71
ViT-Base	28.44	0.8501	244.31
ViT-Large	<u>28.56</u>	<u>0.8518</u>	798.11
ViT-Small (Ours)	**30.14**	**0.8600**	**58.86**

5.1 Evaluations on the Encoder Network

In our method, the encoder network is used to infer the distribution of degeneration factors. First, we conducted ablations on the structures of encoder architecture. The configurations of variant models including: 1) VGG-19; 2) ResNet34; 3) ViT-base; 4) ViT-Large; 5) a ViT variant model proposed by us: ViT-Small. The original ViT stacks multiple layers of transformer encoders and embeds the input image patches into a high-dimensional vector space, which makes its parameters very large. To make the network more lightweight, we design the ViT-Small, which simplifies the original transformer structure. We reduce the stacking layers of the encoder from 12 (ViT-Base) or 24 (ViT-Large) to 4, the embedding dimension of the image patches from 768 (ViT-Base) or 1024 (ViT-Large) to 512, and set the number of heads of the multi-head attention mechanism to 8.

The quantitative results are shown in Table 3. The CNN-based architectures achieve similar performance. However, they are worse than the three ViT structures, which indicates that the self-attention mechanism of ViT can better learn the distribution of degeneration factors in the latent space. Meanwhile, we also noticed that the parameter amount of ViT-Small is much lower than the other four structures. The lightweight ViT not only did not weaken the powerful representation ability but also made the model better. This indicates that this lightweight variant of vision transformer in the inference network is effective.

5.2 Evaluations on the Reconstruction Loss Function

We also explore the influence of different reconstruction loss functions in the optimization process. The reconstruction loss directly measures the quality of the cloud removal effect. Therefore, choosing a good measurement criterion plays a crucial role in the training process.

We compare the impact of MSE and SmoothL1 (beta = 0.5) loss function and verify the boosting effect of the edge loss. For a quick comparative experiment, the models with different loss functions are trained for 150 epochs. The experimental results are shown in Fig. 7. It can be seen that the SmoothL1 loss function achieves better optimization results in PSNR and SSIM during the training process. The SSIM shows that the optimization results are significantly improved

Table 4. Ablation studies on the reconstruction loss function.

	SmoothL1	MSE	Edge Loss	PSNR↑	SSIM↑
1	–	✓	–	27.14	0.8293
2	✓	–	–	27.57	0.8302
3	–	✓	✓	27.70	0.8417
4	✓	–	✓	**27.83**	**0.8421**

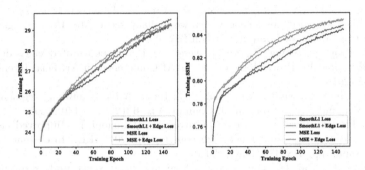

Fig. 7. Graph of PSNR and SSIM with different objective function during training process.

after adding the edge loss, which demonstrates the edge loss can promote the optimization of the network.

We also tested the generalization performance to verify that achieving superior performance on the training set is not due to overfitting. It can be seen from Table 4 that the model trained with SmoothL1 joint edge loss on the test set also has better PSNR and SSIM scores. At the same time, the higher SSIM shows that the edge loss can make the model pay more attention to the detailed textures.

6   Conclusion

In this paper, we propose a thin cloud removal network based on CVAE and tackle single image de-clouding from the perspective of uncertainty analysis. The novelty of the proposed algorithm is that it can achieve one-to-many mapping, and can generate multiple clear and reasonable images corresponding to a single cloud image. Moreover, we construct a large-scale dataset from the real world to overcome the shortcomings of synthetic datasets that cannot fully represent real scenes. Both quantitative and qualitative experimental results show the superiority of our proposed method and demonstrate that considering uncertainty has great potential to improve the thin cloud removal algorithm.

Acknowledgements. This work was supported in part by the National Key Research and Development Program of China under Grant 2019YFC1510905 and in part by the National Natural Science Foundation of China under Grant 61871011.

References

1. Li, B., et al.: Benchmarking single-image dehazing and beyond. IEEE Trans. Image Process. **28**(1), 492–505 (2018)
2. Zhang, Z., Zhao, L., Liu, Y., Zhang, S., Yang, J.: Unified density-aware image dehazing and object detection in real-world hazy scenes. In: Proceedings of the Asian Conference on Computer Vision (2020)
3. Li, B., Peng, X., Wang, Z., Xu, J., Feng, D.: End-to-end united video dehazing and detection. In: Proceedings of the AAAI Conference on Artificial Intelligence, vol. 32 (2018)
4. Tu, Z., Chen, X., Yuille, A.L., Zhu, S.C.: Image parsing: unifying segmentation, detection, and recognition. Int. J. Comput. Vis. **63**(2), 113–140 (2005)
5. Tarel, J.P., Hautiere, N., Cord, A., Gruyer, D., Halmaoui, H.: Improved visibility of road scene images under heterogeneous fog. In: 2010 IEEE Intelligent Vehicles Symposium, pp. 478–485. IEEE (2010)
6. Sakaridis, C., Dai, D., Van Gool, L.: Semantic foggy scene understanding with synthetic data. Int. J. Comput. Vis. **126**(9), 973–992 (2018)
7. Richter, R.: A spatially adaptive fast atmospheric correction algorithm. Int. J. Remote Sens. **17**(6), 1201–1214 (1996)
8. Vermote, E.F., Tanré, D., Deuze, J.L., Herman, M., Morcette, J.J.: Second simulation of the satellite signal in the solar spectrum, 6s: an overview. IEEE Trans. Geosci. Remote Sens. **35**(3), 675–686 (1997)
9. He, K., Sun, J., Tang, X.: Single image haze removal using dark channel prior. IEEE Trans. Pattern Anal. Mach. Intell. **33**(12), 2341–2353 (2010)
10. Xu, M., Deng, F., Jia, S., Jia, X., Plaza, A.J.: Attention mechanism-based generative adversarial networks for cloud removal in landsat images. Remote Sens. Environ. **271**, 112902 (2022)
11. Li, W., Li, Y., Chen, D., Chan, J.C.W.: Thin cloud removal with residual symmetrical concatenation network. ISPRS J. Photogramm. Remote. Sens. **153**, 137–150 (2019)
12. Zhou, Y., Jing, W., Wang, J., Chen, G., Scherer, R., Damaševičius, R.: MSAR-DefogNet: lightweight cloud removal network for high resolution remote sensing images based on multi scale convolution. IET Image Proc. **16**(3), 659–668 (2022)
13. Zi, Y., Xie, F., Zhang, N., Jiang, Z., Zhu, W., Zhang, H.: Thin cloud removal for multispectral remote sensing images using convolutional neural networks combined with an imaging model. IEEE J. Sel. Top. Appl. Earth Observations Remote Sens. **14**, 3811–3823 (2021)
14. Cai, B., Xu, X., Jia, K., Qing, C., Tao, D.: DehazeNet: an end-to-end system for single image haze removal. IEEE Trans. Image Process. **25**(11), 5187–5198 (2016)
15. Li, B., Peng, X., Wang, Z., Xu, J., Feng, D.: AOD-Net: all-in-one dehazing network. In: Proceedings of the IEEE International Conference on Computer Vision, pp. 4770–4778 (2017)
16. Qin, M., Xie, F., Li, W., Shi, Z., Zhang, H.: Dehazing for multispectral remote sensing images based on a convolutional neural network with the residual architecture. IEEE J. Sel. Top. Appl. Earth Observations Remote Sens. **11**(5), 1645–1655 (2018)

17. Zheng, J., Liu, X.Y., Wang, X.: Single image cloud removal using U-net and generative adversarial networks. IEEE Trans. Geosci. Remote Sens. **59**(8), 6371–6385 (2020)
18. Chavez, P.S., Jr.: An improved dark-object subtraction technique for atmospheric scattering correction of multispectral data. Remote Sens. Environ. **24**(3), 459–479 (1988)
19. Fattal, R.: Dehazing using color-lines. ACM Trans. Graph. (TOG) **34**(1), 1–14 (2014)
20. Berman, D., Avidan, S., et al.: Non-local image dehazing. In: Proceedings of the IEEE Conference on Computer Vision and Pattern Recognition, pp. 1674–1682 (2016)
21. Xu, M., Pickering, M., Plaza, A.J., Jia, X.: Thin cloud removal based on signal transmission principles and spectral mixture analysis. IEEE Trans. Geosci. Remote Sens. **54**(3), 1659–1669 (2015)
22. Mao, X., Shen, C., Yang, Y.B.: Image restoration using very deep convolutional encoder-decoder networks with symmetric skip connections. In: Advances in Neural Information Processing Systems, vol. 29 (2016)
23. Singh, P., Komodakis, N.: Cloud-GAN: cloud removal for sentinel-2 imagery using a cyclic consistent generative adversarial networks. In: 2018 IEEE International Geoscience and Remote Sensing Symposium, IGARSS 2018, pp. 1772–1775. IEEE (2018)
24. Ren, W., Liu, S., Zhang, H., Pan, J., Cao, X., Yang, M.-H.: Single image dehazing via multi-scale convolutional neural networks. In: Leibe, B., Matas, J., Sebe, N., Welling, M. (eds.) ECCV 2016. LNCS, vol. 9906, pp. 154–169. Springer, Cham (2016). https://doi.org/10.1007/978-3-319-46475-6_10
25. Makarau, A., Richter, R., Müller, R., Reinartz, P.: Haze detection and removal in remotely sensed multispectral imagery. IEEE Trans. Geosci. Remote Sens. **52**(9), 5895–5905 (2014)
26. Narasimhan, S.G., Nayar, S.K.: Vision and the atmosphere. Int. J. Comput. Vis. **48**(3), 233–254 (2002)
27. Dosovitskiy, A., et al.: An image is worth 16×16 words: transformers for image recognition at scale. arXiv preprint arXiv:2010.11929 (2020)
28. Hu, J., Shen, L., Sun, G.: Squeeze-and-excitation networks. In: Proceedings of the IEEE Conference on Computer Vision and Pattern Recognition, pp. 7132–7141 (2018)
29. Pan, H.: Cloud removal for remote sensing imagery via spatial attention generative adversarial network. arXiv preprint arXiv:2009.13015 (2020)
30. Zhang, X., Wang, T., Wang, J., Tang, G., Zhao, L.: Pyramid channel-based feature attention network for image dehazing. Comput. Vis. Image Underst. **197**, 103003 (2020)
31. Isola, P., Zhu, J.Y., Zhou, T., Efros, A.A.: Image-to-image translation with conditional adversarial networks. In: Proceedings of the IEEE Conference on Computer Vision and Pattern Recognition, pp. 1125–1134 (2017)
32. Yu, W., Zhang, X., Pun, M.O., Liu, M.: A hybrid model-based and data-driven approach for cloud removal in satellite imagery using multi-scale distortion-aware networks. In: 2021 IEEE International Geoscience and Remote Sensing Symposium IGARSS, pp. 7160–7163. IEEE (2021)
33. Wang, Z., Bovik, A.C., Sheikh, H.R., Simoncelli, E.P.: Image quality assessment: from error visibility to structural similarity. IEEE Trans. Image Process. **13**(4), 600–612 (2004)

34. Mittal, A., Soundararajan, R., Bovik, A.C.: Making a "completely blind" image quality analyzer. IEEE Signal Process. Lett. **20**(3), 209–212 (2012)
35. Mittal, A., Moorthy, A.K., Bovik, A.C.: No-reference image quality assessment in the spatial domain. IEEE Trans. Image Process. **21**(12), 4695–4708 (2012)
36. Kingma, D.P., Ba, J.: Adam: a method for stochastic optimization. arXiv preprint arXiv:1412.6980 (2014)

Blind Image Super-Resolution with Degradation-Aware Adaptation

Yue Wang[1], Jiawen Ming[1], Xu Jia[1(✉)], James H. Elder[2], and Huchuan Lu[1(✉)]

[1] Dalian University of Technology, Dalian 116024, China
{xjia,lhchuan}@dlut.edu.cn
[2] York University, Toronto M3J 1P3, Canada

Abstract. Most existing super-resolution (SR) methods are designed to restore high resolution (HR) images from certain low resolution (LR) images with a simple degradation, *e.g.* bicubic downsampling. Their generalization capability to real-world degradation is limited because it often couples several degradation factors such as noise and blur. To solve this problem, existing blind SR methods rely on either explicit degradation estimation or translation to bicubicly downsampled LR images, where inaccurate estimation or translation would severely deteriorate the SR performance. In this paper, we propose a plug-and-play module, which could be applied to any existing image super-resolution model for feature-level adaptation to improve the generalization ability to real-world degraded images. Specifically, a degradation encoder is proposed to compute an implicit degradation representation with a ranking loss based on the degradation level as supervision. The degradation representation then works as a kind of condition and is applied to the existing image super-resolution model pretrained on bicubicly downsampled LR images through the proposed region-aware modulation. With the proposed method, the base super-resolution model could be fine-tuned to adapt to the condition of degradation representation for further improvement. Experimental results on both synthetic and real-world datasets show that the proposed image SR method with compact model size performs favorably against state-of-the-art methods. Our source code is publicly available at https://github.com/wangyue7777/blindsr_daa.

Keywords: Blind super-resolution · Multiple unknown degradations · Feature-level adaptation · Ranking loss · Region-aware modulation

1 Introduction

Single Image Super-Resolution (SISR) aims at predicting high-resolution (HR) images with high-frequency details from their corresponding low-resolution (LR)

Partially supported by the Natural Science Foundation of China, No. 62106036, and the Fundamental Research Funds for the Central University of China, DUT21RC(3)026.

Supplementary Information The online version contains supplementary material available at https://doi.org/10.1007/978-3-031-26313-2_5.

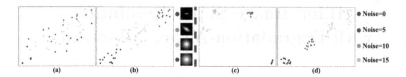

Fig. 1. An illustration of the degradation representation supervised by contrastive loss in [28] (a, c), and the proposed ranking loss (b, d) with different blur kernels (left) and noise levels (right) on Set14. Ranking loss can not only separate different degradations, but also provide information of degradation level.

images. Inspired by the success of deep learning, numerous existing SR methods [2,14,21] apply CNN-based models to effectively restore the HR image based on a fixed and known degradation (*e.g.* bicubic downsampling). However, these methods may have limited generalization to real-world situation where multiple degradations with unknown blur, downsampler, and noise are coupled together.

To address the SR problem with multiple degradations, several non-blind and blind SR approaches have been proposed. Most non-blind methods [3,23,31,34] usually require both LR image and its explicit ground-truth degradation as inputs to predict the corresponding HR image. While most blind methods [13,19,22] conduct the explicit degradation estimation first and then combine with non-blind SR methods to restore HR images. However, when dealing with unknown degradation at inference stage, it may be difficult for these non-blind and blind approaches to give reasonable performance. Inaccurate explicit degradation would seriously deteriorate the performance of HR image restoration.

Instead of explicitly estimating degradation of an LR image, a new attempt called DASR [28] has been made to implicitly learn degradation representation in feature space with a degradation encoder following contrastive learning fashion [6,12] for blind SR. Such degradation representation can distinguish various degradations and lead to a degradation-aware SR model. However, the degradation encoder is only taught to distinguish one from the other without being aware of whether its degradation is heavier than the other, which is more important in adjusting an SR model to adapt to certain degradation.

On the other hand, designing and training powerful SR models for bicubic downsampling degradation has already cost a lot of human and computation resources. However, data distribution gap between bicubicly downsampled images and images with more practical degradations, prevents those existing pretrained SR models from being generalized well to LR images with multiple degradations. There have been several works [15,24] that take advantages of these existing SR models pretrained on bicubicly downsampled images to promote the development of SR models for real-world degradations. Image translation techniques [9,16,38] are employed to convert images of interesting degradations to bicubicly downsampled ones and then those converted images are fed to existing pretrained SR models for HR restoration. However, the imperfect translation would cause performance drop in the process of restoring HR image and produce many artifacts.

In this work, we propose a plug-and-play module for blind SR, which can be applied to any existing SR models pretrained on bicubicly downsampled data. It provides degradation-aware feature-level adaptation to improve the generalization ability to real-world degraded images. It consists of three components: the pretrained SR model, a degradation encoder followed by a ranker, and a degradation-aware modulation module. Specifically, the degradation encoder computes a latent degradation representation such that the SR model can be adapted to various degradation. Ranking loss is imposed on top to make correct decision on estimating the degree of degradation in an image as illustrated in Fig. 1. To make an existing SR model adapt to various degradations, the degradation representation works as a condition to apply the proposed degradation-aware modulation to the intermediate features of SR model. Even if the degradation is spatially-invariant, different types of textures may have different sensitivity to the degradation. Hence, the modulation is designed to be region-aware and sample-specific. It allows a region in an LR image to be super-resolved adaptively not only to different degradations but also to content of the image. To further improve its performance, the pretrained SR model is fine-tuned together with the degradation encoder and modulation module. With an existing pretrained light-weight SR model as our SR model, we can obtain a compact SR model that performs favorably against existing blind SR models of larger model size.

Main contributions of this work are three-fold.

- We come up with a novel plug-and-play module for blind SR. It can provide degradation-aware feature-level adaptation for any existing SR network pretrained with the degradation of only bicubic downsampling to improve the generalization ability to various degraded images.
- We propose a ranking loss for extracting degradation representation with information of the degradation degree, and a dynamic region-aware modulation for adaptation on intermediate features within the pretrained SR network.
- Our method has relatively compact model size and performs favorably against the state-of-the-art SR methods on both synthetic and real-world datasets.

2 Related Work

SR with a Simple Degradation. Early SR methods focus on LR images with a simple degradation, *e.g.* bicubic downsampling. Since [7], numerous SR methods apply CNN-based networks to improve performance. [21,36] enhance the results by utilizing deep residual networks with excessive convolutions layers. [14,18] design lightweight networks for SR to save the computational costs, while preserving good SR quality. However, these methods can not generalize well on real-world LR images which couples multiple unknown degradations.

SR with Various Degradations. To address this problem, several non-blind methods [3,23,31,34] have been proposed to use the explicit ground-truth degradation as inputs for HR restoration. However, they have limited applications since the explicit ground-truth degradation may be unknown during inference.

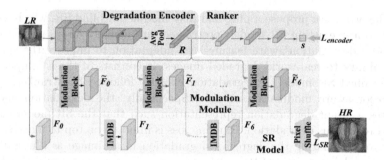

Fig. 2. The structure of our overall method. It contains a degradation encoder with a ranker; an SR model pretrained on bicubicly downsampled LR images; and a degradation-aware modulation module with several modulation blocks.

Recently, blind SR methods have been investigated to avoid requiring the explicit ground-truth degradation as input during inference. Several methods [13,19,20, 22] apply the explicit degradation estimation for assisting the HR restoration. [19] first predicts the kernel from LR image, and then applies a non-blind SR method using both the estimated kernel and LR image as inputs. [13] adopts a deep alternating network where the kernel estimation and HR restoration can be alternately and repeatedly optimized. Meanwhile, [15] estimates the correction filter and [24] uses Generative Adversarial Network (GAN) for image translation to transfer the LR image to look like a bicubicly downsampled one, which can then be fed to any existing SR model pretrained on bicubicly downsampled LR images for HR restoration. However, these non-blind methods are sensitive to the degradation estimation or image translation so that any errors happened in these processes would severely deteriorate the SR performance. A novel strategy for blind SR is to learn an implicit degradation representation [28] with contrastive learning, and build a fixed SR structure with dozens of modulation blocks for generating HR image with specific information of degradation.

Meanwhile, blind SR methods with other alternative ways have been proposed. [29,32,37] try to improve the generalization capability of any SR models by generating a large number of synthetic data for training. Specially, [29,32] design practical degradation models by considering the real-life degradation processes, while [37] uses GAN [10] to generate realistic blur-kernels. The self-supervised internal learning can also be used for blind SR [25,26]. [25] applies zero-shot learning by training a small image-specific CNN at test time, while [26] further applies meta-transfer learning [8] to decrease the gradient steps.

In this paper, we propose a novel flexible plug-and-play module for blind SR. It can be applied on any existing SR networks pretrained with the degradation of only bicubic downsampling to improve its generalization ability to real-world degraded images. Our method requires implicit degradation representation learning for degradation-aware modulation with two improvements. Firstly, we use a ranking loss instead of contrastive learning, which can provide the degree level of a degradation. Secondly, we propose a region-aware modulation instead of uniformly modulating features on all spatial positions.

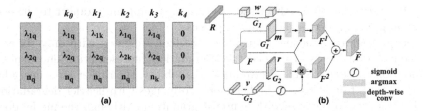

Fig. 3. Details of the proposed method. (a) Data preparation for training degradation encoder. Two kinds of patches are cropped from an HR image to apply various degradations and form q and k_i. (b) The structure of degradation-aware modulation block. It consists of two types of dynamic region-aware modulation: a depth-wise convolution and a channel-wise attention.

3 Method

3.1 Problem Formulation

In this work, we focus on blind super-resolution with various unknown degradations. The degradation model can be formulated as:

$$I^{LR} = (I^{HR} \otimes kernel) \downarrow_{sf} + noise, \qquad (1)$$

where I^{HR} is the original HR image, I^{LR} is the degraded LR image. $kernel$, $noise$, $\downarrow_{sf}$ and $\otimes$ denote the blur kernel, noise, downsampling operation with scaling factor of sf and convolution operation. Following [28], we apply bicubic downsampling, the anisotropic Gaussian kernels and Additive White Gaussian Noise to synthesize LR images for training. The anisotropic Gaussian kernel we use is characterized by a Gaussian probability density function $N(0, \Sigma)$, which means it has zero mean and varying covariance matrix Σ. Therefore, the blur kernel can be determined by two eigenvalues λ_1, λ_2, and rotation angle θ of its Σ. The Additive White Gaussian Noise can be determined by its noise level n.

Given an existing SR model pretrained on LR-HR pairs with only bicubic downsampling as degradation, the goal of our method is to adapt this pretrained SR model to work on images with various unknown degradations. To achieve this purpose, we introduce a framework which consists of three parts: a pretrained base SR model, a light degradation encoder with ranker, and a degradation-aware modulation module with several light modulation blocks. The structure of this end-to-end system is shown in Fig. 2.

3.2 Weakly Supervised Degradation Encoder

Instead of explicitly estimating parameters for various degradations, the goal of a degradation encoder is to distinguish various degradations and to make estimation about degradation levels. A very recent work called DASR [28] makes initial attempt in computing degradation representation by means of contrastive learning. However, the degradation representation can only distinguish various degradations among images but can not tell which image is more severely degraded than the other. To address this issue, we propose to append a ranker to the end of degradation encoder in the training process.

Both degradation encoder and ranker are light-weighted with only six and four convolution layers. To make the degradation representation encoded by degradation encoder of high discriminative capability, the ranker after degradation encoder is taught to give higher scores to images with heavier degradation and lower scores to the ones with lighter degradation. Although the model does not need exact degradation parameters as supervision, it requires order relation between a pair of images on level of degradation. Therefore, we need to prepare images with various degradation levels to train degradation encoder and ranker.

Data Preparation. According to Eq. 1, when generating I^{LR} from I^{HR}, the degradation is determined by four parameters: $\lambda_1, \lambda_2, \theta$ for blur, and n for noise. Here we use λ_1, λ_2 and n to determine the ranking order of different degradations since degradation with larger values of them would have higher degree level. While θ only affects the rotation, not the degree of degradation.

For each I^{HR}, we randomly extract two types of patches to apply various degradations. The first kind of patch is used to generate a query LR image q, and the second kind of patch is used to generate five key LR images as k_i for calculating the loss for encoder, where $i \in \{0, 1 \ldots 4\}$. Two sets of degradation parameters are randomly selected for query patches and key patches, which are indicated as $P_q = \{\lambda_{1q}, \lambda_{2q}, n_q\}$ and $P_k = \{\lambda_{1k}, \lambda_{2k}, n_k\}$. P_q is used as the degradation parameters for generating q and k_0 separately for two patches so that these two LR images contain different contents but the same degradation. Then, we generate degraded key patches k_i ($i \in \{1, 2, 3\}$) by P_{k_i}, where $P_{k_i}[i] = P_k[i]$ and the other two parameters remain the same as P_q, so that only one parameter of k_i is different from q. Finally, we generate k_4 by using only bicubic downsampling as degradation. It is used as a baseline for other LR images with degradation indicated as $P_{k_4} = \{0, 0, 0\}$ since it does not have any blur and noise. The degradation parameters of q and all k_i are shown in Fig. 3(a).

Ranking-Based Supervision. The degradation encoder and ranker produce both degradation representations and ranking scores for the generated LR images. The degradation representations are indicated as $R_q \in \mathbb{R}^C$ and $R_{k_i} \in \mathbb{R}^C$ which are used for modulation, while the ranking scores s_q and s_{k_i} are just numbers for calculating the loss for encoder.

First of all, we calculate the ranking loss by q, k_1, k_2 and k_3 in a pair-wise manner. Given q and each k_i, here $i \in \{1, 2, 3\}$, only the value of i-th parameter for the degradation is different. So it is easy to decide the ground-truth ranking order for these two images as:

$$\begin{cases} s_q < s_{k_i} & if \quad P_q[i] < P_{k_i}[i] \\ s_q > s_{k_i} & if \quad P_q[i] > P_{k_i}[i] \end{cases} \qquad (2)$$

Therefore, we train our degradation encoder by a margin-ranking loss [35] to guide the output ranking scores to have the right order:

$$L_{rank_1} = \sum_{i=1}^{3} max(0, (s_q - s_{k_i}) * \gamma + \varepsilon)$$

$$where \quad \begin{cases} \gamma = 1 & if \quad P_q[i] < P_{k_i}[i] \\ \gamma = -1 & if \quad P_q[i] > P_{k_i}[i] \end{cases}$$

(3)

where γ indicates the ground-truth order between q and k_i, ε is the margin which controls the distance between two scores. By forcing the ranking scores to have the right order, it encourages the degradation representations to encode information about degradation and its level for later degradation-aware modulation. With an appropriate margin ε, our ranking loss can also encourage distinguishing degradation representations between LR images degraded in different ways.

Meanwhile, we also force LR images with the same degradation to have the same ranking score. It is achieved by using L1 loss ($L1$) to supervise the ranking score s_q and s_{k_0} of q and k_0 to have the same value:

$$L_{eq} = L1(s_{k_0}, s_q)$$

(4)

We then use k_4 as a baseline which has lower scores than q and all other k_i, and has no difference on degradation with bicubicly downsampling LR images:

$$L_{rank_2} = \sum_{i=0}^{3} max(0, (s_{k_i} - s_{k_4}) * -1 + \varepsilon)$$
$$+ max(0, (s_q - s_{k_4}) * -1 + \varepsilon)$$

(5)

$$L_{k_4} = L1(s_{k_4}, 0).$$

(6)

The overall loss for degradation encoder includes the above mentioned losses:

$$L_{encoder} = L_{rank_1} + \beta_1 L_{rank_2} + \beta_2 L_{k_4} + \beta_3 L_{eq}$$

(7)

where β_1, β_2, β_3 are hyper-parameters to combine these losses.

3.3   Degradation-Aware Modulation

Basic SR Model. We first introduce the basic SR model to be modulated. In this work, we take a lightweight super-resolution network IMDN [14] as the basic model. It is composed of six information multi-distillation blocks (IMDBs) and gives reasonable performance on bicubicly downsampled images. To show that the proposed method is able to work on any existing SR model, we do not make any changes on top of IMDN. For the above-mentioned generated LR images, we only use q as input for HR restoration for efficiency. Then we denote $F_l \in \mathbb{R}^{C \times H_l \times W_l}$ as the feature of q within IMDN, where $l \in \{0, 1, ...6\}$. H_l, W_l are the resolution of F_l and C is the feature dimensionality. Here, $F_l, l \in \{1, 2, ...6\}$ indicates the feature output from the l-th IMDB, and F_0 indicates the feature before the first IMDB. Specifically, the pretrained IMDN is fine-tuned together with training the degradation encoder and modulation module for better performance.

Modulation Module. To adapt each feature F_l of q in SR model, we design a modulation module which consists of seven modulation blocks. These modulation blocks are separately inserted into IMDN, so that each block is used to modulate one feature of q before and after each IMDB. Meanwhile, each modulation block uses information of degradation degree from q's degradation representation R for adapting F_l.

We notice that DASR applies two kinds of modulations in one modulation block, a depth-wise convolution and a channel-wise attention. The first one takes the degradation representation R as input and predicts one convolutional kernel $w_l \in \mathbb{R}^{C \times 1 \times 3 \times 3}$. w_l is then used as the parameters of a 3×3 depth-wise convolution on F_l to process F_l^1. The second one also takes R as input to predict one channel-wise modulation coefficient $v_l \in \mathbb{R}^C$. v_l is then used to rescale different channel components for all spatial positions of F_l to produce F_l^2. F_l^1 and F_l^2 are added together to form the adapted feature. Both two modulations in DASR assume the degradation equally affects all spatial positions of one image so that they only learn one set of w_l and v_l for all spatial positions.

However, even though by applying a spatially-invariant degradation for all spatial positions in an HR image, the degradation may have different impacts on different spatial positions. It is mainly because different types of textures have different sensitivity to the degradation. For example, positions which present the contour of an object would contain more high-frequency information. More information loss may occur on these positions when applying the degradation to HR image. Consider that, it would be better to design a region-wise and sample-specific modulation. Therefore, we propose an efficient region-aware modulation by modifying the modulation based on DRConv [5] (Fig. 3(b)).

Region-Aware Modulation. For the first kind of modulation, instead of only learning one convolution kernel for all positions in F_l, we follow DRConv to learn G_1 filter kernels from degradation representation R and denote them as w_l^g, $g \in \{1, 2, \cdots, G_1\}$. G_1 is the number of kernels in this kind of modulation. Each filter kernel $w_l^g \in \mathbb{R}^{C \times 1 \times 3 \times 3}$ is only applied to a selected number of spatial positions instead of all positions in F_l. We then learn a series of guided masks $m_l^g \in \mathbb{R}^{H_l \times W_l}$ which divide all spatial positions in F_l to G_1 groups. Each mask represents one region of F_l with a selected number of positions. Here, we learn these spatial-wise masks from F_l to focus on the characteristic of the feature to be modulated. In this way, only the g-th kernel is applied on the selected positions in g-th mask, so that different positions from F_l would adaptively select different kernels to apply. To maintain the efficiency, we also apply the idea of depth-wise convolution as DASR. The c-th dimensionality of output feature map F_l^1 can be expressed as follow where (h, w) is one point in selected positions in m_l^g:

$$F_l^1{}_{(h,w,c)} = F_{l(h,w,c)} * w_l^g{}_{(c)}$$
$$(h, w) \in m_l^g \tag{8}$$

The channel-wise attention modulation can also be modified in the same way to achieve a dynamic region-aware modulation. It means that we can also predict G_2 channel-wise coefficients from R and denote them as v_l^g, $g \in \{1, 2, \cdots, G_2\}$. G_2 is the number of channel-wise coefficients for this modulation. Each $v_l^g \in \mathbb{R}^C$ is also only applied to a selected number of spatial positions in F_l according to a new series of guided masks $r_l^g \in \mathbb{R}^{H_l \times W_l}$ which divide all positions in F_l to G_2 groups. The c-th dimensionality of output feature map F_l^2 is expressed as:

$$F_l^2{}_{(h,w,c)} = F_{l(h,w,c)} \times v_l^g{}_{(c)}$$
$$(h, w) \in r_l^g \tag{9}$$

Here (h, w) is one of the points in selected positions in r_l^g.

We obtain the adapted feature by combining the modulated features from two kinds of modulations. By modifying the original modulation to be in a region-aware way, we can achieve an efficient pixel-wise modulation. Same as DASR, we apply the two kinds of above-mentioned modulation twice in each modulation block, while for simplicity, we only show the structure of applying them once in Fig. 3(b). The final adapted feature from i-th modulation block is denoted as $\widetilde{F}_i$ and is used as the input to the $(i + 1)$-th IMDB in the SR model to predict the SR image. The loss function on SR is:

$$L_{SR} = L1(SR, HR) \tag{10}$$

And the overall loss function is as follow:

$$L_{overall} = L_{SR} + \alpha * L_{encoder} \tag{11}$$

With the help of modulation module, the output SR image is specifically predicted based on the degradation of the input LR image. It helps to improve the generalization of the overall structure to work for not only the multiple degradations in training set, but also any unknown degradations in testing set.

4   Experiments

4.1   Datasets

Following [28], we use 800 training HR images in DIV2K [1] and 2650 training images in Flickr2K [27] and apply Eq. 1 to synthesize LR images, which form LR-HR pairs as our training set. Specifically, we apply the anisotropic Gaussian kernels, bicubic downsampler and additive white Gaussian noise in Eq. 1. For bicubic downsampler, the scaling factor sf is set to 4 for $\times 4$ SR. For anisotropic Gaussian kernels, the kernel size is fixed to 21×21, the ranges of eigenvalues λ_1 and λ_2 are set to $[0.2, 4.0)$, and the range of rotation angle θ is set to $[0, \pi)$. For additive white Gaussian noise, the range of noise level n is set to $[0, 25)$.

During inference, we use HR images from benchmark dataset Set14 [30] and also apply Eq. 1 to synthesize LR images as [28]. These LR-HR pairs are used as

Table 1. Quantitive results ($\times 4$ SR) on in-domain synthetic test sets. The best two results are in Red and Blue. We also present the number of parameters (Params) and Flops.

Method	Params (M)	Flops (G)	$\lambda_1/\lambda_2/\theta$ n	2.0/0.5/0 PSNR	SSIM	2.0/1.0/10 PSNR	SSIM	3.5/1.5/30 PSNR	SSIM	3.5/2.0/45 PSNR	SSIM	3.5/2.0/90 PSNR	SSIM
DnCNN+IKC	6.0	24.3	10	26.00	0.6874	26.06	0.6837	24.56	0.6281	24.44	0.6190	24.49	0.6201
			15	25.53	0.6659	25.50	0.6619	24.23	0.6134	24.11	0.6049	24.12	0.6040
DnCNN+DAN	5.0	81.1	10	25.78	0.6783	25.70	0.6722	24.23	0.6174	24.05	0.6069	24.12	0.6086
			15	25.36	0.6596	25.25	0.6533	23.98	0.6055	23.81	0.5962	23.86	0.5973
DnCNN +CF+RCAN	26.3	68.1	10	25.15	0.6781	25.12	0.6747	23.85	0.6210	23.60	0.6100	23.58	0.6099
			15	24.56	0.6545	24.48	0.6492	23.40	0.6012	23.22	0.5914	23.05	0.5894
DnCNN+SRMDNF +Predictor	2.2	9.1	10	25.97	0.6843	25.78	0.6747	24.14	0.6149	23.92	0.6032	23.98	0.6046
			15	25.55	0.6656	25.38	0.6577	23.94	0.6052	23.74	0.5952	23.79	0.5965
DnCNN+MANet	10.6	40.8	10	20.20	0.5023	20.33	0.5091	21.12	0.5329	21.18	0.5332	20.92	0.5207
			15	20.23	0.5034	20.36	0.5089	21.09	0.5291	21.13	0.5284	20.86	0.5175
BSRNet	16.7	73.5	10	25.59	0.6803	25.57	0.6772	24.69	0.6430	24.61	0.6369	24.63	0.6362
			15	24.39	0.6493	24.37	0.6460	23.67	0.6156	23.55	0.6097	23.61	0.6111
DASR	6.0	13.1	10	26.58	0.7030	26.49	0.6960	25.62	0.6624	25.44	0.6538	25.43	0.6527
			15	26.04	0.6827	25.93	0.6764	25.10	0.6434	24.94	0.6350	24.91	0.6346
Ours	2.9	6.2	10	26.58	0.7008	26.47	0.6939	25.62	0.6616	25.48	0.6538	25.42	0.6523
			15	26.04	0.6815	25.94	0.6752	25.12	0.6436	24.97	0.6358	24.93	0.6347

our synthetic testing set to conduct experiments with various unknown degradations. Meanwhile, we enlarge the range of three parameters of degradation, λ_1, λ_2 and n during testing. We also use RealSR [4] testing set to further evaluate the performance of our method on real-world LR images. It contains 100 HR images and their corresponding LR images taken from real world.

4.2   Implementation Details

Our model is implemented based on the Pytorch toolbox and trained on one GTX 3090 GPU. The batch size and the patch size of LR images are set to 32 and 48×48 during training. We also use random rotation and flipping as the data augmentation technique during training to avoid overfitting. In our experiments, we set $\alpha = 0.2$, $\beta_1 = 0.2$, $\beta_2 = 2$, $\beta_3 = 5$, $\varepsilon = 0.5$, $G_1 = G_2 = 4$. For the optimizer, we adopt Adam [17]. The overall network is trained in two stages. For stage one, we only train the degradation encoder with ranker by optimizing Eq. 7 for 100 epochs. The initial learning rate is set to 10^{-4} and decreased with the power of 0.1 after 60 epochs. For stage two, we freeze the ranker while training all the rest parts by optimizing Eq. 11 for 700 epochs. The initial learning rate is set to 10^{-4} and decreased to half after every 125 epochs.

4.3   Comparison with State-of-the-Art Methods

To verify the effectiveness of our proposed blind SR method with degradation-aware adaptation, we compare our method with 7 state-of-art SR methods, including one non-blind SR method: SRMDNF [34]; three blind SR methods with explicit degradation estimation: IKC [11], DAN [13], MANet [19]; one

Table 2. Quantitive results ($\times 4$ SR) on out-domain synthetic test sets and real world test set (RealSR). The best two results are in Red and Blue.

Method	Params (M)	Flops (G)	Out-domain $\lambda_1/\lambda_2/\theta$												RealSR	
			2.0/1.0/10		3.5/1.5/30		3.5/2.0/45		3.5/4.5/60		4.5/5.0/120		5.0/5.0/180			
		n	PSNR	SSIM	PSNR	SSIM	PSNR	SSIM	PSNR	SSIM	PSNR	SSIM	PSNR	SSIM	PSNR	SSIM
DnCNN +IKC	6.0	24.3	24.22	0.6152	23.30	0.5801	23.20	0.5732	22.29	0.5412	21.94	0.5286	21.86	0.5248		
			23.49	0.5941	22.79	0.5640	22.68	0.5588	21.89	0.5305	21.57	0.5189	21.51	0.5163	27.19	0.7833
			22.85	0.5751	22.23	0.5491	22.13	0.5446	21.43	0.5192	21.21	0.5104	21.12	0.5080		
DnCNN +DAN	5.0	81.1	24.16	0.6128	23.20	0.5775	23.10	0.5712	22.21	0.5400	21.84	0.5280	21.78	0.5248		
			23.47	0.5928	22.72	0.5630	22.61	0.5580	21.83	0.5306	21.52	0.5198	21.45	0.5173	27.80	0.7877
			22.85	0.5751	22.19	0.5490	22.09	0.5447	21.39	0.5199	21.17	0.5121	21.09	0.5095		
DnCNN +CF+RCAN	26.3	68.1	23.25	0.5973	22.49	0.5604	22.28	0.5491	21.41	0.5088	21.05	0.4902	21.03	0.4883		
			22.47	0.5724	21.94	0.5371	21.78	0.5313	21.10	0.4951	20.71	0.4745	20.60	0.4696	27.72	0.7825
			21.89	0.5500	21.34	0.5177	21.29	0.5119	20.75	0.4797	20.37	0.4643	20.27	0.4562		
DnCNN +SRMDNF +Predictor	2.2	9.1	24.28	0.6174	23.20	0.5799	23.11	0.5741	22.17	0.5414	21.81	0.5292	21.75	0.5259		
			23.54	0.5956	22.73	0.5664	22.62	0.5611	21.81	0.5331	21.49	0.5219	21.43	0.5196	27.62	0.7789
			22.87	0.5772	22.18	0.5516	22.08	0.5472	21.37	0.5230	21.14	0.5148	21.06	0.5122		
DnCNN +MANet	10.6	40.8	20.37	0.5052	20.89	0.5169	20.93	0.5170	20.80	0.5045	20.81	0.5042	20.77	0.5023		
			20.37	0.5035	20.73	0.5111	20.79	0.5116	20.64	0.5005	20.62	0.4991	20.58	0.4976	oom	oom
			20.28	0.5007	20.60	0.5059	20.58	0.5055	20.39	0.4944	20.42	0.4942	20.34	0.4920		
BSRNet	16.7	73.5	21.44	0.5871	21.01	0.5644	20.92	0.5609	20.51	0.5405	20.34	0.5317	20.28	0.5284		
			19.95	0.5519	19.77	0.5380	19.70	0.5342	19.38	0.5176	19.29	0.5114	19.22	0.5085	27.35	0.8071
			18.99	0.5250	18.78	0.5121	18.76	0.5107	18.58	0.4979	18.43	0.4933	18.46	0.4920		
DASR	6.0	13.1	24.67	0.6320	23.87	0.6011	23.81	0.5963	22.95	0.5650	22.45	0.5471	22.36	0.5430		
			23.65	0.5969	23.06	0.5701	23.02	0.5672	22.27	0.5396	21.88	0.5239	21.79	0.5194	27.80	0.7934
			22.82	0.5693	22.42	0.5480	22.36	0.5439	21.69	0.5174	21.49	0.5094	21.33	0.5045		
Ours	2.9	6.2	24.73	0.6335	23.95	0.6041	23.89	0.5995	22.96	0.5663	22.46	0.5483	22.36	0.5441		
			23.93	0.6061	23.33	0.5814	23.22	0.5760	22.42	0.5475	22.00	0.5319	21.91	0.5278	27.84	0.8024
			23.16	0.5719	22.62	0.5491	22.54	0.5452	21.79	0.5196	21.56	0.5117	21.42	0.5058		

blind SR with image translation: CF [15]; one blind SR method with implicit degradation representation learning: DASR [28]; and one blind SR method with enlarged synthetic training data: BSRNet [32]. Specifically, IKC, DAN, MANet and SRMDNF are designed to handle images with only blur kernel and down-sampling as degradation without noise. We notice that DASR tests this kind of SR model by first denoising the testing LR images using DnCNN [33]. For a fair comparison, we follow the same strategy to test these four methods and Predictor of IKC is used to estimate blur kernels for SRMDNF. Meanwhile, [32] focuses on improving perceptual quality by training SR model with adversarial loss. Here, we compare with its non-GAN version (BSRNet) for fairness.

Comparison on Synthetic Data. During training, we set ranges to the four degradation parameters, λ_1, λ_2, n and θ, the same as DASR for generating LR images. While at inference time, we enlarge the ranges of λ_1, λ_2, n to generate more testing data. The testing LR images with degradation parameters within the training ranges are considered as in-domain data, and the testing LR images with degradation parameters out of the training ranges are considered as out-domain data compared to the training data. Here, we present the comparison of in-domain and out-domain data in Table 1 and Table 2. We also analyze the efficiency of each method by presenting the number of parameters and FLOPs.

According to Table 1, our method can achieve comparable results on in-domain test data with DASR even though it has only half the model size and FLOPs of DASR, which indicates the effectiveness of our method. Meanwhile, both DASR and our method can perform much better than all other methods, which indicates the advantage of degradation-aware adaptation and latent degradation representation learning for blind SR.

The performance of out-domain test data in Table 2 also shows that our method as well as DASR can be superior to other methods. Meanwhile, with the help of the proposed ranking loss and region-aware modulation, our method achieves better results than DASR on these out-domain test data. It means that our method has a better generalization ability on LR images with unseen degradations, which have different kernels and noises compared to training data. We also present some qualitative examples in Fig. 4(a)(b) for both in-domain and out-domain data. Compared to other methods, our method tends to generate clearer textures with less artifacts.

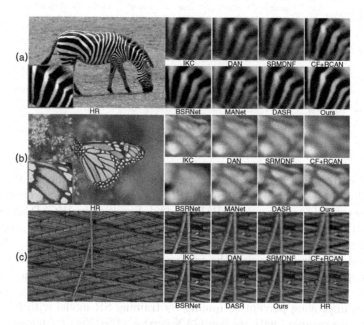

Fig. 4. Visual results (×4 SR) on (a) in-domain, (b) out-domain synthetic test data, and (c) RealSR test data. Zoom in for better visual comparison.

Especially, our method has a relatively compact model size and FLOPs by using IMDN as SR model, which indicates the efficiency of our method. Our FLOPs is the smallest among all methods, while our number of parameters is only slightly larger than SRMDNF, a light-weighted non-blind SR method which does not require any degradation learning. Note that CF+RCAN is larger since RCAN is a heavier SR model, CF itself has much smaller model size. However, it requires image-specific training at testing period which is different from others.

Comparison on Real-World Data. To further show the generalization ability of all methods on real-world situation, we directly test all models trained with synthetic data on RealSR without re-training or fine-tuning on any real-world data. The comparisons are presented in Table 2. It indicates that our method can perform favorably against other methods in most cases, which proves our method can also generalize well on real-world data which is entirely different from the training data. Qualitative examples are presented in Fig. 4(c).

4.4 Ablation Study

Study on Each Component. Here, we present the ablation study to show the improvement of our proposed components. It can be separated into three parts: the loss for degradation encoder; the type of modulation; and the training strategy for base SR model. Model-1 represents the original IMDN which is pre-trained on bicubicly downsampling images without using degradation encoder and modulation. For Model-2, 3, 5, we fine-tune IMDN while applying different kinds of degradation-aware modulation. We try two kinds of the losses for degradation encoder, 'CL' is the contrastive learning loss in [28] while 'RL' is the proposed ranking loss. For the type of modulation, we try 'UM', the uniform modulation in [28] where the same modulation parameter is used for features among all spatial positions, and 'RM', the proposed region-aware modulation. For Model-4, we fix the original IMDN and only train the degradation encoder as well as modulation module for degradation-aware modulation. Table 3 shows the training strategy for each model and quantitative results on both synthetic data ($\lambda_1 = 2.0, \lambda_2 = 5.0, \theta = 90, n = 0$) and RealSR. Model-5 is our final model.

Table 3. Ablation study on different components on synthetic data (2.0/5.0/90/0) and real data. The best results are in Red.

Method	Encoder		Modulation		SRNet	Set14		RealSR	
	+CL	+RL	+UM	+RM	Fix	PSNR	SSIM	PSNR	SSIM
Model-1					√	23.47	0.6004	27.65	0.7796
Model-2	√		√			24.86	0.6525	27.76	0.7931
Model-3		√	√			24.98	0.6590	27.79	0.7991
Model-4		√		√	√	24.37	0.6355	27.79	0.8001
Model-5		√		√		25.08	0.6602	27.84	0.8024

We notice that by applying different kinds of modulation, all models can achieve improvements compared to Model-1 (original IMDN). It indicates that degradation-aware modulation does improve the generalization ability of SR model. However, different kinds of degradation-aware modulation would also affect the performance. Improvements from Model-2 to Model-3 show that 'RL', ranking loss which learns the degradation degree can perform better than 'CL', which can only distinguish one degradation from the other. Meanwhile, from Model-3 to Model-5, the improvements show that 'RM', region-aware modulation which allows different regions in feature to choose different parameters for modulation is better than 'UM'. Moreover, even though Model-4 which fixes base SR model during training can achieve improvements compared to Model-1 by applying the same degradation-aware modulation as Model-5, Model-5 by fine-tuning SR model during training gains further enhancements from Model-4.

Table 4. Ablation study with different SR Net on in-domain (3.5/2.0/45/25), out-domain (4.5/5.0/120/5), and real data. The best results are in Red.

Method	IMDN						RCAN						EDSR					
	In-domain		Out-domain		RealSR		In-domain		Out-domain		RealSR		In-domain		Out-domain		RealSR	
	PSNR	SSIM	PSNR	SSIM	PSNR	SSIM	PSNR	SSIM	PSNR	SSIM	PSNR	SSIM	PSNR	SSIM	PSNR	SSIM	PSNR	SSIM
-bic	20.07	0.2845	22.37	0.5156	27.65	0.7796	19.81	0.2728	22.36	0.5116	27.65	0.7797	19.64	0.2574	22.35	0.5098	27.64	0.7793
-ft	24.05	0.6047	23.61	0.5873	27.66	0.7963	24.13	0.6087	23.55	0.5832	27.70	0.7921	24.21	0.6118	23.65	0.5870	27.73	0.7925
-Ours	24.19	0.6094	23.78	0.5934	27.84	0.8024	24.28	0.6133	23.77	0.5921	27.86	0.7939	24.23	0.6117	23.84	0.5952	27.87	0.7934

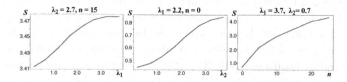

Fig. 5. Curves for ranking scores.

Study on Different SR Net. To show that the proposed structure is more flexible than DASR [28] since it can be applied to other SR models, we also try to implement the same structure to RCAN [36] and EDSR [21]. Here, the number of modulation blocks is set to 11 and 33 for 10 residual group blocks in RCAN and 32 residual blocks in EDSR. The results of in-domain, out-domain and RealSR data are shown in Table 4. It indicates that using the proposed degradation-aware modulation on these three base SR (-Ours) gain improvements compared to their original SR models pretrained on bicubicly downsampled LR images (-bic). We also show the results of simply fine-tuning base SR models on the same training data as '-Ours' without using any degradation-aware modulation (-ft), which achieves worse results especially on out-domain data and RealSR compared to '-Ours'. It indicates that even though '-ft' uses training data with various degradations, it may still limit the generalization ability on unseen degradations without learning an informative degradation representation for applying a modulation specific to the degradation.

Study on Ranking Scores. To prove that the proposed degradation encoder with ranker can produce ranking scores with the right order. We generate a series of synthetic LR images by HR images from RealSR with degradation of using two fixed parameters while altering the third one in λ_1, λ_2 and n. We then produce their ranking scores s by our degradation encoder and ranker and draw curves as in Fig. 5. It shows that by setting larger value for the unfixed parameter, the generated LR image would have larger s.

5 Conclusions

In this paper, we propose a blind SR method with degradation-aware adaptation. It applies a plug-and-play module to improve the generalization capability of an existing SR model pretrained on bicubicly downsampled LR images to real-world degradation. The proposed method consists of three components: the pretrained base SR model, a degradation encoder followed by a ranker, and a degradation-aware modulation module. The degradation encoder extracts a latent degradation representation supervised by ranking loss to estimate the degree of degradation for modulation. The degradation-aware modulation module then uses degradation representation as condition to apply a region-aware and sample-specific adaptation for the intermediate features of SR model. Our method has relatively compact model size and performs favorably against the state-of-the-art SR methods on both synthetic and real-world datasets.

References

1. Agustsson, E., Timofte, R.: NTIRE 2017 challenge on single image super-resolution: dataset and study. In: Proceedings of the IEEE Conference on Computer Vision and Pattern Recognition Workshops, pp. 126–135 (2017)
2. Ahn, N., Kang, B., Sohn, K.A.: Fast, accurate, and lightweight super-resolution with cascading residual network. In: Proceedings of the European Conference on Computer Vision (ECCV), pp. 252–268 (2018)
3. Aquilina, M., Galea, C., Abela, J., Camilleri, K.P., Farrugia, R.A.: Improving super-resolution performance using meta-attention layers. IEEE Signal Process. Lett. **28**, 2082–2086 (2021)
4. Cai, J., Zeng, H., Yong, H., Cao, Z., Zhang, L.: Toward real-world single image super-resolution: a new benchmark and a new model. In: Proceedings of the IEEE/CVF International Conference on Computer Vision, pp. 3086–3095 (2019)
5. Chen, J., Wang, X., Guo, Z., Zhang, X., Sun, J.: Dynamic region-aware convolution. In: Proceedings of the IEEE/CVF Conference on Computer Vision and Pattern Recognition, pp. 8064–8073 (2021)
6. Chen, T., Kornblith, S., Norouzi, M., Hinton, G.: A simple framework for contrastive learning of visual representations. In: International Conference on Machine Learning, pp. 1597–1607. PMLR (2020)
7. Dong, C., Loy, C.C., He, K., Tang, X.: Learning a deep convolutional network for image super-resolution. In: Fleet, D., Pajdla, T., Schiele, B., Tuytelaars, T. (eds.) ECCV 2014. LNCS, vol. 8692, pp. 184–199. Springer, Cham (2014). https://doi.org/10.1007/978-3-319-10593-2_13
8. Finn, C., Abbeel, P., Levine, S.: Model-agnostic meta-learning for fast adaptation of deep networks. In: International Conference on Machine Learning, pp. 1126–1135. PMLR (2017)
9. Ghiasi, G., Lee, H., Kudlur, M., Dumoulin, V., Shlens, J.: Exploring the structure of a real-time, arbitrary neural artistic stylization network. arXiv preprint arXiv:1705.06830 (2017)
10. Goodfellow, I., et al.: Generative adversarial nets. Adv. Neural Inf. Process. Syst. **27** (2014)

11. Gu, J., Lu, H., Zuo, W., Dong, C.: Blind super-resolution with iterative kernel correction. In: Proceedings of the IEEE/CVF Conference on Computer Vision and Pattern Recognition, pp. 1604–1613 (2019)

12. He, K., Fan, H., Wu, Y., Xie, S., Girshick, R.: Momentum contrast for unsupervised visual representation learning. In: Proceedings of the IEEE/CVF Conference on Computer Vision and Pattern Recognition, pp. 9729–9738 (2020)

13. Huang, Y., Li, S., Wang, L., Tan, T., et al.: Unfolding the alternating optimization for blind super resolution. Adv. Neural. Inf. Process. Syst. **33**, 5632–5643 (2020)

14. Hui, Z., Gao, X., Yang, Y., Wang, X.: Lightweight image super-resolution with information multi-distillation network. In: Proceedings of the 27th ACM International Conference on Multimedia, pp. 2024–2032 (2019)

15. Hussein, S.A., Tirer, T., Giryes, R.: Correction filter for single image super-resolution: robustifying off-the-shelf deep super-resolvers. In: Proceedings of the IEEE/CVF Conference on Computer Vision and Pattern Recognition, pp. 1428–1437 (2020)

16. Johnson, J., Alahi, A., Fei-Fei, L.: Perceptual losses for real-time style transfer and super-resolution. In: Leibe, B., Matas, J., Sebe, N., Welling, M. (eds.) ECCV 2016. LNCS, vol. 9906, pp. 694–711. Springer, Cham (2016). https://doi.org/10.1007/978-3-319-46475-6_43

17. Kingma, D.P., Ba, J.: Adam: a method for stochastic optimization. In: The International Conference on Learning Representations (2015)

18. Li, W., Zhou, K., Qi, L., Jiang, N., Lu, J., Jia, J.: LAPAR: linearly-assembled pixel-adaptive regression network for single image super-resolution and beyond. Adv. Neural. Inf. Process. Syst. **33**, 20343–20355 (2020)

19. Liang, J., Sun, G., Zhang, K., Van Gool, L., Timofte, R.: Mutual affine network for spatially variant kernel estimation in blind image super-resolution. In: Proceedings of the IEEE/CVF International Conference on Computer Vision, pp. 4096–4105 (2021)

20. Liang, J., Zhang, K., Gu, S., Van Gool, L., Timofte, R.: Flow-based kernel prior with application to blind super-resolution. In: Proceedings of the IEEE/CVF Conference on Computer Vision and Pattern Recognition, pp. 10601–10610 (2021)

21. Lim, B., Son, S., Kim, H., Nah, S., Mu Lee, K.: Enhanced deep residual networks for single image super-resolution. In: Proceedings of the IEEE Conference on Computer Vision and Pattern Recognition Workshops, pp. 136–144 (2017)

22. Luo, Z., Huang, Y., Li, S., Wang, L., Tan, T.: End-to-end alternating optimization for blind super resolution. arXiv preprint arXiv:2105.06878 (2021)

23. Ma, C., Tan, W., Yan, B., Zhou, S.: Prior embedding multi-degradations super resolution network. Neurocomputing **489**, 534–546 (2022)

24. Rad, M.S., Yu, T., Musat, C., Ekenel, H.K., Bozorgtabar, B., Thiran, J.P.: Benefiting from bicubically down-sampled images for learning real-world image super-resolution. In: Proceedings of the IEEE/CVF Winter Conference on Applications of Computer Vision, pp. 1590–1599 (2021)

25. Shocher, A., Cohen, N., Irani, M.: "zero-shot" super-resolution using deep internal learning. In: Proceedings of the IEEE Conference on Computer Vision and Pattern Recognition, pp. 3118–3126 (2018)

26. Soh, J.W., Cho, S., Cho, N.I.: Meta-transfer learning for zero-shot super-resolution. In: Proceedings of the IEEE/CVF Conference on Computer Vision and Pattern Recognition, pp. 3516–3525 (2020)

27. Timofte, R., Agustsson, E., Van Gool, L., Yang, M.H., Zhang, L.: NTIRE 2017 challenge on single image super-resolution: methods and results. In: Proceedings of the IEEE Conference on Computer Vision and Pattern Recognition Workshops, pp. 114–125 (2017)
28. Wang, L., et al.: Unsupervised degradation representation learning for blind super-resolution. In: Proceedings of the IEEE/CVF Conference on Computer Vision and Pattern Recognition, pp. 10581–10590 (2021)
29. Wang, X., Xie, L., Dong, C., Shan, Y.: Real-ESRGAN: training real-world blind super-resolution with pure synthetic data. In: Proceedings of the IEEE/CVF International Conference on Computer Vision, pp. 1905–1914 (2021)
30. Zeyde, R., Elad, M., Protter, M.: On single image scale-up using sparse-representations. In: Boissonnat, J.-D., et al. (eds.) Curves and Surfaces 2010. LNCS, vol. 6920, pp. 711–730. Springer, Heidelberg (2012). https://doi.org/10.1007/978-3-642-27413-8_47
31. Zhang, K., Gool, L.V., Timofte, R.: Deep unfolding network for image super-resolution. In: Proceedings of the IEEE/CVF Conference on Computer Vision and Pattern Recognition, pp. 3217–3226 (2020)
32. Zhang, K., Liang, J., Van Gool, L., Timofte, R.: Designing a practical degradation model for deep blind image super-resolution. In: Proceedings of the IEEE/CVF International Conference on Computer Vision, pp. 4791–4800 (2021)
33. Zhang, K., Zuo, W., Chen, Y., Meng, D., Zhang, L.: Beyond a gaussian denoiser: residual learning of deep CNN for image denoising. IEEE Trans. Image Process. **26**(7), 3142–3155 (2017)
34. Zhang, K., Zuo, W., Zhang, L.: Learning a single convolutional super-resolution network for multiple degradations. In: Proceedings of the IEEE Conference on Computer Vision and Pattern Recognition, pp. 3262–3271 (2018)
35. Zhang, W., Liu, Y., Dong, C., Qiao, Y.: RankSRGAN: generative adversarial networks with ranker for image super-resolution. In: Proceedings of the IEEE/CVF International Conference on Computer Vision, pp. 3096–3105 (2019)
36. Zhang, Y., Li, K., Li, K., Wang, L., Zhong, B., Fu, Y.: Image super-resolution using very deep residual channel attention networks. In: Proceedings of the European Conference on Computer Vision (ECCV), pp. 286–301 (2018)
37. Zhou, R., Susstrunk, S.: Kernel modeling super-resolution on real low-resolution images. In: Proceedings of the IEEE/CVF International Conference on Computer Vision, pp. 2433–2443 (2019)
38. Zhu, J.Y., Park, T., Isola, P., Efros, A.A.: Unpaired image-to-image translation using cycle-consistent adversarial networks. In: Proceedings of the IEEE International Conference on Computer Vision, pp. 2223–2232 (2017)

Multi-Branch Network with Ensemble Learning for Text Removal in the Wild

Yujie Hou[1], Jiwei Chen[1], and Zengfu Wang[1,2(✉)]

[1] School of Information Science and Technology, University of Science and Technology of China, Hefei, China
{houyj1219,cjwbdw06}@mail.ustc.edu.cn, zfwang@ustc.edu.cn
[2] Institute of Intelligent Machines, Chinese Academy of Sciences, Hefei, China

Abstract. The scene text removal (STR) is a task to substitute text regions with visually realistic backgrounds. Due to the diversity of scene text and the intricacy of background, earlier STR approaches may not successfully remove scene text. We discovered that different networks produce different text removal results. Thus, we present a novel STR approach with a multi-branch network to entirely erase the text while maintaining the integrity of the backgrounds. The main branch preserves high-resolution texture information, while two sub-branches learn multi-scale semantic features. The complementary erasure networks are integrated with two ensemble learning fusion mechanisms: a feature-level fusion and an image-level fusion. Additionally, we propose a patch attention module to perceive text location and generate text attention features. Our method outperforms state-of-the-art approaches on both real-world and synthetic datasets, improving PSNR by 1.78 dB in the SCUT-EnsText dataset and 4.45 dB in the SCUT-Syn dataset.

1 Introduction

The text information that appears in natural scene images is referred to as scene text [16]. Scene text such as license plate numbers and phone numbers may be captured inadvertently when taking a picture [10]. With the development of text detection and recognition technology, such sensitive information could be easily gathered when posting scene images on the Internet. Concealing sensitive information is in high demand to reduce the danger of privacy disclosure. Recent deep learning-based text detection and recognition approaches require a huge number of training data, but manual labeling is time-consuming as well as costly. To fill this gap, the STR is used to generate a synthetic scene text dataset by erasing the text in the image and swapping it for the new text with new content. It might be viewed as a novel method to produce high-quality synthetic datasets for scene text detection and recognition.

Numerous STR techniques in deep learning have been proposed and demonstrated promising performance in recent years (see Sect. 2), yet there still exist

---

Supplementary Information The online version contains supplementary material available at https://doi.org/10.1007/978-3-031-26313-2_6.

|(a) Image|(b) Ground-Truth|(c) EraseNet 28.00 dB|(d) MBE **31.92 dB**|
|(e) Image|(f) Ground-Truth|(g) EraseNet 28.02 dB|(h) MBE **37.10 dB**|

Fig. 1. Examples of text removal in the wild. Qualitative comparisons and quantitive results of PSNR (higher is better) given by the Erasenet [18] and the MBE are shown in the last two columns. Best view with zoom-in.

multi-scale text inexhaustive erasure problem and the background texture excessive erasure problem in real-world text removal. For example, tiny scene texts are difficult to be removed, and symbolic patterns may be deleted incorrectly (see Fig. 1c and Fig. 1g). We analyze previous methods to identify the bottlenecks that restrain the performance. To begin with, a large number of STR methods [2,16,28,37] employ a two-stage paradigm that divides the procedure into a text detection phase and a text removal phase. The divide-and-conquer idea is straightforward, but the two-stage model is vulnerable in a long-range inference. Any mistake that appeared in the text detection process would directly influence the text removal results in the second stage. Second, one STR network is insufficient to capture all text variance in natural scenarios, since different scenes have texts with different fonts, sizes, colors, and illuminations.

To ameliorate the above-mentioned issues, we present a novel framework called Multi-Branch Network with Ensemble Learning (MBE). Rather than dividing the STR into two cascaded steps (text detection stage and text removal stage), we build an ensemble learning model that consists of three parallel STR branches to generate complementary erasure results. The main branch contains a feature fusion high-resolution network (FFHRNet) for retaining complex background texture and the two sub-branches work on hierarchical patch pictures for learning multi-scale semantic features using a U-Net framework. The visualization output of the main branch in Fig. 2d demonstrates that the FFHRNet is capable of keeping high-resolution backgrounds but leaves rough text sketches. The two sub-branches are prone to entirely erasing the text region, but the non-text patterns are also erased (in Fig. 2b and Fig. 2c).

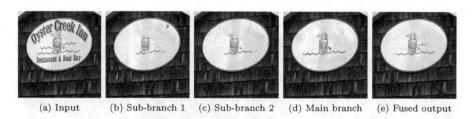

(a) Input   (b) Sub-branch 1   (c) Sub-branch 2   (d) Main branch   (e) Fused output

Fig. 2. Visualization of intermediate and final results from the MBE. The sub-branch network which extracts multi-scale semantic features is prone to excessively erase non-text regions. The main branch leaves the remains of rough text sketches. The fused result achieves the best performance in erasing scene texts and maintaining the integrity of non-text areas.

Intuitively, combining the complementary outputs from all branches can increase the MBE's stability and performance, resulting in better text-removed results. To do this, we propose two fusion procedures that utilize the strengths of all branches. First, we propose an implicit fusion technique called crossing branch feature fusion (CBF) for fusing multiple branches at the feature level. In terms of CBF, one branch combines several semantic features from other branches. The multi-scale semantic features can enhance the text erasure performance at various font sizes. The patch attention module (PAM) can perceive text locations through a simple segmentation and generate text attention features. Second, a convolutional LSTM module (CLSTM) is proposed as an explicit fusion method to fuse the text-erased results at the image level. The CLSTM can preserve the correct text erasure regions in all outputs while discarding the broken background (refer to Fig. 2e).

Extensive experiments are conducted on both the real-world dataset, SCUT-EnsText [18] and the synthetic dataset, SCUT-Syn [39]. Our MBE outperforms the state-of-the-art method in PSNR by 1.78 dB and 4.45 dB on the two datasets, respectively. The contributions are summarized as follows:

- We propose a multi-branch network with ensemble learning (MBE) for STR, that employs ensemble learning to train three STR branches to learn complimentary erasure outcomes and merges all STR branches via an elaborate fusion process to improve the overall model's reliability and performance.
- The three branches are designed to produce complementary outputs for the model ensemble. The main branch preserves high-resolution information, and two sub-branches learn multi-scale semantic features on patch-level images.
- We propose two fusion strategies to fully exploit the inherent advantages of three branches. An implicit fusion approach assists one branch in fusing semantic and attention features from another branch. An explicit fusion approach combines all branches' suboptimal outputs into the final results.

- The quantitative and qualitative results on both the SCUT-EnsText [18] and the SCUT-Syn [39] datasets indicate that our method outperforms the previous state-of-the-art STR method by a large margin.

2   Related Work

Traditional text concealment approaches use image processing to make the text region hard to be detected and recognized. Frome *i.e.* [4] employ a Gaussian filter to blur text region in Google Street View. Inai *i.e.* [10] submerge the scene text by degrading the readability of characters. They use exemplar-based image inpainting to damage the stroke structure. These traditional methods have limitations on complex scenarios, *e.g.* complicated backgrounds, or perspective distortion, and they fail to fill the text region with a plausible background.

Inspired by the notable success of deep learning, novel methods are proposed to conceal the scene text. Nakamura *i.e.* [24] first design an automatic scene text eraser that converts the text erasure problem into an image transformation problem. They use neural networks to learn the transformation function between the scene text images and non-text images without the annotations for the text locations. EnsNet [39] uses a lateral connection structure to integrate high-level semantics and low-level spatial information. Four loss functions are proposed to improve the reality of filling backgrounds. The early methods are lightweight as well as fast but often left noticeable text remnants.

A couple of two-step approaches decouple the scene text removal into two sub-tasks: the text detection task and the text removal task [2,16,28,37]. The text position predicted in the first stage guides the second stage where to erase, and the then text region is filled with a meaningful background. However, if text detection is incorrect, it will degrade the text removal results by leaving text remnants or breaking the integrity of the non-text region. Thus, two-stage STR methods might cause apparent drawbacks and generate low-quality text-removed images. Benefiting from the development of generative adversarial network (GAN) [6,15,22], image restoration methods achieve significant improvement in generating local textures. Erasenet [18] proposes a coarse-to-fine generator network with a local-global discriminator network. In [2], they connect two GAN-based frameworks to refine text removal results at the stroke level. Though the GAN-based methods might improve the erasure quality, the training process is not stable and heavy.

3   Multi-Branch Network with Ensemble Learning

3.1   Overall Architecture

The motivation of our method is that different STR branches can produce complementary text removal results, and it is reasonable to combine them for a better text-removed image. To acquire complementary results, we propose three text removal branches in our method. The main branch (FFHRNet) preserves fine

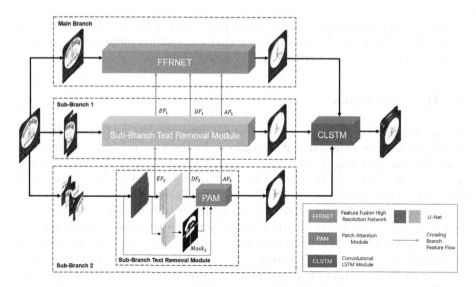

Fig. 3. An overview of our model. The black bold arrows represent the main branch, sub-branch 1, and sub-branch 2, respectively. Sub-branch 1 uses two non-overlapping patch images as input and sub-branch 2 uses four non-overlapping patch images as input. The red arrows represent the crossing branch feature fusion. AF: Attention Feature. EF: Encoder Feature. DF: Decoder Feature. (Color figure online)

textures from the original resolution image. The sub-branches operate on patch-hierarchical images for learning multi-scale semantic features via an encoder-decoder architecture. Following that, we combine the three branches with the CFB as a feature fusion module and the CLSTM as an image fusion module for the model ensemble.

3.2 Main Branch Network

Exiting STR approaches [2,18,32,39] almost follow the U-Net framework. Due to the repetitive usage of scale variation procedures in U-Net, the text-erased results are prone to damage the integrity of the background and details of local texture from the original picture. Thus, our main branch employs the feature fusion high-resolution network (FFHRNet), which is inspired by HRNet [5,27] and the channel attention mechanism [40], to retain high-resolution representations. A high-resolution branch (the black bold arrow in the Fig. 4) and three downsampling branches make up the FFHRNet. The high-resolution branch includes no downsampling or upsampling operations to generate texturally-enriched representations and gradually adds low-resolution feature representations from lower branches to fuse multi-scale information. To adaptively re-calibrate the feature map in the channel dimension, channel attention blocks [40] have been implemented in the high-resolution branch.

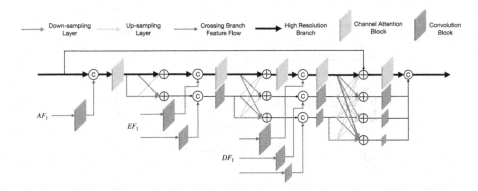

Fig. 4. The feature fusion high-resolution network (FFHRNet). The red-bold arrows illustrate how and where to fuse features from sub-branch 1. (Color figure online)

Attention features (AF_1), encoder features (EF_1) and decoder features (DF_1) from sub-branch 1 are gradually transferred to the FFHRNet, according to the crossing branch feature fusion process (see Sect. 3.4). The AF_1, which carries text location information, is concatenated with feature maps in the high-resolution branch after being scaled by a convolution block. The EF_1 and DF_1 are fused with FFHRNet in the same way.

3.3 Sub-branch Network

Encoder-Decoder Network. The two sub-branch networks, which mainly contain an encoder-decoder network [25] and a PAM, capture the text in scene images and wipe them as precisely as possible. Scene text in the wild has varied scales, which may give rise to failures in text detection, so we separate the input image into several non-overlapping patches to develop a multi-patch hierarchy learning model, which is akin to [26,36,38]. The patch-level inputs compared to the original image considerably lighten the sub-branch network and naturally provide multi-scale semantic information. We also utilize the skip connection technique [19] in the encoder-decoder network to link the downsampling layer and the upsampling layer to reduce information loss. In the U-Net module, the patch images first map to low-resolution representations and then progressively recover to the original resolution by applying several reverse mappings. Annotations for text location are not available in the model inference phase, thus we train another decoder module [18] after the encoder module of U-Net to determine text positions. The binary masks ($Mask_1$ and $Mask_2$) roughly segment scene texts and non-text background (0 for text and 1 for background), which is supervised by dice loss Eq. (3). The PAM then uses the text mask to compute the attention feature.

Patch Attention Module (PAM). The goal of PAM is to enhance the text position response in the feature map. As illustrated in Fig. 5, we element-wise multiply the input decoder feature $DF \in \mathbb{R}^{H \times W \times C}$ from early encoder-decoder

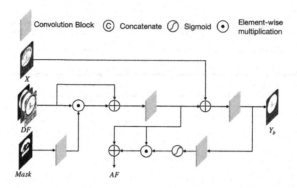

Fig. 5. The architecture of patch attention module (PAM).

network with the binary mask $M \in \mathbb{R}^{H \times W \times 1}$ where H, W denotes the height and width dimension of feature map, and C is the number of channel. Then, the new feature map containing both multi-scale semantic features and text location information is added to the original input X as a residual part to obtain the text removal output Y_b in the sub-branch. To get the attention feature AF, we import the output Y_b to a convolution layer followed by the sigmoid activation, and then we element-wise multiply the activated feature map with the previous feature map as an attention-guided residual, which is added back to the previous feature map. The attention mechanisms could suppress the less informative features and only retain the useful parts. Finally, the attention feature representation AF will be passed to other branches for information fusion.

3.4   Crossing Branch Feature Fusion (CBF)

The CBF is presented as a method for implicitly fusing three STR branches at the feature level. From the main branch (top) to the sub-branch (bottom), the input image is gradually split into smaller patches, and we fuse the features in a down-top pathway to merge low-resolution, semantically strong features with high-resolution, semantically weak features. The red arrows in Fig. 3 indicate two paths of feature transmission: from sub-branch 2 to sub-branch 1 (CBF_1), and from sub-branch 1 to the main branch (CBF_2). The attention feature AF_2 from sub-branch 2 concatenates with the patch-level input image X_1 after convolution block resizing, and the encoder and decoder feature EF_2, DF_2 are imported as supplementary inputs into the U-Net in sub-branch 1. We transmit the feature maps from all encoder layers and decoder layers in the U-Net of sub-branch 2, which means $EF_2 = \{EF_{2a}, EF_{2b}, EF_{2c}\}$, $DF_2 = \{DF_{2a}, DF_{2b}, DF_{2c}\}$. In CBF_1, the multi-scale semantic features from sub-branch 2 are progressively imported to the same-scale encoder-decoder layers in sub-branch 1 to improve the scene text erasure performance at any text size. In CBF_2, the encoder and decoder features EF_1, DF_1 and the attention feature AF_1 from sub-branch 1 are transmitted to the main branch following the same setting in CBF_1.

The method of feature fusion across all STR branches has several advantages. First, it reduces the vulnerability of the feature by repeated use of up- and down-sampling operations in the encoder-decoder network, and the results are more robust when the model confronts information loss due to various interferences. Second, the feature of one branch containing multi-scale semantic information and text location information can help enrich the feature of the other branches. Third, the network optimization procedure becomes more stable as it eases the flow of information, thereby allowing us to train three complementary STR networks and the CLSTM successfully without a model collapse. Additionally, the ablation experiment in Sect. 4.3 demonstrates the effectiveness of CBF in text erasing performance.

3.5   Convolutional LSTM Module (CLSTM)

The CLSTM module [9,35] is another fusion mechanism to explicitly merge multiple branches at the image level. We stack the text removal results from three branches into a sequence pattern, and the CLSTM could predict the next images of the sequence data as our fused output. Due to the gate cell mechanism, the fused outputs can retain correct erasure results from complementary branches while discarding the incorrect erasure sections.

3.6   Train Strategy

For training our MBE, we use the scene text image X, text-removed ground-truth I_{gt}, and text mask ground-truth M as inputs. We optimize our method with the Charbonnier loss [3,21], Edge loss, and Dice loss. The details of our loss functions are as follows.

Because of the multi-branch framework, the Charbonnier loss and Edge loss penalize all branch outputs. The subscript i (from 1 to 3) in Eq. (1) and Eq. (2) denotes the main branch, sub-branch 1, and sub-branch 2, respectively. The Charbonnier loss is defined as:

$$L_{Char} = \sum_{i=1}^{3} \sqrt{\|Y_i - I_{gt}\|^2 + \varepsilon^2} \tag{1}$$

where Y_i represents the text-erased outputs from different branch networks. The Charbonnier loss has a constant parameter ε, which is set to 10^{-3} in our experiments.

The Edge loss is defined as:

$$L_{Edge} = \sum_{i=1}^{3} \sqrt{\|\triangle Y_i - \triangle I_{gt}\|^2 + \varepsilon^2} \tag{2}$$

where $\triangle$ denotes the Laplacian operator. ε is set to 10^{-3} in our experiments.

Table 1. Ablation study on different components of the proposed MBE on SCUT-EnsText. FFHRNet: feature fusion high-resolution network. SB$_1$: sub-branch network 1. SB$_2$: sub-branch network 2. CBF$_1$: crossing branch feature fusion (SB$_2$ to SB$_1$). CBF$_2$: crossing branch feature fusion (SB$_1$ to FFHRNet). PAM: patch attention module. CLSTM: convolutional LSTM module.

FFHRNet	SB$_1$	SB$_2$	CBF$_1$	CBF$_2$	PAM	CLSTM	PSNR (↑)	MSSIM (↑)	AGE (↓)	pEPs (↓)	pCEPs (↓)
✓	✗	✗	✗	✗	✗	✗	31.2012	0.9575	2.8951	0.0235	0.0162
✓	✓	✓	✗	✗	✗	✗	34.2082	0.9690	2.1542	0.0146	0.0098
✓	✓	✓	✓	✗	✗	✗	34.3908	0.9699	2.1129	0.0140	0.0094
✓	✓	✓	✓	✓	✗	✗	34.5285	0.9684	2.1059	0.0142	0.0094
✓	✓	✓	✓	✓	✓	✗	34.6652	0.9705	2.0835	0.0139	0.0094
✓	✗	✓	✓	✓	✓	✓	34.7209	0.9708	2.0877	0.0134	0.0090
✓	✓	✗	✓	✓	✓	✓	34.7084	0.9710	2.1162	0.0136	0.0093
✓	✓	✓	✗	✗	✓	✓	34.2236	0.9698	2.1854	0.0147	0.0107
✓	✓	✓	✓	✗	✓	✓	34.3568	0.9705	2.1235	0.0135	0 0092
✓	✓	✓	✗	✓	✓	✓	34.7896	0.9730	2.0594	**0.01239**	**0.0083**
✓	✓	✓	✓	✓	✗	✓	34.2552	0.9686	2.2819	0.0153	0.0106
✓	✓	✓	✓	✓	✓	✗✗	34.6652	0.9705	2.0835	0.0139	0.0094
✓	✓	✓	✓	✓	✓	✓	**35.0304**	**0.9731**	**2.0232**	0.01282	0.0088

The Dice loss in Eq. (3) is proposed for mask segmentation to learn the text location. It measures the proportion of correctly predicted pixels to the sum of the total pixels of both prediction and ground truth. The Dice loss can be formulated as:

$$L_{Dice} = 1 - \frac{2\sum_{x,y}(S_{x,y}) \times (M_{x,y})}{\sum_{x,y}(S_{x,y})^2 + \sum_{x,y}(M_{x,y})^2} \tag{3}$$

where S represents the predicted mask from the decoder module and M represents the text mask ground-truth. $S_{x,y}$ and $M_{x,y}$ denote the pixel value at point x, y.

Finally, we sum three loss functions together to form the total loss of our MBE, which is defined as Eq. (4):

$$L_{Total} = L_{Char} + \lambda L_{Edge} + \mu L_{Dice} \tag{4}$$

where the λ is set to 0.05 and μ is set to 0.105.

4   Experiments and Analysis

4.1   Datasets and Evaluation Protocol

Datasets. We use the images from SCUT-EnsText [18] and SCUT-Syn [39] dataset to train our method. These two datasets are widely applied in previous STR methods, and we test our approach by following the same method in [18]. The SCUT-EnsText is a real-world dataset including 2,749 training images and 813 test images, and the SCUT-Syn is a synthetic dataset containing 8000 training images and 800 test images with a size of 512 × 512. A scene text image is

Table 2. Quantitative comparison of our method and start-of-the-art methods on SCUT-EnsText and SCUT-Syn datasets. The Best and second best scores are highlighted and underlined, respectively.

Methods	SCUT-EnsText					SCUT-Syn				
	PSNR (↑)	MSSIM (↑)	AGE (↓)	pEPs (↓)	pCEPs (↓)	PSNR (↑)	MSSIM (↑)	AGE (↓)	pEPs (↓)	pCEPs (↓)
Bain [2]	15.9399	0.5706	24.8974	0.3282	0.2123	20.83	0.8319	10.5040	0.1021	0.5996
Pixel2Pixel [11]	26.6993	0.8856	6.0860	0.0480	0.0337	26.67	0.9108	5.4678	0.0473	0.0244
SceneTextEraser [24]	25.4651	0.9014	6.0069	0.0532	0.0296	25.40	0.9012	9.4853	0.0553	0.0347
EnsNet [39]	29.5382	0.9274	4.1600	0.0307	0.0136	37.36	0.9644	1.7300	0.0069	0.0020
Zdenek [37]	–	–	–	–	–	37.46	0.9810	–	–	–
MTRNet [29]	–	–	–	–	–	29.71	0.9443	–	–	–
MTRNet++ [28]	24.6145	0.8990	11.3669	0.1459	0.0869	34.55	<u>0.9845</u>	–	–	–
EraseNet [18]	32.2976	0.9542	3.1264	0.0192	0.0110	38.32	0.9765	1.5982	0.0048	<u>0.0004</u>
PERT [32]	<u>33.2492</u>	<u>0.9695</u>	<u>2.1833</u>	<u>0.0136</u>	**0.0088**	<u>39.40</u>	0.9787	<u>1.4149</u>	<u>0.0045</u>	0.0006
MBE (Ours)	**35.0304**	**0.9731**	**2.0594**	**0.01282**	**0.0088**	**43.85**	**0.9864**	**0.9356**	**0.0013**	**0.00004**

processed into a 1-2-4 multi-patch model for multi-branch input shown in Fig. 3. The notation 1-2-4 indicates the number of non-overlapping image patches from the coarsest level to the finest level.

Evaluation Protocol. We adopt the same evaluation metrics in [18,39] to comprehensively evaluate the text erasure performance, which includes peak signal to noise ratio (PSNR), multi-scale structural similarity (MSSIM) [33], an average of the gray level absolute difference (AGE), percentage of error pixels (pEPs) and percentage of clustered error pixels (pCEPS).

4.2   Implementation Details

The MBE is an end-to-end trained model implemented in Pytorch. Vertical and horizontal flips are randomly applied as data augmentation. We use the Adam optimizer [17] with an initial learning rate of 2×10^{-4} and apply the cosine annealing strategy [20] to steadily decrease the learning rate to 1×10^{-6}.

4.3   Ablation Study

In this subsection, we investigate the effect of each component in our proposed MBE step by step. The number of branch networks, the cross branch feature fusion (CBF), the patch attention module (PAM), and the convolutional LSTM module (CLSTM) are the focus of our study. Evaluations are performed on the real-world SCUT-EnsText dataset. The quantitative results are shown in Table 1 which demonstrates that the MBE outperforms all inferior models.

Number of Branch Networks. This subsection identifies the number of branch networks that perform optimally. We gradually increase the number of sub-branches from 0 to 3. The sub-branch 3 takes eight non-overlapping patch images as input. By integrating sub-branch 1 and sub-branch 2 into the FFHR-Net, our model achieves a higher performance than the previous model demonstrated in the Table 1. When the sub-branch 1 or sub-branch 2 modules are

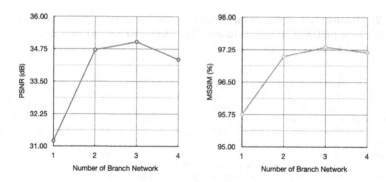

Fig. 6. PSNR *vs.* Number of branch networks and MSSIM *vs.* Number of branch networks. Our method achieves the best performance when we set three branches.

removed from our final model, the inferior model's PSNR performance decreases from 35.03 dB to 34.72 dB and 34.70 dB, respectively. However, when we continue to insert the sub-branch into the overall model, both PSNR and MISSM deteriorate (Fig. 6). This demonstrates that we cannot fuse branch networks infinitely to enhance the model's performance. Excessive branches would obstruct the ensemble model and need extra calculations during training. Because a network with a large number of branches is hard to train as a multi-task learning, the entire model is not stable during optimization. As a result, the generated outcomes are worse than before. In brief, our method employs a single main branch and two sub-branches.

Cross Branch Feature Fusion. To demonstrate the effect of our proposed CBF on model fusion, we divide the CBF into two components (CBF_1 and CBF_2) and test them separately. CBF_1 combines the features of sub-branch 1 with features of sub-branch 2, and CBF_2 combines the features of the main branch with the features of sub-branch 1. The ablation research in Table 1 shows that the PSNR climbs from 34.20 dB to 34.39 dB and subsequently to 34.52 dB when we gradually add the CBF_1 and CBF_2 module to the model. When either CBF_1 or CBF_2 is removed from our final model, the inferior model performs poorly on most of the criteria. The two ablation studies demonstrate that both the two feature fusion mechanisms can significantly improve STR performance.

PAM and CLSTM. We remove the PAM in both sub-branches to verify the effectiveness of text location information for text removal. In the Table 1, we observe that the previous model produces better results after adding the PAM and the MBE model decreases by a large margin when the PAM is removed. The CLSTM combines text-erased outputs from all branch networks. Our model with CLSTM has a considerable improvement of 0.36 dB in PSNR compared to the model without it. The visualization results in Fig. 2d show that the fused output contains both the text-erased results in the sub-branch outputs and the integrity of the background in the main branch output.

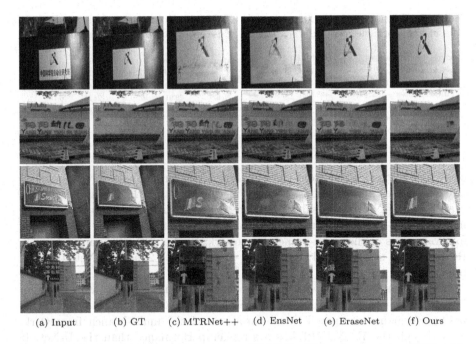

(a) Input   (b) GT   (c) MTRNet++   (d) EnsNet   (e) EraseNet   (f) Ours

Fig. 7. Examples of text erased image on SCUT-EnsText of comparing MBE with previous methods. Best viewed with zoom-in.

4.4   Comparison with State-of-the-Art Methods

In this section, we verify the effectiveness of MBE by comparing our method against recent state-of-the-art approaches on the SCUT-EnsText and the SCUT-Syn datasets. The results are shown in Table 2. The MBE almost achieves the best performance in all metrics on two datasets. Compared to the current best STR method, PERT [32], we obtain a performance gain of 1.78 dB on the SCUT-EnsText dataset and 4.45 dB on the SCUT-Syn dataset in PSNR.

Figure 7 illustrates visualization results to compare our MBE with other methods. MTRNet++ [28] and EnsNet [39] cannot exhaustively remove text with arbitrary orientations or irregular fonts, and cause the outputs with rough text sketches. EraseNet [18] has higher text removal performance than MTR-Net++ and EnsNet, but some non-text patterns are wiped because of failures in text detection. In addition, small-size texts can not be perfectly removed. Our method alleviates the aforementioned problems. Scene texts in various scales are removed, and the complex backgrounds are reserved.

4.5   The Effectiveness of Complementary Multi-Branch Network

The three branches in MBE are designed for learning complementary text-removal functions so that the final fused results achieve the best performance

Table 3. Ablation study on different modules in multi-branch network.

Multiple branch framework	PSNR (↑)	MSSIM (↑)
ResNet-101 + UNet + UNet	34.2614	0.9657
FFHRNet + ResNet101 + UNet	34.4316	0.9711
FFHRNet + UNet + ResNet-101	33.5561	0.9678
ResNet-101+ResNet-101+ResNet-101	32.1547	0.9452
FFHRNet + UNet + UNet	**35.0304**	**0.9731**

Table 4. Robustness study on SCUT-EnsText with various degraded inputs.

Degradation	EraseNet [18]		MBE	
	PSNR (↑)	MSSIM (↑)	PSNR (↑)	MSSIM (↑)
Blur	25.92	0.80	26.04	0.82
Noise	23.91	0.70	24.85	0.78
Rain	27.51	0.87	28.04	0.90

compared to the output from the individual STR branch. To verify the effectiveness of the complementary network mechanism, the FFHRNet in the main branch and U-Net in the sub-branch are replaced with another strong benchmark, ResNet-101 [8] to form an irrelevant multi-branch network. We compare four variations of the multi-branch framework: ResNet-101 in the main branch, ResNet-101 in sub-branch 1, ResNet-101 in sub-branch 2, and ResNet-101 in all branches.

Experimental results with various multi-branch networks are shown in Table 3. We observe that the complementary framework in MBE achieves the best performance compared to all variations of the multi-branch framework, even though the ResNet-101 has a stronger performance than the U-Net. It implies that simply fusing multiple modules instead of considering the relationship among multiple branches can not enhance the text removal results. As a brief conclusion, we use the FFHRNet and U-Net as a backbone to construct the multiple complementary branches framework for ensemble learning.

4.6 Robustness Analysis

We demonstrate our method's robustness in this experiment with three degraded image approaches on the SCUT-EnsText: blurry image, noisy image, and rainy image. To create blurry photos, we use a Gaussian filter with a kernel size of 5×5. We add Gaussian noise with a mean of 0.5 and a variation of 0.1 to generate noisy photos. To create rainy images, we multiplied the length of Gaussian noise by 10 and rotated them 45° to simulate the direction of rain in nature.

As shown in Table 4, it demonstrates our method achieves higher performance in both PSNR and MSSIM than EraseNet. This proves that the ensemble learning in our method can improve the model's robustness when facing interference factors and information loss.

4.7 Synthetic Data via STR for Scene Text Recognition

Since MBE can provide reliable performance on text removal, we extend it to generate a synthetic dataset via replacing the background inpainting module in the SRNet [34] with MBE (SR-MBENet). The SRNet can replace a text in the source image with another one while retaining the styles of both the background and the original text. We collect 50000 real-world data from [13,14,23,30] as

Table 5. Scene text recognition accuracy results on 4 benchmark test datasets. We train DTRB with three synthetic datasets.

Model	Train data	IC13 [14]	IC15 [13]	IIIT [23]	SVT [31]
DTRB [1]	MJSyn [12]+SynText [7]	**93.6**	77.6	87.9	**87.5**
DTRB [1]	Synth-data 1 (SRNet)	87.2	64.0	84.6	77.1
DTRB [1]	Synth-data 2 (SR-MBENet)	93.1	**78.2**	**89.5**	86.7

style images and generate 20 text-swapped images from a single style image to construct our synthetic dataset via SR-MBENet. We train the scene text recognition [1] with three synthetic datasets to analyze the effect of our method by the recognition performance and follow the same evaluation protocol in [1].

In Table 5, we find that the synthetic dataset generated by SRNet might decrease the model performance compared to the baseline (MJSyn [12] +SynText [7]). The reason for it might be that the texts with rare font shapes failed to transfer to new text or the complex text structures are hard to erase leading to noise labels. The SR-MBENet can improve the quality of synthetic datasets by alleviating the second problem. Thus, the model trained with our proposed dataset achieves the highest performance on two benchmarks.

5   Conclusion

We propose a novel method for the STR task by training multiple complementary STR models and combining them for a better result with ensemble learning to solve the multi-scale text erasure problem and background destruction problem. Combining a diverse set of individual STR models can also improve the stability of the overall model, leading to more reliable results than individual models. To ensure synergy between reciprocal branches, we propose a crossing branch feature fusion guideline to help features flow in all branches. The intermediate outputs from different branches are fused in a fusion module for final results. Our model achieves significant performance gains compared to previous STR methods on both the real-world dataset and the synthetic dataset. In the future, we will extend the MBE to a novel scene text editing method that can swap text in scene images with another one while maintaining a realistic look. We believe the new synthetic dataset can fill the gap of shortage in a reliable, large-scale scene text dataset.

Acknowledgments. This work was supported by the Strategic Priority Research Program of the Chinese Academy of Sciences (XDC08020400).

References

1. Baek, J., et al.: What is wrong with scene text recognition model comparisons? Dataset and model analysis. In: Proceedings of the IEEE/CVF International Conference on Computer Vision, pp. 4715–4723 (2019)

2. Bian, X., Wang, C., Quan, W., Ye, J., Zhang, X., Yan, D.M.: Scene text removal via cascaded text stroke detection and erasing. arXiv preprint arXiv:2011.09768 (2020)
3. Charbonnier, P., Blanc-Feraud, L., Aubert, G., Barlaud, M.: Two deterministic half-quadratic regularization algorithms for computed imaging. In: Proceedings of 1st International Conference on Image Processing, vol. 2, pp. 168–172. IEEE (1994)
4. Frome, A., et al.: Large-scale privacy protection in google street view. In: 2009 IEEE 12th International Conference on Computer Vision, pp. 2373–2380. IEEE (2009)
5. Geng, Z., Sun, K., Xiao, B., Zhang, Z., Wang, J.: Bottom-up human pose estimation via disentangled keypoint regression. In: Proceedings of the IEEE/CVF Conference on Computer Vision and Pattern Recognition, pp. 14676–14686 (2021)
6. Goodfellow, I., et al.: Generative adversarial nets. Adv. Neural Inf. Process. Syst. **27** (2014)
7. Gupta, A., Vedaldi, A., Zisserman, A.: Synthetic data for text localisation in natural images. In: Proceedings of the IEEE Conference on Computer Vision and Pattern Recognition, pp. 2315–2324 (2016)
8. He, K., Zhang, X., Ren, S., Sun, J.: Deep residual learning for image recognition. In: Proceedings of the IEEE Conference on Computer Vision and Pattern Recognition, pp. 770–778 (2016)
9. Hochreiter, S., Schmidhuber, J.: Long short-term memory. Neural Comput. **9**(8), 1735–1780 (1997)
10. Inai, K., Pålsson, M., Frinken, V., Feng, Y., Uchida, S.: Selective concealment of characters for privacy protection. In: 2014 22nd International Conference on Pattern Recognition, pp. 333–338. IEEE (2014)
11. Isola, P., Zhu, J.Y., Zhou, T., Efros, A.A.: Image-to-image translation with conditional adversarial networks. In: Proceedings of the IEEE Conference on Computer Vision and Pattern Recognition, pp. 1125–1134 (2017)
12. Jaderberg, M., Simonyan, K., Vedaldi, A., Zisserman, A.: Synthetic data and artificial neural networks for natural scene text recognition. arXiv preprint arXiv:1406.2227 (2014)
13. Karatzas, D., et al.: ICDAR 2015 competition on robust reading. In: 2015 13th International Conference on Document Analysis and Recognition (ICDAR), pp. 1156–1160. IEEE (2015)
14. Karatzas, D., et al.: ICDAR 2013 robust reading competition. In: 2013 12th International Conference on Document Analysis and Recognition, pp. 1484–1493. IEEE (2013)
15. Karras, T., Aila, T., Laine, S., Lehtinen, J.: Progressive growing of GANs for improved quality, stability, and variation. arXiv preprint arXiv:1710.10196 (2017)
16. Keserwani, P., Roy, P.P.: Text region conditional generative adversarial network for text concealment in the wild. IEEE Trans. Circ. Syst. Video Technol. **32**, 3152–3163 (2021)
17. Kingma, D.P., Ba, J.: Adam: a method for stochastic optimization. arXiv preprint arXiv:1412.6980 (2014)
18. Liu, C., Liu, Y., Jin, L., Zhang, S., Luo, C., Wang, Y.: EraseNet: end-to-end text removal in the wild. IEEE Trans. Image Process. **29**, 8760–8775 (2020)
19. Long, J., Shelhamer, E., Darrell, T.: Fully convolutional networks for semantic segmentation. In: Proceedings of the IEEE Conference on Computer Vision and Pattern Recognition, pp. 3431–3440 (2015)
20. Loshchilov, I., Hutter, F.: SGDR: Stochastic gradient descent with warm restarts. arXiv preprint arXiv:1608.03983 (2016)

21. Mehri, A., Ardakani, P.B., Sappa, A.D.: MPRNet: multi-path residual network for lightweight image super resolution. In: Proceedings of the IEEE/CVF Winter Conference on Applications of Computer Vision, pp. 2704–2713 (2021)

22. Mirza, M., Osindero, S.: Conditional generative adversarial nets. arXiv preprint arXiv:1411.1784 (2014)

23. Mishra, A., Alahari, K., Jawahar, C.: Scene text recognition using higher order language priors. In: BMVC-British machine vision conference. BMVA (2012)

24. Nakamura, T., Zhu, A., Yanai, K., Uchida, S.: Scene text eraser. In: 2017 14th IAPR International Conference on Document Analysis and Recognition (ICDAR), vol. 1, pp. 832–837. IEEE (2017)

25. Ronneberger, O., Fischer, P., Brox, T.: U-net: convolutional networks for biomedical image segmentation. In: Navab, N., Hornegger, J., Wells, W.M., Frangi, A.F. (eds.) MICCAI 2015. LNCS, vol. 9351, pp. 234–241. Springer, Cham (2015). https://doi.org/10.1007/978-3-319-24574-4_28

26. Suin, M., Purohit, K., Rajagopalan, A.: Spatially-attentive patch-hierarchical network for adaptive motion deblurring. In: Proceedings of the IEEE/CVF Conference on Computer Vision and Pattern Recognition, pp. 3606–3615 (2020)

27. Sun, K., Xiao, B., Liu, D., Wang, J.: Deep high-resolution representation learning for human pose estimation. In: Proceedings of the IEEE/CVF Conference on Computer Vision and Pattern Recognition, pp. 5693–5703 (2019)

28. Tursun, O., Denman, S., Zeng, R., Sivapalan, S., Sridharan, S., Fookes, C.: MTR-Net++: one-stage mask-based scene text eraser. Comput. Vis. Image Underst. **201**, 103066 (2020)

29. Tursun, O., Zeng, R., Denman, S., Sivapalan, S., Sridharan, S., Fookes, C.: MTR-Net: a generic scene text eraser. In: 2019 International Conference on Document Analysis and Recognition (ICDAR), pp. 39–44. IEEE (2019)

30. Veit, A., Matera, T., Neumann, L., Matas, J., Belongie, S.: COCO-text: dataset and benchmark for text detection and recognition in natural images. arXiv preprint arXiv:1601.07140 (2016)

31. Wang, K., Babenko, B., Belongie, S.: End-to-end scene text recognition. In: 2011 International Conference on Computer Vision, pp. 1457–1464. IEEE (2011)

32. Wang, Y., Xie, H., Fang, S., Qu, Y., Zhang, Y.: A simple and strong baseline: progressively region-based scene text removal networks. arXiv preprint arXiv:2106.13029 (2021)

33. Wang, Z., Bovik, A.C., Sheikh, H.R., Simoncelli, E.P.: Image quality assessment: from error visibility to structural similarity. IEEE Trans. Image Process. **13**(4), 600–612 (2004)

34. Wu, L., et al.: Editing text in the wild. In: Proceedings of the 27th ACM International Conference on Multimedia, pp. 1500–1508 (2019)

35. Xingjian, S., Chen, Z., Wang, H., Yeung, D.Y., Wong, W.K., Woo, W.C.: Convolutional LSTM network: a machine learning approach for precipitation nowcasting. In: Advances in Neural Information Processing Systems, pp. 802–810 (2015)

36. Zamir, S.W., et al.: Multi-stage progressive image restoration. In: Proceedings of the IEEE/CVF Conference on Computer Vision and Pattern Recognition, pp. 14821–14831 (2021)

37. Zdenek, J., Nakayama, H.: Erasing scene text with weak supervision. In: Proceedings of the IEEE/CVF Winter Conference on Applications of Computer Vision, pp. 2238–2246 (2020)

38. Zhang, H., Dai, Y., Li, H., Koniusz, P.: Deep stacked hierarchical multi-patch network for image deblurring. In: Proceedings of the IEEE/CVF Conference on Computer Vision and Pattern Recognition, pp. 5978–5986 (2019)

39. Zhang, S., Liu, Y., Jin, L., Huang, Y., Lai, S.: EnsNet: ensconce text in the wild. In: Proceedings of the AAAI Conference on Artificial Intelligence, vol. 33, pp. 801–808 (2019)
40. Zhang, Y., Li, K., Li, K., Wang, L., Zhong, B., Fu, Y.: Image super-resolution using very deep residual channel attention networks. In: Proceedings of the European Conference on Computer Vision (ECCV), pp. 286–301 (2018)

Lightweight Alpha Matting Network Using Distillation-Based Channel Pruning

Donggeun Yoon[1] , Jinsun Park[2] , and Donghyeon Cho[1(✉)]

[1] Chungnam National University, Daejeon, Republic of Korea
202250187@o.cnu.ac.kr, cdh12242@cnu.ac.kr
[2] Pusan National University, Busan, Republic of Korea
jspark@pusan.ac.kr

Abstract. Recently, alpha matting has received a lot of attention because of its usefulness in mobile applications such as selfies. Therefore, there has been a demand for a lightweight alpha matting model due to the limited computational resources of commercial portable devices. To this end, we suggest a distillation-based channel pruning method for the alpha matting networks. In the pruning step, we remove channels of a student network having fewer impacts on mimicking the knowledge of a teacher network. Then, the pruned lightweight student network is trained by the same distillation loss. A lightweight alpha matting model from the proposed method outperforms existing lightweight methods. To show superiority of our algorithm, we provide various quantitative and qualitative experiments with in-depth analyses. Furthermore, we demonstrate the versatility of the proposed distillation-based channel pruning method by applying it to semantic segmentation.

Keywords: Matting · Channel pruning · Knowledge distillation

1 Introduction

The purpose of a natural image matting (*i.e.*, alpha matting) is to estimate the transparency of the user-specified foreground in an image. The alpha matting is formally defined as follows [12]:

$$I = \alpha F + (1 - \alpha)B, \tag{1}$$

where I, F and B are the observed color image, foreground, background, respectively. Also, α is transparency (*i.e.*, alpha matte). The natural image matting is a highly ill-posed problem because it needs to estimate F, B, and α simultaneously from an input color image I and a trimap providing known foreground and

---

Project page is at https://github.com/DongGeun-Yoon/DCP.

Supplementary Information The online version contains supplementary material available at https://doi.org/10.1007/978-3-031-26313-2_7.

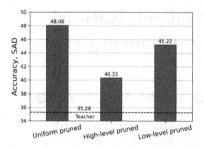 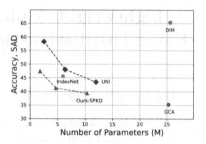

Fig. 1. (Left) Comparison of arbitrarily pruned models. The high-level pruned model removes channels from the high-level layers, and the low-level pruned model removes the channels from the low-level layers. (Right) Trade-offs between accuracy and model size. Circle dots show results of original models. Squares and triangles denote results of pruned GCA models using uniform pruning and our method, respectively.

background pixels. Traditional approaches for natural image matting are categorized into affinity-based and sampling-based methods. Affinity-based methods [1, 4,5,11,20,27,28,43,55] propagate alpha values from known regions to pixels in unknown regions by analyzing statistical correlation among pixels. Meanwhile, sampling-based methods [7,8,16,19,25,40,41,48] construct foreground and background color sample sets using pixels in known areas, then estimates alpha values in unknown regions. However, these algorithms often rely on strong assumptions such as local smoothness [28] or sparsity of foreground and background colors [48].

Since the advent of large-scale image matting datasets such as Adobe-1k [50], deep learning-based matting algorithms been actively studied [2,9,10,30,34,35, 37,42,44,46]. These methods outperform conventional ones remarkably. Usually, the alpha matting networks are based on U-Net [38] or fully-convolutional networks (FCN) [33]. For better performance, the number of layers or channels can be increased and also auxiliary modules can be added to baseline networks. However, this leads to the increased computational costs and memory requirements that can be problematic for mobile applications. Recently, a lightweight alpha matting network based on similarity-preserving knowledge distillation (SPKD) [52] was introduced to resolve these issues. It successfully transfers similarities of features from the teacher network to the student network, which make the student network achieves much better performance than the baseline student network trained from scratch.

However, it is still an open problem that which architecture is the best one for the lightweight student network for natural image matting. It can be seen from the left of Fig. 1 that the performance varies greatly depending on which layer the channels are removed from. Note that the high-level pruned model has fewer parameters than the low-level pruned model. Also, as shown in right of Fig. 1, there is a trade-off between performance and model size, thus it is important to find an proper network architecture. To find the optimal lightweight network architecture, various network pruning techniques can be applied. Although it has been actively studied in the field of classification, it has not been dealt with much in the reconstruction problem including alpha matting. Recently, channel pruning methods for semantic segmentation task were introduced in [6,21], but they mainly focus on preserving high-level semantic information rather than low-level fine structures that are crucial for the natural image matting problems.

To focus on low-level fine details during the channel pruning, we borrow the power of a pre-trained high-performance matting network which well preserves fine details. In other words, in this paper, we present a distillation-based channel pruning method that removes the channels having a low impact in mimicking the pre-trained teacher network. In the pruning phase, we induce the sparsity of the scaling factor of the batch normalization (BN) layer as in [6,21,31] and additionally apply distillation loss with a powerful pre-trained teacher model that is capable of precisely guiding a student network to preserve fine structural details in its prediction. In the training phase, we train the pruned lightweight network by the same distillation loss used in the pruning stage. Note that proposed method can make existing lightweight model (*i.e.*, IndexNet) even lighter.

Our contributions can be summarized as follows. (i) We introduce a novel channel pruning method for the natural image matting problem. To our best knowledge, this is the first attempt to apply the network pruning technique for the alpha matting problem. (ii) By utilizing a distillation loss within the channel pruning step, we succeed in finding a lightweight alpha matting network that can recover fine details. (iii) Our pruned network outperforms other baseline pruning approaches on two publicly available alpha matting datasets (Adobe-1K, Distinctions-646) while having a comparable number of parameters. In addition, we provide various ablation studies for a deeper understanding.

2   Related Works

2.1   Natural Image Matting

Most image matting techniques can be categorized into affinity-based and color sampling-based methods. In affinity-based methods, statistical affinity is analyzed among the local and non-local neighbors to propagate values of alpha to the unknown areas from the known regions. Levin *et al.* [28] introduced the closed-form solution based on matting Laplacian using the linear color model. For handling high resolution images, He *et al.* [20] proposed efficient method to solve a large kernel matting Laplacian. Furthermore, Lee and Wu [27] introduced non-local matting propagating alpha values across non-local neighboring pixels. Chen *et al.* [4] suggested the KNN matting which uses only k-nearest non-local neighbors to propagate alpha values. In addition, Chen *et al.* [5] utilized both local and non-local smoothness prior and Aksoy *et al.* [1] proposed multiple definitions of affinity for natural image matting.

The color sampling-based methods find foreground and background colors from constructed color sampler sets, then estimate alpha values in unknown regions. Bayesian matting [12] utilizes statistical models to analyze pixels in unknown regions. Robust matting [48], shared matting [16] and weighted color and texture matting [41] select the best color samples based on their own designed cost functions that take into account spatial, photometric, or texture information. He *et al.* [19] proposed a randomized searching method to use global samples in the known areas to find the best combination of foreground and background colors. Shahrian *et al.* [40] constructed comprehensive color sample sets to cover broad color variations using Gaussian Mixture Model (GMM). Karacan *et al.* [25] choose colors of foreground and background based on sparse representation.

After large-scale alpha matting datasets were published [37,50], a lot of deep learning-based works have been introduced. Xu *et al.* [50] proposed a simple two-stage network for natural image matting. Lutz *et al.* [35] applied adversarial training for obtaining visually appealing alpha matte results. To preserve details of alpha mattes, Hao *et al.* [34] introduced IndexNet including indices-guided unpooling operation. In addition, contextual attention [30] and hierarchical attention [37] mechanisms were proposed for the matting problem. Yu *et al.* [53] proposed mask-guided matting leveraging a progressive refinement network with a general coarse mask as guidance. Although the performance of alpha matting has been substantially improved, there are still not many studies on lightening alpha matting networks. Recently, Yoon *et al.* [52] succeeded to utilize knowledge distillation (KD) to obtain the lightweight deep-CNN model for alpha matting. They reduce the number of channels with a fixed ratio, therefore, the optimal channel reduction ratio should be determined empirically.

2.2 Network Pruning

The purpose of the network pruning is to reduce redundancies in the over-parameterized deep CNN models for fast run-time while maintaining performance. In general, network pruning is divided into unstructured pruning [14,18, 36,45] which requires special libraries or hardware, and structured pruning [3, 29,31,49] which is relatively easy to implement. In this subsection, we focus on structured pruning that is more relevant to our work. Wen *et al.* [49] proposed a Structured Sparsity Learning (SSL) method to sparsify structures including filters, channels, or layers by using group sparsity regularization. Li *et al.* [29] introduced a method to remove channels having small incoming weights in a trained deep CNN model. Changpinyo *et al.* [3] deactivate connections between filters in convolutional layers to obtain smaller networks. Liu *et al.* [31] proposed the network slimming method to explicitly impose channel-wise sparsity in the deep CNN model using scaling factors in batch normalization. Gao *et al.* [15] proposed a feature boosting and suppression (FBS) method to dynamically remove and boost channels according to the inputs using auxiliary connections. Despite many pruning studies, most of them focus on the classification task. Fortunately, pruning techniques for semantic segmentation have begun to be introduced recently. Chen *et al.* [6] suggested a channel pruning method for semantic segmentation based on multi-task learning. Furthermore, He *et al.* [21] proposed context-aware channel pruning method by leveraging the layer-wise channels interdependency. However, pruning researches for matting network have not been addressed yet.

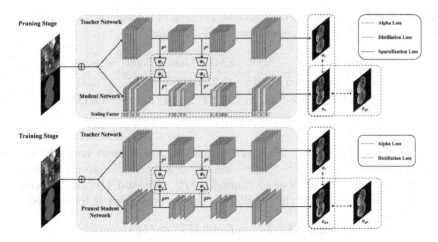

Fig. 2. In the pruning stage, the student network is lightweighted using scaling factor sparsification loss and distillation loss with pre-trained teacher model. In the training stage, the same distillation loss is used to train the pruned student network.

Since the estimation of the fine structures in alpha mattes are the most important objective of the matting network, a powerful pruning technique suitable for this purpose is strongly required. To this end, we present a distillation-based channel pruning technique that exploits a powerful pre-trained alpha matting model suitable for recovering low-level fine details.

3   Proposed Approach

In this section, we briefly describe the basics of KD and motivation of using KD for network pruning. Then, we introduce the distillation-based channel pruning method for sparsifying alpha matting network, and explain a method for training pruned lightweight model with KD. We use the same distillation method for both pruning and training stages, even though it is also possible to utilize different methods. Related experiments are provided by the ablation studies. Overview of our distillation-based channel pruning and training is illustrated in Fig. 2.

3.1   Knowledge Distillation

Knowledge distillation (KD) [23] is a technique supervising a small student model by a larger teacher model. The main purpose of KD is to transfer rich feature representations of the large model trained by the huge amount of data into the small model. Therefore, it is very useful when there is a lack of training data or limited computational resources and memory of the devices.

Table 1. The first row: model with channels removed from low-level layers. The second row: model with channels removed from high-level layers.

Methods	MSE	SAD	Grad	Conn	#Param
Low-level pruned	0.012	45.22	24.85	39.77	22.63M
High-level pruned	**0.011**	**40.33**	**20.34**	**35.48**	**8.83M**

Mathematically, feature maps of the teacher and student networks in i-th layer are denoted as $F_i^t \in \mathbb{R}^{C_i^t \times H_i^t \times W_i^t}$ and $F_i^s \in \mathbb{R}^{C_i^s \times H_i^s \times W_i^s}$, respectively. Note that $\{C_i^t, C_i^s\}$ are the number of channels, $\{H_i^t, H_i^s\}$ and $\{W_i^t, W_i^s\}$ represent the spatial size. Generally, the distillation loss for each layer is formulated as

$$\mathcal{L}_{KD}(F_i^t, F_i^s) = \mathcal{L}_F(\Phi_t(F_i^t), \Phi_s(F_i^s)), \tag{2}$$

where, $\mathcal{L}_F(\cdot)$ is a similarity function, $\Phi_t(\cdot)$ and $\Phi_s(\cdot)$ are feature transform functions for the teacher and student networks. According to the purpose of distillation, appropriate $\mathcal{L}_F(\cdot)$, $\Phi_t(\cdot)$ and $\Phi_s(\cdot)$ should be designed.

3.2 Motivation

Over the recent years, various KD methods have been introduced [17, 22, 23, 47, 51], but most of them arbitrarily set the architecture of the student network. Therefore, they do not ensure whether the student network is optimal for both distillation and the given tasks. For example, the importance of each channel in the layers of a deep CNN model may be different, therefore, reducing the number of channels uniformly for all the layers is sub-optimal obviously. We believe that it is also important for the alpha matting task to find the optimal student model.

To confirm this, we perform a preliminary experiment using GCA [30] as a baseline matting model. First, we divide the encoder of GCA model into two groups: low-level layers (conv1-conv3) and high-level layers (conv4-conv5). Then, we apply uniform 50% channel pruning to low-level and high-level layers separately, and then obtain two different pruned networks. The ratios of the removed channel parameters to the whole encoder are 12.75% in low-level and 37.25% in high-level layers, respectively. In other words, more parameters are eliminated from the high-level layers rather than the low-level ones. Using these two uniformly pruned GCA models, we verified the alpha matting performance on the Adobe-1k dataset [50]. As reported in Table 1, the model removing channels of high-level layers (the second row) prunes more channels than the model removing channels of low-level layers (the first row) but achieves better performance. The number of network parameters is also much less. As a result, it can be seen that the channels of low-level layers have more influence on the alpha matting performance. Regarding that the high-level pruned network has achieved better performance, this result implies that the channel distributions of the original and optimal pruned models might be different significantly and the low-level layers are highly important in the alpha matting problem.

Therefore, in this paper, we propose a method to find a student network model that can well receive low-level knowledge from a large-capacity teacher network. To this end, we introduce a distillation-aware pruning loss in the pruning stage to create an optimal lightweight network for alpha matting.

3.3 Pruning with KD

Inspired by [31], we adopt a channel pruning method based on the sparsification of scaling factors in batch normalization (BN) layers. BN layer is used in most deep CNN models for better generalization and fast convergence. Formally, the BN layer is defined as follows:

$$y = \gamma \frac{x - \mu}{\sqrt{\sigma^2 + \epsilon}} + \beta, \tag{3}$$

where x and y are input and output of BN layer, and μ and σ are mean and standard deviation of the input mini-batch features, and ϵ is a small constant. γ and β are the learnable scaling and shifting factors. In [31], the scaling factor γ in the BN layer is considered as the measure for the importance of each channel. In other words, a channel with a very small γ is regarded as the layer which does not contribute significantly to the final prediction. Therefore, enforcing sparsification on the scaling factors eases the identification of prunable layers.

Similarly, our pruning method trains a target student network with sparsification loss and distillation loss, then remove channels with small scaling factors in BN layers. We adopt the same alpha matting model for both teacher and student networks. For the network pruning, only parameters of the student network are updated while those of the teacher network are fixed. The final loss includes alpha prediction, channel sparsification, and distillation losses as follows:

$$\mathcal{L}_P = \lambda_1 \mathcal{L}_\alpha(\alpha_s, \alpha_{gt}) + \lambda_2 \mathcal{L}_\alpha(\alpha_s, \alpha_t) + \lambda_3 \sum_{\gamma \in \zeta} |\gamma| + \lambda_4 \sum_{i \in \eta} \mathcal{L}_{KD}(F_i^t, F_i^s), \tag{4}$$

where $\mathcal{L}_\alpha(\cdot)$ is the vanilla alpha prediction loss introduced in [50], and α_s, α_t, α_{gt} are alpha matte prediction results from the student network and the teacher network, and ground truth, respectively. ζ is the set of scaling factors over all the BN layers and η is the index set of layers utilized for distillation loss. λ_1, λ_2, λ_3, and λ_4 are balancing factors for each term. Note that the distillation loss is used only for the encoder part.

In (4), the gamma value γ corresponding to the importance score can be estimated significantly differently depending on the distillation loss, which means that different pruned networks can be created. Therefore, we adopt several recent KD methods to be utilized in the proposed channel pruning method as follows:

- **Neuron Selectivity Transfer (NST):** Huang and Wang proposed NST [24] that aligns the distribution of spatial neuron activations between teacher and student networks. To this end, NST minimizes maximum mean discrepancy (MMD) distance between activations of teacher and student networks.

Thus, $\Phi(\cdot)$ in (2) is a certain function for kernel trick which projects samples into a higher dimensional feature space. Also, $\mathcal{L}_F(\cdot)$ is distance (*i.e.*, L_2 distance) between means of projected features of teacher and student networks.

- **Overhaul of Feature Distillation (OFD):** Heo *et al.* [22] investigated various aspects of the existing feature distillation methods and suggested OFD that is a simple but effective distillation method. In particular, $\Phi_t(\cdot)$ in (2) is a margin ReLU function while $\Phi_s(\cdot)$ is a regressor consisting of a 1×1 convolution layer. Also, $\mathcal{L}_F(\cdot)$ in (2) is a partial L_2 distance.
- **Similarity-Preserving Knowledge Distillation (SPKD):** The SPKD-based distillation method makes the pairwise similarity of the student network similar to that of the teacher network. In [47], batch similarity for the classification task is used while spatial and channel similarity for the regression task is utilized in [26,52]. Thus, $\Phi(\cdot)$ in (2) is a function of making pairwise similarities and $\mathcal{L}_F(\cdot)$ is the L_2 distance.

After training with distillation loss as in (4), we prune the target student network based on scaling factors of BN layers. The smaller the scaling factor is, the less impact it has on the output of the layer, thus we remove the channels with a lower scaling factor than a threshold. To eliminate M channels, we adopt the M-th smallest scaling factor as the threshold. At this point, thresholds of the encoder and decoder are obtained separately since distillation loss is only used in the encoder. After pruning, we can get the compact lightweight alpha matting network, which is suitable to get fine details by KD.

3.4   Training with KD

By the aforementioned our distillation-based channel pruning, the architecture of a lightweight student network can be obtained. In [32], the network structure itself is considered more important than the remaining parameters after pruning. In other words, the fine-tuned model and the trained from scratch model achieve similar result, or even the trained from scratch model performs better. Thus, we train the pruned network from scratch again by applying KD using the teacher network based on the loss function defined as follows:

$$\mathcal{L}_T = w_1 \mathcal{L}_\alpha(\alpha_{\mathrm{ps}}, \alpha_{\mathrm{gt}}) + w_2 \mathcal{L}_\alpha(\alpha_{\mathrm{ps}}, \alpha_{\mathrm{t}}) + w_3 \sum_{i \in \eta} \mathcal{L}_{KD}(F_i^t, F_i^{ps}), \qquad (5)$$

where α_{ps} is a prediction of the pruned student network and F_i^{ps} is feature maps in the i-th layer of the pruned student network. w_1, w_2, and w_3 are balancing factors for each term in (5). Unlike (4), sparsification loss is not included, and the pruned student network is used. We use the same distillation loss as the pruning step, but other distillation losses can be used.

4   Experimental Results

In this section, we evaluate the proposed distillation-based channel pruning method both quantitatively and qualitatively. We validate our method on various teacher models including GCA [30], DIM [50], and IndexNet [34], and also

Table 2. Quantitative evaluation by GCA-50% model on the benchmark.

Dataset	Methods		MSE	SAD	Grad	Conn	#Param	FLOPs
	KD	Prune						
Adobe-1k	Unpruned(teacher)		0.009	35.28	16.92	35.53	25.27M	11.19G
	–	UNI	0.017	52.61	34.27	46.24	6.35M	**2.90G**
	–	NS	0.017	51.57	28.70	45.66	**4.30M**	6.84G
	–	FBS	0.013	45.09	22.87	39.39	7.11M	**2.90G**
	–	CAP	0.014	48.55	26.01	42.76	5.13M	6.50G
	NST	NS	0.020	58.10	36.78	51.80	**4.30M**	6.84G
	NST	Ours	0.017	53.47	30.59	47.37	5.80M	7.02G
	OFD	NS	0.014	46.96	24.16	41.93	**4.30M**	6.84G
	OFD	Ours	0.012	43.15	21.79	37.66	5.13M	6.48G
	SPKD	NS	0.012	42.69	21.88	37.54	**4.30M**	6.84G
	SPKD	Ours	**0.011**	**41.26**	**21.42**	**35.87**	4.66M	6.74G
Disticntions-646	Unpruned (teacher)		0.025	27.60	15.82	22.03	25.27M	11.19G
	–	UNI	0.037	37.83	26.35	28.36	6.35M	**2.90G**
	–	NS	0.028	31.45	20.47	25.69	**3.99M**	6.41G
	–	FBS	**0.024**	28.61	**17.36**	23.52	7.11M	**2.90G**
	–	CAP	0.026	29.23	18.59	23.85	5.30M	6.36G
	NST	NS	0.038	36.13	24.33	28.20	**3.99M**	6.41G
	NST	Ours	0.035	36.58	23.69	27.42	4.93M	6.16G
	OFD	NS	0.026	28.45	19.86	23.22	**3.99M**	6.41G
	OFD	Ours	**0.024**	**27.12**	**17.36**	22.03	5.03M	6.22G
	SPKD	NS	**0.024**	27.88	18.33	22.46	**3.99M**	6.41G
	SPKD	Ours	**0.024**	27.31	17.81	**21.90**	4.24M	6.72G

provide various ablation studies. Finally, we show that the proposed algorithm can be utilized for the other task such as semantic segmentation.

4.1 Implementation Details

In most experiments, we adopt GCA matting as a baseline alpha matting network. In order to evaluate our distillation-based channel pruning method, we use two public benchmark datasets: Adobe-1k [50] and Distinctions-646 [37]. Since Distinctions-646 test set does not provide official trimaps, we generate trimaps from ground truth alpha matte using dilation with kernel size 10. The evaluation metrics for all quantitative experiments are mean squared error (MSE), sum of absolute difference (SAD), gradient error (Grad), connectivity (Conn), the number of network parameters (#Param) and floating-point-opertions (FLOPs). We use activations of the last four layers in the encoder for computing distillation loss as in [52] for a fair comparison.

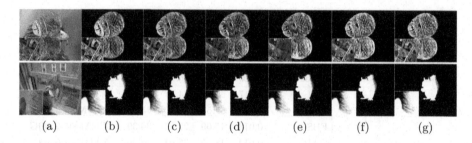

(a)   (b)   (c)   (d)   (e)   (f)   (g)

Fig. 3. Qualitative image matting results by GCA. (a) Input images. (b) Ground truths. (c) UNI. (d) NS [31]. (e) CAP [21]. (f) NS-SPKD. (g) Ours-SPKD.

Table 3. Quantitative results by DIM-50% model on the Adobe-1k.

Methods		MSE	SAD	Grad	Conn	#Param	FLOPs
KD	Prune						
Unpruned (teacher)		0.021	65.37	33.20	67.58	25.58M	24.51G
–	UNI	0.049	114.02	78.89	122.00	6.40M	6.19G
–	NS	0.052	120.82	83.10	129.70	6.32M	7.65G
–	FBS	0.052	110.22	83.14	118.60	6.92M	6.19G
–	CAP	0.040	101.77	63.93	108.61	**4.08M**	**4.26G**
NST	NS	0.033	94.31	55.48	100.67	6.32M	7.65G
NST	Ours	0.032	89.83	49.04	95.20	5.98M	11.23G
OFD	NS	0.029	76.74	42.45	79.86	6.32M	7.65G
OFD	Ours	0.032	76.71	43.86	80.61	7.97M	17.61G
SPKD	NS	0.029	76.73	42.70	80.77	6.32M	7.65G
SPKD	Ours	**0.027**	**73.67**	**40.78**	**76.58**	7.81M	12.53G

4.2   Quantitative Comparisons

We quantitatively verify our distillation-based channel pruning and training methods on Adobe-1k and Distinctions-646 datasets. We adopt the aforementioned NST [24], OFD [22], and SPKD [52] as KD methods for both pruning and training stages. For comparison, uniform channel pruning (UNI), network slimming (NS) [31], feature boosting and suppression (FBS) [15], and context-aware pruning (CAP) [21] are chosen. As reported in Table 2, the number of parameters in all student networks and FLOPs are much smaller than that of a teacher network (about 16–25% parameters and 60% FLOPs). Although our pruned model sometimes has more parameters or more FLOPs than other pruned models (UNI, NS, FBS and CAP), the alpha matting performance is far superior to their performances. Also, our distillation-based channel pruning method achieves better performance than NS regardless of distillation types. Note that we utilize the same KD method in the training step for both our pruning method and NS. Usually, performance is slightly higher when SPKD is used than OFD. However,

Table 4. Quantitative results by IndexNet-25% model on the Adobe-1k.

Methods		MSE	SAD	Grad	Conn	#Param	FLOPs
KD	Prune						
Unpruned (teacher)		0.013	45.61	27.06	43.79	8.15M	5.64G
–	UNI	0.027	65.21	42.56	66.83	3.49M	**3.22G**
–	NS	0.026	65.45	40.79	67.11	4.21M	5.34G
–	FBS	0.020	56.43	34.41	56.78	4.05M	**3.22G**
–	CAP	0.018	53.32	35.17	53.41	4.07M	5.38G
NST	NS	0.020	57.04	33.99	57.49	4.21M	5.34G
NST	Ours	0.019	54.21	28.14	53.57	**4.02M**	4.95G
OFD	NS	0.017	52.13	29.99	51.76	4.21M	5.34G
OFD	Ours	0.015	47.24	**24.42**	46.26	4.41M	5.13G
SPKD	NS	0.016	50.35	27.21	49.86	4.21M	5.34G
SPKD	Ours	**0.014**	**47.06**	25.98	**45.77**	5.09M	5.21G

when NST is used, the performance is lower than the existing pruning that does not include KD in the training step. It indicates that the type of distillation loss is also an important factor for both the pruning and training.

To verify the generality of our method, the same experiments are performed using DIM and IndexNet as backbone models instead of GCA matting. Similar to the case of GCA matting, the best performance is achieved with SPKD as reported in Table 3 and Table 4. A different point from the case of GCA matting is that comparable performance was achieved even when using NST. Note that the original IndexNet is already a lightweight model because it is based on MobileNetv2 [39], but it can be even lighter by applying our channel pruning.

4.3 Qualitative Comparisons

Figure 3 shows the qualitative performance of our method. We compare our results obtained using SPKD with results from existing pruning algorithms. Examples contain various object structures: short hair, overlapped color distribution (*squirrel*) and transparency (*glass*). As expected, the results of the existing pruning methods are over-smoothed as shown in the (*glass*) example of Fig. 3-(d, e). In this example, UNI produces a better result than NS and CAP. Overall, results using distillation loss in the pruning step (Fig. 3-(f)) show stable and visually pleasing predictions. Moreover, our final results using the SPKD in both pruning and training step (Fig. 3-(g)) provide the best predictions with fine details preserved.

4.4 Ablation Studies

Different Distillation for Pruning and Training. Since it is possible to utilize different distillation losses for pruning and training stages, it is meaningful

Table 5. Ablation study on various combinations of methods for distillation and pruning method. All evaluations are conducted by GCA-50% model on the Adobe-1k.

Methods		MSE	SAD	Grad	Conn
KD	Prune				
NST	+NST	0.017	53.47	30.59	47.37
	+OFD	0.018	53.70	30.85	46.78
	+SPKD	0.019	56.85	35.94	49.30
OFD	+NST	0.012	44.09	21.91	39.24
	+OFD	0.012	43.15	21.79	37.66
	+SPKD	0.013	44.14	23.51	39.82
SPKD	+NST	0.013	43.98	23.65	38.82
	+OFD	**0.011**	42.07	21.51	36.58
	+SPKD	**0.011**	**41.26**	**21.42**	**35.87**

Table 6. Results according to various pruning ratios. All evaluations are conducted by GCA-model with SPKD on the Adobe-1k.

Methods	MSE	SAD	Grad	Conn	#Param
UNI-30%	0.012	43.46	23.78	38.61	12.00M
UNI-50%	0.015	48.06	30.28	42.81	6.35M
UNI-70%	0.019	58.26	33.53	50.77	2.50M
Ours-30%	**0.010**	**39.38**	**19.45**	**34.80**	10.37M
Ours-50%	0.011	41.26	21.42	35.87	4.66M
Ours-70%	0.014	47.36	25.87	42.02	**1.80M**

to explore whether it is better to use different distillation losses in pruning and training steps or to use the same distillation loss. To this end, we performed experiments on all combinations of NST, OFD, and SPKD in the pruning and training phases. As reported in Table 5, we can achieve better performance when the same distillation loss is used in the pruning and training phases. Even more, in the student model pruned with NST, it is better to use NST in the training stage than OFD and SPKD, which are more advanced distillation techniques. These results are reasonable because the student network architecture obtained by a specific KD method will have a high chance to be more effective for the same distillation method than the other ones.

Pruning Ratio. We analyze our distillation-based pruning according to pruning ratios. We compare the results of the model in which the number of channels is reduced by 30%, 50%, and 70% using the our method, and the model uniformly reduced in the same proportion. For all cases, we use the same SPKD as distillation loss for training step. As in Table 6, the pruned models whose channels are reduced by 70% and 50% using our method achieve better performance and fewer network parameters than the model uniformly pruned by 50%.

Table 7. Results of training our pruned model from scratch without distillation.

Prune	MSE	SAD	Grad	Conn
+NST	**0.017**	**54.02**	**31.50**	**47.45**
+OFD	**0.017**	56.44	33.10	49.39
+SPKD	**0.017**	56.88	32.62	50.09

Table 8. Comparisons of Running Time (RT) per image on DIM model.

Method	MSE	SAD	#Param	FLOPs	RT (ms)
Unpruned	0.021	65.37	25.58M	24.51G	11.33
UNI	0.049	114.02	6.40M	6.19G	3.80
NS	0.052	110.22	6.32M	7.65G	3.87
CAP	0.040	101.77	**4.08M**	**4.26G**	**3.50**
Ours (NST)	0.032	89.83	5.98M	11.23G	5.53
Ours (OFD)	0.032	76.71	7.97M	17.61G	5.67
Ours (SPKD)	**0.027**	**73.67**	7.81M	12.53G	5.64

Training from Scratch without KD. To analyze the effect of paired distillation loss for both the pruning and training stages, we train our pruned model from scratch without KD. As reported in Table 7, our pruned model achieves slightly worse performance than models pruned by UNI, NS, and CAP when trained without KD in the training phase. Therefore, we conclude that our distillation-based channel pruning is more beneficial when it is combined with the proper distillation method during the training.

Running Time. We measure the running time of the each pruned model using Adobe-1k dataset. As reported in Table 8, the performance (MSE, SAD) of our method with SPKD is quite close to those of unpruned teacher model while it runs twice faster than the teacher model. The existing methods (UNI, NS, CAP) are faster than our method, but the performance (MSE, SAD) is very poor.

Application on Semantic Segmentation. Our distillation-based channel pruning technique is applicable not only to alpha matting but also to other tasks. Therefore, in this subsection, we verify whether the proposed method is effective for semantic segmentation. For experiments, we adopt PSPNet-50 [54] as a baseline model and test our method on Pascal VOC 2012 validation set [13]. We utilize the mean Intersection over Union (mIoU), and pixel accuracy (Acc.) as evaluation metrics.

As reported in Table 9, the proposed distillation-based channel pruning method achieves superior performance compared to the other existing channel pruning methods. Note that the performance of the pruned model by the NS is similar to our method when KD is applied, but the pruned model by our method has much fewer parameters. Also, as shown in Fig. 4, our channel pruning method produces a visually more pleasing result compared to the other channel pruning techniques.

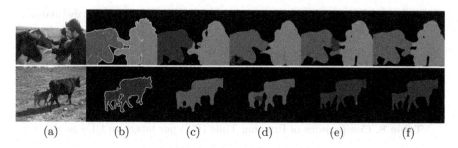

(a)   (b)   (c)   (d)   (e)   (f)

Fig. 4. Example of semantic segmentation results on PASCAL VOC2012 validation set. (a) Input images. (b) Ground truths. (c) NS. (d) CAP. (e) NS-OFD. (f) Ours-OFD.

Table 9. Semantic segmentation results by 50% pruned PSPNet-50.

Methods		mIoU	Acc.	#Param	Methods		mIoU	Acc.	#Param
KD	Prune				KD	Prune			
Unpruned (teacher)		78.02	95.13	49.1M	NST	NS	60.67	90.80	26.5M
					NST	Ours	60.81	90.69	22.0M
–	UNI	51.40	88.05	**12.3M**	OFD	NS	62.45	90.69	26.5M
–	NS	41.78	85.24	26.5M	OFD	Ours	**63.48**	**90.85**	21.7M
–	FBS	53.62	88.75	19.7M	SPKD	NS	58.26	89.55	26.5M
–	CAP	53.61	88.58	22.2M	SPKD	Ours	58.20	89.18	21.9M

5   Conclusion

We have proposed a distillation-based channel pruning method for lightening a deep image matting network. In the pruning step, we train a student network that has the same architecture with a teacher network using the distillation-based sparsification loss. Then, we remove channels that have low scaling factor of BN layer. Finally, we train the pruned student network using the same distillation loss utilized in the pruning step. Experimental results demonstrate that our distillation-based channel pruning method successfully reduces the number of parameters. The lightweight network obtained by the proposed method achieves significantly better performance than other lightweight networks with similar capacity. We analyze the proposed channel pruning technique through extensive ablation studies.

Acknowledgements. This work was partly supported by Institute of Information & communications Technology Planning & Evaluation (IITP) grant funded by the Korea government (MSIT) (No. RS-2022-00155857, Artificial Intelligence Convergence Innovation Human Resources Development (Chungnam National University)) and the National Research Foundation of Korea (NRF) grant funded by the Korea government (MSIT, No. 2021R1A4A1032580 and No. 2022R1C1C1009334).

References

1. Aksoy, Y., Aydin, T.O., Pollefeys, M.: Designing effective inter-pixel information flow for natural image matting. In: Proceedings of Computer Vision and Pattern Recognition (CVPR) (2017)
2. Cai, S., et al.: Disentangled image matting. In: Proceedings of International Conference on Computer Vision (ICCV) (2019)
3. Changpinyo, S., Sandler, M., Zhmoginov, A.: The power of sparsity in convolutional neural networks. ArXiv abs/1702.06257 (2017)
4. Chen, Q., Li, D., Tang, C.K.: KNN matting. In: Proceedings of Computer Vision and Pattern Recognition (CVPR) (2012)
5. Chen, X., Zou, D., Zhou, S.Z., Zhao, Q., Tan, P.: Image matting with local and nonlocal smooth priors. In: Proceedings of Computer Vision and Pattern Recognition (CVPR) (2013)
6. Chen, X., Wang, Y., Zhang, Y., Du, P., Xu, C., Xu, C.: Multi-task pruning for semantic segmentation networks. ArXiv abs/2007.08386 (2020)
7. Cho, D., Kim, S., Tai, Y.-W.: Consistent matting for light field images. In: Fleet, D., Pajdla, T., Schiele, B., Tuytelaars, T. (eds.) ECCV 2014. LNCS, vol. 8692, pp. 90–104. Springer, Cham (2014). https://doi.org/10.1007/978-3-319-10593-2_7
8. Cho, D., Kim, S., Tai, Y.W., Kweon, I.S.: Automatic trimap generation and consistent matting for light-field images. IEEE Trans. Pattern Anal. Mach. Intell. (TPAMI) 39(8), 1504–1517 (2016)
9. Cho, D., Tai, Y.W., Kweon, I.S.: Deep convolutional neural network for natural image matting using initial alpha mattes. IEEE Trans. Image Process. (TIP) 28(3), 1054–1067 (2018)
10. Cho, D., Tai, Y.-W., Kweon, I.: Natural image matting using deep convolutional neural networks. In: Leibe, B., Matas, J., Sebe, N., Welling, M. (eds.) ECCV 2016. LNCS, vol. 9906, pp. 626–643. Springer, Cham (2016). https://doi.org/10.1007/978-3-319-46475-6_39
11. Choi, I., Lee, M., Tai, Y.-W.: Video matting using multi-frame nonlocal matting laplacian. In: Fitzgibbon, A., Lazebnik, S., Perona, P., Sato, Y., Schmid, C. (eds.) ECCV 2012. LNCS, vol. 7577, pp. 540–553. Springer, Heidelberg (2012). https://doi.org/10.1007/978-3-642-33783-3_39
12. Chuang, Y.Y., Curless, B., Salesin, D.H., Szeliski, R.: A Bayesian approach to digital matting. In: Proceedings of Computer Vision and Pattern Recognition (CVPR) (2001)
13. Everingham, M., Eslami, S.M.A., Gool, L.V., Williams, C.K.I., Winn, J.M., Zisserman, A.: The pascal visual object classes challenge: a retrospective. Int. J. Comput. Vision 111, 98–136 (2014)
14. Frankle, J., Carbin, M.: The lottery ticket hypothesis: finding sparse, trainable neural networks. In: International Conference on Learning Representations (2019)
15. Gao, X., Zhao, Y., Łukasz Dudziak, Mullins, R., zhong Xu, C.: Dynamic channel pruning: feature boosting and suppression. In: International Conference on Learning Representations (2019)
16. Gastal, E.S.L., Oliveira, M.M.: Shared sampling for real-time alpha matting. In: Eurographics (2010)
17. Ge, S., Zhao, S., Li, C., Li, J.: Low-resolution face recognition in the wild via selective knowledge distillation. IEEE Trans. Image Process. (TIP) 28(4), 2051–2062 (2019)

18. Han, S., Pool, J., Tran, J., Dally, W.J.: Learning both weights and connections for efficient neural networks. In: Proceedings of Neural Information Processing Systems (NeurIPS), pp. 1135–1143 (2015)
19. He, K., Rhemann, C., Rother, C., Tang, X., Sun, J.: A global sampling method for alpha matting. In: Proceedings of Computer Vision and Pattern Recognition (CVPR) (2011)
20. He, K., Sun, J., Tang, X.: Fast matting using large kernel matting laplacian matrices. In: Proceedings of Computer Vision and Pattern Recognition (CVPR) (2010)
21. He, W., Wu, M., Liang, M., Lam, S.K.: CAP: context-aware pruning for semantic segmentation. In: Proceedings of Winter Conference on Applications of Computer Vision (WACV), pp. 960–969 (2021)
22. Heo, B., Kim, J., Yun, S., Park, H., Kwak, N., Choi, J.Y.: A comprehensive overhaul of feature distillation. In: Proceedings of International Conference on Computer Vision (ICCV) (2019)
23. Hinton, G., Vinyals, O., Dean, J.: Distilling the knowledge in a neural network. In: Proceedings of Neural Information Processing Systems Workshops (NeurIPSW) (2015)
24. Huang, Z., Wang, N.: Like what you like: knowledge distill via neuron selectivity transfer. ArXiv abs/1707.01219 (2017)
25. Karacan, L., Erdem, A., Erdem, E.: Image matting with kl-divergence based sparse sampling. In: Proceedings of International Conference on Computer Vision (ICCV) (2015)
26. Ko, S., Park, J., Chae, B., Cho, D.: Learning lightweight low-light enhancement network using pseudo well-exposed images. IEEE Signal Process. Lett. (SPL) **29**, 289–293 (2022)
27. Lee, P., Wu, Y.: Nonlocal matting. In: Proceedings of Computer Vision and Pattern Recognition (CVPR) (2011)
28. Levin, A., Lischinski, D., Weiss, Y.: A closed-form solution to natural image matting. IEEE Trans. Pattern Anal. Mach. Intell. (TPAMI) **30**(2), 0162–8828 (2008)
29. Li, H., Kadav, A., Durdanovic, I., Samet, H., Graf, H.P.: Pruning filters for efficient convnets. In: International Conference on Learning Representation (ICLR) (2017)
30. Li, Y., Lu, H.: Natural image matting via guided contextual attention. In: Association for the Advancement of Artificial Intelligence (AAAI) (2020)
31. Liu, Z., Li, J., Shen, Z., Huang, G., Yan, S., Zhang, C.: Learning efficient convolutional networks through network slimming. In: Proceedings of International Conference on Computer Vision (ICCV), pp. 2736–2744 (2017)
32. Liu, Z., Sun, M., Zhou, T., Huang, G., Darrell, T.: Rethinking the value of network pruning. In: ICLR (2019)
33. Long, J., Shelhamer, E., Darrell, T.: Fully convolutional networks for semantic segmentation. In: Proceedings of Computer Vision and Pattern Recognition (CVPR), pp. 3431–3440 (2015)
34. Lu, H., Dai, Y., Shen, C., Xu, S.: Indices matter: learning to index for deep image matting. In: Proceedings of International Conference on Computer Vision (ICCV) (2019)
35. Lutz, S., Amplianitis, K., Smolic, A.: AlphaGAN: generative adversarial networks for natural image matting. In: British Machine Vision Conference (BMVC) (2018)
36. Molchanov, D., Ashukha, A., Vetrov, D.: Variational dropout sparsifies deep neural networks. In: Proceedings of International Conference on Machine Learning (ICML), pp. 2498–2507 (2017)
37. Qiao, Y., et al.: Attention-guided hierarchical structure aggregation for image matting. In: Proceedings of Computer Vision and Pattern Recognition (CVPR) (2020)

38. Ronneberger, O., Fischer, P., Brox, T.: U-net: convolutional networks for biomedical image segmentation. In: Navab, N., Hornegger, J., Wells, W.M., Frangi, A.F. (eds.) MICCAI 2015. LNCS, vol. 9351, pp. 234–241. Springer, Cham (2015). https://doi.org/10.1007/978-3-319-24574-4_28

39. Sandler, M., Howard, A., Zhu, M., Zhmoginov, A., Chen, L.C.: MobileNetv 2: Inverted residuals and linear bottlenecks. In: Proceedings of the IEEE Conference on Computer Vision and Pattern Recognition (CVPR) (2018)

40. Shahrian, E., Rajan, D., Price, B., Cohen, S.: Improving image matting using comprehensive sampling sets. In: Proceedings of Computer Vision and Pattern Recognition (CVPR) (2013)

41. Shahrian, E., Rajan, D.: Weighted color and texture sample selection for image matting. In: Proceedings of Computer Vision and Pattern Recognition (CVPR) (2012)

42. Shen, X., Tao, X., Gao, H., Zhou, C., Jia, J.: Deep automatic portrait matting. In: Leibe, B., Matas, J., Sebe, N., Welling, M. (eds.) ECCV 2016. LNCS, vol. 9905, pp. 92–107. Springer, Cham (2016). https://doi.org/10.1007/978-3-319-46448-0_6

43. Sun, J., Jia, J., Tang, C.K., Shum, H.Y.: Poisson matting. ACM Trans. Graph. (ToG) **23**(3), 315–321 (2004)

44. Sun, Y., Tang, C.K., Tai, Y.W.: Semantic image matting. In: Proceedings of the IEEE/CVF Conference on Computer Vision and Pattern Recognition (CVPR), pp. 11120–11129 (2021)

45. Tanaka, H., Kunin, D., Yamins, D.L., Ganguli, S.: Pruning neural networks without any data by iteratively conserving synaptic flow. In: Larochelle, H., Ranzato, M., Hadsell, R., Balcan, M.F., Lin, H. (eds.) Advances in Neural Information Processing Systems, vol. 33, pp. 6377–6389. Curran Associates, Inc. (2020)

46. Tang, J., Aksoy, Y., Oztireli, C., Gross, M., Aydin, T.O.: Learning-based sampling for natural image matting. In: Proceedings of Computer Vision and Pattern Recognition (CVPR) (2019)

47. Tung, F., Mori, G.: Similarity-preserving knowledge distillation. In: Proceedings of International Conference on Computer Vision (ICCV) (2019)

48. Wang, J., Cohen, M.F.: Optimized color sampling for robust matting. In: Proceedings of Computer Vision and Pattern Recognition (CVPR) (2007)

49. Wen, W., Wu, C., Wang, Y., Chen, Y., Li, H.: Learning structured sparsity in deep neural networks. In: Proceedings of Neural Information Processing Systems (NeurIPS) (2016)

50. Xu, N., Price, B.L., Cohen, S., Huang, T.S.: Deep image matting. In: Proceedings of Computer Vision and Pattern Recognition (CVPR) (2017)

51. Yim, J., Joo, D., Bae, J., Kim, J.: A gift from knowledge distillation: Fast optimization, network minimization and transfer learning. In: Proceedings of Computer Vision and Pattern Recognition (CVPR) (2017)

52. Yoon, D., Park, J., Cho, D.: Lightweight deep CNN for natural image matting via similarity-preserving knowledge distillation. IEEE Signal Process. Lett. **27**, 2139–2143 (2020)

53. Yu, Q., et al.: Mask guided matting via progressive refinement network. In: Proceedings of Computer Vision and Pattern Recognition (CVPR), pp. 1154–1163 (2021)

54. Zhao, H., Shi, J., Qi, X., Wang, X., Jia, J.: Pyramid scene parsing network. In: Proceedings of the IEEE Conference on Computer Vision and Pattern Recognition (CVPR) (2017)

55. Zheng, Y., Kambhamettu, C.: Learning based digital matting. In: Proceedings of International Conference on Computer Vision (ICCV) (2009)

AutoEnhancer: Transformer on U-Net Architecture Search for Underwater Image Enhancement

Yi Tang[1]([✉]), Takafumi Iwaguchi[1], Hiroshi Kawasaki[1], Ryusuke Sagawa[2], and Ryo Furukawa[3]

[1] Kyushu University, Fukuoka, Japan
tang.yi.727@m.kyushu-u.ac.jp, {iwaguchi,kawasaki}@ait.kyushu-u.ac.jp
[2] National Institute of Advanced Industrial Science and Technology, Tokyo, Japan
ryusuke.sagawa@aist.go.jp
[3] Kindai University, Higashi-osaka, Japan
furukawa@hiro.kindai.ac.jp

Abstract. Deep neural architecture plays an important role in underwater image enhancement in recent years. Although most approaches have successfully introduced different structures (e.g., U-Net, generative adversarial network (GAN) and attention mechanisms) and designed individual neural networks for this task, these networks usually rely on the designer's knowledge, experience and intensive trials for validation. In this paper, we employ Neural Architecture Search (NAS) to automatically search the optimal U-Net architecture for underwater image enhancement, so that we can easily obtain an effective and lightweight deep network. Besides, to enhance the representation capability of the neural network, we propose a new search space including diverse operators, which is not limited to common operators, such as convolution or identity, but also transformers in our search space. Further, we apply the NAS mechanism to the transformer and propose a selectable transformer structure. In our transformer, the multi-head self-attention module is regarded as an optional unit and different self-attention modules can be used to replace the original one, thus deriving different transformer structures. This modification is able to further expand the search space and boost the learning capability of the deep model. The experiments on widely used underwater datasets are conducted to show the effectiveness of the proposed method. The code is released at https://github.com/piggy2009/autoEnhancer.

Keywords: Underwater image enhancement · Neural architecture search · Transformer

1 Introduction

Image enhancement which aims to improve the quality and recover the original information content by giving a low-quality image is a fundamental technique

Supplementary Information The online version contains supplementary material available at https://doi.org/10.1007/978-3-031-26313-2_8.

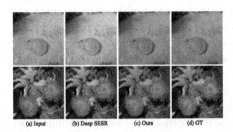

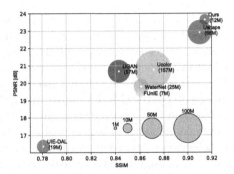

Fig. 1. Illustration of different enhancement methods. (a) Input images. (b) results from Deep SESR enhancer [18]. (c) Our enhanced images. (d) Ground truths.

Fig. 2. Comparisons with state-of-the-art enhancers in terms of PSNR metric (Y axis), SSIM metric (X axis) and parameters (circular area) on UIEB dataset. Ours is competitive against WaterNet [28], FUnIE [19], UGAN [9], UIE-DAL [40], Ucolor [27] and Ushape [35].

for image/video processing, such as video tracking [41], object recognition [19], and so on. Recently, image enhancement technologies are usually deployed in autonomous vehicles to assist the driving at night and in extreme weather [25] or remotely operated underwater vehicle (ROV) to explore marine life and protect ecosystem [23]. Accordingly, underwater image enhancement (UIE) has recently become an interesting and meaningful research topic in computer vision tasks. However, UIE is still very challenging, because the underwater scenario is complex and diverse. For example, due to the different underwater depths, the collected images are suffering from different visual qualities, especially image brightness, which is significantly decreased with the depth. Additionally, the objects in underwater scenes are diverse. The stones, animals and plants present different colors or textures by the strong absorption and scattering, which also increases the difficulty for the enhancement algorithms to recover their original appearance from underwater scenarios.

Early approaches [6,8,26] mainly rely on a physical model, called Retinex theory [24], whose purpose is to estimate an accurate medium transmission. Then, the quality degradation values can be deduced by the medium transmission. These methods are able to improve the quality of some images in simple scenes like the shallow sea and weak ambient light. However, facing complex cases, such as turbid water, and extremely dark, these physical model-based methods always fail to estimate medium transmission, even these basic physical models are not always correct in some complicated scenes.

To enhance the image quality of severe conditions, many deep learning-based methods have been proposed [9,18,28] in the underwater image enhancement. Since it is difficult to prepare sufficient labeled data in underwater scenes, weakly supervised strategy [29] or generative adversarial network (GAN) [19,20] is used at the early stage. However, these deep models are still difficult to recover the objects' color in some complex scenes. As shown in Fig. 1, Deep SESR, which is a

GAN-based method [18], cannot accurately restore the color of marine organisms. Recently, as U-Net architecture is able to effectively encode multi-level features for clear image reconstruction and easy implementation, most of the existing methods adopt this structure as a base network, and then design some specific modules for UIE. For example, the tailored attention module [27] and transformer module [35] are applied to the U-Net architecture. These modules are effective to boost performance, but their specific structures mainly rely on designers' experience and the heavy computational cost of repeated trials for validation. Additionally, in order to achieve competitive performance, the tailored modules are more and more complicated and significantly increase the parameters of models. The performance and model size of recent methods are shown in Fig. 2.

To balance the model performance and scale of parameters, our key insight is to leverage the strategy of neural architecture search (NAS) to automatically design an optimal U-Net framework for image enhancement instead of heavy structure validation experiments. First, we propose a new search space for our enhancement network. Different from [44, 48] our search space is not limited to the common and lightweight operators, such as convolution, dilated convolution, etc., but also includes transformer module. Second, we propose a selectable transformer module, whose original multi-head self-attention is regarded as an optional unit, so that we can apply the NAS strategy to automatically search for an optimal self-attention module (e.g., shuffle attention [49], efficient channel attention [37]) and then to further improve the feature representation capability of the proposed network. In order to decrease the scale of parameters and use arbitrary input size, we apply convolution rather than a fully-connected operator to encode features in our selectable transformer module. Third, to allow our network to learn more color information, we introduce the images from different color spaces (i.e., RGB and Lab) as the network inputs, so that more robust color features can be extracted to improve the quality of images in the severe conditions. In the end, the contributions of our method are summarized as follows:

- We introduce a practical solution to apply Neural Architecture Search (NAS) to automatically build an end-to-end U-Net deep network for underwater image enhancement, especially for severely color degraded images.
- We present a new search space, where we are not limited to applying lightweight operators and further propose a selectable transformer module. This module grants the neural network substantial learning capability by automatically selecting suitable self-attention operators in the proposed network.
- The proposed architecture is able to encode the features from different color spaces to improve the adaptation and generalization. Besides, the comprehensive experiments prove that the proposed approach achieves competitive performance in different scenarios with the less parameters.

2   Related Works

2.1   Image Enhancement

The development of image enhancement can be briefly divided into two phases. In the first phase, most of the approaches exploit physical models (e.g., Retinex model [11]) to enhance image quality. For example, Ancuti et al. [2] propose a fusion-based model, which first tries to obtain the color-corrected and contrast-enhanced versions of an underwater image and then compute the corresponding weight maps to generate the final fusion result. Ancuti et al. modify the fusion model [2] and further propose a multi-scale fusion strategy for underwater image enhancement in [1]. Additionally, dynamic pixel range stretching [17], pixel distribution adjustment [12] and color correction algorithm [2] are used in underwater scenario. In [36], blurriness prior is proposed to improve the image quality but fails to recover the original color of underwater objects. These approaches can improve the quality of images to some extent, but their robustness is weak when dealing with difficult scenes. Moreover, most of these methods are suffering from heavy computation, thus affecting the efficiency of their models.

With the wide deployment of deep learning models, the community of image enhancement enters the second phase. Especially, after the proposal of fully convolutional networks (FCN) and U-Net structure, more are more efficient deep learning-based methods [3,21,34,42,46] are introduced into this community. For example, WaterGAN [30] proposes to combine GAN and U-Net to solve the problem of underwater image enhancement. Meanwhile, Li et al. [29] also propose a GAN-based weakly supervised deep models for this task. After that, Yang et al. [45] further uses conditional GAN (cGAN) to improve the image quality. GANs are widely applied to this task because there are few labeled datasets in the underwater image enhancement. It is very hard to simulate a similar underwater scenario to collect the low-quality images as inputs and its corresponding high-quality images as ground truths. Therefore, GAN is usually used with weakly supervised training strategies for deep network training. After that, WaterNet [28] not only proposes a gated fusion U-Net-based model but also collects a dataset called UIEB in this community. Moreover, their method for data collecting is novel. They try to use different enhancement methods to improve the quality of underwater images. Then, some volunteers will pick the best enhanced result as the ground truth. Following this pipeline, Ushape [35] collects a large underwater dataset, which contains 5004 images with labels. Moreover, Ushape presents a new U-Net, which includes two different transformer modules to learn robust image color and space information.

In summary, U-Net architecture is widely used in underwater image enhancement. The reasons are two-fold: 1) It can effectively extract color, content and texture features of underwater images. Then, these features are very useful to remove the noise and reconstruct a clear image by using the end-to-end U-Net architecture. 2) U-Net structure is easy to implement and extend. Generally, new modules can be directly inserted into this architecture. However, due to the diverse and complex underwater scenes, recent methods have to design more complex modules in U-Net. They are effective but increase the complexity of the models as well. Different from the existing methods that focus on designing a specific deep network, we introduce NAS to automatically obtain the optimal network for the underwater image enhancement.

2.2 Neural Architecture Search

The purpose of NAS is to automatically design neural networks. Early methods often use reinforcement learning [50] or evolution algorithms [43]. However, these methods require massive computing resources and cost much time during the searching. To alleviate this burden, Liu et al. [33] proposed DARTS. This method assigns weights to different operators, and then the gradient descent algorithm (SGD) is used to simultaneously optimize the corresponding parameters of different operators. DARTS is able to relieve some computation burden, but the consumption of resources is still heavy. After that, Guo et al. [14] propose a single path one-shot, namely SPOS. SPOS decouples network searching into supernet training and subnet searching. Firstly, a supernet that contains all of the optional operators should be built. Then, an evolutionary algorithm is used to search for suitable operators by using the trained supernet. Since only one path can be activated during a training iteration, the consumption of resources is much smaller than DARTS. Based on the above previous NAS models, many methods [4,13,32] adopt it to search high-performance deep networks. For example, LightTracker [44] introduce SPOS to search a lightweight tracker for industrial deployments in the object tracking task. Auto-MSFNet [48] proposes a NAS-based multi-scale fusion network for salient object detection.

3 Preliminaries

Before the introduction of the proposed method, we give a short instruction for neural architecture search (NAS). Generally, in order to strengthen the learning capability of the neural network, a complex topological structure, including lots of multiple branches or skip connections, will be introduced in the search space. However, this kind of NAS will cost a lot of computation resources and increase search time. In this paper, to balance the resources and network performance, we introduce some prior knowledge of network design and restrict the topology of neural networks. Recently, the U-Net framework is straightforward and widely deployed in the community of image enhancement. We also adopt this model and then search its specific operators/layers. To obtain the optimal subnet, we exploit One-Shot NAS [14] as our search strategy. The reason is that One-Shot NAS can save computation resources (especially GPU memory), and is easier to converge than the previous method [33].

Specifically, One-Shot NAS is regarding all network structures as different subnets of a supernet and shares their corresponding weights between the structures with the same operators/layers. The entire process of One-Shot NAS includes three stages: supernet training, subnet searching and subnet retraining. In the first stage, the supernet $N(S, W)$ is built with the search space S and network parameters W, which are shared by all the architecture candidates. We firstly need to train this supernet and obtain all the optimized parameters by using the training set:

$$W^* = \arg\min_{W} L_{train}(N(S, W)), \tag{1}$$

where L_{train} is the loss function in the training stage and W^* is the optimized parameters after minimizing the loss function.

During the subnet searching, we can use the trained supernet to search the optimal subnet s^* on the validation set:

$$s^* = \arg\max_{s \in S} Acc_{val}(N(s, W^*(s))), \tag{2}$$

where Acc_{val} represents the accuracy of subnets on the validation set based on the trained supernet with its parameters W^*. During the search stage, we choose subnets by different sampling algorithms, such as random sampling. In this paper, we follow [44] to use evolutionary algorithms.

In the final stage, the optimal subnet $M(\cdot, \cdot)$ needs to be re-trained by using the input data X from the training set to obtain the final optimized parameter $W^{'}$:

$$W^{'} = \arg\min_{W} L_{train}(M(X; W)), \tag{3}$$

4   The Proposed Method

Our NAS-based enhancement network inherits the widely used U-Net architecture, which consists of two components: encoder and decoder. Different from the previous U-Net architectures, the original residual structures or convolution blocks are replaced by the proposed NAS blocks so that the network can automatically select the most suitable operators and learn robust and reliable features for image enhancement. Figure 3 shows the proposed NAS-based framework. Given the low-quality image, its two color spaces, namely RGB and Lab images, are fed into the proposed network. In the encoder, multi-level features are extracted by using downsampling operation and different receptive fields. Then, these features are further upsampled and fused to recover the final enhanced image in the decoder.

4.1   Overall Pipeline

Given the underwater image $I^j \in R^{H \times W \times 3}$, where $H \times W$ represents the size of the image, j denotes the color space, we use its RGB and Lab, two different color spaces to extract features. The input images are fed into the network, which consists of different NAS blocks. For each block, as shown in Fig. 3 (a), there is a convolution operator for adjusting the channel number and a choice layer for operator selection. We also employ a skip connection in the NAS block to accelerate network convergence. This whole process can be written as below:

$$F_i^j = Conv(F_{i-1}^j)$$
$$F_{i+1}^j = op(F_i^j) + F_i^j, \qquad op \in S, \tag{4}$$

where $op(\cdot)$ is an optional operation and S denotes its corresponding search space. $Conv(\cdot)$ represents the convolutional operation with kernel 3×3.

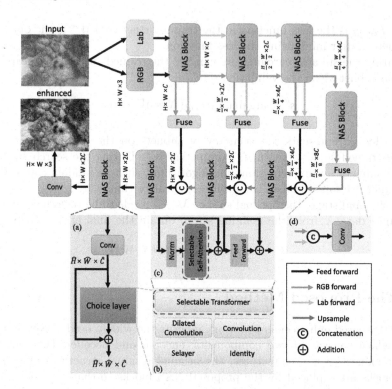

Fig. 3. The proposed framework for network searching. In the encoder, the proposed NAS blocks are employed to extract multi-level features from the image with multi-color spaces. In the decoder, we recover the enhanced images by gradually fusing the multi-level features. The core modules include: (a) NAS Block. (b) Search Space. (c) Selectable Transformer. (d) Feature fusion from two color spaces.

F_{i-1}^j, F_i^j, F_{i+1}^j are the feature maps from previous, current and next NAS block, respectively. Taking the first NAS block as an example, the previous feature maps F_0^j, namely the input image $I^j \in R^{H \times W \times 3}$ are fed into the network. Then, through the convolution, we can obtain the feature map $F_1^j \in R^{H \times W \times C}$, whose channel number is C. After that, the feature maps are fed into the choice layer and generate the output $F_2^j \in R^{H \times W \times C}$ for the next block. Notice that the NAS blocks in the encoder are used to extract the features from RGB and Lab color spaces. In the training phase, the parameters of the same operator are shared in a NAS block.

As shown in Fig. 3, starting from the input with $H \times W$, the size is downsampled to half of the original one and the channel number is increased to double by using pixel-unshuffle [38]. As we introduce two color spaces, their features at the same level are integrated before upsampling. Figure 3 (d) shows its structure:

$$F_i = Conv(\|_{j \in \Omega} F_i^j), \tag{5}$$

where $||$ is the concatenation operation. Ω refers to the color spaces, including RGB and Lab color spaces in our framework.

In the decoder, the fusing feature maps from the different color spaces are further concatenated with the decoder features by skip connections to recover gradually the original resolution by the pixel-shuffle operations [38]. In the end, an extra convolution with kernel 1×1 is used to generate the final enhanced image.

4.2   Search Space

The search space contains all possible candidate operators. Traditional search space [44,50] only uses some basic operators, such as convolution, pooling, etc. These operators cannot fully discover spatial and color information from the network inputs. In this paper, we further expand the search space, which includes conventional operators, such as convolution, identity, and introduce some new operators like transformer. The specific content is shown in Fig. 3 (b). It contains identity, convolution with 3×3 kernels, dilated convolution with 3×3 kernels and 2 dilations, squeeze-and-excitation block [16] and the proposed selectable transformer.

The previous transformer modules like Vision Transformer (VIT) [7] or Class-Attention in Image Transformers (CaiT) [39] try to encoder their features by image patches and fully-connected layers, which are very useful to extract robust information. However, due to the deployment of fully-connected operators in their structures, the input feature maps need to be resized into a fixed dimension. Moreover, with the increase of input size, the computation complexity grows dramatically as well. In the UIE community, Ushape [35] extends VIT structure and designs two different transformers for feature embedding, but the existing issues are still not alleviated. Each image is warped into a fixed size to meet the requirement of their tailored transformer structures. In real scenes, the images are collected by arbitrary resolutions. If the input image is with high-resolution, the computation complexity can be too heavy to be deployed in some embedded hardware. Some content information may be lost by directly warping the images.

In this paper, inspired by [15,47], we modify the original transformer structure. First, the fully-connected operators in the transformer are replaced by the convolutions. Second, we apply self-attention across channels rather than the spatial dimension, thus generating the attention map in the global context. Therefore, the feature maps with arbitrary sizes can be directly fed into the proposed transformer module. Besides, the computation complexity and the scale of parameters can be decreased remarkably. Further, combining with the NAS strategy, we design a selectable multi-head self-attention module (SMHSA) (shown in Fig. 3 (c)), where we introduce different self-attention mechanisms, including shuffle attention [49], double attention [10], spatial group-wise enhance [31], efficient channel attention [37], thus deriving different transformer structures. Besides, this modification can further expand the search space and boost the feature representation capability of the proposed network. The selectable transformer can be formulated as:

$$\hat{F}_i = op_a(Ln(F_i)) + F_i \quad op_a \in S_a$$
$$F_{i+1} = FF(Ln(\hat{F}_i)) + \hat{F}_i, \tag{6}$$

where $F_i, \hat{F}_i, F_{i+1} \in R^{\hat{H} \times \hat{W} \times \hat{C}}$ represent the input, intermediate and output feature maps of the proposed selectable transformer. The size of the feature maps will not be changed through the proposed NAS block. $Ln(\cdot)$ is the layer normalization. $op_a(\cdot)$ denotes the optional self-attention operators, whose S_a is the subset the proposed the search space S, namely $S_a \subset S$. $FF(\cdot)$ refers to the feed-forward structure, whose fully-connected layers are also replaced by convolutions. To the end, the search space contains 9 operators, including (1) identity (Id), (2) convolution with 3×3 kernels $(Conv)$, (3) dilated convolution with 3×3 kernels and 2 dilations $(Dconv)$, (4) squeeze-and-excitation block [16] (SE), (5) transformer with transposed attention [47] (T_{ta}), (6) transformer with shuffle attention [49] (T_{sa}), (7) transformer with spatial group-wise enhance attention [31] (T_{sge}), (8) transformer with double attention [5] (T_{da}) and (9) transformer with efficient channel attention [37] (T_{eca}).

4.3   Network Optimization

In our framework, following the Eq. 1 and Eq. 3, we need to optimize the supernet and optimal subnet. For the objective function, we employ a combining loss for network optimization. Given the low-quality image $I \in R^{H \times W \times 3}$ and its corresponding high-quality image $G \in R^{H \times W \times 3}$, the proposed network can generate the predicted image $P \in R^{H \times W \times 3}$. Then, the combining loss can be formulated as:

$$L = \alpha * ||G - P||_1 + \beta * ||G - P||_2 + \gamma * \sum_k ||\varphi(G) - \varphi(P)||_1, \tag{7}$$

From Eq. 7, we can see that three different loss functions are jointly used to optimize the network. The first term $|| \cdot ||_1$ represents L1 loss, which computes the absolute distances between the true value and the predicted value in each pixel. The second term $|| \cdot ||_2$ is L2 loss. It is used to minimize the error by using the squared distance. The purpose of the L1 and L2 loss functions is to optimize the low-frequency regions. To process the high-frequency information and retain the image style, we introduce perceptual loss, namely the third term in Eq. 7. $\varphi(\cdot)$ denotes the embedding function, which is the output of the k-th layer in VGG-16. Additionally, to balance the magnitude of the loss values, we introduce three loss weights α, β, γ for each term.

5   Experiments

5.1   Experimental Setting

Datasets. In this paper, in order to validate the scalability and adaptation of the proposed approach, we introduce three underwater datasets and one low-light dataset in the evaluation experiments. These datasets are described as follows:

Underwater Image Enhancement Benchmark (UIEB) [28]. This dataset contains 890 paired images, but their high-quality images are generated by enhancement methods. Concretely, several enhancement methods are employed to process the low-quality images to generate the enhanced ones. After that, some volunteers will manually choose the best as the final high-quality one. In experiments, the images of UIEB are divided into the training set and testing set, in which 800 and 90 paired images are included, respectively.

Large-Scale Underwater Image (LSUI) [35]. The collection of this dataset almost follows the rule of UIEB, but LSUI is much larger than UIEB. In order to satisfy the training requirements, LSUI collects 5004 underwater images and their corresponding high-quality images. For the setting in [35], 4500 paired images are used for training. The remaining 504 images are used for testing.

Enhancement of Underwater Visual Perception (EUVP) [19]. It contains large-scale paired and unpaired collections for underwater images. These images are captured from different cameras, such as GoPro, AUV's uEye cameras, ROV's HD camera and etc. EUVP also collects some video frames from a few publicly available YouTube videos. Totally, the paired images contain 11435, 570, and 515 pairs for the training, validation, and testing, respectively. Due to the low resolution of the images in this dataset, we mainly use their test set for evaluation in our experiments.

Evaluation Metrics. In this paper, for objective comparison, we introduce two full reference evaluation measures: Peak Signal to Noise Ratio (PSNR) and Structure SIMilarity index (SSIM). They can measure color and structural similarity between the enhanced images and ground truths. Both of their scores are higher the better.

5.2   Implementation Details

In this paper, we adopt PyTorch to implement the proposed approach. For our network training, we use the Adam optimizer to minimize the loss function with an initial learning rate of 1.0×10^{-4}. The learning rate follows the "poly" adjustment policy so that it can be gradually decreased during the network training. For data augmentation, we use random cropping and random horizontal flipping. The input images are cropped into 256×256 and the value of image pixels is normalized to [0,1]. As the supernet training needs a GPU with large memory, we use a PC with an NVIDIA RTX A6000 GPU. The batch size can be set to 10. To balance their loss values, we introduce loss weights α, β, γ for L1, L2 and perceptual loss, respectively. In our experiments, we set them as 0.25, 1, and 0.2. As shown in Fig. 3, the channel number of the feature maps is the multiple of C, we set it to 48 in the current network. For the network testing, our network does not need to resize the images to a fixed resolution. The images of any size can be directly fed into our network.

The proposed method needs to search optimal subnet by a validation set. For the training data, there is a little different from the setting in [35]. We randomly

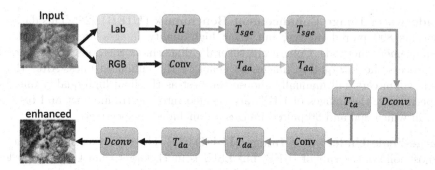

Fig. 4. The optimal network after subnet searching. During the searching, we can automatically obtain the specific operators to extract features from the RGB and Lab images in the encoder. For clear presentation, this figure only shows the chosen operators after network searching. Please understand it together with Fig. 3 and Sect. 4.2.

choose 100 images from the training set for validation. Therefore, we totally use 4400, 100, and 504 images in LSUI dataset for training, validation and testing. More specifically, we firstly use 4400 images for supernet training. Then, the 100 images are exploited for subnet searching, thus obtaining the optimal subnet. The specific structure is shown in Fig. 4. After that, the subnet is retrained by the training set. Finally, we evaluate the subnet and report the experimental results on the underwater testing set of UIEB (90 paired images), LSUI (504 paired images) and EUVP (515 paired images), respectively.

5.3 Comparisons with the State-of-the-Arts

Table 1 firstly reports the quantitative results on UIEB dataset. In this table, all of the state-of-the-arts are deep learning-based methods. Notice that the proposed approach can achieve the best performance for both PSNR and SSIM metrics. Especially for the PSNR metric, our method obtains performance gains of 2.54 dB over Ushape [35]. Their model also introduces a transformer to encode the deep features. Although the performance of Ushape is competitive, the input images have to be resized to a fixed resolution. The reason is that their transformer still employs linear operators. Moreover, their transformer is based on fully-connected operators, so their model size is much higher than ours. RCTNet [22] obtains favorable performance on PSNR and SSIM as well. Moreover, its model also accepts images with an arbitrary size, but our PSNR and SSIM are better, which provides a substantial gain of 2.18 dB on PSNR. Table 2 shows the results on LSUI dataset. This dataset contains diverse underwater scenes and object categories, so it is more difficult and challenging. As we can see, without warping the input image and their corresponding ground truths, our PSNR can still reach 26.13 dB, which obtains significant gains of 1.97 dB over Ushape, the original state-of-the-art method. Table 3 presents the experimental results on EUVP dataset. This is an early dataset and mainly collects colorful underwater creatures. Our method still outperforms significantly the other methods in PSNR. For example, ours can surpass the previous best RCTNet [22] by 3.13 dB and the GAN-based Deep SESR

Table 1. Quantitative comparison on the UIEB underwater dataset.

Method	Param	PSNR	SSIM
WaterNet [28]	25M	19.81	0.8612
FUnIE [19]	7M	19.45	0.8602
UGAN [9]	57M	20.68	0.8430
UIE-DAL [40]	19M	16.37	0.7809
Ucolor [27]	157M	20.78	0.8713
RCTNet[a] [22]	–	22.45	0.8932
Ushape [35]	66M	22.91	0.9100
Ours	12M	**25.45**	**0.9231**

[a] Their code is not released. We cannot obtain their accurate the scale of parameter.

Table 2. Quantitative comparison on the LSUI underwater dataset.

Method	Param	PSNR	SSIM
WaterNet [28]	25M	17.73	0.8223
FUnIE [19]	7M	19.37	0.8401
UGAN [9]	57M	19.79	0.7843
UIE-DAL [40]	19M	17.45	0.7912
Ucolor [27]	157M	22.91	0.8902
Ushape [35]	66M	24.16	**0.9322**
Ours	12M	**26.13**	0.8608

[18] by 5.35 dB. In our network, we mainly exploit effective but lightweight operators to construct the proposed search space. Moreover, after removing the fully-connected layers in the transformer, the network parameters can be dramatically decreased. Finally, our scale of parameters achieves 12M, which is competitive against the other state-of-the-arts as well.

Figure 5 exhibits the visual comparison between the proposed method and the state-of-the-arts on underwater scenes. The shipwreck (the first row) demonstrates that the underwater images may suffer from multiply noises, such as color distortion, blurring, splotchy textures, etc. The previous approaches are able to eliminate some noise and recover the original content to some extent. However, their enhanced images still exist respective drawbacks. For example, FUnIE [19] remove major distorted colors, but the left bottom and right bottom corner still exist the irradicable noise region. WaterNet [28] and Ushape [35] can recover the content and texture of the original image, but the color style of the entire image is changed. Compared with their enhanced images, our result not only restores the image content but also retains the color style as much as possible.

5.4 Ablation Study

In this section, to validate the effectiveness of the different components, we design the ablation studies. Table 4 shows the experimental results. First, we validate

Table 3. Quantitative comparison on the EUVP underwater dataset.

Method	Param	PSNR	SSIM
WaterNet [28]	25M	20.14	0.6802
FUnIE [19]	7M	23.40	0.8420
UGAN [9]	57M	23.49	0.7802
Deep SESR [18]	3M	24.21	0.8401
RCTNet [22]	–	26.43	**0.8912**
Ours	12M	**29.56**	0.8818

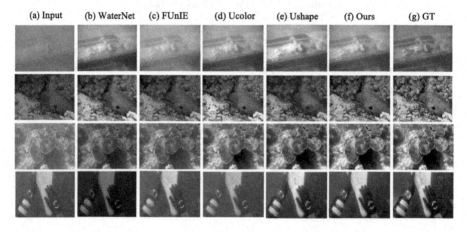

Fig. 5. Visual comparison on underwater dataset. (a) input images with low-light quality. (b) WaterNet [28]. (c) FUnIE [19] (d) Ucolor [27]. (e) Ushape [35] (f) Our enhanced images. (g) Ground truths.

the proposed transformer module, namely the selectable transformer. We train the supernet without the proposed transformer and then search for the corresponding optimal subnet, whose performance is evaluated on three underwater datasets. As shown in Table 4, without the transformer module, the measures of PSNR and SSIM are decreased dramatically. For instance, its PSNR drops by 2.61 dB, 0.91 dB and 1.41 dB on UIEB, LSUI, EUVP datasets, respectively. It is an enormous degradation. Second, we validate the effectiveness of multi-color spaces. In our framework, we use RGB and Lab two color spaces. Here, we retain RGB images to extract features and remove Lab color space. According to the results, we can see the Lab images are useful in the neural network. With the Lab color space, we can boost the PSNR from 23.69 dB to 25.45 dB on UIEB and the SSIM from 0.8666 to 0.8818 on the EUVP dataset. Although the improvement is less than the transformer modules, multi-color space is an effective part for the image enhancement task. Third, we evaluate the skip connection setting in our network. As shown in our framework, we introduce a skip connection into the proposed NAS block. The network performance will be reduced when this operation is not employed in the NAS block. For example, the PSNR and SSIM are decreased by 1.44 dB and 0.0106 on the LSUI dataset, respectively. These experiments denote that all of the proposed components are effective to enhance the quality of images.

Table 4. Effectiveness of different modules on three datasets by using PSNR and SSIM evaluation metrics. We validate the proposed search space, multi-color spaces inputs and skip connection in our NAS block.

Modules	UIEB		LSUI		EUVP	
	PSNR	SSIM	PSNR	SSIM	PSNR	SSIM
Full modules	25.45	0.9231	26.13	0.8608	29.56	0.8818
w/o Transformer	22.02	0.8705	25.12	0.8425	27.80	0.8624
w/o Multi-color spaces	23.69	0.8965	25.70	0.8551	28.03	0.8666
w/o Skip connection	22.82	0.8926	25.39	0.8546	28.12	0.8712

Table 5. Effectiveness of different loss functions on three datasets.

Training setting	UIEB		LSUI		EUVP	
	PSNR	SSIM	PSNR	SSIM	PSNR	SSIM
Full Loss Functions	25.45	0.9231	26.13	0.8608	29.56	0.8818
w/o L1 Loss	23.16	0.9028	25.70	0.8432	28.27	0.8578
w/o L2 Loss	23.29	0.9022	25.80	0.8551	28.73	0.8724
w/o Perceptual Loss	22.95	0.8960	25.51	0.8575	28.20	0.8720

For the network optimization, we introduce three different loss functions: L1, L2 and perceptual loss. Table 5 shows the quantitative results by using different losses to train the network. We gradually remove L1, L2 and perceptual loss to optimize the network. From the results, we can see that all of them are useful to boost network performance. Among them, the perceptual loss can retain the original style and high-frequency information, so it is more effective to improve the quality of images.

From the our final structure (see Fig. 4), we can observe: 1) The different deriving transformers have been chosen in the final structure, denoting those different operators can explore larger feature spaces and can generate more suitable feature representations for the underwater image enhancement, 2) the transformer modules are mainly chosen in the deep layers, revealing that transformers might be most suitable to encode the high-level features, and 3) using different operators are more effective than sharing the same modules for different input data, namely RGB and Lab images.

6 Conclusions

In this paper, we employ neural architecture search (NAS) technology to propose a NAS-based U-Net framework. It is able to automatically design a deep model so that it can process severely degraded images, such as turbid water or extremely dark scenes. Moreover, we introduce a search space including the common operators and the proposed selectable transformer module, which assigns the substantial learning capability to our deep model. Besides, the proposed architecture can exploit the multi-color spaces for the underwater scenarios. Finally, the extensive experiments demonstrate that the proposed framework can obtain an optimal neural network and achieve competitive performance on the widely used datasets.

References

1. Ancuti, C.O., Ancuti, C., De Vleeschouwer, C., Bekaert, P.: Color balance and fusion for underwater image enhancement. IEEE Trans. Image Process. **27**(1), 379–393 (2017)
2. Ancuti, C., Ancuti, C.O., Haber, T., Bekaert, P.: Enhancing underwater images and videos by fusion. In: Proceedings of the IEEE Conference on Computer Vision and Pattern Recognition, pp. 81–88. IEEE (2012)
3. Chen, Y.S., Wang, Y.C., Kao, M.H., Chuang, Y.Y.: Deep photo enhancer: Unpaired learning for image enhancement from photographs with gans. In: Proceedings of the IEEE Conference on Computer Vision and Pattern Recognition, pp. 6306–6314 (2018)
4. Chen, Y., Yang, T., Zhang, X., Meng, G., Xiao, X., Sun, J.: Detnas: Backbone search for object detection. In: Advances in Neural Information Processing Systems, vol. 32 (2019)
5. Chen, Y., Kalantidis, Y., Li, J., Yan, S., Feng, J.: A 2-nets: Double attention networks. In: Advances in Neural Information Processing Systems, vol. 31 (2018)
6. Chiang, J.Y., Chen, Y.C.: Underwater image enhancement by wavelength compensation and dehazing. IEEE Trans. Image Process. **21**(4), 1756–1769 (2011)
7. Dosovitskiy, A., et al.: An image is worth 16x16 words: Transformers for image recognition at scale. arXiv preprint arXiv:2010.11929 (2020)
8. Drews, P.L., Nascimento, E.R., Botelho, S.S., Campos, M.F.M.: Underwater depth estimation and image restoration based on single images. IEEE Comput. Graph. Appl. **36**(2), 24–35 (2016)
9. Fabbri, C., Islam, M.J., Sattar, J.: Enhancing underwater imagery using generative adversarial networks. In: Proceedings of the IEEE International Conference on Robotics and Automation, pp. 7159–7165. IEEE (2018)
10. Fu, J., et al.: Dual attention network for scene segmentation. In: Proceedings of the IEEE/CVF conference on computer vision and pattern recognition, pp. 3146–3154 (2019)
11. Fu, X., Zhuang, P., Huang, Y., Liao, Y., Zhang, X.P., Ding, X.: A retinex-based enhancing approach for single underwater image. In: Proceedings of the IEEE International Conference on Image Processing, pp. 4572–4576. IEEE (2014)
12. Ghani, A.S.A., Isa, N.A.M.: Underwater image quality enhancement through integrated color model with rayleigh distribution. Appl. Soft Comput. **27**, 219–230 (2015)

13. Ghiasi, G., Lin, T.Y., Le, Q.V.: Nas-fpn: Learning scalable feature pyramid architecture for object detection. In: Proceedings of the IEEE/CVF Conference on Computer Vision and Pattern Recognition, pp. 7036–7045 (2019)
14. Guo, Z., et al.: Single path one-shot neural architecture search with uniform sampling. In: Vedaldi, A., Bischof, H., Brox, T., Frahm, J.-M. (eds.) ECCV 2020. LNCS, vol. 12361, pp. 544–560. Springer, Cham (2020). https://doi.org/10.1007/978-3-030-58517-4_32
15. Hassani, A., Walton, S., Shah, N., Abuduweili, A., Li, J., Shi, H.: Escaping the big data paradigm with compact transformers. arXiv preprint arXiv:2104.05704 (2021)
16. Hu, J., Shen, L., Sun, G.: Squeeze-and-excitation networks. In: Proceedings of the IEEE conference on computer vision and pattern recognition, pp. 7132–7141 (2018)
17. Iqbal, K., Odetayo, M., James, A., Salam, R.A., Talib, A.Z.H.: Enhancing the low quality images using unsupervised colour correction method. In: Proceedings of the IEEE International Conference on Systems, Man and Cybernetics, pp. 1703–1709. IEEE (2010)
18. Islam, M.J., Luo, P., Sattar, J.: Simultaneous enhancement and super-resolution of underwater imagery for improved visual perception. arXiv preprint arXiv:2002.01155 (2020)
19. Islam, M.J., Xia, Y., Sattar, J.: Fast underwater image enhancement for improved visual perception. IEEE Robot. Autom. Lett. 5(2), 3227–3234 (2020)
20. Kim, G., Kwon, D., Kwon, J.: Low-lightgan: Low-light enhancement via advanced generative adversarial network with task-driven training. In: Proceedings of the IEEE International Conference on Image Processing, pp. 2811–2815. IEEE (2019)
21. Kim, H.-U., Koh, Y.J., Kim, C.-S.: PieNet: personalized image enhancement network. In: Vedaldi, A., Bischof, H., Brox, T., Frahm, J.-M. (eds.) ECCV 2020. LNCS, vol. 12375, pp. 374–390. Springer, Cham (2020). https://doi.org/10.1007/978-3-030-58577-8_23
22. Kim, H., Choi, S.M., Kim, C.S., Koh, Y.J.: Representative color transform for image enhancement. In: Proceedings of the IEEE/CVF International Conference on Computer Vision, pp. 4459–4468 (2021)
23. Kimball, P.W., et al.: The artemis under-ice auv docking system. J. Field Robot. 35(2), 299–308 (2018)
24. Land, E.H.: The retinex theory of color vision. Sci. Am. 237(6), 108–129 (1977)
25. Lee, Y., Jeon, J., Ko, Y., Jeon, B., Jeon, M.: Task-driven deep image enhancement network for autonomous driving in bad weather. In: Proceedings of the IEEE International Conference on Robotics and Automation, pp. 13746–13753. IEEE (2021)
26. Li, C.Y., Guo, J.C., Cong, R.M., Pang, Y.W., Wang, B.: Underwater image enhancement by dehazing with minimum information loss and histogram distribution prior. IEEE Trans. Image Process. 25(12), 5664–5677 (2016)
27. Li, C., Anwar, S., Hou, J., Cong, R., Guo, C., Ren, W.: Underwater image enhancement via medium transmission-guided multi-color space embedding. IEEE Trans. Image Process. 30, 4985–5000 (2021)
28. Li, C., et al.: An underwater image enhancement benchmark dataset and beyond. IEEE Trans. Image Process. 29, 4376–4389 (2019)
29. Li, C., Guo, J., Guo, C.: Emerging from water: Underwater image color correction based on weakly supervised color transfer. IEEE Signal Process. Lett. 25(3), 323–327 (2018)
30. Li, J., Skinner, K.A., Eustice, R.M., Johnson-Roberson, M.: Watergan: unsupervised generative network to enable real-time color correction of monocular underwater images. IEEE Robot. Autom. Lett. 3(1), 387–394 (2017)

31. Li, X., Hu, X., Yang, J.: Spatial group-wise enhance: Improving semantic feature learning in convolutional networks. arXiv preprint arXiv:1905.09646 (2019)
32. Liu, C., et al.: Auto-deeplab: Hierarchical neural architecture search for semantic image segmentation. In: Proceedings of the IEEE/CVF Conference on Computer Vision and Pattern Recognition, pp. 82–92 (2019)
33. Liu, H., Simonyan, K., Yang, Y.: Darts: Differentiable architecture search. arXiv preprint arXiv:1806.09055 (2018)
34. Park, J., Lee, J.Y., Yoo, D., Kweon, I.S.: Distort-and-recover: Color enhancement using deep reinforcement learning. In: Proceedings of the IEEE Conference on Computer Vision and Pattern Recognition, pp. 5928–5936 (2018)
35. Peng, L., Zhu, C., Bian, L.: U-shape transformer for underwater image enhancement. arXiv preprint arXiv:2111.11843 (2021)
36. Peng, Y.T., Cosman, P.C.: Underwater image restoration based on image blurriness and light absorption. IEEE Trans. Image Process. $26(4)$, 1579–1594 (2017)
37. Wang, Q., Wu, B., Zhu, P., Li, P., Zuo, W., Hu, Q.: Eca-net: Efficient channel attention for deep convolutional neural networks. In: Proceedings of the IEEE Conference on Computer Vision and Pattern Recognition (2020)
38. Shi, W., et al.Real-time single image and video super-resolution using an efficient sub-pixel convolutional neural network. In: Proceedings of the IEEE Conference on Computer Vision and Pattern Recognition, pp. 1874–1883 (2016)
39. Touvron, H., Cord, M., Sablayrolles, A., Synnaeve, G., Jégou, H.: Going deeper with image transformers. In: Proceedings of the IEEE/CVF International Conference on Computer Vision, pp. 32–42 (2021)
40. Uplavikar, P.M., Wu, Z., Wang, Z.: All-in-one underwater image enhancement using domain-adversarial learning. In: Proceedings of the IEEE Conference on Computer Vision and Pattern Recognition Workshops, pp. 1–8 (2019)
41. Uzair, M., Brinkworth, R.S., Finn, A.: Bio-inspired video enhancement for small moving target detection. IEEE Trans. Image Process. 30, 1232–1244 (2020)
42. Wang, R., Zhang, Q., Fu, C.W., Shen, X., Zheng, W.S., Jia, J.: Underexposed photo enhancement using deep illumination estimation. In: Proceedings of the IEEE/CVF Conference on Computer Vision and Pattern Recognition, pp. 6849–6857 (2019)
43. Xie, L., Yuille, A.: Genetic cnn. In: Proceedings of the IEEE International Conference on Computer Vision, pp. 1379–1388 (2017)
44. Yan, B., Peng, H., Wu, K., Wang, D., Fu, J., Lu, H.: Lighttrack: Finding lightweight neural networks for object tracking via one-shot architecture search. In: Proceedings of the IEEE/CVF Conference on Computer Vision and Pattern Recognition, pp. 15180–15189 (2021)
45. Yang, M., et al.: Underwater image enhancement based on conditional generative adversarial network. Signal Process.: Image Commun. 81, 115723 (2020)
46. Yang, W., Wang, S., Fang, Y., Wang, Y., Liu, J.: From fidelity to perceptual quality: A semi-supervised approach for low-light image enhancement. In: Proceedings of the IEEE/CVF Conference on Computer Vision and Pattern Recognition, pp. 3063–3072 (2020)
47. Zamir, S.W., Arora, A., Khan, S., Hayat, M., Khan, F.S., Yang, M.H.: Restormer: Efficient transformer for high-resolution image restoration. arXiv preprint arXiv:2111.09881 (2021)
48. Zhang, M., Liu, T., Piao, Y., Yao, S., Lu, H.: Auto-msfnet: Search multi-scale fusion network for salient object detection. In: Proceedings of the ACM International Conference on Multimedia, pp. 667–676 (2021)

49. Zhang, Q.L., Yang, Y.B.: Sa-net: Shuffle attention for deep convolutional neural networks. In: Proceedings of the IEEE International Conference on Acoustics, Speech and Signal Processing, pp. 2235–2239. IEEE (2021)
50. Zoph, B., Le, Q.V.: Neural architecture search with reinforcement learning. arXiv preprint arXiv:1611.01578 (2016)

Multi-granularity Transformer for Image Super-Resolution

Yunzhi Zhuge[1] and Xu Jia[2(✉)]

[1] The University of Adelaide, Adelaide, Australia
[2] School of Artificial Intelligence, Dalian University of Technology, Dalian, China
xjia@dlut.edu

Abstract. Recently, transformers have made great success in computer vision. Thus far, most of those works focus on high-level tasks, e.g., image classification and object detection, and fewer attempts were made to solve low-level problems. In this work, we tackle image super-resolution. Specifically, transformer architectures with multi-granularity transformer groups are explored for complementary information interaction, to improve the accuracy of super-resolution. We exploit three transformer patterns, *i.e.*, the window transformers, dilated transformers and global transformers. We further investigate the combination of them and propose a **Multi-granularity Transformer** (MugFormer). Specifically, the window transformer layer is aggregated with other transformer layers to compose three transformer groups, namely, Local Transformer Group, Dilated Transformer Group and Global Transformer Group, which efficiently aggregate both local and global information for accurate reconstruction. Extensive experiments on five benchmark datasets demonstrate that our MugFormer performs favorably against state-of-the-art methods in terms of both quantitative and qualitative results.

1 Introduction

Single Image Super-resolution (SISR) is a low-level computer vision task where high-resolution (HR) images are recovered from their low-resolution (LR) counterparts. It often serves as an important pre-processing or intermediate step in many computer vision techniques to solve other problems, *e.g.*, Semantic Segmentation [37], Object Detection [15] and Text Recognition [40]. As one LR input can be associated with multiple HR images, SISR is an ill-posed problem.

Early methods of SISR rely on interpolation (*e.g.*, bicubic interpolation and discrete wavelet transform) and regularisation. In the past decade, convolutional neural networks (CNNs) have become the standard model for computer vision tasks due to their representational capability. Many CNN based SISR methods [22,49,50] have been proposed. These techniques learn a non-linear mapping between LR input and HR output; outperform traditional methods by a large margin. However, convolution operations are limited to information processing in local neighborhood, restricting the capability of CNN-based models to capturing long-range relationships among pixels, which could provide important internal prior for this task.

Supplementary Information The online version contains supplementary material available at https://doi.org/10.1007/978-3-031-26313-2_9.

Another series of techniques combine Non-local Attention with CNN models to achieve SISR [22,27,28,49]. In RNAN [49], each attention block contains one trunk branch and one local mask branch which concentrate on local structures and long-range dependencies respectively. CSNLN [28] studies cross-scale feature correlation of images by learning to mine long-range dependencies between LR features and larger-scale HR patches. However, limited by the computational cost of Non-local attention, those methods are typically inefficient and hard to deploy.

Transformer [35] models have been dominating the field of natural language processing and many studies have demonstrated their ability on vision problems [3,13,34]. For instance, Swin Transformer [24] outperforms state-of-the-art methods by a large margin on image classification, object detection and segmentation. Inspired by the success of vision transformer, some recent works also apply them to low-level vision tasks [5,20,43,51]. Among them, IPT [5] is the pioneering work in which a standard transformer architecture is utilized; aiming at solving multiple restoration problems with large-scale pre-training. Uformer [43] and SwinIR [20] are built on Swin Transformers. The former combines a Swin Transformer with Unet [31], while the latter leverages deep residual connections [21,42,50] to stack several Swin Transformer layers inside each residual block. Although these methods achieve robust results on a series tasks including image super-resolution, image denoising and deraining, directly applying transformers to SISR still has some limitations. (1) The receptive field of local self-attention is restricted to a patch window, preventing the model from building long-range dependencies. (2) Although global self-attention is able to capture context of arbitrary distances, the computational cost can hardly be afforded.

In this work we propose a novel transformer-based method, named **Multi-granularity Transformer** (MugFormer), which efficiently aggregate both local and global information in an image to enhance details while maintaining relatively low computational cost. Specifically, a MugFormer block, the major component of the model, is composed of three groups of transformer layers, *i.e.*, Local Transformer Groups (LTGs), Dilated Transformer Groups (DTGs) and Global Transformer Groups (GTGs). An LTG comprises a Window Transformer Layer and a shifted Window Transformer Layer. The Window Transformer Layer computes self-attention among pixels within a local neighborhood, hence the LTGs are able to aggregate sufficient local information. In a DTG, the shifted Window Transformer Layer is replaced by a Dilated Transformer Layer which is able to capture long-distance relationship among pixels, hence able to aggregate non-local information in a larger range. A GTG consists of a Window Transformer Layer and a Global Transformer Layer. In the Global Transformer Layer, self-attention is computed based on patches instead of pixels, *i.e.*, both queries and keys are computed features for patches. In this way, the GTGs can efficiently integrate information at larger scale from the whole image. By stacking several MugFormer blocks, the model is able to make full use of external and internal priors to recover details in an image. A series of ablative models are designed and compared to demonstrate the effectiveness of the proposed method. In the comparisons with state-of-the-art methods, it shows favorable performance against them.

In summary, the main contributions of our work are three-fold:

- We propose three transformer groups, *i.e.*, Local Transformer Group (LTG), Dilated Transformer Group (DTG) and Global Transformer Group (GTG), which are capable of capturing context of different ranges for accurate image SR.

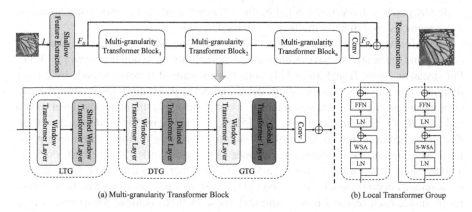

(a) Multi-granularity Transformer Block   (b) Local Transformer Group

Fig. 1. The architecture of the proposed MugFormer. (a) is the structure of a Multi-granularity Transformer Block and (b) shows the detailed components inside a Local Transformer Group.

- We analysis the characteristics of transformer block and explore the complementarity between them. Exhaustive experiments demonstrate that our arrangement, *i.e.*, from local to global could obtain optimal results.
- Our **Multi**-granularity Trans-**former** (MugFormer) outperforms the state-of-the-art methods on multiple image SR benchmarks.

2 Related Work

2.1 Image Super-Resolution

The rapid development of digital devices has increased the demand for high-quality graphics. Image restoration algorithms are often used on edge devices to overcome optical hardware bottlenecks. Early approaches are model-based which formulate image restoration as optimization problems [12,14]. Recently, convolutional neural networks have been applied to image restoration and inspired many leaning-based approaches [11], the results of which are much better than the model-based ones. Dong *et al.* [11] first proposed to solve image super resolution. In [18,21,50], deep residual and dense connections are exploited to learn hierarchical features for more effective representation. Considering that images might fall into uneven distribution, some recent works [27,28,50,52] use attention mechanisms to focus learning on challenging areas and capture realtionships across longer distances. Syed *et al.* [46] proposed a multi-scale architecture which extracts and aggregates spatially-precise information in high-resolution and contextual information in low-resolution simultaneously. In [27], deep feature pixels are partitioned into groups and then attention is only calculated within the group, which significantly reduces the computational cost while forcing the module to focus on informative area

2.2 Vision Transformer

Transformer [35] was first applied on natural language processing (NLP) tasks [10,30]. Motivated by the success of transformers in NLP, a variety of transformer models have been proposed to solve visual tasks, *e.g.*, image classification [8,13,34], object detection [3,19,53], image segmentation [36,44] and video understanding [1]. Seminally, ViT [13] first uses stacked transformer encoders to classify images. To do this input images are partitioned into non-overlapping patches which are used as tokens. This adaptation of transformers surpasses state-of-the-art convolutional architectures on image classification. However, the astonishing performance of this work is due to a hyperscale training dataset (JFT-300M). Touvron *et al.* [34] introduced an additional distillation token with hard-label distillation that achieves comparable results when training on much smaller datasets (ImageNet-1K). Some recent works [7,24,38,39] focus on general backbone design, leading to more flexibility in downstream tasks, *e.g.*, object detection and semantic/instance segmentation.

Inspired by the successful adaptations of transformers to vision task, several works have applied transformers to image restoration [5,20,43]. IPT [5] aims to solve different restoration problems with a multi-task transformer framework. Controversially, IPT is pre-trained on ImageNet and its performance is influenced more by training data quantity than network architecture. Uformer [43] explores several designs which combine window self-attention [24] with UNet [31]. SwinIR [20] stacks window transformer blocks into a deep network. However, both Uformer and SwinIR calculate self-attention in non-overlapping windows, failing to capture patterns between distant tokens. These studies apply traditional transformer blocks to image restoration tasks without modification. In this work, we analyse the characteristics of transformer structures and how they relate to image SR. From this we propose a multi-granularity transformer architecture for image SR.

3   Methodology

In standard transformers the computational complexity of self-attention grows quadratically with input size, which becomes a serious problem when applied to image restoration tasks. Image restoration tasks such as image super-resolution often require high resolution images as inputs for decent performance, making the application of self-attention computationally infeasible. Window-based self-attention [24] is utilized in SwinIR [20] and Uformer [43] to achieve trade-offs between accuracy and computational complexity. However, window-based self-attention limits feature extraction to a local receptive field. Although shifted window partitioning and layer stacking help expanding the receptive field of a window, interactions among distant elements in the input fail to be modelled, especially for high-resolution inputs. In this work, we propose multi-granularity transformer blocks which are able to extract local information and global context in a unified network. The multi-granularity transformer block is composed of three transformer groups with different granularity, *i.e.*, Local Transformer Group, Dilated Transformer Group and Global Transformer Group. Each transformer group captures different patterns of texture from local to global which complement one another.

3.1 Overview

The overall pipeline of our proposed MugFormer is shown in Fig. 1. It is composed of three main parts: a shallow CNN stem, a multi-granularity feature enhancement module and an upsampling module. Following the practices of previous work [20,21,48], a single convolutional layer is used to extract shallow features:

$$F_0 = H_{SF}(I), \tag{1}$$

where $F_0 \in \mathbb{R}^{H \times W \times C}$ and $I \in \mathbb{R}^{H \times W \times C'}$ are the extracted shallow features and input image respectively. $H_{SF}(\cdot)$ is a 3×3 convolutional layer. F_0 is then fed to a more powerful feature extraction module, producing feature maps $F_{HF} \in \mathbb{R}^{H \times W \times C}$ as

$$F_{HF} = H_{MF}(F_0), \tag{2}$$

where $H_{MF}(\cdot)$ is the multi-granularity feature enhancement module, which is formed by stacking K Multi-granularity Transformer Blocks (MGTBs). The feature extraction procedure of k-th MGTB can be described as

$$F_k = H_{MGTB_k}(F_{k-1}) = H_{MGTB_k} \\ (H_{MGTB_{k-1}}(\dots H_1(F_0)\dots)), \tag{3}$$

where $MGTB_k(\cdot)$ is the k-th MGTB, F_{k-1} and F_k represent the input and output respectively. At the end of each MGTB we attach a convolutional layer with structured inductive bias after the transformers. Due to the important role of skip connections in both CNNs [50] and transformers [35], they are also adopted here to stabilise training and promote information propagation:

$$F_{HD} = H_{CONV}(F_K) + F_0, \tag{4}$$

where H_{CONV} represents a 3×3 convolutional layer and F_{HD} is the output of the last MGTB. The specific design of Multi-granularity Transformer Block will be detailed later in Sect. 3.2. Finally, the high-resolution output I_{HR} is obtained via the reconstruction module as

$$I_{HR} = H_{REC}(F_{HD}), \tag{5}$$

where $H_{REC}(\cdot)$ represents the reconstruction operation which first upsamples features via a sub-pixel layer [32] and then produces the final super-resolution result with an additional convolutional layer. The network is trained end-to-end with L_1 reconstruction loss.

3.2 Multi-granularity Transformer Block

Recent works [4,7,45] has demonstrated that using both global and local information in transformer models helps achieving better performance. Motivated by them, we further explore the interaction of tokens in transformers. Specifically, we examine three patterns, *i.e.*, window transformers, dilated transformers and global transformers. As shown in Fig. 1(a), a MGTB is composed of a Local Transformer Group, a Dilated

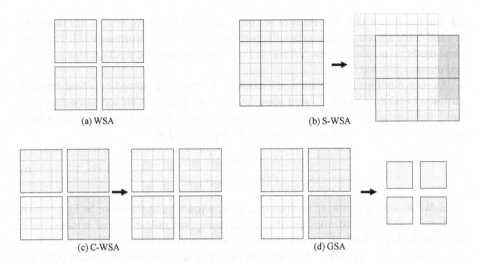

(a) WSA

(b) S-WSA

(c) C-WSA

(d) GSA

Fig. 2. Schematic views of the self-attentions used in the proposed three transformer groups.

Transformer Group, a Global Transformer Group and a convolutional layer. Each group contains two consecutive transformer layers and one convolutional layer is added before the residual connection.

Local Transformer Group. Motivated by previous work which reduce the computational cost of transformers by executing self-attention calculation within non-overlapped windows [24], we follow the practice of Swin Transformer [24] to build our Local Transformer Group, which is composed of Window Transformer Layer and shifted Window Transformer Layer. As shown in Fig. 2(a), window self-attention (WSA) evenly divides an input of size $H \times W \times C$ into $\frac{HW}{M^2}$ windows, each of which corresponds to an $M \times M$ patch. Self-attention is computed for all pixels in local neighborhood. Thus, the computational cost of the self-attention is $\mathcal{O}(4HWC^2 + 2HWCM^2)$. This modification makes computation linear with respect to input resolution rather than quadratic, which is the case in standard self-attention $\mathcal{O}(H^2W^2C)$. In a separated window, the details of MSA can be formulated as

$$\text{MultiHead}(Q, K, V) = \text{Concat}(H_0, , ...H_n)W^O, \tag{6}$$

$$Head_j = \text{Attention}(QW_j^Q, KW_j^K, VW_j^V), \tag{7}$$

where $Q, K, V \in \mathbb{R}^{n \times d}$ are the embeddings of key, query and value, and $W^O \in \mathbb{R}^{C \times C}$, $W_j^Q \in \mathbb{R}^{C \times d}, W_j^K \in \mathbb{R}^{C \times d}$ and $W_j^V \in \mathbb{R}^{C \times d}$ are linear projection matrices. n represents number of heads in the attention layer and d, which is equal to $\frac{C}{n}$, is the dimension of each head. Previous work added relative positional bias to each head which changes the attention map representation to:

$$\text{Attention}(Q, V, K) = \text{Softmax}(QK^T/\sqrt{d} + B)V, \tag{8}$$

where $Q, K, V \in \mathbb{R}^{M^2 \times d}$ denote the $query$, key and $value$ in the self-attention module respectively; d is the dimension of $query$ and key. $B \in \mathbb{R}^{G^2 \times G^2}$ is a relative positional bias matrix. In our task, the sizes of testing images and training images are inconsistent and using a fixed-sized matrix will result in sub-optimal performance [8]. Thus, we adopt dynamic positional bias (DPB) [41] of which the relative position bias is generated dynamically via MLPs.

As shown in Fig. 1(b), window self-attention (WSA) is followed by a feed-forward network (FFN) composed of two Linear layers using ReLU as an activation function. Layer normalisation (LN) is applied to inputs before WSA and the FFN. The whole process of Window Transformer Layer can be represented as

$$Z = \mathrm{WSA}(\mathrm{LN}(Z)) + Z,$$
$$Z = \mathrm{FFN}(\mathrm{LN}(Z)) + Z. \tag{9}$$

In WSA, self-attention is computed in each window and therefore lacks between window interactions. To alleviate this shortcoming we utilise shifted window self-attention (S-WSA) [24]. This method adopts a window partitioning strategy to establish dependency across windows. As shown in Fig. 2(b), window partition starts from the top-left which displaces the windows by $(\lfloor \frac{M}{2} \rfloor, \lfloor \frac{M}{2} \rfloor)$ pixels from the regularly partitioned windows. Although S-WSA can enable some connection between windows, it only models interactions between locally connected windows; failing to capture important long-range dependencies.

Table 1. Ablation study on the compositions of each transformer block. We report the PSNR results on Manga109 (4×). The performance increases significantly when both three transformers are adopted, comparing with the baseline which only contains WSA-WSA/GSA-GSA Transformer Groups.

WSA-WSA transformer group	✓							
GSA-GSA transformer group		✓						
Local transformer group			✓			✓		✓
Dilated transformer group				✓			✓	✓
Group transformer group					✓	✓	✓	✓
PSNR	31.65	31.48	31.72	31.73	31.70	31.80	31.78	**31.86**

Dilated Transformer Group. To resolve the limited receptive field in Local Transformer Group, we sample features to obtain a dispersed input for self-attention; similar to atrous convolution [6]. This forms the basis for the Dilated Transformer Group which includes pixels from further away into the computation of self-attention. As shown in Fig. 1(a), a Dilated Transformer Group contains one Window Transformer Layer and one Dilated Transformer Layer. In the computation of dilated self-attention (DSA), the receptive field is expanded by sampling tokens with a large interval rate. For an input of spatial dimension $\lfloor H, W \rfloor$, we sample $\frac{HW}{M^2}$ windows at $I = (\frac{H}{M}, \frac{W}{M})$ intervals. Figure 2(c) shows an example of DSA when $I = (2, 2)$. Tokens from different locations are effectively reallocated, enabling long-range connections between distant features. It is worth mentioning that DSA establishes hierarchical connections of tokens while maintaining equal computational cost as WSA.

Global Transformer Group. Although Local and Dilated Transformer Groups enable inter-token relationship modelling for short and long distant regions respectively, the self-attention calculation is still limited to a patch. To further expand the receptive field, we introduce global self-attention (GSA). GSA computes self-attention between each patch in the image, as shown in Fig. 2(d). Similar to PVT2 [38], GSA reduces the computational cost by decreasing the spatial scale of *key* and *value* with global average pooling before calculating self-attention. We set the down-sampling size R to the window size in WSA. Thus, the computation cost of GSA is $\mathcal{O}(HWCR^2)$. GSA efficiently allows dependency modelling between tokens extracted across the whole image; an important ability for discovering and modelling large scale similarities in image patterns.

3.3 Comparisons with SwinIR

SwinIR is based on the Swin Transformer, which is composed of local window self-attention layers and different windows are connected via window partitioning. However, there are essential differences between Swin Transformer and SwinIR. Swin Transformer is a hierarchical architecture in which the receptive field size expands as features are down-sampled. When the input resolution is 224×224, the features in the last stage have been down-sampled to 7×7, which is equal to the window size. In contrast, the resolution throughout SwinIR remains unchanged. This makes SwinIR prone to relying on local dependencies due to its limited receptive field, especially for high resolution scenes.

Our method investigates information of different ranges by novel combinations of WSA, S-WSA, DSA and GSA, which effectively exploits the local and global context for better results.

4   Experiments

In this section, we elaborate on the datasets, implementation details and experiments to evaluate the efficacy of MugFormer.

4.1   Datasets and Evaluation Metrics.

Following [21,28,50], 800 images from DIV2K [33] training set are used to train MugFormer. We choose 5 standard benchmarks: Set5 [2], Set14 [47], B100 [25], Urban100 [17] and Manga109 [26] as our testing sets with three upscaling factors: $\times 2$, $\times 3$ and $\times 4$. We transform SR outputs into YCbCr space and evaluate performance with PSNR and SSIM metrics on Y channel.

4.2   Implementation Details

The implementation details of our MugFormer is specified here. In Local, Dilated and Global Transformer Groups, we set the number of attention heads and dimensions to 6 and 180 respectively. These hyperparameters maintaining comparable parameters and

FLOPs with SwinIR. We set the window size of WSA, S-WSA, DSA, and the down-sampling size of GSA to 8. The number of Multi-granularity Transformer Blocks is set to 6.

During training, paired images are augmented by randomly applying rotations of 90°, 180° or 270° and horizontally flipping. Each mini-batch contains 16 LR patches and with size 64×64. We optimize the model using Adam with hyperparameters $\beta_1 = 0.9$, $\beta_2 = 0.999$ and $\epsilon = 1e - 8$. The initial learning rate is set to $1e - 4$ and is reduced by half when iterations reach $\{250000, 400000\}$. The training is done on two Nvidia TITAN RTX GPUs.

Table 2. Ablation study on influence of the transformer blocks orders w.r.t. the peformence.

Methods	PSNR	SSIM
GTG⟶ LTG ⟶ DTG	31.79	0.9226
GTG⟶ DTG ⟶ LTG	31.78	0.9224
LTG⟶ GTG ⟶ DTG	31.83	0.9230
DTG⟶ GTG ⟶ LTG	31.83	0.9228
DTG ⟶ LTG ⟶ GTG	31.84	0.9230
LTG ⟶ DTG ⟶ GTG	**31.86**	**0.9233**

Table 3. Ablation studies on investigating the impact of transformer blocks.

Group numbers	Parameters (M)	FLOPs (G)	Set5	Set14	B100	Urban100	Manga109
n = 2	4.51	159.92	32.63	28.79	27.75	26.75	31.33
n = 3	6.40	220.18	32.70	28.86	27.81	26.90	31.57
n = 4	8.29	280.45	32.75	28.89	27.83	26.99	31.70
n = 5	10.19	340.71	32.82	28.94	27.86	27.07	31.79
n = 6	12.10	400.97	32.86	29.03	27.88	27.16	31.8

4.3   Ablation Study

MugFormer is primarily composed of three transformer groups, discussed in Sect. 3. In this section we conduct ablative experiments to analyze and verify the effectiveness of the proposed architectural units. To begin with, we analyse the efficacy of each transformer group. Then, we illustrate that our arrangement, *i.e.*, from local to global, achieves optimal results.

Multi-granularity Transformer Group. To demonstrate that each transformer group contributes to the final results, we conduct a series experiments on Manga109 and the results are shown in Table 1. WSA-WSA Transformer Group and GSA-GSA Transformer Group denote that the transformer group is composed of two consecutive window transformer layers or global transformer layers respectively. WSA-WSA Transformer Group compute self-attention in windows without connections between them;

Table 4. Quantitative comparisons (PSNR/SSIM) with BI degradation on benchmark datasets. Best and second best results are highlighted with red and blue colors, respectively.

Method	Scale	Set5		Set14		B100		Urban100		Manga109	
		PSNR	SSIM	PSNR	SSIM	PSNR	SSIM	PSNR	SSIM	PSNR	SSIM
EDSR [21]	×2	38.11	0.9602	33.92	0.9195	32.32	0.9013	32.93	0.9351	39.10	0.9773
DBPN [16]	×2	38.09	0.9600	33.85	0.9190	32.27	0.9000	32.55	0.9324	38.89	0.9775
RDN [50]	×2	38.24	0.9614	34.01	0.9212	32.34	0.9017	32.89	0.9353	39.18	0.9780
RCAN [48]	×2	38.27	0.9614	34.12	0.9216	32.41	0.9027	33.34	0.9384	39.44	0.9786
NLRN [22]	×2	38.00	0.9603	33.46	0.9159	32.19	0.8992	31.81	0.9249	-	-
RNAN [49]	×2	38.17	0.9611	33.87	0.9207	32.32	0.9014	32.73	0.9340	39.23	0.9785
SAN [9]	×2	38.31	0.9620	34.07	0.9213	32.42	0.9028	33.10	0.9370	39.32	0.9792
RFANet [23]	x2	38.26	0.9615	34.16	0.9220	32.41	0.9026	33.33	0.9389	39.44	0.9783
HAN [29]	×2	38.27	0.9614	34.16	0.9217	32.41	0.9027	33.35	0.9385	39.46	0.9785
NLSA [27]	×2	38.34	0.9618	34.08	0.9231	32.43	0.9027	33.42	0.9394	39.59	0.9789
SwinIR [20]	×2	38.35	0.9620	34.14	0.9227	32.44	0.9030	33.40	0.9393	39.60	0.9792
Ours	×2	38.38	0.9622	34.19	0.9232	32.46	0.9031	33.43	0.9395	39.64	0.9785
Ours+	×2	38.43	0.9624	34.28	0.9236	32.50	0.9233	33.52	0.9399	39.71	0.9789
EDSR [21]	×3	34.65	0.9280	30.52	0.8462	29.25	0.8093	28.80	0.8653	34.17	0.9476
RDN [50]	×3	34.71	0.9296	30.57	0.8468	29.26	0.8093	28.80	0.8653	34.13	0.9484
RCAN [48]	×3	34.74	0.9299	30.65	0.8482	29.32	0.8111	29.09	0.8702	34.44	0.9499
NLRN [22]	×3	34.27	0.9266	30.16	0.8374	29.06	0.8026	27.93	0.8453	-	-
RNAN [49]	×3	34.66	0.9290	30.52	0.8462	29.26	0.8090	28.75	0.8646	34.25	0.9483
SAN [9]	×3	34.75	0.9300	30.59	0.8476	29.33	0.8112	28.93	0.8671	34.30	0.9494
RFANet [23]	x3	34.79	0.9300	30.67	0.8487	29.34	0.8115	29.15	0.8720	34.59	0.9506
HAN [29]	×3	34.75	0.9299	30.67	0.8483	29.32	0.8110	29.10	0.8705	34.48	0.9500
NLSA [27]	×3	34.85	0.9306	30.70	0.8485	29.34	0.8117	29.25	0.8726	34.57	0.9508
SwinIR [20]	×3	34.89	0.9312	30.77	0.8503	29.37	0.8124	29.29	0.8744	34.74	0.9518
Ours	×3	34.93	0.9318	30.87	0.8520	29.40	0.8132	29.38	0.8756	34.89	0.9521
Ours+	×3	34.98	0.9321	30.92	0.8527	29.42	0.8135	29.48	0.8769	35.01	0.9528
EDSR [21]	×4	32.46	0.8968	28.80	0.7876	27.71	0.7420	26.64	0.8033	31.02	0.9148
DBPN [16]	×4	32.47	0.8980	28.82	0.7860	27.72	0.7400	26.38	0.7946	30.91	0.9137
RDN [50]	×4	32.47	0.8990	28.81	0.7871	27.72	0.7419	26.61	0.8028	31.00	0.9151
RCAN [48]	×4	32.63	0.9002	28.87	0.7889	27.77	0.7436	26.82	0.8087	31.22	0.9173
NLRN [22]	×4	31.92	0.8916	28.36	0.7745	27.48	0.7306	25.79	0.7729	-	-
RNAN [49]	×4	32.49	0.8982	28.83	0.7878	27.72	0.7421	26.61	0.8023	31.09	0.9149
SAN [9]	×4	32.64	0.9003	28.92	0.7888	27.78	0.7436	26.79	0.8068	31.18	0.9169
RFANet [23]	×4	32.66	0.9004	28.88	0.7894	27.79	0.7442	26.92	0.8112	31.41	0.9187
HAN [29]	×4	32.64	0.9002	28.90	0.7890	27.80	0.7442	26.85	0.8094	31.42	0.9177
NLSA [27]	×4	32.59	0.9000	28.87	0.7891	27.78	0.7444	26.96	0.8109	31.27	0.9184
SwinIR [20]	×4	32.72	0.9021	28.94	0.7914	27.83	0.7459	27.07	0.8164	31.67	0.9226
Ours	×4	32.86	0.9037	29.03	0.7931	27.88	0.7468	27.16	0.8168	31.86	0.9233
Ours+	×4	32.92	0.9041	29.09	0.7940	27.90	0.7474	27.23	0.8194	31.99	0.9245

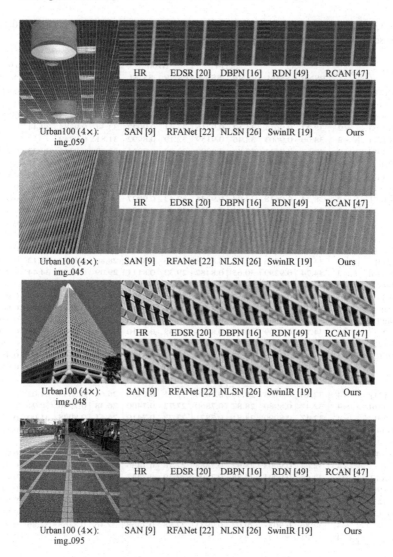

Fig. 3. Visual comparisons for 4× SR with BI degradation on Urban100 dataset.

only extracting local information. In contrast, GSA-GSA Transformer Group contains group transformer layers that capture global context. In the first two columns, we observe that both transformers using purely local or global information perform relatively poorly on Manga109(4x), the PSNR of which are 31.65 dB and 31.48 dB respectively. In columns 3–5, the transformer blocks are made with LTGs, DTGs and GTGs respectively. Steady improvement in PSNR is observed as transformer layers model increasing global relationships. Columns 6–7 contain results from transformer blocks consisting of two LTGs/DTGs and one GTG. We find that both combinations increase

PSNR, demonstrating that context of different ranges are important when learning to perform single image SR. In the last column where all transformer groups are combined, PSNR is improved from 31.80 dB to 31.86 dB eventually.

Table 5. Quantitative comparisons (PSNR/SSIM) with BD degradation on benchmark datasets. Best and second best results are highlighted with red and blue colors, respectively.

Method	Scale	Set5		Set14		B100		Urban100		Manga109	
		PSNR	SSIM	PSNR	SSIM	PSNR	SSIM	PSNR	SSIM	PSNR	SSIM
Bicubic	×3	28.78	0.8308	26.38	0.7271	26.33	0.6918	23.52	0.6862	25.46	0.8149
VDSR [18]	×3	33.25	0.9150	29.46	0.8244	28.57	0.7893	26.61	0.8136	31.06	0.9234
RDN [50]	×3	34.58	0.9280	30.53	0.8447	29.23	0.8079	28.46	0.8582	33.97	0.9465
RCAN [48]	×3	34.70	0.9288	30.63	0.8462	29.32	0.8093	28.81	0.8647	34.38	0.9483
SAN [9]	×3	34.75	0.9290	30.68	0.8466	29.33	0.8101	28.83	0.8646	34.46	0.9487
RFANet [23]	×3	34.77	0.9292	30.68	0.8473	29.34	0.8104	28.89	0.8661	34.49	0.9492
HAN [29]	×3	34.76	0.9294	30.70	0.8475	29.34	0.8106	28.99	0.8676	34.56	0.9494
Ours	×3	34.92	0.9309	30.91	0.8501	29.42	0.8127	29.29	0.8726	34.95	0.9513
Ours+	×3	34.95	0.9311	30.95	0.8505	29.44	0.8130	29.38	0.8740	35.07	0.9518

Influence of Transformer Block Numbers. We show the influence of transformer block numbers in Table 3. It can be observed that PSNR, parameters and FLOPs increase steadily as the number of transformer blocks growths, demonstrating that a trade-off between performance and computational cost can be achieved by adaptively changing the number of transformer blocks.

Influence of Transformer Sequences. As is introduced in Sect. 3, self-attention is calculated in a hierarchical manner from local to global in each transformer block of Mug-Former. To verify that this arrangement is optimal, we evaluate the PSNR of transformer groups with different group orderings on Manga109. As shown in Table 2, peak performance is reached when we cascading transformer groups by LTG, DTG and GTG. Other permutations result in PSNR dropping from 0.02 dB to 0.07 dB.

4.4 Results with Bicubic (BI) Degradation

To verify the effectiveness of MugFormer, we compare our method to 10 others, *i.e.*, EDSR [21], DBPN [16], RDN [50], RCAN [48], NLRN [22], RNAN [49], SAN [9], RFANet [23], NLSA [27] and SwinIR [20]. Following [9,20,21], we apply the self-ensemble strategy to further boost performance which is denoted as Ours+.

Quantitative Results. In Table 4, we compare the PSNR and SSIM results for various scaling factors. Compared with other methods, MugFormer achieves the best results on all benchmark datasets at all scales, except for SSIM on Manga109 (2×). In particular, our method increases the PSNR by 0.14 dB and 0.19 dB over SwinIR on Set5 and Manga109 at 4× scale. This illustrates that the proposed multi-granularity transformer block could efficiently contextualising information extracted from different ranges to achieve more accurate results. When applying the self-ensemble strategy, PSNR is further improved by 0.06 dB and 0.13 dB respectively.

Qualitative Results. In Fig. 3, we show the outputs of a series SR method on the Urban100 benchmark dataset at 4× scale. Our method achieves more visually pleasant results than other methods on a variety of patterns. The textures in 'img_045' are challenging, most other methods either suffer from distortions or fail to restore fine details. Our method recovers the high frequency details clearly and produces less blurring artifacts. 'img_048' contains repeated patterns that demonstrate MugFormer's ability of exploiting different context ranges to produce fine results. In 'img_095', MugFormer recover the edges of the irregular tiles clearly whereas the results produced by other methods are blurred in different levels. Several other methods, *e.g.*, RCAN, RFANet and SwinIR deform the original structure; while our method can keep the shape intact and produce more fidelity results than others.

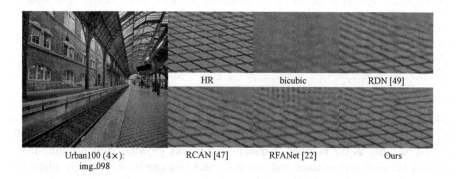

Fig. 4. Visual comparisons for 4× SR with BI degradation on Urban100 dataset.

4.5 Results with Blur-downscale (BD) Degradation

We qualitatively and quantitatively compare the results on benchmark datasets with blur-down degradation (BD), which is a common practice in some recent works [9, 48,50]. In Fig. 4, we can observe that compared with bicubic upsampling, RDN [50], RCAN [48] and RFANet [23], out method restore the shape of tiles more clearly. In Table 5, we observe that our method outperforms all other methods by a large margin on the benchmark datasets. The performance gap between MugFormer and other methods is further enlarged when the self-ensemble strategy is used, *e.g.*, Ours+ exceeds RFANet by 0.39 dB on Urban100 and 0.58 dB on Manga109. The above comparative analysis demonstrates that our method is robust to BD degradation.

4.6 Complexity Analysis

We compare the model size, FLOPs and PSNR with several SR methods to analyse model complexity in Table 6. MugFormer uses significantly less parameters and FLOPs than both EDSR and HAN while achieving better PSNR scores. Specifically, HAN would consume 1679.72 GFLOPs when the input size is $160 \times 160 \times 3$, which is 4 times more than ours. SwinIR has slightly less parameters than our method (11.94 M vs. 12.10 M), while its PSNR score is much worse (31.67 dB vs. 31.86 dB). The above analysis demonstrate that comparing with previous state-of-the-art methods, our MugFormer achieves better results without paying additional computational cost.

Table 6. Parameters, FLOPs and PSNR scores on Manga109 with $4\times$ factor. The FLOPs are calculated with input size $160 \times 160 \times 3$.

Methods	Parameters (M)	FLOPs (G)	PSNR (dB)
EDSR [21]	43.09	1287.03	31.02
RCAN [48]	15.59	408.53	31.22
HAN [29]	64.19	1679.72	31.42
SwinIR [20]	11.94	410.86	31.67
Ours	12.10	400.97	31.86

5 Conclusion

Recent works have validated that vision transformer can achieve state-of-the-art results on low-level vision tasks. However, none of them have been able to exploit the full range of contextual information available when calculating self-attention. In this work, we propose a **mu**lti-granularity transformer (MugFormer) capable of solving single image super-resolution. Specifically, transformer blocks in MugFormer are composed of three transformer groups with different receptive field sizes: Local Transformer Group, Dilated Transformer Group and Global Transformer Group. Local Transformer Group and Dilated Transformer Group both exchange tokens between neighbouring windows; the former performs on adjacent windows while the latter shuffles them by sampling tokens across the image at fixed intervals. Finally, Global Transformer Group builds connection between all tokens. Experiments demonstrate that the integration of multiple transformer groups achieves state-of-the-art results on benchmark datasets.

Acknowledgement. The research was partially supported by the Natural Science Foundation of China, No. 62106036, and the Fundamental Research Funds for the Central University of China, DUT21RC(3)026.

References

1. Arnab, A., Dehghani, M., Heigold, G., Sun, C., Lučić, M., Schmid, C.: ViViT: a video vision transformer. arXiv preprint arXiv:2103.15691 (2021)
2. Bevilacqua, M., Roumy, A., Guillemot, C., Alberi-Morel, M.L.: Low-complexity single-image super-resolution based on nonnegative neighbor embedding. In: Proceedings of the British Machine Vision Conference (2012)
3. Carion, N., Massa, F., Synnaeve, G., Usunier, N., Kirillov, A., Zagoruyko, S.: End-to-end object detection with transformers. In: Vedaldi, A., Bischof, H., Brox, T., Frahm, J.-M. (eds.) ECCV 2020. LNCS, vol. 12346, pp. 213–229. Springer, Cham (2020). https://doi.org/10.1007/978-3-030-58452-8_13

4. Chen, B., et al.: GLiT: neural architecture search for global and local image transformer. In: Proceedings of the IEEE International Conference on Computer Vision (2021)
5. Chen, H., et al.: Pre-trained image processing transformer. In: Proceedings of the IEEE Conference on Computer Vision and Pattern Recognition, pp. 12299–12310 (2021)
6. Chen, L.C., Papandreou, G., Kokkinos, I., Murphy, K., Yuille, A.L.: DeepLab: Semantic image segmentation with deep convolutional nets, atrous convolution, and fully connected CRFs. IEEE Trans. Pattern Anal. Mach. Intell. **40**(4), 834–848 (2018)
7. Chu, X., et al.: Twins: revisiting spatial attention design in vision transformers. In: Proceedings of the Advances in Neural Information Processing Systems (2021)
8. Chu, X., et al.: Conditional positional encodings for vision transformers. arXiv preprint arXiv:2102.10882 (2021)
9. Dai, T., Cai, J., Zhang, Y., Xia, S.T., Zhang, L.: Second-order attention network for single image super-resolution. In: Proceedings of the IEEE Conference on Computer Vision and Pattern Recognition, pp. 11065–11074 (2019)
10. Devlin, J., Chang, M.W., Lee, K., Toutanova, K.: BERT: pre-training of deep bidirectional transformers for language understanding. arXiv preprint arXiv:1810.04805 (2018)
11. Dong, C., Loy, C.C., He, K., Tang, X.: Learning a deep convolutional network for image super-resolution. In: Fleet, D., Pajdla, T., Schiele, B., Tuytelaars, T. (eds.) ECCV 2014. LNCS, vol. 8692, pp. 184–199. Springer, Cham (2014). https://doi.org/10.1007/978-3-319-10593-2_13
12. Dong, W., Zhang, L., Shi, G., Li, X.: Nonlocally centralized sparse representation for image restoration. IEEE Trans. Image Process. **22**(4), 1620–1630 (2012)
13. Dosovitskiy, A., et al.: An image is worth 16×16 words: transformers for image recognition at scale. In: Proceedings of the International Conference on Learning Representation (2021)
14. Elad, M., Aharon, M.: Image denoising via sparse and redundant representations over learned dictionaries. IEEE Trans. Image Process. **15**(12), 3736–3745 (2006)
15. Haris, M., Shakhnarovich, G., Ukita, N.: Task-driven super resolution: object detection in low-resolution images. arXiv preprint arXiv:1803.11316 (2018)
16. Haris, M., Shakhnarovich, G., Ukita, N.: Deep back-projection networks for super-resolution. In: Proceedings of the IEEE Conference on Computer Vision and Pattern Recognition, pp. 1664–1673 (2018)
17. Huang, J.B., Singh, A., Ahuja, N.: Single image super-resolution from transformed self-exemplars. In: Proceedings of the IEEE Conference on Computer Vision and Pattern Recognition, pp. 5197–5206 (2015)
18. Kim, J., Lee, J.K., Lee, K.M.: Accurate image super-resolution using very deep convolutional networks. In: Proceedings of the IEEE Conference on Computer Vision and Pattern Recognition, pp. 1646–1654 (2016)
19. Li, Y., Mao, H., Girshick, R., He, K.: Exploring plain vision transformer backbones for object detection. In: Avidan, S., Brostow, G., Cissé, M., Farinella, G.M., Hassner, T. (eds.) Computer Vision – ECCV 2022. ECCV 2022. LNCS, vol 13669, pp. 280–296. Springer, Cham. https://doi.org/10.1007/978-3-031-20077-9_17
20. Liang, J., Cao, J., Sun, G., Zhang, K., Van Gool, L., Timofte, R.: SwinIR: image restoration using swin transformer. arXiv preprint arXiv:2108.10257 (2021)
21. Lim, B., Son, S., Kim, H., Nah, S., Mu Lee, K.: Enhanced deep residual networks for single image super-resolution. In: Proceedings of the IEEE Conference on Computer Vision and Pattern Recognition Workshop, pp. 136–144 (2017)
22. Liu, D., Wen, B., Fan, Y., Loy, C.C., Huang, T.S.: Non-local recurrent network for image restoration. In: Proceedings of the Advance in Neural Information Processing Systems (2018)

23. Liu, J., Zhang, W., Tang, Y., Tang, J., Wu, G.: Residual feature aggregation network for image super-resolution. In: Proceedings of the IEEE Conference on Computer Vision and Pattern Recognition, pp. 2359–2368 (2020)
24. Liu, Z., et al.: Swin transformer: hierarchical vision transformer using shifted windows. In: Proceedings of the IEEE/CVF International Conference on Computer Vision, pp. 10012–10022 (2021)
25. Martin, D., Fowlkes, C., Tal, D., Malik, J.: A database of human segmented natural images and its application to evaluating segmentation algorithms and measuring ecological statistics. In: Proceedings of the IEEE International Conference on Computer Vision, vol. 2, pp. 416–423. IEEE (2001)
26. Matsui, Y., et al.: Sketch-based manga retrieval using manga109 dataset. J. Multimed. Tools Appl. **76**(20), 21811–21838 (2017)
27. Mei, Y., Fan, Y., Zhou, Y.: Image super-resolution with non-local sparse attention. In: Proceedings of the IEEE Conference on Computer Vision and Pattern Recognition, pp. 3517–3526 (2021)
28. Mei, Y., Fan, Y., Zhou, Y., Huang, L., Huang, T.S., Shi, H.: Image super-resolution with cross-scale non-local attention and exhaustive self-exemplars mining. In: Proceedings of the IEEE Conference on Computer Vision and Pattern Recognition, pp. 5690–5699 (2020)
29. Niu, B., et al.: Single image super-resolution via a holistic attention network. In: Vedaldi, A., Bischof, H., Brox, T., Frahm, J.-M. (eds.) ECCV 2020. LNCS, vol. 12357, pp. 191–207. Springer, Cham (2020). https://doi.org/10.1007/978-3-030-58610-2_12
30. Raffel, C., et al.: Exploring the limits of transfer learning with a unified text-to-text transformer. arXiv preprint arXiv:1910.10683 (2019)
31. Ronneberger, O., Fischer, P., Brox, T.: U-net: convolutional networks for biomedical image segmentation. In: Navab, N., Hornegger, J., Wells, W.M., Frangi, A.F. (eds.) MICCAI 2015. LNCS, vol. 9351, pp. 234–241. Springer, Cham (2015). https://doi.org/10.1007/978-3-319-24574-4_28
32. Shi, W., et al.: Real-time single image and video super-resolution using an efficient sub-pixel convolutional neural network. In: Proceedings of the IEEE Conference on Computer Vision and Pattern Recognition, pp. 1874–1883 (2016)
33. Timofte, R., Agustsson, E., Van Gool, L., Yang, M.H., Zhang, L.: NTIRE 2017 challenge on single image super-resolution: Methods and results. In: Proceedings of the IEEE Conference on Computer Vision and Pattern Recognition Workshop, pp. 114–125 (2017)
34. Touvron, H., Cord, M., Douze, M., Massa, F., Sablayrolles, A., Jégou, H.: Training data-efficient image transformers & distillation through attention. In: Proceedings of the International Conference on Machine Learning, pp. 10347–10357. PMLR (2021)
35. Vaswani, A., et al.: Attention is all you need. In: Proceedings of the Advances in Neural Information Processing Systems, pp. 5998–6008 (2017)
36. Wang, H., Zhu, Y., Adam, H., Yuille, A., Chen, L.C.: Max-deeplab: end-to-end panoptic segmentation with mask transformers. In: Proceedings of the IEEE Conference on Computer Vision and Pattern Recognition, pp. 5463–5474 (2021)
37. Wang, L., Li, D., Zhu, Y., Tian, L., Shan, Y.: Dual super-resolution learning for semantic segmentation. In: Proceedings of the IEEE Conference on Computer Vision and Pattern Recognition, pp. 3774–3783 (2020)
38. Wang, W., et al.: PVTv 2: improved baselines with pyramid vision transformer. arXiv preprint arXiv:2106.13797 (2021)
39. Wang, W., et al.: Pyramid vision transformer: a versatile backbone for dense prediction without convolutions. In: Proceedings of the IEEE International Conference on Computer Vision (2021)

40. Wang, W., et al.: Scene text image super-resolution in the wild. In: Vedaldi, A., Bischof, H., Brox, T., Frahm, J.-M. (eds.) ECCV 2020. LNCS, vol. 12355, pp. 650–666. Springer, Cham (2020). https://doi.org/10.1007/978-3-030-58607-2_38

41. Wang, W., Yao, L., Chen, L., Cai, D., He, X., Liu, W.: CrossFormer: a versatile vision transformer based on cross-scale attention. arXiv preprint arXiv:2108.00154 (2021)

42. Wang, X., et al.: ESRGAN: enhanced super-resolution generative adversarial networks. In: Proceedings of the European Conference on Computer Vision Workshop (2018)

43. Wang, Z., Cun, X., Bao, J., Liu, J.: UFormer: a general U-shaped transformer for image restoration. arXiv preprint arXiv:2106.03106 (2021)

44. Xie, E., Wang, W., Yu, Z., Anandkumar, A., Alvarez, J.M., Luo, P.: SegFormer: simple and efficient design for semantic segmentation with transformers. arXiv preprint arXiv:2105.15203 (2021)

45. Yang, J., et al.: Focal self-attention for local-global interactions in vision transformers. In: Proceedings of the Advances in Neural Information Processing Systems (2021)

46. Zamir, S.W., et al.: Learning enriched features for real image restoration and enhancement. In: Vedaldi, A., Bischof, H., Brox, T., Frahm, J.-M. (eds.) ECCV 2020. LNCS, vol. 12370, pp. 492–511. Springer, Cham (2020). https://doi.org/10.1007/978-3-030-58595-2_30

47. Zeyde, R., Elad, M., Protter, M.: On single image scale-up using sparse-representations. In: Boissonnat, J.-D., Chenin, P., Cohen, A., Gout, C., Lyche, T., Mazure, M.-L., Schumaker, L. (eds.) Curves and Surfaces 2010. LNCS, vol. 6920, pp. 711–730. Springer, Heidelberg (2012). https://doi.org/10.1007/978-3-642-27413-8_47

48. Zhang, Y., Li, K., Li, K., Wang, L., Zhong, B., Fu, Y.: Image super-resolution using very deep residual channel attention networks. In: Proceedings of the European Conference on Computer Vision, pp. 286–301 (2018)

49. Zhang, Y., Li, K., Li, K., Zhong, B., Fu, Y.: Residual non-local attention networks for image restoration. In: Proceedings of the International Conference on Learning Representation (2019)

50. Zhang, Y., Tian, Y., Kong, Y., Zhong, B., Fu, Y.: Residual dense network for image super-resolution. In: Proceedings of the IEEE Conference on Computer Vision and Pattern Recognition, pp. 2472–2481 (2018)

51. Zhao, D., Li, J., Li, H., Xu, L.: Hybrid local-global transformer for image dehazing. arXiv preprint arXiv:2109.07100 (2021)

52. Zhao, H., Kong, X., He, J., Qiao, Yu., Dong, C.: Efficient image super-resolution using pixel attention. In: Bartoli, A., Fusiello, A. (eds.) ECCV 2020. LNCS, vol. 12537, pp. 56–72. Springer, Cham (2020). https://doi.org/10.1007/978-3-030-67070-2_3

53. Zhu, X., Su, W., Lu, L., Li, B., Wang, X., Dai, J.: Deformable DETR: deformable transformers for end-to-end object detection. arXiv preprint arXiv:2010.04159 (2020)

Structure Representation Network and Uncertainty Feedback Learning for Dense Non-uniform Fog Removal

Yeying Jin[1($\boxtimes$)] , Wending Yan[1,3] , Wenhan Yang[2] , and Robby T. Tan[1,3]

[1] National University of Singapore, Singapore, Singapore
{jinyeying,e0267911}@u.nus.edu, robby.tan@nus.edu.sg
[2] Nanyang Technological University, Nanyang, China
wenhan.yang@ntu.edu.sg
[3] Yale-NUS College, Singapore, Singapore
robby.tan@yale-nus.edu.sg

Abstract. Few existing image defogging or dehazing methods consider dense and non-uniform particle distributions, which usually happen in smoke, dust and fog. Dealing with these dense and/or non-uniform distributions can be intractable, since fog's attenuation and airlight (or veiling effect) significantly weaken the background scene information in the input image. To address this problem, we introduce a structure-representation network with uncertainty feedback learning. Specifically, we extract the feature representations from a pre-trained Vision Transformer (DINO-ViT) module to recover the background information. To guide our network to focus on non-uniform fog areas, and then remove the fog accordingly, we introduce the uncertainty feedback learning, which produces uncertainty maps, that have higher uncertainty in denser fog regions, and can be regarded as an attention map that represents fog's density and uneven distribution. Based on the uncertainty map, our feedback network refines our defogged output iteratively. Moreover, to handle the intractability of estimating the atmospheric light colors, we exploit the grayscale version of our input image, since it is less affected by varying light colors that are possibly present in the input image. The experimental results demonstrate the effectiveness of our method both quantitatively and qualitatively compared to the state-of-the-art methods in handling dense and non-uniform fog or smoke.

1 Introduction

Atmospheric particles, such as fog, haze, dust and smoke particles, can degrade the visibility of a scene significantly as shown in Fig. 1. These particles can be modeled as [3]:

$$\mathbf{I}(\mathbf{x}) = \mathbf{J}(\mathbf{x})t(\mathbf{x}) + (1 - t(\mathbf{x}))\,\mathbf{A}, \qquad (1)$$

Our data and code is available at: https://github.com/jinyeying/FogRemoval.

Supplementary Information The online version contains supplementary material available at https://doi.org/10.1007/978-3-031-26313-2_10.

L. Wang et al. (Eds.): ACCV 2022, LNCS 13843, pp. 155–172, 2023.
https://doi.org/10.1007/978-3-031-26313-2_10

| Input | Ours | D4'22 [1] | DeHamer'22 [2] |

Fig. 1. Visual comparisons of different methods: the state-of-the-art CNN-based method [1] and transformer-based method [2] in dense and/or non-uniform fog.

where $\mathbf{I}$ is an observed RGB color vector, $\mathbf{x}$ is the pixel location. $\mathbf{J}$ is the scene radiance. $\mathbf{A}$ is the atmospheric light, and t is the transmission. The first term is called direct attenuation, and the second term is called airlight. Transmission t can be modeled as $t(\mathbf{x}) = \exp(\beta(\mathbf{x})d(\mathbf{x}))$, where β is the particle attenuation factor that depends on the density of the particle distribution and the size of particles; while d is the depth of the scene with respect to the camera. Most existing methods assume the uniformity of the particle distributions, which means they assume β to be independent from $\mathbf{x}$. Note that, in this paper, we deal with fog, haze, atmospheric dust and smoke that can be dense and/or non-uniform. However, for clarity, we write fog to represent them.

Many methods have been proposed to deal with fog degradation. Existing fully supervised CNN-based methods [4–10] require clean ground truths, which are intractable to obtain particularly for non-uniform fog. Synthetic images, unfortunately, cannot help that much for dense and/or non-uniform fog. Synthesizing non-uniform fog is difficult and computationally expensive, and dense synthetic fog has significant gaps with real dense fog. Semi-supervised methods [11–14] adopt the domain adaptation. However, the huge domain gap between synthetic and real dense and/or non-uniform fog images is not easy to align. Unsupervised methods [1,15–18] make use of statistical similarity between unpaired training data, and are still less effective compared with semi-supervised or supervised methods. Importantly, unsupervised methods can generate hallucinations, particularly in dense fog areas. Recently, ViT-based dehazing methods [2,19] have been proposed; however, memory and computation complexity slow down the convergence [20], causing unreliable performance on real-world high-resolution non-uniform fog images.

In this paper, our goal is to remove fog, particularly dense or non-uniform fog, or a combination of the two (dense and non-uniform). Unlike non-dense uniform fog, where the human visual perception can still discern the background scenes, dense and/or non-uniform fog significantly weakens the information of the background scenes (see Fig. 1). To achieve our goal, first, we exploit the representation extracted from DINO-ViT [21], a self-supervised pre-trained model in order to recover background structures. DINO-ViT captures visual representations from data, e.g., scene structure representations, based on self-similarity prior [22]. Second, since the recovery of the $\mathbf{A}$ is challenging [23], to avoid the direct recovery of **A**, we introduce a grayscale feature multiplier to learn fog degradation in an end-to-end manner. Grayscale images are less affected by multi-colored light sources (skylight, sunlight, or cars' headlights, etc.) as well as the colors of the particle scattered lights (whitish for fog, yellowish or reddish for haze or atmospheric dust or smoke). We can multiply the grayscale features and our feature multiplier (derived from the model in Eq. (1)), to ensure our features are unaffected by the airlight and thus are more reliable when applied to our multiplier consistency loss.

Third, we propose an uncertainty-based feedback learning that allows our network to pay more attention to regions that are still affected by fog based on our uncertainty predictions, iteratively. Since the network usually has high uncertainty on the dense fog regions (because background information is washed out by the fog and the input image contains less background information in those regions), we can use an uncertainty map as an attention cue to guide the network to differentiate dense fog region from the rest of input image. In one iteration, if our output still contains fog in some regions, the uncertainty map will indicate those regions, and in the next iteration, our method will focus on these regions to further defog them.

To sum up, our main contributions and novelties are as follows:

- To the best of our knowledge, our method is the first single-image defogging network that performs robustly in dense non-uniform fog, by combining structure representations from ViT and features from CNN as feature regularization. Thus, the background information under fog can be preserved and extracted.
- We propose the grayscale feature multiplier that acts as feature enhancement and guides our network to learn to extract clear background information.
- We introduce the uncertainty feedback learning in our defogging network, which can refine the defogging results iteratively by focusing on areas that still suffer from fog.

Experimental results show that our method is effective in removing dense and/or non-uniform fog images, outperforming the state-of-the-art methods both quantitatively and qualitatively.

2   Related Works

Non-learning methods introduced priors from the atmosphere scattering model. Tan [24] estimates the airlight to increase contrast, Fattal [25] estimates transmission, which is statistical uncorrelated to surface shading, He et al. [26] introduce the dark channel prior, Berman et al. [27] propose a haze-line constraint, and Meng et al. [28] estimate transmission using its minimum boundary.

CNN-based methods allow faster results [29–32]. DehazeNet [4] and MSCNN [33] use CNN, DCPDN [6] trains densely connected pyramid network to estimate transmission map. AODNet [5], GFN [34,35] applies CGAN, EPDN [7] applies pix2pix, they end-to-end output clear images. Griddehazenet [8] designs

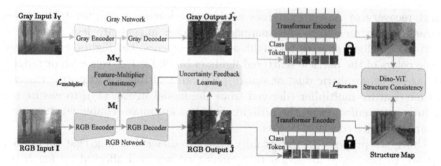

Fig. 2. The pipeline of our network, which consists of (i) grayscale feature multiplier (top left), (ii) structure representation network (right), and (iii) uncertainty feedback learning (middle). The grayscale feature multiplier ($\mathbf{M_Y}$) provides features (red) from CNN, and guides the RGB network to enhance features. The structure representation network provides structure representations (purple) from fixed and pre-trained DINO-ViT, to recover background information. (Color figure online)

attention-based [36] grid network, MSBDN [9] designs boosted multi-scale decoder, FFA-Net [37] proposes feature fusion attention network, AECR-Net [10] applies contrastive learning. Few fully-supervised methods [38–40] are proposed to deal with Dense-Haze [41]. All these methods employ fully supervised learning and hence require ground truths to train their networks. However, obtaining a large number of real dense or non-uniform fog images and their corresponding ground truths is intractable. Semi-supervised methods [11–14] have been introduced, unfortunately, they still suffer from gaps between synthetic and real fog images. Unsupervised methods [1,15–18] are mainly CycleGAN-based. However, the generated images can easily render artefacts (structures that are not originally in the input image) when unpaired training data is used. Though all these methods perform well on normal fog dataset, they are CNN-based, and tend to perform poorly on dense and non-uniform fog [2] since CNN fails to model long-range pixel dependencies [42].

Recently, ViT-based dehazing [2,19] has made progress. DehazeFormer [19] is trained on synthetic fog images (RESIDE outdoor dataset [43]), which are not realistic and cause unreliable performance on real-world fog images. DeHamer [2] combines CNN and Transformer for image dehazing; however, memory and computation complexity slow down the convergence [20], causing inefficient performance on real-world high resolution fog images. In contrast, our method exploits features from both ViT and CNN.

3   Proposed Method

Figure 2 shows the pipeline of our architecture, which consists of three parts: (i) grayscale feature multiplier, (ii) structure representation network, and (iii) uncertainty feedback learning. Since grayscale images are less affected by multi-colored light sources and colorful particle scattered lights, we develop a grayscale

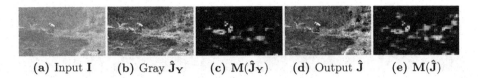

(a) Input I   (b) Gray $\hat{\mathbf{J}}_{\mathbf{Y}}$ (c) $\mathbf{M}(\hat{\mathbf{J}}_{\mathbf{Y}})$ (d) Output $\hat{\mathbf{J}}$ (e) $\mathbf{M}(\hat{\mathbf{J}})$

Fig. 3. Visualization of the features extracted from the grayscale feature multiplier. (a) Input fog image $\mathbf{I}$, (b) Grayscale output image $\hat{\mathbf{J}}_{\mathbf{Y}}$, (c) Sample feature map for $\hat{\mathbf{J}}_{\mathbf{Y}}$, (d) Output fog-free image $\hat{\mathbf{J}}$, and (e) Sample feature map for $\hat{\mathbf{J}}$. We can observe that features in (c) for the grayscale fog images are less affected by fog, and can effectively guide the features in (e) owing to our multiplier consistency loss.

network to guide our RGB network. Hence, in our pipeline, we have two parallel subnetworks: one for processing the grayscale input image, and the other one for processing the RGB input image.

3.1 Grayscale Feature Multiplier

Feature Multiplier. Dense and/or non-uniform fog suffers from low contrast and degraded features. To extract clear background features, we design a subnetwork to predict the amount by which these features should be enhanced. Considering the fog model in Eq. (1) and to avoid the challenges of predicting atmosphere light $\mathbf{A}$ [23], we turn the relationship between fog $\mathbf{I}$ and clear images $\mathbf{J}$ into a multiplier relationship: $\mathbf{J}(\mathbf{x}) = \mathbf{I}(\mathbf{x})\mathbf{M}(\mathbf{x})$, which is called $\mathbf{M}$ feature multiplier [44], where $\mathbf{M}(\mathbf{x}) = \frac{\mathbf{I}(\mathbf{x}) + t(\mathbf{x})\mathbf{A} - \mathbf{A}}{\mathbf{I}(\mathbf{x})t(\mathbf{x})}$.

The feature multiplier $\mathbf{M}$ depends on atmospheric light $\mathbf{A}$ and transmission $t(\mathbf{x})$, which are both unknown. Moreover, $\mathbf{A}$ is an RGB color vector; implying that in order to estimate $\mathbf{M}$, there are four unknowns in total for each pixel: 3 for the RGB values of $\mathbf{A}$ and 1 for t. These unknowns influence the accuracy of the network in learning the correct value of $\mathbf{M}$. To overcome the difficulty, we propose to employ a grayscale feature multiplier, where all variables in the grayscale feature multiplier become scalar variables. Consequently, the number of unknowns the network needs to learn is reduced to only two variables for each pixel: $t(\mathbf{x})$ and $\mathbf{A}$. Note that, to avoid the direct recovery of $\mathbf{A}$, our network implicitly includes $\mathbf{A}$ in the feature multiplier.

Grayscale-Feature Multiplier. We feed the grayscale image, $\mathbf{I}_{\mathbf{Y}}$, to our grayscale encoder, which estimates the grayscale feature multiplier $\mathbf{M}_{\mathbf{Y}}$. We multiply grayscale features and $\mathbf{M}_{\mathbf{Y}}$ before feeding them to our grayscale decoder. We train the grayscale network independently from the RGB network, using both synthetic and unpaired real images. Once the grayscale network is trained, we freeze it, and employ it as the guidance for training the RGB network.

As for the RGB network, the RGB encoder takes the RGB image as input, $\mathbf{I}$, and estimates the color feature multiplier $\mathbf{M}_{\mathbf{I}}$. Having estimated $\mathbf{M}_{\mathbf{I}}$, we multiply it with the RGB features and feed the multiplied features to our RGB decoder. As shown in Fig. 2, we constrain the learning process of our RGB network by

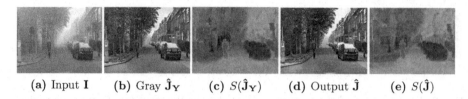

(a) Input $\mathbf{I}$ (b) Gray $\hat{\mathbf{J}}_{\mathbf{Y}}$ (c) $S(\hat{\mathbf{J}}_{\mathbf{Y}})$ (d) Output $\hat{\mathbf{J}}$ (e) $S(\hat{\mathbf{J}})$

Fig. 4. Visualization of structure representations. (a) Input fog image $\mathbf{I}$, (b) Grayscale output image $\hat{\mathbf{J}}_{\mathbf{Y}}$, (c) DINO-ViT keys for $\hat{\mathbf{J}}_{\mathbf{Y}}$, (d) Output fog-free image $\hat{\mathbf{J}}$, and (e) DINO-ViT keys for $\hat{\mathbf{J}}$. We can observe that DINO-ViT representations in (c) capture structure scene/object parts (*e.g.* cars, trees, buildings), and are less affected by fog.

imposing a consistency loss between the grayscale feature multiplier, $\mathbf{M_Y}$, and the RGB feature multiplier $\mathbf{M_I}$. We call this loss a multiplier consistency loss.

Multiplier Consistency Loss. To constrain the RGB feature multiplier $\mathbf{M_I}$, we utilize the grayscale feature multiplier $\mathbf{M_Y}$ as guidance. Based on the Gray World assumption [45], we define the multiplier consistency loss as:

$$\mathcal{L}_{\text{multiplier}} = \|\mathbf{M_I} - \mathbf{M_Y}\|_2 , \tag{2}$$

where $\mathbf{M_I}$ and $\mathbf{M_Y}$ are the feature multipliers of the RGB and grayscale images. To construct this loss, first, we train our grayscale network independently from our RGB network. By training the grayscale network on both synthetic and real images, $\mathbf{M_Y}$ is optimized. Once the training is completed, we freeze the grayscale network. Subsequently, we train our RGB network.

In this training stage, the network losses are the same as those in the grayscale network, except all the images used to calculate the losses are now RGB images. Unlike the training process of the grayscale network, however, we need to apply the multiplier consistency loss $\mathcal{L}_{\text{multiplier}}$ to train the RGB network. Note that, the reason we use the loss to enforce $\mathbf{M_I}$ and $\mathbf{M_Y}$ to be close, and do not use $\mathbf{M_Y}$ as the feature multiplier for the RGB network (i.e., $\mathbf{M_I} = \mathbf{M_Y}$) is because we intend to train the RGB convolution layers; so that, in the testing stage, we do not need the grayscale network.

3.2   Structure Representation Network

A few methods [22,46–48] have exploited self-similarity-based feature descriptors to obtain structure representations. Unlike these methods, to reveal the clear background structures, we use deep spatial features obtained from DINO-ViT [49], which has been proven to learn meaningful visual representations [50]. Moreover, these powerful representations are shared across different object classes. Specifically, we use keys' self-similarity in the attention model, at the deepest transformer layer. In Fig. 4, we show the Principal Component Analysis (PCA) visualization of the keys' self-similarity and demonstrate the three top components as RGB at layer 11 of DINO-ViT. As one can observe, the structure

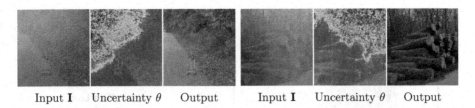

Input **I**   Uncertainty θ Output   Input **I**   Uncertainty θ Output

Fig. 5. Uncertainty maps of O-HAZE [51] dataset. The (b) uncertainty map indicates the fog intensity.

representations capture the clear background parts, which helps the network significantly preserve the background structures.

Dino-ViT Structure Consistency Loss. Our Dino-ViT structure consistency loss encourages the deep-structure representations of the RGB output to be similar to the grayscale features, since the grayscale features are robust to fog:

$$\mathcal{L}_{\text{structure}} = \left\| S(\hat{\mathbf{J}}) - S(\hat{\mathbf{J}}_{\mathbf{Y}}) \right\|_F , \tag{3}$$

where S is the self-similarity descriptor, defined by the difference in the self-similarity of the keys extracted from the attention module, with $n \times n$ dimension, where n is the number of patches. $\|\cdot\|_F$ is the Frobenius norm. The self-similarity descriptor is defined as:

$$S(\hat{\mathbf{J}})_{ij} = \text{cos-sim}(k_i(\hat{\mathbf{J}}), k_j(\hat{\mathbf{J}})) = 1 - \frac{k_i(\hat{\mathbf{J}}) \cdot k_j(\hat{\mathbf{J}})}{\left\| k_i(\hat{\mathbf{J}}) \right\| \cdot \left\| k_j(\hat{\mathbf{J}}) \right\|}, \tag{4}$$

where $\text{cos-sim}(\cdot)$ is the cosine similarity between keys, k_i are the spatial keys.

3.3 Uncertainty Feedback Learning

Uncertainty Map. The main challenge of dealing with dense non-uniform fog distributions is how to differentiate the dense fog regions from the light fog regions. To address this problem, we exploit an uncertainty map as an attention map to guide the network to differentiate dense fog regions from the rest of the input image. Since the network produces higher uncertainty for the denser fog regions. Each value in the uncertainty map represents the confidence of the defogging operation at the corresponding pixel (i.e. the variance). The higher the value, the more uncertain the network's prediction for that pixel.

To generate an uncertainty map together with the defogged result, we add a multi-task decoder to our network. Note that the defogged result and the uncertainty map are decoded from the same features, since there is only one encoder. We assume that the defogged output $\hat{\mathbf{J}}$ follows a Laplace distribution,

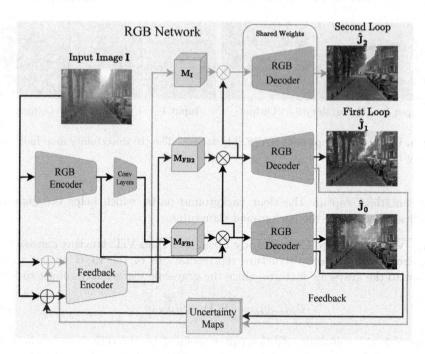

Fig. 6. Architecture of the uncertainty feedback learning. This network refines the performance of the RGB network.

where the mean of this distribution is the clear ground truth $\mathbf{J}^{gt}$ [52,53]. Under this assumption, we can define a likelihood function as follows:

$$p(\mathbf{J}^{gt}|\mathbf{I}) = \frac{1}{2\theta}\exp(-\frac{\left\|\hat{\mathbf{J}} - \mathbf{J}^{gt}\right\|_1}{\theta}),\tag{5}$$

where θ is the variance of the Laplace distribution. In our implementation, we define this variance as the uncertainty of the defogged output $\hat{\mathbf{J}}$. Therefore, Eq. (5) includes both outputs generated by our multi-task network. Taking the logarithm of both sides of Eq. (5) and maximizing it, we can obtain: $\arg\max_\theta \ln p(\mathbf{J}^{gt}|\mathbf{I}) = -\frac{\left\|\hat{\mathbf{J}}-\mathbf{J}^{gt}\right\|_1}{\theta} - \ln\theta.$

For the first term in this likelihood $-\frac{\left\|\hat{\mathbf{J}}-\mathbf{J}^{gt}\right\|_1}{\theta}$, we simply convert the negative sign to positive and put it into the loss function. The second term $-\ln\theta$, we convert it to $\ln(\theta + 1)$ to avoid negative infinity when θ is zero. Hence, the uncertainty loss we will minimize is expressed as follows:

$$\mathcal{L}_{\text{unc}} = \frac{\left\|\hat{\mathbf{J}} - \mathbf{J}^{\text{gt}}\right\|_1}{\theta} + \ln(\theta + 1).\tag{6}$$

Uncertainty Feedback Learning. Unfortunately, the results of our baseline network might still suffer from the remaining fog. There are two possible reasons.

First, the effectiveness of our multiplier consistency loss depends on the grayscale network's performance. While we can see in our ablation studies that this grayscale guidance improves the defogging performance, the grayscale network cannot completely remove fog all the time. Second, our discriminative loss cannot fully suppress fog for any input image, since we do not have paired training ground truths for real images.

To address this problem, we introduce uncertainty feedback learning, which the architecture is shown in Fig. 6. We provide our network extra attention to the different densities of fog based on our network-generated uncertainty maps. Specifically, we introduce uncertainty feedback learning to make our network focus on areas where fog is still visible and to defog these areas iteratively. In one iteration, if our output still contains fog in some regions, then the uncertainty map will indicate those regions, and in the next iteration, our method will focus on these regions to further defog them.

As shown in Fig. 6, we feedforward the uncertainty map together with the input image into the feedback encoder, producing a new feedback feature multiplier $\mathbf{M_{FB}}$. We multiply this multiplier with the RGB features, and feed the multiplication result to the RGB decoder, generating the enhanced output, $\hat{\mathbf{J}}_1$. To train our RGB network and the feedback network, we use real images (that do not have ground truths) and apply only the discriminative loss. We compute the loss of this output $\hat{\mathbf{J}}_i$ (where i is the index of the iterations) with the same loss functions as the initial output image $\hat{\mathbf{J}}$, and backpropagate the errors. We iterate this process a few times to obtain the final output. The number of iterations is constrained by the GPU memory. From our experiments, we found that the uncertainty map tends to be unchanged after two or three iterations.

3.4 Overall Losses

In training our network, we use both synthetic images with ground truths and real images without ground truths. For both the grayscale and RGB networks, we feedforward a set of synthetic images into the network, which outputs the predicted clear synthetic images. For the same batch, we feedforward a set of real images into the network, producing the predicted real images. Having obtained the predicted clear images of both the synthetic and real images, we then train the discriminators in the grayscale channel of the grayscale and RGB networks. Training discriminators requires a set of reference images, which must be real and clear (without fog). Our reference images include the ground truth images of the synthetic fog images (paired), and other real images that with no correlation to our input images (unpaired).

We multiply each loss function with its respective weight, and sum them together to obtain our overall loss function:

$$\mathcal{L} = \lambda_m \mathcal{L}_{\text{multiplier}} + \lambda_s \mathcal{L}_{\text{structure}} + \lambda_u \mathcal{L}_{\text{unc}} + \mathcal{L}_{\text{MSE}} + \lambda_d \mathcal{L}_{\text{dis}}, \qquad (7)$$

where λ are the weights for the respective losses. $\lambda_m = 1$, $\lambda_u = 1$, their values are obtained empirically. $\lambda_s = 0.1$, $\lambda_d = 0.005$, their values are followed default

Table 1. Quantitative results on Dense-HAZE, NH-HAZE, O-HAZE and self-collected smoke datasets.

Method	Dense-HAZE [41]		NH-HAZE [56]		O-HAZE [51]		SMOKE	
	PSNR↑	SSIM↑	PSNR↑	SSIM↑	PSNR↑	SSIM↑	PSNR↑	SSIM↑
DCP [26]	10.06	0.39	10.57	0.52	16.78	0.65	11.26	0.26
DehazeNet [4]	13.84	0.43	16.62	0.52	17.57	0.77	–	–
AODNet [5]	13.14	0.41	15.40	0.57	15.03	0.54	–	–
GDN [8]	–	–	–	–	23.51	**0.83**	15.19	0.53
MSBDN [9]	15.37	0.49	19.23	0.71	24.36	0.75	13.19	0.34
FFA-Net [37]	14.39	0.45	19.87	0.69	22.12	0.77	–	–
AECR-Net [10]	15.80	0.47	19.88	**0.72**	–	–	–	–
DeHamer'22 [2]	16.62	**0.56**	20.66	0.68	17.02	0.43	13.31	0.28
Ours	**16.67**	0.50	**20.99**	0.61	**24.61**	0.75	**18.83**	**0.62**

setting. $\mathcal{L}_{\text{MSE}}$ is the Mean Squared Error (MSE) loss (applied only to synthetic images), $\mathcal{L}_{\text{dis}}$ is the discriminative loss.

4   Experimental Results

Implementation. We use two sets of data to train our networks: real fog images and reference clear images, synthetic fog images and their ground truth. For the real fog images, we train on self-collected and Internet fog images. For the clear reference images, we collect clear images from Google Street View and Internet. For synthetic training images, we render fog images (Eq. 1) from clear images, taken from Cityscapes [55], which provides 2,975 pairs of RGB images and their disparity maps. Subsequently, we fine-tune the model on different datasets. For self-collected smoke images, we fine-tune the model on the 110 self-collected smoke images and clean pairs, and 100 unpaired Internet clean references. We also collect 12 other pairs of fog data for evaluation. Our data is publicly available.

Datasets. We collected real smoke data by ourselves. We used a fog machine to generate fog, where we fixed the camera pose to record fog images and their paired ground truth. Ancuti et al. [51] propose the O-HAZE dataset consisting of 45 pairs of hazy/clear scenes using a smoke generator to simulate the atmospheric scattering effect in the real world. Using the same smoke generator equipment, Ancuti et al. [41] also propose the Dense-HAZE and NH-HAZE [56,57], which both consist of 55 pairs of hazy/clear scenes, 45 training, 5 validation and 5 test images. The scenes in the Dense-HAZE and NH-HAZE datasets are similar to the O-Haze dataset, but the smoke density is much higher and more non-homogeneous.

Baselines. We evaluate our method against the non-learning method Non-Local Image Dehazing (NLD) [27], state-of-the-art transformer-based dehazing

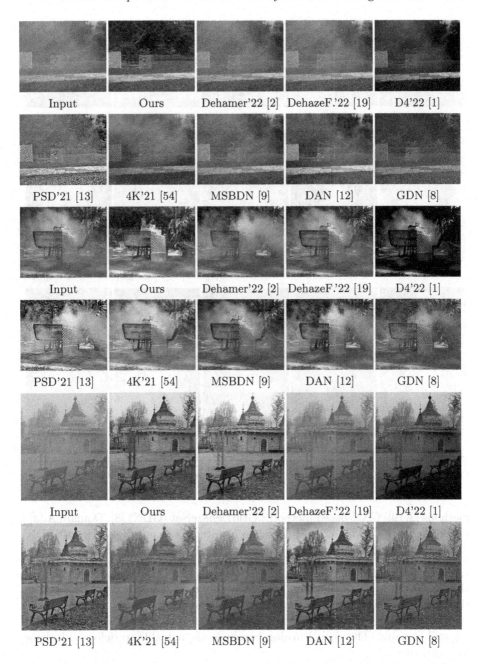

Fig. 7. Qualitative evaluation results on real fog machine and O-Haze [51] images.

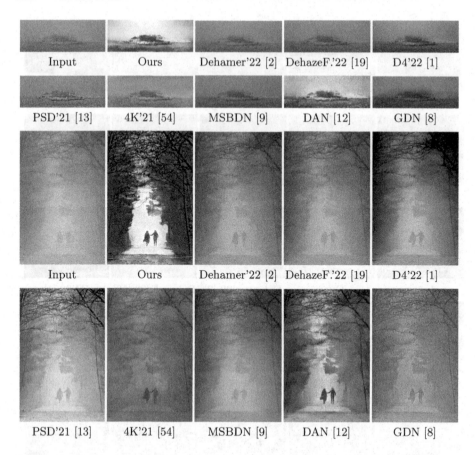

Fig. 8. Comparison results on commonly used test foggy images. (a) Input images. (b) Our results. (c)~(g) Results of the state-of-the-art methods.

methods [2,19], CNN-based methods: GridDehazeNet (GDN) [8], Domain Adaptation Network (DAN) [12], Multi-Scale Boosted Dehazing Network (MSBDN) [9], 4KDehazing (CVPR21) [54], PSD (CVPR21) [13], D4 (CVPR22) [1], etc.

Qualitative Comparisons. Comparisons on the self-collected fog and O-HAZE dataset are shown in Fig. 7. The baseline methods do not perform well on the images. Some results are too dark, and some still have fog left. Also, since the generated fog is not uniform in the Dense-Haze and NH-Haze datasets, some fog still remains. The deep learning baselines are not able to defog such dense fog adequately.

Figures 8 to 9 show the input dense non-uniform fog images, our defogging results, and the results of the state-of-the-art methods. Due to the uniform and/or severe fog density, the input images are degraded by multiple factors like blur, contrast, sharpness, and color distortion. As shown in the figures, our method outperforms the state-of-the-art methods on real dense fog images.

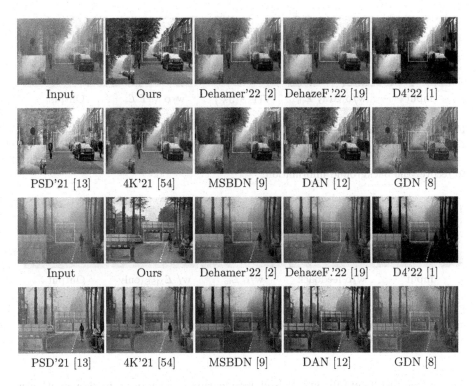

Fig. 9. Comparison results on real dense fog images. (a) Input images. (b) Our results. (c)~(g) Results of the state-of-the-art methods. Our results show better visibility.

Quantitative Comparisons. We also conduct quantitative evaluations on O-HAZE, NH-Haze and Dense-Haze, which are shown in Table 1. We measure the restoration performance using the Peak Signal-to-Noise Ratio (PSNR) and the Structural Similarity (SSIM); higher is better. Our method achieves the best PSNR, SSIM performance.

4.1 Ablation Studies

We conduct ablation studies to analyze the characteristics of the proposed algorithm. We first evaluate the grayscale feature multiplier, if the grayscale network is removed, the RGB network will have no guidance from grayscale and the results are shown in Fig. 10b. To show the effectiveness of using ViT, we remove the structure consistency loss, the results are shown in Fig. 10d. We then remove the uncertainty feedback network from our model. After training with the same semi-supervised training strategy and the same loss functions, the results are shown in Fig. 11b. We can observe that the results are not as effective as those using the feedback network. In Fig. 11c, we replace our multiplier generator with the normal generator. Therefore, we can observe more fake content, such as the fake leaves on the tree. Finally, Fig. 11d shows the results of using the MSE loss only.

| Input | w/o Gray $\mathcal{L}_{\mathrm{m}}$ | ViT $S(\hat{\mathbf{J}}_{\mathbf{Y}})$ | w/o ViT $\mathcal{L}_{\mathrm{s}}$ | Output |

Fig. 10. Ablation studies on (b) without using our grayscale multiplier consistency loss $\mathcal{L}_{\mathrm{multiplier}}$, and (d) without using our Dino-ViT structure consistency loss $\mathcal{L}_{\mathrm{structure}}$. (e) is our final output. (c) shows DINO-ViT capture scene structure, helping the network to recover the background information.

| Input | w/o feedback | w/o $\mathcal{L}_{\mathrm{m}}$ | w/ $\mathcal{L}_{\mathrm{MSE}}$ only | Output |

Fig. 11. Ablation studies on (b) without uncertainty feedback network; (c) without multiplier consistency loss; (d) defogging results from our model with the MSE loss only. (e) is our final output.

The typical results of fully supervised deep learning methods trained on synthetic images are unsatisfactory. Some fog still remains, details are lost, and some regions are considerably dark.

5   Conclusion

We have proposed a learning-based defogging method that targets dense and/or non-uniform fog. Our method combines the structure representations from ViT and the features from CNN as feature regularization that can guide our network to recover background information. Our pipeline consists of a grayscale network and an RGB network. We introduced the grayscale feature multiplier, which is designed to enhance features. Aside from the new structure loss and multiplier consistency loss, we also introduced uncertainty feedback learning that refines the performance of the RGB generator network. Experimental results show that our method works for dense and/or non-uniform fog, and outperforms the state-of-the-art methods.

Acknowledgment. This research/project is supported by the National Research Foundation, Singapore under its AI Singapore Programme (AISG Award No: AISG2-PhD/2022-01-037[T]), and partially supported by MOE2019-T2-1-130. Wenhan Yang's research is supported by Wallenberg-NTU Presidential Postdoctoral Fellowship. Robby T. Tan's work is supported by MOE2019-T2-1-130.

References

1. Yang, Y., Wang, C., Liu, R., Zhang, L., Guo, X., Tao, D.: Self-augmented unpaired image dehazing via density and depth decomposition. In: Proceedings of the IEEE/CVF Conference on Computer Vision and Pattern Recognition, pp. 2037–2046 (2022)
2. Guo, C.L., Yan, Q., Anwar, S., Cong, R., Ren, W., Li, C.: Image dehazing transformer with transmission-aware 3d position embedding. In: Proceedings of the IEEE/CVF Conference on Computer Vision and Pattern Recognition, pp. 5812–5820 (2022)
3. Koschmieder, H.: Theorie der horizontalen Sichtweite. Number V. 2 in Beiträge zur Physik der freien Atmosphäre. Keim & Nemnich (1924)
4. Cai, B., Xu, X., Jia, K., Qing, C., Tao, D.: Dehazenet: an end-to-end system for single image haze removal. IEEE Trans. Image Process.ing 25, 5187–5198 (2016)
5. Li, B., Peng, X., Wang, Z., Xu, J., Feng, D.: Aod-net: All-in-one dehazing network. In: Proceedings of the IEEE International Conference on Computer Vision, pp. 4770–4778 (2017)
6. Zhang, H., Patel, V.M.: Densely connected pyramid dehazing network. In: Proceedings of the IEEE Conference on Computer Vision and Pattern Recognition, pp. 3194–3203 (2018)
7. Qu, Y., Chen, Y., Huang, J., Xie, Y.: Enhanced pix2pix dehazing network. In: Proceedings of the IEEE/CVF Conference on Computer Vision and Pattern Recognition, pp. 8160–8168 (2019) 8160–8168
8. Liu, X., Ma, Y., Shi, Z., Chen, J.: Griddehazenet: Attention-based multi-scale network for image dehazing. In: Proceedings of the IEEE/CVF International Conference on Computer Vision, pp. 7314–7323 (2019)
9. Dong, H., et al.: Multi-scale boosted dehazing network with dense feature fusion. In: Proceedings of the IEEE/CVF Conference on Computer Vision and Pattern Recognition, pp. 2157–2167 (2020)
10. Wu, H., et al.: Contrastive learning for compact single image dehazing. In: Proceedings of the IEEE/CVF Conference on Computer Vision and Pattern Recognition, pp. 10551–10560 (2021)
11. Li, L., et al.: Semi-supervised image dehazing. IEEE Trans. Image Process. 29, 2766–2779 (2019)
12. Shao, Y., Li, L., Ren, W., Gao, C., Sang, N.: Domain adaptation for image dehazing. In: Proceedings of the IEEE/CVF Conference on Computer Vision and Pattern Recognition, pp. 2808–2817 (2020)
13. Chen, Z., Wang, Y., Yang, Y., Liu, D.: Psd: Principled synthetic-to-real dehazing guided by physical priors. In: Proceedings of the IEEE/CVF Conference on Computer Vision and Pattern Recognition, pp. 7180–7189 (2021)
14. Li, Y., Chang, Y., Gao, Y., Yu, C., Yan, L.: Physically disentangled intra-and inter-domain adaptation for varicolored haze removal. In: Proceedings of the IEEE/CVF Conference on Computer Vision and Pattern Recognition, pp. 5841–5850 (2022)
15. Huang, L.Y., Yin, J.L., Chen, B.H., Ye, S.Z.: Towards unsupervised single image dehazing with deep learning. In: 2019 IEEE International Conference on Image Processing (ICIP), IEEE, pp. 2741–2745 (2019)
16. Golts, A., Freedman, D., Elad, M.: Unsupervised single image dehazing using dark channel prior loss. IEEE Trans. Image Process. 29, 2692–2701 (2019)
17. Li, B., Gou, Y., Gu, S., Liu, J.Z., Zhou, J.T., Peng, X.: You only look yourself: unsupervised and untrained single image dehazing neural network. Int. J. Comput. Vis. 129, 1754–1767 (2021)

18. Zhao, S., Zhang, L., Shen, Y., Zhou, Y.: Refinednet: a weakly supervised refinement framework for single image dehazing. IEEE Trans. Image Process. **30**, 3391–3404 (2021)
19. Song, Y., He, Z., Qian, H., Du, X.: Vision transformers for single image dehazing. arXiv preprint arXiv:2204.03883 (2022)
20. Zhu, X., Su, W., Lu, L., Li, B., Wang, X., Dai, J.: Deformable detr: Deformable transformers for end-to-end object detection. arXiv preprint arXiv:2010.04159 (2020)
21. Caron, M., Touvron, H., Misra, I., Jégou, H., Mairal, J., Bojanowski, P., Joulin, A.: Emerging properties in self-supervised vision transformers. In: Proceedings of the IEEE/CVF International Conference on Computer Vision, pp. 9650–9660 (2021)
22. Shechtman, E., Irani, M.: Matching local self-similarities across images and videos. In: 2007 IEEE Conference on Computer Vision and Pattern Recognition, pp. 1–8 IEEE (2007)
23. Sulami, M., Geltzer, I., Fattal, R., Werman, M.: Automatic recovery of the atmospheric light in hazy images. In: IEEE International Conference on Computational Photography (ICCP) (2014)
24. Tan, R.T.: Visibility in bad weather from a single image. In: 2008 IEEE Conference on Computer Vision and Pattern Recognition, pp. 1–8 IEEE (2008)
25. Fattal, R.: Single image dehazing. ACM Trans. Graph. (TOG) **27**, 1–9 (2008)
26. He, K., Sun, J., Tang, X.: Single image haze removal using dark channel prior. IEEE Trans. Patt. Anal. Mach. Intell. **33**, 2341–2353 (2010)
27. Berman, D., Treibitz, T., Avidan, S.: Single image dehazing using haze-lines. IEEE Trans. Patt. Anal. Mach. Intell. **42**, 720–734 (2018)
28. Meng, G., Wang, Y., Duan, J., Xiang, S., Pan, C.: Efficient image dehazing with boundary constraint and contextual regularization. In: Proceedings of the IEEE International Conference on Computer Vision, pp. 617–624 (2013)
29. Li, Y., You, S., Brown, M.S., Tan, R.T.: Haze visibility enhancement: a survey and quantitative benchmarking. Comput. Vis. Image Understand. **165**, 1–16 (2017)
30. Ye, T., et al.: Perceiving and modeling density is all you need for image dehazing. arXiv preprint arXiv:2111.09733 (2021)
31. Lin, B., Zhang, S., Bao, F.: Gait recognition with multiple-temporal-scale 3d convolutional neural network. In: ACM MM (2020)
32. Lin, B., Zhang, S., Yu, X.: Gait recognition via effective global-local feature representation and local temporal aggregation. In: ICCV (2021)
33. Ren, W., Liu, S., Zhang, H., Pan, J., Cao, X., Yang, M.-H.: Single image dehazing via multi-scale convolutional neural networks. In: Leibe, B., Matas, J., Sebe, N., Welling, M. (eds.) ECCV 2016. LNCS, vol. 9906, pp. 154–169. Springer, Cham (2016). https://doi.org/10.1007/978-3-319-46475-6_10
34. Ren, W., et al.: Gated fusion network for single image dehazing. In: Proceedings of the IEEE Conference on Computer Vision and Pattern Recognition, pp. 3253–3261 (2018)
35. Li, R., Pan, J., Li, Z., Tang, J.: Single image dehazing via conditional generative adversarial network. In: Proceedings of the IEEE Conference on Computer Vision and Pattern Recognition, pp. 8202–8211 (2018)
36. Jin, Y., Sharma, A., Tan, R.T.: Dc-shadownet: Single-image hard and soft shadow removal using unsupervised domain-classifier guided network. In: Proceedings of the IEEE/CVF International Conference on Computer Vision, pp. 5027–5036 (2021)

37. Qin, X., Wang, Z., Bai, Y., Xie, X., Jia, H.: Ffa-net: feature fusion attention network for single image dehazing. Proc. AAAI Conf. Artif. Intell. **34**, 11908–11915 (2020)
38. Dudhane, A., Singh Aulakh, H., Murala, S.: Ri-gan: An end-to-end network for single image haze removal. In: Proceedings of the IEEE Conference on Computer Vision and Pattern Recognition Workshops(2019)
39. Bianco, S., Celona, L., Piccoli, F., Schettini, R.: High-resolution single image dehazing using encoder-decoder architecture. In: Proceedings of the IEEE Conference on Computer Vision and Pattern Recognition Workshops (2019)
40. Morales, P., Klinghoffer, T., Jae Lee, S.: Feature forwarding for efficient single image dehazing. In: Proceedings of the IEEE Conference on Computer Vision and Pattern Recognition Workshops (2019)
41. Ancuti, C.O., Ancuti, C., Sbert, M., Timofte, R.: Dense-haze: A benchmark for image dehazing with dense-haze and haze-free images. In: IEEE International Conference on Image Processing (ICIP), IEEE **2019**, 1014–1018 (2019)
42. Dosovitskiy, A., et al.: An image is worth 16x16 words: Transformers for image recognition at scale. arXiv preprint arXiv:2010.11929 (2020)
43. Li, B., et al.: Benchmarking single-image dehazing and beyond. IEEE Trans. Image Process. **28**, 492–505 (2018)
44. Li, R., Tan, R.T., Cheong, L.F., Aviles-Rivero, A.I., Fan, Q., Schonlieb, C.B.: Rainflow: Optical flow under rain streaks and rain veiling effect. In: Proceedings of the IEEE International Conference on Computer Vision, pp. 7304–7313 (2019)
45. Buchsbaum, G.: A spatial processor model for object colour perception. J. Franklin Inst. **310**, 1–26 (1980)
46. Zheng, C., Cham, T.J., Cai, J.: The spatially-correlative loss for various image translation tasks. In: Proceedings of the IEEE/CVF Conference on Computer Vision and Pattern Recognition, pp. 16407–16417 (2021)
47. Kolkin, N., Salavon, J., Shakhnarovich, G.: Style transfer by relaxed optimal transport and self-similarity. In: Proceedings of the IEEE/CVF Conference on Computer Vision and Pattern Recognition, pp. 10051–10060 (2019)
48. Jin, Y., Yang, W., Tan, R.T.: Unsupervised night image enhancement: When layer decomposition meets light-effects suppression. arXiv preprint arXiv:2207.10564 (2022)
49. Tumanyan, N., Bar-Tal, O., Bagon, S., Dekel, T.: Splicing vit features for semantic appearance transfer. In: Proceedings of the IEEE/CVF Conference on Computer Vision and Pattern Recognition, pp. 10748–10757 (2022)
50. Amir, S., Gandelsman, Y., Bagon, S., Dekel, T.: Deep vit features as dense visual descriptors. arXiv preprint arXiv:2112.05814 (2021)
51. Ancuti, C.O., Ancuti, C., Timofte, R., De Vleeschouwer, C.: O-haze: a dehazing benchmark with real hazy and haze-free outdoor images. In: Proceedings of the IEEE Conference on Computer Vision and Pattern Recognition Workshops, pp. 754–762 (2018)
52. Kendall, A., Gal, Y.: What uncertainties do we need in bayesian deep learning for computer vision? In: Advances in Neural Information Processing Systems, vol. 30 (2017)
53. Ning, Q., Dong, W., Li, X., Wu, J., Shi, G.: Uncertainty-driven loss for single image super-resolution. Adv. Neural Inform. Process. Syst. **34**, 16398–16409 (2021)
54. Zheng, Z., et al.: Ultra-high-definition image dehazing via multi-guided bilateral learning. In: 2021 IEEE/CVF Conference on Computer Vision and Pattern Recognition (CVPR), pp. 16180–16189. IEEE (2021)

55. Cordts, M., et al.: The cityscapes dataset for semantic urban scene understanding. In: Proceedings of the IEEE Conference on Computer Vision and Pattern Recognition, pp. 3213–3223 (2016)
56. Ancuti, C.O., Ancuti, C., Timofte, R.: Nh-haze: An image dehazing benchmark with non-homogeneous hazy and haze-free images. In: Proceedings of the IEEE/CVF Conference on Computer Vision and Pattern Recognition workshops, pp. 444–445 (2020)
57. Ancuti, C.O., Ancuti, C., Vasluianu, F.A., Timofte, R.: Ntire 2020 challenge on nonhomogeneous dehazing. In: Proceedings of the IEEE/CVF Conference on Computer Vision and Pattern Recognition Workshops, pp. 490–491 (2020)

DualBLN: Dual Branch LUT-Aware Network for Real-Time Image Retouching

Xiang Zhang[1] , Chengzhe Lu[1] , Dawei Yan[1] , Wei Dong[1(✉)] ,
and Qingsen Yan[2(✉)]

[1] Xi'an University of Architecture and Technology, Xi'an, China
dongwei156@outlook.com
[2] Northwestern Polytechnical University, Xi'an, China
qingsenyan@gmail.com

Abstract. The 3D Lookup Table (3D LUT) is an efficient tool for image retouching tasks, which models non-linear 3D color transformations by sparsely sampling them into a discrete 3D lattice. We propose **DualBLN** (Dual Branch LUT-aware Network) which innovatively incorporates the data representing the color transformation of 3D LUT into the real-time retouching process, which forces the network to learn the adaptive weights and the multiple 3D LUTs with strong representation capability. The estimated adaptive weights not only consider the content of the raw input but also use the information of the learned 3D LUTs. Specifically, the network contains two branches for feature extraction from the input image and 3D LUTs, to regard the information of the image and the 3D LUTs, and generate the precise LUT fusion weights. In addition, to better integrate the features of the input image and the learned 3D LUTs, we employ bilinear pooling to solve the problem of feature information loss that occurs when fusing features from the dual branch network, avoiding the feature distortion caused by direct concatenation or summation. Extensive experiments on several datasets demonstrate the effectiveness of our work, which is also efficient in processing high-resolution images. Our approach is not limited to image retouching tasks, but can also be applied to other pairwise learning-based tasks with fairly good generality. Our code is available at https://github.com/120326/DualBLN.

Keywords: 3D lookup table · Photo retouching · Color enhancement

1 Introduction

Along with the promotion of digital image technology, it is common for people to use cameras or cell phones to take photos and record beautiful moments.

This work is supported by the Fundamental Research Funds for the Central Universities (No. D5000220444) and the Natural Science Basic Research Program of Shaanxi (2021JLM-16) and the Yulin Science and Technology Plan Project (CXY-2020-063).

Supplementary Information The online version contains supplementary material available at https://doi.org/10.1007/978-3-031-26313-2_11.

L. Wang et al. (Eds.): ACCV 2022, LNCS 13843, pp. 173–189, 2023.
https://doi.org/10.1007/978-3-031-26313-2_11

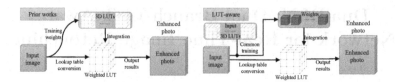

Fig. 1. Comparison between previous works and our method. Previous works (left) only uses images as the only input to the network when training the model, while our LUT-aware (right) applies look-up table information on the input side.

However, most people will press the shutter randomly and the photos taken will be affected by external factors such as weather and time of day, and the original photos taken directly may have darker or overly bright areas. Due to this, the photos directly generated by the shooting equipment still need further post-processing to improve their visual quality. The retouching process requires the use of professional software that is very difficult to start, requires sufficient expertise reserves, and is quite time-consuming. These problems directly lead to the high threshold and tedious work for manual photo retouching.

The simplest solution for this task can be achieved to some extent by expert pre-stored color filters, but the poor generalization of fixed retouching methods is not a good solution. The 3D lookup table is a mapping relationship that can handle low-quality images well. The areas near the edges of the lookup table can be targeted for color conversion of light and dark areas to reduce noise and achieve better mapping results. However, the internal parameters of the lookup table depend on the expert's preset, and it is complex to target the optimization for a specific image. In recent years, combining traditional photo retouching techniques with deep learning has gained attention in academia. For example, Zeng et al. [45] combined multiple lookup tables with convolutional neural networks to propose an image-adaptive 3D lookup table method. Based on this, Liang et al. [24] focused on portrait photo retouching by segmenting foreground portraits and rear scenes, then realizing weighted optimization of different regions to give more attention to portrait regions. However, previous works are not flexible enough to use the information of 3DLUT for fusion.

Benefiting from the above works, we believe that lookup table parameters are a non-negligible element in image retouching tasks. No model directly uses the 3D LUT itself as a learnable object but only optimizes the parameters inside the 3D LUT using an optimizer from the field of deep learning to learn a pre-processed 3D LUT model for image retouching task. When performing transformations related to image modification, the network needs to know the internal data of the lookup table to perform targeted optimization. In other words, passively changing the lookup table parameters based on the model retouching results is not the optimal solution for image retouching since the information about these parameters is not fully used in the learning model.

To alleviate this problem, we propose the dual branch LUT-aware network named DualBLN which consists of image branch and LUT branch. In Fig. 2, the image input branch is used to process unretouched raw images. This branch

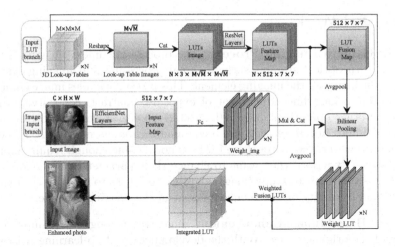

Fig. 2. Schematic diagram of the framework of the network structure. Given an unre-touched input image, it is passed through the classifier network and used to generate weights and fuse the N LUTs after flattening.

focuses on three dimensions: network depth, width and image resolution, using EfficientNet [33] to extract features from the images and generate weights for the initial fusion of lookup table information. The LUT input branch is the module responsible for processing the 3D LUTs fed into the network. The 3D lookup table data is converted into 2D data that approximates the shape of the input image and fed into ResNet [12] with the fully connected layer removed for the generation of the feature map and the initial fusion with the image weights, resulting in the LUT fusion map. The inclusion of lookup table parameters allows for an adaptive image modification model based on LUT perception and thus generates more accurate lookup table fusion weights. To make the features fused as much as possible and retain the information, bilinear pooling [25] is used to generate 3D LUT fusion weights. Multiplied using the outer product at each location of the feature map and pooled across locations to combine the feature information. The outer product captures the pairwise correlations between feature channels and can model the interactions between dual branch features.

The contributions of this paper are as follows:

- In order to better utilize the internal information of the lookup table to achieve more exquisite image retouching effects, we propose a new two-branch network structure named DualBLN, which innovatively uses the LUT as part of the input to implement an adaptive LUT-aware model structure.
- In an effort to reasonably fuse the two intermediate feature matrices generated by the bifurcated structure, bilinear pooling is used for feature fusion to reduce the negative effects of two different feature matrices that are too different and also to improve the overall robustness of the model.
- Extensive experiments are conducted on three datasets. The results demonstrate that our method is reasonable and efficient.

2   Related Work

LUT in Camera Imaging Process. The process of camera imaging is very complex, with optical systems such as signal processing and imaging systems focusing the image on the imaging element. This process includes image enhancement modules, including adjustment of exposure, contrast, color style, and a number of other operations [3,5,8,20,21,23,27,29,43]. According to [16], most of these modules in real systems use a common technique, namely LUT (Lookup table). However, the use of these LUTs is not flexible enough require manual debugging by experts if they want to change their parameters. Therefore, [45] used this as their hair to study image adaptive 3D LUTs to improve the expressiveness and flexibility of photo enhancement in the imaging pipeline.

Learning-Based Image Enhancement. Image retouching aims to improve the quality of the original image. With the development of deep learning networks, significant progress has been made in this task [4,7,11,14,17–19,28,30,32,35,41, 46]. Gharbi *et al.* proposed the HDRNet [7] that put most of the computation on downsampled images. It can be regarded as a masterpiece along the lines of a bilateral filter. He *et al.* [11] proposed the CSRNet that extracted global features with normal CNN and modulated the features after 1×1 convolution. CSRNet [11] used an end-to-end approach that is easy to train.

Image restoration [3,6,10,26,36,42,44,47] aims to remove image distortions caused by various situations. Since manual retouching requires a mass of expert knowledge and subjective judgment, many learning-based image restoration methods have emerged recently. Wang *et al.* [36] proposed a neural network for photo enhancement using deep lighting estimation to fix underexposed photos. Recently Mahmoud *et al.* [1] proposed a model that can perform multi-scale exposure correction for images. Guo *et al.* [9] proposed a model based on a luminance enhancement curve, which is iterated continuously to achieve gradual contrast and luminance enhancement of low-light images. As for the noise reduction task, Huang *et al.* [13] presented a model which generates two independent noise-bearing images of similar scenes to train the noise-reduction network.

Some researchers [17,28,38–40] have adapted the network structure to pursue the enhancement of the original image. In addition to expert retouching, Han-Ul *et al.* [18] developed PieNet to solve the problem of personalization in image enhancement. These works demonstrate that image enhancement has splendid results based on paired datasets. However, the collection of paired datasets is expensive. Therefore, image enhancement methods based on unpaired datasets started to receive attention. Some GAN-based methods [4,14] do not require pairs of input and target images. Meanwhile, Jongchan *et al.* [30] proposed the Distort-and-Recover method focusing on image color enhancement, which only required high-quality reference images for training. While existing image enhancement models have good generality, our work focuses on exploring the role of look-up table information in the network architecture, a novel approach that makes it an under-explored task.

Deep Learning Methods with 3D LUT. In previous studies, Zeng *et al.* [45] combined the deep learning-based weight predictor and 3D LUT for the first time, which achieved outstanding results. Then, multiple look-up tables were dynamically combined to capture image characteristics and perform the enhancement. [45] was a representative work that combined the deep learning paradigm with the traditional image enhancement paradigm, which presented the community with a new perspective on how to implement image enhancement. Although the most significant contribution of Liang *et al.* [24] is to provide a high-quality paired portrait photo retouch dataset, they changed the network architecture to use ResNet [12] instead of the simple CNN in the network of Zeng *et al.* [45] as an image classifier and achieved some improvements in the results, which inspired us to replace some of the structures in the network, allowing the final generation of more reasonable weights for fusing LUTs. Subsequently, Jo *et al.* [15] implemented a similar look-up process from input to output values by training a deep super-resolution network and transferring the output values of the deep learned model into the LUT. Wang *et al.* [37] further optimized the whole structure by employing UNet to generate the output of the encoding part as the weights for fusing multiple LUTs and using the output of the decoding part as the spatially-aware weights for the whole image to further optimize the interpolation results of the 3D LUT.

3   Methodology

3.1   3D LUT of Traditional Image Enhancement

Originally a traditional technique widely used in the field of screen color imaging display, 3D LUT has been combined with deep learning in recent years to perform image enhancement work.

As shown in Fig. 3(a), it can be simply interpreted as a 3D lattice consisting of three 1D LUTs, corresponding to the RGB color channels, and a total of M^3 elements. The input RGB value is mapped in three dimensions according to a look-up table to obtain the converted color. The input image is defined as I, and the converted image is O through the look-up table, then the conversion process can be expressed by the formula:

$$O_{(i,j,k)} = \varphi(I_{(i,j,k)}^R, I_{(i,j,k)}^G, I_{(i,j,k)}^B), \tag{1}$$

where (i, j, k) are the coordinates corresponding to the pixel color of the image in RGB space, and φ is defined as the conversion method from the input color value to the output color value. Usually, M is usually set to 33 in practice, and the range of coordinates (0 to 255) taken under the three channels is much larger than the set value M. As shown in Fig. 3(b), the introduction of trilinear interpolation can solve this problem. In this strategy, the LUT can be flattened and fed into the network, we make $M = 36$, and this part of the work will be described in detail in the following.

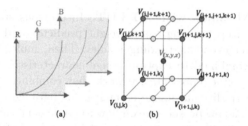

Fig. 3. (a) The 3D LUT is a cube containing M^3 nodes, but each coordinate system can be regarded as a separate 1D LUT. (b) The trilinear interpolation can compensate for the problem of an insufficient range of coordinates, and calculate the values of other points in the cube by giving the values of the vertices.

3D LUT is applied to conventional camera imaging to improve the image quality of the camera and also to reduce the effect of color difference between various devices. For image retouching tasks, the part of the lookup table that is closer to the black area inside the lookup table specializes in color mapping the dark areas of the original image, improving the details in dark scenes, and achieving better visual effects. Correspondingly, the part of the lookup table closer to white is also good at handling overexposed areas of the image. For other normal imaging areas, color conversion can also become more in line with human visual preferences. In summary, 3D LUT is a very suitable color conversion model for our work, as it can repair defects in photos and make images more brilliant.

The retouching style of the image shifts with the content of the shot, so a single 3D LUT does not work well with a wide variety of photos. As the prior art in 3D LUT paper, we use fused 3D LUTs, *i.e.*, we fuse multiple LUTs according to the weights generated by the classifier and thus achieve differentiation of retouching results.

3.2   Proposed Method

Retouching images using 3D LUTs is efficient and fast, and the individual pixel color values of an image are found and mapped to produce a retouched image. Our model uses a two-branch network to train weights and fuse multiple 3D LUTs based on these weights to achieve a differentiated retouching result. The network contains two starting points, corresponding to the dual branches in the architecture, for input photos and lookup tables, respectively. Thus it can be subdivided into four segments based on their functions: *the input image branch module, the input LUT branch module, the feature map fusion module, and the weighted fusion of 3D LUTs module.*

Image Input Branch. Unretouched images are essential as the input to the network, and traditional deep learning methods generate weights directly from the input images for subsequent weighted fusion. We adopt EfficientNet [33] as the network layer of the image input branch, but we additionally reserve the middle feature map for the subsequent feature map fusion module, in addition to generating weights for fusing LUTs.

Input LUT Branch. Since the structure of a 3D LUT is different from that of a 2D image, an additional deformation operation is required before feeding it into the network, which simply means flattening the data into a picture-like storage pattern and feeding the flattened LUTs image into the network as input. ResNet [12] is chosen as the network architecture for this branch, but we remove the final fully connected layer and keep only the LUT feature maps up to the middle, which is fused according to the weights generated by the image input branch to produce the final LUT fusion map.

Feature Map Fusion. The previous two branching modules ensure that the dimensions of the feature maps fed into the fusion module are the same. For the two feature maps extracted from Image and 3D LUT, the vector of the two fused features is obtained by bilinear pooling [25], which is used to generate the final weights and used to weight the different 3D LUTs.

Weighted Fusion of 3D LUTs. This is the most intuitive part of image retouching, the original image is directly fused with the weighted 3D LUT to find the mapping relationship in the lookup table pixel by pixel, and finally, the image is mapped into a retouched and enhanced photo with better visual effect.

3.3 The Image Processing Module

Simply using the set ResNet [12] does not achieve the best classification results, and if we want to further improve the accuracy of the classifier for image classification, it is a good way to replace it with EfficientNet [33], which is more suitable for image classification, it explores the effects of input resolution, depth, and width of the network, and uses Neural Architecture Search to search for a rationalized configuration of the above three parameters, which improves the image classification accuracy while achieving a smaller parameter computation. Considering all aspects, EfficientNet [33] is more suitable for our task and can be used for image processing to obtain intermediate feature matrices that are more conducive to subsequent computations and more accurate classification weights.

However, EfficientNet [33] is still not perfect. In our experiments, we found that although it looks fast and lightweight, it is very memory cost in practice. However, this problem can be avoided by reasonable settings.

EfficientNet [33] contains a total of eight branching categories from B0 to B7, and the accuracy of the classification and the number of parameters required for calculation are increasing in order. After consideration, we choose B0 as our image classifier, although the other models have better accuracy, their increased computational cost cannot be ignored. Considering the memory usage and the fact that B0 already has very good training results, this choice is an extremely cost-effective optimization decision.

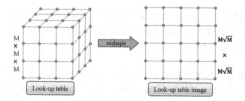

Fig. 4. A simple illustration of a look-up table directly subjected to reshapee operation to obtain a flattened LUT-image that can be fed into a neural network.

3.4 The LUT-Aware Module

Look-up tables (LUTs) are widely used for color correction and grading, but they are essentially a mapping of data between RGB values, with the coordinates still storing the RGB three-channel color values. In terms of data type, it is identical to the image that is fed into the network, the differences is that the image is a two-dimensional plane. Theoretically, just as a three-channel RGB image can be used as the input to a deep learning network, the data in the 3D LUT can also be fed to the network. In short, we believe that drawing the information from the 3D LUTs into the network can help the network to estimate better.

As shown in Fig. 4, before training, we set N 3D LUTs, each of which has a parametric number of M^3. We noted that the data in the form of 3D storage cannot be fed directly into the network for learning, but could be converted into a form similar to an image. This is the reason why we change the value of M to 36, under which the data can be directly expanded into a plane, and this step can be expressed by the formula:

$$LUT_{orig}(M^3) \xrightarrow{flatten} LUT_{flat}(M\sqrt{M} \times M\sqrt{M}), \tag{2}$$

where LUT_{orig} is the original 3D LUT storage form, and LUT_{flat} is the flattened storage form. We call it LUT image because it has a similar appearance to the image. Obviously after this step, the idea of feeding the look-up table into the network learning becomes possible.

As for how to handle the 3D LUT after the transformation, we chose an incomplete ResNet [12] as the network model. Since the current module only needs to obtain feature maps for the fusion module afterward, the network model does not need the final fully connected layer for outputting weights. In addition, ResNet [12] is mature enough, which is very friendly used in this task. After the network layer, the LUT feature map is obtained.

Although it is possible to use the LUT feature map for the subsequent feature map fusion module, it will eventually produce poor fusion results because of the large gap between the image and the LUT feature maps. In order to reduce the gap between the feature maps, we fuse the LUT feature maps initially according to the image weights to ensure the effectiveness of the subsequent feature map fusion module. The effects of this section will be compared and analyzed in the subsequent experimental section (see Sect. 4.3).

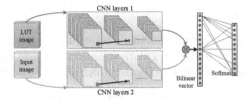

Fig. 5. Bilinear pooling is mainly used for feature fusion, for features x and y extracted from the same sample, the two features are fused by bilinear pooling to obtain the vector. The final output of the learned weights through the fully connected layer.

3.5 Feature Fusion Using Bilinear Pooling

Our network is constructed with two different inputs, the image, and the LUT image. The overall framework is shown in Fig. 2, we keep the feature map before feeding it to the fully connected layer for subsequent operations; the LUTs Feature Map is combined with the weights generated by the image classifier and fused into a LUT fusion map with the same size as the Input Feature Map, which is further mingled with it by averaging pooling and bilinear pooling [25]. For image $\mathcal{I}$ and 3D LUT $\mathcal{L}$ at the position l of two features $f_{img} \in \mathbb{R}^{T \times M}$ and $f_{lut} \in \mathbb{R}^{T \times N}$, the bilinear pooling can be expressed by the following equation:

$$
\begin{aligned}
b(l, \mathcal{I}, \mathcal{L}, f_{img}, f_{LUT}) &= f_{img}^T(\mathcal{I}) f_{LUT}(\mathcal{L}) && \in \mathbb{R}^{M \times N}, \\
\xi(\mathcal{I}, \mathcal{L}) &= \sum_l b(l, \mathcal{I}, \mathcal{L}, f_{img}, f_{LUT}) && \in \mathbb{R}^{M \times N}, \\
x &= vec(\xi(\mathcal{I}, \mathcal{L})) && \in \mathbb{R}^{MN \times 1}, \\
y &= sign(x)\sqrt{|x|} && \in \mathbb{R}^{MN \times 1}, \\
z &= y/\|y\|_2 && \in \mathbb{R}^{MN \times 1}.
\end{aligned}
\tag{3}
$$

Intuitively, bilinear pooling [25] is the bilinear fusion of two features to obtain the matrix b. Sum pooling, or max pooling, is performed on b at all positions, after which the matrix ξ is obtained, and then, ξ is expanded into a vector, which is called the bilinear vector x. After the moment normalization operation on x, we could get smoothed feature y, and after further L2 normalization operation, the fused feature z is obtained.

Besides, we have considered other possibilities - whether it is possible to use a simpler approach (e.g. matrix stitching or element summation). But experience and experiments led us to conclude that bilinear pooling, which is specifically made for feature fusion, is more effective than the simple approach.

At this point, we can simply use the fully connected layer to generate weights that can be better fused against the original lookup table rather than just through optimization methods. Extensive experiments (see Sect. 4.2) have shown that our proposed LUT-aware module can significantly improve image enhancement, not only for optimal retouching, but also for other image-related tasks, and has shown advantageous results on several datasets.

3.6   Loss Function

As we adopt the look-up table paradigm to retouch photos, we follow [45], adopt the MSE loss $\mathcal{L}_{mse}$, the smooth regularization loss $\mathcal{R}_s$ and monotonicity regularization loss $\mathcal{R}_m$ as the basic loss terms, which can be calculated as:

$$\mathcal{L}_{LUT} = \mathcal{L}_{mse} + \lambda_s \mathcal{R}_s + \lambda_m \mathcal{R}_m, \tag{4}$$

where λ_s and λ_m are trade-off coefficients, we follow [45] and set $\lambda_s = 1 \times 10^{-4}$, $\lambda_m = 10$. The MSE Loss $\mathcal{L}_{mse}$ ensures the content consistency between enhancing result and target photo. Smooth regularization $\mathcal{R}_s$ and monotonicity regularization $\mathcal{R}_m$ are used to ensure the retouching process of the LUT are smoothed and monotonic, and the relative brightness and saturation of the input RGB values are maintained, ensuring natural enhancement results.

4   Experiments

4.1   Experiment Setups

Datasets. We complete all experiments and compare the data on PPR10K [24], MIT-Adobe FiveK [2], and HDR+ [10] datasets, respectively. PPR10K [24] contains high-quality raw portrait photos and its corresponding retouched result pairs. We use randomly scrambled, a-expert-retouched, low-resolution photos for training according to the authors' recommendation, and divide the dataset into a training set with 8875 photos, and a test set with 2286 photos. Also, to demonstrate that our work can be used for high-resolution photos, the PPR10K-HR dataset are used. MIT-Adobe FiveK [2] is a database often used in many studies on image enhancement and image retouching, and we set 4500 converted photos for training and the remaining 500 for testing. The HDR+ dataset [10] is a continuous shooting dataset collected by Google Camera Group to study high dynamic range (HDR) and low-light imaging of mobile cameras, and we use this dataset to study the generalizability of the model.

Implementation Details. We perform our experiments on NVIDIA RTX 3090 GPUs with Pytorch framework [31]. The number of parameters in the model is only 13.18M, and it takes only 13 ms to retouch a single image (360P). All of the training photos are LR photos, so as to improve the training speed, and the testing photos include HR photos (4K~8K) and LR photos (360P). We follow the data augment setting in [24]. We use Adam [22] as the network optimizer and the learning rate is fixed at 1×10^{-4} following [45].

Evaluation Metrics. Three metrics are employed to evaluate the performance of different methods quantitatively. In addition to the basic $PSNR$ and $SSIM$, the color difference between the retouched photo R and the target photo T is defined as the L2-distance in CIELAB color space with

$$\Delta E_{ab} = \| R^{Lab} - T^{Lab} \|_2 . \tag{5}$$

Table 1. Comparison of photo enhancement results on several different datasets. The ↑ and ↓ denote that larger or smaller is better.

Method	Dataset	$PSNR \uparrow$	$\Delta E_{ab} \downarrow$	$SSIM \uparrow$	Method	Dataset	$PSNR \uparrow$	$\Delta E_{ab} \downarrow$	$SSIM \uparrow$
Dis-Rec [30]	FiveK	21.98	10.42	0.856	Camera Raw	HDR+	19.86	14.98	0.791
HDRNet [7]	FiveK	24.32	8.49	0.912	UPE [4]	HDR+	21.21	13.05	0.816
DeepLPF [28]	FiveK	24.73	7.99	0.916	DPE [36]	HDR+	22.56	10.45	0.872
CSRNet [11]	FiveK	25.17	7.75	**0.924**	HDRNet [7]	HDR+	23.04	8.97	0.879
3D LUT [45]	FiveK	25.21	7.61	0.922	3D LUT [45]	HDR+	23.54	7.93	**0.885**
Ours	FiveK	**25.42**	**7.29**	0.917	Ours	HDR+	**23.77**	**7.89**	0.866

Method	Dataset	$PSNR \uparrow$	$\Delta E_{ab} \downarrow$	$PSNR^{HC} \uparrow$	Method	Dataset	$PSNR \uparrow$	$\Delta E_{ab} \downarrow$	$PSNR^{HC} \uparrow$
HDRNet [7]	PPR-a	23.93	8.70	27.21	HDRNet [7]	PPR-b	23.96	8.84	27.21
CSRNet [11]	PPR-a	22.72	9.75	25.90	CSRNet [11]	PPR-b	23.76	8.77	27.01
3D LUT [45]	PPR-a	25.64	6.97	28.89	3D LUT [45]	PPR-b	24.70	7.71	27.99
HRP [24]	PPR-a	25.99	6.76	28.29	HRP [24]	PPR-b	25.06	7.51	28.36
Ours	PPR-a	**26.51**	**6.45**	**29.74**	Ours	PPR-b	**25.40**	**7.24**	**28.66**
HDRNet [7]	PPR-c	24.08	8.87	27.32	HDRNet [7]	PPR-HR	23.06	9.13	26.58
CSRNet [11]	PPR-c	23.17	9.45	26.47	CSRNet [11]	PPR-HR	22.01	10.20	25.19
3D LUT [45]	PPR-c	25.18	7.58	28.49	3D LUT [45]	PPR-HR	25.15	7.25	28.39
HRP [24]	PPR-c	25.46	7.43	28.80	HRP [24]	PPR-HR	25.55	7.02	28.83
Ours	PPR-c	**25.89**	**7.21**	**29.15**	Ours	PPR-HR	**26.21**	**6.62**	**29.44**

In the training part of the implementation, we use $PSNR$ as the only filtering metric, based on which the model corresponding to the epoch with the highest score is selected for testing, while the metrics ΔE_{ab} and $SSIM$ are computed only in the testing part. In general, a better $PSNR$ will correspond to a better ΔE_{ab} and $SSIM$ score, as this represents a better learning outcome of the model and a higher quality of the augmented picture.

4.2 Visualization of Results

Quantitative Comparisons. Table 1 reports the comparison of our proposed work with state-of-the-art methods. We obtained the results of these methods using the code and default configuration provided by the existing methods, it can be visually seen from the data presented in the table that with the introduction of LUT-aware, the values of the metrics $PSNR$ and $SSIM$ have improved more apparently, while the ΔE_{ab} metric is well optimized, and these data show the effectiveness of our work.

Qualitative Comparisons. The effectiveness of our work can be clearly seen by comparing the photos before and after the optimization of each dataset. Among Fig. 6, our output is the closest to the target photos provided in the dataset, not only in terms of visual effect but also in terms of indicators that demonstrate the validity of our work. For the two most obvious image retouching datasets, PPR10K [24] and MIT-Adobe FiveK [2], our method is more friendly to non-professionals than manually adjusting image parameters. On the HDR+ dataset [10], there are still some gaps compared to the targets provided in the dataset, especially in the case of severe underexposure, and our enhancement results are not natural. This may be due to not taking into account the local contextual information. In future work, we will consider solving such problems.

Table 2. (a)(b) The effect of the size and number of each LUT cell of the 3D LUT was verified. (c) A comparison test of three combined methods of feature maps output by two CNN layers. (d) A comparison experiment of two CNN layers in the network architecture. (e) Comparative experiments demonstrate which of the two feature map fusion methods is more effective. All experiments are trained on the PPR10K [24].

(a)	M	N	$PSNR$	ΔE_{ab}	$SSIM$	(c)	$Method$	$PSNR$	ΔE_{ab}	$SSIM$
	36	3	26.09	6.72	0.915		Cat	25.62	7.12	0.901
	36	4	26.17	6.55	0.921		Add	25.52	7.27	0.899
	36	5	**26.51**	**6.45**	**0.916**		Bilinear Pooling	**26.51**	**6.45**	**0.916**
	36	6	26.33	6.50	0.912	(d)	$Network$	$PSNR$	ΔE_{ab}	$SSIM$
	36	7	26.16	6.70	0.915		2 ResNet	25.84	7.04	0.903
(b)	M	N	$PSNR$	ΔE_{ab}	$SSIM$		ResNet + EfficientNet	25.90	6.97	0.907
	16	5	26.03	6.72	0.911		EfficientNet + ResNet	**26.51**	**6.45**	**0.916**
	25	5	26.23	6.62	0.915		2 EfficientNet	25.93	6.93	0.911
	36	**5**	**26.51**	**6.45**	**0.916**	(e)	$Method$	$PSNR$	ΔE_{ab}	$SSIM$
	49	5	26.14	6.67	0.909		Direct Fusion	25.94	7.01	0.909
	64	5	26.23	6.64	0.914		Pre-weighted Fusion	**26.51**	**6.45**	**0.916**

4.3 Ablation Study

We conduct extensive ablation experiments on the PPR10K dataset [24] to determine the validity of the components and verify the influence of each parameter, and analyze the effects of each component of our model.

Efficacy of Each Component. As shown in Table 2, we chose to use the model in 3D LUT [45] as the baseline model in our experiments and deploy the LUT-aware model on it, and design the ablation experiments. From the experimental data, we try to identify the most suitable experimental setup on all three different metrics. In addition, we enumerated four different ways of using CNN layers and apply them to both the input image and the input LUT, comparing four sets of experiments. The results demonstrate that the combination of using the EfficientNet [33] layer for image input and ResNet [12] for LUT input is the most reasonable and effective.

In [34], layers were designed for image classification and explores the effects of input resolution, depth, and width of the network at the same time, while the LUT-transformed input does not have a resolution as a feature-level meaning. Therefore, more suitable for using the ResNet [12] layer, which has better generalization. In contrast, if the ResNet [12] layer is used for both CNN layers, although it does reduce the training cost substantially, the training results become unsatisfactory. Although there is an improvement compared to the baseline, this proves that the LUT is valuable as an input, but it is obvious that the feature matrix after EfficientNet [33] layer processing has better training effect.

As future research continues, network architectures more suitable for LUT-aware models than EfficientNet [33] layer and ResNet [12] layer may emerge, but the flexibility of the model makes network replacement feasible and convenient, which makes our approach not limited to the performance of the classifier at the moment, but constantly evolving and improving.

Feature Fusion Method. In the previous section, we illustrate that the LUT-aware model uses two different CNN layers, which means that our model architecture has two intermediate feature matrices corresponding to the two inputs.

After the LUTs image is passed through ResNet [12] Layers, the first intermediate feature (LUT feature map) on the lookup table is generated. According to our initial idea, we can directly fuse the double matrix with the features at this point, however, this does not prove to be reasonable. We first perform a weight-based feature map fusion before the feature map fusion. The results of the comparison experiments are shown in Table 2, and the results after the initial fusion are much better than the direct fusion, which proves that our design reasonably eliminates the difference between the image information and the lookup table information and makes the subsequent fusion more effective.

In order to subsequently generate 3D LUT fusion weights, we need to fuse the two feature matrices and put them into the subsequent fully connected layer to learn the fusion weights. We initially consider simply using splicing (cat) or summing (add) to process the matrix data, but the results were unsatisfactory. Therefore, to solve this problem, bilinear pooling [25] is introduced to better handle the fusion operation of feature matrix. The experimental results in Table 2 show that the combination of bilinear pooling [25] can achieve better optimization results, and the improvement is surprising.

However, with the introduction of bilinear pooling, the fully connected layer where our network finally generates the weights becomes more cumbersome. This is due to the fact that bilinear pooling is different from simple splicing or element summing, which makes the dimensionality of the matrix grow substantially.

As scientific research progresses, many contributions have been made to related research. When introducing bilinear pooling into our design, many variants were considered, but this would make the already cumbersome weight output layer more complex and would have limited improvement in the final result. The most original architecture of bilinear pooling [25] was finally adopted.

The Parameter of 3D LUTs. In order to ensure that the experiment settings are appropriate, we change the dimension of LUT for different experiments while keeping other conditions constant. Results of the experiments are shown in Table 2. The ablation results indicate that the most suitable number of 3D LUTs is 5, while the suitable dimension is 36.

Theoretically, the number and size of LUT become relatively larger will have a more detailed mapping of pixel values and thus achieve better retouching. However, a more moderate choice would achieve more desirable results. In fact, if the number N is set too much, it will make the network layer generate too much weight on the image, which is close to the weight generated by image classification and will trigger overfitting-like results, affecting the final fusion effect instead. Besides, the LUT size M is due to the refinement of the interpolation algorithm, which means finer inputs will sightly improve the accuracy, and the larger size of LUT, the more difficult for model learning.

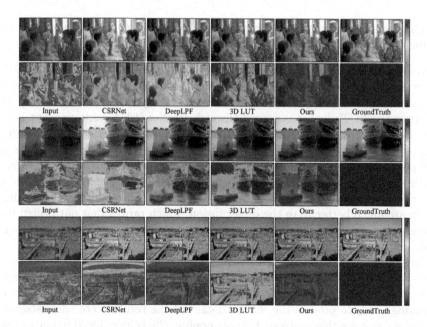

Fig. 6. Qualitative comparisons with corresponding error maps on the FiveK dataset [2] for photo retouching. Blue indicates good effect and red indicates large differences. Our model has the best visualization with the output image closest to the target images. (Color figure online)

5   Conclusion

Since the existing deep learning work on image enhancement based on 3D LUT simply uses the look-up table as a parameter for optimization, ignoring that the look-up table itself is also valuable information that can be sent to the network input port for training, this paper designs a lightweight LUT-aware module, which feeds the 3D LUT into the network module as a parameter after a reasonable deformation. In order to obtain more accurate and reasonable adaptive fusion LUT weights. In addition, we improve the network architecture necessary for training the model, so that the input images and the look-up table information can be effectively combined. Since the final training result contains only one image classifier and some 3D LUTs fused based on the classification results, our approach still maintains the advantage of lightweight look-up table-based photo enhancement. Extensive experiments on several different datasets demonstrate that our approach is effective and can be applied to other image enhancement tasks (*e.g.* low-light enhancement) rather than being limited to image retouching tasks. It is worth mentioning that the unintended using of our method for surveillance may violate personal privacy. In the future, we consider applying this work to other areas as the next research direction, such as image denoising, underwater image enhancement, and super-resolution.

References

1. Afifi, M., Derpanis, K.G., Ommer, B., Brown, M.S.: Learning multi-scale photo exposure correction. In: CVPR, pp. 9157–9167 (2021)
2. Bychkovsky, V., Paris, S., Chan, E., Durand, F.: Learning photographic global tonal adjustment with a database of input/output image pairs. In: CVPR 2011, pp. 97–104. IEEE (2011)
3. Cai, J., Gu, S., Zhang, L.: Learning a deep single image contrast enhancer from multi-exposure images. IEEE TIP **27**(4), 2049–2062 (2018)
4. Chen, Y.S., Wang, Y.C., Kao, M.H., Chuang, Y.Y.: Deep photo enhancer: Unpaired learning for image enhancement from photographs with gans. In: ICCV, pp. 6306–6314 (2018)
5. Finlayson, G.D., Trezzi, E.: Shades of gray and colour constancy. In: Color and Imaging Conference. vol. 2004, pp. 37–41. Society for Imaging Science and Technology (2004)
6. Fu, L., et al.: Auto-exposure fusion for single-image shadow removal. In: CVPR, pp. 10571–10580 (2021)
7. Gharbi, M., Chen, J., Barron, J.T., Hasinoff, S.W., Durand, F.: Deep bilateral learning for real-time image enhancement. ACM TOG **36**(4), 1–12 (2017)
8. Gijsenij, A., Gevers, T., Van De Weijer, J.: Computational color constancy: survey and experiments. IEEE Trans. Image Process. **20**(9), 2475–2489 (2011)
9. Guo, C.G., et al.: Zero-reference deep curve estimation for low-light image enhancement. In: CVPR, pp. 1780–1789 (2020)
10. Hasinoff, S.W., et al.: Burst photography for high dynamic range and low-light imaging on mobile cameras. ACM TOG **35**(6), 1–12 (2016)
11. He, J., Liu, Y., Qiao, Yu., Dong, C.: Conditional sequential modulation for efficient global image retouching. In: Vedaldi, A., Bischof, H., Brox, T., Frahm, J.-M. (eds.) ECCV 2020. LNCS, vol. 12358, pp. 679–695. Springer, Cham (2020). https://doi.org/10.1007/978-3-030-58601-0_40
12. He, K., Zhang, X., Ren, S., Sun, J.: Deep residual learning for image recognition. In: Proceedings of the IEEE Conference on Computer Vision and Pattern Recognition, pp. 770–778 (2016)
13. Huang, T., Li, S., Jia, X., Lu, H., Liu, J.: Neighbor2neighbor: Self-supervised denoising from single noisy images. In: CVPR, pp. 14781–14790 (2021)
14. Ignatov, A., Kobyshev, N., Timofte, R., Vanhoey, K., Van Gool, L.: Dslr-quality photos on mobile devices with deep convolutional networks. In: ICCV, pp. 3277–3285 (2017)
15. Jo, Y., Kim, S.J.: Practical single-image super-resolution using look-up table. In: CVPR, pp. 691–700 (2021)
16. Karaimer, H.C., Brown, M.S.: A software platform for manipulating the camera imaging pipeline. In: Leibe, B., Matas, J., Sebe, N., Welling, M. (eds.) ECCV 2016. LNCS, vol. 9905, pp. 429–444. Springer, Cham (2016). https://doi.org/10.1007/978-3-319-46448-0_26
17. Kim, H.-U., Koh, Y.J., Kim, C.-S.: Global and local enhancement networks for paired and unpaired image enhancement. In: Vedaldi, A., Bischof, H., Brox, T., Frahm, J.-M. (eds.) ECCV 2020. LNCS, vol. 12370, pp. 339–354. Springer, Cham (2020). https://doi.org/10.1007/978-3-030-58595-2_21
18. Kim, H.-U., Koh, Y.J., Kim, C.-S.: PieNet: personalized image enhancement network. In: Vedaldi, A., Bischof, H., Brox, T., Frahm, J.-M. (eds.) ECCV 2020. LNCS, vol. 12375, pp. 374–390. Springer, Cham (2020). https://doi.org/10.1007/978-3-030-58577-8_23

19. Kim, H., Choi, S.M., Kim, C.S., Koh, Y.J.: Representative color transform for image enhancement. In: ICCV, pp. 4459–4468 (2021)
20. Kim, S.J., Lin, H.T., Lu, Z., Süsstrunk, S., Lin, S., Brown, M.S.: A new in-camera imaging model for color computer vision and its application. IEEE Trans. Pattern Anal. Mach. Intell. **34**(12), 2289–2302 (2012)
21. Kim, Y.T.: Contrast enhancement using brightness preserving bi-histogram equalization. IEEE Trans. Consum. Electron. **43**(1), 1–8 (1997)
22. Kingma, D.P., Ba, J.: Adam: A method for stochastic optimization. ICLR (2015)
23. Li, J., Han, K., Wang, P., Liu, Y., Yuan, X.: Anisotropic convolutional networks for 3d semantic scene completion. In: Proceedings of the IEEE/CVF Conference on Computer Vision and Pattern Recognition, pp. 3351–3359 (2020)
24. Liang, J., Zeng, H., Cui, M., Xie, X., Zhang, L.: Ppr10k: A large-scale portrait photo retouching dataset with human-region mask and group-level consistency. In: CVPR, pp. 653–661 (2021)
25. Lin, T.Y., RoyChowdhury, A., Maji, S.: Bilinear cnn models for fine-grained visual recognition. In: Proceedings of the IEEE International Conference on Computer Vision, pp. 1449–1457 (2015)
26. Liu, H., Wan, Z., Huang, W., Song, Y., Han, X., Liao, J.: Pd-gan: Probabilistic diverse gan for image inpainting. In: CVPR, pp. 9371–9381 (2021)
27. Mantiuk, R., Daly, S., Kerofsky, L.: Display adaptive tone mapping. In: ACM SIGGRAPH 2008 papers, pp. 1–10 (2008)
28. Moran, S., Marza, P., McDonagh, S., Parisot, S., Slabaugh, G.: Deeplpf: Deep local parametric filters for image enhancement. In: CVPR, pp. 12826–12835 (2020)
29. Mukherjee, J., Mitra, S.K.: Enhancement of color images by scaling the dct coefficients. IEEE Trans. Image Process. **17**(10), 1783–1794 (2008)
30. Park, J., Lee, J.Y., Yoo, D., Kweon, I.S.: Distort-and-recover: Color enhancement using deep reinforcement learning. In: CVPR, pp. 5928–5936 (2018)
31. Paszke, A., et al.: Pytorch: an imperative style, high-performance deep learning library. NeurIPS **32**, 8026–8037 (2019)
32. Song, Y., Qian, H., Du, X.: Starenhancer: Learning real-time and style-aware image enhancement. In: ICCV, pp. 4126–4135 (2021)
33. Tan, M., Le, Q.: EfficientNet: Rethinking model scaling for convolutional neural networks. In: Chaudhuri, K., Salakhutdinov, R. (eds.) Proceedings of the 36th International Conference on Machine Learning. Proceedings of Machine Learning Research, vol. 97, pp. 6105–6114. PMLR (09–15 Jun 2019)
34. Tan, M., Le, Q.: Efficientnet: Rethinking model scaling for convolutional neural networks. In: International Conference on Machine Learning, pp. 6105–6114. PMLR (2019)
35. Wang, P., Liu, L., Shen, C., Shen, H.T.: Order-aware convolutional pooling for video based action recognition. Pattern Recogn. **91**, 357–365 (2019)
36. Wang, R., Zhang, Q., Fu, C.W., Shen, X., Zheng, W.S., Jia, J.: Underexposed photo enhancement using deep illumination estimation. In: CVPR, pp. 6849–6857 (2019)
37. Wang, T., et al.: Real-time image enhancer via learnable spatial-aware 3d lookup tables. In: ICCV, pp. 2471–2480 (2021)
38. Yan, Q., et al.: High dynamic range imaging via gradient-aware context aggregation network. Pattern Recogn. **122**, 108342 (2022)
39. Yan, Q., et al.: Attention-guided network for ghost-free high dynamic range imaging. In: Proceedings of the IEEE/CVF Conference on Computer Vision and Pattern Recognition, pp. 1751–1760 (2019)

40. Yan, Q., Gong, D., Zhang, Y.: Two-stream convolutional networks for blind image quality assessment. IEEE Trans. Image Process. **28**(5), 2200–2211 (2018)
41. Yan, Q., Zhang, L., Liu, Y., Zhu, Y., Sun, J., Shi, Q., Zhang, Y.: Deep hdr imaging via a non-local network. IEEE Trans. Image Process. **29**, 4308–4322 (2020)
42. Yu, L., Yang, Y., Huang, Z., Wang, P., Song, J., Shen, H.T.: Web video event recognition by semantic analysis from ubiquitous documents. IEEE Trans. Image Process. **25**(12), 5689–5701 (2016)
43. Yuan, L., Sun, J.: Automatic exposure correction of consumer photographs. In: Fitzgibbon, A., Lazebnik, S., Perona, P., Sato, Y., Schmid, C. (eds.) ECCV 2012. LNCS, vol. 7575, pp. 771–785. Springer, Heidelberg (2012). https://doi.org/10.1007/978-3-642-33765-9_55
44. Zamir, S.W., et al.: Multi-stage progressive image restoration. In: CVPR, pp. 14821–14831 (2021)
45. Zeng, H., Cai, J., Li, L., Cao, Z., Zhang, L.: Learning image-adaptive 3d lookup tables for high performance photo enhancement in real-time. IEEE TPAMI (2020)
46. Zhang, Z., Jiang, Y., Jiang, J., Wang, X., Luo, P., Gu, J.: Star: A structure-aware lightweight transformer for real-time image enhancement. In: ICCV, pp. 4106–4115 (2021)
47. Zheng, Z., Ren, W., Cao, X., Wang, T., Jia, X.: Ultra-high-definition image hdr reconstruction via collaborative bilateral learning. In: ICCV, pp. 4449–4458 (2021)

CSIE: Coded Strip-Patterns Image Enhancement Embedded in Structured Light-Based Methods

Wei Cao, Yuping Ye, Chu Shi, and Zhan Song[(✉)]

Guangdong-Hong Kong-Macao Joint Laboratory of Human-Machine Intelligence-Synergy Systems, Shenzhen Institute of Advanced Technology, Chinese Academy of Sciences, Shenzhen 518055, China
{w.cao,yp.ye,chu.shi,zhan.song}@siat.ac.cn

Abstract. When a coded strip-patterns image (CSI) is captured in a structured light system (SLs), it often suffers from low visibility at low exposure settings. Besides degrading the visual perception of the CSI, this poor quality also significantly affects the performance of 3D model reconstruction. Most of the existing image-enhanced methods, however, focus on processing natural images but not CSI. In this paper, we propose a novel and effective CSI enhancement (CSIE) method designed for SLs. More concretely, a bidirectional perceptual consistency (BPC) criterion, including relative grayscale (RG), exposure, and texture level priors, is first introduced to ensure visual consistency before and after enhancement. Then, constrained by BPC, the optimization function estimates solutions of illumination with piecewise smoothness and reflectance with detail preservation. With well-refined solutions, CSIE results can be achieved accordingly and further improve the details performance of 3D model reconstruction. Experiments on multiple sets of challenging CSI sequences show that our CSIE outperforms the existing used for natural image-enhanced methods in terms of 2D enhancement, point clouds extraction (at least 17% improvement), and 3D model reconstruction.

1 Introduction

Undoubtedly, vision-based 3D reconstruction technology plays an essential role in the development of AR/VR innovations such as the metaverse. While reconstructing an object's 3D surface profiles in active or passive projection coding mode is fundamental and critical to numerous vision-based 3D reconstruction systems, such as binocular stereo vision [18], laser scanning [26], time-of-flight [6], and structured light systems (SLs) [13,24] etc. Among those systems, SLs in active projection coding mode has gained wide applications in industrial and commercial fields due to their superior advantages, such as highly accurate and dense 3D reconstruction results. Complete SLs typically consists of a projector for projecting coded strip-patterns and a camera for capturing the coded

---

W. Cao and Y. Ye—These authors contributed equally to this work.

L. Wang et al. (Eds.): ACCV 2022, LNCS 13843, pp. 190–205, 2023.
https://doi.org/10.1007/978-3-031-26313-2_12

strip-patterns image (CSI), respectively. Ideally, SLs usually use CSI and system calibration parameters to decode the depth information of the target under high exposure settings and then use the triangulation principle [12] to achieve accurate estimation of the 3D point coordinates on the surface of the projected object. However, in the high-speed reconstruction of structured light, the exposure time of a camera needs to be synchronized with that of the projector, i.e., a smaller exposure time setting can support reconstruction at a high frame rate. In other words, the extremely low exposure setting of a camera under high-frame-rate reconstruction makes the coded strips in the CSI bury in the dark and difficult to distinguish, further resulting in poor reconstructed 3D results, such as loss of local details and decrease in accuracy. Obviously, the underexposure problem on the CSI introduced at low exposure settings not only reduces the coded strips' discriminability but also seriously affects the 3D reconstruction performance of object surfaces.

It is worth noting that the existing enhancement methods mainly including three categories, i.e., model-free methods [1,4,21], model-based methods [2,7,8,10,11,22,25,28,32], and deep learning-based methods [5,19,30,31], have been developed to address underexposure problem in natural images. However, to the best of our knowledge, there is almost no enhancement method specifically designed to address the underexposure problem in CSI under fixed exposure settings within SLs. Specifically, model-free methods are generally simple and effective, but will wash out details and cause oversaturation problems. Model-based methods mostly work according to the simplified Retinex theory assumption that a captured image P can be decomposed into reflectance component R and illumination component L by $P = R \circ L$, where $\circ$ denotes pixel-wise multiplication. Although such methods have been shown to have impressive enhancement effects in recent years, they are typically accompanied by overexposure issues in local regions. Deep learning-based methods rely on complex network structures and synthetic samples, which will increase high hardware resources and time costs in training and will reduce the generalizing ability of multi-scenario applications in terms of the network. More importantly, the methods mentioned above serve natural images, not CSI. Therefore, the core idea of most these methods, although not all, does not consider CSI's inherent properties.

In this paper, we propose a novel method, i.e., CSIE, for underexposed enhancement of CSI in SLs under a fixed low exposure setting. Our work is mainly inspired by an interesting observation: maintaining the visual consistency before and after enhancement can effectively avoid the disruption of regular coded strip patterns within CSI. Inspired by this observation, a valid criterion, bidirectional perceptual consistency (BPC), is first proposed to describe how to guarantee visual perceptual consistency between before and after enhancement. Then, we turn the underexposed enhancement problem into an optimization problem based on the Retinex model for decomposing the illumination and reflectance components under the constraints of the BPC priors. With well-refined illumination and reflectance components, the enhanced CSI results can be obtained accordingly, and further embedded in SLs methods can reconstruct more 3D profiles of objects' surfaces. In particular, the work in this paper has the following **contributions:** 1) We propose a novel CSIE method. To the best of our knowledge, this is the first time that CSIE is embedded in SLs methods to address underexposure problems in CSI under fixed exposure settings. 2) We define BPC (a simple and intuitive criterion including three consistency priors) in CSIE, which explicitly describes how to avoid breaking the visual perceptual consistency that exists in the CSI before and after enhancement. 3) We design BPC-constrained illumination and reflectance estimation via a variational optimization decomposition function, to achieve enhanced CSI results with high visibility and high signal-to-noise ratios. 4) We introduce a block coordinate descent (BCD) [27] technique to solve the convex problem contained in the designing optimization function. Finally, we evaluate the proposed method that includes a comparison with several state-of-the-art image enhancement methods on both multiple CSI sequences captured by SLs and the 3D reconstruction method of [24]. Experiments demonstrate that the proposed method achieves well enhancement effect in enhancing the visual quality for 2D CSI and simultaneously improves the performance of 3D surface reconstruction.

2   Related Work

Model-Free Methods. Directly linearly amplifying the intensity of an underexposed image is probably the most straightforward way to recover detail in dark regions. However, this operation comes with a thorny problem, i.e., the pixels in the relatively bright regions may increase the risk of saturation and thus wash out corresponding details. Although the histogram equalization (HE) method can alleviate the above problems by forcing the enhanced intensities of input in a normalized manner, it may lead to noise amplification and distortion appearance. To be more wise, an improved version of HE, content and variational contrast (CVC) [4] enhancement, attempts to improve contrast by introducing different regularization terms on the histogram. It may very likely fall into the trouble of overexposure/underexposure enhancement due to ignoring the contrast change caused by real illumination.

Model-Based Methods. Jobson et al. [14,15] did early works based on the Retinex model yet exhibited more unrealistic results in the output. Fu et al. [7] proposed a simultaneous illumination and reflectance estimation (SIRE) method to realize enhancement in logarithmic space, but the reflectance component in it has the problem of detail loss. Thereafter, Fu et al. [8] developed a weighted variational model (WVM) to improve the variation of gradient magnitudes in bright regions. Since the anisotropic smoothness assumption is ignored, the illumination decomposed by the model may fall into erroneous estimation around non-contiguous regions. Guo et al. [10] estimated the initial illumination map from the input and refined it by retaining only the main structural information. This method does well in dealing with underexposed images with globally uniform illumination, however, produces an overexposure issue when processing ones with non-uniform illumination. To this end, Zhang et al. [32] designed the high-quality exposure correction (HQEC) method, which estimates reasonable illumination to solve the above problem by considering the visual similarity between input and output. The limitation of this method is the blindness of the noise, leading to results with a low SNR in underexposed situations. Considering this limitation, Cai et al. [2] and Hao et al. [11] presented the joint intrinsic-extrinsic prior (JieP) model and the gaussian total variation (GTV) model, respectively, to achieve a balance between visual enhancement and noise compression. However, both optimized models suffer from over-smoothing in the illumination and reflectance, and the latter's piecewise smoothness constraint on the reflectance component makes the model ineffective for enhancing images with extremely low exposure. Different from JieP, Ren et al. [22] proposed the joint denoising and enhancement (JED) method by considering an additional detail enhancement term on the reflectance component, but it also induces local distortion on that. In addition, Xu et al. [28] proposed a structure and texture aware retinex (STAR) model in recent years, which designed an exponential filter through local derivatives and used it to constraint for illumination and reflectance components, respectively. Because of the constraint of local partial derivatives, the coded structures of underexposed CSI face destroyed problems. It is worth noting that Song et al. [25] developed the HDR-based method to improve CSI for alleviating the local underexposure and overexposure problems caused by the high reflectivity of the object surface in the CSI. Different from CSIs (captured with a fixed exposure setting) used in our method, the HDR-based method [25] obtains the solution that requires at least three CSIs (captured with different exposure settings by the same camera under the same scene).

Deep Learning-Based Methods. Chen et al. [5] proposed a low-light enhancement method with low photon counts and low SNRs based on the fully convolutional networks in an end-to-end training way. However, the input of network training is raw sensor data, which is difficult to obtain and causes a high training cost. Lore et al. [19] developed a depth encoder to enhance contrast, but its enhanced results only have well performance in noise reduction. Inspired by neurobiological observations, Zhan et al. [31] designed a feature-linking model (FLM) by utilizing the spike times of encoded information, which can preserve information and enhance image detail information simultaneously. Afterward, Zhan et al. [30] also presented a linking synaptic computation network (LSCN) that generates detail-enhanced results, but its noise amplifying problem is obvious. However, almost none of the above methods are suitable for CSI enhancement, mainly due to their enhanced networks being designed for natural images and not considering the regular encoded information in CSI.

3 Proposed Method

In this section, we describe the proposed novel CSIE method for enhancing CSI. We first introduce one Retinex-based model decomposition problem and then restraint it by defining the BPC criterion, including three consistency priors

(RG, exposure, texture). Jointing the above priors, we further proposed an optimization function that is designed for decomposing illumination and reflectance components in CSI, respectively. Finally, we use an efficient BCD technique to extract solutions for the convex optimization function iteratively. With well-refined components in solutions, the enhanced CSI can be obtained accordingly.

3.1 Model Decomposition Problem

Let us recall the Retinex model, a commonly used visual model to estimate the illumination and reflectance components in real scenes for image enhancement. Unlike previous enhancement methods based on this model, we apply it here to the processing of CSI instead of natural images and combine the inherent priors in CSI to formulate the image decomposition problem as the minimization of the following optimization function $F(\cdot, \cdot)$:

$$\min_{R,L} F(R, L) = ||R \circ L - P||_2^2 + \lambda_g f_g + \lambda_e f_e + \lambda_r f_r, \qquad (1)$$

where f_e, f_g and f_r are three different regularization functions, λ_e, λ_g and λ_r are all non-negative balancing weights. $||R \circ L - P||_2^2$, data fidelity term, constraints the product of the illumination and reflectance components to be close to the original CSI.

In general, decomposing an image into illumination and reflectance components is a highly ill-posed problem due to lack of reasonable priors on the components. Appropriate component priors as constraints can reduce the solution space and converge quickly. To this end, we describe the introduced priors about CSI in Eq. (1) in detail below.

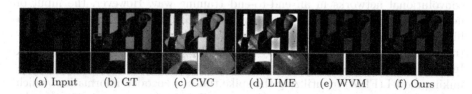

(a) Input   (b) GT   (c) CVC   (d) LIME   (e) WVM   (f) Ours

Fig. 1. Issues existed by previous methods. GT: Ground truth (CSI captured with 2000 ms of exposure value).

3.2 Bidirectional Perceptually Consistency

By observing large numbers of CSI sequences pairs between underexposed and well-exposed, we find that inherent properties (RG (defined as the relative grayscale change of neighboring pixels in the CSI), exposure, texture) existed in underexposed CSI are buried in the dark, which results in SLs method that rely on strip-edge features cannot effectively identify and further significantly affects the 3D reconstructed performance. Compared with the well-exposed CSI (see Fig. 1 (b)), the distortions of relative grayscale, inconsistency of exposure, and loss of details produced by existing methods on the CSI enhancement results are the three main issues. For instance, coded strip features (regular bright-dark order in spatial position) are distorted in the enhanced result by the CVC method due to the damage of the original relative grayscale, as shown in Fig. 1 (c). Texture degradation and loss of details due to local overexposure appear on the LIME method enhancement results, as shown in Fig. 1 (d). The WVM enhancement results have a local over-dark problem caused by inconsistent exposure, while these regions are contrary to the consistent exposure in the input, as shown in Fig. 1 (e). We intuitively believe that the above three issues can well be removed when we use inherent properties to preserve visual consistency before and after enhancement in CSI, as shown in Fig. 1 (f). Additionally, we analyze their plausibility by defining the following three consistency priors (RG, exposure, and texture) in BPC and then verify the effectiveness of those in BPC in Sect. 4.

RG Consistency Prior. One fact is that RG change in CSI is caused by the coded projection, which is an inherent feature belonging to CSI. For instance, we show a synthetic patch with the simulated CSI in Fig. 2 (a), which contains weak textures and strong edges/structures. The RG change, such as the relative grayscale change in the red and blue boxes in Fig. 2 (a), enables the strip-edge at the discontinuous region can be identified by SLs-based method [24] to reconstruct the profile of target surface, which can be regarded as an important prior feature. Intuitively, RG inconsistency, such as smaller or no discontinuity differences, will weaken the discrimination of the strip-edge features on the enhanced CSI, thereby reducing the ability to recover depth information for the SLs-based method. To avoid this issue, we take the preprocessed original CSI (see Fig. 2 (b)) as a prior constraint to ensure global consistency (see Figs. 2 (b) and (c)) between before and after enhancement on the relative grayscale. Mathematically, we express the regularization term as:

$$f_g = ||L - G||_2^2, \tag{2}$$

where $G=wgif(P)$ is the output (see Fig. 2 (b)) smoothed by a weighted guided image filtering [17] operation $wgif(\cdot)$. This regularization term takes into account the balance between RG preservation and noise suppression. Therefore, G as a prior can not only be used to maintain the consistency of RG in the illumination smoothing process but also be regarded as the initial value of illumination to guide its smoothing.

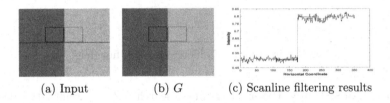

(a) Input   (b) G (c) Scanline filtering results

Fig. 2. Illustration of RG changing.

Exposure Consistency Prior. Exposure consistency emphasizes a reasonable estimation of the illumination distribution. This distribution usually can be understood as piecewise smoothing [7,8,10], which follows the illumination distribution on images captured from the real scene and can help to recover clear details from underexposed regions in CSI. It should be noted that the different existing norms, such as L_1 and L_2, directly employed to constraint illumination will ignore the specificity of CSI, i.e., the structure is buried in the dark or says blind. To alleviate this issue, we use L_γ norm [20] to constrain the illumination gradient to achieve piecewise smoothing and further estimate the illumination with preserved overall structures. Hence, we provide one spatial smoothness regularization term:

$$f_e = ||\nabla L||_\gamma^\gamma, \tag{3}$$

where $|| \cdot ||_\gamma^\gamma$ stands for L_γ norm with $0 \leq \gamma \leq 2$. ∇ is the first-order differential operator contains two directions: ∇_h (horizontal) and ∇_v (vertical). Since the L_γ norm in Eq. (3) will cause a non-smooth optimization problem, a simple numerical approximation is introduced [2,3,11,20] and Eq. (3) can be rewritten as:

$$f_e \approx w||\nabla L||_2^2, \tag{4}$$

where $||\nabla L||_\gamma^\gamma \approx w|||\nabla L||_2^2$ and

$$w \approx \begin{cases} (|\nabla L| + \varepsilon_L)^{\gamma-2}, & 0 < \gamma \leq 2 \\ \begin{cases} \phi^{-2} & \text{if } |\nabla L| < \phi \\ |\nabla L|^{-2} & \text{otherwise} \end{cases}, & \gamma = 0 \end{cases}, \tag{5}$$

ϕ is a small constant (typically $\frac{1}{8}$) used for determining gradient sparsity of illumination. The constant ε_L is a small value (typically 0.0001) to avoid the zero denominator. For approximate operations, please refer to [20,29]. Obviously, this approximation operation, on the one hand, changes the non-smooth L_γ term into L_2 one. On the other hand, it makes the weighted L_2 norm have both abilities that the piecewise smoothness and the L_0 norm pursuit (gradient sparsity), as shown in Fig. 3.

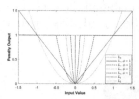

Fig. 3. Distribution of different penalty functions.

Texture Consistency Prior. Existing researches [9,23] regard the decomposed R as the part that can remain unchanged under illumination variations because it contains inherent properties of the object surface, namely edges.

Consistent properties are also included in edges of the captured CSI. So, texture consistency needs to consider the consistency of edge degradation between reflectance component and input before and after the CSI enhancement, which can also be called reflectance gradient degradation prior. In addition, edges, as dependency features that need to be identified in the 3D model reconstruction method [24], should be preserved in the output after CSI enhancement to the greatest extent possible. To this end, we project edges of the noise-reduced original CSI P onto ones of R and express the gradient fidelity term as follows:

$$f_r = ||\nabla R - M||_2^2, \tag{6}$$

where

$$M(\nabla P; \varepsilon_m) := \begin{cases} 0, & |\nabla P| < \varepsilon_m \\ \nabla P, & \text{otherwise}, \end{cases} \tag{7}$$

is a truncated function that only penalizes gradients whose magnitudes are smaller than the small threshold ε_m (typically 1e–5), as shown in Fig. 4. ε_m is used for determining whether there is an edge at a pixel in the CSI. In other words, small ε_m can better preserve textures, and vice versa. So, this regularization term separates the reflectance component (with noise-suppressed and detail-preserved) from CSI by removing small non-zero gradients, i.e., flattening tiny textures/noises.

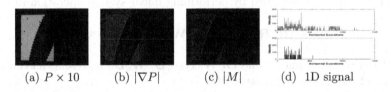

(a) $P \times 10$ (b) $|\nabla P|$ (c) $|M|$ (d) 1D signal

Fig. 4. Illustration of truncated ability in M. For observation easily, the intensity of original CSI P is linearly scaled by 10.

3.3   Exact Solver to Problem (1)

Although the illumination smoothness term constrained by L_γ norm is non-smooth, the results of numerically approximated operation act as a tight surrogate to change the non-smooth L_γ term into a piecewise smooth L_2 one. By doing so, the optimization function in Eq. (1) can be rewritten as the following equivalent form:

$$\min_{R,L} F(R, L) = ||R \circ L - P||_2^2 + \lambda_e w ||\nabla L||_2^2 + \lambda_g ||L - G||_2^2 + \lambda_r ||\nabla R - M||_2^2. \tag{8}$$

One can see that the optimization function in Eq. (8) can be regarded as a problem that only contains two variables (R and L) to solve. Block coordinate descent (BCD) [27] technique is a common choice to solve this problem. To facilitate the solution and analysis, we further divide the objective function in Eq. (8) into two sub-problems corresponding to R and L as follows:

L **sub-problem:** Collecting the L involved terms from Eq. (8) gives the following problem:

$$L_{k+1} = \arg\min_{L} ||R \circ L - P||_2^2 + \lambda_e w ||\nabla L||_2^2 + \lambda_g ||L - G||_2^2. \qquad (9)$$

R **Sub-problem:** With L_{k+1} acquired from the above solution, the minimization corresponding to R in Eq. (8) can be formulated as the following optimization problem:

$$R_{k+1} = \arg\min_{R} ||R \circ L_{k+1} - P||_2^2 + \lambda_r ||\nabla R - M||_2^2. \qquad (10)$$

As can be seen from the two sub-problems above, they are both minimization problems containing only classical least-squares terms and therefore have closed-form global optimal solutions. The solutions are detailed as follows:

a) Solution for (T1): The sub-problem in Eq. (9) can be reformulated in matrix notation as:

$$(\mathbf{R}\circ\mathbf{L}-\mathbf{P})^T(\mathbf{R}\circ\mathbf{L}-\mathbf{P})+\lambda_g(\mathbf{L}-\mathbf{G})^T(\mathbf{L}-\mathbf{G})+\lambda_e(\mathbf{L}^T\mathbf{D}_h^T\mathbf{W}_h\mathbf{D}_h\mathbf{L}+\mathbf{L}^T\mathbf{D}_v^T\mathbf{W}_v\mathbf{D}_v\mathbf{L}), \qquad (11)$$

where $\mathbf{D}_h$ and $\mathbf{D}_v$ are Toeplitz matrices from discrete gradient operators with forward difference, respectively. $\mathbf{W}_h$ and $\mathbf{W}_v$ denote diagonal matrices containing weights w_h and w_v, respectively. The unique solution of the variable $\mathbf{L}$ in Eq. (11) can be easily obtained by performing linear system operation like:

$$\mathbf{L}_{k+1} = (\mathbf{R}_k^T\mathbf{R}_k + \lambda_g\mathbf{1} + \lambda_e\bar{\mathbf{W}}_k)^{-1}(\mathbf{R}_k^T\mathbf{P} + \lambda_g\mathbf{G}), \qquad (12)$$

where $\mathbf{1}$ is an identity matrix and $\mathbf{D}_h^T\mathbf{W}_h\mathbf{D}_h+\mathbf{D}_v^T\mathbf{W}_v\mathbf{D}_v$ represents a symmetric positive definite Laplacian matrix [16].

b) Solution for (T2): Similar to the solution of *(T1)*, the update of the closed-form solution R_{k+1} can be directly obtained by the following operations:

$$\mathbf{R}_{k+1} = (\mathbf{L}_{k+1}^T\mathbf{L}_{k+1} + \lambda_r\bar{\mathbf{V}}_k)^{-1}(\mathbf{L}_{k+1}^T\mathbf{P} + \lambda_r\bar{\mathbf{M}}), \qquad (13)$$

where $\bar{\mathbf{V}} = \mathbf{D}_h^T\mathbf{D}_h+\mathbf{D}_v^T\mathbf{D}_v$. Note that $\bar{\mathbf{M}} = \text{vec}^{-1}(\mathbf{D}_h^T\dot{\mathbf{M}}_h+\mathbf{D}_v^T\dot{\mathbf{M}}_v)$, where $\dot{\mathbf{M}}_h$ and $\dot{\mathbf{M}}_v$ are the vector versions of the corresponding $\mathbf{M}_h$ and $\mathbf{M}_v$, respectively, while $\text{vec}^{-1}(\cdot)$ represents the inverse vectorization operator for reshaping vectors back to their matrix format.

The above iterative estimation is repeated until the convergence conditions $||\mathbf{L}_{k+1} - \mathbf{L}_k||/\mathbf{L}_k \leq \varpi$ and $||\mathbf{R}_{k+1} - \mathbf{R}_k||/\mathbf{R}_k \leq \varpi$ are satisfied or the maximum number of iterations exceeds a preset constant K. The whole iterative optimization process is summarized as Algorithm 1. To further improve the visibility of images, the final enhanced CSI $\mathbf{P}_f$ is achieved by projecting the adjusted illumination back to the reflectance, i.e., $\mathbf{P}_f = \mathbf{R} \circ \mathbf{L}_f$, where $\mathbf{L}_f$ is gamma-corrected (empirically set as 2.2) illumination estimation.

Algorithm 1. Exact Solver to Optimization Problem (8)

Require: The weight coefficients λ_e, λ_g, λ_r; the original CSI **P**, initial illumination map **G**, and truncated result **M**; the positive parameter ϖ and the maximum number of iterations K.

Ensure: Optimal solutions $\mathbf{R}_{k+1}$ and $\mathbf{L}_{k+1}$.

1: initial $\mathbf{L}_0 \leftarrow \mathbf{P}$, $\varpi \leftarrow 0.001$, $k \leftarrow 0$, and $K \leftarrow 20$;
2: **repeat**
3:    Update $\mathbf{L}_{k+1}$ using Eq. (12);
4:    Update $\mathbf{R}_{k+1}$ with $\mathbf{L}_{k+1}$ using Eq. (13);
5:    $k \leftarrow k + 1$;
6: **until** $(\|\mathbf{L}_{k+1} - \mathbf{L}_k\|/\mathbf{L}_k \leq \varpi$ and $\|\mathbf{R}_{k+1} - \mathbf{R}_k\|/\mathbf{R}_k \leq \varpi)$ or $k > K$.

---

4 Experiments

In this section, we run all enhancement experiments using Matlab R2021a on a laptop with Windows 11 OS, 16G RAM and Intel Core i7-2.3 GHz CPU. In our experiments, the parameters λ_e, λ_g, λ_r, ϖ, and γ (in L_γ norm) are empirically set to 0.01, 0.15, 5, 0.001, and 0.6 respectively. In addition, the experimental setup in the SLs' hardware configured with an off-the-shelf projector (TI3010, with resolution 1280×720 pixels, ≤2800 fps) and a camera (BFS-U3-16S2M, with resolution 1440×1080 pixels, USB interface) with 50ms of exposure time, as shown in Fig. 5 (a). Meanwhile, we use the 3D model reconstruction method [24] (for showing the reconstructed 3D model performance of enhanced CSI) and its coding strategy (see Fig. 5 (b)), and implement it by writing C++ in the VS2019 environment. To fully evaluate the proposed method, we test 16 sets CSI sequences of object surfaces with different reflectance under a fixed low exposure setting, such as samples in Fig. 5 (c). Then, we compare proposed CSIE subjectively and objectively with existing state-of-the-art methods, including CVC [4], SIRE [7], WVM [8], LIME [10], JieP [2], JED [22], HQEC [32], GTV [11], STAR [28], and LSCN [30].

(a) SLs   (b) Coding strategy   (c) Testing samples

Fig. 5. Experimental configuration. (a) The SLs consists of an off-the-shelf projector and a camera, and the two devices are synchronized. (b) Coding strategy (with 18 pattern images to be projected) of Gray code combined with binary shifting strip with widths of 4 pixels [24]. (c) Samples from 16 sets of the captured CSI sequences.

Retinex Decomposition. One can observe that visual artifacts appear in the illumination and reflectance components on the SIRE simultaneously, such as the edges of the frog's eyes in Fig. 6 (b). These artifacts are generated due to an unreasonable assumption that illumination is with unconstrained isotropic smoothness. Furthermore, JieP, JED, and STAR all produce strong artifact and over-smoothing problems on the reflectance component, such as the frog's hair and mouth in Figs. 6 (c), (d), and (e). For these visual distortions in the decomposed components, in essence, it is because those methods reduce the ability to discriminate structures-textures at very low exposures. In contrast, the illumination component constrained by the L_γ norm in our method to be as far as possible both removed most of the tiny textures and preserved the prominent structures. Meanwhile, the reflectance component constrained by the L_2 norm in our method to maintain both more textures and details of high-frequency, such as the frog's face in Fig. 6 (f). More importantly, unlike SIRE, thanks to the suppression of noise factors, our model can effectively avoid noise amplification on the reflectance component, which is particularly suitable for recovering the details of underexposed CSI.

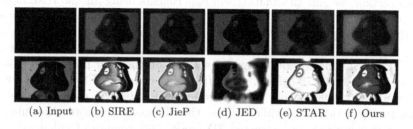

(a) Input   (b) SIRE   (c) JieP   (d) JED   (e) STAR   (f) Ours

Fig. 6. Comparison of several Retinex decomposition results. (a) Input and corresponding ten times intensity levels (used for observation). **Top Row in (b) to (f):** Illumination component. **Bottom Row in (b) to (f):** Reflectance component.

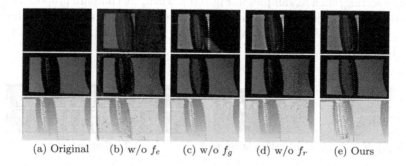

(a) Original   (b) w/o f_e (c) w/o f_g (d) w/o f_r (e) Ours

Fig. 7. Ablation study of different prior on 3D reconstruction performance of the proposed CSIE. (a) The images from the first to the last rows are original CSI, depth maps, and 3D point clouds, respectively. From (b) to (e): The enhanced versions corresponding to (a).

3D Impact of Model with Different Prior. Since RG, exposure, and texture consistency priors have not been adopted in previous Retinex algorithms, we analyze their impacts in the following experiments. Here, we set $\lambda_e = 0$, or

$\lambda_g = 0$, or $\lambda_r = 0$ in (8), respectively, and update them according to Eqs. 9 to 13 describe, and thus have three baselines: CSIE w/o f_e, CSIE w/o f_g and CSIE w/o f_r. From Fig. 7, one can see that CSIE w/o f_e tends to generate visual artifacts on the coded strip at the right black that should not be appeared on the enhanced CSI results. This problem will lead to lots of holes appearing on 2D depth maps and 3D point clouds simultaneously. The bright streaks of CSIE w/o f_g on the enhanced CSI results destroy the coded information at the depth discontinuities, causing the details loss of the screwdriver's local profile on the 2D depth map and 3D point clouds, respectively. However, the increase in point clouds numbers of both demonstrates that the two regularization terms have a positive impact on improving the 3D reconstruction performance of the object surface. For CSIE w/o f_r, the local textures lost in the enhanced CSI results directly lead to the emergence of large numbers of black holes in the 2D depth image, which seriously affects the numbers of 3D point clouds extraction. Obviously, the prior f_r is far more important than the former two for CSI enhancement and 3D reconstruction. By considering three, the proposed CSIE obtains output with pleasing visibility and undistorting coded strip, which not only satisfies the visual expectations (consistency between RG, exposure, and texture) on the enhanced CSI results but also reasonably recovers more useful depth details buried in the dark.

Convergence Behavior. Analyzing the convergence rate of CSIE with different prior from Fig. 8, one can observe that different components with joint priors are faster in convergence rate than ones without λ_e, or λ_g, or λ_r. This is mainly due to the BPC criterion applying the different priors' constraints to reduce the solution space of the objective function. Besides, one can see that the iterative error ϖ for different components with arbitrarily different priors reduces to less than 0.001 in 20 iterations. This favorable convergence performance benefits from the proposed CSIE exact solver converging to global optimal solutions for the problem (8).

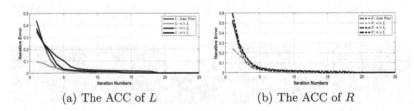

(a) The ACC of L (b) The ACC of R

Fig. 8. Convergence rate of our model with different prior. ACC: Average convergence curves.

Subjective Comparison. For comparison fairness, we use the CSI sequence with 2000 ms of exposure time as the reference (ground truth) instead of the one with 50 ms of that. Figure 9 shows several visual comparisons. From which, we can find that WVM, HQEC, STAR, and GTV cannot effectively recall the information in the dark region on the original CSI, which significantly affects the depth information extraction and the 3D model reconstruction, such as the bells in Fig. 9 (a). This problem is almost always generated, especially on GTV results.

Although the enhanced CSI results of CVC and LSCN exhibit higher visibility in the given cases, the coded features with relatively regular bright-black strips present on them are destroyed. While, unreasonable coded strips indirectly cause both to produce invalid depth and point cloud maps, as shown in the second and three rows in Figs. 9 (a), (b) and (c). As for LIME, it recovers more obvious and high-contrast details, however, its depth and point cloud information will be lost due to amplified noises and overexposed textures on the enhanced CSI results' local regions. In contrast, the enhanced CSI results by CSIE are closer to the ground-truth CSI than other methods, as shown in Figs. 9 (a), (b) and (c). Besides, our method obtains a balanced enhanced performance between depth estimation, point clouds extraction, and 3D model reconstruction benefit from the reasonable consideration of BPC introduced for CSIE.

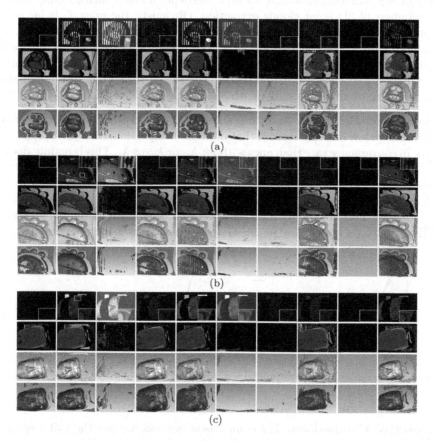

Fig. 9. Result comparison of different methods on CSI. **From Left to Right in Three Cases:** Original CSI, Ground truth, CVC, WVM, LIME, LSCN, HQEC, STAR, GTV, and Ours, respectively. **From Top Row to Bottom Row in Three Cases:** Enhanced results by different methods, corresponding 2D depth map, 3D point clouds, and 3D mesh map, respectively.

Objectively Comparison. Here, we apply four indicators (peak signal-to-noise ratio (PSNR), structural similarity index measure (SSIM), root mean square error (RMSE), and number of points (NPs)) to evaluate the performance of our CSIE objectively. As we can see, our CSIE method performs favorably against existing image enhancement methods adapted to natural images, which shows that the proposed CSIE method has superior performance in terms of structure preservation and noise compression, as shown in Table 1. Additionally, we note that STAR has higher NPs (see Fig. 10), but its other measurement results (with smaller PSNR and SSIM values and larger RMSE values) are less than the performance of our proposed method. It is worth noting that our method ranks second on NPs, but the NPs extracted by our method have better 3D reconstruction performance than the ones extracted by STAR, as shown in Figs. 9 (a), (b) and (c). The main reason is that using local partial derivatives in STAR generates numerous invalid NPs, which in turn recovers more erroneous 3D surface details that do not belong to the object. Obviously, the CSIE method achieves not only higher PSNR and SSIM values but also lower RMSE values in contrast to mentioned above methods, which is highly correlated with its better decomposition of the illumination and reflectance components on the CSI. Overall, the CSIE method not only has a better comprehensive performance compared to other methods, but its results are at least 17% improvements better than the original CSI sequences in terms of NPs extraction.

Table 1. Quantitative measurement results on 16 sets of CSI sequences with a fixed exposure value (50 ms) in terms of average PSNR, SSIM, and RMSE.

Metrics	Original	CVC	WVM	LIME	LSCN	HQEC	STAR	GTV	Ours
PSNR	19.38	15.89	23.55	22.07	19.76	21.82	23.44	19.23	**25.23**
SSIM	0.3969	0.3152	0.7167	0.5602	0.0931	0.6261	0.7858	0.3807	**0.8098**
RMSE	0.1839	0.3979	0.1089	0.1133	0.3271	0.1317	0.1056	0.1817	**0.1009**

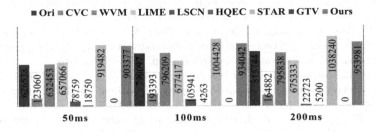

Fig. 10. Quantitative comparison results on 16 sets of CSI sequences with different exposure values (50 ms, 100 ms, and 200 ms) in terms of average NPs.

5   Conclusion

In this paper, we propose a novel CSIE method implemented in a variational optimization decomposition, which can be used for CSI enhancement and further improve the performance of the existing 3D model reconstruction method based on SLs. The proposed CSIE is based on a visually bidirectional perceptual consistency criterion, including RG, exposure, and texture consistency priors. Combined with all priors, the proposed CSIE can simultaneously obtain the illumination component with piecewise smoothness and the reflectance component with detail preservation on the enhanced CSI under a low exposure setting. Experimental results on 2D enhancement and 3D model reconstruction demonstrate that our CSIE outperforms other existing enhancement methods adapted to the natural image in terms of visual enhancement and coded strip feature preservation.

Acknowledgements. This work is supported by the Key-Area Research and Development Program of Guangdong Province, China (2019B010149002).

References

1. Abdullah-Al-Wadud, M., Kabir, M.H., Dewan, M.A.A., Chae, O.: A dynamic histogram equalization for image contrast enhancement. IEEE Trans. Consum. Electron. **53**(2), 593–600 (2007)
2. Cai, B., Xu, X., Guo, K., Jia, K., Hu, B., Tao, D.: A joint intrinsic-extrinsic prior model for retinex. In: IEEE International Conference on Computer Vision, pp. 4000–4009 (2017)
3. Cao, W., Wu, S., Wu, J., Liu, Z., Li, Y.: Edge/structure-preserving texture filter via relative bilateral filtering with a conditional constraint. IEEE Signal Process. Lett. **28**, 1535–1539 (2021)
4. Celik, T., Tjahjadi, T.: Contextual and variational contrast enhancement. IEEE Trans. Image Process. **20**(12), 3431–3441 (2011)
5. Chen, C., Chen, Q., Xu, J., Koltun, V.: Learning to see in the dark. In: IEEE Conference on Computer Vision and Pattern Recognition, pp. 3291–3300 (2018)
6. Cho, H., Kim, S.W.: Mobile robot localization using biased chirp-spread-spectrum ranging. IEEE Trans. Industr. Electron. **57**(8), 2826–2835 (2009)
7. Fu, X., Liao, Y., Zeng, D., Huang, Y., Zhang, X.P., Ding, X.: A probabilistic method for image enhancement with simultaneous illumination and reflectance estimation. IEEE Trans. Image Process. **24**(12), 4965–4977 (2015)
8. Fu, X., Zeng, D., Huang, Y., Zhang, X.P., Ding, X.: A weighted variational model for simultaneous reflectance and illumination estimation. In: IEEE Conference on Computer Vision and Pattern Recognition, pp. 2782–2790 (2016)
9. Grosse, R., Johnson, M.K., Adelson, E.H., Freeman, W.T.: Ground truth dataset and baseline evaluations for intrinsic image algorithms. In: IEEE International Conference on Computer Vision, pp. 2335–2342 (2009)
10. Guo, X., Li, Y., Ling, H.: LIME: low-light image enhancement via illumination map estimation. IEEE Trans. Image Process. **26**(2), 982–993 (2016)
11. Hao, S., Han, X., Guo, Y., Xu, X., Wang, M.: Low-light image enhancement with semi-decoupled decomposition. IEEE Trans. Multimedia **1**(1), 1–14 (2020)
12. Hartley, R., Zisserman, A.: Multiple view geometry in computer vision. Cambridge University Press (2003)
13. Van der Jeught, S., Dirckx, J.J.: Real-time structured light profilometry: a review. Opt. Lasers Eng. **87**, 18–31 (2016)

14. Jobson, D.J., Rahman, Z.u., Woodell, G.A.: A multiscale retinex for bridging the gap between color images and the human observation of scenes. IEEE Trans. Image Process. **6**(7), 965–976 (1997)
15. Jobson, D.J., Rahman, Z.u., Woodell, G.A.: Properties and performance of a center/surround retinex. IEEE Trans. Image process. **6**(3), 451–462 (1997)
16. Krishnan, D., Fattal, R., Szeliski, R.: Efficient preconditioning of Laplacian matrices for computer graphics. ACM Trans. Graph. **32**(4), 1–15 (2013)
17. Li, Z., Zheng, J., Zhu, Z., Yao, W., Wu, S.: Weighted guided image filtering. IEEE Trans. Image Process. **24**(1), 120–129 (2014)
18. Liu, Z., Yin, Y., Wu, Q., Li, X., Zhang, G.: On-site calibration method for outdoor binocular stereo vision sensors. Opt. Lasers Eng. **86**, 75–82 (2016)
19. Lore, K.G., Akintayo, A., Sarkar, S.: LLNet: a deep autoencoder approach to natural low-light image enhancement. Pattern Recogn. **61**, 650–662 (2017)
20. Min, D., Choi, S., Lu, J., Ham, B., Sohn, K., Do, M.N.: Fast global image smoothing based on weighted least squares. IEEE Trans. Image Process. **23**(12), 5638–5653 (2014)
21. Pisano, E.D., et al.: Contrast limited adaptive histogram equalization image processing to improve the detection of simulated spiculations in dense mammograms. J. Digit. Imaging **11**(4), 193–200 (1998)
22. Ren, X., Li, M., Cheng, W.H., Liu, J.: Joint enhancement and denoising method via sequential decomposition. In: IEEE International Symposium on Circuits and Systems, pp. 1–5 (2018)
23. Rother, C., Kiefel, M., Zhang, L., Schölkopf, B., Gehler, P.: Recovering intrinsic images with a global sparsity prior on reflectance. In: Advances in Neural Information Processing Systems 24 (2011)
24. Song, Z., Chung, R., Zhang, X.T.: An accurate and robust strip-edge-based structured light means for shiny surface micromeasurement in 3-D. IEEE Trans. Industr. Electron. **60**(3), 1023–1032 (2012)
25. Song, Z., Jiang, H., Lin, H., Tang, S.: A high dynamic range structured light means for the 3D measurement of specular surface. Opt. Lasers Eng. **95**, 8–16 (2017)
26. Sun, Q., Chen, J., Li, C.: A robust method to extract a laser stripe centre based on grey level moment. Opt. Lasers Eng. **67**, 122–127 (2015)
27. Tseng, P.: Convergence of a block coordinate descent method for nondifferentiable minimization. J. Optim. Theory Appl. **109**(3), 475–494 (2001)
28. Xu, J., et al.: Star: a structure and texture aware Retinex model. IEEE Trans. Image Process. **29**(1), 5022–5037 (2020)
29. Xu, L., Zheng, S., Jia, J.: Unnatural l_0 sparse representation for natural image deblurring. In: IEEE Conference on Computer Vision and Pattern Recognition, pp. 1107–1114 (2013)
30. Zhan, K., Shi, J., Teng, J., Li, Q., Wang, M., Lu, F.: Linking synaptic computation for image enhancement. Neurocomputing **238**, 1–12 (2017)
31. Zhan, K., Teng, J., Shi, J., Li, Q., Wang, M.: Feature-linking model for image enhancement. Neural Comput. **28**(6), 1072–1100 (2016)
32. Zhang, Q., Yuan, G., Xiao, C., Zhu, L., Zheng, W.S.: High-quality exposure correction of underexposed photos. In: ACM International Conference on Multimedia, pp. 582–590 (2018)

Teacher-Guided Learning for Blind Image Quality Assessment

Zewen Chen[1,2], Juan Wang[1], Bing Li[1(✉)], Chunfeng Yuan[1],
Weihua Xiong[4], Rui Cheng[4], and Weiming Hu[1,2,3]

[1] NLPR, Institute of Automation, Chinese Academy of Sciences, Beijing, China
{chenzewen2022,jun_wang}@ia.ac.cn, {bli,cfyuan,wmhu}@nlpr.ia.ac.cn
[2] School of Artificial Intelligence, University of Chinese Academy of Sciences,
Beijing, China
[3] CAS Center for Excellence in Brain Science and Intelligence Technology,
Shanghai, China
[4] Zeku Technology (Shanghai) Corp, Shanghai, China
chengrui@zeku.com

Abstract. The performance of deep learning models for blind image quality assessment (BIQA) suffers from annotated data insufficiency. However, image restoration, as a closely-related task with BIQA, can easily acquire training data without annotation. Moreover, both image semantic and distortion information are vital knowledge for the two tasks to predict and improve image quality. Inspired by these, this paper proposes a novel BIQA framework, which builds an image restoration model as a teacher network (TN) to learn the two aspects of knowledge and then guides the student network (SN) for BIQA. In TN, multi-branch convolutions are leveraged for performing adaptive restoration from diversely distorted images to strengthen the knowledge learning. Then the knowledge is transferred to the SN and progressively aggregated by computing long-distance responses to improve BIQA on small annotated data. Experimental results show that our method outperforms many state-of-the-arts on both synthetic and authentic datasets. Besides, the generalization, robustness and effectiveness of our method are fully validated. The code is available in https://github.com/chencn2020/TeacherIQA.

Keywords: Blind image quality assessment · Image restoration · Prior knowledge

1 Introduction

Image quality assessment (IQA) has been an active topic in image processing. Numerous applications, such as unmanned aerial vehicle, surveillance *et al.*, rise an urgent demand for IQA. Compared with full-reference and reduced-reference IQA, blind IQA (BIQA) receive more attention for removing the dependence on reference images which are even impossible to obtain in real-world applications.

Supplementary Information The online version contains supplementary material available at https://doi.org/10.1007/978-3-031-26313-2_13.

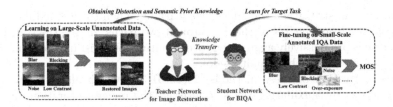

Fig. 1. Workflow of the proposed teacher-guided learning framework for BIQA, which consists of prior knowledge learning and target task learning.

In BIQA methods, the central idea is to extract features from images and map them to an IQA score. Traditional methods rely on handcrafted features to construct BIQA models, which can be divided into nature scene statistic (NSS)-based models [28,29,35] and human visual system (HVS)-related models [19,44, 46]. In recent years, Convolutional Neural Networks (CNNs) become the hotspot of various research fields. The performance of BIQA methods has also been greatly advanced by CNNs. Early CNNs-based BIQA methods [6,33] typically adopt shallow networks to extract low-level features, such as edges, textures and color, which explicitly reflect the distortion information.

However, training a successful deep CNN highly relies on an avalanche of annotated data. For IQA dataset, the labels, *e.g.*, mean opinion scores (MOSs), are obtained through psychophysical experiments. These experiments are expensive and time-consuming, making the acquisition of large-scale annotated data challenging. For this problem, one of seemingly plausible solutions is to combine multiple IQA datasets for training [52]. Unfortunately, IQA datasets have different perceptual scales due to the difference in psychophysical experiments. Using multi-scaled MOSs for training can lead to suboptimal performance. In addition, pre-training has been assumed to be an effective approach to address the lack of training data. Generally, the networks are pre-trained on other datasets or tasks to learn prior knowledge, and then fine-tuned for the target task. For example, some methods [22,25] pre-train the BIQA models to learn the quality rank on vast generated training samples first. Then they fine-tune the models to learn the quality score on standard IQA datasets. However, the models can only learn the perceptual scale of the same distortion type during the quality rank stage. Besides, the pre-trained image classification networks are also popularly used as the feature extractors in many BIQA models [18,39,42,48]. However, recent research [54] has shown that these networks are less adaptable to the BIQA task, since the classification task seldom considers the distortion information.

In order to overcome the bottleneck of insufficient annotated data, this paper proposes a new teacher-guided learning framework for BIQA to obtain the knowledge about image distortions and semantics from a large collection of unannotated data. The workflow of our framework is shown in Fig. 1, where an image restoration model is built as a teacher network (TN) to learn the two aspects of knowledge and then it guides the student network (SN) for the BIQA training on small annotated data. In TN, multi-branch convolutions (MC) are used for capturing fine-grained semantic and distortion information to achieve adaptive restoration and strengthen the knowledge learning. Then the learned knowledge is transferred from the TN to the SN through two paths. In SN, the transferred knowledge is progressively aggregated by computing long-distance responses and finally merged to a global quality score.

The motivation of these methods [20,23,31,34], which also employ image restoration as the auxiliary task, is to leverage the image restoration model to restore reference images to compare with distorted images. These methods are sensitive to the quality of restored images. However, our framework resorts to image restoration for feature learning since the image restoration and IQA tasks share similar knowledge. Our contributions are summarized as follows:

- We propose a new teacher-guided learning framework for BIQA, where a TN is presented to learn prior knowledge about image semantics and distortions from large unannotated data. By inheriting the knowledge from the TN, the SN can learn BIQA more efficiently by only using a small amount of annotated data.
- A multi-branch convolution is presented for the image restorer to capture the fine-grained features to achieve adaptive restoration for different types of distortions, and an attention mechanism is developed for the image quality predictor to aggregate the transferred knowledge for score estimate. Both network designs significantly improve the prediction accuracy for BIQA.
- Experimental results show that our method achieves state-of-the-art performance on both synthetic and authentic datasets. Besides, the generalization, robustness and effectiveness of our model are validated by cross-dataset evaluations, small training data experiments, ablation studies and group maximum differentiation (gMAD) competition.

2   Related Work

For the context of our work, we briefly review related work on blind image quality assessment and learning methods for insufficient data.

2.1   Blind Image Quality Assessment

In the early stage, researchers found out statistical characteristics vary when images are corrupted by different distortions. Thus, a quantity of NSS-based BIQA models were proposed. Saad et al. [35] and Moorthy et al. [29] respectively utilize the NSS model of discrete cosine transform and discrete wavelet transform coefficients to construct BIQA models. Mittal et al. [28] propose to utilize the NSS of locally normalized luminance coefficients to quantify quality scores. Other works attempt to extract HVS-related features, such as NRSL [19], LPSI [44] and M3 [46]. However, when it comes to complex and mixed distortions, the performance of the handcrafted-based BIQA models is far from satisfactory.

In recent years, benefit from the powerful representation ability of CNNs, BIQA methods have achieved impressive results. Kang et al. [12] are the pioneers to use the CNN to predict the quality score. They also propose a multi-task

CNN [13], which predicts the quality score and distortion type simultaneously. These early CNNs-based BIQA methods adopt shallow networks to prevent the over-fitting problem due to the lack of sufficient annotated data. To break through this limitation, some methods [1,39,42,48] adopt pre-trained networks (eg. ResNet [10] and VGG [38]), which are pre-trained on large-scale datasets like ImageNet [4], as the feature extractor. Benefit from the prior knowledge about image semantic information, these BIQA methods achieve a great progress on authentic IQA datasets. However, when it comes to synthetic IQA databases, the performance is far from satisfactory. This is because the pre-trained tasks seldom consider the image distortion information. To make BIQA models more aware of the distortions, some methods combine the image semantics with the distortions. For example, Zhang *et al.* [51] propose a DB-CNN model, where two networks respectively pre-trained for image classification and distortion classification are used as the feature extractor. Zhu *et al.* [54] propose a MetaIQA model. They adopt the meta learning approach to learn a prior knowledge model of various distortions, and then fine-tune the prior model with unknown distortions.

2.2   Learning Methods for Insufficient Data

Training a successful deep CNN largely relies on *supervised learning* that requires a huge number of annotations, which are expensive to obtain. Learning prior knowledge from other datasets or tasks has proven to be effective for improving the performance of target tasks in which the annotated data is not enough. As a result, a series of variant supervised learning methods are born. For example, in *semi-supervised learning* methods [3,47], the model is trained on a fraction of the dataset that is annotated manually first. Then the trained model is used to predict the remaining portion of the unannotated dataset. At last, the model is trained on the full dataset comprising of manually annotated and pseudo annotated data. In the *weakly-supervised learning* method [27], the recognition model is pre-trained with billions of Instagram images with noisy hashtags. Then the model is fine-tuned on annotated ImageNet dataset. For *self-supervised learning* methods, supervisory signals of the partial input is used to learn a better representation of the input. Generally, this is done via a pretext task that applies a transformation to the input image of the target task. The pretext tasks include image colorization [17], orientation [8] and counting visual primitives [30], *etc.* Though the learnt prior knowledge is effective in improving the performance of the target task, Shen *et al.* [37] and He *et al.* [9] demonstrate this benefit is reduced when the pre-training data belongs to a completely different domain.

In this paper, we resort to self-supervised learning (SSL) to address insufficient annotated data. We use image restoration as the pretext task to learn prior knowledge for BIQA. Compared with semi-supervised and weakly-supervised learning, SSL does not require any annotated data. Compared with other pretext tasks, image restoration can provide more related knowledge for BIQA.

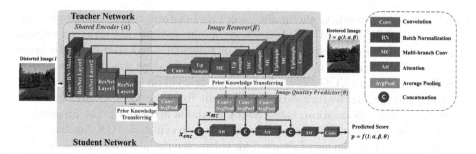

Fig. 2. Overview of our BIQA model, which consists of a teacher network (TN) and a student network (SN)

3 Proposed Method

Figure 2 shows the overview of our framework, which consists of two networks: a teacher network (TN) and a student network (SN). The TN and the SN share a same encoder. In addition, the TN also includes an image restorer, while the SN includes an image quality predictor. The training of our framework is divided into two phases. In the first phase, the TN is trained to learn the knowledge about the semantics and distortions from the image restoration task. In the second phase, the SN inherits the prior knowledge from the TN to learn BIQA on the IQA datasets. In the following, we introduce our method in details.

3.1 Teacher Network Learning from Image Restoration

Pretext Task. Both image semantics and distortions are vital knowledge for BIQA. The purpose of TN is to obtain the two knowledge to guide BIQA learning. Although pre-trained classification networks are equipped with strong semantic perceptual ability, recent research has shown that these networks are less adaptable to BIQA. This can be attributed to that the classification task pays more attention to high-level semantics, which are less sensitive to distortions. In contrast, image restoration requires both high-level and low-level features. On the one hand, low-level details explicitly reflect the distortion type and level. On the other hand, high-level semantics help to infer the distortion information (*eg.*, semantic information helps to judge the smooth area is clean sky or blurry jeans). Both image restoration and BIQA rely on the two aspects of knowledge. From this perspective, the knowledge of the two tasks can be shared. We employ image restoration as the objective task of the TN training.

Distortion-Aware Image Restoration. The TN consists of a shared encoder and an image restorer parameterized by α and β. Given an input image I, the TN aims to recover a high-quality image $\hat{I}$ from I, which is denoted as $\hat{I} = g(I; \alpha, \beta)$. For the encoder, it should have powerful feature representation ability. To this end, we adopt ResNet-50 [10] as the encoder, since it has proven to be an excellent feature extractor by many computer vision tasks. For the image restorer, its responsibility is to infer clean image content from encoder features. However, because of the limited distortion perception and detail synthesis ability of the model, most existing image restoration models only perform well for a specific distortion. For this reason, many restoration models adopt complicated networks, such as multi-level wavelet CNNs [21], scale recurrent network [40] and residual channel attention CNNs [53]. Since image restoration is only used as an auxiliary task in this paper, we do not aim to design a cumbersome network to accurately restore images. We employ a simple effective multi-branch convolutions (MCs), which consist of multiple parallel paths with different sizes of convolution kernels, to deal with various distortions. We first add skip connections to transmit the low-level features of the encoder to the decoder to strengthen the distortion perception ability. Then, the MCs are used to extract the context features and synthesize fine-grained details in multi-resolution receptive fields. The operation can be formulated as follows:

$$f_i = f_l \oplus f_h, \qquad f_o = B_5\left(B_1\left(f_i\right) \oplus B_2\left(f_i\right) \oplus B_3\left(f_i\right) \oplus B_4\left(f_i\right)\right),$$
$$B_i \subseteq \{1 \times 1\,\text{conv}, 3 \times 3\,\text{conv}, 5 \times 5\,\text{conv}, \text{maxPool}\}, \qquad (1 \leq i \leq 5) \tag{1}$$

where f_l and f_h denote features of the encoder and decoder, respectively, the symbol $\oplus$ denotes concatenation, and B_i $(1 \leq i \leq 5)$ denotes the i-th branch[1].

Loss Function. The first phase of our method is to train the TN for image restoration. We combine three losses, including reconstruction loss $\mathcal{L}_{\text{rec}}$, structure loss $\mathcal{L}_{\text{stru}}$ and perceptual loss $\mathcal{L}_{\text{percept}}$, to promote the consistency of the ground truth images I and the restored image $\hat{I}$ in pixel domain, low-level and high-level feature domains, respectively. The loss function is formulated as follows:

$$\mathcal{L}_{\text{TN}}(I, \hat{I}; \alpha, \beta) = \frac{1}{N} \sum_{n=1}^{N} [\varepsilon \mathcal{L}_{\text{rec}}(I, \hat{I}) + \rho \mathcal{L}_{\text{stru}}(I, \hat{I}) + \mu \mathcal{L}_{\text{percept}}(I, \hat{I})],$$
$$= \frac{1}{N} \sum_{n=1}^{N} [\varepsilon ||I - \hat{I}||_1 + \rho(1 - \text{SSIM}(I, \hat{I})) + \mu \sum_{t=1}^{T} \frac{1}{\Theta_t} ||\psi_t(I) - \psi_t(\hat{I})||_1], \tag{2}$$

where the hyper-parameters ε, ρ and μ balance their trade-off, and each loss is normalized by the batch size N. In the second loss, SSIM denotes the Structural Similarity Index [43]. In the third loss, $\psi_t(x)$ denote the t-th layer output of the pretrained VGG-19 network [38] for input x, T is the total number of layers used to calculate $\mathcal{L}_{\text{percept}}$, and Θ_t denote the number of elements in the t-th layer output. Concretely, we extract the 1st–5th pooling layer outputs of the VGG-19.

3.2 Student Network Learning for BIQA

Given an input image I, our BIQA model aims to infer its quality score p, which is modeled as $p = f(I; \Phi)$, where $\Phi = \{\alpha, \beta, \theta\}$ denote the network parameters. Recall that α and β are the parameters of the encoder and the restorer, respectively, which have been well pre-trained on a large collection of distorted and

---

[1] More details about the architecture are provided in the supplementary material.

reference image pairs. While θ is the parameter of the image quality predictor in the SN. The objective of our method in the second phase is to learn θ and fine-tune α and β on the IQA dataset. Benefit from the prior knowledge in α and β, our model can learn Φ more effectively and efficiently only using a small amount of annotated IQA data compared with those which learn Φ from scratch. In the following, we introduce the prior knowledge guided learning in detail.

Prior Knowledge Transferring. During the second phase training, the prior knowledge learned in the first phase is transferred to the image quality predictor from two paths. As shown in Fig. 2, one path is from the encoder, where the features are extracted from its bottleneck layer, denoted as f_{enc}. Another path is from the image restorer. Recall that the MCs are adopted to capture fine-grained context features. Here, we extract its output to the SN, denoted as f_{MC}. The introduction of f_{MC} can effectively reinforce the information lacked in f_{enc} due to the pooling operations in the encoder. In the experimental section, we validate that both the prior knowledge transferring paths and the MCs promote the BIQA performance.

Global Knowledge Aggregation. Given the prior knowledge, the objective of the SN is to extract useful information from the knowledge and map it to the image quality score. It is worth noting that different semantic regions show different responses for the same distortion type and level. As shown in Fig. 3, when the image suffers from the uniformly distributed blur distortion, the textured regions (*e.g.*, flowering shrubs) are affected more seriously than the smooth regions (*e.g.*, sky). When the image suffers from the noise distortion, the responses of these regions are converse. Motivated by this fact, we propose to capture long-distance dependencies for merging the distortion level of each local regions to a global quality score. To achieve this goal, we adopt the self-attention module [41], where three projections are learned to compute distant responses by matrix multiplication. In our framework, f_{enc} is used as the basic image features of the SN, and f_{MC} output from the 1st–3rd MCs are successively transferred to concatenate with f_{enc}. The concatenated features are aggregated using the self-attention module to convert the local features to global quality-related features. By three feature aggregation operations, we obtain a 7×7 feature map (for a 224×224 input). Finally, we adopt three 1×1 convolutions to reduce the channel number and a 7×7 convolution to map the feature map to a quality score.

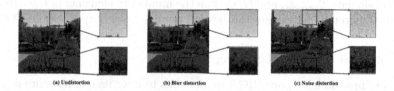

(a) Undistortion   (b) Blur distortion   (c) Noise distortion

Fig. 3. Different semantic regions show different responses for the same distortion. Smooth regions are sensitive to noise, while textured regions are vulnerable to blur.

Loss Function. Let $g = \{g_n \mid n \in [1, N]\}$ and $p = \{p_n \mid n \in [1, N]\}$ denote the ground truth and predicted quality scores of N images, respectively, and the subscript n denotes the n-th image. The optimization objective of the SN is defined as minimizing the ℓ_1 distance between g_n and p_n, that is $\mathcal{L}_{SN}(p, g; \alpha, \beta, \theta) = \frac{1}{N}\sum_n^N |g_n - p_n|$. Based on the loss function, we leverage the ADAM optimizer to update the parameter θ and fine-tune the parameters α and β with a small learning rate at the same time.

4 Experiments

In this section, we introduce experimental datasets, implementations and evaluation metrics first. Then we compare our method with state-of-the-art BIQA methods. Next, ablation studies are presented. Finally, we make a visual analysis and gMAD competitions to compare the robustness of the model.

4.1 Datasets

We trained and evaluated our model on four synthetic IQA datasets, including LIVE [36], CSIQ [16], TID2013 [32] and WED [24], and two authentic datasets, including LIVEC [6] and KonIQ-10K [11]. The LIVE consists of 779 distorted images by adding 5 distortion types on 29 reference images. The CSIQ possesses 866 distorted images derived from 30 reference images and 6 synthetic distortion types. The TID2013 contains 3,000 distortion images generated from 25 high-quality images, 24 distortion types and 5 levels. The WED contains 4,744 pristine natural images, and 94,880 distorted images are created from them with 4 distortion types and 5 levels. The LIVEC and KonIQ-10k contain 1,162 and 10,073 images, respectively, derived from the real world. These images have more complex distortions, making BIQA on the two datasets more challenging.

4.2 Implementations

The First Phase. The training of the TN for image restoration does not require any annotated data. We collect massive images from publicly available datasets. Specifically, We used 4,744 high-quality images of the WED dataset as reference images. Following [22,23,51], we manually added 16 out of a total of 24 distortions (including types of 1, 2, 5–10, 14–19, 22, 23) defined by the TID2013 [32] and 4 levels (including levels of 1–4) on the reference images. We did not add other distortion types to evaluate the generalization ability of our model and we did not use the level 5, which are seriously distorted, leading the model difficult to converge. Consequently, we created 303,616 distorted images. Each distorted image and its corresponding reference image constitute an image pair. Besides, each image is randomly flipped and cropped into 20 patches with the size of 224×224. The TN is trained for 10 epochs with a learning rate of 5×10^{-5} and the batch size N is set to 80. The hyper-parameters of the three loss functions defined in (2) are set to $\varepsilon = 1.0$, $\rho = 0.08$ and $\mu = 1.0$.

The Second Phase. The SN is trained on individual IQA dataset for BIQA. Following existing methods [20,39,51], we randomly flip and crop the input image into 25 patches with the size of 224×224. Each patch keeps the same quality score as the source image. Each dataset is randomly divided into 80% for training and 20% for testing. To ensure that there is no overlapping images between the training and the testing set on synthetic datasets, the dataset is divided according to the reference image. For authentic datasets, there are no reference images, so we divide the dataset according to the distorted image. All the experiments on each dataset are conducted 10 times repeatedly and we choose the model with the lowest validation error. The final result is the median value of the 10 scores. We adopt the Adam optimizer with a learning rate of 6×10^{-6}. The model is optimized for 16 epochs with a batch size of 92. All the experiments are conducted on Pytorch with NVIDIA 3090 GPUs.

Evaluation Metrics. We utilize two metrics to measure the performance of BIQA model: Pearson linear correlation coefficient (PLCC) and Spearman rank order correlation coefficient (SROCC). PLCC measures the linear correlation between the ground truth and predicted scores. SROCC measures the monotonicity between them. Both metrics range from -1 to 1. A higher value indicates a higher performance of the model.

4.3   Comparisons with State-of-the-Arts

A. Comparison Within Individual Datasets
We compare our model with four traditional BIQA, including BRISQUE [28], ILNIQE [50], HOSA [45] and FRIQUEE [7], and eleven CNNs-based BIQA, including BIECON [14], WaDIQaM-NR [2], PQR [49], RankIQA [22], DIQA [15], Hall-IQA [20], DB-CNN [51], MetaIQA [54], HyperIQA [39], AIGQA [23] and VCRNet [31]. The comparisons on five datasets are shown in Table 1, where the two highest scores are marked in black bold and blue bold respectively. Compared with 4 traditional models, our model achieves the best performance on all datasets. Compared with 11 CNNs-based models, our model achieves competitive results on 4 datasets. On the LIVE, our model obtains a slight lower performance, but it still achieves acceptable results with SROCC of 0.962 and PLCC of 0.965. We find that many of the compared models only perform well for authentic or synthetic datasets. For example, HyperIQA achieves excellent scores on authentic datasets, while its performance on synthetic datasets significantly degrades. By contrast, our model reports prominent scores on both datasets. In addition, the VCRNet [31] adopts a similar framework as our model, while its performance is not as excellent as ours. We attribute our advantage to the MC based image restorer and the self-attention based quality predictor, which effectively improve the performance of our model.

B. Comparison on Individual Distortions
In addition, we test the performance of our model on individual distortions. Table 2 lists SROCC on indivisual distortions on TID2013, and the best result for each distortion type is marked in bold. According to Table 2, our full model

Table 1. Performance comparison of BIQA methods on five IQA datasets

Dataset	LIVEC		KonIQ		TID		LIVE		CSIQ	
Model	SROCC	PLCC	SROCC	PLCC	SROCC	PLCC	SROCC	PLCC	SROCC	PLCC
BRISQUE [28]	0.608	0.629	0.665	0.681	0.651	0.573	0.939	0.935	0.746	0.829
ILNIQE [50]	0.432	0.508	0.507	0.523	0.519	0.640	0.902	0.865	0.806	0.808
HOSA [45]	0.640	0.678	0.671	0.694	0.688	0.764	0.946	0.947	0.741	0.823
FRIQUEE [7]	0.720	0.720	–	–	0.669	0.704	0.948	0.962	0.839	0.863
BIECON [14]	0.595	0.613	0.619	0.651	0.717	0.762	0.958	0.960	0.815	0.823
WaDIQaM [2]	0.671	0.680	0.797	0.805	0.787	0.761	0.954	0.963	–	–
PQR [49]	0.857	**0.882**	0.880	0.884	0.740	0.798	0.965	0.971	0.873	0.901
RankIQA [22]	–	–	–	–	0.780	0.799	**0.981**	**0.982**	**0.947**	**0.960**
DIQA [15]	0.703	0.704	–	–	0.825	0.850	0.975	0.977	0.884	0.915
Hall-IQA [20]	–	–	–	–	**0.879**	0.880	**0.982**	**0.982**	0.885	0.910
DB-CNN [51]	0.851	**0.869**	0.880	0.876	0.816	0.865	0.968	0.971	0.946	0.959
MetaIQA [54]	0.835	0.802	0.887	0.850	0.853	–	0.835	0.802	–	–
HyperIQA [39]	**0.859**	**0.882**	**0.906**	**0.917**	0.831	0.833	0.962	0.966	0.923	0.942
AIGQA [23]	0.751	0.761	–	–	0.871	**0.893**	0.960	0.957	0.927	0.952
VCRNet [31]	0.856	0.865	0.894	0.909	0.846	0.875	0.973	**0.974**	0.943	0.955
Ours	**0.861**	**0.882**	**0.910**	**0.916**	**0.920**	**0.932**	0.962	0.965	**0.950**	**0.961**

achieves the best performance on 9 out of 24 distortion types. Although our model does not perform best for the other 15 distortion types, it still surpasses most of the compared models. Moreover, our model obtains the highest average score (AVG) of 0.846 and the lowest standard deviation (STD) of 0.134. This indicates that our model has better stability for different types of distortion.

C. Cross-Dataset Evaluations

We further conduct cross-dataset experiments on three IQA datasets, including TID2013, CSIQ and LIVE. We use one dataset for training and the remaining two datasets for testing. Six state-of-the-art IQA models, including BRISQUE [28], FRIQUEE [7], HOSA [45], DB-CNN [51], HyperIQA [39] and VCRNet [31] are used for comparison. The evaluation results in terms of SROCC are shown in Table 3, where the two highest scores are marked in black bold and blue bold respectively. The TID2013 contains more distortion types and reference images than another two datasets. As shown from Table 3, most models achieve good performance when they are trained on TID2013 and tested on LIVE. On the contrary, when these models are trained on LIVE or CSIQ, their performance on TID2013 is much less satisfying. This indicates that training on the data with more diversities can effectively improve the generalization of the BIQA models. In addition, we observe that the models trained on CSIQ perform well on LIVE. However, the models trained on LIVE show a low performance on CSIQ. Nevertheless, our model ranks the top two among all the compared models. The result validates the good generalization ability of our model.

D. Comparison on Small Training Data

In this section, we conduct experiments to validate the proposed teacher-guided learning framework is effective in small data training. We randomly selected 20%,

Table 2. Performance comparison of individual distortions on TID2013 dataset in terms of SROCC. The bold distortion types are those used in TN learning

Type	BRISQUE	M3 [46]	HOSA	RankIQA	Hall-IQA	DB-CNN	AIGQA	HyperIQA	Full	w/o TNL	w/o MC
#1	0.711	0.766	0.853	0.667	0.923	0.790	**0.932**	0.769	0.907	0.775	0.677
#2	0.432	0.560	0.625	0.620	0.880	0.700	**0.916**	0.613	0.855	0.557	0.490
#3	0.746	0.782	0.782	0.821	0.945	0.826	0.944	0.918	**0.967**	0.925	0.858
#4	0.252	0.577	0.368	0.365	0.673	0.646	0.662	0.448	**0.721**	0.203	0.191
#5	0.842	0.900	0.905	0.760	**0.955**	0.879	0.953	0.839	0.920	0.828	0.718
#6	0.765	0.738	0.775	0.736	0.810	0.708	**0.911**	0.758	0.906	0.736	0.653
#7	0.662	0.832	0.810	0.783	0.855	0.825	0.908	0.828	**0.909**	0.779	0.790
#8	0.871	0.896	0.892	0.809	0.832	0.859	0.917	0.873	**0.939**	0.848	0.808
#9	0.612	0.709	0.870	0.767	**0.957**	0.865	0.914	0.804	0.915	0.836	0.737
#10	0.764	0.844	0.893	0.866	0.914	0.894	**0.945**	0.860	0.913	0.852	0.777
#11	0.745	0.855	0.932	0.878	0.624	0.916	0.932	0.888	**0.950**	0.893	0.843
#12	0.301	0.375	0.747	0.704	0.460	0.772	0.858	0.723	**0.860**	0677	0.685
#13	0.748	0.718	0.701	0.810	0.782	0.773	**0.898**	0.846	0.881	0.817	0.821
#14	0.269	0.173	0.199	0.512	**0.664**	0.270	0.130	0.369	0.575	0.254	0.234
#15	0.207	0.379	0.327	0.622	0.122	0.444	**0.723**	0.428	0.598	0.440	0.418
#16	0.219	0.119	0.233	0.268	0.182	−0.009	**0.554**	0.424	0.434	0.404	0.032
#17	−0.001	0.155	0.294	0.613	0.376	0.548	**0.830**	0.740	0.779	0.617	0.478
#18	0.003	−0.199	0.119	0.662	0.156	0.631	0.689	0.710	**0.858**	0.676	0.395
#19	0.717	0.738	0.782	0.619	0.850	0.711	**0.948**	0.767	0.925	0.788	0.681
#20	0.196	0.353	0.532	0.644	0.614	0.752	**0.886**	0.786	0.855	0.692	0.618
#21	0.609	0.692	0.835	0.800	0.852	0.860	0.897	0.879	**0.938**	0.842	0.824
#22	0.831	0.908	0.855	0.779	**0.911**	0.833	0.908	0.785	0.878	0.740	0.702
#23	0.615	0.570	0.801	0.629	0.381	0.732	**0.889**	0.739	0.876	0.719	0.576
#24	0.807	0.893	0.905	0.859	0.616	0.902	0.908	0.910	**0.944**	0.903	0.873
AVG	0.538	0.597	0.668	0.691	0.681	0.714	0.836	0.738	**0.846**	0.700	0.620
STD	0.281	0.301	0.262	0.151	0.267	0.217	0.182	0.163	**0.134**	0.197	0.228

Table 3. Cross-dataset evaluation

Training	TID2013		CSIQ		LIVE	
Testing	LIVE	CSIQ	LIVE	TID2013	CSIQ	TID2013
BRISQUE	0.790	0.590	0.847	0.454	0.562	0.358
FRIQUEE	0.755	0.635	0.879	0.463	0.722	0.461
HOSA	0.846	0.612	0.773	0.329	0.594	0.361
DB-CNN	**0.891**	**0.807**	0.877	0.540	**0.758**	0.524
HyperIQA	0.834	0.686	0.848	0.481	0.707	0.504
VCRNet	0.822	0.721	**0.886**	**0.542**	**0.768**	0.502
Ours	**0.864**	**0.789**	**0.911**	**0.581**	0.738	**0.658**

Table 4. Ablation studies

Dataset	LIVEC		CSIQ		TID2013	
Methods	SROCC	PLCC	SROCC	PLCC	SROCC	PLCC
w/o path-1	0.853	0.871	**0.953**	**0.962**	0.876	0.894
w/o path-2	0.776	0.846	0.890		0.733	0.779
w/o TNL	0.854	0.875	0.921	0.942	0.764	0.801
w/o MC	0.799	0.821	0.887	0.895	0.692	0.759
w/o Att	0.850	0.871	0.941	0.955	0.865	0.890
Full Model	**0.861**	**0.882**	0.950	0.961	**0.920**	**0.932**

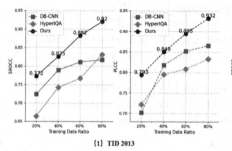
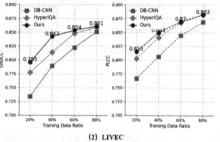

(1) TID 2013   (2) LIVEC

Fig. 4. Performance comparison of small data training on TID2013 and LIVEC.

40%, 60% and 80% images from the TID2013 and LIVEC dataset for training and 20% for testing. The four experiments were repeated 10 to overcome the bias introduced by randomness. The median scores of SROCC and PLCC are reported. Two state-of-the-art IQA models (DB-CNN and HyperIQA) are used for comparison. The SROCC and PLCC curves with respect to the training data ratio on TID2013 and LIVEC datasets. As shown in Fig. 4, as the training data ratio increases, the performance of all models shows an upward trend. Moreover, our model always ranks the top one across all ratios on both datasets.

4.4 Ablation Studies

In order to validate contributions key components make to the proposed method, we train a series of variant models: i) *w/o path-1* and ii) *w/o path-2*, where the first and second prior knowledge path from the encoder and image restorer are removed, respectively; iii) *w/o TNL*, where teacher network learning (TNL) from image restoration is removed; iv) *w/o MC*, where the MC is replaced by three convolutions; v) *w/o Att*, where the self-attention is replaced by a convolution. All parameter settings are kept the same as the full model, as explained in Sect. 4.2. Experimental results on three datasets are presented in Table 4, where the highest scores are marked in bold.

   i) For *w/o path-1* and *w/o path-2*, we can see that the removal of any path degrades the performance on LIVEC and TID2013, especially *w/o path-2*. This shows that the path 2 provides more useful information required by the IQA.
  ii) For *w/o TNL*, we observe the two metrics show a significant decrease on TID2013 by 18.04% and 14.05%, respectively. We speculate that since the TN is pre-trained for learning the distortions defined by on TID2013, the learnt prior knowledge is more beneficial to the IQA performance on TID2013.
 iii) For *w/o MC*, its performance shows a more obvious decease on TID2013, by 24.74% and 17.46% in terms of SROCC and PLCC, respectively. We speculate that this is because the TID2013 contains more various distortion types, which rises a higher requirement to the generalization ability of the model.
  iv) For *w/o Att*, we observe a slight decrease on LIVEC and CSIQ but an obvious decrease on TID2013. We speculate that it is related to our pre-training samples, which are made by imposing distortions defined by TID2013. Consistent data distribution makes it easier to achieve knowledge aggregation.

4.5 The gMAD Competition

To further evaluate the generalization of the proposed method, we conduct gMAD competition [26] on the SPAQ [5] dataset. There are two roles required: an attacker and a defender. The image pairs are selected when one model regards the image pairs with the same quality while the other regards them with different quality. If the image pairs are easy to distinguish, the attacker wins, otherwise, the defender wins. We choose two state-of-the-art BIQA methods HyperIQA [39] and DB-CNN [51] to compare with the proposed method.

Fig. 5. The gMAD competition against HyperIQA [39] and DB-CNN [51] on SPAQ

As shown in Fig. 5, we can see that when our model is the defender (the leftmost four columns), there is no much perception difference in the image pairs selected by the attacker. By contrast, when our model is the attacker (the rightmost four columns), it can easily select the image pairs with obvious quality differences, while the defenders regard these images with similar quality.

4.6   Analysis for the Multi-branch Convolutions

Benefit from the strengthened distortion information by the MC, the image restorer achieves adaptive image restoration for diverse distortions, which further improves the prediction accuracy of IQA scores. Both Table 2 and Table 4 have validated that removing MC degrades the IQA performance. In this section, we make a analysis on the MC and its effect on the image restoration.

Visual Analysis. Recall that f_{enc} and f_{MC} are the transferred knowledge from the TN to the SN. As their attention maps shown in Fig. 6, f_{enc} focuses more on the salient semantic regions, such as the persons in (b) and the elk in (d). In contrast, f_{MC} pays more attention on distorted regions, such as over-exposure sky in (a), (b) and (c), noisy sky in (e) and motion blur in (f). The examples are consistent with our assumptions that f_{enc} has stronger semantic information while the distortion information is more prominent in f_{MC}.

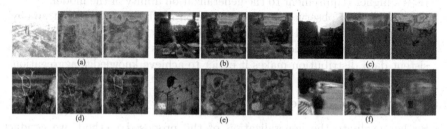

Fig. 6. Attention maps of the feature maps f_{enc} and f_{MC}. The images from left to right are respectively distorted images, attention maps of f_{enc} and f_{MC}.

Image Restoration Performance. In Fig. 7(a), we qualitatively compare the restored results of our full model and the variant *w/o MC* for synthetic

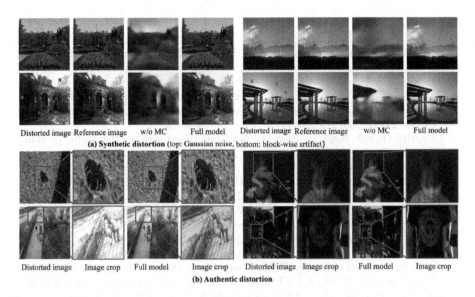

Distorted image Reference image   w/o MC   Full model   Distorted image Reference image   w/o MC   Full model

(a) Synthetic distortion (top: Gaussian noise, bottom: block-wise artifact)

Distorted image   Image crop   Full model   Image crop   Distorted image   Image crop   Full model   Image crop

(b) Authentic distortion

Fig. 7. Restored images by the TN of our variant model *w/o MC* and our full model for (a) synthetic distortion and (b) authentic distortion. (zoom in for more details)

distortions[2]. It can be seen that our full model restores visually pleasing images, while the results of the *w/o MC* suffer from serious blurry artifacts. Moreover, the results measured by PSNR and SSIM show that our full model achieves 28.22 and 0.881, while the *w/o MC* obtains 16.04 and 0.543. Both objective and subjective results validate the effectiveness of the MC in improving the quality of restored images. We also show restored images of our full model for authentic distortions, which are not presented in TN learning. As shown in Fig. 7(b), our full model achieves excellent restoration for the authentic distorted images. Though authentic images are not pre-trained for image restoration, our model is still able to deal with them well, which validates the generalization of our model.

5   Conclusion

This paper proposes a new teacher-guided learning framework for BIQA to break the limitation of insufficient annotated data. In our framework, a multi-branch convolution based TN is presented to learn the prior knowledge from image restoration, and a SN is constructed to learn for BIQA by inheriting the prior knowledge from the TN using the attention mechanism. Experimental results show that our method surpasses many state-of-the-arts on both authentic and synthetic datasets. In addition, cross-dataset evaluations and gMAD competitions prove our method has a good generalization ability. Moreover, ablation studies validate the effectiveness of key components of our method.

---

[2] More restored results are shown in supplementary material.

References

1. Bianco, S., Celona, L., Napoletano, P., Schettini, R.: On the use of deep learning for blind image quality assessment. Signal Image Video Process. **12**(2), 355–362 (2018)
2. Bosse, S., Maniry, D., Müller, K.R., Wiegand, T., Samek, W.: Deep neural networks for no-reference and full-reference image quality assessment. IEEE Trans. Image Process. **27**(1), 206–219 (2017)
3. Chapelle, O., Scholkopf, B., Zien, A.: Semi-supervised learning (Chapelle, O. et al., eds.; 2006)[book reviews]. IEEE Trans. Neural Netw. **20**(3), 542 (2009)
4. Deng, J., Dong, W., Socher, R., Li, L.J., Li, K., Fei-Fei, L.: ImageNet: a large-scale hierarchical image database. In: 2009 IEEE Conference on Computer Vision and Pattern Recognition, pp. 248–255. IEEE (2009)
5. Fang, Y., Zhu, H., Zeng, Y., Ma, K., Wang, Z.: Perceptual quality assessment of smartphone photography. In: Proceedings of the IEEE/CVF Conference on Computer Vision and Pattern Recognition, pp. 3677–3686 (2020)
6. Ghadiyaram, D., Bovik, A.C.: Massive online crowdsourced study of subjective and objective picture quality. IEEE Trans. Image Process. **25**(1), 372–387 (2015)
7. Ghadiyaram, D., Bovik, A.C.: Perceptual quality prediction on authentically distorted images using a bag of features approach. J. Vis. **17**(1), 32 (2017)
8. Gidaris, S., Singh, P., Komodakis, N.: Unsupervised representation learning by predicting image rotations. arXiv preprint arXiv:1803.07728 (2018)
9. He, K., Girshick, R., Dollár, P.: Rethinking ImageNet pre-training. In: Proceedings of the IEEE/CVF International Conference on Computer Vision, pp. 4918–4927 (2019)
10. He, K., Zhang, X., Ren, S., Sun, J.: Deep residual learning for image recognition. In: Proceedings of the IEEE Conference on Computer Vision and Pattern Recognition, pp. 770–778 (2016)
11. Hosu, V., Lin, H., Sziranyi, T., Saupe, D.: KonIQ-10k: an ecologically valid database for deep learning of blind image quality assessment. IEEE Trans. Image Process. **29**, 4041–4056 (2020)
12. Kang, L., Ye, P., Li, Y., Doermann, D.: Convolutional neural networks for no-reference image quality assessment. In: Proceedings of the IEEE Conference on Computer Vision and Pattern Recognition, pp. 1733–1740 (2014)
13. Kang, L., Ye, P., Li, Y., Doermann, D.: Simultaneous estimation of image quality and distortion via multi-task convolutional neural networks. In: 2015 IEEE International Conference on Image Processing (ICIP), pp. 2791–2795. IEEE (2015)
14. Kim, J., Lee, S.: Fully deep blind image quality predictor. IEEE J. Sel. Top. Signal Process. **11**(1), 206–220 (2016)
15. Kim, J., Nguyen, A.D., Lee, S.: Deep CNN-based blind image quality predictor. IEEE Trans. Neural Netw. Learn. Syst. **30**(1), 11–24 (2018)
16. Larson, E.C., Chandler, D.M.: Most apparent distortion: full-reference image quality assessment and the role of strategy. J. Electron. Imaging **19**(1), 011006 (2010)
17. Larsson, G., Maire, M., Shakhnarovich, G.: Colorization as a proxy task for visual understanding. In: Proceedings of the IEEE Conference on Computer Vision and Pattern Recognition, pp. 6874–6883 (2017)
18. Li, D., Jiang, T., Lin, W., Jiang, M.: Which has better visual quality: the clear blue sky or a blurry animal? IEEE Trans. Multimed. **21**(5), 1221–1234 (2018)
19. Li, Q., Lin, W., Xu, J., Fang, Y.: Blind image quality assessment using statistical structural and luminance features. IEEE Trans. Multimed. **18**(12), 2457–2469 (2016)

20. Lin, K.Y., Wang, G.: Hallucinated-IQA: no-reference image quality assessment via adversarial learning. In: Proceedings of the IEEE Conference on Computer Vision and Pattern Recognition, pp. 732–741 (2018)

21. Liu, P., Zhang, H., Zhang, K., Lin, L., Zuo, W.: Multi-level wavelet-CNN for image restoration. In: Proceedings of the IEEE Conference on Computer Vision and Pattern Recognition Workshops, pp. 773–782 (2018)

22. Liu, X., Van De Weijer, J., Bagdanov, A.D.: RankIQA: learning from rankings for no-reference image quality assessment. In: Proceedings of the IEEE International Conference on Computer Vision, pp. 1040–1049 (2017)

23. Ma, J., Wu, J., Li, L., Dong, W., Xie, X., Shi, G., Lin, W.: Blind image quality assessment with active inference. IEEE Trans. Image Process. **30**, 3650–3663 (2021)

24. Ma, K., et al.: Waterloo exploration database: new challenges for image quality assessment models. IEEE Trans. Image Process. **26**(2), 1004–1016 (2016)

25. Ma, K., Liu, W., Liu, T., Wang, Z., Tao, D.: dipIQ: blind image quality assessment by learning-to-rank discriminable image pairs. IEEE Trans. Image Process. **26**(8), 3951–3964 (2017)

26. Ma, K., et al.: Group mad competition-a new methodology to compare objective image quality models. In: Proceedings of the IEEE Conference on Computer Vision and Pattern Recognition, pp. 1664–1673 (2016)

27. Mahajan, D., et al.: Exploring the limits of weakly supervised pretraining. In: Proceedings of the European Conference on Computer Vision (ECCV), pp. 181–196 (2018)

28. Mittal, A., Moorthy, A.K., Bovik, A.C.: No-reference image quality assessment in the spatial domain. IEEE Trans. Image Process. **21**(12), 4695–4708 (2012)

29. Moorthy, A.K., Bovik, A.C.: Blind image quality assessment: from natural scene statistics to perceptual quality. IEEE Trans. Image Process. **20**(12), 3350–3364 (2011)

30. Noroozi, M., Pirsiavash, H., Favaro, P.: Representation learning by learning to count. In: Proceedings of the IEEE International Conference on Computer Vision, pp. 5898–5906 (2017)

31. Pan, Z., Yuan, F., Lei, J., Fang, Y., Shao, X., Kwong, S.: VCRNet: visual compensation restoration network for no-reference image quality assessment. IEEE Trans. Image Process. **31**, 1613–1627 (2022)

32. Ponomarenko, N., et al.: Color image database TID2013: peculiarities and preliminary results. In: European Workshop on Visual Information Processing (EUVIP), pp. 106–111. IEEE (2013)

33. Ponomarenko, N., et al.: Image database TID2013: peculiarities, results and perspectives. Signal Process. Image Commun. **30**, 57–77 (2015)

34. Ren, H., Chen, D., Wang, Y.: RAN4IQA: restorative adversarial nets for no-reference image quality assessment. In: Proceedings of the AAAI Conference on Artificial Intelligence, vol. 32 (2018)

35. Saad, M.A., Bovik, A.C., Charrier, C.: Blind image quality assessment: a natural scene statistics approach in the DCT domain. IEEE Trans. Image Process. **21**(8), 3339–3352 (2012)

36. Sheikh, H.R., Sabir, M.F., Bovik, A.C.: A statistical evaluation of recent full reference image quality assessment algorithms. IEEE Trans. Image Process. **15**(11), 3440–3451 (2006)

37. Shen, Z., Liu, Z., Li, J., Jiang, Y.G., Chen, Y., Xue, X.: Object detection from scratch with deep supervision. IEEE Trans. Pattern Anal. Mach. Intell. **42**(2), 398–412 (2019)

38. Simonyan, K., Zisserman, A.: Very deep convolutional networks for large-scale image recognition. arXiv preprint arXiv:1409.1556 (2014)
39. Su, S., et al.: Blindly assess image quality in the wild guided by a self-adaptive hyper network. In: Proceedings of the IEEE/CVF Conference on Computer Vision and Pattern Recognition (CVPR) (2020)
40. Tao, X., Gao, H., Shen, X., Wang, J., Jia, J.: Scale-recurrent network for deep image deblurring. In: Proceedings of the IEEE Conference on Computer Vision and Pattern Recognition, pp. 8174–8182 (2018)
41. Vaswani, A., et al.: Attention is all you need. In: Advances in Neural Information Processing Systems, vol. 30 (2017)
42. Wang, J., et al.: MSTRIQ: no reference image quality assessment based on swin transformer with multi-stage fusion. In: Proceedings of the IEEE/CVF Conference on Computer Vision and Pattern Recognition, pp. 1269–1278 (2022)
43. Wang, Z., Bovik, A.C., Sheikh, H.R., Simoncelli, E.P.: Image quality assessment: from error visibility to structural similarity. IEEE Trans. Image Process. **13**(4), 600–612 (2004)
44. Wu, Q., Wang, Z., Li, H.: A highly efficient method for blind image quality assessment. In: 2015 IEEE International Conference on Image Processing (ICIP), pp. 339–343. IEEE (2015)
45. Xu, J., Ye, P., Li, Q., Du, H., Liu, Y., Doermann, D.: Blind image quality assessment based on high order statistics aggregation. IEEE Trans. Image Process. **25**(9), 4444–4457 (2016)
46. Xue, W., Mou, X., Zhang, L., Bovik, A.C., Feng, X.: Blind image quality assessment using joint statistics of gradient magnitude and laplacian features. IEEE Trans. Image Process. **23**(11), 4850–4862 (2014)
47. Yalniz, I.Z., Jégou, H., Chen, K., Paluri, M., Mahajan, D.: Billion-scale semi-supervised learning for image classification. arXiv preprint arXiv:1905.00546 (2019)
48. Yang, S., et al.: MANIQA: multi-dimension attention network for no-reference image quality assessment. In: Proceedings of the IEEE/CVF Conference on Computer Vision and Pattern Recognition (CVPR) Workshops, pp. 1191–1200 (2022)
49. Zeng, H., Zhang, L., Bovik, A.C.: A probabilistic quality representation approach to deep blind image quality prediction. arXiv preprint arXiv:1708.08190 (2017)
50. Zhang, L., Zhang, L., Bovik, A.C.: A feature-enriched completely blind image quality evaluator. IEEE Trans. Image Process. **24**(8), 2579–2591 (2015)
51. Zhang, W., Ma, K., Yan, J., Deng, D., Wang, Z.: Blind image quality assessment using a deep bilinear convolutional neural network. IEEE Trans. Circuits Syst. Video Technol. **30**(1), 36–47 (2018)
52. Zhang, W., Zhai, K., Zhai, G., Yang, X.: Learning to blindly assess image quality in the laboratory and wild. In: 2020 IEEE International Conference on Image Processing (ICIP), pp. 111–115. IEEE (2020)
53. Zhang, Y., Li, K., Li, K., Wang, L., Zhong, B., Fu, Y.: Image super-resolution using very deep residual channel attention networks. In: Proceedings of the European conference on computer vision (ECCV), pp. 286–301 (2018)
54. Zhu, H., Li, L., Wu, J., Dong, W., Shi, G.: METAIQA: deep meta-learning for no-reference image quality assessment. In: Proceedings of the IEEE/CVF Conference on Computer Vision and Pattern Recognition, pp. 14143–14152 (2020)

ElDet: An Anchor-Free General Ellipse Object Detector

Tianhao Wang[1], Changsheng Lu[2], Ming Shao[3], Xiaohui Yuan[1],
and Siyu Xia[1(✉)]

[1] School of Automation, Southeast University, Nanjing, China
{wangtianhao,yuanxh,xsy}@seu.edu.cn
[2] College of Engineering and Computer Science, The Australian National University,
Canberra, Australia
Changsheng.Lu@anu.edu.au
[3] Computer and Information Science Department, University of Massachusetts
Dartmouth, Dartmouth, USA
mshao@umassd.edu

Abstract. Ellipse detection is a fundamental task in object shape analysis. Under complex environments, the traditional image processing based approaches may under-perform due to the hand-crated features. Instead, CNN-based approaches are more robust and powerful. In this paper, we introduce an efficient anchor-free data-augmentation based general ellipse detector, termed *ElDet*. Different from existing CNN-based methods, our *ElDet* relies more on edge information which could excavate more shape information into learning. Specifically, we first develop an edge fusion module to composite an overall edge map which has more complete boundary and better continuity. The edge map is treated as augmentation input for our *ElDet* for ellipse regression. Secondly, three loss functions are tailored to our *ElDet*, which are angle loss, IoU loss, and binary mask prediction loss to jointly improve the ellipse detection performance. Moreover, we contribute a diverse ellipse dataset by collecting multiple classes of elliptical objects in real scenes. Extensive experiments show that the proposed ellipse detector is very competitive to state-of-the-art methods.

1 Introduction

Geometric shape is a crucial characteristic to objects and is of great importance for object detection and recognition. In some scenarios, we pay more attention to shape & contour information, such as medical imaging diagnosis [1], object counting [2], and CAD workpieces recognition [3,4]. Existing shape detection methods are mainly based on traditional image processing [5,6], which heavily depend on low-level edge lines and omit physical meanings of objects. Thus, such methods are susceptible to interference from extraneous noisy edges or lines.

Ellipse shape commonly appears in various scenes and can be modelled by 5-D parameters. Compared to other shapes, *e.g.*, rectangle, ellipse presents superior information. Traditional ellipse detection algorithms [5,7] usually build the

L. Wang et al. (Eds.): ACCV 2022, LNCS 13843, pp. 223–238, 2023.
https://doi.org/10.1007/978-3-031-26313-2_14

mathematical model based on segmented edges, contours, and curvatures. These methods have achieved relatively accurate and efficient ellipse detection. However, they require appropriate pre-processing to ensure the quality of ellipse fitting. The most significant pre-processing step used by these methods is edge detection. Current edge detectors will inevitably introduce extraneous lines and noise, which largely affects the subsequent detection. In addition, most of these methods require artificially set some thresholds and other parameters, which is difficult to guarantee the consistency of accuracy and efficiency.

With the rapid development of deep learning, it is apparent that CNN-based methods are more robust and efficient, especially under complex scenes. Recently, approach [8] develops an anchor-based ellipse detector based on Faster R-CNN [9], but it is two-stage and subject to specific object classes. Some researchers suggest that Convolutional Neural Network (CNN) is strongly biased towards textures rather than shapes [10]. Therefore, for class-specific object detection, texture information can indeed play a big role, but for general ellipse detection, edge information is more desirable as it describes the essential geometric shapes.

In addition, multi-task learning (MTL) is important in machine learning [11,12]. Compared to single-task learning (STL), MTL jointly optimize multiple functions with close relevance. During training, the shared and more general representations are learned, thus achieving better generalization during testing. In most of cases, MTL has proved to outperform STL. In this paper, we use the ellipse mask segmentation as a pretext task in addition to ellipse detection task, forming the multi-task learning fashion. The reason behind this is that the edge has close relationship to binary ellipse masks, which both provide shape information crucial to ellipse detection.

We propose a novel data-augmentation based ellipse detector (*ElDet*) in this paper, which is anchor-free, one-stage, and general. Unlike existing CNN-based approaches, we enrich the input with data augmentation by combining edge maps using our *Edge Fusion Module*, which is omitted by EllipseNet [13] and Ellipse R-CNN [14]. The edge information allows our detector to effectively use contour shape information for precise ellipse object detection. Moreover, our model has a potential of detecting various ellipse-shaped objects, regardless of their actual class labels. During regressing the ellipse parameters, elliptic angle is difficult to learn and has a larger impact on rotated object detection. Recent works have proposed new bounding box representations, such as ordered quadrilateral [15]. However, most popular angle regression methods suffer from the problem of boundary discontinuity (*i.e.*, $-\frac{\pi}{2}$ vs. $\frac{\pi}{2}$), which may lead a large and unstable loss. To address this issue, we propose an aspect-ratio based angle loss and a Gaussian distribution based IoU loss. Further, we also add an auxiliary task of binary mask segmentation to fully exploit the edge information from ellipse objects. The contributions are summarized as follows:

1. We propose an anchor-free and general ellipse object detector, which is simple, effective, and capable of being applied to downstream tasks such as irregular-shape object detection.
2. We design an edge fusion module that learns adaptive weight coefficients and fuse multiple edge maps. The obtained fused edge maps will be used for data

augmentation. This module and subsequent detectors together consist of an end-to-end model.

3. We design three dedicated losses for precise ellipse detection including aspect-ratio based angle loss, Gaussian distribution based IoU loss, and binary mask regression loss, which jointly optimizes the *ElDet.*

4. A new ellipse detection dataset collected from real-world scenarios is contributed to enrich the diversity of datasets in the field of ellipse detection.

2 Related Works

2.1 Anchor-Free Object Detector

Anchor boxes are widely used in mainstream detectors, such as Faster R-CNN [9] and YOLOv3 [16]. Anchor-based object detectors are mainly based on anchor boxes which can be considered as pre-designed sliding-windows and proposals. With prior knowledge, anchor boxes significantly improves the accuracy and speed of the predicted object bounding boxes. However, the design of anchor boxes is rather tricked and introduces a large number of hyper-parameters.

To avoid the overwhelming exploration of anchor boxes, anchor-free object detectors are proposed. The anchor-free methods are roughly divided into two branches: i) dense prediction approaches, *e.g.*, DenseBox [17] and FCOS [18]; ii) keypoint-based approaches, *e.g.*, CornerNet [19] and CenterNet, which closely relate to keypoint detection approaches [20,21]. Our method falls into anchor-free keypoint-based category.

CenterNet is one-staged object detector. It treats each object as a point, *i.e.*, center point of the object bounding box. The center point can be regarded as a single shape-agnostic anchor. The detector locates the object center point by keypoint estimation and regress other object attributes directly, such as size, direction, 3-D position and even posture. Moreover, CenterNet does not need Non-Maximum Suppression (NMS) [22], since it only has one positive "anchor" per object. With its minimalist design and great performance, CenterNet is used as basic framework for many anchor-free methods.

2.2 Rotated Object Detection

Classical object detection typically uses a horizontal rectangular box to frame the object position. However, for some scenarios, such as remote sensing object detection and text detection, the object has a rotation angle. Using rotated object detection to precisely locate the object is beneficial to provide more accurate inputs for subsequent tasks such as recognition and analysis. Most rotated object detectors are inherited from traditional anchor-based object detectors by using rotated bounding boxes or quadrangles.

The main problem of rotated object detection is the angle prediction. Gliding Vertex [23] and RSDet [15] represent the bounding box by four corner points and determine the rotation angle by calculating the offset of corner points. CSL [24]

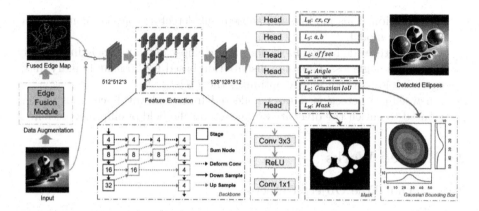

Fig. 1. Overview of the proposed ellipse detector. We use DLA-34 [28] as the back-bone for feature extraction. There are two types of losses, where one is for regressing ellipse parameters, and another, namely, mask segmentation, is auxiliary to promote the performance of ellipse detection.

and DCL [25] transform angle prediction from a regression problem to a classification problem. GWD [26] and KLD [27] convert the rotation regression loss into the distance of two 2-D Gaussian distributions. We also follow rotated object detection and introduce the 2-D Gaussian distribution into ellipse detection.

2.3 Ellipse Detection

Traditional ellipse detection can be roughly divided into three streams, namely, clustering-based, optimization-based, and arc-based methods. Lu *et al.* [7] propose an efficient ellipse detection based on arc support line segment. Recently, CNN-based methods go viral. For instance, Li *et al.* [8] replace the Region Proposal Network (RPN) in Faster R-CNN by a Gaussian Proposal Network (GPN). Ellipse R-CNN [14] presents a two-stage detector based on Mask R-CNN and solves the problem in occluded and cluttered scenes. Apart from these anchor-based detectors, EllipseNet [13] develops an anchor-free ellipse detector in medical images. In this paper, we push further by using edge information and improving the accuracy of angle regression.

3 Proposed Method

3.1 Overview of Framework

As shown in Fig. 1, our framework is developed based on CenterNet [29]. We adapt DLA-34 [28] as the backbone. The goal of the detector is to regress the five parameters of ellipse (x, y, a, b, θ), where (x, y) are the coordinates of the center point, a, b $(a \geq b)$ are the major and minor axis, and $\theta \in [-90, 90)$ is the rotation angle. We introduce edge images as augmented data. To improve

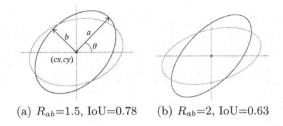

(a) R_{ab}=1.5, IoU=0.78   (b) R_{ab}=2, IoU=0.63

Fig. 2. Influence of aspect ratio R_{ab} on IoU. When the center points overlap, the greater the ratio, the more significant the impact of the angle (The angle of red ellipse is 15°, while the green one is 45°). (Color figure online)

the accuracy of angle regression, we add an angle loss based on the aspect ratio, and use Gaussian Wasserstein distance (GWD) loss. In addition, binary mask segmentation is adopted to enhance the network training.

3.2   Ellipse Parameters Regression

We follow CenterNet in the regression of the center point coordinates, the major and minor axis, and the offset. In particular, focal loss function [30] and smooth-L1 loss function are respectively used to optimize (x, y) and a, b. Size Loss $\mathcal{L}_S$ is used to predict a, b. Given an input image $I \in R^{W \times H \times 3}$ with height H and width W, the predicted heatmap $\hat{Y} \in [0,1]^{\frac{W}{R} \times \frac{H}{R} \times 2}$ represents the probability map of the center point location and Y represents the ground truth heatmap. We set output stride $R = 4$. To reduce the discretization error caused by the output stride, the offset is also predicted and offset loss $\mathcal{L}_O$ is calculated with smooth-L1 loss. The heatmap loss $\mathcal{L}_H$ is obtained as follows:

$$\mathcal{L}_H = \frac{-1}{N} \sum_{xyc} \begin{cases} (1 - \hat{Y}_{xyc})^\alpha log(\hat{Y}_{xyc}), & if \ \ Y_{xyc} = 1 \\ (1 - Y_{xyc})^\beta (\hat{Y}_{xyc})^\alpha \log(1 - \hat{Y}_{xyc}), & others \end{cases} \tag{1}$$

where x, y, c indexes a channel, α and β are hyper-parameters of the focal loss, N is the number of keypoints in image I. Moreover, $\alpha = 2$ and $\beta = 4$.

Among the five parameters of ellipse, rotation angle θ largely affects detection results, especially on IoU, as shown in Fig. 2. Assuming (x, y) are equal, the influence of the angle on IoU relies on the aspect ratio $R_{ab} = a/b$. The greater the ratio, the more significant the impact of the angle. This means it is difficult to predict the rotation angle for a round-like object, and too much attention on the angle of round-like object also raises challenges in the angle regression.

To solve this issue, we add a weight based on aspect ratio to angle loss. The angle loss $\mathcal{L}_\theta$ is reformulated as follows:

$$W_\theta = \begin{cases} 1 & if \ R_{ab} < 1.2 \\ 2 & if \ R_{ab} \geq 1.2, \end{cases} \tag{2}$$

$$\mathcal{L}_\theta = W_\theta * \text{smooth}_{L1}(\theta_p, \theta_g), \tag{3}$$

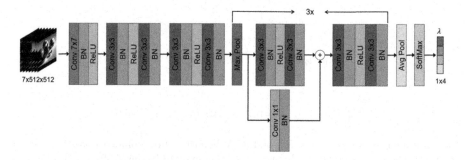

Fig. 3. Network structure of edge fusion module.

where W_θ represents the angle loss weight, θ_p and θ_g are predicted rotation angle value and ground-truth rotation angle value. We use smooth-L1 loss function to calculate the difference between θ_p and θ_g.

3.3 Edge Fusion Module

CNNs are biased towards texture information [10], while ellipse detection relies more on shape information such as contours and edges. Therefore, we introduce edge maps as data augmentation for inputs, and our extensive experiments show that edge maps yield significant improvements for ellipse detection.

Different edge detection methods have their own advantages and yet shortcomings such as sensitivity to noise, positioning, and continuity. In order to obtain high-quality edge maps, we design an adaptive Edge Fusion Module (EFM) for edge maps which are extracted by multiple methods. The EFM is based on ResNet-18 [31] with some modifications, as shown in Fig. 3.

To obtain an overall better edge map, firstly, we extract four edge maps using *Canny* [32], *Sobel* [33], *Laplacian* [34] operators and *AdaptiveThreshold* [35] method. Then we concatenate the RGB image and the four different edge maps by channel and feed them into the EFM to obtain the weight coefficients corresponding to the four edge maps. The final edge map is obtained via the weighted summation:

$$Map = \sum_1^{i=4} \lambda_i \cdot Map_i$$

$$\sum_1^{i=4} \lambda_i = 1 \qquad (4)$$

where Map means final edge map, Map_i means edge maps extracted by four edge detectors and λ_i are their corresponding weights. The fused edge map will be normalized into $[0, 255]$. With this fusion method, we are able to improve the value of the true edge, reduce the interference of noise, and make the contour more complete (Fig. 4).

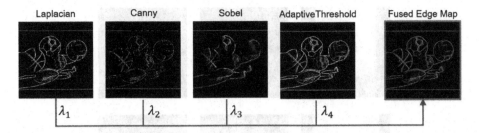

| Laplacian | Canny | Sobel | AdaptiveThreshold | Fused Edge Map |

$\lambda_1 \qquad \lambda_2 \qquad \lambda_3 \qquad \lambda_4$

Fig. 4. Weighted summation of edge maps based on the learned weight coefficients produced by Edge Fusion Module (EFM). The left four different edge maps are extracted by *Laplacian, Canny, Sobel,* and *AdaptiveThreshold*, respectively, and the rightmost is the fused edge map.

Note that we use the edge map as a way of data augmentation, which means that during the training process we input the edge fusion map with probability of 0.5, otherwise we input the RGB image to the subsequent detector.

3.4 Gaussian IoU

As the IoU calculation method for rectangle bounding box is sub-optimal for ellipse detection, we discover that 2-D Gaussian distribution matches ellipse better in shape. In addition, 2-D Gaussian IoU can well integrate into loss functions to address the boundary discontinuity and round-like problem. We simply parameterize a 2-D Gaussian distribution by the mean μ and the covariance matrix Σ in ellipse bounding box $\mathcal{B}(x, y, a, b, \theta)$:

$$
\begin{aligned}
\Sigma^{\frac{1}{2}} &= RSR^T \\
&= \begin{pmatrix} cos\theta & -sin\theta \\ sin\theta & cos\theta \end{pmatrix} \begin{pmatrix} a & 0 \\ 0 & b \end{pmatrix} \begin{pmatrix} cos\theta & sin\theta \\ -sin\theta & cos\theta \end{pmatrix} \\
&= \begin{pmatrix} a \cdot cos^2\theta + b \cdot sin^2\theta & (a-b)cos\theta sin\theta \\ (a-b)cos\theta sin\theta & a \cdot sin^2\theta + b \cdot cos^2\theta \end{pmatrix} \\
\mu &= [x, y]
\end{aligned}
\tag{5}
$$

Further, the Wasserstein distance [36] $\mathbf{W}$ between two Gaussian probabilities $X \sim \mathcal{N}(\mu_1, \Sigma_1)$ and $Y \sim \mathcal{N}(\mu_2, \Sigma_2)$ is expressed as:

$$
\mathbf{W}(\mu; \nu) := \inf \mathbb{E}(||X - Y||_2^2)^{1/2}.
\tag{6}
$$

Consequently, we could compute the IoU loss L_G via Wasserstein distance as:

$$
d^2 = ||\mu_1 - \mu_2||_2^2 + \mathbf{Tr}(\Sigma_1 + \Sigma_2 - 2(\Sigma_1^{1/2}\Sigma_2\Sigma_1^{1/2})^{1/2}),
\tag{7}
$$

where

$$
\mathcal{L}_G = 1 - \frac{1}{1 + log(d^2)},
\tag{8}
$$

Overall, we use IoU loss L_G to measure the error between predicted ellipse and groundtruth ellipse. By optimizing L_G, our model is able to regress ellipse parameters $\mathcal{B}(x, y, a, b, \theta)$.

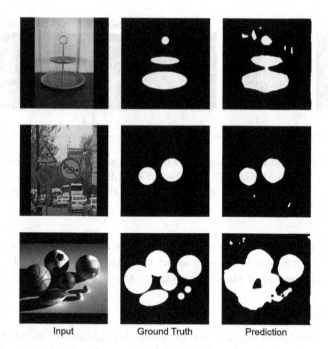

Input   Ground Truth   Prediction

Fig. 5. Results of binary mask prediction. From left to Right are input images, ground truth and prediction of binary masks.

3.5   Ellipse Mask Segmentation

Mask segmentation [37] is able to effectively segment the boundary between the foreground objects and background. Binary masks are more sensitive to the demarcation area of the foreground and background, which can be more conducive to the utilization of elliptical edge information. Based on the idea of parameter sharing in multi-task learning, we introduce ellipse mask segmentation as an auxiliary task. Though it does not directly affect the regression of object parameters, it optimizes deep model parameters in a multi-task learning fashion and forces the model to pay higher attention to the object area. The mask loss $\mathcal{L}_M$ is calculated by binary cross-entropy loss. Some results of ellipse mask segmentation are shown in Fig. 5. Overall, the total loss of our pipeline can be formulated as:

$$\begin{aligned}\mathcal{L} = &\lambda_H \mathcal{L}_H + \lambda_S \mathcal{L}_S + \lambda_O \mathcal{L}_O \\ &+ \lambda_\theta \mathcal{L}_\theta + \lambda_G \mathcal{L}_G + \lambda_M \mathcal{L}_M.\end{aligned} \tag{9}$$

4   Experiments

4.1   General Ellipse Detection Dataset (GED)

To our best knowledge, most of *publicly available* ellipse datasets target for conventional methods. In particular, some samples are not regular ellipses or highly similar. Moreover, their sizes are usually small and may not accommodate deep learning models. Thus, we contribute a new general ellipse detection dataset, termed **GED**, whose images are collected from real-world scenarios. GED consists of **1443** images and each image is manually annotated. The ellipses in GED are relatively regular and have large difference in texture. The classes of elliptic objects are diverse, *e.g.*, ball, wheel, dishes, button.

4.2   Implementation Details

For training, we use weights pre-trained on ImageNet to initialize the backbone DLA-34 [28], and Adam to optimize the networks on a single GeForce RTX 3080 GPU. For edge fusion, four edge detectors are used which are *Laplacian, Canny, Sobel* operators and *adaptiveThreshold*. All the loss weights are set as 0.1, except $\lambda_H = 1, \lambda_G = 15, \lambda_M = 1$. The aspect ratio threshold in angle loss is set to 1.2. First, the threshold of 1.2 is roughly the dividing line of the ellipse from a visual point of view. Second, approximately half of the data has the ratio of the long and short axes smaller than 1.2, while rest larger than that. Since the dataset used by EllipseNet is not open-source, we train the networks on GED and FDDB [38] dataset, respectively. 80% of the images is randomly splitted as training set and the rest as test set. All the images are resized into 512×512. The learning rate is set to be 1.25×10^{-4} and we train 150 epochs in GED dataset while 300 epochs in FDDB dataset. Traditional methods that do not use the GPU are executed on the computer with Inter Core i7-11700k 3.60 GHz.

4.3   Evaluation Metrics

We exploit two evaluation metrics: 1) *AP* over ellipse IoU thresholds, and 2) AP^Θ over ellipse IoU thresholds and angle error thresholds:

$$AP = \sum_{i=1}^{n-1}(r_{i+1} - r_i)P_{interp}(r_{i+1}) \tag{10}$$

$$P_{interp}(r) = \max_{r' \geq r} P(r')$$

where $r_1, r_2, \cdots, r_n$ are the recall value. in ascending order; $P(*)$ means precision and $r(*)$ is recall, which can be computed by:

$$\text{Precision} = \frac{TP}{TP + FP} \tag{11}$$

$$\text{Recall} = \frac{TP}{TP + FN}$$

We focus more on the accuracy of predicted angles by introducing AP^Θ. Considering the influence of round-like problem, we ignore the angle error when the aspect ration is less than 1.2. For example, $AP^{10}_{0.75}$ means that we consider a prediction as a true positive if ellipse IoU is greater than 0.75 and angle error is less than $10°$, or ellipse IoU is greater than 0.75 and aspect ratio is less than 1.2.

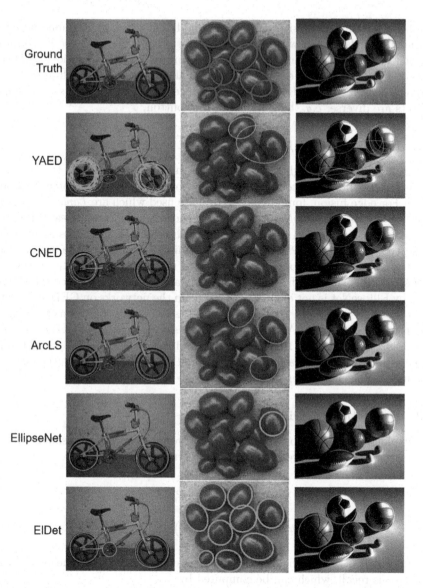

Fig. 6. Qualitative results on GED dataset. The first row shows Groud-truth images; the second to forth rows show the detections by traditional approaches; the results of fifth row is achieved by EllipseNet, which is a CNN-based approach. The last row shows visualization of our method ElDet. As we can see, our approach could successfully detect general elliptic objects.

4.4   Compared Methods

To verify the effectiveness of our *ElDet*, we compare our approach with the CNN based ellipse detection method EllipseNet [13], and also the state-of-the-art

(SOTA) traditional approaches such as YAED [39], CNED [40], and Arc-support Line Segment based method (ArcLS) [7] on GED dataset. Furthermore, we evaluate our method on FDDB dataset to explore the adaptability on downstream tasks.

4.5   Results on GED Dataset

Table 1. Quantitative results on GED dataset. $AP_{0.75}$: True positive when IoU is greater than 0.75. $AP_{0.75}^{10}$: True positive when IoU is greater than 0.75 and angle error is less than 10°.

Methods	$AP_{0.5}$	$AP_{0.5}^{10}$	$AP_{0.75}$	$AP_{0.75}^{10}$	Time/ms
YAED	0.2875	0.2476	0.1942	0.1653	11.14
CNED	0.3691	0.3217	0.3134	0.2748	**9.57**
ArcLS	0.3346	0.3088	0.2312	0.2735	78.23
EllipseNet	0.3138	0.2840	0.1924	0.2735	31.96
ElDet (Ours)	**0.7403**	**0.7215**	**0.5739**	**0.5606**	44.88

Table 1 shows the detailed quantitative results. Our method achieves the best performance with a large margin compared to the state-of-the-art methods. Specifically, on $AP_{0.5}^{10}$ and $AP_{0.75}^{10}$, ElDet achieves 0.7215 and 0.5606 respectively, which indicates our model provides better accuracy of angle regression. Besides, our detection time per image is 34.94 ms on average, which is similar to EllipseNet 31.96 ms. We observe that traditional approaches are highly efficient, though at lower detection accuracy compared to our ElDet. EllipseNet may be more concerned with texture information as traditional CNNs, therefore performs poorly on such a dataset with inconsistent texture information.

Moreover, we visualize some detection examples in Fig. 6 by overlaying the detected ellipses on the original image. From Fig. 6, we observe that our ElDet can handle different situations better and is robust to the interference of complex backgrounds.

Results on FDDB Dataset. ArcLS regresses ellipse based on arc support line segments and requires the objects have elliptic shape. However, the faces in FDDB are not regular ellipses, thus traditional approaches are not suitable for general face detection and we only compare our ElDet with EllipseNet on FDDB dataset.

Table 2 shows the results on FDDB dataset. Our method achieves best scores with 0.8665 on FDDB dataset and outperform EllipseNet by ∼ 3%. The visualizations are shown in Fig. 7. As we can see, our ElDet could address some occlusions and perfectly fit face contours into ellipses. This demonstrates that our framework is rather general in addressing various geometric shapes, and has potential be adapted to various downstream tasks in real-world applications.

| (a) Ground Truth | (b) EllipseNet | (c) ElDet |

Fig. 7. Detection examples on FDDB dataset by our approach.

Table 2. Quantitative results on FDDB dataset.

Methods	$AP_{0.5}$	$AP_{0.5}^{10}$	$AP_{0.75}$	$AP_{0.75}^{10}$	Time/ms
EllipseNet	0.8383	0.6406	0.7788	0.6037	30.91
ElDet	**0.8665**	**0.8181**	**0.8218**	**0.7844**	33.77

Table 3. Quantitative results of different edge maps as data augmentation for our ElDet on GED dataset.

Methods	$AP_{0.5}$	$AP_{0.5}^{10}$	$AP_{0.75}$	$AP_{0.75}^{10}$
Adaptive threshold	0.6599	0.6237	0.5105	0.4850
Sobel	0.7015	0.6650	0.5204	0.4954
Canny	0.7086	0.6705	0.5293	0.5148
Laplacian	0.7018	0.6802	0.5352	0.5270
Fusion	**0.7403**	**0.7215**	**0.5739**	**0.5606**

Comparison of Different Edge Maps. Tabel 3 shows the performance of our ElDet with different edge maps as augmentation input. Among the four individual edge detection methods, *Adaptive Threshold* method is significantly worse than other methods, and Laplacian operator obtained the best performance. Our Edge Fusion Module (EFM) significantly outperforms individual edge map,

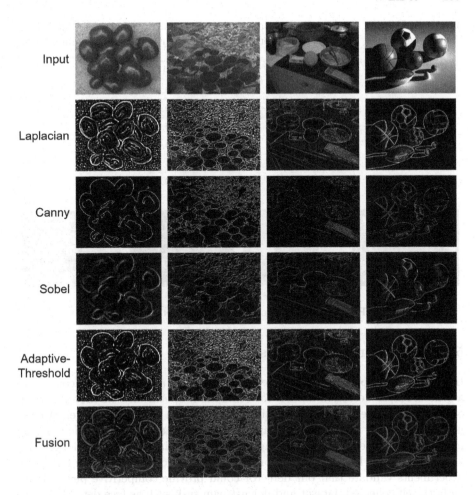

Fig. 8. Qualitative results of different edge extraction methods. From top to bottom are *Input, Laplacian, Canny, Sobel, AdaptiveThreshold* and our *Fusion* maps, respectively.

with an improvement of about 4% in each metric. As shown in Fig. 8, the noise is clearly faded and the edges are relatively clear and complete in our fused edge maps (see last row in Fig. 8), which demonstrates the effectiveness of our EFM.

Ablation Study. Table 4 shows the effects of proposed losses and edge information based data augmentation for ElDet. Firstly, with Gaussian IoU, the performance boosts significantly, *e.g.*, $AP_{0.75}$ increases by 0.09 and $AP_{0.75}^{10}$ increases by 0.14. It shows Gaussian IoU is suitable for object detection with rotation angle. Then, a large margin of improvement can be observed when edge information is added. Finally, when all components including angle loss weight and binary mask prediction are added, the accuracy is further improved.

Table 4. Ablation results on GED dataset. **G:** Gaussian IoU Loss. **W:** Angle Loss Weight. **M:** Ellipse Mask Segmentation. **E:** Edge Map Fusion as Data Augmentation.

Methods	G	W	M	E	$AP_{0.75}$	$AP_{0.75}^{10}$
ElDet	–	–	–	–	0.3624	0.3094
ElDet	✓	–	–	✓	0.4598	0.4439
ElDet	✓	✓	-	-	0.4378	0.4163
ElDet	✓	✓	-	✓	0.4873	0.4571
ElDet	✓	✓	✓	-	0.4513	0.4413
ElDet	✓	✓	✓	✓	**0.5739**	**0.5606**

Fig. 9. Some failure cases of our ElDet method.

5   Conclusion and Discussion

In this paper, we present a simple yet anchor-free ellipse detector and contribute a general ellipse detection dataset for evaluation. Specifically, we first obtain an overall better edge map by edge fusion module which can learn the weight coefficients adaptively and take advantage of the extracted edge information as augmented input. Then, we propose angle loss weight, binary mask prediction loss, and Gaussian IoU loss to jointly improve the CNN model performance. Extensive experiments validate that our detector could provide competitive performance on both self-collected dataset and downstream task such as face detection.

Currently, we believe that our approach still has much space to improve in future research. In some scenarios, our method may fail to detect the ellipses, as shown in Fig. 9. Sometimes the elliptic objects are too large or too small compared to the full image. As a consequence, the detected ellipses have larger deviation to the groundtruth, which possibly is due to the downsampling and model fitting. Moreover, for circular or elliptic objects with overlapping or occlusions, the ellipse regression accuracy may be affected under such situation. It should note that detecting overlapping objects is a common challenge for all anchor-free object detectors. For some complex scenes with low contrast, low illumination, or many ellipses, we observe that ellipse detection is still very challenging.

References

1. Lu, W., Tan, J.: Detection of incomplete ellipse in images with strong noise by iterative randomized hough transform (IRHT). Pattern Recogn. **41**(4), 1268–1279 (2008)

2. Roy, P., Kislay, A., Plonski, P.A., Luby, J., Isler, V.: Vision-based preharvest yield mapping for apple orchards. Comput. Electron. Agric. **164**, 104897 (2019)
3. Lu, C., Wang, H., Gu, C., Wu, K., Guan, X.: Viewpoint estimation for workpieces with deep transfer learning from cold to hot. In: Cheng, L., Leung, A.C.S., Ozawa, S. (eds.) ICONIP 2018. LNCS, vol. 11301, pp. 21–32. Springer, Cham (2018). https://doi.org/10.1007/978-3-030-04167-0_3
4. Lu, C., Gu, C., Wu, K., Xia, S., Wang, H., Guan, X.: Deep transfer neural network using hybrid representations of domain discrepancy. Neurocomputing **409**, 60–73 (2020)
5. Prasad, D.K., Leung, M.K., Cho, S.Y.: Edge curvature and convexity based ellipse detection method. Pattern Recogn. **45**(9), 3204–3221 (2012)
6. Lu, C., Xia, S., Huang, W., Shao, M., Fu, Y.: Circle detection by arc-support line segments. In: 2017 IEEE International Conference on Image Processing (ICIP), pp. 76–80. IEEE (2017)
7. Lu, C., Xia, S., Shao, M., Fu, Y.: Arc-support line segments revisited: an efficient high-quality ellipse detection. IEEE Trans. Image Process. **29**, 768–781 (2019)
8. Li, Y.: Detecting lesion bounding ellipses with gaussian proposal networks. In: Suk, H.-I., Liu, M., Yan, P., Lian, C. (eds.) MLMI 2019. LNCS, vol. 11861, pp. 337–344. Springer, Cham (2019). https://doi.org/10.1007/978-3-030-32692-0_39
9. Ren, S., He, K., Girshick, R., Sun, J.: Faster R-CNN: towards real-time object detection with region proposal networks. IEEE Tran. Pattern Anal. Mach. Intell. **39**(6), 1137–1149 (2017)
10. Geirhos, R., Rubisch, P., Michaelis, C., Bethge, M., Wichmann, F.A., Brendel, W.: ImageNet-trained CNNs are biased towards texture; increasing shape bias improves accuracy and robustness. arXiv preprint arXiv:1811.12231 (2018)
11. Kendall, A., Gal, Y., Cipolla, R.: Multi-task learning using uncertainty to weigh losses for scene geometry and semantics. In: Proceedings of the IEEE Conference on Computer Vision and Pattern Recognition, pp. 7482–7491 (2018)
12. Caruana, R.: Multitask learning. Mach. Learn. **28**(1), 41–75 (1997)
13. Chen, J., Zhang, Y., Wang, J., Zhou, X., He, Y., Zhang, T.: EllipseNet: anchor-free ellipse detection for automatic cardiac biometrics in fetal echocardiography. In: de Bruijne, M., et al. (eds.) MICCAI 2021. LNCS, vol. 12907, pp. 218–227. Springer, Cham (2021). https://doi.org/10.1007/978-3-030-87234-2_21
14. Dong, W., Roy, P., Peng, C., Isler, V.: Ellipse R-CNN: learning to infer elliptical object from clustering and occlusion. IEEE Trans. Image Process. **30**, 2193–2206 (2021)
15. Qian, W., Yang, X., Peng, S., Yan, J., Guo, Y.: Learning modulated loss for rotated object detection. In: Proceedings of the AAAI Conference on Artificial Intelligence, vol. 35, pp. 2458–2466 (2021)
16. Redmon, J., Farhadi, A.: YOLOv3: an incremental improvement. arXiv preprint arXiv:1804.02767 (2018)
17. Huang, L., Yang, Y., Deng, Y., Yu, Y.: DenseBox: unifying landmark localization with end to end object detection. arXiv preprint arXiv:1509.04874 (2015)
18. Tian, Z., Shen, C., Chen, H., He, T.: FCOS: a simple and strong anchor-free object detector. IEEE Trans. Pattern Anal. Mach. Intell. **44**, 1922–1933 (2020)
19. Law, H., Deng, J.: Cornernet: Detecting objects as paired keypoints. In: Proceedings of the European conference on computer vision (ECCV), pp. 734–750 (2018)
20. Lu, C., Koniusz, P.: Few-shot keypoint detection with uncertainty learning for unseen species. In: Proceedings of the IEEE/CVF Conference on Computer Vision and Pattern Recognition (CVPR), pp. 19416–19426 (2022)

21. Cao, Z., Simon, T., Wei, S.E., Sheikh, Y.: Realtime multi-person 2D pose estimation using part affinity fields. In: Proceedings of the IEEE Conference on Computer Vision and Pattern Recognition, pp. 7291–7299 (2017)
22. Neubeck, A., Van Gool, L.: Efficient non-maximum suppression. In: 18th International Conference on Pattern Recognition (ICPR 2006), vol. 3, pp. 850–855. IEEE (2006)
23. Xu, Y., et al.: Gliding vertex on the horizontal bounding box for multi-oriented object detection. IEEE Trans. Pattern Anal. Mach. Intell. **43**(4), 1452–1459 (2020)
24. Yang, X., Yan, J.: Arbitrary-oriented object detection with circular smooth label. In: Vedaldi, A., Bischof, H., Brox, T., Frahm, J.-M. (eds.) ECCV 2020. LNCS, vol. 12353, pp. 677–694. Springer, Cham (2020). https://doi.org/10.1007/978-3-030-58598-3_40
25. Yang, X., Hou, L., Zhou, Y., Wang, W., Yan, J.: Dense label encoding for boundary discontinuity free rotation detection. In: Proceedings of the IEEE/CVF Conference on Computer Vision and Pattern Recognition, pp. 15819–15829 (2021)
26. Yang, X., Yan, J., Ming, Q., Wang, W., Zhang, X., Tian, Q.: Rethinking rotated object detection with gaussian wasserstein distance loss. In: International Conference on Machine Learning, pp. 11830–11841. PMLR (2021)
27. Yang, X., et al.: Learning high-precision bounding box for rotated object detection via Kullback-Leibler divergence. Adv. Neural Inf. Process. Syst. **34**, 18381–18394 (2021)
28. Yu, F., Wang, D., Shelhamer, E., Darrell, T.: Deep layer aggregation. In: Proceedings of the IEEE Conference on Computer Vision and Pattern Recognition, pp. 2403–2412 (2018)
29. Zhou, X., Wang, D., Krähenbühl, P.: Objects as points. arXiv preprint arXiv:1904.07850 (2019)
30. Lin, T.Y., Goyal, P., Girshick, R., He, K., Dollár, P.: Focal loss for dense object detection. In: Proceedings of the IEEE International Conference on Computer Vision, pp. 2980–2988 (2017)
31. He, K., Zhang, X., Ren, S., Sun, J.: Deep residual learning for image recognition. In: Proceedings of the IEEE Conference on Computer Vision and Pattern Recognition, pp. 770–778 (2016)
32. Canny, J.: A computational approach to edge detection. IEEE Trans. Pattern Anal. Mach. Intell. **6**, 679–698 (1986)
33. Gao, W., Zhang, X., Yang, L., Liu, H.: An improved sobel edge detection. In: 2010 3rd International Conference on Computer Science and Information Technology, vol. 5, pp. 67–71. IEEE (2010)
34. Jain, R., Kasturi, R., Schunck, B.G., et al.: Machine Vision, vol. 5. McGraw-Hill, New York (1995)
35. Bradley, D., Roth, G.: Adaptive thresholding using the integral image. J. Graph. Tools **12**(2), 13–21 (2007)
36. Panaretos, V.M., Zemel, Y.: Statistical aspects of wasserstein distances. arXiv preprint arXiv:1806.05500 (2018)
37. He, K., Gkioxari, G., Dollár, P., Girshick, R.: Mask R-CNN. In: Proceedings of the IEEE International Conference on Computer Vision, pp. 2961–2969 (2017)
38. Jain, V., Learned-Miller, E.: FDDB: a benchmark for face detection in unconstrained settings. Technical report, UMass Amherst technical report (2010)
39. Fornaciari, M., Prati, A., Cucchiara, R.: A fast and effective ellipse detector for embedded vision applications. Pattern Recogn. **47**(11), 3693–3708 (2014)
40. Jia, Q., Fan, X., Luo, Z., Song, L., Qiu, T.: A fast ellipse detector using projective invariant pruning. IEEE Trans. Image Process. **26**(8), 3665–3679 (2017)

Truly Unsupervised Image-to-Image Translation with Contrastive Representation Learning

Zhiwei Hong[1], Jianxing Feng[2], and Tao Jiang[1,3(✉)]

[1] Tsinghua University, Beijing 100084, China
hzw17@mails.tsinghua.edu.cn
[2] Haohua Technology Co., Ltd., Shanghai, China
[3] University of California, Riverside, CA 92521, USA
jiang@cs.ucr.edu

Abstract. Image-to-image translation is a classic image generation task that attempts to translate an image from the source domain to an analogous image in the target domain. Recent advances in deep generative networks have shown remarkable capabilities in translating images among different domains. Most of these models either require pixel-level (with paired input and output images) or domain-level (with image domain labels) supervision to help the translation task. However, there are practical situations where the required supervisory information is difficult to collect and one would need to perform truly unsupervised image translation on a large number of images without paired image information or domain labels. In this paper, we present a truly unsupervised image-to-image translation model that performs the image translation task without any extra supervision. The crux of our model is an embedding network that extracts the domain and style information of the input style (or reference) image with contrastive representation learning and serves the translation module that actually carries out the translation task. The embedding network and the translation module can be integrated together for training and benefit from each other. Extensive experimental evaluation has been performed on various datasets concerning both cross-domain and multi-domain translation. The results demonstrate that our model outperforms the best truly unsupervised image-to-image translation model in the literature. In addition, our model can be easily adapted to take advantage of available domain labels to achieve a performance comparable to the best supervised image translation methods when all domain labels are known or a superior performance when only some domain labels are known.

1 Introduction

Image-to-image translation (I2I) is a classic image generation task [25] that attempts to translate an image from the source domain to an analogous image in

---

Supplementary Information The online version contains supplementary material available at https://doi.org/10.1007/978-3-031-26313-2_15.

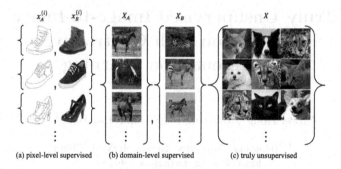

Fig. 1. Different levels of supervision. (**a**) Pixel-level supervision consists of training examples $\{x_A^{(i)}, x_B^{(i)}\}_{i=1}^N$, where $x_A^{(i)}$ and $x_B^{(i)}$ have matching content. (**b**) Domain-level supervision consists of a source set $X_A = \{x_A^{(i)}\}_{i=1}^N$ of images from domain A and a target set $X_B = \{x_B^{(j)}\}_{j=1}^N$ of images from domain B, with no information provided as to which $x_B^{(j)}$ matches each $x_A^{(i)}$. The multi-domain translation scenario is similar. (**c**) A truly unsupervised instance simply consists of a set of images X where neither matching image pairs nor domain information are provided.

the target domain while preserving the content representations. I2I has attracted extensive attention nowadays due to its wide range of applications in many computer vision and image processing tasks such as image synthesis, image style transfer, human pose estimation, *etc.* Thanks to the rapid development of deep neural networks especially generative adversarial networks, image-to-image translation has achieved remarkable progress in the past few years. Isola *et al.* [13] first used a conditional Generative Adversarial Network (cGAN) [23] to perform image-to-image translation with pixel-level supervised input-output image pairs. But the applicability of this method seems to be restricted in many real situations, including image synthesis and style transfer, where such matching image pairs are not available. Therefor, some unsupervised image-to-image translation models such as CycleGAN [35] and UNIT [19] have been proposed to deal with image translation between two domains (*i.e.*, cross-domain image translation) without pixel-level supervision. In addition to cross-domain image translation, many multi-domain image translation models [5,12,18,20,28,31] have been developed in the last few years. Though these models are generally called **unsupervised** in contrast to the pixel-level supervised methods [13,27], they are actually not truly unsupervised, since they implicitly assume that the domain labels of the training images are given *a priori*. However, this assumption may be hard to satisfy in practice when the number of domains and samples increases. In particular, when we are given a large number of images from unknown sources (FFHQ [15]), it might be expensive and difficult to figure out the domain of each image, especially because some of the domain boundaries may be vague. So, the truly unsupervised image-to-image translation problem (where neither pixel-level paired images nor domain labels are available) has been introduced by Kyungjune *et al.* [2] recently. As described in [2], it can help reduce the effort of data annotation for model training and provide robustness against noisy labels produced by a manual labeling process. More importantly, it may also serve as a strong baseline for developing semi-supervised image translation models. Here, we are given two images x_A (the source or content image) and x_B (the reference or style image) and our goal is to translate x_A to an analogous image in the same domain as x_B while preserving its original content. See Fig. 1 for a more detailed illustration of three levels of supervision in image translation. Though a solution to this problem was proposed in [2], it suffers from some serious issues such as the content loss issue discussed in COCO-FUNIT [28]. Since there is no supervision, it is difficult to control what parts of the input style image should be incorporated or transferred into the input content image. Ideally, the transferred information should only include style, such as fur texture and color in animal images. In reality, other types of information such as the pose of objects often get in as well. Hence, how to construct a proper embedding of the reference image is a critical step in truly unsupervised image translation. COCO-FUNIT [28] tried to reduce the style embedding (or code) variance of different input image crops to tackle this problem. More specifically, it utilizes the content embedding of the input content image to normalize the style embedding of the input style image, which helps to improve the translation performance but cannot completely eliminate the confusions between content and style representations.

In this paper, we extend the work in [2] and present a general **C**ontrastive representation learning based truly **UN**supervised **I**mage-to-image **T**ranslation model (**CUNIT**). Our overall method proceeds in three steps. First, we cluster images into (pseudo) domains to create pseudo domain labels for each image. Second, we extract the unique style embedding of the input style image. Finally, we learn to translate images between pseudo domains with the guide of style embeddings and pseudo domain labels. The first two steps are realized by using a style embedding network with two branches (or modules) that output the pseudo domain label and style embedding respectively. Here, pseudo domain labels are generated by a differentiable clustering method based on mutual information maximization [14]. To create the style embedding, a Siamese network architecture [4, 7], which is flexible with batch size and does not require negative samples, is adopted to tackle the content-loss problem discussed in COCO-FUNIT [28]. We try to ensure that the style embedding of an input image is close to those of its augmented versions (*e.g.*, images obtained by RandomResizedCrop [3]) but far from those of other images by using a normalized L_2 distance loss. The clustering and style embedding modules share a common encoder in the style embedding network so both can benefit from each other. To realize the last step of our method, a cGAN is adopted to perform reference-guided image translation. After integrating the style embedding network and cGAN together, our model is able to separate image domains and perform image translation smoothly under a truly unsupervised setting.

Extensive experimental evaluation has been performed on various datasets concerning both cross-domain and multi-domain scenarios. The results demonstrate that our model outperforms the best truly unsupervised I2I model in the literature and is comparable or even superior to the supervised I2I models when the domain labels are fully or partially provided. The major contributions of our work include: **(1)** We extend the work in [2] and present a general model for truly unsupervised image-to-image translation without requiring any explicit supervision (at neither the pixel-level nor domain-level). **(2)** We adopt a new contrastive representation learning architecture to control the style embedding so as to help deal with the style code variance problem [28] and extract better style features. We also introduce a new reconstruction loss to better preserve content features. The superior performance of our model in extensive experiments over the state-of-the-art (SOTA) image-to-image translation methods demonstrate the effectiveness of both above techniques. **(3)** Our model could easily be adapted to take advantage of available domain labels to perform comparably to the best supervised image translation methods when all domain labels are known or significantly better when only some domain labels are known.

2   Related Work

Generative Adversarial Networks. Image generation and synthesis have been widely investigated in recent years. Different from auto-encoder architectures like VAE [17], generative adversarial networks (GANs) [6] play a zero-sum game and is composed of two parts: a generator G and a discriminator D. The generator G is trained to generate samples that are closed to real data from a random variable and D is trained to distinguish whether a sample is generated by G or from real data. Mehdi and Simon proposed conditional GANs [23] (cGANs) to generate data based on a particular condition. To address the stability issues in GANs, Wasserstein-GAN (WGAN) [1] was proposed to optimize an approximation of the Wasserstein distance. To further improve the vanishing and exploding gradient problems of WGAN, Gulrajani *et al.* [8] proposed WGAN-GP that uses gradient penalty instead of the weight clipping to deal with the Lipschitz constraint in WGAN.

Pixel-Level Supervised I2I. Isola *et al.* first proposed Pix2Pix [13] that utilizes a cGAN to do the image translation based on pixel-level supervised input-output image pairs. Following this seminal work, a sequence of I2I models have shown remarkable performance. For example, Wang *et al.* proposed pix2pixHD [32] to learn a mapping that converts a semantic image to a high-resolution photo-realistic image. Park *et al.* proposed SPADE [27] to further improve pix2pixHD on handling diverse input labels and delivering better output quality.

Domain-Level Supervised and Truly Unsupervised I2I. Apart from the above pixel-level supervised I2I, many unsupervised I2I methods have been introduced in the past few years. These so-called unsupervised methods do not need matching image pairs but still explicitly require the image domain information. Here, we call them domain-level supervised methods as opposed to our truly unsupervised setting. Zhu *et al.* proposed CycleGAN [35] to deal with cross-domain I2I with a cycle consistency loss. UNIT [19] tries to learn a one-to-one mapping between two visual domains based on a shared latent space assumption. MUNIT [12] further learns a many-to-many mapping between two visual domains. In MSGAN [21], a simple yet effective regularization term was proposed to address the mode collapse issue in cGANs that improved image diversity without loss of quality. Inspired by few-shot learning, Liu *et al.* proposed FUNIT [20] to learn a style-guided image translation model that can generate translations in unseen domains. COCO-FUNIT [28] further improved FUNIT with a content-conditioned style encoding scheme for style code computation. Note that these methods all require image domain labels for training. Wang *et al.* [33] tried to utilize the noise-tolerant pseudo labeling scheme to reduce the labeling cost at the training process. Recently, Kyungjune *et al.* introduced the first method TUNIT [2] for performing the truly unsupervised I2I task.

Contrastive Representation Learning and Unsupervised Clustering. Unsupervised representation learning aims to extract informative features for downstream tasks without any human supervision. Self-supervised learning represented by contrastive learning has demonstrated its effectiveness and remarkable performance in unsupervised representation learning recently. Different from generative-based models such as the auto-encoder, contrastive learning is a discriminative-based scheme whose core idea is to attract different augmented views of the same image (positive pairs) and repulse augmented views of different images (negative pairs). Based on contrastive learning, SimCLR [3] used very large batch sizes and MoCo [9] built a dynamic dictionary with a queue and a moving-averaged encoder to deal with the memory bank problem [34]. They both require high-quality negative samples to achieve a good performance. Interestingly, subsequent work BYOL [7] suggested that negative samples are not necessary for contrastive learning, and Simsiam [4] claimed that simple Siamese networks can learn informative representations without using negative sample pairs, large batches or momentum encoders. These results have become the new SOTA self-supervised visual representation learning methods. On the other hand, IIC [14] utilized mutual information maximization in an unsupervised manner so that the model clusters images while assigning the images to clusters evenly. In this paper, we integrate both the unsupervised clustering and representation learning methods to deal with the truly unsupervised I2I downstream task.

3 Method

3.1 Overview

Let X be a dataset consisting of images from $K(\geq 2)$ different domains. Suppose that K is unknown and for each image $x_i \in X$, its domain label y_i is also unknown. We use $\hat{K}$ to denote the estimated value of K and treat $\hat{K}$ as a hyper-parameter in training. The goal of (truly) unsupervised image-to-image translation model is to translate a 'content' image x_A from some domain A to an analogous image of some domain B as specified by a reference 'style' image x_B (*i.e.*, the domain that contains x_B), while preserving the content information of x_A. Our model consists of three components: a style embedding network, a

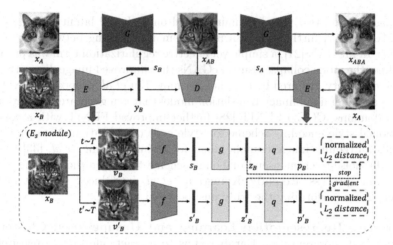

Fig. 2. An overview of the proposed CUNIT framework. The style embedding network E takes a reference image x_B as the input and estimates its pseudo domain label y_B and style embedding s_B. The pseudo domain label y_B is then used to train the domain-specific discriminator D. The style embedding s_B and the gradient feedback from D help the generator network G to translate the input content image x_A to the analogous image x_{AB} in the domain of x_B while preserving the content information of x_A.

conditional generator and a multi-task domain-specific discriminator (as shown in Fig. 2). The style embedding network is the key component that outputs the pseudo domain label y_B and style embedding s_B of the input reference image x_B. Then style embedding s_B is fed into the conditional generator as a 'condition' to guide the translation. The pseudo domain label y_B is fed into the domain-specific discriminator that forces the generator to generate an image with the style (*e.g.* fur texture and color in animal images) of x_B and content (*e.g.* object pose) of x_A. In general, we regard the features of an image that are not affected by various augmentation operations (such as cropping and affine transformations) as its styles while the others as its content. This is reflected in the choice of the loss function for training the contrastive style embedding module E_s (described below).

3.2   The Style Embedding Network

The style embedding network E consists of two branches (or modules) E_y and E_s that output the pseudo domain label y and style embedding s respectively.

Unsupervised Domain Estimation E_y. The domain information, necessary for the subsequent domain-specific discriminator in our model, is unfortunately not available during training. To resolve this issue, we employ an unsupervised clustering approach to produce pseudo domain labels. Many methods have been proposed to deal with unsupervised image clustering with impressive performance in the past few years. Here, we adopt a differentiable clustering method called IIC [14] that maximizes the mutual information (MI) between feature vectors of two images. Given an image x, define $p = E_y(x)$ as the output of E_y, where p represents the probability vector of x over $\hat{K}$ domains. Similarly, we define x^+ and p^+ as the augmented versions of x and p. The mutual information between p and p^+ is thus $I(p, p^+) = H(p) - H(p|p^+)$. The value $I(p, p^+)$ reaches its optimum when the entropy $H(p)$ is maximized and the conditional entropy $H(p|p^+)$ is minimized. By maximizing the mutual information, E_y is encouraged to distribute all images as evenly as possible over $\hat{K}$ domains while assigning paired images (x, x^+) to the same domain. The module E_y is trained via the following objective function:

$$\mathcal{L}_{MI} = -I(\boldsymbol{p}, \boldsymbol{p}^+) = -I(\boldsymbol{P}) = -\sum_{i=1}^{\hat{K}}\sum_{j=1}^{\hat{K}} \boldsymbol{P}_{ij} \ln \frac{\boldsymbol{P}_{ij}}{\boldsymbol{P}_i \boldsymbol{P}_j}, \tag{1}$$

$$s.t. \quad \boldsymbol{P} = \mathbb{E}_{x^+ \sim T(x)|x \sim p_{data}(x)}[E_y(x) \cdot E_y(x^+)^T]$$

where T is a composition of random augmentations such as random cropping and affine transformations. $\boldsymbol{P}_i = \boldsymbol{P}(p = i)$ denotes the $\hat{K}$-dimensional marginal probability vector, and $\boldsymbol{P}_{ij} = \boldsymbol{P}(p = i, \boldsymbol{p}^+ = j)$ denotes the joint probability. (See [14] for more details of this objective function.) Here, the pseudo domain label $y = argmax(E_y(x))$ is generated as a one-hot vector to be fed to the domain-specific discriminator.

Contrastive Style Embedding E_s. To perform reference-guided image translation, a style embedding of the reference image is required for the generator. Inspired by [4,7], we use contrastive learning based on a Siamese architecture to learn the style embedding. As mentioned in the last paragraph of Sect. 2, such a model can learn informative representations without using negative sample pairs, large batches or momentum encoders. The Siamese architecture here is composed of an encoder f, a projector g, and a predictor q. During contrastive learning, the reference image x_B is randomly augmented by two transformations t and t' sampled from a transformation family T (as shown in Fig. 2) to generate two views v_B and v'_B. The transformation family includes widely used augmentations [3], such as RandomResizedCrop, RandomFlip, GaussianBlur, etc. The views v_B and v'_B are encoded by the encoder f to obtain the style embeddings s_B and s'_B. Then, the projector g and predictor q are applied to s_B or s'_B sequentially. For these two augmented views, denote the output of the projector g as $z_B \triangleq f(s_B)$ and $z'_B \triangleq f(s'_B)$ and the output of q as $p_B \triangleq q(z_B)$ and $p'_B \triangleq q(z'_B)$. We force p_B to be similar to z'_B and p'_B to be similar to z_B by minimizing the symmetric loss:

$$\mathcal{L}_{co}^E = \frac{1}{2}||\widetilde{p}_B - \widetilde{z'_B}||_2^2 + \frac{1}{2}||\widetilde{p'_B} - \widetilde{z}_B||_2^2 \tag{2}$$

where $\widetilde{\cdot} \triangleq \frac{\cdot}{||\cdot||_2}$ and $||\cdot||_2$ denotes the l_2 norm. Here, z_B and z'_B are detached from the computational graph before calculating the loss such that the gradient would not back-propagate through z_B and z'_B. In our experiments, the contrastive style embedding module significantly improves the quality of unsupervised image clustering compared to using only IIC [14] due to the shared encoder f between the two modules. A similar phenomenon has also been observed in [2].

3.3   The Image Translation Module

As shown in Fig. 2, the image translation module is in fact a conditional generative adversarial network (cGAN) [23]. It takes both the original source domain image x_A and the style embedding s_B of the reference image x_B as the input to generate x_{AB} that should have the same target domain label y_B as x_B. The style embedding s_B is fed to the decoding layers of G using a multi-scale AdaIN [11] technique. The discriminator D is a multi-task domain-specific discriminator [22] and it takes the pseudo domain label y_B as the input to guide the generator G to produce more realistic images. To train the entire image translation model, three loss functions are adopted. (a) The GAN loss is used to produce more realistic images in the target domain. (b) A style contrastive loss is used to further improve the quality of the generated images and prevent style corruption. (c) An image reconstruction loss is used to help the generated images preserve more content information (*i.e.*, domain-invariant features).

GAN Loss. Given the content image x_A, reference image x_B, pseudo domain label y_B, and style embedding s_B, the GAN is trained with the following objective function:

$$\mathcal{L}_{adv} = \mathbb{E}_{x_B \sim p_{data}(x)}[\log D_{y_B}(x_B)] + \mathbb{E}_{x_A, x_B \sim p_{data}(x)}[\log(1 - D_{y_B}(G(x_A, s_B)))] \quad (3)$$

where $D_{y_B}(\cdot)$ denotes the logits from the domain-specific (y_B) discriminator. Note that there is no direct gradient backward propagation here from the discriminator D to style embedding network E because y_B is a one-hot vector only used to determine which head of the multi-task discriminator D to use.

Style Contrastive Loss. In order to prevent degenerate solutions where the generator ignores the given style embedding s_B and synthesizes a random image of domain B, we impose a style contrastive loss to the generator:

$$\mathcal{L}_{style}^G = \mathbb{E}_{x_A, x_B \sim p_{data}(x)}[-\log \frac{\exp(s_{AB} \cdot s_B)}{\sum_{i=0}^{N} \exp(s_{AB} \cdot s_i^- /\tau)}] \quad (4)$$

where $s_{AB} = E_s(x_{AB}) = E_s(G(x_A, s_B))$ denotes the style embedding of the translated image x_{AB} and s_i^- denotes the negative style embeddings (*i.e.*, style embeddings of other samples in the same mini-batch). This loss forces the generated image x_{AB} to have a dissimilar style to images other than the reference image x_B. It also prevents the encoder from mapping all images to the same style embedding.

Reconstruction Loss. To better preserve the domain-invariant features (*i.e.*, the content information) of the content image x_A, an improved image reconstruction loss with a new term is introduced. The loss is composed of two parts, the self-reconstruction loss $\mathcal{L}_{self\_rec}$ and the cross-reconstruction loss $\mathcal{L}_{cross\_rec}$ (new term, similar to the work in [35]), as follows:

$$\mathcal{L}_{rec} = \mathbb{E}_{x_A \sim p_{data}(x)}[||x_A - G(x_A, s_A)||_1] + \mathbb{E}_{x_A, x_B \sim p_{data}(x)}[||x_A - G(G(x_A, s_B), s_A)||_1] \quad (5)$$

where $\mathcal{L}_{rec} = \mathcal{L}_{self\_rec} + \mathcal{L}_{cross\_rec}$ is intended to minimize the total l_1 distance between the source image x_A and its self-reconstructed image $G(x_A, s_A)$ and between x_A and its cross-reconstructed image $x_{ABA} = G(G(x_A, s_B), s_A)$. The reconstruction loss encourages G to preserve the domain-invariant information (*e.g.*, object pose).

3.4 Overall Training

In our experiment, the unsupervised clustering module E_y and style embedding module E_s share a common encoder f in the style embedding network E so both can benefit from each other. The clustering module may obtain rich features acquired by contrastive representation learning in the style embedding module and improve its accuracy in generating pseudo domain labels. The style embedding module can also extract more domain-specific features and prevent the entire model from collapsing with the help of the clustering module. Once the embedding network E has been sufficiently trained, it can be further refined with the cGAN module jointly to perform image translation as follows. The generator G takes the style embedding extracted from input style image as a reference to translate the input content image to its analog that is expected to be in the same domain as the reference style image. With the adversarial loss feedback from the cGAN, the style embedding network E further improves its learned domain-separating features and extracts style embeddings with richer information that can help the generator G fool the domain-specific discriminator D. After integrating the style embedding network and the cGAN module together, our model is able to separate image domains and perform image-to-image translation successfully under a truly unsupervised setting.

The overall objective for above mentioned style embedding network E, generator G and discriminator D is given by

$$
\begin{aligned}
\mathcal{L}_D &= -\mathcal{L}_{adv} \\
\mathcal{L}_G &= \mathcal{L}_{adv} + \lambda^G_{style}\mathcal{L}^G_{style} + \lambda_{rec}\mathcal{L}_{rec} \\
\mathcal{L}_E &= \mathcal{L}_G + \lambda_{MI}\mathcal{L}_{MI} + \lambda_{co}\mathcal{L}^E_{co}
\end{aligned}
\tag{6}
$$

where λ^G_{style}, λ_{rec}, λ_{MI}, and λ^E_{co} are weights for balancing different loss terms. More details about these parameters are given in the supplementary materials.

4 Experiments

In this section, we evaluate our model on both domain-labeled data and unlabeled data under different experimental settings (*i.e.*, cross-domain and multidomain). The performance of our method is compared both quantitatively and qualitatively with that of the representative (and SOTA) published methods. The experiments are grouped according to (1) truly unsupervised settings and (2) semi-supervised settings when some (but not all) domain labels are available. We also perform ablation studies to assess the impact of the proposed objective functions, training strategy and choice of domain numbers.

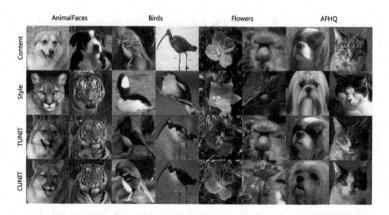

Fig. 3. Truly unsupervised image-to-image translation results on different datasets.

Datasets. To evaluate performance on multi-domain image translation, we use the following three popular labeled datasets: AnimalFaces [20], Birds [30] and Flowers [24]. Following the strategies in [2], we select ten classes from each of the three dataset, referred to as *AnimalFaces-10*, *Birds-10* and *Flowers-10*. When these datasets are used in truly unsupervised image translation, their the domain labels are simply masked. For cross-domain image translation evaluation, we use the dataset Summer2Winter and Dog2Cat from CycleGAN [35]. For data without domain labels, a high quality AFHQ [5] dataset is adopted. AFHQ involves roughly three groups of animals (cats, dogs and wild animals), where each group consists of diverse breeds/species with different styles but the exact domain labels are not provided.

Evaluation Metrics and Compared Methods. We consider the following three metrics, *Inception Score (IS)* [29], the mean of class-wise *Fréchet Inception Distance (mFID)* [10] and *Translation Accuracy (Acc)* [20] in our experiments. The IS and mFID scores have been widely used in GAN-based image analyses to evaluate the generated image quality and diversity. The smaller an mFID score is, the better the performance is, which is the opposite for IS scores. The Acc score is used to evaluate whether a model is able to generate images of the same style as the target domain. It is a percent number between 0 and 100%. For experiments under truly unsupervised situation, we compare our model with TUNIT [2]. To the best of our knowledge, TUNIT is the only method that has been proposed in the literature to address the truly unsupervised I2I problem. For multi-domain supervised or semi-supervised image translation (where some but not all domain labels are given), we compare our model with COCO-FUNIT [28], SEMIT [33], Kim *et al.* [16] and TUNIT. Note that both TUNIT and our model can be easily adapted to take advantage of the available domain labels in their loss functions. We also compare our model with CycleGAN [35], UNIT [19], MSGAN [21], CUT [26] and COCO-FUNIT in cross-domain image translation task.

4.1 Truly Unsupervised Image-to-Image Translation

To verify that our proposed method is able to handle truly unsupervised image-to-image translation well, we evaluate our model on the datasets AnimalFaces-10, Birds-10, Flowers-10, and AFHQ. During the training, the domain labels of the first three datasets are masked as mentioned before. However, the labels are used later on for quantitative evaluation. Since AFHQ has three groups of images (cat, dog and wild), we train a separate model for each group. For all experiments on truly unsupervised image translation, we use TUNIT as the baseline and we set the number of clusters $\hat{K} = 10$ for all models as done in [2].

Table 1. Quantitative evaluation of our model under truly unsupervised setting on different datasets with comparison to TUNIT [2]. The arrows indicate the directions of more desired values.

Dataset	Method	mFID $\downarrow$	IS $\uparrow$	Acc $\uparrow$
AnimalFaces-10	TUNIT	47.9	26.6	84.2
	CUNIT	45.2	28.9	88.3
Birds-10	TUNIT	82.3	73.8	62.2
	CUNIT	74.6	78.4	67.5
Flowers-10	TUNIT	67.3	48.7	65.8
	CUNIT	60.7	52.3	70.3

Figure 3 and Table 1 show the visual results and quantitative evaluation of CUNIT and TUNIT on the four datasets. From the images in Fig. 3, we observe that CUNIT is able to capture more subtle style features (*e.g.* the fur textures of cats and dogs and the color information of birds and flowers) than TUNIT. More visual results can be found in the supplementary materials. Table 1 shows that CUNIT outperforms TUNIT by 5.6%, 8.6% and 5% in terms of mFID, IS and Acc, respectively, on AnimalFaces-10. On the datasets Birds-10 and Flowers-10, CUNIT outperformed TUNIT by at least 6% with respect to all evaluation metrics. Because the AFHQ dataset has no ground truth domain labels, we are not able to provide the quantitative scores on AFHQ. In summary, these experimental results suggest that our model outperforms TUNIT significantly in truly unsupervised image-to-image translation.

4.2 Domain-Level Supervised or Semi-Supervised Image Translation

Cross-Domain (Supervised) Image Translation. Recall that Cycle-GAN [35] adopts a cycle-consistency loss and UNIT [19] makes a shared-latent space assumption to learn a mapping between two visual domains, and both are representative models in cross-domain I2I. MSGAN [21] further improves the diversity of the generated images without loss of quality using a simple yet

Table 2. Quantitative evaluation (based on mFID) of our model with comparison to other methods in cross-domain image-to-image translation.

Method	CycleGAN [35]	UNIT [19]	MSGAN [21]	CUT [26]	COCO-FUNIT [28]	CUNIT (ours)
Summer2Winter	78.7	73.6	66.4	58.4	55.9	53.3
Dog2Cat	85.7	79.3	71.5	68.6	66.1	63.8

Table 3. Quantitative evaluation (based on mFID) in multi-domain semi-supervised image-to-image translation with partial domain labels available during training.

Method	AnimalFaces-10				Birds-10				Flowers-10			
	20%	40%	60%	80%	20%	40%	60%	80%	20%	40%	60%	80%
COCO-FUNIT [28]	104.8	85.9	75.3	59.6	129.5	108.7	98.3	82.9	128.6	105.2	87.5	70.4
SEMIT [33]	53.3	52.1	50.5	49.7	87.4	85.2	83.9	82.6	73.1	71.3	69.8	68.5
Kim et al. [16]	47.3	46.1	45.4	44.7	79.1	77.4	75.8	74.6	64.9	63.3	62.4	61.2
TUNIT [2]	46.2	46.2	45.9	45.6	80.5	80.1	79.6	79.5	65.7	65.4	64.9	65.0
CUNIT (ours)	44.9	44.1	44.3	43.9	73.8	73.2	73.5	72.9	59.8	59.6	59.1	58.9

effective regularization term and has achieved impressive performance on cross-domain I2I. CUT [26] introduces contrastive learning to I2I successfully. COCO-FUNIT is the SOTA multi-domain image translation model that could also be applied in the cross-domain situation. We compare CUNIT with all above methods on the Summer2Winter and Dog2Cat datasets. Table 2 shows that CUNIT outperforms CycleGAN, UNIT, MSGAN, CUT, and COCO-FUNIT by 32% and 25%, 27% and 19%, 19% and 10%, 8% and 7%, and 4% and 3% in terms of mFID on the two datasets, respectively. Hence, CUNIT can generate images with more diversity and better quality than the SOTA cross-domain image translation methods. Some supportive visual results are given in supplementary Fig. S5.

Multi-domain Semi-supervised Image Translation with Partial Domain Labels. Since there are only two domains in cross-domain image translation, it is relatively easy to separate the domains and extract style embeddings for CUNIT. Now we evaluate the model's performance on multiple domains and compare it with the SOTA multi-domain image translation models COCO-FUNIT [28] (supervised), Kim et al. [16] and SEMIT [33] (semi-supervised), and TUNIT [2]. Recall that COCO-FUNIT is a domain-level fully supervised model while CUNIT and TUNIT are truly unsupervised. However, the latter two models can be easily modified to take advantage of the available labels as detailed below. In many practical situations, there may be a large number of images but only a few of them have domain labels. So, we also conduct a semi-supervised experiment as in [2] to test how these models perform when partial domain labels are provided.

The datasets AnimalFaces-10, Birds-10 and Flowers-10 are used in the experiment. Let X be a (whole) dataset. We separate X into the labeled part $X_{labeled}$

Table 4. Ablation study on various components of CUNIT and training strategies using the AnimalFaces-10 dataset.

Configuration	mFID ↓	IS ↑	Acc ↑
CUNIT w\joint	45.2	28.9	88.3
CUNIT w\sequential	45.8	28.1	87.8
CUNIT w\o $\mathcal{L}_{co}$	48.5	26.5	83.4
CUNIT w\o $\mathcal{L}_{style}^{G}$	47.6	27.4	86.3
CUNIT w\o $\mathcal{L}_{rec}$	47.9	27.2	85.9
CUNIT w\o $\mathcal{L}_{cross\_rec}$	46.7	27.8	86.9

Table 5. Quantitative evaluation (based on mFID) of our model using different pseudo domain numbers $\hat{K}$ on AnimalFaces-10.

$\hat{K}$	1	4	7	10	13	16	20	30	50
mFID ↓	91.4	62.3	51.4	45.2	46.6	47.5	48.5	50.7	54.3

and unlabeled part $X_{unlabeled}$ with a ratio $\alpha = |X_{labeled}|/|X|$. Under this semi-supervised setting, we add an additional cross-entropy loss term to our model between the ground truth domain labels and pseudo domain labels estimated by the style embedding network on data $X_{labeled}$. The ground truth domain labels in $X_{labeled}$ are also used for training the domain-specific discriminator. A similar modification is also applied to TUNIT. In this experiment, we set the ratio α to 20%, 40%, 60%, and 80% as in [2]. The results are shown in Table 3. The performance of COCO-FUNIT significantly decays quickly when α decreases while CUNIT, TUNIT, Kim et al. [16] and SEMIT remain relatively stable. Although the latter four methods are more robust, CUNIT still outperforms the other three methods significantly in terms of mFID on all three datasets and under all ratios of α. This experiment shows that CUNIT can be easily adapted to the semi-supervised image translation scenario when some domain labels are available with a performance superior to the existing methods. Some supportive visual results are given in supplementary Fig. S6.

4.3 Some Analyses of the Proposed Model

In this section, we analyze the impact of our proposed objective functions, training strategy and choice of domain numbers on the performance of CUNIT.

Ablation Study. In Table 4, we ablate various components of our model and measure their impact on performance in truly unsupervised image-to-image translation on the AnimalFaces-10 dataset. We observe that joint training of the style embedding network and image translation network has a better performance than training the two models sequentially. The loss $\mathcal{L}_{co}$ is the most important one among the three loss terms ($\mathcal{L}_{co}$, $\mathcal{L}_{style}^{G}$ and $\mathcal{L}_{rec}$), which improved mFID by 3.3(6.8%), IS by 2.4(9%) and Acc by 4.9%. We also observe that the mFID score of CUNIT without using the cross-reconstruction loss term $\mathcal{L}_{cross\_rec}$ in Eq. 5 was 46.7 on the AnimalFaces-10 dataset (vs 45.2 with the term), which clearly demonstrates the effectiveness of this new term. The results indicate that CUNIT has benefited a lot from the jointly trained style embedding network based on contrastive representation learning.

Sensitivity to $\hat{K}$. The hyper-parameter $\hat{K}$ (the number of pseudo domains used in training) may influence how CUNIT clusters the images and hence its performance in truly unsupervised I2I. We test CUNIT on the AnimalFaces-10 dataset with different values of $\hat{K}$ and summarize its performance in Table 5. As expected, the model achieves the best performance in terms of mFID when $\hat{K}$ is the same as the real domain numbers K ($K = 10$ in AnimalFaces-10). Moreover, when $\hat{K}$ slightly larger than K, the model still performed reasonably well. The (simple) experiment suggests that CUNIT has a relatively robust performance as long as estimated $\hat{K}$ is near or slightly larger than the true K. More discussions concerning both K and $\hat{K}$ can be found in supplementary Sect. 2.

Limitation of CUNIT. The above results demonstrate that our model CUNIT performs very well in reference-guided image translation under truly unsupervised, semi-supervised or even supervised settings when the number of domains is not very large. It would be interesting to know if this advantage of CUNIT remains true when the number of domains is very large. Supplementary Table S1 shows a comparison of CUNIT, TUNIT and COCO-FUNIT on the AnimalFaces dataset with various values of K, where CUNIT and TUNIT are trained without domain labels and COCO-FUNIT is trained with full labels. On AnimalFaces-10, CUNIT achieves a comparable performance as COCO-FUNIT (45.2 vs 44.8 in mFID) and outperforms TUNIT (47.9) by 5.6%. However, on AnimalFaces-149, the performance of both CUNIT and TUNIT drop significantly (106.9 and 106.3, respectively) compared with COCO-FUNIT (92.4). Because mFID measures the difference in feature distributions between the generated images and training images, the results suggest that, as K increases, it is very hard for the unsupervised methods to infer domain labels for images consistent with the true domain labels. Hence, CUNIT is more suitable in image translation applications where the domain numbers are not that large. More detailed analysis on how the number of domains K affects the performance of our model can be found in supplementary Subsect. 2.2 and Table S1.

5   Conclusion

Most of the existing I2I methods either require pixel-level or domain-level supervision to help the translation task. In this paper, we present a truly unsupervised I2I model, CUNIT, to perform image translation without requiring any supervision. The model consists of a style embedding network that extracts the domain and style information of the input style image with contrastive representation learning and an image translation module based on cGANs that actually carries out the reference-guided image translation. The embedding network and translation module are integrated together for training and benefit from each other, which enables CUNIT to successfully separate image domains and perform translation between these domains. Extensive experimental evaluation has been performed on various datasets concerning both cross-domain and multi-domain image translation. The results demonstrate that our model outperforms the best truly unsupervised I2I model in the literature (TUNIT). In addition, our model can be easily adapted to take advantage of the available domain labels to achieve a performance comparable to the best supervised image translation methods when all domain labels are known or a superior performance when only some (but not all) domain labels are provided. Therefor, we believe that CUNIT has great potentials in many practical image translation applications.

Acknowledgments. This work was supported in part by the National Key Research and Development Program of China grant 2018YFC0910404.

References

1. Arjovsky, M., Chintala, S., Bottou, L.: Wasserstein generative adversarial networks. In: International Conference on Machine Learning, pp. 214–223 (2017)
2. Baek, K., Choi, Y., Uh, Y., Yoo, J., Shim, H.: Rethinking the truly unsupervised image-to-image translation. In: Proceedings of the IEEE/CVF International Conference on Computer Vision, pp. 14154–14163 (2021)
3. Chen, T., Kornblith, S., Norouzi, M., Hinton, G.: A simple framework for contrastive learning of visual representations. In: International Conference on Machine Learning, pp. 1597–1607. PMLR (2020)
4. Chen, X., He, K.: Exploring simple Siamese representation learning. In: Proceedings of the IEEE/CVF Conference on Computer Vision and Pattern Recognition, pp. 15750–15758 (2021)
5. Choi, Y., Uh, Y., Yoo, J., Ha, J.W.: StarGAN v2: diverse image synthesis for multiple domains. In: Proceedings of the IEEE/CVF Conference on Computer Vision and Pattern Recognition, pp. 8188–8197 (2020)
6. Goodfellow, I., et al.: Generative adversarial nets. In: Advances in Neural Information Processing Systems, pp. 2672–2680 (2014)
7. Grill, J.B., et al.: Bootstrap your own latent: a new approach to self-supervised learning. arXiv preprint arXiv:2006.07733 (2020)
8. Gulrajani, I., Ahmed, F., Arjovsky, M., Dumoulin, V., Courville, A.C.: Improved training of wasserstein GANs. In: Advances in Neural Information Processing Systems, pp. 5767–5777 (2017)
9. He, K., Fan, H., Wu, Y., Xie, S., Girshick, R.: Momentum contrast for unsupervised visual representation learning. In: Proceedings of the IEEE/CVF Conference on Computer Vision and Pattern Recognition, pp. 9729–9738 (2020)
10. Heusel, M., Ramsauer, H., Unterthiner, T., Nessler, B., Hochreiter, S.: GANs trained by a two time-scale update rule converge to a local nash equilibrium. In: Advances in Neural Information Processing Systems 30 (2017)
11. Huang, X., Belongie, S.: Arbitrary style transfer in real-time with adaptive instance normalization. In: Proceedings of the IEEE International Conference on Computer Vision, pp. 1501–1510 (2017)

12. Huang, X., Liu, M.-Y., Belongie, S., Kautz, J.: Multimodal unsupervised image-to-image translation. In: Ferrari, V., Hebert, M., Sminchisescu, C., Weiss, Y. (eds.) ECCV 2018. LNCS, vol. 11207, pp. 179–196. Springer, Cham (2018). https://doi.org/10.1007/978-3-030-01219-9_11

13. Isola, P., Zhu, J.Y., Zhou, T., Efros, A.A.: Image-to-image translation with conditional adversarial networks. In: Proceedings of the IEEE Conference on Computer Vision and Pattern Recognition, pp. 1125–1134 (2017)

14. Ji, X., Henriques, J.F., Vedaldi, A.: Invariant information clustering for unsupervised image classification and segmentation. In: Proceedings of the IEEE/CVF International Conference on Computer Vision, pp. 9865–9874 (2019)

15. Karras, T., Laine, S., Aila, T.: A style-based generator architecture for generative adversarial networks. In: Proceedings of the IEEE/CVF Conference on Computer Vision and Pattern Recognition, pp. 4401–4410 (2019)

16. Kim, K., Park, S., Jeon, E., Kim, T., Kim, D.: A style-aware discriminator for controllable image translation. In: Proceedings of the IEEE/CVF Conference on Computer Vision and Pattern Recognition, pp. 18239–18248 (2022)

17. Kingma, D.P., Welling, M.: Auto-encoding variational bayes. arXiv preprint arXiv:1312.6114 (2013)

18. Lin, J., Xia, Y., Liu, S., Zhao, S., Chen, Z.: ZstGAN: an adversarial approach for unsupervised zero-shot image-to-image translation. Neurocomputing **461**, 327–335 (2021)

19. Liu, M.Y., Breuel, T., Kautz, J.: Unsupervised image-to-image translation networks. In: Advances in neural information processing systems, pp. 700–708 (2017)

20. Liu, M.Y., et al.: Few-shot unsupervised image-to-image translation. In: Proceedings of the IEEE/CVF International Conference on Computer Vision, pp. 10551–10560 (2019)

21. Mao, Q., Lee, H.Y., Tseng, H.Y., Ma, S., Yang, M.H.: Mode seeking generative adversarial networks for diverse image synthesis. In: Proceedings of the IEEE/CVF Conference on Computer Vision and Pattern Recognition, pp. 1429–1437 (2019)

22. Mescheder, L., Geiger, A., Nowozin, S.: Which training methods for GANs do actually converge? In: International Conference on Machine Learning, pp. 3481–3490. PMLR (2018)

23. Mirza, M., Osindero, S.: Conditional generative adversarial nets. arXiv preprint arXiv:1411.1784 (2014)

24. Nilsback, M.E., Zisserman, A.: Automated flower classification over a large number of classes. In: 2008 Sixth Indian Conference on Computer Vision, Graphics & Image Processing, pp. 722–729. IEEE (2008)

25. Pang, Y., Lin, J., Qin, T., Chen, Z.: Image-to-image translation: Methods and applications. arXiv preprint arXiv:2101.08629 (2021)

26. Park, T., Efros, A.A., Zhang, R., Zhu, J.Y.: Contrastive learning for unpaired image-to-image translation. In: Vedaldi, A., Bischof, H., Brox, T., Frahm, J.M. (eds.) Computer Vision – ECCV 2020. ECCV 2020. Lecture Notes in Computer Science, vol. 12354, pp. 319–345 Springer, Cham (2020). https://doi.org/10.1007/978-3-030-58545-7_19

27. Park, T., Liu, M.Y., Wang, T.C., Zhu, J.Y.: Semantic image synthesis with spatially-adaptive normalization. In: Proceedings of the IEEE/CVF Conference on Computer Vision and Pattern Recognition, pp. 2337–2346 (2019)

28. Saito, K., Saenko, K., Liu, M.-Y.: COCO-FUNIT: few-shot unsupervised image translation with a content conditioned style encoder. In: Vedaldi, A., Bischof, H., Brox, T., Frahm, J.-M. (eds.) ECCV 2020. LNCS, vol. 12348, pp. 382–398. Springer, Cham (2020). https://doi.org/10.1007/978-3-030-58580-8_23

29. Salimans, T., Goodfellow, I., Zaremba, W., Cheung, V., Radford, A., Chen, X.: Improved techniques for training GANs. Adv. Neural. Inf. Process. Syst. **29**, 2234–2242 (2016)
30. Van Horn, G., et al.: Building a bird recognition app and large scale dataset with citizen scientists: the fine print in fine-grained dataset collection. In: Proceedings of the IEEE Conference on Computer Vision and Pattern Recognition, pp. 595–604 (2015)
31. Wang, M., et al.: Example-guided style-consistent image synthesis from semantic labeling. In: Proceedings of the IEEE/CVF Conference on Computer Vision and Pattern Recognition, pp. 1495–1504 (2019)
32. Wang, T.C., Liu, M.Y., Zhu, J.Y., Tao, A., Kautz, J., Catanzaro, B.: High-resolution image synthesis and semantic manipulation with conditional GANs. In: Proceedings of the IEEE Conference on Computer Vision and Pattern Recognition, pp. 8798–8807 (2018)
33. Wang, Y., Khan, S., Gonzalez-Garcia, A., van de Weijer, J., Khan, F.S.: Semi-supervised learning for few-shot image-to-image translation. In: Proceedings of the IEEE/CVF Conference on Computer Vision and Pattern Recognition, pp. 4453–4462 (2020)
34. Wu, Z., Xiong, Y., Yu, S.X., Lin, D.: Unsupervised feature learning via non-parametric instance discrimination. In: Proceedings of the Ieee Conference On Computer Vision and Pattern Recognition, pp. 3733–3742 (2018)
35. Zhu, J.Y., Park, T., Isola, P., Efros, A.A.: Unpaired image-to-image translation using cycle-consistent adversarial networks. In: Proceedings of the IEEE International Conference on Computer Vision, pp. 2223–2232 (2017)

MatchFormer: Interleaving Attention in Transformers for Feature Matching

Qing Wang, Jiaming Zhang, Kailun Yang$^{(\boxtimes)}$, Kunyu Peng,
and Rainer Stiefelhagen

Karlsruhe Institute of Technology, Karlsruhe, Germany
kailun.yang@kit.edu
https://github.com/jamycheung/MatchFormer

Abstract. Local feature matching is a computationally intensive task at the subpixel level. While *detector-based* methods coupled with feature descriptors struggle in low-texture scenes, CNN-based methods with a sequential *extract-to-match* pipeline, fail to make use of the matching capacity of the encoder and tend to overburden the decoder for matching. In contrast, we propose a novel hierarchical *extract-and-match* transformer, termed as *MatchFormer*. Inside each stage of the hierarchical encoder, we interleave self-attention for feature extraction and cross-attention for feature matching, yielding a human-intuitive *extract-and-match* scheme. Such a match-aware encoder releases the overloaded decoder and makes the model highly efficient. Further, combining self- and cross-attention on multi-scale features in a hierarchical architecture improves matching robustness, particularly in low-texture indoor scenes or with less outdoor training data. Thanks to such a strategy, Match-Former is a multi-win solution in efficiency, robustness, and precision. Compared to the previous best method in indoor pose estimation, our lite MatchFormer has only 45% GFLOPs, yet achieves a +1.3% precision gain and a 41% running speed boost. The large MatchFormer reaches state-of-the-art on four different benchmarks, including indoor pose estimation (ScanNet), outdoor pose estimation (MegaDepth), homography estimation and image matching (HPatch), and visual localization (InLoc).

Keywords: Feature matching · Vision transformers

1 Introduction

Matching two or more views of a scene is the core of many basic computer vision tasks, *e.g.*, Structure-from-Motion (SfM) [19,24], Simultaneous Localization and Mapping (SLAM) [4,11], relative pose estimation [16], and visual localization [29,35,44], *etc.* For vision-based matching, classical *detector-based* methods (see Fig. 1(a)), coupled with hand-crafted local features [10,28], are computationally intensive due to the high dimensionality of local features [29,53].

Q. Wang and J. Zhang—Equal contribution.

Supplementary Information The online version contains supplementary material available at https://doi.org/10.1007/978-3-031-26313-2_16.

L. Wang et al. (Eds.): ACCV 2022, LNCS 13843, pp. 256–273, 2023.
https://doi.org/10.1007/978-3-031-26313-2_16

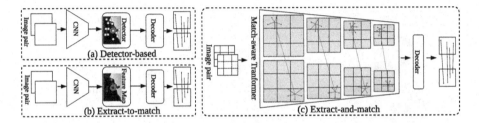

Fig. 1. Feature matching pipelines. While (a) *detector-based* methods coupled with feature descriptors, (b) *extract-to-match* methods fail to make use of the matching capacity of the encoder. Self- and cross-attention are interleaved inside each stage of the match-aware transformer to perform a novel (c) *extract-and-match* pipeline.

Recent works [22,25,40] based on deep learning focus on learning detectors and local descriptors using Convolutional Neural Networks (CNNs). Some partial transformer-based methods [14,34] only design an attention-based decoder and remain the *extract-to-match* pipeline (see Fig. 1(b)). For instance, while COTR [14] feeds CNN-extracted features into a transformer-based decoder, SuperGlue [30] and LoFTR [34] only apply attention modules atop the decoder. Overburdening the decoder, yet neglecting the matching capacity of the encoder, makes the whole model computationally inefficient.

Rethinking local feature matching, in reality, one can perform feature extraction and matching simultaneously by using a pure transformer. We propose an *extract-and-match* pipeline shown in Fig. 1(c). Compared to the *detector-based* methods and the *extract-to-match* pipeline, our new scheme is more in line with human intuition, which learns more respective features of image pairs while paying attention to their similarities [51]. To this end, a novel transformer termed *MatchFormer* is proposed, which helps to achieve multi-wins in precision, efficiency, and robustness of feature matching. For example, compared to LoFTR [34] in Fig. 2, MatchFormer with lower GFLOPs is more robust in low-textured scenes and achieves higher matching number, speed, and accuracy.

More specifically, for improving computational efficiency and the robustness in matching low-texture scenes, we put forward *interleaving* self- and cross-attention in MatchFormer to build a matching-aware encoder. In this way, the local features of the image itself and the similarities of its paired images can be learned simultaneously, so called *extract-and-match*, which relieves the overweight decoder and makes the whole model efficient. The cross-attention arranged in earlier stages of the encoder robustifies feature matching, particularly, in low-texture indoor scenarios or with less training samples outdoors, which makes MatchFormer more suitable for real-world applications where large-scale data collection and annotation are infeasible. To extract continuous patch information and embed location information, a novel *positional patch embedding (PosPE)* method is designed in the matching-aware encoder, which can enhance the detection of low-level features. Additionally, the lite and large versions *w.r.t.* feature resolutions, each with two efficient attention modules [32,41], are fully investigated to overcome the massive calculations in transformers when

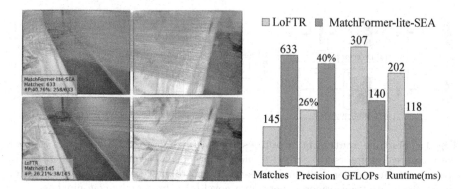

Fig. 2. Comparison between MatchFormer and LoFTR. With 45% GFLOPs of LoFTR, our efficient MatchFormer boosts the running speed by 41%, while delivering more robust matches and a higher matching precision on such a low-texture indoor scenario. Green color in the figure refers to correct matches and red color to mismatches (Color figure online).

dealing with fine features. Furthermore, MatchFormer, with a hierarchical transformer, conducts multi-level feature extraction in the encoder and multi-scale feature fusion in the decoder, which contribute to the robustness of matching. Finally, for the precision, extensive experiments prove that MatchFormer achieves state-of-the-art performances of indoor location estimation on Scan-Net [7], outdoor location estimation on MegaDepth [18], image matching and homography estimation on HPatches [1], and visual localization on InLoc [35].

In summary, the contributions of this paper include:

– We rethink local feature matching and propose a new *extract-and-match* pipeline, which enables synchronization of feature extraction and feature matching. The optimal combination path is delivered when *interleaving* self- and cross-attention modules within each stage of the hierarchical structure to enhance multi-scale features.
– We propose a novel vision transformer, *i.e.*, *MatchFormer*, equipped with a robust hierarchical transformer encoder and a lightweight decoder. Including lite and large versions and two attention modules, four variants of Match-Former are investigated.
– We introduce a simple and effective positional patch embedding method, *i.e.*, *PosPE*, which can extract continuous patch information and embed location information, as well as enhances the detection of low level features.
– MatchFormer achieves state-of-the-art scores on matching low-texture indoor images and is superior to previous *detector-based* and *extract-to-match* methods in pose estimation, homography estimation, and visual localization.

2   Related Work

Local Feature Matching. *Detector-based* methods [6,10,13,23] usually include five steps: detecting interest points, calculating visual descriptors, searching for nearest neighbor matches, rejecting incorrect matches, and estimating geometric transformations. In *extract-to-match* methods [10,17,25,26,30,33,34,37] designed for feature matching, CNNs are normally adopted to learn dense and discriminative features. CAPS [40] fuses multi-resolution features extracted by CNNs and obtains the descriptor of each pixel through interpolation. DSM [36] strengthens detection and refines the descriptors by merging various frames and multiple scales extracted by CNNs. DRC-Net [17] obtains CNN feature maps of two different resolutions, generates two 4D matching tensors, and fuses them to achieve high-confidence feature matching. D2Net [10] obtains valid key points by detecting the local maximum of CNN features. R2D2 [25] adapts dilated convolutions [5,45] to maintain image resolution and predict each key points and descriptors. COTR [14], LoFTR [34], and QuadTree [37] follow sequential *extract-to-match* processing. In this work, we consider that feature extraction and similarity learning through a transformer synchronously, can provide matching-aware features in each stage of the hierarchical structure.

Vision Transformer. Transformer [9] excels at capturing long-distance dependency [39], making it outstanding in vision tasks such as classification [20,38,46], detection [3,41,54], semantic segmentation [42,48,50], image enhancement [49], and image synthesis [12]. For local-feature matching, only attention blocks of transformers have been used in recent works. For example, SuperGlue [30] and LoFTR [34] applied self- and cross-attention to process the features which were extracted from CNNs. Yet, attention can actually function as the backbone module for feature extraction instead of only being used in the decoder for CNNs. This has been verified in ViT [9], but mainly for classification and segmentation tasks [41,50]. It remains unclear whether it is transferable to the image feature matching. When a pure transformer framework is used to process local feature matching, the computation complexity will be exceedingly large. Besides, transformers often lack and miss local feature information [46]. In this paper, we put forward a fully transformer image matching framework. In our model, we design positional patch embedding to enhance the feature extraction and introduce interleaving attention to achieve efficient and robust feature matching.

3   Methodology

3.1   MatchFormer

As illustrated in Fig. 3, MatchFormer employs a hierarchical transformer, which comprises four stages to generate high-resolution coarse and low-resolution fine features for local feature matching. In four stages, the self- and cross-attention are arranged in an *interleaving* strategy. Each stage consists of two components: one *positional patch embedding (PosPE)* module, and a set of efficient attention modules. Then, the multi-scale features are fused by an FPN-like decoder. Finally, the coarse and fine features are passed to perform the coarse-to-fine matching, as introduced in LoFTR [34].

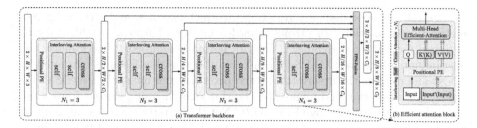

Fig. 3. MatchFormer architecture: (a) The transformer backbone generates high-resolution coarse features and low-resolution fine features; In (b), each attention block has interleaving-arranged self-attention (*w.r.t.* Q, K, V and red arrows) within the *input*, and cross-attention (*w.r.t.* Q, K', V' and alternative green arrows) cross images (*input* and *input'*). Multi-head efficient-attention reduces the computation; Positional Patch Embedding (PE) completes the patch embedding and the position encoding (Color figure online).

Extract-and-Match Pipeline. Unlike the *extract-to-match* LoFTR using attention on a single-scale feature map and only after feature extraction, we combine self- and cross-attention inside the transformer-based encoder and apply on multiple feature scales (see Fig. 1). The combination of two types of attention modules enables the model to extract non-local features via self-attention and explore their similarities via cross-attention simultaneously, so called the *extract-and-match* scheme. As a new matching scheme, however, the difficulty lies in finding an effective and optimal combination strategy while maintaining the efficiency and robustness of the entire model. Thanks to the hierarchy nature of Transformers [9,41], we obtain two insights: (1) As the feature map at the shallow stage emphasizes textural information, *relatively* more self-attention are applied to extract the feature itself on the early stages. (2) As the feature map at the deep stage is biased toward semantic information, *relatively* more cross-attention are developed to explore the feature similarity on the later stages. These two observations lead us to design a novel *interleaving* strategy for joining self- and cross-attention.

Interleaving Self-/Cross-Attention. As shown in Fig. 3(a), the combination of self- and cross-attention modules are set at each stage in an *interleaving* strategy. Each block in Fig. 3(b) contains N attention modules, where each attention module is represented as self-attention or alternative cross-attention according to the input image pair. For self-attention, Q and (K, V) come from the same *input*, so the self-attention is responsible for feature extraction of the image itself. For cross-attention, (K', V') are from another *input'* of the image pair. Thus, the cross-attention learns the similarity of the image pair, resulting a match-aware transformer-based encoder. Within an attention block, self-attended features are extracted, while the similarity of the feature pair is located by the cross-attention. The strategy is more human-intuitive, which learns more respective features of image pairs while paying attention to their similarities.

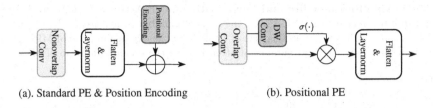

(a). Standard PE & Position Encoding   (b). Positional PE

Fig. 4. Comparison between different patch embedding modules.

Positional Patch Embedding (PosPE). Typical transformers [9], split the image ($H \times W \times 3$) into patches with size of $P \times P$ and then flatten these patches into sequence with a size of $N \times C$, where $N = HW/P^2$. The process is difficult to gather location information around patches. As a result, low-level feature information cannot be acquired directly through the standard process [46], which severely restricts the local feature matching. In the case of standard Patch Embedding (PE) in Fig. 4(a), the independent patch ignores the information around it and requires additional position encoding at the end. Therefore, we propose a simple but effective positional patch embedding (PosPE) method for capturing low feature information with few parameters, as shown in Fig. 4(b). It has a 7×7 convolution layer (with padding 3 and stride 2) in the first stage, and 3×3 convolution layers (all with padding 1 and stride 2) in later stages. A depth-wise 3×3 convolution is added to further enhance local features and encode positional information by its padding operation. The pixel-wise weights are then scaled by a sigmoid function $\sigma(\cdot)$ after the first step of convolution. Besides, our PosPE includes a first overlapping convolution that captures the continuous patch area information. PosPE augments the location information of patches and extracts denser features, which facilitates accurate feature matching.

Preliminaries on Efficient-Attention. After Patch Embedding, the query Q, key K, and value V are obtained, with the same $N \times C$ dimension according to the input resolution $N = H \times W$. The computation of the traditional attention is formulated as: $softmax((QK^T)/\sqrt{d})V$, where $\sqrt{d}$ is the scaling factor. However, the product of QK^T introduces a $O(N^2)$ complexity, which is prohibitive in large image resolutions and makes the model inefficient. To remedy this problem, we apply two kinds of efficient attention, *i.e.*, *Spatial Efficient Attention (SEA)* as in [41,42] or *Linear Attention (LA)* as in [32]. Then, $O(N^2)$ is reduced to $O(N^2/R)$ or $O(N)$. Hence, larger input feature maps can be well handled and processed while using a pure transformer-based encoder in the feature matching task.

Multi-scale Feature Fusion. Apart from the interleaving combination, there are four different stages in our hierarchical transformer encoder, in which the feature resolution shrinks progressively. Different from previous works [14,17] considering only the single-scale feature, MatchFormer fuses multi-scale features to generate dense and match-aware features for feature matching. As shown in Fig. 3(a), we flexibly adopt an FPN-like decoder in our architecture, because it can bring two benefits: (1) generating more robust coarse- and fine features for promoting the final matching; (2) creating a lightweight decoder without making the whole model computationally complex.

Table 1. MatchFormer-lite and -large with Linear Attention (LA) and Spatial Efficient Attention (SEA). C: the channel number of feature $\boldsymbol{F}$; K, S and P: the patch size, stride, and padding size of PosPE; E: the expansion ratio of MLP in an attention block; A: the head number of attention; R: the down-scale ratio of SEA.

Stage	MatchFormer-lite		MatchFormer-large		N_i
F_1	$H/4 \times W/4$	$K = 7, S = 4, P = 3, E = 4$	$H/2 \times W/2$	$K = 7, S = 2, P = 3, E = 4$	
	$C_1 = 128$	**LA:** $A = 8$; **SEA:** $A = 1, R = 4$	$C_1 = 128$	**LA:** $A = 8$; **SEA:** $A = 1, R = 4$	$\times 3$
F_2	$H/8 \times W/8$	$K = 3, S = 2, P = 1, E = 4$	$H/4 \times W/4$	$K = 3, S = 2, P = 1, E = 4$	
	$C_2 = 192$	**LA:** $A = 8$; **SEA:** $A = 2, R = 2$	$C_2 = 192$	**LA:** $A = 8$; **SEA:** $A = 2, R = 2$	$\times 3$
F_3	$H/16 \times W/16$	$K = 3, S = 2, P = 1, E = 4$	$H/8 \times W/8$	$K = 3, S = 2, P = 1, E = 4$	
	$C_3 = 256$	**LA:** $A = 8$; **SEA:** $A = 4, R = 2$	$C_3 = 256$	**LA:** $A = 8$; **SEA:** $A = 4, R = 2$	$\times 3$
F_4	$H/32 \times W/32$	$K = 3, S = 2, P = 1, E = 4$	$H/16 \times W/16$	$K = 3, S = 2, P = 1, E = 4$	
	$C_4 = 512$	**LA:** $A = 8$; **SEA:** $A = 8, R = 1$	$C_4 = 512$	**LA:** $A = 8$; **SEA:** $A = 8, R = 1$	$\times 3$
Output	Coarse: $H/4 \times W/4, 128$		Coarse: $H/2 \times W/2, 128$		
	Fine: $H/8 \times W/8, 192$		Fine: $H/8 \times W/8, 256$		

3.2 Model Settings

MatchFormer Variants. MatchFormer is available with its *lite* and *large* versions, as presented in Table 1. For the MatchFormer-lite models, we pick a lower resolution setting, which greatly increases the matching efficiency and ensures a certain matching accuracy. Therefore, we set MatchFormer-lite 4-stage features in the respective resolution of $\frac{1}{r_i} \in \{\frac{1}{4}, \frac{1}{8}, \frac{1}{16}, \frac{1}{32}\}$ of the input. To promote context learning for matching, feature embeddings with higher channel numbers are beneficial, which are set as $C_i \in \{128, 192, 256, 512\}$ for four stages. In the MatchFormer-large models, higher resolution feature maps facilitate accurate dense matching. Hence, the $\frac{1}{r_i}$ and C_i are set as $\{\frac{1}{2}, \frac{1}{4}, \frac{1}{8}, \frac{1}{16}\}$ and $\{128, 192, 256, 512\}$ for the large MatchFormer.

Attention Module Variants. To fully explore the proposed *extract-and-match* scheme, each of the two MatchFormer variants has two attention variants. Here, we mainly investigate Linear Attention (LA) and Spatial Efficient Attention (SEA). Thus, there are four versions of MatchFormer as presented in Table 1. We found that they have different capabilities for recognizing features, making them suitable for various tasks. In the local feature matching, the density of features is different indoors and outdoors. We study the two kinds of attention in indoor (in Sect. 4.2) and outdoor (in Sect. 4.3) pose estimation, respectively.

4   Experiments

4.1   Implementation and Datasets

ScanNet. We use ScanNet [7] to train our indoor models. ScanNet is an indoor RGB-D video dataset with 2.5 million views in 1,513 scans with ground-truth poses and depth maps. The lack of textures, the ubiquitous self-similarity, and the considerable changes in viewpoint make ScanNet a challenging dataset for indoor image matching. Following [30], we select 230 million image pairs with the size of 640×480 as the training set and 1,500 pairs as the testing set.

Table 2. Indoor pose estimation on ScanNet. The AUC of three different thresholds and the average matching precision (P) are evaluated.

Method	Pose estimation AUC (%)			P
	@5°	@10°	@20°	
ORB [28]+GMS [2] CVPR'17	5.21	13.65	25.36	72.0
D2-Net [10]+NN CVPR'19	5.25	14.53	27.96	46.7
ContextDesc [22]+RT [21] CVPR'19	6.64	15.01	25.75	51.2
SP [8]+NN CVPRW'18	9.43	21.53	36.40	50.4
SP [8]+PointCN [43] CVPR'18	11.40	25.47	41.41	71.8
SP [8]+OANet [47] ICCV'19	11.76	26.90	43.85	74.0
SP [8]+SuperGlue [30] CVPR'20	16.16	33.81	51.84	84.4
LoFTR [34] CVPR'21	22.06	40.80	57.62	87.9
LoFTR [34]+QuadTree [37] ICLR'22	23.90	43.20	60.30	89.3
MatchFormer-lite-LA	20.42	39.23	56.82	87.7
MatchFormer-lite-SEA	22.89	42.68	60.66	89.2
MatchFormer-large-LA	24.27	43.48	60.55	89.2
MatchFormer-large-SEA	**24.31**	**43.90**	**61.41**	**89.5**

MegaDepth. Following [10], we use MegaDepth [18] to train our outdoor models, which has 1 million internet images of 196 scenarios, and their sparse 3D point clouds are created by COLMAP [31]. We use $38,300$ image pairs from 368 scenarios for training, and the same $1,500$ testing pairs from [34] for evaluation.

Implementation Settings. On the indoor dataset ScanNet, MatchFormer is trained using Adam [15] with initial learning rate and batch size, setting for the lite version at 3×10^{-3} and 4, and for the large version at 3×10^{-4} and 2. In the case of the outdoor dataset MegaDepth, MatchFormer is trained using Adam with initial learning rate and batch size, setting for the lite version at 3×10^{-3} and 2, and for the large version at 3×10^{-4} and 1. To compare LoFTR and MatchFormer at different data scales on outdoor pose estimation task, both use 8 A100 GPUs, otherwise use 64 A100 GPUs following LoFTR [34]. We perform Image Matching, Homography Estimation, and InLoc Visual Localization experiments using the model trained with MatchFormer-large-LA on MegaDepth.

4.2 Indoor Pose Estimation

Indoor pose estimation is highly difficult due to wide areas devoid of textures, a high degree of self-similarity, scenes with complicated 3D geometry, and frequent perspective shifts. Faced with all these challenges, MatchFormer with interleaved self- and cross-attention modules still functions well as unfolded in the results.

Fig. 5. Qualitative visualization of MatchFormer and LoFTR [34]. MatchFormer achieves higher matching numbers and more correct matches in low-texture scenes.

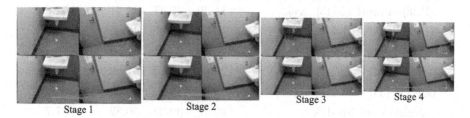

Fig. 6. Visualization of self- and cross-attention at 4 stages of MatchFormer. Cross-attention focuses on learning the similarity across paired images and gradually refines the matching range, while self-attention focuses on detecting features of the image itself and enabling long-range dependencies.

Metrics. Following [30], we provide the area under the cumulative curve (AUC) of the pose error at three different thresholds ($5°, 10°, 20°$). The camera pose is recovered by using RANSAC. We report the matching precision (P), the probability of a true match if its epipolar is smaller than 5×10^{-4}.

Quantitative Results. As shown in Table 2, MatchFormer demonstrates exceptional performance on the low-texture indoor pose estimation task. The matching precision (P) of MatchFormer-large-SEA reaches the state-of-the-art level of 89.5%. Benefiting from the *extract-and-match* strategy, MatchFormer-large-SEA can bring +5.1% improvement over the *detector-based* SuperGlue, +1.6% over the *extract-to-match* LoFTR. Pose estimation AUC of MatchFormer is also significantly superior to *detector-based* SuperGlue. Compared to LoFTR, MatchFormer provides a more pronounced pose estimation AUC by boosting (+2.25%, +3.1%, +3.79%) at three thresholds of ($5°, 10°, 20°$). The LoFTR model is recently adapted by a complex decoder with QuadTree Attention [37]. However, MatchFormer maintains its lead (+0.41%, +0.70%, +1.11%) with the *extract-and-match* strategy. Additionally, compared to LoFTR, our lightweight MatchFormer-lite-SEA has only 45% GFLOPs, yet achieves a +1.3% precision gain and a 41% running speed boost. More details of the efficiency comparison will be presented in Table 7. Comparing SEA and LA, we found that the spatial scaling operation in SEA has benefits in handling low-texture features, thus it is more suited for indoor scenes and provides better results.

Table 3. Outdoor pose estimation on MegaDepth. † represents training on different percentages of datasets, which requires 8 GPUs for training.

Method	Data percent	Pose estimation AUC (%)			P
		@5°	@10°	@20°	
SP [8]+SuperGlue [30] cvpr'20	100%	42.18	61.16	75.95	–
DRC-Net [17] NeurIPS'20	100%	27.01	42.96	58.31	–
LoFTR [34] cvpr'21	100%	52.80	69.19	81.18	94.80
MatchFormer-lite-LA	100%	48.74	65.83	78.81	97.55
MatchFormer-lite-SEA	100%	48.97	66.12	79.07	97.52
MatchFormer-large-LA	100%	**52.91** (+0.11)	**69.74** (+0.55)	**82.00** (+0.82)	**97.56** (+2.76)
Robustness with less training data and fewer GPU resources:					
LoFTR†	10%	38.81	54.53	67.04	83.64
MatchFormer†	10%	42.92 (+4.11)	58.33 (+3.80)	70.34 (+3.30)	85.08 (+1.44)
LoFTR†	30%	47.38	64.77	77.68	91.94
MatchFormer†	30%	49.53 (+2.15)	66.74 (+1.97)	79.43 (+1.75)	94.28 (+2.34)
LoFTR†	50%	48.68	65.49	77.62	92.54
MatchFormer†	50%	50.13 (+1.45)	66.71 (+1.22)	79.01 (+1.39)	94.89 (+2.35)
LoFTR†	70%	49.08	66.03	78.72	93.86
MatchFormer†	70%	51.22 (+2.14)	67.44 (+1.41)	79.73 (+1.01)	95.75 (+1.89)
LoFTR†	100%	50.85	67.56	79.96	95.18
MatchFormer†	100%	**53.28** (+2.43)	**69.74** (+2.18)	**81.83** (+1.87)	**96.59** (+1.41)

Qualitative Results. The indoor matching results are in Fig. 5. In challenging feature-sparse indoor scenes, it can reliably capture global information to assure more matches and high accuracy. Thus, the pose solved by matching prediction has a lower maximum angle error (ΔR) and translation error (Δt). Due to the hierarchical transformer and interleaving-attention design, the receptive field of MatchFormer exceeds that of CNN-based methods. It confirms that applying cross-attention modules earlier for learning feature similarity robustifies low-texture indoor matching, which is in line with our *extract-and-match* pipeline.

Self- and Cross-Attention Visualization. To further investigate the effectiveness of interleaving attention in MatchFormer, the features of self- and cross-attention modules in four stages are shown in Fig. 6. Self-attention connects obscure points with surrounding points, while cross-attention learns relationship between points across images. Specifically, self-attention enables the query point to associate surrounding textural features in the shallow stage, and it enables the query point to connect to semantic features in the deep stage. As the model deepens, cross-attention will narrow the range of query points detected across images, rendering the matching much easier and more fine-grained. Finally, these four stages of features are blended, empowering the model to perform accurate feature matching in low-texture scenes.

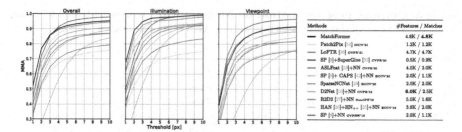

Fig. 7. Image matching on HPatches. The mean matching accuracy (MMA) at thresholds from $[1, 10]$ pixels, and the number of matches and features are reported.

4.3 Outdoor Pose Estimation

Outdoor pose estimation presents unique challenges compared to indoors. In particular, outdoor scenes have greater variations in lighting and occlusion. Still, Matchformer achieves outstanding performance in outdoor scenes.

Metrics. We present the same AUC of the pose error as in the indoor pose estimation task. The matching precision pipolar distance threshold is 1×10^{-4}.

Results. As shown in Table 3, MatchFormer noticeably surpasses the *detector-based* SuperGlue and DRC-Net, as well as the *extract-to-match* LoFTR. Our MatchFormer-lite-LA model also achieves great performance. It can deliver a higher matching precision (P) with 97.55%, despite being much lighter. Note that MatchFormer-large-SEA using the partially optimized SEA will raise an out-of-memory issue. Here, we recommend to use the memory-efficient LA in the high-resolution outdoor scenes. Our MatchFormer-large-LA model achieves consistent state-of-the-art performances on both metrics of AUC and P.

Robustness and Resource-Efficiency. It is reasonable to evaluate the robustness of the model when only less training data and fewer training resources are available in practical applications. Therefore, we further train MatchFormer-large-LA and LoFTR (marked with † in Table 3) using different percentages of datasets and on fewer resources with 8 GPUs. First, compared to LoFTR†, MatchFormer† obtains consistent improvements on different constrained data scales, *i.e.*, the first $\{10, 30, 50, 70, 100\}$ percentages of the original dataset. It proves that MatchFormer has more promise in data-hungry real-world applications. Second, training with the same 100% data on different GPU resources, LoFTR† has $(-1.95\%, -1.63\%, -1.22\%)$ performance drops at three AUC thresholds of $(5°, 10°, 20°)$ when using 8 GPUs instead of 64 GPUs. In contrast, MatchFormer maintains the stable and surprising accuracy, which shows that our method is more resource-friendly and easier to reproduce.

4.4 Image Matching

Metrics. On the standard image matching task of HPatches sequences based on sequences with illumination or viewpoint change, we evaluate MatchFormer by

Table 4. Homography estimation on HPatches. † represents training on different percentages of datasets, which requires 8 GPUs for training.

Method	Data percent	Overall Accuracy (%, $\epsilon < 1/3/5$ px)	Illumination	Viewpoint	#Matches
SP [8] CVPRW'18	100%	0.46/0.78/0.85	0.57/0.92/0.97	0.35/0.65/0.74	1.1K
D2Net [10] CVPR'19	100%	0.38/0.71/0.82	0.66/0.95/**0.98**	0.12/0.49/0.67	2.5K
R2D2 [25] NeurIPS'19	100%	0.47/0.77/0.82	0.63/0.93/**0.98**	0.32/0.64/0.70	1.6K
ASLFeat [23] CVPR'20	100%	0.48/0.81/0.88	0.62/0.94/**0.98**	0.34/0.69/0.78	2.0K
ASLFeat [23] CVPR'20 + ClusterGNN [33]	100%	0.51/0.83/0.89	0.61/**0.95**/**0.98**	0.42/0.72/**0.82**	–
SP [8] + SuperGlue [30] CVPR'20	100%	0.51/0.82/0.89	0.60/0.92/**0.98**	0.42/0.71/0.81	0.5K
SP [8] + CAPS [40] ECCV'20	100%	0.49/0.79/0.86	0.62/0.93/**0.98**	0.36/0.65/0.75	1.1K
SP [8] + ClusterGNN [33] CVPR'22	100%	0.52/**0.84**/**0.90**	0.61/0.93/**0.98**	**0.44**/**0.74**/0.81	–
SIFT + CAPS [40] ECCV'20	100%	0.36/0.77/0.85	0.48/0.89/0.95	0.26/0.65/0.76	1.5K
SparseNCNet [27] ECCV'20	100%	0.36/0.65/0.76	0.62/0.92/0.97	0.13/0.40/0.58	2.0K
Patch2Pix [52] CVPR'21	100%	0.50/0.79/0.87	0.71/**0.95**/**0.98**	0.30/0.64/0.76	1.3K
LoFTR [34] CVPR'21	100%	**0.55**/0.81/0.86	0.74/**0.95**/**0.98**	0.38/0.69/0.76	4.7K
MatchFormer	100%	**0.55**/0.81/0.87	**0.75**/**0.95**/**0.98**	0.37/0.68/0.78	**4.8K**
Robustness with less training data and fewer GPU resources:					
LoFTR†	10%	0.50/0.78/0.84	0.74/0.95/**0.98**	0.28/0.63/0.71	3.6K
MatchFormer†	10%	0.50/0.78/0.84	0.72/0.93/0.97	0.30/0.64/0.71	4.0K
LoFTR†	30%	0.52/0.80/0.86	0.74/0.96/**0.98**	0.32/**0.66**/0.74	4.1K
MatchFormer†	30%	**0.57**/**0.81**/0.86	**0.78**/**0.97**/**0.98**	**0.36**/**0.66**/0.74	4.4K
LoFTR†	50%	0.52/0.79/0.85	0.73/0.95/**0.98**	0.32/0.65/0.73	4.1K
MatchFormer†	50%	0.54/0.78/0.85	0.75/0.95/**0.98**	0.35/0.62/0.74	**4.5K**
LoFTR†	70%	0.52/0.79/0.85	0.74/0.94/**0.98**	0.31/0.64/0.73	4.1K
MatchFormer†	70%	0.55/0.79/0.86	0.76/0.94/**0.98**	0.35/0.64/0.75	**4.5K**
LoFTR†	100%	0.52/0.79/0.86	0.74/0.93/**0.98**	0.32/0.65/0.74	4.2K
MatchFormer†	100%	0.54/0.79/**0.87**	0.74/0.95/**0.98**	**0.36**/**0.66**/**0.77**	**4.5K**

detecting correspondences between pairs of input images. Following the experimental setup of Patch2Pix [52], we report the mean matching accuracy (MMA) at thresholds from $[1, 10]$ pixels, and the number of matches and features.

Results. Figure 7 illustrates the results for the experiments with illumination and viewpoint changes, along with the MMA. Under varying illumination conditions, our method provides the best performance. On overall (the threshold ≤3 pixels), Matchformer performs optimally at precision levels. While other methods can only account for lighting changes or viewing angles changes, MatchFormer is reasonably compatible and maintains its functionality when the viewpoint changes. Thanks to the match-aware encoder, a larger number of features and matches, both 4.8K, are obtained. The results reveal the effectiveness of our *extract-and-match* strategy for image matching.

4.5   Homography Estimation

Metrics. To evaluate how the matches contribute to the accuracy of the geometric relations estimation, we assess MatchFormer in the homography estimation on HPatches benchmark [1]. The proportion of accurately predicted homographies with an average corner error distance less than 1/3/5 pixels is reported.

Table 5. Visual localization on InLoc. We report the percentage of correctly localized queries under specific error thresholds, following the HLoc [29] pipeline.

Method	Localized queries (%, 0.25 m/0.5 m/1.0 m, 10°)	
	DUC1	DUC2
SP [8] + NN cvprw'18	40.4/58.1/69.7	42.0/58.8/69.5
D2Net [10] + NN cvpr'19	38.4/56.1/71.2	37.4/55.0/64.9
R2D2 [25] + NN NeurIPS'19	36.4/57.6/74.2	45.0/60.3/67.9
SP [8] + SuperGlue [30] cvpr'20	49.0/68.7/80.8	53.4/**77.1**/82.4
SP [8] + CAPS [40] + NN eccv'20	40.9/60.6/72.7	43.5/58.8/68.7
SP [8] + ClusterGNN [33] cvpr'22	47.5/69.7/79.8	53.4/**77.1**/84.7
ASLFeat [23] + SuperGlue [30] cvpr'20	51.5/66.7/75.8	53.4/76.3/84.0
ASLFeat [23] + ClusterGNN [33] cvpr'22	**52.5**/68.7/76.8	55.0/76.0/82.4
SIFT + CAPS [40] + NN eccv'20	38.4/56.6/70.7	35.1/48.9/58.8
SparseNCNet [27] eccv'20	41.9/62.1/72.7	35.1/48.1/55.0
Patch2Pix [52] cvpr'21	44.4/66.7/78.3	49.6/64.9/72.5
LoFTR-OT [34] cvpr'21	47.5/72.2/84.8	54.2/74.8/**85.5**
MatchFormer	46.5/**73.2**/**85.9**	**55.7**/71.8/81.7

Results. As shown in Table 4, the large-LA MatchFormer achieves excellent performance on the HPatches benchmark in homography estimation. It reaches the best level in the face of illumination variations, delivering the accuracy of $(0.75, 0.95, 0.98)$ at 1/3/5 pixel errors. Additionally, MatchFormer obtains highest number of matches with 4.8K. To evaluate the robustness and resource-efficiency, we also execute experiments with varying dataset percentages in Table 4. Compared to LoFTR†, MatchFormer† performs significantly better in homography experiments, and is relatively unaffected by the limited training data. MatchFormer trained with 30% data has a better performance in illumination variations. One reason is that the accuracy of the geometry relation estimation is related to accurate matches, as well as the distribution and number of matches [52]. Training with fewer GPUs on 100% data, while LoFTR† has noticeable performance drops, MatchFormer† maintains stable performance and requires fewer training resources for success. These experiments sufficiently prove that our new *extract-and-match* pipeline has higher robustness than the *extract-to-match* one used in previous methods.

4.6   Visual Localization on InLoc

Metrics. A robust local feature matching method ensures accurate visual localization. To evaluate our local feature matching method MatchFormer, we test it on the InLoc [35] benchmark for visual localization. Referring to SuperGlue [30], we utilize MatchFormer as the feature matching step to complete the visual localization task along the localization pipeline HLoc [29].

Results. As shown in Table 5, on the InLoc benchmark for visual localization, MatchFormer reaches a level comparable to the current state of art methods SuperGlue and LoFTR. Interleaving attention in the MatchFormer backbone

Table 6. Ablation study with different structures, attention arrangements and PEs.

Method	Self	Cross	PosPE	StdPE	Pose estimation AUC (%)			P
					@5°	@10°	@20°	
LoFTR [34] cvpr'21					15.47	31.72	48.63	82.6
❶ Convolution					7.36	18.17	32.21	76.1
❷ Self-only	✓				9.48	22.68	38.10	81.3
❸ Cross-only		✓			13.88	29.98	46.89	84.4
❹ Sequential	✓	✓			14.75	31.03	48.27	85.0
❺ Sequential	✓	✓	✓		17.32	34.85	52.71	85.8
❻ Interleaving	✓	✓		✓	16.53	34.63	52.31	85.9
❼ Interleaving	✓	✓	✓		18.01	35.87	53.46	86.7

Table 7. Efficiency analysis. Runtime in ms, GFLOPs @ 640×480.

Method	#Params	GFLOPs	Runtime	P
LoFTR [34]	11	307	202	87.9
LoFTR [34]+QuadTree [37]	13	393	234	89.3
MatchFormer-lite-LA	22	97	140	87.7
MatchFormer-large-LA	22	389	246	87.8
MatchFormer-lite-SEA	23	140	118	89.2
MatchFormer-large-SEA	23	414	390	89.5

enables robust local feature matching in indoor scenes with large low-texture areas and repetitive structures.

4.7 MatchFormer Structural Study

Performing the *extract-and-match* strategy in a pure transformer, the layout between self- and cross-attention co-existing inside each stage of MatchFormer is a critical point to achieve efficient and robust feature matching. The structural study is conducted to explore the sweet spot to arrange attention modules.

Ablation Study of Interleaving. To verify the rationality of the model design, models in Table 6 are ablated according to different backbone structures, attention arrangements and patch embedding modules. Models are trained with 10% data of ScanNet. Such a setting is one for efficiency and another is that the robustness between models is validated with less training data. By comparing ❶ and ❷, we establish that the transformer with self-attention significantly improves the matching precision (P, +5.2%) compared to utilizing the convolutional extractor, which shows the long-range dependency can robustify the local feature matching. While the structure in ❷ contains only self-attention in between, the structure in ❸ with cross-attention can bring a +3.1% performance gain, which demonstrates the benefits of leaning feature similarity inside a transformer. The sequential structures (❹❺) apply pure self-attention in the early stages and pure cross-attention in the later stages, while our interleaving structures (❻❼) apply mix self-/cross-attention in each stage. Our structures improve the overall performance, which adaptively inserts self-/cross-attention in multi-scale stages, and it is in line with our statement about the *extract-and-match* strategy in transformers. The comparison between ❹ and ❺ indicates that the proposed PosPE is capable of completing the fixed position encoding and it comes with a +0.8% gain. Our PosPE in ❼ can enhance the accuracy by +0.8% compared with standard PE (StdPE) in ❻, demonstrating that PosPE is more robust. Our interleaving model in ❼ surpasses LoFTR by a large margin (+4.1% @ P), indicating that MatchFormer is more robust, not only in low-texture indoor scenes, but also with less training data.

Feature Maps Comparison. As shown in Fig. 8, we visualize the feature maps of the ablation experiment ❷ and ❼ of Table 6. In both shallow and deep lay-

shallow layer   deep layer   weights

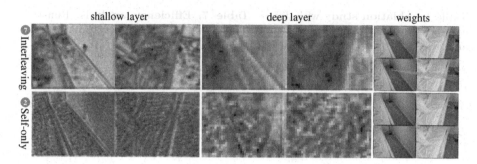

Interleaving

Self-only

Fig. 8. Feature maps comparison between interleaving and self-only attention in shallow and deep layers (from the last layer of the stage-2 and stage-3, respectively).

ers, our interleaving attention structure enables MatchFormer to capture dense features and learn feature similarities, such as the paired regions highlighted in yellow. The model with only self-attention tends to extract features in each individual image and neglects the matching-aware features across images, *i.e.*, without cross-attention weights. As a result, the self-attention model without cross-attention model will be incapable of matching local features when the image features are sparse (*i.e.*, low-texture scenes).

Runtime and Efficiency Analysis. Aside from verifying the effectiveness of arranging self- and cross-attention in an interleaving manner, MatchFormer is still supposed to be computationally efficient. The comparisons of efficiency results including the #Parameters (M), GFLOPs, and runtime (ms) are detailed in Table 7. Based on a 3080Ti GPU, MatchFormer is compared against the previous transformer-based LoFTR. We quantify the average runtime it takes for MatchFormer to complete a single image pair on the ScanNet test set, which includes 1, 500 pairs of images in the resolution of 640 × 480. MatchFormer-lite-SEA is clearly much faster, speeding up the matching process by 41%, although a higher number of parameters is required. Additionally, we compute the GFLOPs of the two approaches to determine their computing costs and storage demands. The GFLOPs of MatchFormer-lite-SEA are only 45% of those of LoFTR. Yet, our model achieves a +1.3% precision gain. Thanks to interleaving self- and cross-attention in between, our lite and large MatchFormers achieve state-of-the-art performances with respect to previous methods on various tasks.

5   Conclusions

Rethinking local feature matching from a novel *extract-and-match* perspective with transformers, we propose the MatchFormer framework equipped with a matching-aware encoder by interleaving self- and cross-attention for performing feature extraction and feature similarity learning synchronously. MatchFormer circumvents involving a complex decoder as used in the *extract-to-match* methods and adopts a lightweight FPN-like decoder to fuse multi-scale features.

Experiments show that MatchFormer achieves state-of-the-art performances in indoor and outdoor pose estimation on the ScanNet and MegaDepth benchmarks, and in both homography estimation and image matching on the HPatches benchmark, as well as in visual localization on the InLoc benchmark.

References

1. Balntas, V., Lenc, K., Vedaldi, A., Mikolajczyk, K.: HPatches: a benchmark and evaluation of handcrafted and learned local descriptors. In: CVPR (2017)
2. Bian, J., Lin, W.Y., Matsushita, Y., Yeung, S.K., Nguyen, T.D., Cheng, M.M.: GMS: grid-based motion statistics for fast, ultra-robust feature correspondence. In: CVPR (2017)
3. Carion, N., Massa, F., Synnaeve, G., Usunier, N., Kirillov, A., Zagoruyko, S.: End-to-end object detection with transformers. In: Vedaldi, A., Bischof, H., Brox, T., Frahm, J.-M. (eds.) ECCV 2020. LNCS, vol. 12346, pp. 213–229. Springer, Cham (2020). https://doi.org/10.1007/978-3-030-58452-8_13
4. Chen, H., Hu, W., Yang, K., Bai, J., Wang, K.: Panoramic annular SLAM with loop closure and global optimization. Appl. Opt. **60**, 6264–6274 (2021)
5. Chen, L.C., Papandreou, G., Kokkinos, I., Murphy, K., Yuille, A.L.: DeepLab: semantic image segmentation with deep convolutional nets, atrous convolution, and fully connected CRFs. IEEE Trans. Pattern Anal. Mach. Intell. **40**, 834–848 (2018)
6. Cheng, R., Wang, K., Lin, L., Yang, K.: Visual localization of key positions for visually impaired people. In: ICPR (2018)
7. Dai, A., Chang, A.X., Savva, M., Halber, M., Funkhouser, T., Nießner, M.: ScanNet: richly-annotated 3D reconstructions of indoor scenes. In: CVPR (2017)
8. DeTone, D., Malisiewicz, T., Rabinovich, A.: SuperPoint: self-supervised interest point detection and description. In: CVPRW (2018)
9. Dosovitskiy, A., et al.: An image is worth 16×16 words: transformers for image recognition at scale. In: ICLR (2021)
10. Dusmanu, M., et al.: D2-net: a trainable CNN for joint detection and description of local features. In: CVPR (2019)
11. Engel, J., Koltun, V., Cremers, D.: Direct sparse odometry. IEEE Trans. Pattern Anal. Mach. Intell. **40**, 611–625 (2018)
12. Esser, P., Rombach, R., Ommer, B.: Taming transformers for high-resolution image synthesis. In: CVPR (2021)
13. Fang, Y., Wang, K., Cheng, R., Yang, K.: CFVL: a coarse-to-fine vehicle localizer with omnidirectional perception across severe appearance variations. In: IV (2020)
14. Jiang, W., Trulls, E., Hosang, J., Tagliasacchi, A., Yi, K.M.: COTR: correspondence transformer for matching across images. In: ICCV (2021)
15. Kingma, D.P., Ba, J.: Adam: a method for stochastic optimization. In: ICLR (2015)
16. Li, S., Yuan, L., Sun, J., Quan, L.: Dual-feature warping-based motion model estimation. In: ICCV (2015)
17. Li, X., Han, K., Li, S., Prisacariu, V.: Dual-resolution correspondence networks. In: NeurIPS (2020)
18. Li, Z., Snavely, N.: MegaDepth: learning single-view depth prediction from internet photos. In: CVPR (2018)
19. Lindenberger, P., Sarlin, P.E., Larsson, V., Pollefeys, M.: Pixel-perfect structure-from-motion with featuremetric refinement. In: ICCV (2021)

20. Liu, Z., et al.: Swin transformer: hierarchical vision transformer using shifted windows. In: ICCV (2021)
21. Lowe, D.G.: Distinctive image features from scale-invariant keypoints. Int. J. Comput. Vis. **60**, 91–110 (2004)
22. Luo, Z., et al.: ContextDesc: local descriptor augmentation with cross-modality context. In: CVPR (2019)
23. Luo, Z., et al.: ASLFeat: learning local features of accurate shape and localization. In: CVPR (2020)
24. Ma, W.C., Yang, A.J., Wang, S., Urtasun, R., Torralba, A.: Virtual correspondence: humans as a cue for extreme-view geometry. In: CVPR (2022)
25. Revaud, J., De Souza, C., Humenberger, M., Weinzaepfel, P.: R2D2: reliable and repeatable detector and descriptor. In: NeurIPS (2019)
26. Revaud, J., Leroy, V., Weinzaepfel, P., Chidlovskii, B.: PUMP: pyramidal and uniqueness matching priors for unsupervised learning of local descriptors. In: CVPR (2022)
27. Rocco, I., Arandjelović, R., Sivic, J.: Efficient neighbourhood consensus networks via submanifold sparse convolutions. In: Vedaldi, A., Bischof, H., Brox, T., Frahm, J.-M. (eds.) ECCV 2020. LNCS, vol. 12354, pp. 605–621. Springer, Cham (2020). https://doi.org/10.1007/978-3-030-58545-7_35
28. Rublee, E., Rabaud, V., Konolige, K., Bradski, G.: ORB: an efficient alternative to SIFT or SURF. In: ICCV (2011)
29. Sarlin, P.E., Cadena, C., Siegwart, R., Dymczyk, M.: From coarse to fine: robust hierarchical localization at large scale. In: CVPR (2019)
30. Sarlin, P.E., DeTone, D., Malisiewicz, T., Rabinovich, A.: SuperGlue: learning feature matching with graph neural networks. In: CVPR (2020)
31. Schonberger, J.L., Frahm, J.M.: Structure-from-motion revisited. In: CVPR (2016)
32. Shen, Z., Zhang, M., Zhao, H., Yi, S., Li, H.: Efficient attention: attention with linear complexities. In: WACV (2021)
33. Shi, Y., Cai, J.X., Shavit, Y., Mu, T.J., Feng, W., Zhang, K.: ClusterGNN: cluster-based coarse-to-fine graph neural network for efficient feature matching. In: CVPR (2022)
34. Sun, J., Shen, Z., Wang, Y., Bao, H., Zhou, X.: LoFTR: detector-free local feature matching with transformers. In: CVPR (2021)
35. Taira, H., et al.: InLoc: indoor visual localization with dense matching and view synthesis. In: CVPR (2018)
36. Tang, S., Tang, C., Huang, R., Zhu, S., Tan, P.: Learning camera localization via dense scene matching. In: CVPR (2021)
37. Tang, S., Zhang, J., Zhu, S., Tan, P.: Quadtree attention for vision transformers. In: ICLR (2022)
38. Touvron, H., Cord, M., Douze, M., Massa, F., Sablayrolles, A., Jégou, H.: Training data-efficient image transformers & distillation through attention. In: ICML (2021)
39. Vaswani, A., et al.: Attention is all you need. In: NeurIPS (2017)
40. Wang, Q., Zhou, X., Hariharan, B., Snavely, N.: Learning feature descriptors using camera pose supervision. In: Vedaldi, A., Bischof, H., Brox, T., Frahm, J.-M. (eds.) ECCV 2020. LNCS, vol. 12346, pp. 757–774. Springer, Cham (2020). https://doi.org/10.1007/978-3-030-58452-8_44
41. Wang, W., et al.: Pyramid vision transformer: a versatile backbone for dense prediction without convolutions. In: ICCV (2021)
42. Xie, E., Wang, W., Yu, Z., Anandkumar, A., Alvarez, J.M., Luo, P.: SegFormer: simple and efficient design for semantic segmentation with transformers. In: NeurIPS (2021)

43. Yi, K.M., Trulls, E., Ono, Y., Lepetit, V., Salzmann, M., Fua, P.: Learning to find good correspondences. In: CVPR (2018)

44. Yoon, S., Kim, A.: Line as a visual sentence: context-aware line descriptor for visual localization. IEEE Robot. Autom. Lett. **6**, 8726–8733 (2021)

45. Yu, F., Koltun, V.: Multi-scale context aggregation by dilated convolutions. In: ICLR (2016)

46. Yuan, L., et al.: Tokens-to-token ViT: training vision transformers from scratch on ImageNet. In: ICCV (2021)

47. Zhang, J., et al.: Learning two-view correspondences and geometry using order-aware network. In: ICCV (2019)

48. Zhang, J., Yang, K., Constantinescu, A., Peng, K., Müller, K., Stiefelhagen, R.: Trans4Trans: efficient transformer for transparent object segmentation to help visually impaired people navigate in the real world. In: ICCVW (2021)

49. Zhang, Z., Jiang, Y., Jiang, J., Wang, X., Luo, P., Gu, J.: STAR: a structure-aware lightweight transformer for real-time image enhancement. In: ICCV (2021)

50. Zheng, S., et al.: Rethinking semantic segmentation from a sequence-to-sequence perspective with transformers. In: CVPR (2021)

51. Zhong, G., Pun, C.M.: Subspace clustering by simultaneously feature selection and similarity learning. Knowl. Based Syst. **193**, 105512 (2020)

52. Zhou, Q., Sattler, T., Leal-Taixe, L.: Patch2Pix: epipolar-guided pixel-level correspondences. In: CVPR (2021)

53. Zhou, Z., Wu, Q.M.J., Wan, S., Sun, W., Sun, X.: Integrating SIFT and CNN feature matching for partial-duplicate image detection. IEEE Trans. Emerg. Topics Comput. Intell. **4**, 539–604 (2020)

54. Zhu, X., Su, W., Lu, L., Li, B., Wang, X., Dai, J.: Deformable DETR: deformable transformers for end-to-end object detection. In: ICLR (2021)

SG-Net: Semantic Guided Network for Image Dehazing

Tao Hong⬤, Xiangyang Guo⬤, Zeren Zhang⬤, and Jinwen Ma$^{(\boxtimes)}$⬤

Department of Information and Computational Sciences, School of Mathematical Sciences and LMAM, Peking University, Beijing 100871, China
{paul.ht,guoxy}@pku.edu.cn, Eric_Zhang@stu.pku.edu.cn,
jwma@math.pku.edu.cn

Abstract. From traditional handcrafted priors to learning-based neural networks, image dehazing technique has gone through great development. In this paper, we propose an end-to-end Semantic Guided Network (SG-Net (Codebase page: https://github.com/PaulTHong/Dehaze-SG-Net)) for directly restoring the haze-free images. Inspired by the high similarity (mapping relationship) between the transmission maps and the segmentation results of hazy images, we found that the semantic information of the scene provides a strong natural prior for image restoration. To guide the dehazing more effectively and systematically, we utilize the information of semantic segmentation with three easily portable modes: Semantic Fusion (SF), Semantic Attention (SA), and Semantic Loss (SL), which compose our Semantic Guided (SG) mechanisms. By embedding these SG mechanisms into existing dehazing networks, we construct the SG-Net series: SG-AOD, SG-GCA, SG-FFA, and SG-AECR. The outperformance on image dehazing of these SG networks is demonstrated by the experiments in terms of both quantity and quality. It is worth mentioning that SG-FFA achieves the state-of-the-art performance.

Keywords: Image dehazing · Semantic attention · Perception loss

1 Introduction

As a representative task with lots of application value in low-level computer vision, image dehazing has attracted the interest of many researchers in recent years. Like other similar tasks such as image denoising, image deraining, *etc.*, image dehazing can be summarized as an image restoration problem. The atmosphere scattering model [17,19] is formulated as:

$$\boldsymbol{I}(x) = \boldsymbol{J}(x)t(x) + \boldsymbol{A}(1 - t(x)) \tag{1}$$

where $\boldsymbol{I}(x)$ and $\boldsymbol{J}(x)$ are the degraded hazy image and the target haze-free image respectively. $\boldsymbol{A}$ is the global atmosphere light, and $t(x)$ is the medium

Supplementary Information The online version contains supplementary material available at https://doi.org/10.1007/978-3-031-26313-2_17.

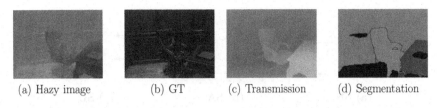

(a) Hazy image   (b) GT   (c) Transmission   (d) Segmentation

Fig. 1. Visualization of a sample from NYUv2. We can observe the high similarity (mapping relationship) between the transmission map and the segmentation result, which inspires our exploration on semantic guidance for image dehazing.

transmission map. Moreover, we have $t(x) = e^{-\beta d(x)}$ with β and $d(x)$ being the atmosphere scattering parameter and the scene depth, respectively. Since the transmission map $t(x)$ and the atmosphere light A are often unknown in real scenarios, image dehazing is an ill-posed problem. Therefore the core challenge is to estimate $t(x)$ and A properly, then we can restore the haze-free image as:

$$J(x) = \frac{I(x) - A}{t(x)} + A \qquad (2)$$

We can divide dehazing methods into two classes, traditional prior-based methods and learning-based methods. Classic traditional methods include DCP [11], BCCR [18], CAP [35], *etc.* With the rise of deep learning, many neural network methods are successively proposed, such as DehazeNet [3], MSCNN [21], AOD-Net [13], GCA-Net [4], -FFANet [20], AECR-Net [31]. Driven by the supervised data, these networks are well designed to fulfill the dehazing task, each with pros and cons.

Figure 1 displays one sample from NYUv2 [25]. As we can see, the transmission map and the semantic segmentation [10] result of this hazy image are highly related. From formula (1) we know that the transmission map $t(x)$ is dependent on the scene depth $d(x)$, while one object in the segmentation result often has similar $d(x)$. The ideal estimated maps of haze-free images shall be smooth in the regions of the same object and only discontinuous across the boundaries of different objects. The semantic segmentation information of images seems to provide a relatively accurate prior for this requirement, by building a mapping relationship with the transmission map. Cheng *et al.* firstly clarified to use semantic information to resolve image dehazing, but calling ordinary convolutional feature maps as semantic module and color module [9] is far-fetched. Song *et al.* proposed a multi-task network for semantic segmentation and dehazing [26], while it is not very targeted and requires a higher resource consumption. Ren *et al.* proposed to incorporate global semantic priors as input to regularize the transmission maps for video dehazing [22], whose effectiveness is partly due to the coherent similarity between video frames. This work enlightens us to migrate to image dehazing and fulfill semantic guidance more abundantly. Zhang *et al.* proposed a semantic-aware dehazing network with adaptive feature fusion [34], but this approach requires the ground-truth semantic label.

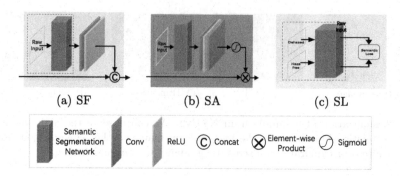

Fig. 2. Semantic Fusion (left), Semantic Attention (middle) and Semantic Loss (right). Note that the module in the red dotted rectangle is shared in one network. (Color figure online)

Therefore the key challenge is how to fit the mapping relationship from semantic segmentation to haze transmission with accurately guided tools, rather than negative interference. Apart from feature fusion, attention is considered to be an effective mechanism for neural network learning to be in line with human learning. The attention mechanism [28,29,32] has been researched in detail in the design of neural networks, and is widely applied in Natural Language Processing and Computer Vision. The FFA-Net proposes a feature attention module, which combines the Channel Attention (CA, the gated fusion module of GCA-Net is just a kind of CA) and Pixel Attention (PA) in channel-wise and pixel-wise features, respectively. The excellent performance of FFA-Net inspires us the great potential of attention for integrating semantic information. Furthermore, based on the reconstruction loss between dehazed and haze-free images, we propose a new kind of semantic perception loss to regularize their feature maps through semantic segmentation, resulting in finer dehazed results.

Elegantly combining semantic information with attention mechanism, perception loss, *etc.*, we propose a comprehensive Semantic Guided Network, *i.e.* SG-Net, from two perspectives: network structure and learning course. We mainly adopt three operation modes to fulfill semantic guidance, whose schematics are shown in Fig. 2. SF plus SA improves the network structure, while SL facilitates the optimization process.

– **Semantic Fusion (SF):** Incorporate feature maps of semantic segmentation as new branches into current dehazing networks. Fusion makes shallow features propagation more directional and effective.
– **Semantic Attention (SA):** Directly transfer the feature maps of semantic segmentation as attention. Refine high-level features more specifically at the pixel level.
– **Semantic Loss (SL):** Impose constraints on the perception loss between the semantic segmentation feature maps of dehazed and haze-free images. Optimize towards a more semantic-aware direction.

In the experiments, we choose four representative networks as baselines, *i.e.* AOD-Net, GCA-Net, FFA-Net and AECR-Net, respectively. For the first three networks, the dehazing effect gradually increases in order, while the inference time consumption also gradually increases. After adding our SG mechanisms, we get a stronger SG-Net series, named SG-AOD, SG-GCA, SG-FFA and SG-AECR, respectively.

The main contributions of our work are as follows:

- We propose a novel end-to-end network to restore haze-free images, outperforming existing methods both in quantity and quality, of which SG-FFA gets the state-of-the-art performance.
- We elaborately design SF, SA, and SL to give full play to the guidance of semantic information. With the detailed exploration of cooperative strategies, these operation modes aggregate dehazing effects from different scales and levels.
- Our simple but efficient SG mechanisms can be embedded into the existing network series at will, improving accuracy while only adding a little extra time consumption.

2 Related Work

2.1 Image Dehazing

As introduced in the previous section, image dehazing has evolved from traditional prior-based methods to learning-based methods. The dark channel prior (DCP) [11] is a brilliant discovery. Moreover, the boundary constraint and contextual regularization (BCCR) [18] and color attenuation prior (CAP) [35] are successively proposed.

As for neural network methods, they usually adopt an encoder-decoder structure to learn restoration. AOD-Net [13] directly generates the clean image through a lightweight CNN, named All-in-One Dehazing Network. GCA-Net [4] means Gated Context Aggregation Network, which adopts the smoothed dilation convolution [30] to help remove the gridding artifacts, and leverages a gated sub-network to fuse the features from different levels. As for FFA-Net [20], *i.e.* Feature Fusion Attention Network, it combines Channel Attention with Pixel Attention mechanism. AECR-Net [31] proposes a contrastive regularization built upon contrastive learning to exploit both the information of hazy images and clear images as negative and positive samples, respectively. And Chen *et al.* proposed a Principled Synthetic-to-real Dehazing (PSD) framework [8], *i.e.* a synthetic data pre-trained backbone, followed by unsupervised fine-tuning with real hazy images. In addition to the synthetic hazy image pairs, Yang *et al* proposed a disentangled dehazing network to generate realistic haze-free images only using unpaired supervision [33], which leads to a new challenge. In this paper, we focus on dehazing with supervised mode.

2.2 Semantic Segmentation

Semantic segmentation aims to cluster image pixels of the same object class with assigned labels. The general semantic segmentation architecture can be considered as an encoder-decoder network. The encoder is usually a pre-trained classification network, like ResNet [12]. And the task of the decoder is to semantically project the discriminable features (lower resolution) learned by the encoder into the pixel space (higher resolution) to obtain a dense classification.

The classic development path of semantic segmentation networks includes FCN [16], U-Net [23], DeepLab series: v1 [5], v2 [6], v3 [7], RefineNet [15], and MTI-Net [27] *etc.* We adopt RefineNet as the semantic segmentation branch unless otherwise specified.

3 Proposed Method

For dehazing task, the hazy image and the haze-free image are usually denoted as I and J. Denoting the whole dehazing network as $\mathcal{D}$, then in general it is optimized towards

$$\min \; \mathcal{L}\left(\mathcal{D}(I), J\right) \tag{3}$$

where $\mathcal{L}$ is the defined restoration loss function.

Our semantic guidance works on network $\mathcal{D}$ in the form of SF and SA, and works on loss $\mathcal{L}$ in the form of SL, respectively. Combining the power of designing network constructs and loss functions, our SG-Net series takes advantage of semantic information to perform well in image dehazing.

3.1 Semantic Fusion and Semantic Attention

To illustrate SF and SA in detail, we can refer to Fig. 2. Feed the raw hazy input to the pretrained semantic segmentation network (denoted as $\mathcal{S}$), then it exports the semantic feature maps ($\mathcal{S}(\cdot)$ stands for the output logits of the last layer). Note that in one whole network, all the SG branches share the same $\mathcal{S}$, therefore we just need to generate the semantic feature maps once and then impose different operations on them.

Denote the convolution layer, ReLU activation function, Sigmoid activation function as Conv, δ, σ, and denote the operation of concatenation, element-wise sum, element-wise product as $\cup$, $\oplus$, $\otimes$, respectively. Besides, denote the middle feature maps from the baseline network branch as F (size $C \times H \times W$), then we can fulfill SF and SA function by operation $\cup$ and $\otimes$, as shown below, where S_F and S_A are generated feature maps from the corresponding SG mechanisms.

Semantic Fusion

$$S_F = \delta(\mathrm{Conv}(\mathcal{S}(I))) \tag{4}$$

$$\check{F} = F \cup S_F \tag{5}$$

Let the size of F and S_F be $C_1 \times H \times W$ and $C_2 \times H \times W$ respectively, then the size of $\check{F}$ is $(C_1 + C_2) \times H \times W$. If the size $H \times W$ of F and S_F are different, we only need to add an upsampling or downsampling in the SF branch, so as the SA branch. Removing all other elements and only leaving the concatenation will degenerate SF into an ordinary skip-layer connection.

Semantic Attention

$$S_A = \sigma(\text{Conv}(\delta(\text{Conv}(\mathcal{S}(I))))) \tag{6}$$

$$\tilde{F} = F \otimes S_A \tag{7}$$

The size of S_A is $1 \times H \times W$. Note that the size of Channel Attention (CA) and Pixel Attention (PA) in FFA-Net [20] are $C \times 1 \times 1$ and $1 \times H \times W$, respectively. And the formula of PA can be expressed as:

$$P_A = \sigma(\text{Conv}(\delta(\text{Conv}(F)))) \tag{8}$$

$$\tilde{F} = F \otimes P_A \tag{9}$$

The key difference between SA and PA is the source of attention. Generating attention through the pretrained semantic segmentation network fully excavates the semantic prior information, leading the dehazing networks to learn the transmission map more specifically. It can be seen from the visualization analysis in Sect. 4.5 that after a relatively deep stage of feature propagation, the PA only focuses on the local edges of objects, while our SA still has an accurate grasp of the global contour.

As for the general usage strategy of SG mechanisms, we recommend **adopting SF for shallow feature maps and SA for deep feature maps**. SF and SA could be considered as guiding from channel-wise (coarse) and pixel-wise (fine) levels, respectively. Since the $\mathcal{S}(I)$ is more matched with shallow F, so concatenating them with high-level deep F at the back layer is not very appropriate. In that case, the element-wise product provides accurate and efficient semantic guidance at pixel-level to make up for deep F. In addition, we recommend **adopting SF at a relatively low-resolution scale** if there is a downsampling operation in the networks. We infer that a low-resolution scale could alleviate the mismatches between S_F and F, especially for the object edges. More specifically quantified, we recommend placing one or two SF in the front and center (denoting the number of whole layers as n, then we may consider the layer of $[\frac{n}{2}]$, where $[]$ is a rounding operation), and placing one SA in the back (e.g. $n-3$). A more detailed exploration on the design of SG mechanisms can refer to Sect. 4.4, including multi-branch strategy, fusion position, *etc.*

3.2 Semantic Loss

For the common reconstruction loss of image dehazing, we adopt residual learning rather than directly learning the haze-free images since the former

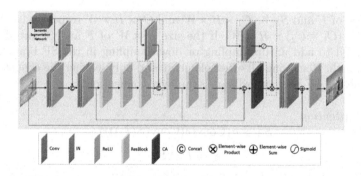

Fig. 3. SG-AOD network architecture.

learning method is more effective. Hence, the restoration loss function is cal-culated between the network output $\mathcal{D}(I)$ and residual $J - I$.

$$
\begin{aligned}
r &= J - I \\
\hat{r} &= \mathcal{D}(I) \\
\mathscr{L}_{\text{rec}} &= ||\hat{r} - r||_1
\end{aligned}
\tag{10}
$$

where $|| \cdot ||_1$ is the L1 norm. Through the experiments, we discover that L1 loss performs better than L2 loss, especially when comparing SSIM (Structural Similarity) metrics.

What's more, we propose a new kind of semantic perception loss. To strengthen the semantic relationship between haze-free and dehazed images, we apply a regularization on their feature maps through the pretrained semantic segmentation network, *i.e.* $\mathcal{S}(\mathcal{D}(I))$ and $\mathcal{S}(J)$:

$$
\mathscr{L}_{\text{sem}} = ||\mathcal{S}(\mathcal{D}(I)) - \mathcal{S}(J)||_1
\tag{11}
$$

where $\mathcal{S}(\cdot)$ could be considered to be substituted by features $\mathcal{S}_i(\cdot)$ from different stages i.

Then, we can combine the reconstruction loss and semantic loss to get our final loss function as

$$
\mathscr{L} = \mathscr{L}_{\text{rec}} + \lambda_{\text{sem}}\mathscr{L}_{\text{sem}}
\tag{12}
$$

where λ_{sem} is an adjustable positive weight. Note that the AECR-Net has also adopted an extra contrastive loss $\mathscr{L}_{\text{con}}$ [31], thus our SG-AECR loss composes of three parts:

$$
\mathscr{L} = \mathscr{L}_{\text{rec}} + \lambda_{\text{con}}\mathscr{L}_{\text{con}} + \lambda_{\text{sem}}\mathscr{L}_{\text{sem}}
\tag{13}
$$

where λ_{con} is also a positive weight. The experiments indicate that our semantic loss brings a significant promotion, especially on SSIM metrics. For more detailed results, please refer to Sect. 4.4.

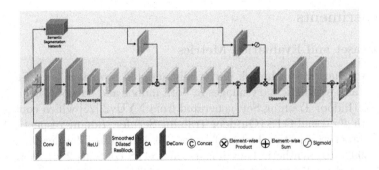

Fig. 4. SG-GCA network architecture.

3.3 SG-Net Series

Firstly, we take AOD-Net as an example to give a detailed introduction of SG-AOD, as shown in Fig. 3. Then we can easily master the other members of SG-Net series: SG-GCA, SG-FFA and SG-AECR. They are shown in Fig. 4 and Appendix, respectively. Each of them can be considered as a combination of the baseline network and the SG module.

SG-AOD. Embedding our proposed SG module into the baseline AOD-Net, then the SG-AOD network architecture can be seen in Fig. 3 (SL is not presented, the same as below). Dividing this network into two parts, the lower part is the baseline AOD-Net (grey background), and the upper part is the SG module (green background). Focusing on the SG module, the red cube represents the semantic segmentation network. The SG module has two different kinds of branches, which exactly correspond to the two different semantic guided modes: 2 SFs and 1 SA, as shown in the blue and green dotted rectangle, respectively.

SG-GCA. Speaking of the SG-GCA, the baseline GCA-Net adopts the smoothed dilated convolution and a downsampling-upsampling framework. On the basis of it, we add an SF branch and an SA branch at the downsampling scale as the SG module, then SG-GCA is constructed.

SG-FFA. As for the SG-FFA, the baseline FFA-Net fully adopts the CA and PA modules. In addition to the final CA and PA, every block in the group structure contains a pair of CA and PA (3 groups contain 19 blocks). We add 2 SF branches in front of the G-1 and G-2 modules. Besides, we update the last PA and the PA of G-3 to SA, as indicated by the red dotted line.

SG-AECR. The baseline AECR-Net consists of autoencoder-like downsampling-upsampling framework and contrastive regularization, and the former includes 6 FA blocks, 1 DFE module, and 2 adaptive mixup operations. We add an SF branch after the 3rd FA block and add an SA branch after the DFE module.

4   Experiments

4.1   Dataset and Evaluation Metrics

The image dehazing benchmark universally adopted nowadays is RESIDE [14], which contains synthetic hazy images in both indoor and outdoor scenarios. We adopt ITS (Indoor Training Set, generated from NYUv2 [25] which contains the scene depth $d(x)$) and OTS (Outdoor Training Set) for training respectively, and SOTS (Synthetic Objective Test Set) for test. ITS contains 1399 clean images and 13990 (1399 × 10) synthetic hazy images, and OTS contains 2061 clean images and 72135 (2061 × 35) synthetic hazy images. SOTS contains 500 indoor images and 500 outdoor images. The synthesis method is setting different atmosphere light A and scattering parameter β within a certain range.

To further evaluate the robustness of dehazing models in the real-world scene, we also adopt two challenging real-world datasets: Dense-Haze [1] and NH-HAZE (Non-Homogeneous HAZE) [2]. The haze of Dense-Haze is very heavy and the haze of NH-HAZE is not uniformly distributed. These two datasets both contain 55 1200 × 1600 size images, consisting of 45 training images, 5 validation images and 5 test images. Following the division of AECR-Net, the size of training set and test set are 40 and 5 for Dense-Haze, while 45 and 5 for NH-HAZE.

As for the evaluation metrics, we adopt the common PSNR (Peak Signal to Noise Ratio) and SSIM (Structural Similarity).

4.2   Implementation Details

We finish the experiments on NVIDIA GPU (Tesla V100) by PyTorch framework. The configuration of our SG-Net series that does not appear in the detailed description (please refer to the Appendix) is just the same as the baseline networks. All the SG-Nets adopt Adam as optimizer with momentum $\beta_1 = 0.9$, $\beta_2 = 0.999$. Unless otherwise specified, our utilized semantic segmentation model is RefineNet: RF-LW-ResNet-50. As for the loss weight λ_{sem}, we adjust it so that the reconstruction loss and weighted semantic loss are about at the same level.

4.3   Quantitative and Qualitative Evaluation

As Table 1 shows, we choose the classic DCP method and four representative networks, *i.e.* AOD, GCA, FFA, AECR, to make comparisons. For a certain type of network, from the baseline network to our SG-Net, PSNR and SSIM both gradually get varying degrees of improvement, which strongly demonstrates the effectiveness of our proposed SG mechanisms. During our research, the investigated state-of-the-art methods are FFA-Net on RESIDE, and AECE-Net on Dense-Haze and NH-HAZE, respectively. Our SG-FFA still gets some breakthroughs to reach a new state-of-the-art performance. After increasing the training batch from 2 to 5 with the same iteration, FFA gets further promotion on (PSNR, SSIM) for indoor SOTS: $(38.61, 0.9913)$ of FFA-Net and $(39.18, 0.9932)$ of SG-FFA. It should be noted that the performance on dataset ITS is almost

Table 1. Quantitative comparisons on different datasets for different dehazing methods.

Methods	Indoor SOTS		Outdoor SOTS		Dense-Haze		NH-HAZE	
	PSNR	SSIM	PSNR	SSIM	PSNR	SSIM	PSNR	SSIM
DCP	16.62	0.8179	19.13	0.8148	–	–	–	–
AOD-Net	21.30	0.8251	25.78	0.9293	–	–	–	–
SG-AOD	**23.33**	**0.8707**	**26.18**	**0.9362**	–	–	–	–
GCA-Net	27.79	0.9452	28.39	0.9500	–	–	–	–
SG-GCA	**29.78**	**0.9621**	**29.15**	**0.9593**	–	–	–	–
FFA-Net	36.39	0.9886	31.69	**0.9800**	–	–	–	–
SG-FFA	**37.56**	**0.9915**	**32.11**	0.9791	–	–	–	–
AECR-Net	33.34	0.9824	–	–	14.43	0.4450	18.50	0.6562
SG-AECR	**33.67**	**0.9832**	–	–	**14.91**	**0.4641**	**18.68**	**0.6609**

the same as the reported performance in the original paper of FFA-Net, but the performance on OTS drops a lot. So we have to take the run result as the real baseline and then adopt SG modules on it for a fair comparison. Similarly, with the open-source code from the authors of AECR-Net [31], we are still not able to reach the best level reported in the paper. So we need to reproduce the code as a baseline to make a comparison, and would not claim the outperformance as new state-of-the-art performance. Our SG-AECR beats the AECR-Net on all three datasets, which once again reveals the effectiveness of semantic guidance for image dehazing. Dense-Haze and NH-HAZE are far more challenging than RESIDE, thus common networks such as AOD-Net behave not well on them. Thanks to the power of contrastive regularization, AECR-Net could get relatively better results.

Furthermore, we display the qualitative comparisons for different dehazing methods here. In Fig. 5, the top 2 rows correspond to the ITS-trained models, while the bottom 4 rows correspond to the OTS-trained models. We can observe that DCP suffers from severe color distortion because of their underlying prior assumptions. AOD-Net is often unable to entirely remove the haze and tends to output low-brightness images. GCA-Net is unsatisfactory at processing high-frequency detail such as textures and edges. Compared to the baseline series, our SG-Net series is superior in detail maintenance and color fidelity, such as the sky region. Concentrating on the last pumpkin image, our SG-FFA has the most obvious dehazing effect, especially on the ground surface. And zooming in on the red wall area of the first image, the white haze of SG-FFA is the weakest, close to nothing. Some visualization results of SG-AECR are shown in Fig. 6. We can observe the superiority of our SG-AECR over AECR-Net, for example, the string 'OUTDOOR' on the ping pong table in the 3th column of images. More quantitative and qualitative results (including training curve, *etc.*) are demonstrated in the Appendix.

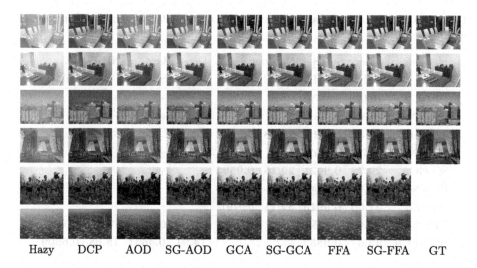

Hazy   DCP   AOD   SG-AOD   GCA   SG-GCA   FFA   SG-FFA   GT

Fig. 5. Qualitative comparisons on SOTS (the top 2 rows for indoor and the middle 2 rows for outdoor) and real-world hazy images (the bottom 2 rows, without corresponding ground truth images) for different dehazing methods. Zoom in on the green rectangle area for more details. (Color figure online)

Fig. 6. Qualitative comparisons on indoor SOTS, Dense-Haze and NH-HAZE (corresponding in column order, two columns each) for our SG-AECR. Zoom in on the green rectangle area for more details. (Color figure online)

4.4   Ablation Study

To further analyze the function of SG mechanisms, we make a comprehensive ablation study as shown in Table 2. Without any mechanism corresponds to the baseline models, and including SA module means replacing PA with SA. Taking SG-AOD and SG-GCA on ITS as examples, SA and SF both bring promotion and the appropriate combination of them with SL achieves better performance. From PA to SA, the more specific guidance of semantic feature maps and their superiority as attention are fully embodied. Moreover, the flexible transplantation of SG mechanisms is worth mentioning.

Table 2. Ablation analysis with different SG mechanisms on indoor SOTS.

SA			✓		✓	✓
SF				✓	✓	✓
SL						✓
SG-AOD	PSNR	21.30	22.07	23.14	23.24	**23.33**
	SSIM	0.8251	0.8360	0.8432	0.8468	**0.8707**
SG-GCA	PSNR	27.79	28.28	28.98	29.06	**29.78**
	SSIM	0.9452	0.9475	0.9493	0.9531	**0.9621**

Table 3. Ablation analysis of different SF positions on indoor SOTS for SG-AOD.

SF Position	None	c1+r1	c1+r3	cr+r3+r7	c2+r3+r7	r3+r7	r1+r3	r1+r3+r5
PSNR	21.30	**23.23**	23.14	22.93	22.60	22.40	23.02	22.27
SSIM	0.8251	**0.8585**	0.8432	0.8322	0.8403	0.8260	0.8312	0.8271

And we briefly introduce the design details of SG mechanisms here. For SA, we increase the convolutional layer from 1 to 2 (with a 0.81 increase of PNSR in a set of AOD-ITS comparative experiments, abbreviated as PSNR ↑ 0.81, the same as below). For SF, if a multi-branch strategy is adopted, we add independent SF branches instead of sharing the same SF parameters (PSNR ↑ 0.26). These modifications bring positive effects because the fitting capacity of the network has been further strengthened. Besides, the concatenation position of SF is carefully explored. For SG-AOD, adding another SF branch after the 7th ResBlock brings a negative effect (PSNR ↓ 0.21). For SG-GCA, embedding SF branch before downsampling does not perform better than embedding after downsampling (PSNR ↓ 0.39). These phenomena reflect that the semantic fusion is more suitable for shallow feature maps and relatively low-resolution scales, which is consistent with our inference. Denoting the layers of SG-AOD as c1–c2 (convolution layer), r1–r7 (residual layer) in order, a more detailed exploration is shown in Table 3 (without SA and SL). We can see the superiority of front c1 over back r7, *etc.*

On the other hand, we have mentioned that we set the SL weight λ_{sem} to satisfy that the reconstruction loss and weighted semantic loss are about at the same order of magnitude. Therefore, the network will take into account the guidance of these loss functions with nearly equal importance when training. Following this simple and effective selection principle, we have already achieved good results. As for different semantic weights λ_{sem}, we make a simple study on ITS for SG-AOD. From Table 4 we can see that our semantic loss has a significant promotion on dehazing effect, especially on SSIM metrics.

Table 4. Ablation analysis of different SL weights on indoor SOTS for SG-AOD.

SL Weight	0	0.0005	0.001	0.003	0.005
PSNR	23.24	22.82	22.81	**23.33**	23.20
SSIM		0.8468	0.8540	0.8639	0.8707	**0.8747**

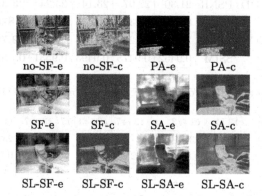

no-SF-e   no-SF-c   PA-e   PA-c

SF-e   SF-c   SA-e   SA-c

SL-SF-e   SL-SF-c   SL-SA-e   SL-SA-c

Fig. 7. Visual comparisons on middle feature maps between AOD-Net (top) and our SG-AOD (middle without SL and bottom with SL). The feature map of SF is from the first convolution module after SF module, and PA is equivalent to no-SA. For a clearer observation, *e* and *c* mean *histogram equalization* and *colormap*, respectively.

4.5   Visualization Analysis

As Fig. 7 shows, still taking the demo image in Fig. 1 as an example, we display the middle feature maps from the same position for comparison, with or without semantic guidance (results of SG-GCA are in the Appendix). The feature maps with SG mechanisms contain more details and fit the contour of objects better, thus generating more smooth and accurate dehazed results. We have also tried to implement a visual explanation with Grad-CAM [24], which uses the Gradient-weighted Class Activation Mapping to produce a coarse localization map to highlight the important regions. Yet the results is not as ideal as in Fig. 7. We infer that the dehazing task is not like a classification task which only focuses on partial saliency regions.

4.6   Segmentation Model

We mainly adopt the RF-LW-ResNet-50 trained on NYUv2 dataset as the semantic segmentation model. On ITS, from NYU-Res50 to the relatively stronger NYU-Res152, there is not much difference in the dehazing metrics. We infer that the improved dehazing effect is mainly due to our proposed SG mechanisms, that is, how to better impose semantic guidance, while the impact of segmentation models is relatively slight. Though the images of OTS do not seem to be very consistent with NYUv2-trained segmentation model, their segmentation results still play a good role in the SG-Nets. Moreover, substituting

Table 5. Time (training and inference) and parameter analysis.

Methods	AOD		GCA		FFA		AECR	
	Base	SG	Base	SG	Base	SG	Base	SG
Train (h)	3.2	4.1	22.6	25.3	193.4	181.2	40.1	47.2
Infer (s)	0.16	0.19	0.30	0.32	0.47	0.49	0.39	0.46
#Params (M)	0.62	0.66	0.71	0.72	4.46	4.49	2.61	3.93

PASCAL_VOC-trained model (21 classes) for NYUv2-trained model partially improves the dehazing metrics on OTS, because PASCAL_VOC is more consistent with outdoor images. For more details on the exploration of segmentation models such as the superiority of soft logits over hard outputs, please refer to the Appendix.

4.7 Efficiency Analysis

Finally, we give simple comparisons of training time (on ITS), inference time (per image on average, on SOTS), and parameters between our SG-Nets and the baseline series, as shown in Table 5. Note that the time consumption corresponds to 1 GPU, and the parameters of pretrained semantic segmentation model are not counted. We can see that the efficient SG mechanism does not bring a lot of extra time and space consumption, which are mainly dominated by the segmentation model. Thus pre-storing the semantic segmentation feature maps of the training data can save the training time if needed. And it is worth noting that the training time of SG-FFA is less than FFA-Net. This is due to that we replace many SAs with PAs, while the input channel numbers of SA's 2 layers are less than PA's, [40, 5] *versus* [64, 8].

5   Conclusion

In this paper, we have proposed an end-to-end Semantic Guided Network for image dehazing. Semantic guidance is fulfilled with three simple yet effective designs: Semantic Fusion, Semantic Attention and Semantic Loss. The outperformance over existing methods is demonstrated both in quantity and quality. And our SG mechanisms could be flexibly embedded into a certain network so that a better tradeoff between accuracy and speed would be sought. In future work, it is worth studying to further explore the explanation of semantic mechanism (similar function of field depth or edge contour) and extend it to other low-level vision tasks.

Acknowledgements. This work was supported by the Natural Science Foundation of China under grant 62071171.

References

1. Ancuti, C.O., Ancuti, C., Sbert, M., Timofte, R.: Dense-haze: a benchmark for image dehazing with dense-haze and haze-free images. In: 2019 IEEE International Conference on Image Processing (ICIP), pp. 1014–1018. IEEE (2019)
2. Ancuti, C.O., Ancuti, C., Timofte, R.: NH-HAZE: an image dehazing benchmark with non-homogeneous hazy and haze-free images. In: Proceedings of the IEEE/CVF Conference on Computer Vision and Pattern Recognition Workshops, pp. 444–445 (2020)
3. Cai, B., Xu, X., Jia, K., Qing, C., Tao, D.: Dehazenet: an end-to-end system for single image haze removal. IEEE Trans. Image Process. **25**(11), 5187–5198 (2016)
4. Chen, D., et al.: Gated context aggregation network for image dehazing and deraining. In: 2019 IEEE Winter Conference on Applications of Computer Vision (WACV), pp. 1375–1383. IEEE (2019)
5. Chen, L.C., Papandreou, G., Kokkinos, I., Murphy, K., Yuille, A.L.: Semantic image segmentation with deep convolutional nets and fully connected crfs. arXiv preprint arXiv:1412.7062 (2014)
6. Chen, L.C., Papandreou, G., Kokkinos, I., Murphy, K., Yuille, A.L.: Deeplab: semantic image segmentation with deep convolutional nets, atrous convolution, and fully connected crfs. IEEE Trans. Pattern Anal. Mach. Intell. **40**(4), 834–848 (2017)
7. Chen, L.C., Papandreou, G., Schroff, F., Adam, H.: Rethinking atrous convolution for semantic image segmentation. arXiv preprint arXiv:1706.05587 (2017)
8. Chen, Z., Wang, Y., Yang, Y., Liu, D.: PSD: principled synthetic-to-real dehazing guided by physical priors. In: Proceedings of the IEEE/CVF Conference on Computer Vision and Pattern Recognition, pp. 7180–7189 (2021)
9. Cheng, Z., You, S., Ila, V., Li, H.: Semantic single-image dehazing. arXiv preprint arXiv:1804.05624 (2018)
10. Garcia-Garcia, A., Orts-Escolano, S., Oprea, S., Villena-Martinez, V., Garcia-Rodriguez, J.: A review on deep learning techniques applied to semantic segmentation. arXiv preprint arXiv:1704.06857 (2017)
11. He, K., Sun, J., Tang, X.: Single image haze removal using dark channel prior. IEEE Trans. Pattern Anal. Mach. Intell. **33**(12), 2341–2353 (2010)
12. He, K., Zhang, X., Ren, S., Sun, J.: Deep residual learning for image recognition. In: Proceedings of the IEEE Conference on Computer Vision and Pattern Recognition, pp. 770–778 (2016)
13. Li, B., Peng, X., Wang, Z., Xu, J., Feng, D.: AOD-Net: all-in-one dehazing network. In: Proceedings of the IEEE International Conference on Computer Vision, pp. 4770–4778 (2017)
14. Li, B., et al.: Reside: a benchmark for single image dehazing. arXiv preprint arXiv:1712.04143 1 (2017)
15. Lin, G., Milan, A., Shen, C., Reid, I.: RefineNet: multi-path refinement networks for high-resolution semantic segmentation. In: Proceedings of the IEEE Conference on Computer Vision and Pattern Recognition, pp. 1925–1934 (2017)
16. Long, J., Shelhamer, E., Darrell, T.: Fully convolutional networks for semantic segmentation. In: Proceedings of the IEEE Conference on Computer Vision and Pattern Recognition, pp. 3431–3440 (2015)
17. McCartney, E.J.: Optics of the atmosphere: scattering by molecules and particles. New York (1976)
18. Meng, G., Wang, Y., Duan, J., Xiang, S., Pan, C.: Efficient image dehazing with boundary constraint and contextual regularization. In: Proceedings of the IEEE International Conference on Computer Vision, pp. 617–624 (2013)

19. Narasimhan, S.G., Nayar, S.K.: Vision and the atmosphere. Int. J. Comput. Vis. **48**(3), 233–254 (2002)
20. Qin, X., Wang, Z., Bai, Y., Xie, X., Jia, H.: FFA-Net: feature fusion attention network for single image dehazing. In: Proceedings of the AAAI Conference on Artificial Intelligence, vol. 34, pp. 11908–11915 (2020)
21. Ren, W., Liu, S., Zhang, H., Pan, J., Cao, X., Yang, M.-H.: Single image dehazing via multi-scale convolutional neural networks. In: Leibe, B., Matas, J., Sebe, N., Welling, M. (eds.) ECCV 2016. LNCS, vol. 9906, pp. 154–169. Springer, Cham (2016). https://doi.org/10.1007/978-3-319-46475-6_10
22. Ren, W., et al.: Deep video dehazing with semantic segmentation. IEEE Trans. Image Process. **28**(4), 1895–1908 (2018)
23. Ronneberger, O., Fischer, P., Brox, T.: U-Net: convolutional networks for biomedical image segmentation. In: Navab, N., Hornegger, J., Wells, W.M., Frangi, A.F. (eds.) MICCAI 2015. LNCS, vol. 9351, pp. 234–241. Springer, Cham (2015). https://doi.org/10.1007/978-3-319-24574-4_28
24. Selvaraju, R.R., Cogswell, M., Das, A., Vedantam, R., Parikh, D., Batra, D.: Gradcam: visual explanations from deep networks via gradient-based localization. In: Proceedings of the IEEE International Conference on Computer Vision, pp. 618–626 (2017)
25. Silberman, N., Hoiem, D., Kohli, P., Fergus, R.: Indoor segmentation and support inference from RGBD images. In: Fitzgibbon, A., Lazebnik, S., Perona, P., Sato, Y., Schmid, C. (eds.) ECCV 2012. LNCS, vol. 7576, pp. 746–760. Springer, Heidelberg (2012). https://doi.org/10.1007/978-3-642-33715-4_54
26. Song, T., Jang, H., Ha, N., Yeon, Y., Kwon, K., Sohn, K.: Deep multi-task network for simultaneous hazy image semantic segmentation and dehazing. J. Korea Multimedia Soci. **22**(9), 1000–1010 (2019)
27. Vandenhende, S., Georgoulis, S., Van Gool, L.: MTI-Net: multi-scale task interaction networks for multi-task learning. In: Vedaldi, A., Bischof, H., Brox, T., Frahm, J.-M. (eds.) ECCV 2020. LNCS, vol. 12349, pp. 527–543. Springer, Cham (2020). https://doi.org/10.1007/978-3-030-58548-8_31
28. Vaswani, A., et al.: Attention is all you need. In: Advances in Neural Information Processing Systems, pp. 5998–6008 (2017)
29. Wang, X., Girshick, R., Gupta, A., He, K.: Non-local neural networks. In: Proceedings of the IEEE Conference on Computer Vision and Pattern Recognition, pp. 7794–7803 (2018)
30. Wang, Z., Ji, S.: Smoothed dilated convolutions for improved dense prediction. In: Data Mining and Knowledge Discovery, pp. 1–27 (2021)
31. Wu, H., et al.: Contrastive learning for compact single image dehazing. In: Proceedings of the IEEE/CVF Conference on Computer Vision and Pattern Recognition, pp. 10551–10560 (2021)
32. Xu, K., et al.: Show, attend and tell: neural image caption generation with visual attention. In: International Conference on Machine Learning, pp. 2048–2057. PMLR (2015)
33. Yang, X., Xu, Z., Luo, J.: Towards perceptual image dehazing by physics-based disentanglement and adversarial training. In: Proceedings of the AAAI Conference on Artificial Intelligence, vol. 32 (2018)
34. Zhang, S., et al.: Semantic-aware dehazing network with adaptive feature fusion. IEEE Trans. Cybernet. **53**, 454–467 (2021)
35. Zhu, Q., Mai, J., Shao, L.: A fast single image haze removal algorithm using color attenuation prior. IEEE Trans. Image Process. **24**(11), 3522–3533 (2015)

Self-Supervised Dehazing Network Using Physical Priors

Gwangjin Ju[1], Yeongcheol Choi[2], Donggun Lee[1], Jee Hyun Paik[2],
Gyeongha Hwang[3], and Seungyong Lee[1(✉)]

[1] POSTECH, Pohang, Korea
{gwangjin,dalelee,leesy}@postech.ac.kr
[2] POSCO ICT, Pohang, Korea
{ycchoi,jeehyun100}@poscoict.com
[3] Yeungnam University, Gyeongsan, Korea
ghhwang@yu.ac.kr

Abstract. In this paper, we propose a lightweight self-supervised dehazing network with the help of physical priors, called *Self-Supervised Dehazing Network (SSDN)*. SSDN is a modified U-Net that estimates a clear image, transmission map, and atmospheric airlight out of the input hazy image based on the Atmospheric Scattering Model (ASM). It is trained in a self-supervised manner, utilizing recent self-supervised training methods and physical prior knowledge for obtaining realistic outputs. Thanks to the training objectives based on ASM, SSDN learns physically meaningful features. As a result, SSDN learns to estimate clear images that satisfy physical priors, instead of simply following data distribution, and it becomes generalized well over the data domain. With the self-supervision of SSDN, the dehazing performance can be easily finetuned with an additional dataset that can be built by simply collecting hazy images. Experimental results show that our proposed SSDN is lightweight and shows competitive dehazing performance with strong generalization capability over various data domains.

1 Introduction

Vision systems are applied to many tasks like autonomous driving, factory safety surveillance, etc. However, haze artifacts reduce the scene visibility, and the performance of vision systems could be degraded by reduced visibility. Dehazing can help vision systems become robust by reducing haze from the scene.

One of the popular approaches in the dehazing task is prior-based. Most of the existing prior-based dehazing methods are based on Atmospheric Scattering Model (ASM) [17]. Prior-based methods remove haze by estimating the transmission map, which reflects the amount of haze in the image. Since the methods are based on physical properties, they show stable performance over a variety of domains with different image contents (Fig. 1).

Supplementary Information The online version contains supplementary material available at https://doi.org/10.1007/978-3-031-26313-2_18.

(a)   (b)   (c)

Fig. 1. Dehazed results of (a) input images by (b) DehazeNet [4] and (c) our method. While our method is trained on the indoor dataset in a self-supervised manner, it shows comparative performance to DehazeNet which is trained on the outdoor dataset in a supervised manner.

Recently, deep learning based dazing methods are proposed, which utilize powerful CNNs. Early method [4] estimates the transmission map of ASM using CNN. Most deep learning-based dehazing methods are image-to-image translation approaches like pix2pix [11] and estimate the clear image directly from a hazy image. More recently, an unsupervised image-to-image translation approach [5] has been proposed using cycle consistency from CycleGAN [27]. Deep learning-based methods show high performance in the trained domains and run fast by GPU acceleration.

Although many approaches are proposed for dehazing, they have limitations. Most prior-based methods are not designed to utilize GPU, so they run slowly compared to deep learning-based methods. They also show lower performance compared to data-driven methods. Deep learning-based methods show high performance but their performance degrades a lot when the data domain changes. Moreover, building datasets is difficult because acquiring both hazy and clear images with the same view is almost infeasible.

In this paper, inspired by [18] and [17], we propose *Self-Supervised Dehazing Network (SSDN)*. SSDN estimates disentangled clear image, transmission map, and atmospheric airlight out of a hazy image. In the training phase, SSDN learns to satisfy the ASM by reconstructing the hazy image from outputs. To make the output of SSDN realistic, we exploit physical prior knowledge such as Dark Channel Prior [10], total variation [21], the relation between hazy and clear images in color space, and local variance.

To the best of our knowledge, this research is the first attempt to merge physical prior knowledge and self-supervision on the dehazing task. SSDN has several advantages that compensate limitations of other approaches. First, SSDN dehazes images based on ASM, which is physically meaningful and explainable than other deep learning-based methods. Second, SSDN is implemented as a lightweight CNN, enabling application to real-time systems. Third, SSDN is well generalized over data domains thanks to physical prior knowledge. Lastly, it is easy to build a dataset for SSDN training by simply collecting hazy images without corresponding clear images. With these advantages, SSDN can be applied to practical vision systems, especially real-time ones due to its lightweight structure and stable performance over various data domains.

In summary, our method merges physical prior knowledge with self-supervised learning to resolve limitations of previous dehazing methods, such as long execution time, different performance over domains, and laborious dataset building.

2   Related Work

2.1   Prior-Based Methods

Prior-based methods perform dehazing based on the observed characteristics of hazy images. Most of those method utilizes Atmospheric Scattering Model [17] that models hazy image based on physics-based knowledge.

One of the most representative methods is the Dark Channel Prior (DCP) [10]. DCP assumes that at least one of the R, G, and B channel values tends to be very low for clear images. The Color Attenuation Prior (CAP) [28] assumes that the difference between saturation and value channel in HSV space is proportional to the amount of haze. In [3], the Non-local Color Prior (NCP) is proposed, which is based on the observation that a clear image consists of a small number of clusters in the RGB color space.

Most prior-based methods are straightforward and more accessible than deep learning-based approaches. Furthermore, those methods show strong domain generalization capability. However, the dehazing performance of prior-based methods is lower than most of the supervised deep learning-based methods.

2.2   Supervised Learning Methods

Recently, the dehazing task was successfully performed using supervised deep learning methods. These methods exploit a paired dataset of hazy and clear images to learn to generate clear images from given hazy images.

DehazeNet [4] takes a hazy image as input and estimates the transmission map. The estimated transmission map is then used with ASM to dehaze the hazy image. Feature Fusion Attention Network (FFANet) [19] improved the dehazing performance by proposing specialized modules for dehazing, such as channel attention and pixel attention modules. In the supervised learning methods, the dehazing performance has been improved thanks to the recent advances of deep learning architectures [13, 16, 25].

Supervised deep learning methods have demonstrated high dehazing performance and showed fast inference speed based on GPU acceleration. However, recent deep learning-based methods are getting to use larger and more complex networks, and performing them on low-end devices, e.g., embedded systems for autonomous driving, would not be easy. In addition, it is challenging to build a paired dataset needed for supervised learning methods. Lastly, these methods may show poor generalization capability due to the dependency on the dataset.

2.3 Unsupervised Learning Methods

Recently unsupervised learning methods have been proposed to perform dehazing without a paired dataset to overcome the difficulty of dataset construction. Cycle-Dehaze [5] uses cycle consistency loss [27] to train a dehazing network on an unpaired dataset. D^4 (Dehazing via Decomposing transmission map into Density and Depth) [24] utilizes depth estimation with ASM to build cycle consistency. These methods need no paired dataset but still, it needs both clean and hazy image sets.

DDIP [7] and You Only Look Yourself (YOLY) [15] perform dehazing based on ASM. They optimize a network from scratch for each hazy image, without using any dataset. As these methods perform optimization for a single image, they are free from domain change and show better performance than other prior-based methods. However, they take seconds or even minutes to remove haze from an image, which makes them hard to be used for real-time vision systems.

3   Physical Priors

In this section, we describe physical priors used for our proposed framework. We first describe priors proposed in previous works and then propose several priors for the dehazing task based on ASM.

3.1   Conventional Priors

Atmospheric Scattering Model. ASM [17] represents the scattering of scene radiance by the particle in the atmosphere as the following equation:

$$I = JT + A(1 - T), \tag{1}$$

where I, J, T, and A denote hazy image, clear scene radiance, transmission map, and atmospheric airlight, respectively. For a hazy image $I \in \mathbb{R}^{H \times W \times C}$, we assume the transmission is a multi-channel map $T \in \mathbb{R}^{H \times W \times C}$ and the airlight A is homogeneous, i.e. $A \in \mathbb{R}^{1 \times 1 \times C}$.

Dark Channel Prior. DCP [10] estimates the transmission map based on the observation that the pixel intensity of at least one channel among RGB channel is close to 0 in a clear image. It can be represented as follow:

$$T_{DCP} = 1 - \min_c(\min_{y \in \Omega(x)} (\frac{I^c(y)}{A^c})),$$

(2)

where c denotes a RGB color channel and $\Omega(x)$ is the window of each pixel.

Total Variation Prior. Total variation prior [21] has been used for various image restoration tasks. It is based on the observation that a clear image tends to have a quite low total variation (nearly 0) which can be represented as follow:

$$TV(I) = \sum_{i,j} |I_{i+1,j} - I_{i,j}| + |I_{i,j+1} - I_{i,j}| \approx 0,$$

(3)

where $I_{i,j}$ denotes the pixel value of I at coordinate (i, j).

3.2   Our Proposed Priors

In ASM, a hazy image is represented as an interpolation between a clear image and airlight, and it is known that airlight is close to white. We propose several priors on hazy and clear images with this property.

In RGB color space, the pixel intensity of the hazy image I is higher than that of the clear image J as I is closer to white than J due to the interpolation in ASM:

$$J < I.$$

(4)

In HSV color space, we derive priors on value (brightness) and saturation channels. For value (brightness) channel, the pixel value of a hazy image is higher than that of the clear image, again due to the interpolation in ASM. For saturation channel, the saturation of hazy image is lower than that of a clear image, as mixture with white reduces the saturation.

$$J_{value} < I_{value},$$

(5)

$$J_{sat} > I_{sat},$$

(6)

where x_{value} is value channel and x_{sat} is saturation channel in HSV space.

The homogeneous airlight A makes the contrast of a hazy image lower than a clear image. Hence, the local variance of the hazy image is lower than that of the clear image as follow:

$$var(J) > var(I),$$

(7)

where $var(x)$ is a local variance operator that computes the variance of each color channel in a local window centered at x.

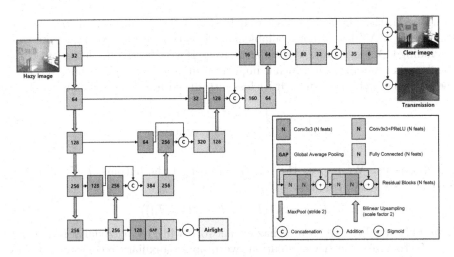

Fig. 2. Overall framework of our proposed SSDN. Given a hazy image, SSDN estimates clear image, transmission map, and airlight separately.

4   Self-Supervised Dehazing Network

Our self-supervised learning framework for dehazing has been inspired by CVF-SID [18] but contains important differences to exploit ASM and physical priors of hazy images. Unlike the denoising problem that CVF-SID handles by simply exploiting reconstruction loss and variance norm, the dehazing task needs to consider a complicated haze structure. So we exploit several physical priors described in Sect. 3 to train our Self-Supervised Dehazing Network (SSDN) based on ASM.

4.1   Overall Framework

Our proposed SSDN is a multi-variate function, and the structure of SSDN is a modified U-Net [20] as shown in Fig. 2. The output of SSDN is given by:

$$\hat{J}, \hat{T}, \hat{A} = SSDN(I), \tag{8}$$

where

- $\hat{J} \in \mathbb{R}^{H \times W \times C}$ is the estimated clear image.
- $\hat{T} \in \mathbb{R}^{H \times W \times C}$ is the estimated transmission map.
- $\hat{A}$ is the estimated airlight. It assumed to be homogeneous, i.e. $\hat{A} \in \mathbb{R}^{1 \times 1 \times C}$. It is estimated by the lowest level feature map followed by global average pooling, a fully-connected layer, and a Sigmoid layer.

4.2   Self-Supervised Dehazing Losses

In this section, we describe the training objectives used in the proposed framework. The framework performs dehazing by exploiting the reconstruction loss using ASM, the physical priors based loss, and the regularization loss. In our framework, GAN loss is not available since it is trained only with hazy images. Excluding GAN loss makes the quantitative performance slightly lower but helps the domain generalization which is important in practical applications. $Sl1(x)$ in the following sections is smooth L1 loss introduced in [8] and defined as below.

$$Sl1(x) = \begin{cases} 0.5(x)^2, & \text{if } |x| < 1 \\ |x| - 0.5, & \text{otherwise.} \end{cases} \tag{9}$$

ASM Losses. We impose the constraint so that the outputs $\hat{J}$, $\hat{T}$, and $\hat{A}$ of SSDN satisfy ASM as follow:

$$L_{rec} = Sl1(I - (\hat{J}\hat{T} + \hat{A}(1 - \hat{T}))). \tag{10}$$

If we only use Eq. (10), the dehazing network will give a trivial solution, i.e. $\hat{J} = I$. To avoid the trivial solution, we propose auxiliary reconstruction loss exploiting Eq. (2):

$$L_{DCPrec} = Sl1(I - (\hat{J}T_{DCP} + A_{max}(1 - T_{DCP}))), \tag{11}$$

where A_{max} denotes the maximum pixel value of I of each channel and T_{DCP} is described in Eq. (2). When the input of SSDN is $\hat{J}$, the clear image output should be the same as the input and the transmission map output should be 1 as follow:

$$\hat{J}_J, \hat{T}_J, \hat{A}_J = SSDN(\hat{J}),$$
$$L_{Jrec} = Sl1(\hat{J}_J - \hat{J}) + Sl1(\hat{T}_J - 1). \tag{12}$$

Since $\hat{A}$ is the homogeneous airlight, if we use it as the input of SSDN, the airlight output is the same to the input and the transmission output should be 0.

$$\hat{J}_A, \hat{T}_A, \hat{A}_A = SSDN(\hat{A}),$$
$$L_{Arec} = Sl1(\hat{A}_A - \hat{A}) + Sl1(\hat{T}_A). \tag{13}$$

Additionally, we propose a self-augmentation loss inspired by [18] as follow:

$$T' = \hat{T} + N(0, \sigma_T^2),$$
$$A' = \hat{A} + N(0, \sigma_A^2),$$
$$I' = \hat{J}T' + A'(1 - T'),$$
$$\hat{J}_{aug}, \hat{T}_{aug}, \hat{A}_{aug} = SSDN(I'),$$
$$L_{aug} = Sl1(I' - (\hat{J}_{aug}\hat{T}_{aug} + \hat{A}_{aug}(1 - \hat{T}_{aug}))), \tag{14}$$

where $N(\mu, \sigma^2) \in \mathbb{R}^{1 \times 1 \times C}$ is a Gaussian noise for homogeneous changes of T and A, while σ_T^2 and σ_A^2 are hyperparameters. Applying homogeneous changes helps the self-augmented data $\hat{J}_{aug}$ to be physically plausible augmentations.

Overall, the loss exploiting ASM is represented as follow:

$$L_{ASM} = \lambda_{rec}L_{rec} + \lambda_{DCPrec}L_{DCPrec} + \lambda_{Jrec}L_{Jrec} + \lambda_{Arec}L_{Arec} + \lambda_{aug}L_{aug}, \tag{15}$$

where each λ is a weight hyperparameter for each loss term.

Prior Losses. In this section, we define the loss functions reflecting the priors described in Sect. 3 so that the clear image output $\hat{J}$ of SSDN is close to the real clear image.

First, we use Eq. (2) as a guidance for $\hat{T}$. To reduce halo artifact, Ω in Eq. (2) is set to 1×1. Since DCP may make wrong estimation of the transmission map in a bright scene, such as a white wall in an indoor or city scene, we multiply T_{DCP} on loss term to impose low weight on those cases.

$$L_{DCP} = Sl1((\hat{T} - T_{DCP})T_{DCP}), \tag{16}$$

where T_{DCP} is defined in Eq. (2). Secondly, we define the total variation prior described in Eq. (3) to the clear image output $\hat{J}$.

$$L_{TV} = Sl1(TV(\hat{J})). \tag{17}$$

We implement the priors described in Eqs. (4), (5), and (6) as the following loss terms:

$$L_{PI} = Sl1(\max(\hat{J} - I, 0)), \tag{18}$$

$$L_{value} = Sl1(\max(\hat{J}_{value} - I_{value}, 0)), \tag{19}$$

$$L_{sat} = Sl1(\max(I_{sat} - \hat{J}_{sat}, 0)). \tag{20}$$

The local variance prior described in Eq. (7) is implemented as a loss term as follow:

$$L_{var} = Sl1(\max(var(I) - var(\hat{J}), 0)). \tag{21}$$

We avoid overdehazing and make the output close to the clear image by applying $\max(*, 0)$ in Eqs. (18), (19), (20), and (21). Lastly, we define the loss for the airlight from the observation that the airlight is similar to the highest pixel value of the hazy image:

$$L_A = Sl1(\hat{A} - max(I)). \tag{22}$$

Overall, the loss function reflecting the priors is represented as follow:

$$\begin{aligned} L_{prior} =& \lambda_{DCP}L_{DCP} + \lambda_{TV}L_{TV} + \lambda_{PI}L_{PI} + \\ & \lambda_{value}L_{value} + \lambda_{sat}L_{sat} + \lambda_{var}L_{var} + \lambda_A L_A. \end{aligned} \tag{23}$$

where each λ is a weight hyperparameter for each loss term.

Regularization. We apply the regularization so that the output of the network has appropriate values. First, we define the identity loss to prevent that the clear image output $\hat{J}$ is quite different from I as follow:

$$L_{idt} = Sl1(\hat{J} - I). \tag{24}$$

Secondly, we impose regularization on the estimated transmission map. In general, the transmission map is known to be smooth. Moreover, since the scattering coefficient is similar in the range of the visual light, the transmission should be close to gray. The regularization for the transmission is given by:

$$L_{Tgray} = Sl1(\hat{T} - mean_c(\hat{T})),$$
(25)

$$L_{Tsmooth} = Sl1(\hat{T} - BoxFilter(\hat{T})),$$
(26)

where $mean_c(x)$ is a channelwise mean operator for pixel x.

Merging each regularization, the final regularization loss function is defined as:

$$L_{reg} = \lambda_{idt}L_{idt} + \lambda_{Tgray}L_{Tgray} + \lambda_{Tsmooth}L_{Tsmooth},$$
(27)

where each λ is a weight hyperparameter for each loss term.

Total Loss. The final objective function is given by:

$$L = L_{ASM} + L_{prior} + L_{reg}.$$
(28)

5   Experiments

5.1   Implementation Details

We implement SSDN based on U-Net but replaced normal convolutions and ReLUs with residual blocks and PReLUs, respectively. For a lightweight framework, we reduce the number of channels and apply channel reductions to skip connections and decoder outputs as shown in Fig. 2.

In the training phase, we randomly crop each image from the dataset to a patch with size of 128×128. To obtain the effect of extending the dataset, we apply random horizontal flip as data augmentation. For the update of network parameters, Adam optimizer [12] with a learning rate of 1e-4 is used with batch size of 32 on two TITAN XPs.

There are hyperparameters in Eq. (28). We empirically set them: $\{\lambda_{rec}, \lambda_{DCPrec}, \lambda_{Tgray}, \lambda_{Tsmooth}, \lambda_{var}\}$ to 1, $\{\lambda_{Jrec}, \lambda_{Arec}, \lambda_{aug}, \lambda_{DCP}, \lambda_{idt}\}$ to 0.1, $\{\lambda_{TV}, \lambda_{PI}, \lambda_{value}, \lambda_{sat}, \lambda_A\}$ to 0.01. In Eq. (14), we define the values of hyperparameters as $\sigma_T^2 = 0.3$ and $\sigma_A^2 = 0.2$.

5.2   Datasets

We conduct experiments on both indoor and outdoor scenes. For the indoor case, we train SSDN with RESIDE standard [14] indoor training set. Indoor set of the Synthetic Objective Testing Set (SOTS) from RESIDE standard is selected as the indoor test set. We refer to SSDN trained on RESIDE standard as *ours-indoor*.

For the outdoor case, we train SSDN with RESIDE beta [14] Outdoor Training Set (OTS). The synthetic set of Hybrid Subjective Testing Set (HSTS) from RESIDE standard is selected as the outdoor test set. We refer to SSDN trained on OTS as *ours-outdoor*.

Table 1. Comparison in terms of computational cost on 620 × 460 images.

Metrics	Supervised Method			
	DehazeNet [4]	MSBDN-DFF [9]	DW-GAN [6]	TBDN [26]
FLOPs (GMACs)	–	183.62	150.61	396.96
Params (M)	–	31.35	51.51	50.35
Exec time (s)	1.05	0.03	0.05	0.06
Metrics	Prior-Based	Unsupervised		Self-Supervised
	DCP	DDIP	YOLY	Ours
FLOPs (GMACs)	–	–	–	**94.53**
Params (M)	–	–	–	**16.62**
Exec time (s)	0.05	~600	~30	**0.008**

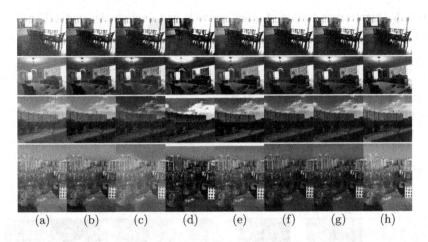

(a)   (b)   (c)   (d)   (e)   (f)   (g)   (h)

Fig. 3. Dehazing results of ours and other methods. The first two rows from SOTS indoor, the other two from the HSTS. (a) Input hazy images, (b) DehazeNet, (c) DCP, (d) DDIP, (e) YOLY, (f) *ours-indoor*, (g) *ours-outdoor*, and (h) GT clean images.

5.3   Results

Baselines. To compare the performance of our method, we select diverse approaches to dehazing. For the supervised method, we select DehazeNet [4], MSBDN-DFF [9], DW-GAN [6], and TBDN [26]. The performance of [6] and [26] on HSTS are not reported on their paper. We train them on OTS and test on HSTS as *ours-outdoor*. Hence, the results of [6] and [26] on Table 3 may not be the best for them. For the prior-based method, we select DCP [10], which is the representative method in that area. Lastly, for unsupervised methods, we select DDIP [7] and YOLY [15], which optimizes a neural network on each image.

Experiment Results. Comparisons on computational cost are shown in Table 1. For an image with the size of 620 × 460, YOLY and DDIP take about few minutes and supervised methods take fractions of a second. On the other hand, our method takes about 0.008 s on a TITAN XP since it requires only a single

Table 2. Quantitative results of other methods and ours on the synthetic indoor dehazing test set (SOTS).

Metrics	Supervised Method			
	DehazeNet [4]	MSBDN-DFF [9]	DW-GAN [6]	TBDN [26]
PSNR	21.14	33.79	35.94	**37.61**
SSIM	0.847	0.984	0.986	**0.991**

Metrics	Prior-Based	Unsupervised		Self-Supervised	
	DCP	DDIP	YOLY	*ours-indoor*	*ours-outdoor*
PSNR	16.62	16.97	19.41	19.56	19.51
SSIM	0.818	0.714	0.833	0.833	0.827

Table 3. Quantitative results of other methods and ours on the synthetic outdoor dehazing test set (HSTS).

Metrics	Supervised Method			
	DehazeNet [4]	MSBDN-DFF [9]	DW-GAN [6]	TBDN [26]
PSNR	24.48	**31.71**	30.67	27.22
SSIM	0.915	0.933	**0.973**	0.916

Metrics	Prior-Based	Unsupervised		Self-Supervised	
	DCP	DDIP	YOLY	*ours-indoor*	*ours-outdoor*
PSNR	14.84	20.91	23.82	19.47	19.84
SSIM	0.761	0.884	0.913	0.859	0.851

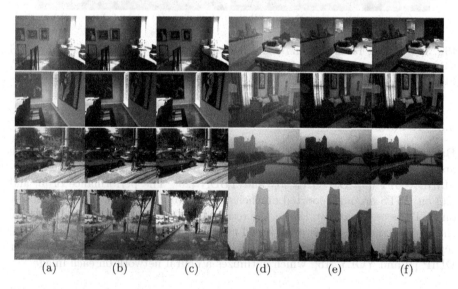

(a) (b) (c) (d) (e) (f)

Fig. 4. More dehazing results on SOTS dataset by our proposed SSDN. (a), (d) input hazy images, (b), (e) output dehazed images, and (c), (f) GT clear images. For upper two rows, the images are sampled from SOTS indoor set and dehazed using *ours-indoor*, SOTS outdoor set and *ours-outdoor* for lower two rows.

Table 4. Result of ablation study. For each experiment setting, PSNR and SSIM is measured between the output and SOTS indoor dataset. The first row, *hazy-clear* shows the PSNR and SSIM between hazy and clear images in the dataset.

Experiment name	Experiment setting	PNSR	SSIM
–	hazy-clear	11.97	0.6934
Model 1	L_{rec} (Eq. (10))	11.59	0.6896
Model 2	L_{ASM} (Eq. (15))	9.08	0.2821
Model 3	L_{ASM}, L_{prior} (Eqs. (15), (23))	8.60	0.3012
Model 4	L (Eq. (28))	19.35	0.8304

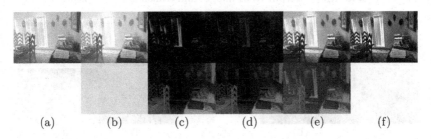

(a)   (b)   (c)   (d)   (e)   (f)

Fig. 5. Results of ablation study. (a) input hazy image, (b) *Model 1*, (c) *Model 2*, (d) *Model 3*, (e) *Model 4* and (f) the GT clear image. The top row shows the RGB image, and the bottom shows the estimated transmission map.

CNN forward operation. It shows that SSDN can be combined into real-time vision systems without losing real-time property while others cannot.

The quantitative comparisons of each baseline and our methods are shown in Tables 2, 3 and Fig. 3. Our methods show worse performance than supervised methods and similar performance compared to DCP, DDIP, and YOLY. However, our methods show a good generalization property since SSDN learns physical prior knowledge that can be commonly applied to general hazy images.

More dehazed results on SOTS indoor and outdoor dataset by our proposed SSDN are shown in Fig. 4.

Ablation Study. In this section, we show the effect of loss terms (Eqs. (10), (15), and (23)) by ablation study. The results are shown in Table 4 and Fig. 5. *Model 1* outputs an image same to the input, a trivial solution. *Model 2* avoids a trivial solution but it does not properly learn dehazing, especially for bright scene such as white wall (Fig. 5 (c)). *Model 3* handles bright scene and dehazes better than *Model 2* by applying low weights to white regions and using other prior losses such as L_{prior} (Eq. (23)) (Fig. 5 (d)). L_{reg} (Eq. (27)) makes *Model 4* avoid over-dehazing of *Model 3* to produce a clear dehazed image.

Real World Examples. As shown in Fig. 6, the proposed method works on real-world hazy images although it has been trained only on a synthetic dataset. In Fig. 6 (b), *ours-indoor* shows the strong generalization capability.

Fig. 6. Dehazing results on real hazy images using SSDN. Both cases show competitive performance. (a) input hazy images, (b), (c) output RGB images and transmission maps of *ours-indoor*, and (d), (e) output RGB images and transmission maps of *ours-outdoor*.

Fig. 7. Dehazing results on real extremely hazy images using SSDN. *ours-outdoor* does not work properly while finetuned *ours-outdoor* shows better performance. (a) input hazy images, (b), (c) output RGB images and transmission maps of *ours-outdoor*, and (d), (e) output RGB images and transmission maps of finetuned *ours-outdoor*.

Despite the generalization capability of SSDN, extremely hazy images is too different from trained images. In this case, the performance of SSDN can be easily improved by finetuning process with additional hazy images. Figure 7 (d) shows the results of finetuned *ours-outdoor* with 110 real-world extremely hazy images.

Vision System Application. To show that SSDN can make the vision system robust to haze, we choose the depth estimation task as an exemplar case. We use LapDepth [23], a depth estimation framework trained on Make3D dataset [22]. To simulate hazy weather, we synthesize hazy images out of Make3D test set. To synthesize hazy images, we extract the transmission maps and airlights based on DCP from O-HAZE [2] and NH-HAZE [1]. Then, we apply ASM on RGB images of Make3D. In this strategy, we successfully transfer realistic haze from O-HAZE and NH-HAZE to Make3D dataset with this process as shown in Fig. 8.

In Table 5, LapDepth shows large performance degradation on hazy images. SSDN can compensate for the performance degradation while it had little effect on execution time, taking about 0.005 s even on images with the size of 1704 × 2272 with a TITAN XP. For comparison, we finetune LapDepth on our

Fig. 8. Haze synthesis results on Make3D dataset and its dehazed result using SSDN. (a), (d) original clear images, (b), (e) synthesized hazy images, and (c), (f) dehazed results by *ours-outdoor*.

Table 5. Depth estimation results of LapDepth on each experiment setting.

Experiment setting	Dataset	SSDN	RMSE	SSIM
LapDepth	Clear images		8.76	0.94
LapDepth	Hazy images		11.32	0.92
LapDepth	Hazy images	✓	9.85	0.92
Finetuned LapDepth	Clear images		9.16	0.93
Finetuned LapDepth	Hazy images		9.09	0.94

synthesized hazy images. It shows better performance on hazy images, while it makes a degraded performance on clear images. On the other hand, SSDN does not affect the performance for the clear weather case. It shows that our proposed SSDN is a practical method for assisting existing vision systems.

6 Conclusion

SSDN disentangles a hazy image into a clear image, transmission map, and atmospheric airlight based on ASM. To the best of our knowledge, it is the first approach to merging physical prior knowledge and self-supervision for the dehazing task. The proposed method shows competitive dehazing performance to other prior-based methods or unsupervised methods while running extremely faster than them. Our proposed SSDN shows strong generalization capability and it can be more stable over various domains by finetuning with simply gathered additional hazy images. We also showed that SSDN can make existing vision systems robust to hazy images. Experimental results show that our proposed SSDN is a practical dehazing method for real-time vision systems.

Acknowledgements. We would like to thank the anonymous reviewers for their constructive comments. This work was supported by IITP grants (SW Star Lab, 2015-0-00174; AI Innovation Hub, 2021-0-02068; AI Graduate School Program (POSTECH), 2019-0-01906), KOCCA grant (R2021040136), NRF grant (NRF-2021R1F1A1048120) from Korea government (MSIT and MCST), and POSCO ICT COMPANY LTD.

References

1. Ancuti, C.O., Ancuti, C., Timofte, R.: NH-HAZE: an image dehazing benchmark with non-homogeneous hazy and haze-free images. In: Proceedings of the IEEE/CVF Conference on Computer Vision and Pattern Recognition (CVPR) Workshops (2020)
2. Ancuti, C.O., Ancuti, C., Timofte, R., De Vleeschouwer, C.: O-haze: a dehazing benchmark with real hazy and haze-free outdoor images. In: Proceedings of the IEEE Conference on Computer Vision and Pattern Recognition (CVPR) Workshops (2018)
3. Berman, D., treibitz, T., Avidan, S.: Non-local image dehazing. In: Proceedings of the IEEE Conference on Computer Vision and Pattern Recognition (CVPR) (2016)
4. Cai, B., Xu, X., Jia, K., Qing, C., Tao, D.: Dehazenet: an end-to-end system for single image haze removal. IEEE Trans. Image Process. **25**(11), 5187–5198 (2016)
5. Engin, D., Genc, A., Kemal Ekenel, H.: Cycle-dehaze: enhanced cyclegan for single image dehazing. In: Proceedings of the IEEE Conference on Computer Vision and Pattern Recognition (CVPR) Workshops (2018)
6. Fu, M., Liu, H., Yu, Y., Chen, J., Wang, K.: DW-GAN: a discrete wavelet transform gan for nonhomogeneous dehazing. In: Proceedings of the IEEE Conference on Computer Vision and Pattern Recognition (CVPR) Workshops (2021)
7. Gandelsman, Y., Shocher, A., Irani, M.: Double-dip: unsupervised image decomposition via coupled deep-image-priors. In: Proceedings of the IEEE/CVF Conference on Computer Vision and Pattern Recognition (CVPR) (2019)
8. Girshick, R.: Fast r-cnn. In: Proceedings of the 2015 IEEE International Conference on Computer Vision (ICCV) (2015)
9. Hang, D., et al.: Multi-scale boosted dehazing network with dense feature fusion. In: Proceedings of the IEEE/CVF Conference on Computer Vision and Pattern Recognition (CVPR) (2020)
10. He, K., Sun, J., Tang, X.: Single image haze removal using dark channel prior. In: IEEE Conference on Computer Vision and Pattern Recognition, pp. 1956–1963 (2009). https://doi.org/10.1109/CVPR.2009.5206515
11. Isola, P., Zhu, J.Y., Zhou, T., Efros, A.A.: Image-to-image translation with conditional adversarial networks. In: Proceedings of the IEEE Conference on Computer Vision and Pattern Recognition (CVPR) (2017)
12. Kingma, D.P., Ba, J.: Adam: a method for stochastic optimization. In: 3rd International Conference on Learning Representations (ICLR) (2015)
13. Li, B., Peng, X., Wang, Z., Xu, J., Feng, D.: AOD-Net: all-in-one dehazing network. In: Proceedings of the IEEE International Conference on Computer Vision (ICCV), pp. 4780–4788 (2017). https://doi.org/10.1109/ICCV.2017.511
14. Li, B., et al.: Benchmarking single-image dehazing and beyond. IEEE Trans. Image Process. **28**(1), 492–505 (2019)
15. Li, B., Gou, Y., Gu, S., Liu, J.Z., Zhou, J.T., Peng, X.: You only look yourself: unsupervised and untrained single image dehazing neural network. Int. J. Comput. Vis. **129**(5), 1754–1767 (2021). https://doi.org/10.1007/s11263-021-01431-5
16. Liu, J., Wu, H., Xie, Y., Qu, Y., Ma, L.: Trident dehazing network. In: Proceedings of the IEEE/CVF Conference on Computer Vision and Pattern Recognition (CVPR) Workshops, pp. 430–431 (2020)
17. Narasimhan, S.G., Nayar, S.K.: Vision and the atmosphere. Int. J. Comput. Vis. **48**(3), 233–254 (2002)

18. Neshatavar, R., Yavartanoo, M., Son, S., Lee, K.M.: CVF-SID: cyclic multi-variate function for self-supervised image denoising by disentangling noise from image. In: Proceedings of the IEEE/CVF Conference on Computer Vision and Pattern Recognition (CVPR), pp. 17583–17591 (2022)
19. Qin, X., Wang, Z., Bai, Y., Xie, X., Jia, H.: FFA-Net: feature fusion attention network for single image dehazing. In: Proceedings of the AAAI Conference on Artificial Intelligence, vol. 34, pp. 11908–11915 (2020)
20. Ronneberger, O., Fischer, P., Brox, T.: U-Net: convolutional networks for biomedical image segmentation. In: Navab, N., Hornegger, J., Wells, W.M., Frangi, A.F. (eds.) MICCAI 2015. LNCS, vol. 9351, pp. 234–241. Springer, Cham (2015). https://doi.org/10.1007/978-3-319-24574-4_28
21. Rudin, L.I., Osher, S., Fatemi, E.: Nonlinear total variation based noise removal algorithms. Physica D **60**(1–4), 259–268 (1992). https://doi.org/10.1016/0167-2789(92)90242-F
22. Saxena, A., Sun, M., Ng, A.Y.: Make3D: learning 3D scene structure from a single still image. IEEE Trans. Pattern Anal. Mach. Intell. **31**(5), 824–840 (2009). https://doi.org/10.1109/TPAMI.2008.132
23. Song, M., Lim, S., Kim, W.: Monocular depth estimation using laplacian pyramid-based depth residuals. IEEE Trans. Circuits Syst. Video Technol. **31**(11), 4381–4393 (2021)
24. Yang, Y., Wang, C., Liu, R., Zhang, L., Guo, X., Tao, D.: Self-augmented unpaired image dehazing via density and depth decomposition. In: Proceedings of the IEEE/CVF Conference on Computer Vision and Pattern Recognition (CVPR), pp. 2037–2046 (2022)
25. Yu, Y., Liu, H., Fu, M., Chen, J., Wang, X., Wang, K.: A two-branch neural network for non-homogeneous dehazing via ensemble learning. In: Proceedings of the IEEE/CVF Conference on Computer Vision and Pattern Recognition (CVPR) Workshops, pp. 193–202 (2021)
26. Yu, Y., Liu, H., Fu, M., Chen, J., Wang, X., Wang, K.: A two-branch neural network for non-homogeneous dehazing via ensemble learning. In: Proceedings of the IEEE Conference on Computer Vision and Pattern Recognition (CVPR) Workshops (2021)
27. Zhu, J.Y., Park, T., Isola, P., Efros, A.A.: Unpaired image-to-image translation using cycle-consistent adversarial networks. In: Proceedings of the IEEE International Conference on Computer Vision (ICCV) (2017)
28. Zhu, Q., Mai, J., Shao, L.: A fast single image haze removal algorithm using color attenuation prior. IEEE Trans. Image Process. **24**(11), 3522–3533 (2015). https://doi.org/10.1109/TIP.2015.2446191

LHDR: HDR Reconstruction for Legacy Content Using a Lightweight DNN

Cheng Guo[1,2(✉)] 🔟 and Xiuhua Jiang[1,2]

[1] State Key Laboratory of Media Convergence and Communication,
Communication University of China, Beijing, China
{jiangxiuhua,guocheng}@cuc.edu.cn
[2] Peng Cheng Laboratory, Shenzhen, China

Abstract. High dynamic range (HDR) image is widely-used in graphics and photography due to the rich information it contains. Recently the community has started using deep neural network (DNN) to reconstruct standard dynamic range (SDR) images into HDR. Albeit the superiority of current DNN-based methods, their application scenario is still limited: (1) heavy model impedes real-time processing, and (2) inapplicable to legacy SDR content with more degradation types. Therefore, we propose a lightweight DNN-based method trained to tackle legacy SDR. For better design, we reform the problem modeling and emphasize degradation model. Experiments show that our method reached appealing performance with minimal computational cost compared with others.

Keywords: High dynamic range · Legacy content · Degradation model

1 Introduction

Image's dynamic range is defined as the ratio of maximum recorded luminance to the minimum. As name implies, high dynamic range (HDR) image is able to simultaneously envelop rich information in both bright and dark areas, making it indispensable in photography and image-based lighting [1], etc. The common way to obtain an HDR image is fusing multiple standard dynamic range (SDR) images with different exposure, i.e. multi-exposure fusing (MEF) [2]. And recently the community has begun to use deep neural network (DNN) [3–8] to tackle motion and misalignment between different SDR exposures.

While most MEF HDR imaging method is intended to be integrated in camera pipeline for taking new HDR photo, there is a considerable amount of legacy SDR content containing unreproducible historical scenes to be applied in HDR application. Those legacy content has limited dynamic range due to the imperfection of old imaging pipeline, and most importantly, no multi-exposure counterpart to be directly fused into HDR. In this case, we could only manage to recover HDR content from a single SDR image, which is called inverse tone-mapping (ITM) [9] or single-image HDR reconstruction (SI-HDR) [10].

Supplementary Information The online version contains supplementary material available at https://doi.org/10.1007/978-3-031-26313-2_19.

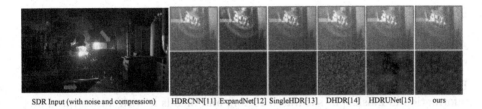

SDR Input (with noise and compression)   HDRCNN[11] ExpandNet[12] SingleHDR[13]   DHDR[14]   HDRUNet[15]   ours

Fig. 1. Current HDR reconstruction methods struggle to handle SDR with noise and compression. In the green and red boxes are tone-mapped reconstructed HDR. (Color figure online)

Different from MEF HDR imaging where full dynamic range is already covered in multiple SDR input, SI-HDR is an ill-posed problem since a method is supposed to recover the lost information by the reduction of dynamic range, etc. Fortunately, DNN has been proven effective in other ill-posed low-level vision tasks, hence researchers have begun to involve it in SI-HDR [11–15]. DNN-based SI-HDR could better infer lost information e.g. those by highlight saturation, since DNN is able to aggregate and process semantic context.

Albeit the success of current DNN-based SI-HDR, there are still 2 aspects to be considered: First, while legacy SDR content is susceptible to noise and compression, to the best of our knowledge, there is no DNN-based method motivated to jointly tackle both of them. Hence, current methods struggle to deal with legacy SDR with noise and compression, as Fig. 1 shows. Second, many method exploit a bulky DNN, which will hinder their real-time processing and deployment on devices with limited computational resources.

Therefore, our task is to design a lightweight DNN capable of handling legacy SDR with noise and compression. Our lightweight approach partly lies in pointwise and group convolution. Meanwhile, to teach the DNN with recovery ability, corresponding degradation should be correctly set in training. To this end, we clarify what kind of degradations are to be recovered by a reformed problem modeling based on camera pipeline [16]. This problem modeling also helps us derive a DNN with modules customized to specific types of degradation.

In the following paper, we first conclude related works from several aspects, then describe the DNN design containing problem modeling and network modules, and finally introduce our training strategy including degradations. Experiment will show that our method outperforms both DNN-based state-of-the-art (SOTA) and non-DNN method [17] on both simulated and real legacy content. Finally, ablation studies are conducted to validate the effectiveness of our ideas.

Our contributions are:

- To the best of our knowledge, making the first attempt handling legacy SDR content with both noise and compression in DNN-based SI-HDR.
- Lightening the DNN to facilitate its practical application.
- Reforming SI-HDR problem modeling by a precise camera pipeline, and emphasizing the impact of degradation model which has long been understated.

2   Related Work

All following methods start from a single SDR image, yet they markedly differ regarding whether it directly outputs an HDR image.

Direct Approach. The initiator of DNN-based SI-HDR [11] reconstruct lost information in mask-split saturated region, and blends it with unsaturated area expanded by inverse camera response function (CRF). [12] first apply non-UNet DNN with multiple branches in different receptive field. [13] model SI-HDR with preliminary 3-step camera pipeline, and assign 4 sub-networks to hierarchically resolve them. [14] introduce more mechanisms: partial convolution from inpainting and gram matrix loss from style transfer. [15] append their UNet with an extra branch to involve input prior in spatial feature modulation. Ideas of other direct approach [18–33] are omitted here, and will be detailed later if involved.

Indirect Approach. Recovering lost information makes SI-HDR more challenging than MEF HDR imaging, hence some methods mitigate this difficulty indirectly. Common idea [34–38] is to transfer single SDR image into multi-exposure SDR sequence to be later merged into HDR using traditional MEF algorithm. Other ideas include: learning the relationship between fixed and real degradation [39], non-I2I (image-to-image) histogram learning [40], using spatial adaptive convolution whose per-pixel weight is predicted by DNN [41], and polishing the result of 3 traditional ITM operators [42]. We take direct approach since indirect one conflicts with the goal of efficient design.

2.1   Lightweight SI-HDR

Lightweight/efficient DNN has long received attention academically and industrially in other low-level vision tasks, e.g. super-resolution [43,44], denoising [45], and even MEF HDR imaging [8]. Yet, few efforts are made in SI-HDR:

Preliminary attempts are made in [23] and [36] where feedback/recursive DNN module with shared parameters is used to reduce total number of DNN parameters (#param), however, only #param is reduced while computational cost is not. To be deployed on mobile platform, [32] reduce computational cost by changing some parameter precision from float32 to int8. [33] apply a similar scheme as [11] but use group convolution to lighten their DNN. [42] is efficient mainly due to its pre/post-processing: their DNN only needs to polish single luminance channel resulting from existing methods.

Their efficiency is manifested in #param, number of multiply-accumulate operations (MACs), and runtime, which will be detailed in experiment part.

2.2   Problem Modeling of SI-HDR

SI-HDR belongs to restoration problem, even using 'black box' DNN, some methods still try to figure out exact degradations to restore. They assign specific degradation with a single step of sub-network and resolve them hierarchically.

Some methods divide their steps subjectively: [27] into 'denoising and expo-sure adjustment' and tone expansion; [29] into dequantization and hallucination; while that of [30] are linearization, hallucination, and refinement.

Few are based on formulating a camera pipeline: [10] divide the task into inverting CRF, bit-depth expansion, and under&over-exposure reconstruction, while steps of [13] are dequantization, linearization, hallucination, and refine-ment. All these step divisions or problem modeling could not cover both noise and compression from legacy SDR, our 'target audience'.

2.3 SI-HDR for Legacy Content

Non-DNN method [17] share the same hypothesis that legacy SDR content is susceptible to noise and quantization artifact, and uses filter to mitigate them. Though DNN has been widely studied in SI-HDR, denoising, and compression artifact removal separately, no DNN-based method is motivated to jointly handle all 3 tasks. Yet, there do exist methods tackling up to 2 of them simultaneously:

Joint SI-HDR and Compression Artifact Removal. [11] provide an alter-native checkpoint trained with JPEG compressed SDR whose quality factor (QF) $\sim U(30, 100)$ while [21] is trained with JPEG degradation with QF $\sim U(10, 70)$.

Joint SI-HDR and Denoising. Input SDR images in the training set of NTIRE HDR Challenge [8,46] contain zero-mean additive Gaussian camera noise, consequently all methods there will learn to jointly denoise. However, only [15,27] etc. belongs to SI-HDR, while the rest are MEF HDR imaging.

2.4 HDR Degradation Model

From the above section, we know that only when specific degradation is added in training, the DNN will learn a corresponding restoration ability. Different from conventional image/video, there are exclusive steps in HDR-to-SDR degradation model due to their dynamic range discrepancy:

Table 1. HDR-exclusive degradation models used by related works.

Type	Used by	Nonlinearity	Under-$\sim$	Over-exp. truncate
Simulated shot	[11, 14, 25, 28] [31, 33, 39]	virtual CRF w. rand. param.	×	histogram fraction $\sim U(5\%, 15\%)$
	[13, 29, 34]	rand. real CRFs	rand. exposure adjust.	
	[30]	fixed CRF		
	[21]	'virtual cam.'	×	value $\sim U(0, 10\%)$
	[15, 27] etc.	gamma 2.2 ± 0.7	fixed exposure adjust.	
Trad. TMO	[12]	rand. param. TMOs	value $\sim U(0, 15\%)$	
	[41]		×	×
	[26, 32]	fixed param. TMOs	×	×
Mid. exp. SDR	[19, 22, 40, 42]	fixed	✓	✓

First, nonlinearity between HDR and SDR is a monotonically increasing one-to-one mapping that itself will not introduce degradation. However, it substantially diverse between real-world cameras, and is measured as CRF [10]. Second, over/under-exposure truncation is to simulate the limited dynamic range of SDR. As in Table 1, there are 3 common practices to conduct above degradation:

'Simulated shot' means getting input SDR by applying virtual camera on the luminance recorded in label HDR. 'Trad. TMO' is for traditional tone mapping operator (TMO) converting label HDR into input SDR. Finally, 'Mid. exp. SDR' starts from a multi-exposure SDR sequence, where middle-exposure (EV=0) SDR is taken as input, meanwhile the whole sequence is merged as label HDR.

We argue that not all of them are favorable to SI-HDR training. For example, the motive of TMO is the exact opposite of degradation in that TMO dedicate to preserver as much information from HDR. In this case, DNN is not likely to learn adequate restoration ability since input SDR is also of high quality (see later experiment). Such analysis serves as the guidance of our training strategy.

3   Proposed Method

3.1   Problem Modeling

As mentioned above, problem modeling is to figure out what degradations are to be restored, so we can (1) apply DNN mechanism tailored for specific degradation, and (2) arrange degradations correctly when training. Similar to [13], we model the SI-HDR task as the reverse of HDR-to-SDR camera pipeline. Since their preliminary model could not envelop the source of noise and compression in legacy content, and the potential color space discrepancy between SDR and HDR (e.g. some HDR data [47,48] is in camera RGB primaries rather than sRGB), we derive a more comprehensive model from a precise camera pipeline [16].

As in Fig. 2, our model consist of 6 steps with various degradations introduced sequentially. After determining 5 degradations and totally 7 operations to resolve in SI-HDR (nonlinearity and CST is not degradation, but do need an operation to reverse), one option is following [13] i.e. executing each step sequentially. However, cascaded sub-networks will make our method bulky thus conflicting with lightweight design ([13] is the slowest one, see Table 3). Hence, inspired

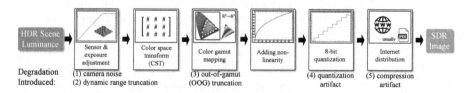

Fig. 2. Our problem modeling: SI-HDR is treated as the inverse of camera pipeline from linear HDR luminance to nonlinear SDR. See supplementary material for detailed derivation.

by the taxonomy of traditional SI-HDR/EO (expansion operator), we turn to analyze each operation and divide them into 2 categories:

Global Operations. CST and nonlinearity belong to global operation where neighboring pixels are not involved in its reversion. Also, it's proven in [49] that both CST and nonlinearity can be approached by a multi-layer perceptron (MLP) on multiple channels of single pixel.

Local Operations. The rest are 'local' operations where different extent of neighboring context is required in their reversion: From other low-level vision tasks e.g. denosing and compression artifact removal etc. we know that recovering (1) (3) (4) (5) in Fig. 2 only require the help of adjacent (small-scale) information. While under&over-exposure reconstruction is more challenging since it requires long-distance dependency, similar as image inpainting.

3.2 DNN Structure

Since there are 2 distinct types of operation/degradation to resolve, we assign 2 steps of sub-network with different customized structure.

Global Network. While most DNN structures are capable of global operation, we adopt minimum-overhead MLP adhering to lightweight principle. Here, image per-pixel MLP is implemented by 4-layer point-wise (1×1) convolution.

In bottom Fig. 3(a), prior with spatial-overall information is used to remedy insufficient receptive-filed. Here, different from [30]/[31] whose prior is segmentation/attention map respectively, ours is input SDR itself depending on what prior information we need. Specifically, we need information of overall luminance/pixel energy. For example, an bright image should require less expansion in SI-HDR,

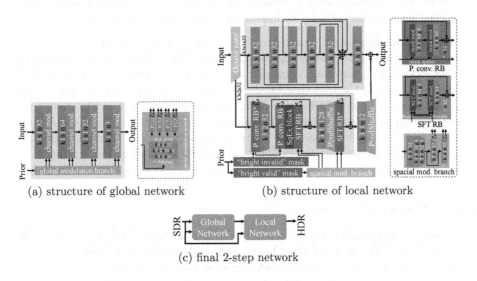

(a) structure of global network   (b) structure of local network

(c) final 2-step network

Fig. 3. DNN structure of proposed method.

and such prior will help the DNN to understand this. Finally, modulation branch will process prior to $\alpha_{scale}, \beta_{bias} \in \mathbb{R}^{c \times 1 \times 1}$ for modulation:

$$modulation(\mathbf{x}) = \alpha_{scale} \odot \mathbf{x} + \beta_{bias}, \mathbf{x} \in \mathbb{R}^{c \times h \times w} \tag{1}$$

where $\odot$ is channel-wise multiply. $\alpha_{scale}, \beta_{bias} \in \mathbb{R}^{c \times 1 \times 1}$ rather than $\mathbb{R}^{c \times h \times w}$ since it's only supposed to contain spatial-global information. The superiority of prior's shape and type has been respectively proven in [15] and [49].

Local network is responsible for inverting all local operations. We split it into 2 branches according to 2 scales of operation. In top Fig. 3(b), we use a 5-layer densely-connected convolution block with small receptive-filed to deal with small-scale local operations. For large-scale under&over-exposure reconstruction, we apply a 2-level encoder-decoder containing residual blocks (RB) to establish long-range dependency, at bottom Fig. 3(b). We also utilize 2 types of soft-mask to ameliorate DNN's over-exposure recover capability:

$$\begin{cases} mask_{bright\ valid}(\mathbf{p}) = max(0, (\mathbf{p} - t)/(1 - t)) \\ mask_{bright\ invalid}(\mathbf{p}) = max((\mathbf{p} - 1)/(t - 1), 1) \end{cases}, t = 0.9, \mathbf{p} \in [0, 1] \tag{2}$$

Here, prior ($\mathbf{p}$) cooperates with 2 kind of masks which aims to endow DNN with different spatial emphasis on over-exposed areas. Hence, the prior is also set to input SDR itself containing luminance information from where over-exposure can be inferred. Specifically, since the surrounding of saturated area is helpful for its recover (consider the case of center saturated direct illuminant), we put $mask_{bright\ valid}$ before spatial modulation (SFT [50]) branch to reweight pixels there. SFT can also be expressed as Eq. 1, but with $\alpha_{scale}, \beta_{bias} \in \mathbb{R}^{c \times h \times w}$ and $\odot$ for pixel-wise multilpy. Yet, saturated area itself is of no useful information for its recover, we therefore multiply tensor with $mask_{bright\ invalid}$ before convolution (partial convolution [51]), to exclude it from deep feature generation.

Lightweight Modules. Apart from 1×1 convolution in global network with less #param, we also change half of the convolution layers in local network's UNet branch to group (= 4) convolution. The main contributor of lightweight design lies, yet, in the idea that low-level vision task donot have an appetite for model complexity/depth. Finally, as in Fig. 3(c), global and local network are integrated into a 2-step network. We put local network first since we empirically found it resulting more accurate color reproduction. Also, all activations are leaky rectified linear unit (leakyReLU) except the last layer (ReLU), hence we remove all normalization layers to fully utilize the nonlinear tail of leakyReLU.

3.3 Training Strategy

We adopt supervised training where input SDR and target HDR are required. As mentioned above, both HDR-exclusive and conventional degradations in input SDR images are crucial for the DNN's learned recover capability.

Table 2. Statistics of SDR images ($\mathbf{x}'$) in candidate training set. Average portion (avg.) of under/over-exposure pixels (i) reflects the extent of HDR-exclusive degradation, its standard deviation (stdev.) stands for the degradation diversity. Note that over-exposure value (val.) of [46] is 248 i.e. $\nexists\ \mathbf{x}'_i \in (248, 255]$.

Category	Data set	Resolution	#pair	SDR under-exp. pixel			SDR over-exp. pixel		
				val.	avg.(%)	stdev.	val.	avg.(%)	stdev.
Simulated shot	[3]	1.5k	74	0	0	N/A	255	3.533	0.0535
	[13]	512	9786		6.365	0.1673		8.520	0.1888
	[46]	HD	1494		8.840	0.0766	248	4.711	0.0497
Mid. exp. SDR	[47]	>4k	105		1.709	0.0647	255	4.355	0.0821
	[42]	6k	400		1.200	0.0373		1.081	0.0191

Dataset with HDR-Exclusive Degradation. Many previous works have released their training set in the form of HDR-SDR pairs, which means HDR-exclusive degradations are already contained. Those datasets have crafted highly-diversified scenes, and are generated by 1 of the 3 ways in Table 1. As analyzed there, 'Trad. TMO' is not beneficial, hence we exclude all such training set from candidate. In Table 2, we quantify the statistics of degraded SDR images in candidate training set. We finally mix NTIRE [46] and Fairchild [47] Dataset based on such statistics: that their over&under-exposure degradation is of appropriate extent and diversity. Meanwhile, the HDR-SDR nonlinearity in [47] is fixed, this is remedied since that of [46] is diversified, as in Table 1. Their ratio in final training patches (sized 600 × 600, total 6060) is about 11:4 (NTIRE:Fairchild).

Conventional degradations are to simulate the characteristics of legacy SDR. We conduct them on off-the-shelf SDR images from above datasets: From [16] we know that camera noise is first gathered at sensor's linear RAW response, while compression is lastly added before storage. Hence, we first linearize SDR image and then simulate it to camera RAW RGB primaries, before adding Poisson-Gaussian camera noise whose distribution is simplified to heteroscedastic Gaussian with $\sigma \sim U(0.001, 0.003)$. Then, the image is transferred back to sRGB, before adding compression. Like [52], we use double JPEG compression to simulate multiple internet transmissions of legacy content, but we use a more realistic model where the first QF$\sim U(60, 80)$ and the second QF is fixed 75 but on rescaled image patches. See supplementary material for detail.

Data pre&post-processing can make pixel value of linear HDR more evenly-distributed thus easier for DNN to understand. While various non-linear pre-processing e.g. μ-law etc. are widely exploited [11,14,18,19,21,22,24,28,31], we choose a simple-yet-effective gamma pre-processing: All label HDR images ($\mathbf{y}$) are normalized by their maximum recorded luminance, then transferred to non-linear domain (denote with superscript $'$) before sending to DNN, i.e.

$$\mathbf{y}' = (\frac{\mathbf{y}}{max(\mathbf{y})})^\gamma, \gamma = 0.45 \tag{3}$$

In this case, we append post-processing $\bar{\mathbf{y}} = \bar{\mathbf{y}}'^{1/0.45}$ on DNN's output HDR image ($\bar{\mathbf{y}}'$) during inference phase, to bring it back to linear domain.

Loss Function. Our 'l_1' and 'l_g' (gradient loss) can both be formulated as average element(i)-wise distance: $\frac{1}{n}\sum_{i=1}^{n}||f(\bar{\mathbf{y}}_i') - f(\mathbf{y}_i')||_1$ where $f()$ is non-op for 'l_1', and a discrete differential operator (outputting $\mathbb{R}^{2\times3\times h\times w}$ where 2 means gradient map on both horizontal and vertical direction) for 'l_g'. The latter is added to highlight the local structure perturbation brought by noise and compression artifact. Final loss are empirically set to: $l_1 + 0.1 \times l_g$. All DNN parameters are Kaiming initialized and optimized by AdAM with learning rate starting from 2×10^{-4} and decaying to half every 2.5×10^5 iters. More training details can be found in supplementary material.

4 Experiments

Criteria. According to the motive of our SI-HDR method, we focus on 3 aspects: (1) Recovery ability of lost information in saturated area, (2) lumiance estimation accuracy and (3) restoration capability of conventional degradations. The first two apply to all SI-HDR methods, while the last one is our emphasis.

Moreover, as reported by [10] and [53], current pixel-distance-based metrics tend to make an assessment paradoxical to subjective result. Hence, we introduce more detailed portrait to assess (1) and (3), while metrics are still used for (2).

4.1 Comparison with SOTA

Our method is compared with 8 others including 7 DNN-based and 3 with lightweight motive, as listed in Table 3. We use PSNR, SSIM and 'quality correlate' from HDR visual difference predictor 3 (VDP) [54] for quantitative analysis.

On Simulated Legacy SDR. The test set consists of 95 simulated legacy SDR images from same dataset and extent of degradation as in training. Note that some methods will inevitably struggle to handle SDR with noise and compression, since they are not trained so. Yet, we didn't re-train them because it's not our work to compensate for their insufficiency in training strategy e.g. [12] has weaker over-exposure recovery ability mainly due to HDR-exclusive degradation in training set. Still, for a fair comparison, for methods not trained to handle such conventional degradations, we first process input SDR with pre-trained auxiliary DNN to mitigate compression artifact ($\star$) [55] and/or noise ($\dagger$) [56].

In Table 3, our method got the highest metrics with minimal runtime and second least #param and MACs. As reported by [10], the main contributor to an appealing score lies in method's estimation accuracy of nonlinearity/CRF. This idea can be confirmed by the heatmap in Fig. 4(b) where each method's luminance distribution correspond with metrics. Therefore, we turn to assess degradation recovery ability by detailed visual comparison in Fig. 4(a). As seen, our method is able to suppress noise and compression while recover adequate information from dark&saturated areas.

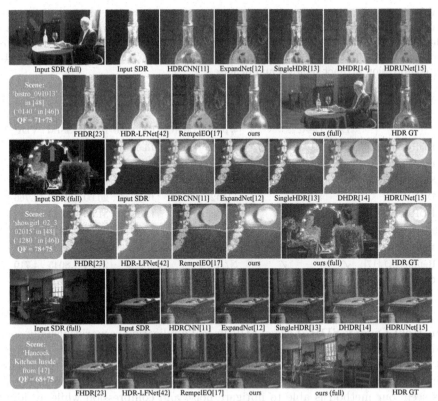

(a) Detailed comparison. All HDR images/patches in relative linear luminance are visualized by MATLAB tone-mapping operator (TMO) 'localtonemap'. We select this TMO since it preserves local contrast thus detail information in both dark and bright areas become more conspicuous.

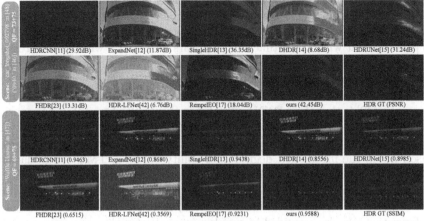

(b) Recovered HDR luminance, visualized by MATLAB heatmap 'turbo'. Closer luminance distribution with GT means better for IBL [1] application.

Fig. 4. Results on simulated legacy SDR input.

Table 3. Quantitative comparison of all competitors. Note that MACs and runtime (both for $\mathbb{R}^{3 \times 1080 \times 1920}$ input) are counted only within DNN, and on desktop computer with i7-4790k CPU and GTX1080 GPU, respectively. Superscript$^{1/2/3}$ stands for Tensorflow/PyTorch/MATLAB implementation, 'DeC.' and 'DeN.' is respectively for compression artifact removal and denoise.

Method	Designed to		Lightw. Motive	Overhead			Metrics		
	DeC	DeN		#param	MACs	Runtime	PSNR	SSIM	VDP
HDRCNN [11]	✓	×†	×	31799k	2135G	15.54 s^1	32.40	.8181	5.806
ExpandNet [12]	×*	×†	×	457k	508G	0.88 s^2	20.47	.5915	4.653
SingleHDR [13]	×*	×†	×	30338k	1994G	41.98 s^1	35.52	.9100	6.231
DHDR [14]	×*	×†	×	51542k	597G	10.49 s^2	20.00	.4760	4.766
HDRUNet [15]	×*	✓	×	1651k	741G	1.51 s^2	31.06	.7638	5.688
FHDR [23]	×*	×†	✓	571k	2368G	10.60 s^2	20.26	.4374	4.985
HDR-LFNet [42]	×*	×†	✓	**203k**	**47.7G**	2.94 s^2	25.73	.4536	4.791
RempelEO [17]	✓	✓	✓	N/A		6.75 s^3	24.14	.8045	4.710
Ours	✓	✓	✓	225k	162G	**0.53 s^2**	**38.12**	**.9515**	**7.173**

On Real Legacy SDR. Legacy SDR in real application scenarios usually contains an unknown degree of (blind) degradation. Here, each method is tested on 51 real legacy SDR images from old movies, photographs, and TV programs. Since there is no GT counterpart, we only provide visual comparison in Fig. 5. As seen, our method is able to mitigate noise and compression while avoiding producing artifacts at dark area which is more susceptible to noise.

Analysis. First, albeit some methods hold lightweight motive, they still take long a time to run because: only #param is reduced while MACs is not [23]; most runtime is spent in data pre/post-processing outside the DNN [42].

Meanwhile, from Fig. 4 we can see that most competitors fail to jointly denoise and remove compression artifact even with the help of auxiliary DNN (*/†), and result with less artifact only appears in [11]/[15] which is also respectively trained with corresponding degradation. This confirms the significance conventional degradation in training set.

Also, some methods [12, 42] underperform reconstructing over-exposure area. Reason for [42] is that their DNN just polishes the result of traditional expansion operators (EOs), from where the lost information was never recovered. For [12], the only competitor who is trained with 'Trad. TMO' dataset (see Table 1), reason lies in the insufficient degradation ability of 'Trad. TMO' 'degradation'. This proves the importance of HDR-exclusive degradation model.

The importance of degradation model etc. will be further proved in ablation studies below. More heuristics analysis, visual results, and detailed experiment configuration are also provided in supplementary material.

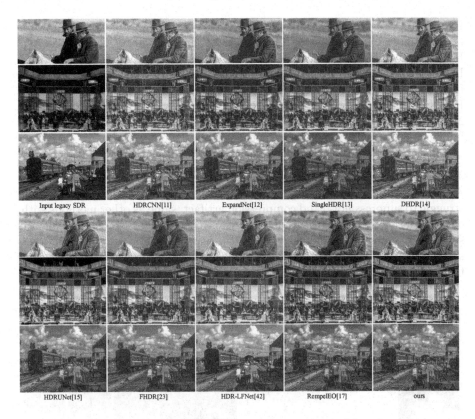

Fig. 5. Results on real legacy SDR input, tone-mapped for visualize.

4.2 Ablation Studies

In this section, we start to verify the effectiveness of some key ingredients of our method, including training configuration and DNN structure.

① **On HDR-exclusive degradation.** In Sect. 2.4&3.3, we argue that a lower degree of over/under-exposure degradation of training SDR tend to endow

Table 4. Metrics of ablation studies. 'Con. deg.' stands for conventional degradations i.e. camera noise and JPEG compression as in Sect. 3.3.

Ablation configuration				Overhead			Metrics		
No.	DNN struct.	Training set	Con. deg.	#param	MACs	Runtime	PSNR	SSIM	VDP
unchanged (denote with -)				225k	162G	0.53 s	38.12	.9515	7.173
①	-	change to [42]	-				29.55	.7123	5.370
②	-	-	w/o				37.16	.8403	6.786
③	w/o. P.C	-	-	337k	206G	0.66 s	36.29	.8112	6.603
④	w/o. G.C	-	-	555k	207G	0.69 s	38.85	.9570	7.191

DNN with less recovery ability. From Table 2 we know that the proportion of over/under-exposure pixels in current training set [46,47] is about 2–9%. Here, keeping other variables unchanged, we replace the training set with HDR-LFNet [42] whose SDR over/under-exposure pixels only account about 1% of the image (see Table 2). As anticipated, when trained with sparingly-degraded SDR, Fig. 6(a)(2) recover far less content in over&under-exposed areas than (a)(3). Meanwhile, metrics in Table 4① drop significantly since DNN learned a different lumiance value distribution from another training set.

② **On conventional degradations.** Here, we remove all camera noise and JPEG compression, to see if DNN still learn corresponding restoration ability. As in Fig. 6(b)(2), without extra degradations in training set, our method also struggle to suppress noise and compression artifact, same as other methods without conventional training degradation. Also, in Table 4②, PSNR drop slightly since the training set is unchanged, thus the learned pixel energy distribution is still accurate. While the decline of SSIM and VDP-Q is relatively larger since the local structure is perturbed by noise and compression artifact.

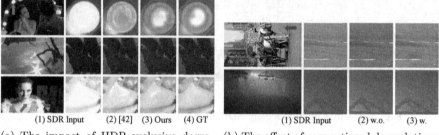

(a) The impact of HDR-exclusive degradation on over-(green arrow) and under-exposure(red arrow) recovery ability.

(b) The effect of conventional degradations on artifact restoration capability.

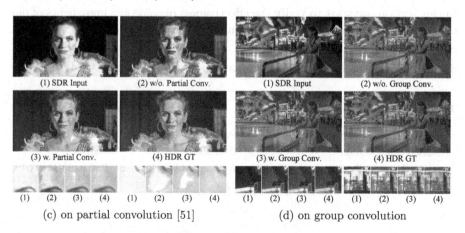

(c) on partial convolution [51]

(d) on group convolution

Fig. 6. Visual demonstration of ablation studies.

③ **On partial convolution and bright invalid mask.** They are claimed as another contributor to DNN's over-exposure recover ability, apart from HDR-exclusive degradation above. Here, we show their indispensability by replacing it with a symmetric structure of decoder, i.e. 'P.conv. RB' at bottom Fig. 3(b) are replaced with 'SFT RB'. In this case, to-be-recover saturated pixels in Fig. 6(c) tend to spread, and metrics also suffer a decline as 'w/o. PC' in Table 3③ shows. The immediate effect proves their ability to exclude useless saturated pattern hence better intermediate deep feature will be generated for the decoder's reconstruction. This is the exact reason why they are placed at encoder rather than decoder end.

④ **On group convolution.** Lightweight DNN has been proven of adequate capability for other low-level vision tasks [8,43–45]. Therefore, we want to check if this also makes sense in SI-HDR. Group convolution (G.C.) is one of the contributor of lightweight design, here we depict if it will deteriorate the DNN's performance. By comparing Table 3④ we know that lightening DNN using group convolution do cause a slight decline on metrics, however, will lead to few noticeable difference in visual result, as Fig. 6(d) shows.

5 Conclusion

Legacy SDR content contains classic historical scenes that cannot be reproduced, and, however, limited dynamic range and degradations brought by old imaging system and multiple transmissions. This formulates an ill-posed problem, SI-HDR, when we want to put those legacy content into HDR application.

The community has begun to take advantage of DNN in SI-HDR problem. We also used DNN but handled more specific problems that hinder current DNN-based methods from real-world deployment: we designed a more lightweight DNN and trained it with elaborately designed degradations. Meanwhile, we reformed SI-HDR problem modeling to better derive DNN structure and arrange degradations correctly. Experiments show that our method is readily applicable to both synthetic and real legacy SDR content. Ablation studies also reveal some factor that will significantly impact the performance of SI-HDR method, including degradation model which has long been understated. Our code is available[1].

Despite the preliminary step we made towards legacy-content-applicable SI-HDR, its cross-degradation generalizability still call for improvement: First, our method perform well on degraded legacy content, but not on clean SDR. Specifically, it tend to vanish/over-smooth high-frequency detail which is mistaken as degraded pattern. This issue also occurs in [15] etc. and should be considered by all legacy-SDR-oriented SI-HDR methods.

Acknowledgements. This work was supported by the PCL2021A10-1 Project of Peng Cheng Laboratory.

---

[1] https://www.github.com/AndreGuo/LHDR.

References

1. Reinhard, E., Heidrich, W., Debevec, P., et al.: High Dynamic Range Imaging: Acquisition, Display, and Image-Based Lighting. Morgan Kaufmann, Burlington (2010)
2. Debevec, P.E., Malik, J.: Recovering high dynamic range radiance maps from photographs. In: Proceedings of SIGGRAPH 1997, pp. 369–378 (1997)
3. Kalantari, N.K., Ramamoorthi, R., et al.: Deep high dynamic range imaging of dynamic scenes. ACM Trans. Graph. **36**, 144–1 (2017)
4. Wu, S., Xu, J., et al.: Deep high dynamic range imaging with large foreground motions. In: Proceedings of ECCV, pp. 117–132 (2018)
5. Yan, Q., Gong, D., Shi, Q., et al.: Attention-guided network for ghost-free high dynamic range imaging. In: Proceedings of CVPR, pp. 1751–1760 (2019)
6. Yan, Q., Zhang, L., Liu, Y., et al.: Deep HDR imaging via a non-local network. IEEE Trans. Image Process. **29**, 4308–4322 (2020)
7. Chen, G., Chen, C., Guo, S., et al.: HDR video reconstruction: a coarse-to-fine network and a real-world benchmark dataset. In: Proceedings of CVPR, pp. 2502–2511 (2021)
8. Pérez-Pellitero, E., et al.: NTIRE 2022 challenge on high dynamic range imaging: methods and results. In: Proceedings of CVPR, pp. 1009–1023 (2022)
9. Banterle, F., Ledda, P., Debattista, K., et al.: Inverse tone mapping. In: Proceedings of the 4th International Conference on Computer Graphics and Interactive Techniques in Australasia and Southeast Asia, pp. 349–356 (2006)
10. Eilertsen, G., Hajisharif, S., et al.: How to cheat with metrics in single-image HDR reconstruction. In: Proceedings of ICCV, pp. 3998–4007 (2021)
11. Eilertsen, G., Kronander, J., et al.: HDR image reconstruction from a single exposure using deep CNNs. ACM Trans. Graph. **36**, 1–15 (2017)
12. Marnerides, D., Bashford-Rogers, T., et al.: ExpandNet: a deep convolutional neural network for high dynamic range expansion from low dynamic range content. Comput. Graph. Forum **37**, 37–49 (2018)
13. Liu, Y.L., Lai, W.S., et al.: Single-image HDR reconstruction by learning to reverse the camera pipeline. In: Proceedings of CVPR, pp. 1651–1660 (2020)
14. Santos, M.S., Ren, T.I., Kalantari, N.K.: Single image HDR reconstruction using a CNN with masked features and perceptual loss. ACM Trans. Graph. **39**, 80–1 (2020)
15. Chen, X., Liu, Y., et al.: HDRUNet: single image HDR reconstruction with denoising and dequantization. In: Proceedings of CVPR, pp. 354–363 (2021)
16. Karaimer, H.C., Brown, M.S.: A software platform for manipulating the camera imaging pipeline. In: Leibe, B., Matas, J., Sebe, N., Welling, M. (eds.) ECCV 2016. LNCS, vol. 9905, pp. 429–444. Springer, Cham (2016). https://doi.org/10.1007/978-3-319-46448-0_26
17. Rempel, A.G., Trentacoste, M., et al.: Ldr2Hdr: on-the-fly reverse tone mapping of legacy video and photographs. ACM Trans. Graph. **26**, 39-es (2007)
18. Zhang, J., Lalonde, J.F.: Learning high dynamic range from outdoor panoramas. In: Proceedings of ICCV, pp. 4519–4528 (2017)
19. Jang, H., et al.: Inverse tone mapping operator using sequential deep neural networks based on the human visual system. IEEE Access **6**, 52058–52072 (2018)
20. Moriwaki, K., Yoshihashi, R., et al.: Hybrid loss for learning single-image-based HDR reconstruction. arXiv preprint: arXiv:1812.07134 (2018)

21. Wang, C., Zhao, Y., Wang, R.: Deep inverse tone mapping for compressed images. IEEE Access **7**, 74558–74569 (2019)

22. Soh, J.W., Park, J.S., Cho, N.I.: Joint high dynamic range imaging and super-resolution from a single image. IEEE Access **7**, 177427–177437 (2019)

23. Khan, Z., Khanna, M., Raman, S.: FHDR: HDR image reconstruction from a single LDR image using feedback network. In: Proceedings of GlobalSIP, pp. 1–5. IEEE (2019)

24. Marnerides, D., Bashford-Rogers, T., Debattista, K.: Deep HDR hallucination for inverse tone mapping. Sensors **21**, 4032 (2021)

25. Ye, N., Huo, Y., et al.: Single exposure high dynamic range image reconstruction based on deep dual-branch network. IEEE Access **9**, 9610–9624 (2021)

26. Lee, B.D., Sunwoo, M.H.: HDR image reconstruction using segmented image learning. IEEE Access **9**, 142729–142742 (2021)

27. A Sharif, S., Naqvi, R.A., et al.: A two-stage deep network for high dynamic range image reconstruction. In: Proceedings of CVPR, pp. 550–559 (2021)

28. Zhang, Y., Aydın, T.: Deep HDR estimation with generative detail reconstruction. Comput. Graph. Forum **40**, 179–190 (2021)

29. Liu, K., Cao, G., et al.: Lightness modulated deep inverse tone mapping. arXiv preprint: arXiv:2107.07907 (2021)

30. Raipurkar, P., Pal, R., Raman, S.: HDR-cGAN: single LDR to HDR image translation using conditional GAN. In: Proceedings of 12th Indian Conference on Computer Vision, Graphics and Image Processing, pp. 1–9 (2021)

31. Yu, H., Liu, W., et al.: Luminance attentive networks for HDR image and panorama reconstruction. Comput. Graph. Forum (40), 181–192 (2021)

32. Borrego-Carazo, J., Ozay, M., et al.: A mixed quantization network for computationally efficient mobile inverse tone mapping. arXiv preprint: arXiv:2203.06504 (2022)

33. Wu, G., Song, R., et al.: LiTMNet: a deep CNN for efficient HDR image reconstruction from a single LDR image. Pattern Recogn. **127**, 108620 (2022)

34. Endo, Y., Kanamori, Y., Mitani, J.: Deep reverse tone mapping. ACM Trans. Graph. **36**, 177-1 (2017)

35. Lee, S., An, G.H., et al.: Deep chain HDRI: reconstructing a high dynamic range image from a single low dynamic range image. IEEE Access **6**, 49913–49924 (2018)

36. Lee, S., An, G.H., Kang, S.J.: Deep recursive HDRI: inverse tone mapping using generative adversarial networks. In: Proceedings of ECCV, pp. 596–611 (2018)

37. Jo, S.Y., Lee, S., et al.: Deep arbitrary HDRI: inverse tone mapping with controllable exposure changes. IEEE Trans. Multimedia **24**, 2713–2726 (2021)

38. Banterle, F., Marnerides, D., et al.: Unsupervised HDR imaging: what can be learned from a single 8-bit video? arXiv preprint: arXiv:2202.05522 (2022)

39. Kinoshita, Y., Kiya, H.: iTM-net: deep inverse tone mapping using novel loss function considering tone mapping operator. IEEE Access **7**, 73555–73563 (2019)

40. Jang, H., et al.: Dynamic range expansion using cumulative histogram learning for high dynamic range image generation. IEEE Access **8**, 38554–38567 (2020)

41. Cao, G., Zhou, F., et al.: A brightness-adaptive kernel prediction network for inverse tone mapping. Neurocomputing **464**, 1–14 (2021)

42. Chambe, M., Kijak, E., et al.: HDR-LFNet: inverse tone mapping using fusion network. HAL preprint: 03618267 (2022)

43. Zhang, K., et al.: AIM 2020 challenge on efficient super-resolution: methods and results. In: Bartoli, A., Fusiello, A. (eds.) ECCV 2020. LNCS, vol. 12537, pp. 5–40. Springer, Cham (2020). https://doi.org/10.1007/978-3-030-67070-2_1

44. Li, Y., et al.: NTIRE 2022 challenge on efficient super-resolution: methods and results. In: Proceedings of CVPR, pp. 1062–1102 (2022)
45. Ignatov, A., et al.: Fast camera image denoising on mobile GPUs with deep learning, mobile AI 2021 challenge: report. In: Proceedings of CVPR, pp. 2515–2524 (2021)
46. Pérez-Pellitero, E., et al.: NTIRE 2021 challenge on high dynamic range imaging: dataset, methods and results. In: Proceedings of CVPR, pp. 691–700 (2021)
47. Fairchild, M.D.: The HDR photographic survey. In: Color and Imaging Conference 2007, pp. 233–238 (2007)
48. Froehlich, J., Grandinetti, S., et al.: Creating cinematic wide gamut HDR-video for the evaluation of tone mapping operators and HDR-displays. In: Digital Photography X, vol. 9023, pp. 279–288 (2014)
49. Liu, Y., He, J., et al.: Very lightweight photo retouching network with conditional sequential modulation. arXiv preprint: arXiv:2104.06279 (2021)
50. Wang, X., Yu, K., et al.: Recovering realistic texture in image super-resolution by deep spatial feature transform. In: Proceedings of CVPR, pp. 606–615 (2018)
51. Liu, G., Reda, F.A., et al.: Image inpainting for irregular holes using partial convolutions. In: Proceedings of ECCV, pp. 85–100 (2018)
52. Jiang, J., Zhang, K., Timofte, R.: Towards flexible blind jpeg artifacts removal. In: Proceedings ICCV, pp. 4997–5006 (2021)
53. Hanji, P., Mantiuk, R., Eilertsen, G., Hajisharif, S., Unger, J.: Comparison of single image HDR reconstruction methods-the caveats of quality assessment. In: Proceedings of SIGGRAPH 2022, pp. 1–8 (2022)
54. Wolski, K., Giunchi, D., et al.: Dataset and metrics for predicting local visible differences. ACM Trans. Graph. 37, 1–14 (2018)
55. Mathworks: JPEG image deblocking using deep learning. (https://www.mathworks.com/help/images/jpeg-image-deblocking-using-deep-learning.html)
56. Zhang, K., Zuo, W., et al.: Beyond a gaussian denoiser: residual learning of deep CNN for image denoising. IEEE Trans. Image Process. 26, 3142–3155 (2017)

NoiseTransfer: Image Noise Generation with Contrastive Embeddings

Seunghwan Lee and Tae Hyun Kim[✉]

Department of Computer Science, Hanyang University, Seoul, Korea
{seunghwanlee,taehyunkim}@hanyang.ac.kr

Abstract. Deep image denoising networks have achieved impressive success with the help of a considerably large number of synthetic train datasets. However, real-world denoising is a still challenging problem due to the dissimilarity between distributions of real and synthetic noisy datasets. Although several real-world noisy datasets have been presented, the number of train datasets (*i.e.*, pairs of clean and real noisy images) is limited, and acquiring more real noise datasets is laborious and expensive. To mitigate this problem, numerous attempts to simulate real noise models using generative models have been studied. Nevertheless, previous works had to train multiple networks to handle multiple different noise distributions. By contrast, we propose a new generative model that can synthesize noisy images with multiple different noise distributions. Specifically, we adopt recent contrastive learning to learn distinguishable latent features of the noise. Moreover, our model can generate new noisy images by transferring the noise characteristics solely from a single reference noisy image. We demonstrate the accuracy and the effectiveness of our noise model for both known and unknown noise removal.

Keywords: Image denoising · Image noise generation

1 Introduction

Noise is a common artifact in imaging systems; thus, accurately modeling the noise is an important task for many image-processing and computer vision applications. To remove the noise in an image, several statistical noise models have been adopted in the literature. The most simple, widely used noise models are additive white Gaussian noise and Poisson noise. However, in a real-world scenario, image noise does not follow Gaussian and Poisson distributions [3,31], and these simple statistical noise models cannot accurately capture the noise characteristic of real noise which includes signal-dependent and signal-independent components. Moreover, developing a noise model that can simulate complex real-world noise process is very difficult because complicated processing steps

---

Code is available at https://github.com/shlee0/NoiseTransfer.

Supplementary Information The online version contains supplementary material available at https://doi.org/10.1007/978-3-031-26313-2_20.

L. Wang et al. (Eds.): ACCV 2022, LNCS 13843, pp. 323–339, 2023.
https://doi.org/10.1007/978-3-031-26313-2_20

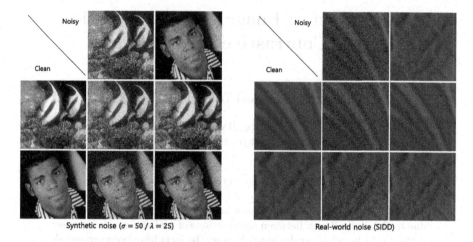

Fig. 1. Examples of generated noisy images. Our proposed model can generate a noisy version of a clean image by transferring noise information in the reference noisy image. **(Left)** Synthetic noise (*i.e.*, Gaussian noise ($\sigma = 50$) (2nd column) and Poisson noise ($\lambda = 25$) (3rd column)) generation results. **(Right)** Real-world noise generation results from the Smartphone Image Denoising Dataset (SIDD) [3]. Noisy images generated in an unpaired manner can have different noise levels that do not exist in the original dataset.

of an imaging pipeline include various noise models, such as photon noise, read noise, and spatially correlated noise. Conventional denoising networks that show promising results in removing noise from known distribution (*e.g.*, Gaussian) frequently fail in dealing with real noise from an unknown distribution due to these limitations.

Collecting real-world datasets that include pairs of clean and real-noisy images can solve these problems. However, the noise distributions of conventional cameras are different from one another, so we need to acquire a large amount of labelled real-world dataset, which is very time-consuming. This problem stimulates the need for synthetic, but realistic noise generation system to avoid taking pairs of clean and noisy pictures. Recently, several generative adversarial network (GAN)-based noise models have been proposed to model the complex real-world noise in a data-driven manner better. Since Chen *et al.* [12] has proposed a generative model to synthesize zero-mean noise, recent models [2,9–11,19,20,24,36] made many attempts to generate signal-dependent noise by considering a clean image as a conditional input.

Despite this encouraging progress, there are still some steps to move forward for image noise generation. Typically, generative models have difficulty in controlling the specific type of noise during synthesizing. In other words, which types of noise will be realized is not predictable at the inference if generator is trained with a large of noise distributions. In addition, this randomness increases if the training dataset includes several different noise types. A naïve, straightforward solution would be to train multiple generators independently to handle multiple noise models. Alternatively, image metadata such as camera-ISO and the raw Bayer pattern can be utilized to avoid this hassle. However, this external data is not always available (*e.g.*, images from unknown resources).

In this work, we propose a novel generative noise model, which can allow multiple different types of noise models. We transfer the noise characteristics within a given reference noisy image to corrupt freely available clean images, and we synthesize new noisy images in this manner. Moreover, our model requires only the noisy image itself without demanding any external information (*e.g.*, metadata). Specifically, we train our discriminator to distinguish the distribution of each noise from the others in a self-supervised manner by adopting a contrastive learning. Then, our generator learns to synthesize a new noisy image using the noise information extracted from the discriminator. With this strategy, we can perform noise generation with paired or unpaired images, and Fig. 1 presents some examples. We demonstrate that our generative noise model can handle a wide range of noise distributions, and the conventional denoising networks trained with our newly synthesized noisy images can remove the real noise much better than existing generative noise models. The main contributions of our work are summarized as follows:

- We propose a novel generative noise model that can handle diverse noise distributions with a single noise generator without additional meta information.
- Our model exploits the representation power of the contrastive learning. To the best of our knowledge, our model is the first approach which utilizes contrastive noise embedding to control the type of noise to be generated.
- Extensive experiments demonstrate that our model achieves state-of-the-art performance in noise generation and is applicable for image denoising.

2 Related Work

2.1 Contrastive Learning

The contrastive learning mechanism introduced by [16] learns similar/dissimilar representations in a self-supervised manner from positive/negative pairs. In the works of instance discrimination [8,35], a query and a key form a positive pair if they originate from the same image and form a negative pair if otherwise. It is known that more negative samples can yield better representation ability, and a large number of negative samples can be maintained in a batch [13] or dynamic dictionary updated by a momentum-based key encoder [18].

After the contrastive learning has shown powerful representation ability in several downstream tasks, it has been integrated with the GAN framework as an auxiliary task. For instance, contrastive learning could relieve forgetting problem of discriminator [14,26], and improve image translation quality by maximizing mutual information of corresponding patches in different domains [17,30]. ContraGAN [22] improved image generation quality by incorporating data-to-data relations as well as data-to-class relations into discriminator. ContraD [21] empirically showed that training the GAN discriminator jointly with the augmentation techniques used in the literature of contrastive learning benefits the task of the discriminator. Moreover, contrastive learning can learn content-invariant degradation representation by constructing image pairs with the same degradation as positive examples. Recently, DASR [33] and AirNet [27] utilized learned degradation representation for image restoration. Different from previous works, our work studies image noise synthesis conditional on degradation representation learned through contrastive learning.

2.2 Generative Noise Model

To address the limitations of simple synthetic noise models, considerable effort has been devoted to numerous generative noise models to synthesize complex noise for the real-world image denoising problem. Particularly, recent generative noise models yield signal-dependent noise given a clean image. Some approaches require metadata (e.g., smartphone code, ISO level, and shutter speed) as an additional input to generate noise from a specific distribution [2,11,24]. However, these approaches assume that the metadata is available, which might not be common in the real scenario (e.g., internet images and pictures), and the use of this additional information limits the usage of the generative noise model in practice. Unlike existing generative models, our model extracts noise representation from an input noisy image itself without relying on the metadata, and thus allows us to use any noisy image as a reference. Then, our generator synthesizes new noisy images based on noise information of the reference noisy image, such that we can easily predict which type of noise will be realized.

3   Proposed Method: NoiseTransfer

Our generative noise model synthesizes new noisy images by transferring the noise of a reference noisy image to other clean images. Specifically, our discriminator takes a single reference noisy image as an input and outputs noise embeddings that represent noise characteristics of the reference noisy image. Then, our generator synthesizes new noisy images by corrupting clean images available for free using the given noise embeddings that we dub NoiseTransfer. Figure 2 depicts the overview of the proposed NoiseTransfer scheme.

3.1   Noise Discrimination with Contrastive Learning

Capturing different characteristics for different noises is essential to keep the noise information distinct. Therefore, we train our discriminator through contrastive learning to learn distinguishable noise embeddings of each noise, and we follow MoCo [18] framework: dynamic dictionary holding a large number of

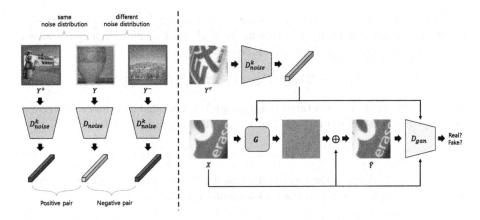

Fig. 2. Our discriminator consists of two branches with shared intermediate convolutional modules for each forward operation denoted by D_{noise} and D_{gan} respectively. **(Left)** An illustration of our noise representation learning scheme. Two noisy images sampled from the same noise distribution form a positive and, in different cases, a negative. **(Right)** Overall flow of the proposed NoiseTransfer. Our noise generator takes a clean image X and noise embeddings $D_{noise}^k(Y^r)$ where Y^r is a reference noisy image.

negative samples and momentum-based key network. Then, a form of a contrastive loss function, called InfoNCE [29], can be written with cosine similarity $s(u, v) = u \cdot v / \|u\|_2 \|v\|_2$ for encoded embeddings u and v as follows:

$$L_{\mathrm{Con}}(q, k^+, Q) =$$
$$- \log \frac{\exp(s(q, k^+)/\tau)}{\exp(s(q, k^+)/\tau) + \sum\limits_{k^- \in Q} \exp(s(q, k^-)/\tau)}, \qquad (1)$$

where q, k^+, and k^- denote the embeddings of a query, positive key, and negative key, respectively; Q denotes a queue containing negative keys; and τ is a temperature hyperparameter. Equation 1 pulls embeddings of the q close to those of the k^+ and pushes them apart from those of the k^-.

In our work, as shown in Fig. 2 (Left), we construct a positive pair of noisy images if they are sampled from the same noise distribution and a negative pair, otherwise. Then, the contrastive loss for noise discrimination can be formulated as follows:

$$L_{noise}^D = \mathbb{E}[L_{\mathrm{Con}}(D_{noise}(Y), D_{noise}^k(Y^+), Q)], \qquad (2)$$

where Y^+ denotes a noisy image that has the same noise distribution to that of another noisy image Y. Note that we encodes the keys (k^+ and k^-) with momentum-based key network D_{noise}^k. We assume that embeddings in Q are from noisy images whose noise distributions are different from that of Y. Equation 2 encourages our discriminator to learn distinguishable noise representation for each different noise.

Our final goal is to synthesize a new noisy image $\tilde{Y}$ through a generator, which has the same noise distribution as the real one Y. Thus, we derive another contrastive loss for the generator as follows:

$$L_{noise}^G = \mathbb{E}[L_{\text{Con}}(D_{noise}(\tilde{Y}), D_{noise}^k(Y^+), Q)]. \tag{3}$$

Note that, in Eq. 3, our generated noisy image $\tilde{Y}$ is encoded as a query. Moreover, we adopt a feature matching loss [32] to stabilize training as follows:

$$L_{noise}^{FM} = \|m_{noise}(Y) - m_{noise}(\tilde{Y})\|_1, \tag{4}$$

where $m_{noise}(\cdot)$ denotes the intermediate feature maps before pooling operation in the D_{noise} (please refer to the supplement for details).

3.2 Noise Generation with Contrastive Embeddings

Given a clean image X and a reference noisy image Y^r, our generator learns to synthesize a new noisy image $\tilde{Y}$ which is a noisy version of X and has the same noise distribution as Y^r. The generation process is described in Fig. 2 (Right). Reference noisy image Y^r is encoded by D_{noise}^k, and noise embeddings $D_{noise}^k(Y^r)$ that contain noise representation of the Y^r are fed to our generator. This approach enables our model to handle a wide range of noise distributions with a single generator. To generate realistic noisy images, our model performs adversarial training. The adversarial losses [15] for our model are defined as follows:

$$\begin{aligned} L_{gan}^D &= -\mathbb{E}[log(D_{gan}(R))] - \mathbb{E}[log(1 - D_{gan}(F)] \\ L_{gan}^G &= -\mathbb{E}[log(D_{gan}(F))], \end{aligned} \tag{5}$$

where R denotes a set of $X, D_{noise}^k(Y^r)$, and Y, whereas F includes $\tilde{Y}$ instead of Y. Our generator synthesizes noisy images with different kinds of noise distribution based on the $D_{noise}^k(Y^r)$, even with the same clean image X. Thus, our discriminator distinguishes whether the input noisy image is real or fake considering the X and $D_{noise}^k(Y^r)$. Similar to Eq. 4, we adopt feature matching loss for stable adversarial training as follows:

$$L_{gan}^{FM} = \|m_{gan}(Y) - m_{gan}(\tilde{Y})\|_1, \tag{6}$$

where $m_{gan}(\cdot)$ denotes feature maps before the last convolution layer in the D_{gan}. Finally, we utilize L_1 reconstruction loss $L_{recon} = \|GF(Y) - GF(\tilde{Y})\|_1$ with the Gaussian filter GF as used in [36] to enforce statistical features of noise distribution. Then, we define the final objective functions for our model as follows:

$$\begin{aligned} L_{\text{D}} &= L_{noise}^D + L_{gan}^D \\ L_{\text{G}} &= L_{noise}^G + L_{gan}^G + \\ &\quad \lambda_{noise}^{FM} L_{noise}^{FM} + \lambda_{gan}^{FM} L_{gan}^{FM} + \lambda_{recon} L_{recon}, \end{aligned} \tag{7}$$

where λ_{noise}^{FM}, λ_{gan}^{FM}, and λ_{recon} control the weights of the associated terms.

Fig. 3. Visual results of noise generation on the SIDD validation set. The corresponding noise is displayed below for each noisy image. **Left to Right**: CA-NoiseGAN [11], DANet [36], GDANet [36], NoiseGAN [9], C2N [20], NoiseTransfer (Ours), Noisy, Clean.

3.3 Discussion

Our model has several advantages compared with existing noise generators. [9] trained 17 different generators to handle numerous camera models and ISO levels. This solution could be straightforward to cover various noise distributions, but training multiple generators for each different noise lacks practicality. To compensate this, image metadata of a noisy image can be exploited to sample a specific noise type [2, 11, 24]. However, such external information is not always available in the real-world. PNGAN [10] requires pre-trained networks for training. Specifically, it uses a camera pipeline modeling network [37] to generate a noisy image that is further refined by generator. It also employs a pre-trained

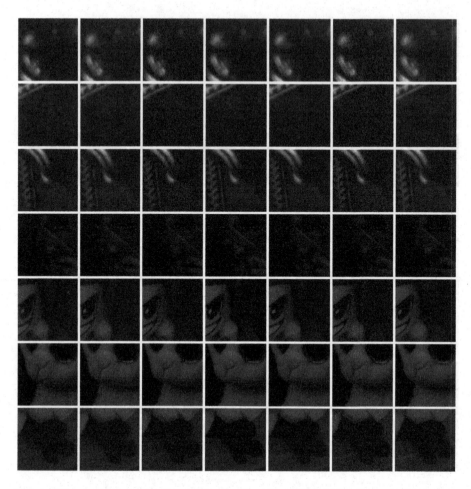

Fig. 4. Visual results for real noise removal on the SIDD validation set (first three rows) and SIDD+ set (last four rows). **Left to Right**: RIDNet results trained by DANet [36], GDANet [36], C2N [20], CycleISP [37], NoiseTransfer (Ours), and Noisy and Clean image.

denoising network as the regularizer. This strategy makes the generated noisy image distribution dependent on pre-trained networks, which may not be suitable in several cases. Although C2N [20] takes random vector that determines the property of synthesized noise, we do not know which value should be used for the random vector when a particular type of noise is required. Compared with these models, our model can handle numerous noise distributions with a single generator, and does not need external resources, and synthesizes a desired noise by transferring the noise information from a reference noisy image.

4 Experiments

4.1 Implementation Details

We train our NoiseTransfer model by using various synthetic and real noisy images. First, for real-world noise, we use the SIDD-Medium dataset [3] following previous works [2,11,20,36]. In this case, two different patches are randomly selected from the same noisy image to get Y and Y^r. For synthetic noise, we sample noise from Gaussian distribution ($\sigma \in [0, 70]$), Poisson distribution ($\lambda \in [5, 100]$), and the combined Poisson-Gaussian distribution ($\sigma \in [0, 70]$ and $\lambda \in [5, 100]$). Then, we acquire synthetic noisy images by corrupting clean images in the DIV2K training set [4] and SIDD-Meidum set using the noise from these synthetic distributions. We use 32 mini-batch of 96×96 patches for training. Each mini-batch includes 16 patches from the SIDD-Medium set and 16 patches corrupted with synthetic noise distributions. We apply data augmentation (flip and rotation) to diversify train images. The noise embedding vector (*i.e.*, outcome by D_{noise}) has 128-dimension, the size of the queue is set to 4096, and temperature parameter τ is set to 0.1 [23]. $\lambda_{noise}^{FM}, \lambda_{gan}^{FM}$, and λ_{recon} are equally set to 100. We use Adam optimizer [25] with an learning rate of 1e−4, $\beta_1 = 0.5$, and $\beta_2 = 0.99$. We also apply L2 regularization with regularization factor 1e−7. Our discriminator and generator are updated 2,000 times during one epoch, and training for 200 epochs takes approximately a week on two Tesla V100 GPUs. We provide more details including network configurations and additional experimental results in the supplement.

4.2 Noisy Image Generation

We first measure the accuracy of the generated noisy images. To do so, we use Average KL Divergence (AKLD) value [36] and Kolmogorov-Smirnov (KS) test value[1] [9] for quantitative evaluation, and compare the results with DANet [36], GDANet [36], C2N [20], and CycleISP [37] in Table 1. Note that, DANet trained only with the SIDD-Medium dataset outperforms GDANet [36] trained with three different real-noise datasets (SIDD-Medium, Poly [34], and RENOIR [5]). The results demonstrate that GDANet does not handle the specific noise better in the SIDD dataset than DANet. CycleISP [37] samples random noise considering specific camera settings; hence, it is unlikely that distribution of the randomly sampled noise matches to that of noise within a specific noisy image. By contrast, our NoiseTransfer which is trained with multiple different noise models can deal with the specific noise by transferring the noise characteristics within the reference noisy image, because our model utilizes noisy images as the reference $\tilde{Y}$ as well as clean images. This advantage allows our model to obtain the best performance among the compared models. However, it is worth mentioning that better AKLD/KS values do not always imply higher denoising performance as will be described in Sect. 4.3. AKLD/KS values compute the

---

[1] Histograms are computed with 256 bins evenly distributed in $[-256, 256]$.

distance of pixel value distributions of two images, thus, we cannot predict how realistic generated noisy image is with only those values.

Figure 3 presents visual comparisons of generated noisy images. The visual results show that our NoiseTransfer can synthesize more realistic and desirable noise than other models which frequently generate unexpected patterns. Note that CA-NoiseGAN [11] conducts noise generation with raw images[2], and NoiseGAN [9] only covers four ISO levels (400–3200), thus, we provide only visual comparisons with these approaches.

Table 1. AKLD/KS test values on the SIDD validation and SIDD+ datasets. The best values are highlighted in bold.

Dataset	SIDD validation		SIDD+	
Metric	AKLD↓	KS↓	AKLD↓	KS↓
DANet	0.2117	0.0732	0.4144	0.1468
GDANet	0.2431	0.1079	0.4744	0.2557
C2N	0.3138	0.1499	0.2882	**0.1330**
CycleISP	0.6881	0.1743	0.9412	0.1743
Ours	**0.1655**	**0.0617**	**0.2324**	0.1537

4.3 Real Noise Denoising

To more accurately validate the quality of generated noisy images, we evaluate the applicability of our NoiseTransfer in real-world image denoising. In this work, we choose lightweight yet effective RIDNet [6] as a baseline denoising network. For a fair comparison, all generative noise models are evaluated by measuring the denoising performance of RIDNet. Following previous works [2,11,20,36], we use images from SIDD [3] for training and validation. The ground-truth clean images and the corresponding generated noisy images are used to train RIDNet. We do not include the ground-truth noisy images in the dataset when training the denoiser to evaluate generative noise models. For our NoiseTransfer, we randomly select a clean image X and choose another random noisy image as the reference Y^r from the SIDD-Medium dataset to render a new noisy patch $\tilde{Y}$.

We evaluate the real noise removal performance on the SIDD validation, SIDD+ [1], and DND benchmark [31] datasets. In Table 2, we measure the denoising performance in terms of PSNR and SSIM values, and denoising results by RIDNet trained with generated noisy images from DANet, GDANet, C2N, CycleISP, and our NoiseTransfer are compared. We also present the result when the ground-truth noisy images are used instead of generated images (RIDNet+GT). Note that C2N [20] got the best KS value on SIDD+ in Table 1, but PSNR/SSIM values are lower than other models. This result shows AKLD/KS

---

[2] For visualization, the camera pipeline matlab code (https://github.com/AbdoKa mel/simple-camera-pipeline) is used.

values do not always hint at higher denoising performance as stated in Sect. 4.2. Our outstanding denoising results show that RIDNet trained with generated noisy images by our NoiseTransfer is generally applicable for real-world denoising. Notably, our method got comparable denoising performance with 'RIDNet+GT', especially on SIDD+, and this result is not surprising in this field. For example, NoiseFlow [2] achieved better performance when using generated images during training rather than the ground-truth real images for raw image denoising (refer to Table. 3 in [2]). This is due to the small number of real GT samples in the training dataset. Figure 4 shows visual denoising results on the SIDD validation and SIDD+ datasets.

Moreover, we plot changes of PSNR values by RIDNet during training on the SIDD validation and SIDD+ datasets in Fig. 5. Particularly, we observe that when the RIDNet is trained with noisy images generated by either GDANet or DANet, the denoiser is overfitted after some iterations and PSNR values drops. We believe this overfitting problem can be caused by unrealistic patterns that GDANet and DANet produce as shown in Fig. 3. Note that CycleISP is not a generative model and instead injects synthetic realistic noise, so RIDNet trained with noisy images synthesized by CycleISP does not suffer from the overfitting problem. However it provides limited performance because CycleISP considers predetermined shot/read noise factors for specific camera settings to inject random noise, which may not follow distribution of real noise. In contrast, RIDNet trained with images by our NoiseTransfer results show promising denoising results on several datasets (more than 0.5 dB compared with CycleISP on average).

Table 2. Denoising results in terms of PSNR/SSIM values on the various real-world noise datasets. 'GT' denotes the ground-truth noisy images. Red and Blue denote the best and second values.

Dataset	SIDD validation	SIDD+	DND
RIDNet + DANet	35.91/0.8762	34.64/0.8600	37.54/0.9292
RIDNet + GDANet	36.58/0.8851	35.22/0.8844	37.13/0.9345
RIDNet + C2N	31.87/0.7274	34.22/0.8290	35.41/0.9032
RIDNet + CycleISP	38.09/0.9095	35.49/0.9006	38.95/0.9485
RIDNet + NoiseTransfer	38.57/0.9112	36.30/0.9095	39.15/0.9492
RIDNet + GT	39.14/0.9155	36.21/0.9057	39.35/0.9502

4.4   Synthetic Noise Denoising

Finally, we evaluate the applicability of our NoiseTransfer in removing synthetic noise. To do so, we first generate noisy images which include noise from known distributions using our NoiseTransfer. Specifically, we use randomly selected clean image in the DIV2K training set as X, and add synthetic noise into another clean image for the reference noisy image Y^r. We add one of Gaussian noise

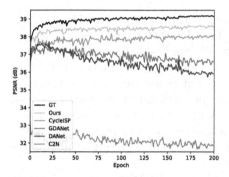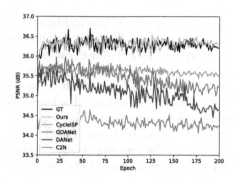

Fig. 5. PSNR value changes during training on the SIDD validation set (Left) and SIDD+ (Right). Denoising performance trained by GT noisy images, NoiseTransfer (Ours), CycleISP, GDANet, DANet, and C2N are compared.

Table 3. PSNR/SSIM results of synthetic noise removal on the BSDS500 dataset. 'GT' denotes the ground-truth noisy images. 'N2G$_g$' and 'N2G$_p$' denote two independently trained networks for Gaussian and Poisson noise respectively. For a random noise level, we report an average of 10 trials. Red and Blue denote the best and second values respectively.

Noise type	Gaussian		Poisson		Poisson-Gaussian	
Noise level	Fixed ($\sigma = 25$)	Random ($\sigma \in [0, 50]$)	Fixed ($\lambda = 30$)	Random ($\lambda \in [5, 50]$)	Fixed ($\lambda = 30, \sigma = 25$)	Random ($\lambda \in [5, 50], \sigma \in [0, 50]$)
RIDNet + N2G$_g$	31.21/0.8806	32.82/0.8818	30.28/0.8702	29.52/0.8464	28.80/0.8276	28.15/0.8070
RIDNet + N2G$_p$	31.17/0.8792	32.74/0.8825	30.31/0.8703	29.56/0.8477	28.93/0.8301	28.32/0.8106
RIDNet + NoiseTransfer	31.27/0.8834	32.76/0.8872	30.58/0.8735	29.95/0.8530	29.16/0.8344	28.71/0.8190
RIDNet + GT	31.48/0.8868	33.20/0.8913	30.74/0.8774	30.20/0.8608	29.31/0.8375	28.85/0.8212

($\sigma \in [0, 50]$) and Poisson noise ($\lambda \in [5, 50]$) following N2G [28]. Additionally, we also add noise from Poisson-Gaussian distribution ($\sigma \in [0, 50], \lambda \in [5, 50]$) to confirm that our NoiseTransfer can generate diverse noises well. The new noisy image $\tilde{Y}$ is synthesized with X and Y^r, and RIDNet is trained with pairs of clean image X and generated noisy image $\tilde{Y}$. In Fig. 6, we present examples of our generated noisy images from known distributions, and we see that our model can synthesize signal-independent noise as well as signal-dependent one.

To quantitatively measure the denoising performance, we use BSDS500 dataset [7] as testset and degrade images in the BSDS500 by adding noise from known distributions, and then put them into RIDNet as input. Denoisng performance of RIDNet trained with noisy images by N2G [28], our NoiseTransfer, and the ground-truth noisy images are compared in Table 3. Note that N2G does not generate noise, but instead extracts noise by denoising the input noisy image. It also adopts a bernoulli random mask to destroy residual structure in the noise, and then the masked noise is used to corrupt other clean images. In Table 3, N2G exhibits favorable performance when the noise type in N2G training matches the noise type in the test noisy image, but it reveals a slight performance drop against other types of noise. In other words, N2G$_g$ shows slightly better denoising results for Gaussian noise removal and N2G$_p$ for Poisson noise removal. This result implies that we may need to train multiple networks separately for each noise distribution (*e.g.*, separated two networks for Gaussian and Poisson). By contrast, our NoiseTransfer shows consistently better denoising performance for several types of noise with a single generator, thus, our method does not require multiple generators independently trained for each noise type.

Fig. 6. Examples of synthetic noise generation. (a) Ground-truth noisy image. (b) Generated noisy image by NoiseTransfer (Ours). (c)–(d) Noise added in (a) and (b), respectively.

4.5   Ablation Study

In this work, we introduced contrastive losses for our NoiseTransfer. Thus, we provide ablation study with and without using the additional contrastive losses during training. We compare the accuracy of the generated noisy images in terms of AKLD and KS value. Figure 7 obviously shows the effect of contrastive learning for image noise generation of our model[3]. First, without L_{noise}^{D} which is the crux of our approach, we found the noise generation performance is very poor, and the model diverged after 14 epochs (Green). This result demonstrates that learning distinguishable noise representation is crucial for our single generator to cover different kinds of noise distributions. Next, with L_{noise}^{D}, we could see

---

[3] It compares the results for the first 60 training epochs, but is sufficient to confirm the effect of the proposed losses, allowing fair and efficient ablations.

much better training results, but still have unstable performance early in training (Blue). Finally, we can achieve more training stability and better performance when we explicitly guide our generator to synthesize a new noisy image with the same noise distribution to that of the Y^r with additional losses L_{noise}^G and L_{noise}^{FM} (Red).

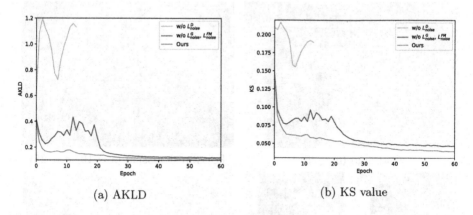

(a) AKLD   (b) KS value

Fig. 7. AKLD and KS test values for the first 60 training epochs. (Green) Trained without L_{noise}^D. This model diverged after 14 epochs. (Blue) Trained without L_{noise}^G and L_{noise}^{FM}. (Red) Our final NoiseTransfer. (Color figure online)

5   Conclusion

In this work, we proposed a novel noisy image generator trained with contrastive learning. Different from existing works, our discriminator learns distinguishable noise representation for each different noise, which is the core of our method. Thus, ours can extract noise characteristics from an input reference noisy image and generate new noisy images by transferring the specific noise to clean images. This approach enables our generator to synthesize noisy images based on the noise information both in a paired or unpaired manner. Consequently, our model can handle multiple noise distributions with a single generator. Experiments demonstrate that the proposed generative noise model can produce more accurate noisy images than conventional methods and the applicability for image denoising.

Acknowledgements. This work was supported by Samsung Electronics Co., Ltd, and Samsung Research Funding Center of Samsung Electronics under Project Number SRFCIT1901-06.

References

1. Abdelhamed, A., Afifi, M., Timofte, R., Brown, M.S.: NTIRE 2020 challenge on real image denoising: dataset, methods and results. In: Proceedings of the IEEE Conference on Computer Vision and Pattern Recognition Workshops (CVPRW) (2020)
2. Abdelhamed, A., Brubaker, M.A., Brown, M.S.: Noise flow: noise modeling with conditional normalizing flows. In: Proceedings of the IEEE International Conference on Computer Vision (ICCV) (2019)
3. Abdelhamed, A., Lin, S., Brown, M.S.: A high-quality denoising dataset for smartphone cameras. In: Proceedings of the IEEE Conference on Computer Vision and Pattern Recognition (CVPR) (2018)
4. Agustsson, E., Timofte, R.: NTIRE 2017 challenge on single image super-resolution: dataset and study. In: Proceedings of the IEEE Conference on Computer Vision and Pattern Recognition Workshops (CVPRW) (2017)
5. Anaya, J., Barbu, A.: Renoir-a dataset for real low-light image noise reduction. J. Vis. Commun. Image Represent. **51**, 144–154 (2018)
6. Anwar, S., Barnes, N.: Real image denoising with feature attention. In: Proceedings of the IEEE International Conference on Computer Vision (ICCV) (2019)
7. Arbelaez, P., Maire, M., Fowlkes, C., Malik, J.: Contour detection and hierarchical image segmentation. PAMI **33**(5), 898–916 (2011). https://doi.org/10.1109/TPAMI.2010.161
8. Bachman, P., Hjelm, R.D., Buchwalter, W.: Learning representations by maximizing mutual information across views. In: Advances in Neural Information Processing Systems (NIPS) (2019)
9. Henz, B., Gastal, E.S.L., Oliveira, M.M.: Synthesizing camera noise using generative adversarial networks. IEEE Trans. Vis. Comput. Graph. **27**(3), 2123–2135 (2021). https://doi.org/10.1109/TVCG.2020.3012120
10. Cai, Y., Hu, X., Wang, H., Zhang, Y., Pfister, H., Wei, D.: Learning to generate realistic noisy images via pixel-level noise-aware adversarial training. In: Beygelzimer, A., Dauphin, Y., Liang, P., Vaughan, J.W. (eds.) Advances in Neural Information Processing Systems (NIPS) (2021)
11. Chang, K.-C., et al.: Learning camera-aware noise models. In: Vedaldi, A., Bischof, H., Brox, T., Frahm, J.-M. (eds.) ECCV 2020. LNCS, vol. 12369, pp. 343–358. Springer, Cham (2020). https://doi.org/10.1007/978-3-030-58586-0_21
12. Chen, J., Chen, J., Chao, H., Yang, M.: Image blind denoising with generative adversarial network based noise modeling. In: Proceedings of the IEEE Conference on Computer Vision and Pattern Recognition (CVPR), pp. 3155–3164 (2018)
13. Chen, T., Kornblith, S., Norouzi, M., Hinton, G.: A simple framework for contrastive learning of visual representations. In: International Conference on Machine Learning (ICML), pp. 1597–1607. PMLR (2020)
14. Chen, T., Zhai, X., Ritter, M., Lucic, M., Houlsby, N.: Self-supervised GANs via auxiliary rotation loss. In: Proceedings of the IEEE Conference on Computer Vision and Pattern Recognition (CVPR), pp. 12154–12163 (2019)
15. Goodfellow, I., et al.: Generative adversarial nets. In: Advances in Neural Information Processing Systems (NIPS), vol. 27. Curran Associates, Inc. (2014)
16. Hadsell, R., Chopra, S., LeCun, Y.: Dimensionality reduction by learning an invariant mapping. In: Proceedings of the IEEE Conference on Computer Vision and Pattern Recognition (CVPR), vol. 2, pp. 1735–1742. IEEE (2006)

17. Han, J., Shoeiby, M., Petersson, L., Armin, M.A.: Dual contrastive learning for unsupervised image-to-image translation. In: Proceedings of the IEEE Conference on Computer Vision and Pattern Recognition Workshops (CVPRW) (2021)
18. He, K., Fan, H., Wu, Y., Xie, S., Girshick, R.: Momentum contrast for unsupervised visual representation learning. In: Proceedings of the IEEE Conference on Computer Vision and Pattern Recognition (CVPR), pp. 9729–9738 (2020)
19. Hong, Z., Fan, X., Jiang, T., Feng, J.: End-to-end unpaired image denoising with conditional adversarial networks. In: Association for the Advancement of Artificial Intelligence (AAAI), vol. 34, pp. 4140–4149 (2020)
20. Jang, G., Lee, W., Son, S., Lee, K.M.: C2N: practical generative noise modeling for real-world denoising. In: Proceedings of the IEEE International Conference on Computer Vision (ICCV), pp. 2350–2359 (2021)
21. Jeong, J., Shin, J.: Training GANs with stronger augmentations via contrastive discriminator. In: Proceedings of the International Conference on Learning Representations (ICLR) (2021)
22. Kang, M., Park, J.: ContraGAN: contrastive learning for conditional image generation. In: Advances in Neural Information Processing Systems (NIPS), vol. 33, pp. 21357–21369. Curran Associates, Inc. (2020)
23. Khosla, P., et al.: Supervised contrastive learning. In: Advances in Neural Information Processing Systems (NIPS), vol. 33, pp. 18661–18673. Curran Associates, Inc. (2020)
24. Kim, D.W., Ryun Chung, J., Jung, S.W.: GRDN: grouped residual dense network for real image denoising and GAN-based real-world noise modeling. In: Proceedings of the IEEE Conference on Computer Vision and Pattern Recognition Workshops (CVPRW) (2019)
25. Kingma, D.P., Ba, J.: Adam: a method for stochastic optimization. In: Proceedings of the International Conference on Learning Representations (ICLR) (2015)
26. Lee, K.S., Tran, N.T., Cheung, N.M.: Infomax-GAN: improved adversarial image generation via information maximization and contrastive learning. In: IEEE/CVF Winter Conference on Applications of Computer Vision (WACV), pp. 3942–3952 (2021)
27. Li, B., Liu, X., Hu, P., Wu, Z., Lv, J., Peng, X.: All-in-one image restoration for unknown corruption. In: Proceedings of the IEEE/CVF Conference on Computer Vision and Pattern Recognition (CVPR), pp. 17452–17462 (2022)
28. Lin, H., Zhuang, Y., Huang, Y., Ding, X., Liu, X., Yu, Y.: Noise2Grad: extract image noise to denoise. In: Zhou, Z.H. (ed.) IJCAI, pp. 830–836. IJCAI (2021). https://doi.org/10.24963/ijcai.2021/115
29. Oord, A.V.D., Li, Y., Vinyals, O.: Representation learning with contrastive predictive coding. arXiv preprint arXiv:1807.03748 (2018)
30. Park, T., Efros, A.A., Zhang, R., Zhu, J.-Y.: Contrastive learning for unpaired image-to-image translation. In: Vedaldi, A., Bischof, H., Brox, T., Frahm, J.-M. (eds.) ECCV 2020. LNCS, vol. 12354, pp. 319–345. Springer, Cham (2020). https://doi.org/10.1007/978-3-030-58545-7_19
31. Plotz, T., Roth, S.: Benchmarking denoising algorithms with real photographs. In: Proceedings of the IEEE Conference on Computer Vision and Pattern Recognition (CVPR), pp. 1586–1595 (2017)
32. Salimans, T., et al.: Improved techniques for training GANs. In: Advances in Neural Information Processing Systems (NIPS), vol. 29. Curran Associates, Inc. (2016)
33. Wang, L., et al.: Unsupervised degradation representation learning for blind super-resolution. In: Proceedings of the IEEE Conference on Computer Vision and Pattern Recognition (CVPR) (2021)

34. Xu, J., Li, H., Liang, Z., Zhang, D., Zhang, L.: Real-world noisy image denoising: a new benchmark. arXiv preprint arXiv:1804.02603 (2018)
35. Ye, M., Zhang, X., Yuen, P.C., Chang, S.F.: Unsupervised embedding learning via invariant and spreading instance feature. In: Proceedings of the IEEE Conference on Computer Vision and Pattern Recognition (CVPR) (2019)
36. Yue, Z., Zhao, Q., Zhang, L., Meng, D.: Dual adversarial network: toward real-world noise removal and noise generation. In: Vedaldi, A., Bischof, H., Brox, T., Frahm, J.-M. (eds.) ECCV 2020. LNCS, vol. 12355, pp. 41–58. Springer, Cham (2020). https://doi.org/10.1007/978-3-030-58607-2_3
37. Zamir, S.W., et al.: CycleiSP: real image restoration via improved data synthesis. In: Proceedings of the IEEE Conference on Computer Vision and Pattern Recognition (CVPR) (2020)

MVFI-Net: Motion-Aware Video Frame Interpolation Network

Xuhu Lin[1], Lili Zhao[1,2], Xi Liu[1], and Jianwen Chen[1(✉)]

[1] University of Electronic Science and Technology of China, Chengdu 611731, China
chenjianwen@uestc.edu.cn
[2] China Mobile Research Institute, Beijing 100032, China
zhaoliliyjy@chinamobile.com

Abstract. Video frame interpolation (VFI) is to synthesize the intermediate frame given successive frames. Most existing learning-based VFI methods generate each target pixel by using the warping operation with either one predicted kernel or flow, or both. However, their performances are often degraded due to the issues on the limited direction and scope of the reference regions, especially encountering complex motions. In this paper, we propose a novel motion-aware VFI network (MVFI-Net) to address these issues. One of the key novelties of our method lies in the newly developed warping operation, *i.e.*, *motion-aware convolution* (MAC). By predicting multiple extensible temporal motion vectors (MVs) and filter kernels for each target pixel, the direction and scope could be enlarged simultaneously. Besides, we first attempt to incorporate the pyramid structure into the kernel-based VFI, which can decompose large motions into smaller scales to improve the prediction efficiency. The quantitative and qualitative experimental results have demonstrated the proposed method delivers the state-of-the-art performance on the diverse benchmarks with various resolutions. Our codes are available at https://github.com/MediaLabVFI/MVFI-Net.

Keywords: Video frame interpolation · Video processing

1 Introduction

Video frame interpolation (VFI) has been greatly demanded in many applications such as frame-rate up conversion [4,5], slow-motion generation [19,35,39] and video compression [10,16], etc. In recent years, deep learning shows its strong capacity in a series of low-level tasks, some learning-based VFI methods have been subsequently developed [2,7,21,29,31,33,34,37,40,41], which can be viewed as a two-stage process: 1) motion estimation (ME), *i.e.*, for the output pixels, finding their reference regions in reference frames; 2) motion compensation (MC), *i.e.*, synthesizing the output pixels based on ME (Fig. 1).

Among the existing methods, one popular strategy is to conduct the optical flow estimation as ME (*e.g.*, [2,29,33,34,41]). However, the optical flow estimator

L. Wang et al. (Eds.): ACCV 2022, LNCS 13843, pp. 340–356, 2023.
https://doi.org/10.1007/978-3-031-26313-2_21

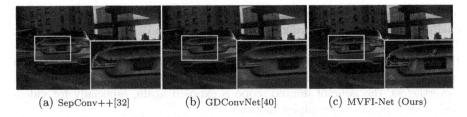

(a) SepConv++[32]   (b) GDConvNet[40]   (c) MVFI-Net (Ours)

Fig. 1. Results of frame interpolation on UHD videos with large motion. The interpolated frame by using our proposed MVFI-Net is sharper with more texture details than those generated by the state-of-the-art kernel-based methods, *e.g.*, SepConv++ [32] and GDConvNet [40].

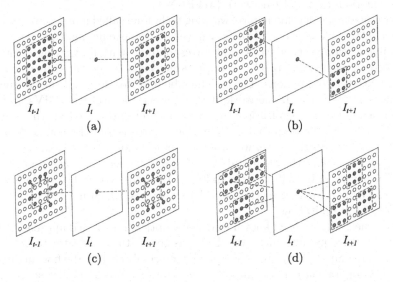

Fig. 2. Comparisons between the mainstream methods and our work. (a) The kernel-based method (*e.g.*, SepConv [31]); (b) The method based on the kernel and flow (*e.g.*, SDC-Net [37]); (c) DSepConv [7]; (d) The proposed MAC.

will impose much computational complexity into the VFI algorithms, and the quality of the interpolated frame largely depends on the quality of flows [46]. Besides, the flow-based methods more consider the most related pixel in reference frame, while ignoring the influence of surrounding pixels, which could result in the limited direction issues.

Instead of using optical flows, some kernel-based VFI methods are developed (*e.g.*, [7,21,31,37,40]), which can be viewed as a convolution process. SepConv [31] estimated a separable kernel for each location, and then convolved these kernels with the corresponding reference regions to predict the output pixels. However, it can not deal with the motions beyond the kernel size since its scope is fixed and limited, as demonstrated in Fig. 2(a). In this case, SDC-Net [37] proposed a spatially-displaced convolution which predicted one flow and one kernel for each location, as shown in Fig. 2(b). Then, the scope could be enlarged based on flow information, but the direction is still limited. Recently, DSepConv [7] utilized a separably deformable convolution to expand the direction of the reference regions [seeing Fig. 2(c)]. The work [21] provided the version without weight sharing as an independent warping operation namely AdaCoF. Nevertheless, the issue of limited scope is exposed again, especially for videos with a large number of complex motions.

Based on the above-mentioned discussions, there are two issues existing in VFI: 1) the direction and scope of reference regions are limited and hard to be loosed simultaneously; 2) kernel-based methods are non-robust for complex motions. To tackle the aforementioned issues, we propose a novel VFI method namely motion-aware VFI network (MVFI-Net).

For issue 1), we develop a novel warping technique called motion-aware convolution (MAC), which is one of the key novelties. In specific, multiple temporally extensible motion vectors (MVs) and corresponding spatially-varying kernels are predicted for each target pixel. Then the target pixel is calculated by convolving kernels with selected regions. The rationale behind this design is that during the motion estimation via the network, it may be possible to search MVs in a very small range and later synthesize the current pixel only based on the adjacent pixels. Obviously, the performance would be largely degraded while dealing with complex motion. In this case, we propose a motion-aware extension mechanism to adaptively extend the temporal MVs for a wider search range, and improve the efficiency of VFI. As illustrated in Fig. 2(d), compared to the previous works, MAC can explore more directions and larger scopes, which has the potential to overcome both limitations.

For issue 2), it has been known that many optical flow-based approaches have used the feature pyramid network (FPN) as the feature extractor to get multi-scale feature maps, which can be warped by internally scaling the flow in different sizes. This operation can decompose large motions into a smaller scale, which facilitates more accurate motion estimation. Thus, it is highly desirable to bring FPN into kernel-based VFI methods. However, for warping multi-scale feature maps, kernels with various sizes are required. This means that large memory is demanded, which is impractical. To solve this problem, we propose a two-stage warping strategy to warp reference frames and multi-scale features, while exploiting a frame synthesis network to mix these information for generating high-quality frame. Experimental results show that our design can improve the robustness and performance of VFI with complex motion.

Our contributions can be summarized as follows: 1) A novel warping technique MAC is proposed to simultaneously alleviate the issues of limited direction and scope of reference regions; 2) We propose a two-stage warping strategy to firstly integrate the pyramid structure into the kernel-based VFI method; 3) The proposed method delivers the state-of-the-art results on several benchmarks with various resolutions.

2 Related Work

In this section, we briefly review the works about VFI. The VFI methods can be mainly divided into three categories: 1) the phase-based methods (*e.g.*, [26,27]), 2) the optical flow-based methods (*e.g.*, [2,3,9,22,23,28,29,33,34,41]), and 3) the kernel-based methods (*e.g.*, [7,8,21,31,32,40]).

Phase-Based VFI. It is commonly-known that images can be transformed to the frequency field by Fourier Transform, and this operation has been used into VFI by [26,27]. Specifically, they utilized a Phase-Net to conduct the motion estimation by the linear combinations of wavelets, which achieved competitive inference time. However, it is difficult for this category of methods to process the large motion on the high frequency components, usually imposing artifacts and pixel disappearance.

Optical Flow-Based VFI. In recent years, the deep learning-based optical flow estimation [13,17,36,44,45] has delivered impressive quality on motion estimation. Therefore, the optical flow estimation has been used in many subsequently developed VFI approaches (*e.g.*, [2,3,15,19,29,33,34]). For example, in [29], the interpolated frame I_t is synthesized by forward warping the input consecutive frames (I_0 and I_1) with their features, under the guidance of the estimated optical flows $t \cdot F_{0 \to 1}$ and $(1 - t) \cdot F_{1 \to 0}$ via softmax splatting and a frame synthesis network. Instead of using the forward-warping method, another trend in this research have exploited the backward-warping strategy (*e.g.*, [2,3,19,33]). It is well-known that for these backward warping-based methods, the flows from the target frame to the bi-directional reference frames, denoted as $F_{t \to 0}$ and $F_{t \to 1}$, are unavailable. To address this issue, the algorithms presented in [3,19] approximated $F_{t \to 0}$ and $F_{t \to 1}$ by linearly combining bi-directional optical flows based on the target time step t. However, such motion estimation is under a basic assumption that the motion is linear and symmetric. Therefore, it can not model complex motions in real-world videos, and any initial errors imposed by flow estimation would be inevitably propagated to the subsequent processing procedures. More recently, the work proposed in [15] directly predicted the intermediate flow via a teacher-student net architecture without any prior bi-directional flow estimation. For the asymmetric motions in real-world videos, a bi-directional correlation volume algorithm [34] is proposed to modify intermediate flows, respectively, which achieves the state-of-the-art performance.

Kernel-Based VFI. Consider that incredibly extra cost would be introduced for predicting prior optical flow, some works (*e.g.*, [7,8,21,30–32]) attempt to directly synthesize the pixel by spatially-varying convolution. For example, the work in [30] synthesized a target pixel by predicting kernels with the size of 41×41 for two reference frames, and then convolved them with the reference pixels. However, a huge amount of memory is required to store the kernels with such large size. In this case, [31,32] decomposed the convolutional kernels into two one-dimensional vectors, and then used outer product to obtain the final kernel. These two methods save much memory but can not handle videos with large motions beyond the limited kernel size. To address this issue, an added kernel is estimated for each flow to collect local appearance information [37]. Moreover, inspired by deformable convolution, [8,40] predicted weight-sharing offsets for each element of kernels, and thus irregular motions could be described. In [21], the degree of freedom of square kernel is further improved, while it is still limited by reference scopes. Obviously, compared to optical flow-based VFI approaches, the existing kernel-based methods have drawbacks in motion estimation due to lack of prior motion guidance. Moreover, it is hard to introduce the pyramid structure into kernel-based VFI methods. This is because unlike the optical flow, if kernels are down-sampled, their weights would change completely, and there is no one-to-one correspondence between pixels. Fortunately, our work can fill up this gap.

3   Method

In this section, we first present the problem statement, and then we give an overview of our MVFI-Net. Later, more details of each module will be provided, respectively.

3.1   Problem Statement

VFI is to synthesize the temporally-consistent middle frame I_1 between two consecutive frames I_0 and I_2. An essential step is to find a transformation function $\mathcal{T}(\cdot)$ to warp reference frames based on the motion estimation (ME) results $\{\theta_0, \theta_2\}$. Therefore, the procedure of VFI can be formulated as

$$I_1 = \mathcal{T}_{\theta_0}(I_0) + \mathcal{T}_{\theta_2}(I_2). \tag{1}$$

However, it is commonly-known that some undesirable artifacts could be yielded during the aforementioned linear combination, when the target pixel is only visible in one of reference frames. This phenomenon is called as the occlusion issue. In this case, we define a soft mask [8,21] $M \in [0,1]^{H \times W}$ to tackle this problem, where $[H, W]$ is the target frame size. Then, Eq. (1) can be modified as

$$I_1 = M \odot \mathcal{T}_{\theta_0}(I_0) + (J - M) \odot \mathcal{T}_{\theta_2}(I_2), \tag{2}$$

where $\odot$ is element-wise multiplication, and $J \in R^{H \times W}$ is a matrix where each element is equal to one.

3.2   Overall Architecture

The pipeline of the proposed MVFI-Net is shown in Fig. 3, which is mainly composed of four modules: a motion estimation network MENet ($\mathcal{U}$), a novel warping technique motion-aware convolution MAC ($\mathcal{M}$), a context-pyramid feature extractor ($\mathcal{C}$) and a frame synthesis network ($\mathcal{G}$). In specific, $\mathcal{U}$ first takes two reference frames I_0 and I_2 as inputs to predict temporal MVs $\{F_{10}, F_{12}\}$, kernel weights $\{K_{10}, K_{12}\}$ and the aforementioned mask M. Concurrently, the weight-sharing $\mathcal{C}$ extracts multi-scale feature maps of $\{I_0, I_2\}$, $i.e.$, $\{c_0^0, c_0^1, c_0^2\}$ for I_0

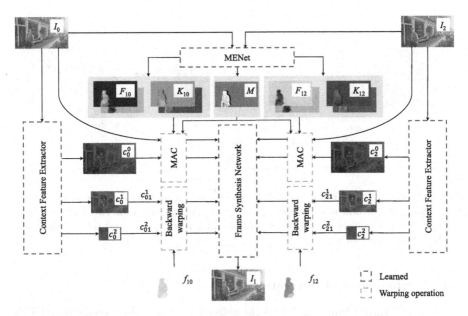

Fig. 3. The overview of our proposed MVFI-Net. The network takes two consecutive frames I_0 and I_2 as inputs, and finally generates the middle frame I_1. Note that green dotted line box represents the parameters of this part will be updated by gradient descent methods, while the gray one means non-parametric warping operation. (Color figure online)

and $\{c_2^0, c_2^1, c_2^2\}$ for I_2. Then, the proposed two-stage warping strategy is used to align these feature maps and reference frames with time step 1. Particularly, $\mathcal{M}$ is adopted to warp $\{I_0, I_2\}$ and feature maps at the first pyramid layer $\{c_0^0, c_2^0\}$. Next, instead of predicting multi-scale kernels, the flow information $\{f_{10}, f_{12}\}$, called as *sumflow*, is calculated by weighted summation of $\{F_{10}, F_{12}\}$ along the channel axis, respectively. Later, lower-resolution feature maps $\{c_0^1, c_0^2, c_2^1, c_2^2\}$ are backward warped to the middle ones $\{c_{01}^1, c_{21}^1, c_{01}^2, c_{21}^2\}$ with the guidance of $\{f_{10}, f_{12}\}$ which are internally scaled to the corresponding size. Finally, the interpolated frame I_1 will be synthesized by $\mathcal{G}$. More details will be analyzed next.

3.3 Motion Estimation Network

As illustrated in Fig. 4, MENet $(\mathcal{U})$ is designed based on the U-Net [38] architecture, followed by nine parallel sub-nets, which are used to predict five elements: the bi-directional temporal MVs ($F_{10} = [u_{10}, v_{10}]$, $F_{12} = [u_{12}, v_{12}]$), filter kernels ($K_{10} = [k_{10}^u, k_{10}^v]$, $K_{12} = [k_{12}^u, k_{12}^v]$) and the soft mask M, where u and v represent the horizontal and vertical direction, respectively. Each prediction process $\mathcal{X}$ can be formulated by

$$\mathcal{X} = \mathcal{U}(Cat[I_0, I_2]),\qquad(3)$$

where $Cat[\cdot]$ is the concatenation operation along the channel axis.

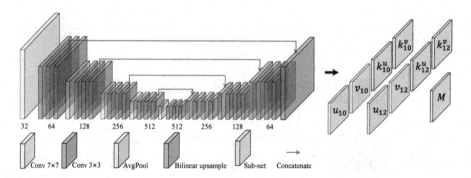

Fig. 4. Our designed MENet. Notably, each sub-net (gray box) consists of three 3×3 convolution layers and one bilinear up-sampling layer. Note that the weights across sub-nets are not sharing. Therefore, temporal MVs, filter kernels and the soft mask are predicted independently.

3.4 Motion-Aware Convolution

Let $\bar{\bar{I}}$ be the target frame and I be the reference frame. Most kernel-based VFI methods (*e.g.*, [31,32]) assume that $\mathcal{T}(\cdot)$ is conducted by using the spatially-varying convolution, which is described as

$$\bar{\bar{I}}(x,y) = \sum K(x,y) \odot P_I(x,y), \tag{4}$$

where $P_I(x,y)$ is the patch centered at (x,y) in I, and the sum ($\sum$) represents the summation of all elements in Hadamard product.

Besides, $K(x,y)$ is a 2D filter kernel obtained by the outer product of two 1D vectors, which is computed as

$$K(x,y) = k^v(k^u)^T \tag{5}$$

However, for these methods, the direction and scope of reference regions are limited, and thus they fail to handle large motion beyond the kernel size. In this case, we attempt to predict multiple extensible temporal MVs for each location, and the corresponding Eq. (4) can be modified as

$$\bar{\bar{I}}(x,y) = \sum_{l=0}^{L-1} \sum K^l(x,y) \odot P_I(x + u^l(x,y) + d_u(l), y + v^l(x,y) + d_v(l)), \tag{6}$$

where $u^l(x,y)$ and $v^l(x,y)$ are horizontal and vertical components of the lth temporal MV, respectively, and L denotes the amount of temporal MVs. $d_u(l)$ and $d_v(l)$ are offset biases, which are adaptively calculated by our proposed motion-aware extension mechanism (MAEM) [see Fig. 5(b) top]. $d_u(l)$ can be formulated as

$$d_u(l) = l \cdot sign(u^l(x,y)), \|u^l(x,y)\| \geq \gamma, \tag{7}$$

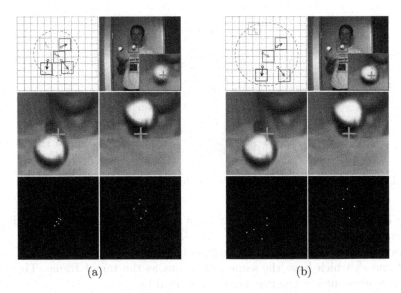

(a)   (b)

Fig. 5. Visualization of the effect of using the traditional dilation mechanism (TDM) and our MAEM on the search range. The first row displays the toy examples and qualitative results given by two methods, and the second row depicts the co-location patches of two reference frames, where the pink cross denotes the co-location position of the target pixel. The third row describes the endpoint of each temporal MV from start point. (a) The result by using TDM. (b) The result by replacing TDM with our MAEM. It can be seen that our MAEM can extend the search range effectively. (Color figure online)

where $sign(\cdot)$ is the signal function, while γ is the preset threshold and we empirically set $\gamma = 1$. Note that $d_v(l)$ can be calculated in the same way. The motivation behind it is that we find the traditional dilation mechanism [see Fig. 5(a) top] fails to handle irregular motions due to its fixed dilation coefficient. To address this issue, we propose motion-aware extension mechanism (MAEM), which is able to adaptively extend temporal MV by modifying its start position on the basis of initial prediction. As shown in Fig. 5, our method can capture more accurate MVs and deliver the higher quality frame.

3.5 Multi-scale Feature Aggregation

Context-Pyramid Feature Extractor. Consider that the features of frames in VFI tasks are different from those in classification tasks. Motivated by [29], we optimize a feature extractor ($\mathcal{C}$) from scratch, rather than using the existing pre-trained model (*e.g.*, VGG [42] and Resnet [14]). As depicted in Fig. 6, the features can be obtained by

$$c_t^s = \mathcal{C}(I_t)^s, \tag{8}$$

where s is the scale of pyramid, and t is the time step of reference frames.

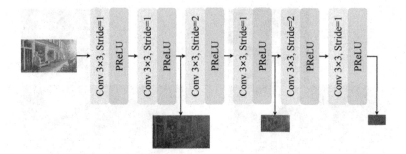

Fig. 6. The architecture of the weight-sharing context feature extractor.

As discussed previously, extremely large memory is required while predicting different kernels (*e.g.*, $H \times W$, $\frac{H}{2} \times \frac{W}{2}$, $\frac{H}{4} \times \frac{W}{4}$) for each scale feature map, which is impractical for applications. To address this issue, we only apply MAC ($\mathcal{M}$) for c_0^0 and c_2^0 which have the same resolutions as the target frame. Then, the warped feature map of the first layer is obtained by

$$c_1^0 = M \odot \mathcal{M}_{F_{10};K_{10}}(c_0^0) + (J - M) \odot \mathcal{M}_{F_{12};K_{12}}(c_2^0). \tag{9}$$

For c_t^1 and c_t^2, we first calculate the *sumflow* (f_{10} and f_{12}) through the predicted temporal MVs as

$$f_{10} = Cat[\sum_l^{L-1} u_{10}^l(x,y) + d_{u_{10}}(l), \sum_l^{L-1} v_{10}^l(x,y) + d_{v_{10}}(l)]. \tag{10}$$

f_{12} can be computed by the same way.

Then the backward warping operation [18] is used for the temporal alignment, which is described as

$$\begin{aligned} c_{01}^s &= backwarp((f_{10})^{\downarrow s}, c_0^s), \\ c_{21}^s &= backwarp((f_{12})^{\downarrow s}, c_2^s), \end{aligned} \tag{11}$$

where $\downarrow s$ denotes that sumflow has been downsampled to the same size with s^{th} feature map.

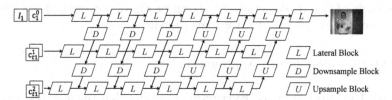

Fig. 7. The structure of the frame synthesis network.

Frame Synthesis Network. The modified version of Grid-Net [28] is used as our frame synthesis network. As depicted in Fig. 7, the inputs of the network are warped frame I_1 and feature maps $\{c_1^0, c_{01}^1, c_{21}^1, c_{01}^2, c_{21}^2\}$, and the output is the final interpolated frame.

4   Experiments

4.1   Datasets and Implementation Details

We select four benchmarks with various video resolutions for comparison, which are Vimeo90K [47] (448×256), UCF101 [24,43] (256×256), Middlebury [1] (640×480) and SNU-FILM [11] (1280×720). We next describe our training details for MVFI-Net.

Loss Functions. To evaluate the difference between the interpolated frame I_1 and its ground truth I_{gt}, we combine Charbonnier penalty function [6] with the gradient loss [25], which can facilitate generating a sharper frame.

$$\mathcal{L}_d = \lambda_1 \mathcal{L}_{char} + \lambda_2 \mathcal{L}_{gdl}, \tag{12}$$

where we empirically set $\lambda_1 = 1$, $\lambda_2 = 1$.

Training Strategy. We train the MVFI-Net for 150 epochs on the Vimeo90K training triplets, and use AdaMax [20] optimization with $\beta_1 = 0.9$, $\beta_2 = 0.999$, where the initial learning rate is set as 0.001. Note that the learning rate will be decreased by a factor of 0.5 when the validation loss does not decrease for five epochs.

Table 1. Quantitative comparisons on three benchmarks. We also calculate the inference time and MACs on Middlebury [1] 'Urban' set. All methods are tested on one NVIDIA 2080Ti GPU. For a fair comparison, each method is only trained on Vimeo90K triplets [47] by taking only two frames as reference.

	Vimeo90K [47]		UCF101 [24,43]		Middlebury [1]			Runtime	MACs
	R	SSIM	PSNR	SSIM	PSNR	SSIM	IE	(seconds)	(T)
SepConv-$\mathcal{L}_1$ [31]	33.86	0.974	34.96	0.966	35.79	0.978	2.25	0.051	0.19
DAIN [2]	34.70	0.979	35.00	0.968	36.70	0.982	2.07	0.130	5.79
CAIN [11]	34.76	0.976	34.98	0.968	35.11	0.974	2.73	0.041	0.42
AdaCoF [21]	34.35	0.974	34.90	0.968	35.72	0.978	2.26	**0.034**	0.37
BMBC [33]	35.06	0.979	35.16	0.968	36.79	0.982	2.06	0.774	2.50
SepConv++ [32]	34.83	0.977	35.27	0.968	37.28	0.984	1.96	0.110	0.14
CDFI [12]	35.17	0.978	35.21	0.967	37.14	0.983	2.01	0.221	0.26
EDSC-$\mathcal{L}_C$ [8]	34.86	0.977	35.17	0.968	36.76	0.982	2.03	0.046	**0.08**
X-VFI [41]	35.07	0.977	35.08	0.968	36.71	0.982	2.05	0.097	0.14
GDConvNet [40]	34.99	0.975	35.16	0.968	35.42	0.978	2.33	1.277	0.87
MVFI-Net$_S$ (ours)	35.71	0.980	35.30	0.968	**37.51**	0.984	**1.93**	0.087	0.35
MVFI-Net$_L$ (ours)	**35.83**	**0.981**	**35.33**	**0.969**	37.48	**0.984**	1.94	0.189	0.49

4.2   Comparison with the State-of-the-Arts

To prove the effectiveness of our proposed algorithm, we compare our method with other competitive works, including SepConv [31], DSepConv [7], DAIN [2], CAIN [11], AdaCoF [21], BMBC [33], SepConv++ [32], CDFI [12], EDSC [8], X-VFI [41] and GDConvNet [40]. For evaluation metrics, we measure the performance of VFI methods in terms of Peak Signal-to-Noise Ratio (PSNR) and Structural Similarity (SSIM). Additionally, we also calculate the widely-used Interpolation Error (IE) on Middlebury-Other set for evaluation. Note that the code of all compared methods are publicly available.

Table 2. Quantitative results of the current competitive kernel-based methods on four settings of SNU-FILM [11].

	Easy		Medium		Hard		Extreme	
	PSNR	SSIM	PSNR	SSIM	PSNR	SSIM	PSNR	SSIM
SepConv-$\mathcal{L}_1$ [31]	39.68	0.990	35.06	0.977	29.39	0.928	24.32	0.856
DSepConv [7]	39.94	0.990	35.30	0.977	29.50	0.925	24.33	0.850
AdaCoF [21]	39.80	0.990	35.05	0.976	29.46	0.925	24.31	0.852
EDSC-$\mathcal{L}_C$ [8]	40.01	0.990	35.36	0.978	29.59	0.927	24.38	0.851
CDFI [12]	40.12	0.991	35.51	0.978	29.73	0.928	24.53	0.848
MVFI-Net$_L$ (ours)	**40.17**	**0.991**	**35.57**	**0.979**	**29.86**	**0.932**	**24.62**	**0.862**

Quantitative Results. We provide two versions of MVFI-Net for comparison, which have different model sizes. Formally, MVFI-Net$_S$ represents five temporal MVs and corresponding 11×11 kernels are predicted, while MVFI-Net$_L$ possesses eleven temporal MVs and the same kernel size. As shown in Table 1, our method is far superior to others on diverse benchmarks in terms of PSNR and SSIM. Compared to the state-of-the-art kernel-based method SepConv++ [32], our lightweight model MVFI-Net$_S$ improves the PSNR by **0.88** dB on Vimeo90K with **1.5×** faster inference speed. Although the fastest VFI approach Ada-CoF [21] is **2.3×** faster than us, MVFI-Net$_S$ gives **1.36** dB improvement on Vimeo90K. Note that the gains are distinct on the other two benchmarks while the MACs are similar. Compared to optical flow-based approaches, we comprehensively provide improvements either objective qualities or inference speed. This result supports that kernel-based approaches could yield impressive results without prior flow estimation.

To further prove that MVFI-Net is more robust for complex motions, we compare it with current competitive kernel-based algorithms on SNU-FILM [11] which is divided into four settings according to motions. From Table 2, it can be obviously found that our proposed MVFI-Net$_L$ delivers better performance on all settings. Generally, it is difficult to retain the structure and shape of objects in the interpolated frame when large motion exists, which imposes artifacts and blurriness with lower SSIM. Nevertheless, MVFI-Net$_L$ partly fixes this defect and supply an impressive result.

Qualitative Results. To verify the subjective quality, we also visually compare MVFI-Net with high-performance VFI approaches. As illustrated in Fig. 8, it can be seen that there are no overshoot artifacts in the frames generated by our method, while others fail. For example, in the third row and fourth row, our method clearly keep the texture details of the airplane head and the wing of the bird, while other methods impose serious artifacts and blur background.

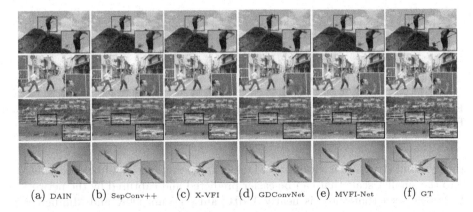

(a) DAIN   (b) SepConv++   (c) X-VFI   (d) GDConvNet   (e) MVFI-Net   (f) GT

Fig. 8. Qualitative comparisons with DAIN [2], SepConv++ [32], XVFI [41] and GDConvNet [40] on the test set of Vimeo90K [47] and SNU-FILM [11] extreme setting, including the large motion and the occlusion issue.

4.3 Ablation Study

In this section, we first conduct ablation studies to demonstrate the effect of our proposed motion-aware extension mechanism (MAEM) and the improvements of introducing the pyramid structure. Then, we design a series of experiments to explore the effectiveness of different amounts of temporal MVs and different kernel sizes. Finally, we attempt to transfer our method to AdaCoF [21], in which multiple flows are predicted for each target pixel, to analyze whether the performance can be improved by our algorithm.

Table 3. Ablation studies of the motion-aware extension mechanism and pyramid architecture.

	MAEM	Pyramid structure	Middlebury [1]			Vimeo90K [47]		Extreme [11]	
			PSNR	SSIM	IE	PSNR	SSIM	PSNR	SSIM
1	✗	✗	36.57	0.981	2.06	34.81	0.976	24.31	0.851
2	✓	✗	36.84	0.983	2.02	34.83	0.976	24.39	0.852
3	✓	✓	**37.51**	**0.984**	**1.93**	**35.71**	**0.980**	**24.46**	**0.860**

MAEM and Pyramid Structure. For a fair comparison, each group is retrained under the same condition without any prior information. We first remove the pyramid structure, and then the final interpolated frame is synthesized by Eq. (2) where $\mathcal{T}(\cdot)$ is MAC. Next, we continue to remove MAEM, temporal MVs are no longer extended according to the initial prediction. From Table 3, it can be observed that our proposed MAEM, which is non-parametric and non-extra inference time cost, provides stable improvements on each benchmark in terms of two evaluation metrics. Besides, it can be demonstrated that

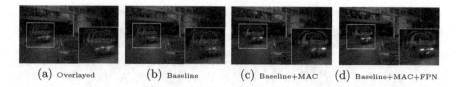

(a) Overlayed   (b) Baseline   (c) Baseline+MAC   (d) Baseline+MAC+FPN

Fig. 9. Qualitative comparisons with Baseline, Baseline+MAC and Baseline+MAC+ FPN. It can be seen that the frame quality is gradually enhanced by our design.

the pyramid structure is vital for VFI, since large motions could be decomposed into the smaller scale that can be easier predicted and captured by the network. It can be seen that there is nearly 1 dB gain on Vimeo90K and Middlebury, while supplying higher structure similarity. We also illustrate a visual result for intuitive comparison in Fig. 9.

Table 4. Ablation studies of the amounts of temporal motion vectors.

	Middlebury [1]			Vimeo90K [47]		Extreme [11]	
	PSNR	SSIM	IE	PSNR	SSIM	PSNR	SSIM
$L = 1$	36.78	0.983	2.01	35.34	0.979	24.37	0.857
$L = 5$	**37.51**	0.984	**1.93**	35.71	0.980	24.46	0.860
$L = 11$	37.48	**0.984**	1.94	**35.83**	**0.981**	**24.62**	**0.862**

Amount of Temporal MVs. As discussed above, more reference pixels are required for complex motions. Therefore, the amount of predicted temporal MVs would directly influence the performance. To verify it, we first set a fixed kernel size $N = 11$, and let the number of temporal MVs be $L \in \{1, 5, 11\}$. As displayed in Table 4, increasing temporal MVs helps the network explore more related regions, and thus the middle frame with a higher quality is synthesized. It should be noted that for Middlebury [1], the model with five temporal MVs is a little better than that with eleven temporal MVs. This can be explained by the fact that the videos in Middlebury usually have small motion. This means that the motion difference between consecutive frames is relatively small. Therefore, redundant temporal MVs may incur dispensable appearance information, leading to undesirable artifacts.

Kernel Size. It has been demonstrated that the quality of the interpolated frame is closely relevant to the size of the adaptive kernel [31]. To explore the effectiveness of the kernel size, we train several models by using the kernels with different sizes. Similar to the above experiments, we fix the number of temporal MVs $L = 5$ and modify the kernel size $N \in \{1, 5, 11\}$. Note that $N = 11$ means the 11×11 kernel is predicted for each target pixel. From Table 5, it can be observed that a larger kernel can facilitate generating a better interpolated result. However, when the kernel becomes larger (i.e., $N = 11$), there is no

Table 5. Ablation studies of kernel size

	Middlebury [1]			Vimeo90K [47]		Extreme [11]	
	PSNR	SSIM	IE	PSNR	SSIM	PSNR	SSIM
$N = 1$	36.82	0.983	2.07	35.45	0.979	24.53	0.860
$N = 5$	37.08	0.984	1.98	35.68	0.980	**24.59**	**0.861**
$N = 11$	**37.51**	**0.984**	**1.93**	**35.71**	**0.980**	24.46	0.860

significant improvements. It is because our proposed MAEM has facilitated capturing motions accurately, while larger kernels have little effect and may impose repetitive local information.

Table 6. Ablation study on transferring our method to AdaCoF [21]

	Middlebury [1]			Vimeo90K [47]		Extreme [11]	
	PSNR	SSIM	IE	PSNR	SSIM	PSNR	SSIM
AdaCoF [21]	35.72	0.978	2.26	34.35	0.974	24.31	0.852
AdaCoF-*ours*	**36.23**	**0.981**	**2.22**	**35.19**	**0.979**	**24.55**	**0.860**

Transferability. In AdaCoF [21], multiple flows are predicted for each target pixel, which is similar to our algorithm. Moreover, they introduce a fixed dilation coefficient to expand the initial point of flow for a wider searching range. As demonstrated above, our MAEM could facilitate more accurate motion estimation and the pyramid structure is vital for VFI. Therefore, we attempt to transfer MAEM and the two-stage warping strategy into AdaCoF to analyze their effectiveness. Table 6 illustrates that our proposed method significantly provides stable gains for AdaCoF on the basis of each benchmark.

5   Conclusion

In this paper, we propose a novel VFI network namely MVFI-Net. There are two novelties: (1) we design an efficient warping technique MAC, where multiple extensible temporal MVs and corresponding filter kernels are predicted for each target pixel, which enlarges the direction and scope of reference region simultaneously; (2) we firstly integrate the pyramid structure into the kernel-based VFI approach, which can decompose complex motions to a smaller scale, improving the efficiency of searching for temporal MVs. Extensive simulations conducted on various datasets have demonstrated that our proposed MVFI-Net is able to consistently deliver the state-of-the-art results in terms of the objective quality and human perception.

References

1. Baker, S., Scharstein, D., Lewis, J., Roth, S., Black, M.J., Szeliski, R.: A database and evaluation methodology for optical flow. Proc. Int. J. Comput. Vis. 1–8 (2007)
2. Bao, W., Lai, W.S., Ma, C., Zhang, X., Gao, Z., Yang, M.H.: Depth-aware video frame interpolation. In: Proceedings of the IEEE/CVF Conference on Computer Vision and Pattern Recognition, pp. 3698–3707 (2019)
3. Bao, W., Lai, W.S., Zhang, X., Gao, Z., Yang, M.H.: Memc-net: motion estimation and motion compensation driven neural network for video interpolation and enhancement. IEEE Trans. Pattern Anal. Mach. Intell. **43**, 933–948 (2019)
4. Bao, W., Zhang, X., Chen, L., Ding, L., Gao, Z.: High-order model and dynamic filtering for frame rate up-conversion. IEEE Trans. Image Process. **27**, 3813–3826 (2018)
5. Castagno, R., Haavisto, P., Ramponi, G.: A method for motion adaptive frame rate up-conversion. IEEE Trans. Circuits Syst. Video Technol. **6**, 436–446 (1996)
6. Charbonnier, P., Blanc-Feraud, L., Aubert, G., Barlaud, M.: Two deterministic half-quadratic regularization algorithms for computed imaging. In: Proceedings of 1st International Conference on Image Processing, pp. 168–172 (1994)
7. Cheng, X., Chen, Z.: Video frame interpolation via deformable separable convolution. In: Proceedings of the AAAI Conference on Artificial Intelligence, pp. 10607–10614 (2020)
8. Cheng, X., Chen, Z.: Multiple video frame interpolation via enhanced deformable separable convolution. IEEE Trans. Pattern Anal. Mach. Intell. **44**, 7029–7045 (2021)
9. Chi, Z., Mohammadi Nasiri, R., Liu, Z., Lu, J., Tang, J., Plataniotis, K.N.: All at once: temporally adaptive multi-frame interpolation with advanced motion modeling. In: Vedaldi, A., Bischof, H., Brox, T., Frahm, J.-M. (eds.) ECCV 2020. LNCS, vol. 12372, pp. 107–123. Springer, Cham (2020). https://doi.org/10.1007/978-3-030-58583-9_7
10. Choi, H., Bajić, I.V.: Deep frame prediction for video coding. IEEE Trans. Circuits Syst. Video Technol. **30**, 1843–1855 (2020)
11. Choi, M., Kim, H., Han, B., Xu, N., Lee, K.M.: Channel attention is all you need for video frame interpolation. In: Proceedings of the AAAI Conference on Artificial Intelligence, pp. 10663–10671 (2020)
12. Ding, T., Liang, L., Zhu, Z., Zharkov, I.: CDFI: compression-driven network design for frame interpolation. In: Proceedings of the IEEE/CVF Conference on Computer Vision and Pattern Recognition, pp. 7997–8007 (2021)
13. Dosovitskiy, A., et al.: FlowNet: learning optical flow with convolutional networks. In: Proceedings of the IEEE Conference on Computer Vision and Pattern Recognition, pp. 2758–2766 (2015)
14. He, K., Zhang, X., Ren, S., Sun, J.: Deep residual learning for image recognition. In: Proceedings of the IEEE Conference on Computer Vision and Pattern Recognition, pp. 770–778 (2016)
15. Huang, Z., Zhang, T., Heng, W., Shi, B., Zhou, S.: RIFE: real-time intermediate flow estimation for video frame interpolation. arXiv preprint arXiv:2011.06294 (2020)
16. Huo, S., Liu, D., Li, B., Ma, S., Wu, F., Gao, W.: Deep network-based frame extrapolation with reference frame alignment. IEEE Trans. Circuits Syst. Video Technol. **31**, 1178–1192 (2021)

17. Ilg, E., Mayer, N., Saikia, T., Keuper, M., Dosovitskiy, A., Brox, T.: FlowNet 2.0: evolution of optical flow estimation with deep networks. In: Proceedings of the IEEE Conference on Computer Vision and Pattern Recognition, pp. 2462–2470 (2017)

18. Jaderberg, M., Simonyan, K., Zisserman, A.: Spatial transformer networks. In: Proceedings of the Advances in Neural Information Processing Systems, pp. 2017–2025 (2015)

19. Jiang, H., Sun, D., Jampani, V., Yang, M.H., Learned-Miller, E., Kautz, J.: Super slomo: high quality estimation of multiple intermediate frames for video interpolation. In: Proceedings of the IEEE Conference on Computer Vision and Pattern Recognition, pp. 3813–3826 (2018)

20. Kingma, D.P., Ba, J.: Adam: a method for stochastic optimization. arXiv preprint arXiv:1412.6980 (2014)

21. Lee, H., Kim, T., Chung, T.Y., Pak, D., Ban, Y., Lee, S.: AdaCof: adaptive collaboration of flows for video frame interpolation. In: Proceedings of the IEEE/CVF Conference on Computer Vision and Pattern Recognition, pp. 5315–5324 (2020)

22. Li, H., Yuan, Y., Wang, Q.: Video frame interpolation via residue refinement. In: IEEE International Conference on Acoustics, Speech and Signal Processing, pp. 2613–2617 (2020)

23. Liu, Y.L., Liao, Y.T., Lin, Y.Y., Chuang, Y.Y.: Deep video frame interpolation using cyclic frame generation. In: Proceedings of the AAAI Conference on Artificial Intelligence (AAAI), pp. 8794–8802 (2019)

24. Liu, Z., Yeh, R.A., Tang, X., Liu, Y., Agarwala, A.: Video frame synthesis using deep voxel flow. In: Proceedings of the IEEE International Conference on Computer Vision, pp. 4473–4481 (2017)

25. Mathieu, M., Couprie, C., LeCun, Y.: Deep multi-scale video prediction beyond mean square error. arXiv preprint arXiv:1511.05440, pp. 1–14 (2016)

26. Meyer, S., Djelouah, A., McWilliams, B., Sorkine-Hornung, A., Gross, M., Schroers, C.: Phasenet for video frame interpolation. In: Proceedings of the IEEE Conference on Computer Vision and Pattern Recognition, pp. 498–507 (2018)

27. Meyer, S., Wang, O., Zimmer, H., Grosse, M., Sorkine-Hornung, A.: Phase-based frame interpolation for video. In: Proceedings of the IEEE Conference on Computer Vision and Pattern Recognition, pp. 1410–1418 (2015)

28. Niklaus, S., Liu, F.: Context-aware synthesis for video frame interpolation. In: Proceedings of the IEEE/CVF Conference on Computer Vision and Pattern Recognition, pp. 1701–1710 (2018)

29. Niklaus, S., Liu, F.: Softmax splatting for video frame interpolation. In: Proceedings of the IEEE/CVF Conference on Computer Vision and Pattern Recognition, pp. 5436–5445 (2020)

30. Niklaus, S., Mai, L., Liu, F.: Video frame interpolation via adaptive convolution. In: Proceedings of the IEEE Conference on Computer Vision and Pattern Recognition, pp. 670–679 (2017)

31. Niklaus, S., Mai, L., Liu, F.: Video frame interpolation via adaptive separable convolution. In: Proceedings of the IEEE International Conference on Computer Vision, pp. 261–270 (2017)

32. Niklaus, S., Mai, L., Wang, O.: Revisiting adaptive convolutions for video frame interpolation. In: Proceedings of the IEEE/CVF Winter Conference on Applications of Computer Vision, pp. 1098–1108 (2021)

33. Park, J., Ko, K., Lee, C., Kim, C.-S.: BMBC: bilateral motion estimation with bilateral cost volume for video interpolation. In: Vedaldi, A., Bischof, H., Brox, T.,

Frahm, J.-M. (eds.) ECCV 2020. LNCS, vol. 12359, pp. 109–125. Springer, Cham (2020). https://doi.org/10.1007/978-3-030-58568-6_7

34. Park, J., Lee, C., Kim, C.S.: Asymmetric bilateral motion estimation for video frame interpolation. In: Proceedings of the IEEE/CVF International Conference on Computer Vision, pp. 14519–14528 (2021)

35. Peleg, T., Szekely, P., Sabo, D., Sendik, O.: IM-Net for high resolution video frame interpolation. In: Proceedings of the IEEE/CVF Conference on Computer Vision and Pattern Recognition, pp. 2393–2402 (2019)

36. Ranjan, A., Black, M.J.: Optical flow estimation using a spatial pyramid network. In: Proceedings of the IEEE Conference on Computer Vision and Pattern Recognition, pp. 4161–4170 (2017)

37. Reda, F.A., Liu, G., Shih, K.J., Kirby, R., Barker, J., Tarjan, D., Tao, A., Catanzaro, B.: SDC-Net: video prediction using spatially-displaced convolution. In: Proceedings of the European Conference on Computer Vision, pp. 718–733 (2018)

38. Ronneberger, O., Fischer, P., Brox, T.: U-Net: convolutional networks for biomedical image segmentation. In: Navab, N., Hornegger, J., Wells, W.M., Frangi, A.F. (eds.) MICCAI 2015. LNCS, vol. 9351, pp. 234–241. Springer, Cham (2015). https://doi.org/10.1007/978-3-319-24574-4_28

39. Shen, W., Bao, W., Zhai, G., Chen, L., Min, X., Gao, Z.: Blurry video frame interpolation. In: Proceedings of the IEEE/CVF Conference on Computer Vision and Pattern Recognition, pp. 5113–5122 (2020)

40. Shi, Z., Liu, X., Shi, K., Dai, L., Chen, J.: Video frame interpolation via generalized deformable convolution. IEEE Trans. Multimedia **20**, 426–436 (2022)

41. Sim, H., Oh, J., Kim, M.: XVFI: extreme video frame interpolation. In: Proceedings of the IEEE/CVF International Conference on Computer Vision, pp. 14469–14478 (2021)

42. Simonyan, K., Zisserman, A.: Very deep convolutional networks for large-scale image recognition. arXiv preprint arXiv:1409.1556 (2014)

43. Soomro, K., Zamir, A.R., Shah, M.: UCF101: a dataset of 101 human actions classes from videos in the wild. arXiv preprint arXiv:1212.0402 (2012)

44. Sun, D., Yang, X., Liu, M.Y., Kautz, J.: PWC-NET: CNNs for optical flow using pyramid, warping, and cost volume. In: Proceedings of the IEEE Conference on Computer Vision and Pattern Recognition, pp. 8934–8943 (2018)

45. Teed, Z., Deng, J.: RAFT: recurrent all-pairs field transforms for optical flow. In: Vedaldi, A., Bischof, H., Brox, T., Frahm, J.-M. (eds.) ECCV 2020. LNCS, vol. 12347, pp. 402–419. Springer, Cham (2020). https://doi.org/10.1007/978-3-030-58536-5_24

46. Wu, Z., Zhang, K., Xuan, H., Yang, J., Yan, Y.: DAPC-Net: deformable alignment and pyramid context completion networks for video inpainting. IEEE Signal Process. Lett. **28**, 1145–1149 (2021)

47. Xue, T., Chen, B., Wu, J., Wei, D., Freeman, W.T.: Video enhancement with task-oriented flow. Proc. Int. J. Comput. Vis. 1106–1128 (2019)

Learning Texture Enhancement Prior with Deep Unfolding Network for Snapshot Compressive Imaging

Mengying Jin, Zhihui Wei, and Liang Xiao

Nanjing University of Science and Technology, Nanjing 210094, China
{jinmengying_maths,gswei}@njust.edu.cn, xiaoliang@mail.njust.edu.cn

Abstract. Coded Aperture Snapshot Spectral Imaging (CASSI) utilizes a two-dimensional (2D) detector to capture three-dimensional (3D) data, significantly reducing the acquisition cost of hyperspectral images. However, such an ill-posed problem desires a reliable decoding algorithm with a well-designed prior term. This paper proposes a decoding model with a learnable prior term for snapshot compressive imaging. We expand the inference obtained by Half Quadratic Splitting (HQS) to construct our Texture Enhancement Prior learning network, TEP-net. Considering the high-frequency information representing the texture can effectively enhance the reconstruction quality. We then propose the residual Shuffled Multi-spectral Channel Attention (Shuffled-MCA) module to learn information corresponding to different frequency components by introducing the Discrete Cosine Transform (DCT) bases. In order to overcome the drawbacks of grouping operations within the MCA module efficiently, we employ the channel shuffle operation instead of a channel-wise operation. Channel shuffle rearranges the channel descriptors, allowing for better extraction of channel correlations subsequently. The experimental results show that our method outperforms the existing state-of-the-art method in numerical indicators. At the same time, the visualization results also show our superior performance in texture enhancement.

Keywords: Coded Aperture Snapshot Spectral Imaging (CASSI) · Deep unfolding · Residual shuffled multi-spectral channel attention · Texture enhancement · Channel shuffle

1 Introduction

Hyperspectral data has been used in a wide range of applications, including agriculture [12], vegetation and water resource studies [6], surveillance [33] and so

This research was funded by the National Natural Science Foundation of China under Grant 61871226; in part by the Fundamental Research Funds for the Central Universities under Grant NO. JSGP202204; in part by the Jiangsu Provincial Social Developing Project under Grant BE2018727.

Supplementary Information The online version contains supplementary material available at https://doi.org/10.1007/978-3-031-26313-2_22.

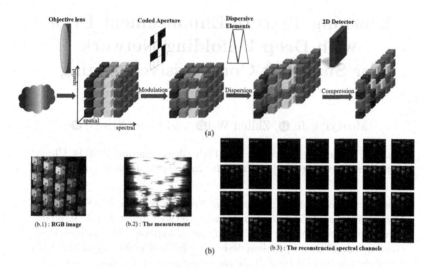

Fig. 1. (a). The data flow of the Coded Aperture Snapshot Spectral Imaging (CASSI) system. (b.1) The RGB image; (b.2) The measurement; (b.3) The reconstructed spectral channels. Color for better view.

on. However, the high spectral resolution of hyperspectral data makes it a certain difficulty in acquisition and storage. Inspired by the theory of compressed sensing, compressed imaging system was developed and is now widely employed for high-speed videos and hyperspectral images. Snapshot Compressive Imaging (SCI) systems combine compressed sensing with optical sensors, i.e., compressing multiple frames of data into a single snapshot measurement, offering the advantages of low cost, low bandwidth, and high speed, and becoming a popular compressed imaging system. As one of the representative SCI systems for hyperspectral image acquisition, the Coded Aperture Snapshot Spectral Imaging (CASSI) [5,22,23] system is of tremendous research value.

The compressed imaging systems always rely on a corresponding decoding algorithm to obtain the original data, and CASSI is no exception. As depicted in Fig. 1, the 3D data is captured by the objective lens first, then modulated by the coded aperture, dispersed by the dispersion element, and finally overlaps on the 2D detector plane. Thereby, it is plagued by several issues that cause the inverse problem under the SCI task to be quite challenging. The conventional model-based computational imaging methods mimic the physical process of imaging and incorporate the prior term in order to compress the solution space. In the selection of the prior items, TwIST [2] utilizes the total variation, whereas DeSCI [11] employs patch-based weighted nuclear norm. These approaches [2,11,29,32] use hand-crafted priors derived from domain knowledge, mainly focusing on extracting generic features, lacking the application of features for the target data itself.

With the development of Convolutional Neural Network(CNN), the CNN-based methods [3,16–18,28] use the powerful learning ability of neural networks to learn features from the data, substantially improving the results. However, they are also being accused of being uninterpretable. Recently, Zhang et al. [34] experimentally demonstrate that neural networks have the capability to express arbitrarily complex functions, which allows CNN to be considered as a learnable proximal operator. This makes it intuitive to think of viewing a deep learning network as a feature prior learning module [37] and combining it with conventional model-based approaches to construct a novel unfolding network for addressing the SCI problem.

Although researchers [34] have proved that CNN can learn arbitrary patterns, including high-frequency information [24], they also confirm that the CNNs tend to learn 'Simple' patterns, i.e., low-frequency information, first. Redundant low-frequency information may affect the propagation of high-frequency information [1]. So treating channels of the input feature equally obviously cannot be a reliable solution. The channel attention [9] offers a workaround by applying channel-wise re-weighting to the input features, which means we can use the channel attention mechanism to enhance the target information that we need selectively.

As stated before, the two-dimensional data acquired by the CASSI system is radially ambiguous, with a significant quantity of missing data. The previous technologies mainly focused on how to recover incomplete data and did not care about the texture information lost, resulting in a lack of clarity. The DGSMP [10] is concerned about this and proposes using a deep unfolding Gaussian Scale Mixed model with spatial adaptation to learn edge texture information and obtain state-of-the-art results.

Motivated by these, this paper will construct an unfolding network for processing SCI tasks with novel texture-enhancement prior learning term. **Firstly**, considering the significance of the texture represented by the high-frequency information for the image recovery effect and the ability of the channel attention mechanism to enhance the information selectively, we introduce a Multi-spectral Channel Attention(MCA) Mechanism for texture learning. **Secondly**, the conventional MCA would assign the same Discrete Cosine Transform(DCT) base to multiple frames in each group after grouping channels. Instead of assigning DCT bases frame by frame [15] resulting in a significant increase in computation, we prefer to introduce a simple and improved method, i.e., channel shuffle. Then, we incorporate the MCA with channel shuffle into a basic residual structure to build the complete texture enhancement prior learning module, so-called the residual Shuffled MCA or SMCA for simplicity. The skipping connections in the residual structure ensure that low-frequency information can propagate backward, allowing the main network to focus on enhancing high-frequency information. **Finally**, we unfolded the data fidelity term into a network form, combined it with the constructed SMCA, and treated it as one stage. Repeating the stage several times will form a complete network. We did a series of experiments and discovered that we received state-of-the-art results on several metrics, with the visualization demonstrating that the texture was successfully enhanced.

The contribution of our work can be summarised as follows:

1. We propose a novel unfolding network with texture enhancement prior learning module for SCI tasks.
2. We introduce MCA to selectively enhance the information corresponding to the different frequencies.
3. We improve the drawback in MCA caused by grouping operation by introducing channel shuffle and coupling the residual structure to construct the Shuffled MCA.
4. Experiments demonstrate the superior performance of our method compared to state-of-the-art methods in terms of numerical evaluation metrics and visualization results.

2   Related Works

Previous Work. As there are arbitrarily many 3D images $\mathcal{X}$ that can be reduced to the same 2D image y, Snapshot Compressive Imaging (SCI) is an ill-conditioned problem. In order to choose the most plausible result among the candidate set, a proper regularization is required. Conventional model-based methods usually use hand-crafted priors, such as TwIST [2] and GAP-TV [32] uses total variation regularization, GMM-online [29] uses Gaussian Mixture Model, DeSCI [11] uses weighted nuclear norm, etc. Although they all have complete theoretical proof but also rely on artificial parameter tuning, while time-consuming, DeSCI requires even hours to process one single image. Neural networks have shown great potential in recent years, with much of the CNN-based works taking recovery to a new level [3,16–18,28]. However, the uninterpretability of CNNs is undesirable given the existence of a complete physical imaging mechanism in computational imaging.

Gregor et al. [7] propose to unfold the inference of conventional model-based methods into neural networks, transforming the methods into parameters learnable while still being interpretable and significantly reducing the time cost. Ista-net [36] and ADMM-net [30] expand the computational flow graph directly into a network and update the parameters efficiently by back propagation. Ma et al. [13] propose Tensor ADMM-net, which further relates the iterative steps with the neural network operations one to one. Zhang et al. [37] then consider using CNN as the prior term of the network. In this paper, we also try to employ CNN, which can fit arbitrary functions, construct the prior learning module, and consider it a learnable proximal operator.

Channel Attention Mechanism. CNNs have achieved impressive outcomes, but they usually treat the channels of the input features equally and ignore the correlation between channels. Squeeze-and-Excitation Network(SENet) [9] believes it is better to directly and explicitly model the dynamic nonlinear dependencies between channels. SENet uses the Global Average Pooling(GAP) operation to 'Squeeze' the information. Otherwise, using the mean value as the feature descriptor has proved that only the lowest frequency information of the image is focused on, while high-frequency information is out of consideration. Thus, CBAM [27] and BAM [19] combine global maximum pooling and GAP to extract richer information. Recently, FcaNet [20] has considered placing the "Squeeze" work under the frequency domain by grouping the input features and then convolving them with the pre-computable 2D DCT bases. They also prove mathematically that when and only when the lowest frequency component in DCT bases is selected, it will be equivalent to the GAP operation.

Channel Shuffle. Grouping operation [26,35] has been widely used in deep learning, effectively processing different components adaptively with less computation. However, grouping operation still leads to information imbalance between groups. In order to address this, ShuffleNet [14,39] introduced the channel shuffle operation to rearrange the channel order after the group convolution, which effectively promotes information fusion between groups. CPN [21] proposed introducing channel shuffle in multi-scale cascaded pyramid networks to enhance the multi-scale information fusion across channels. SA-Net [38] applies the spatial-spectral joint attention mechanism to the grouped data separately and improves the balance between efficiency and performance by applying the channel shuffle operation over the concatenate feature.

3   Proposed Method

3.1   Reconstruction Model with Learnable Prior for CASSI

We assume the expected 3D spectral information is $\mathcal{X} \in \mathbb{R}^{M \times N \times \lambda}$, the 2D measurement captured by the CASSI system is the $y \in \mathbb{R}^{M \times (N+k(\lambda-1))}$, where M and N represent spatial size, the λ is the spectral number, and the k represents the dispersion coefficient caused by the dispersion elements, then we have:

$$y = \Phi \mathcal{X} + n \tag{1}$$

where, $\Phi \in \mathbb{R}^{M \times (N+k(\lambda-1)) \times \lambda}$ is the feed-forward response function describing the physical process in CASSI. n represents the noise.

The reconstruction model corresponding to the Eq. (1) can be written as:

$$\min_{\mathcal{X}} ||y - \Phi \mathcal{X}||_F^2 + \gamma \beta(\mathcal{X}) \tag{2}$$

where $\beta(\cdot)$ is the regularization term and γ is the balance parameter. The Eq. (2) can be written as an unconstrained optimization problem according to the Half Quadratic Splitting (HQS) method:

$$\min_{\mathcal{X},\mathcal{Z}} ||y - \Phi \mathcal{X}||_F^2 + \eta ||\mathcal{X} - \mathcal{Z}||_F^2 + \gamma \beta(\mathcal{Z}) \tag{3}$$

where η is the penalty parameter, $\mathcal{Z}$ is the auxiliary variable. The solution to the Eq. (3) can be split into the following two sub-problems.

$$\mathcal{X}^{k+1} = arg \min_{\mathcal{X}} ||y - \Phi\mathcal{X}||_F^2 + \eta||\mathcal{X} - \mathcal{Z}^k||_F^2 \tag{4}$$

$$\mathcal{Z}^{k+1} = arg \min_{\mathcal{Z}} \eta||\mathcal{X}^{k+1} - \mathcal{Z}||_F^2 + \gamma\beta(\mathcal{Z}) \tag{5}$$

$\mathcal{X}$ **sub-problem**: fixed variable $\mathcal{Z}$, updated variable $\mathcal{X}$. Equation (4) is a least squares problem, and the solution can be given directly in closed form as:

$$\mathcal{X}^{k+1} = (\Phi^T\Phi + \eta\mathcal{I})^{-1}(\Phi^T y + \eta\mathcal{Z}^k) \tag{6}$$

However, it is computationally expensive to calculate the inverse of $\Phi^T\Phi$ directly, so gradient descent is employed here to find the approximate solution of (6) :

$$\mathcal{X}^{k+1} = (1 - \epsilon\eta)\mathcal{X}^k - \epsilon\Phi^T\Phi\mathcal{X}^k + \epsilon\Phi^T y + \epsilon\eta\mathcal{Z}^k \tag{7}$$

where ϵ represents the step size in the gradient descent.

$\mathcal{Z}$ **sub-problem**: fixed variable $\mathcal{X}$, updated variable $\mathcal{Z}$. The formula (5) is a prior term, which can be expressed as a learnable proximal operator:

$$\mathcal{Z}^{k+1} = \mathcal{P}(\mathcal{X}^{k+1}) \tag{8}$$

To solve the Eq. (3) more effectively, we are attempting to convert the model-based method into a learning-based method by extending the inference into a deep neural network. This will allow the method to learn targeted features from the data and apply them to improve performance. In other words, each iteration is viewed as a sub-module of the network, and K consecutive modules are connected in sequence to build the unfolding network. The following section will introduce the proposed texture enhancement prior learning network.

3.2   Texture Enhancement Prior Learning Network: TEP-net

TEP-net consists of three modules, the data fidelity module, the texture enhancement prior learning module (TEP-module), the system forward response and its inverse process learning module. In order to better extract the information, we also proposed a novel residual Shuffled Multi-spectral Channel Attention embedded in the TEP-module, called Shuffled-MCA. Figure 2 demonstrates the construction of the TEP-net.

Learning System Forward Response and Its Inverse. Φ and Φ^T describe the physical imaging processing and its inverse of the CASSI system, which is particularly important in CASSI. Since the network involves multiple multiplication calculations, considering the high computational complexity of tensor multiplication and the fact that the coded aperture varies in different systems and settings. In order to reduce computational complexity and increase the robustness of the system, we follow the design of [10] and use the cascaded residual

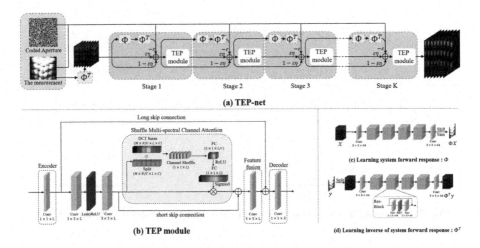

Fig. 2. The structure of the proposed method. (a): The structure of TEP-net. (b): Our proposed residual Shuffled Multi-spectral Channel Attention module for texture enhancement prior learning. (c–d): Structure of the sub-network for learning system forward response and its inverse process: Φ & Φ^T. (c) for learning Φ and (d) for learning Φ^T.

sub-network to learn Φ, Φ^T. It is easy to notice from Fig. 2(a) that $\Phi^T y$ repeatedly occurs in the model. Since the coded aperture Φ_{orig} is known in the actual experiments, to balance performance and effectiveness, we use $\Phi_{orig}^T y$ as input to the model without engaging in additional learning (the top line in Fig. 2(a)).

The Data Fidelity Module. As illustrated in Fig. 2(a), we present this part via a data flow diagram. The network inputs are the measurement y and the $\Phi_{orig}^T y$ reconstructed using the original coded aperture Φ_{orig}. $\Phi_{orig}^T y$ will repeatedly feed into the network as the top line of Fig. 2(a) shows. The measurement y will pass through a randomly initialized Φ^T learning sub-network first. Then, the obtained values $\Phi^T y$ become the initial value of the network.

Learning Texture Enhancement Prior. Conventional hand-crafted priors benefit from domain knowledge with complete theoretical analysis but lack information mining from the target data. Meanwhile, CNNs can fit arbitrary functions and learn from data, allowing CNNs to be viewed as learnable proximal operators. Thus we propose a residual shuffled multi-spectral channel attention sub-network for texture enhancement prior learning, which concatenates a feature extraction term and a shuffled multi-spectral channel attention module with two skip connections.

As shown in Fig. 2(b), the input feature $\mathcal{X}^k \in \mathbb{R}^{M \times N \times \lambda}$ is first encoded by the encoder which is a point-wise convolution with L channels.

$$encoder(\cdot) = conv(\cdot) \tag{9}$$

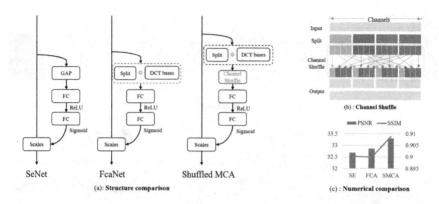

Fig. 3. The comparison of the SENet, FcaNet and the proposed Shuffle-MCA.

Following the encoder is the feature extraction module with a Conv-LeakyReLU-Conv structure. In this module, both convolution kernels are set to 3×3 with L channels. The LeakyReLU is employed as the activation function.

$$Feature(\cdot) = conv(LeakyReLU(conv(encoder(\cdot)))) \qquad (10)$$

After feature extraction, the encoded feature will feed into a regular res-block consisting of the shuffled multi-spectral channel attention module with one short skip connection. The following is a feature fusion block with L convolution kernels, each with a spatial size of 3×3. This feature fusion block can integrate the sum of features with or without passing the module, and then another point-wise convolution is used to decode the feature into the required HSI.

Our network naturally contains skip-connections due to the Eq. (7). Since our TEP-module is based on a residual structure, thus the entire network can be regarded as a simplified Residual-In-Residual structure. As [40] illustrates, these short and long skip connections will allow the low-frequency information to be passed backward through them. The main network will be allowed to concentrate on learning high-frequency information, which is consistent with our intention.

Shuffled Multi-spectral Channel Attention (Shuffled-MCA). We aim to enhance the high-frequency information of the data while completing it. So we try to introduce frequency domain information. We refer to the settings of [20] to set up our shuffled multi-spectral channel attention. The fed feature $\mathcal{X}^K$ is first divided into g groups, i.e., $\mathcal{X}^K = \{\mathcal{X}_0^K, \mathcal{X}_1^K, \cdots, \mathcal{X}_{g-1}^K\}$, each group will be assigned a group of 2D DCT basis generated by one corresponding frequency component. Thus,

$$Freq^i = 2DDCT^{u_i,v_i}(X^i) = \sum_{h=0}^{H-1}\sum_{w=0}^{W-1} X_{:,h,w}^i B_{h,w}^{u_i,v_i} \qquad (11)$$

where $i \in \{0, 1, \cdots, g-1\}$. Then all the $Freq^i$ will be concatenate into one vector, then we got the output of the 'Squeeze' part. By assigning each group with different frequency component, it could effectively weight different information at the same time.

In the previous approaches, the channel descriptors were fed directly into the subsequent 'Excitation' part. However, we assume that although the use of different frequency information is considered, the data within each group still only extracts information under the same frequency component. Therefore, to further improve the 'Squeeze' capability, rather than using channel-wise improvement like [15], we employ the channel shuffle operation and develop the novel *Shuffled Multi-spectral Channel Attention*. Figure 3(a) shows the difference among the structures of our proposed Shuffled-MCA , the original SENet, and FcaNet.

In Fig. 3(b), there is a simple illustration of the actual operation of the channel shuffle. The input feature $\mathcal{F}^n$ will be split into g groups, $\{\mathcal{F}_1^1, \mathcal{F}_2^1, \cdots, \mathcal{F}_i^g\}$, where i represents the number of channels within each group. Then, rearranging the order of $\{\mathcal{F}_1^1, \mathcal{F}_2^1, \cdots, \mathcal{F}_i^g\}$, the output of the channel shuffle would be $\{\mathcal{F}_1^1, \mathcal{F}_1^2, \cdots, \mathcal{F}_1^g, \mathcal{F}_2^1, \cdots, \mathcal{F}_i^g\}$.

We added the channel shuffle operation between 'Squeeze' and 'Excitation'. This operation allows the extraction of information corroding to different frequency components not limited within adjacent channels. By rearranging the order of channel descriptors it will affect the whole data in as extensive a range as possible. We also provide ablation experiments about the embedding strategies of channel shuffle. In Fig. 3(c), the numerical experiments confirm that the channel shuffle operation significantly improves the model's applicability.

4   Experiments

This section will present the details of experiments. First, Sect. 4.1 introduces the database, experimental setup, etc. Section 4.2 offers the results of numerical experiments and the visualization results. Section 4.3 is the ablation experiments related to TEP-net.

4.1   Network Training

In our experiments, two hyperspectral datasets, CAVE [31] and KAIST [4], are used. We select a portion of the data from CAVE for training, and randomly crop out a patch with a spatial scale of 96×96 as one of the training samples. After modulating, the data will be spatially shifted by two-pixel intervals. Then, the spectral dimensions of the shifted data are summed up to produce a two-dimensional measurement of size 96×150 as one of the network input. In order to augment the dataset, each training sample will be randomly flipped or rotated. Meanwhile, 10 images are selected from the KAIST as the test set. For validation purposes, the KAIST will not be present in the training samples. The KAIST images were cropped to a spatial size of 256×256. Also, instead of using the traditional binary mask, the real mask obtained from measurements in the real system was used [16]. To be consistent with the real system, we choose 28 out of 31 bands for the experiments, with a spectral range of 450 nm to 650 nm.

We train the network using an end-to-end training approach, where the training objective is minimizing the Root Mean Square Error (RMSE) between the reconstructed data and the original data. The model is trained by the Adam optimizer with the learning rate 0.001. Given that the network uses ReLU or LeakyReLU as the activation function, the Kaiming Normal [8] was chosen to initialize the convolutional layers. The experiments were implemented by PyTorch and trained with a single Nvidia GeForce RTX 2080Ti. The experiments are set to 200 epochs and take about 20 h.

4.2   Experiment Comparison

We compare various algorithms, including the traditional iterative algorithm: TwIST citech22bioucas2007new, GAP-TV [32], the deep neural networks: TSAnet [16], PnP-DIP [17] and the deep unfolding networks: HSSP [25], DGSMP [10]. For all methods, we use the source code released by the original authors, with TSAnet using their subsequent supplemented PyTorch version, and we rewrite HSSP in PyTorch. All learning-based methods have been retrained using the same training set.

Numerical Results. The Table 1(1) shows the Peak Signal-to-Noise Ratio (PSNR) and Structural Similarity Index (SSIM) results for each image on the KAIST dataset. Our advantage over the iterative algorithm is evident, with a lead of 8.65 dB to 9.95 dB in PSNR and 0.2471 to 0.2488 in SSIM. Moreover, for the learning-based approaches, our method is 6.06 dB, 4.69 dB higher than HSSP and TSAnet in the average PSNR, and is 0.0371 and 0.0694 higher in the average SSIM. Compared to DGSMP, the state-of-the-art method, which is also a deep unfolding network, the PSNR is 3.27 dB higher, and SSIM is 0.037 higher. Due to equipment and time constraints, we only use 30 images from the CAVE dataset to build the training set and use data augmentation to augment the training samples to 5000 per epoch, which may explain the performance degradation of TSAnet and DGSMP. However, our performance also illustrates the proposed method's powerful and robust feature capture capability. DGSMP also claims to work on recovering edges and textures, and the effect shows that introducing frequency information may achieve better quality.

Since we are dealing with a hyperspectral image reconstruction task, we further present the results on four indices, Root Mean Squared Error (RMSE), Erreur Relative Globale Adimensionnelle de Synthèse (ERGAS), Spectral Angle Mapper (SAM), and Universal Image Quality Index(UIQI) in Table 1(2). The SAM describes the level of spectral similarity, which is essential to evaluate the quality of hyperspectral reconstruction tasks, and smaller SAM means better spectral fidelity. Among the seven methods, our method has the smallest SAM value, highlighting our performance on spectral reconstruction. Despite its unsatisfactory indices such as PSNR and SSIM, we also note that the conventional method still has comparable spectral fidelity due to its construction approach from domain knowledge.

Table 1. Numerical experiments on KAIST dataset. Best in bold.

(1) The PSNRs(dB) and SSIMs of seven methods. (In each cell, PSNR is on the left and SSIM is on the right.)

	TwIST [2]	GAP-TV [32]	HSSP [25]	TSAnet [16]	PnP-DIP [17]	DGSMP [10]	Shuffled MCA (ours)
scene01	25.25/0.6665	25.64/0.7451	31.44/0.9207	30.47/0.8616	32.04/0.8646	31.19/0.8715	**33.79/0.9117**
scene02	22.04/0.5541	23.41/0.6052	27.08/0.8664	28.96/0.8071	26.03/0.7136	29.97/0.8457	**33.49/0.9038**
scene03	22.20/0.7415	23.14/0.7639	21.17/0.7937	26.79/0.8553	29.83/0.8259	29.97/0.8682	**33.34/0.9033**
scene04	30.33/0.8134	33.04/0.8620	27.81/0.8576	36.89/0.9241	38.03/0.9268	35.33/0.9216	**40.02/0.9463**
scene05	19.27/0.6411	19.11/0.6684	26.76/0.8902	26.53/0.8261	28.80/0.8438	27.55/0.8357	**30.75/0.8951**
scene06	24.29/0.6529	26.69/0.7430	31.35/**0.9277**	29.21/0.8688	29.43/0.8391	30.54/0.9074	**33.17**/0.9241
scene07	18.26/0.5394	22.10/0.6357	27.97/0.8499	25.68/0.7606	26.84/0.7927	27.86/0.8194	**31.75/0.8870**
scene08	26.13/0.6985	25.23/0.2112	27.60/0.8832	26.57/0.8389	28.24/0.8302	29.51/0.8840	**31.77/0.9015**
scene09	22.18/0.7094	24.30/0.6964	21.58/0.7892	28.23/0.8576	28.78/0.8704	29.86/0.8802	**33.55/0.9137**
scene10	22.60/0.5750	23.95/0.6434	29.73/**0.9387**	26.85/0.7940	27.52/0.7843	28.67/0.8840	**31.46**/0.9015
Average	23.36/0.6592	24.66/0.6575	27.25/0.8717	28.62/0.8394	29.55/0.8291	30.04/0.8718	**33.31/0.9088**

(2) The RMSEs, ERGASs, SAMs and UIQIs of seven methods.

	TwIST [2]	GAP-TV [32]	HSSP [25]	TSAnet [16]	PnP-DIP [17]	DGSMP [10]	Shuffled MCA (ours)
RMSE	27.22	21.43	13.63	10.2	14.24	8.51	**5.85**
ERGAS	119.45	93.54	74.86	50.49	62.87	45.37	**29.88**
SAM	15.54	14.81	20.76	13.4	14.67	13.43	**11.59**
UIQI	0.4247	0.5473	0.6974	0.6648	0.6672	0.7205	**0.7641**

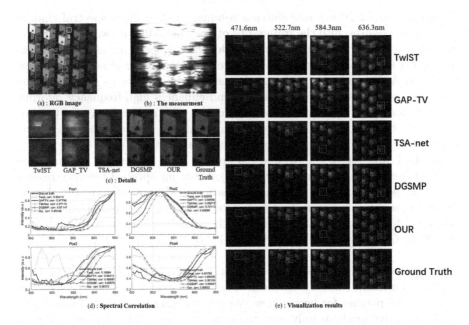

Fig. 4. The visualization results for scene02. (a) The corresponding RGB image. (b) The measurements to be recovered.(c) Zooming in details. (d) Spectral correlation with 4 positions. (e) The visualization results for scene02.

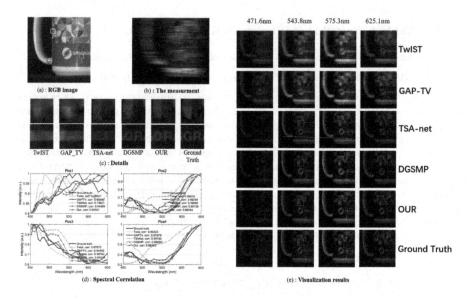

Fig. 5. The visualization results for scene05. (a) The corresponding RGB image. (b) The measurements to be recovered.(c) Zooming in details. (d) Spectral correlation with 4 positions. (e) The visualization results for scene05.

Visualization. TEP-net introduces a residual shuffled multi-spectral channel attention mechanism into the framework of deep unfolding networks and places the hyperspectral image decoding task under the frequency domain. Unlike low-rank theory and CNNs, which tend to deal more with low-frequency information, Shuffle-MCA, by assigning different frequency components to different channels, recovers low-frequency information and enhances high-frequency information synchronously. Therefore, our algorithm can effectively enhance the texture, edges and other regions of the image with significant gradient changes. Fortunately, the visualization supports our hypothesis.

In Fig. 4. and Fig. 5, the (a) and (b) are the RGB images and the measurements of the testing data, respectively. (d) shows our spectral recovery results, and the numerical indicators are the correlation coefficients of each pair of spectral response curves between the recovered data and the real data. Higher values indicate a higher correlation. (e) shows the visualization results obtained by TwIST [2], GAP-TV [32], TSAnet [16], DGSMP [10] and ours TEP-net, respectively.

For demonstration purposes, we select 4 of the 28 bands. They show that the results of our image recovery are much closer to the real data, and to clarify this we also select patches for better view. We are zooming to show that the results of both iterative methods only have the general shape, with TSA-net being too smooth to lose details. Although DGSMP also claims that they are focusing on edge and texture recovering, their results still shows unpleasant artifacts at the edges and are less stable at complex textures. In contrast, our results recover

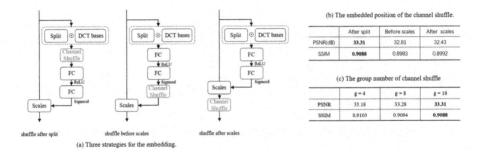

(b) The embedded position of the channel shuffle.

	After split	Before scales	After scales
PSNR(dB)	**33.31**	32.81	32.43
SSIM	**0.9088**	0.8983	0.8992

(c) The group number of channel shuffle

	g = 4	g = 8	g = 16
PSNR	33.18	33.28	**33.31**
SSIM	0.9103	0.9094	**0.9088**

shuffle after split   shuffle before scales   shuffle after scales

(a) Three strategies for the embedding.

Fig. 6. Ablation experiments on the embedding of the channel shuffle.

both edges and appearance well. Texture enhancement does not mean losing the capture of low-frequency information. We assume that the residuals of the sub-network and the self-contained residual structure of the inference process allow low-frequency information to circulate efficiently over the network. It is easy to see that our method still achieves superior performance in smoother areas, such as the bottom of the cup and the side of the cube. More results will show in the supplementary material.

4.3 Ablation Experiments

The Embedding of the Channel Shuffle. In order to solve the imbalance of information extraction due to the grouping, the channel shuffle operation will be added to enhance the network performance. However, it is debatable where to add it, and we finally decided to add it into the middle of 'Squeeze' and 'Excitation'. Hence, it will be more beneficial for information extraction by rearranging channel descriptors obtained by 'Squeeze' and then putting them into 'Excitation' to find the correlation between channels. To verify the effectiveness, we did a set of ablation experiments.

Figure 6. shows the comparison of the three embedding forms. When shuffling after scales, the results dropped, which is because when shuffling after scales, the output feature's channels do not correspond to the residuals anymore, leading to a mixture of non-corresponding information and resulting in an unpleasant consequence. Even though the channel shuffle can always have improvement during the generation of the attention, shuffle before 'Excitation' still got the best performance, which also validates our previous point.

We also offer the selection of hyper-parameters in the channel shuffle, the grouping g. According to Fig. 6.(c), the trends of PSNR and SSIM obtained under different strategies are not consistent, so we chose the strategy $g = 16$ by observing the generated images. The specific reference images are in the supplementary material.

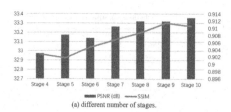 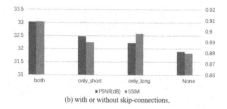

(a) different number of stages.   (b) with or without skip-connections.

Fig. 7. Reconstruction results of (a) different number of stages. (b) with or without skip-connections.

The Number of Stages. In deep unfolding networks, we combine traditional iterative algorithms with deep learning methods, viewing one iteration as one stage, and connecting K stages in series to construct the network. From this perspective, the selection of K is critical, and the selection of K varies in different tasks. Figure 7(a), a larger K may lead to a better results, while takes a much longer to converge. In order to balance computational cost and effectiveness, $K = 8$ is selected for the experiments in this paper.

The Skip-Connections. As we stated previously that our scheme embeds the channel attention mechanism into a residual structure in the hope of propagating low frequency information backwards through the residual skipping connection, in combination with the MCA module to obtain better recovery. In Fig. 7(b), we show the results with or without the skipping connections. We keep the long or short skipping connections alone, or just the backbone network, and there is a decrease in performance, indicating that the residual structure took effect in our task.

5   Conclusion

In this paper, we propose an HQS-based decoding method and expand its inference into a deep unfolding network that can be trained end-to-end for snapshot compressive imaging. Then we propose a residual shuffled MCA sub-network for texture enhancement prior learning and treat it as a learnable proximal operator of the model. By introducing the DCT bases, the model could effectively enhance the information corresponding to the different frequency components. Meanwhile, to overcome the shortcoming caused by the grouping operation within the MCA, we employ the channel shuffle operation to improve the robustness of the network by rearranging the channel descriptors' order. The experiments demonstrate that we have significantly improved the numerical evaluation metrics compared to the state-of-the-art methods. The visualization results also verify the superiority of our texture enhancement learning effect.

References

1. Arpit, D., et al.: A closer look at memorization in deep networks. In: International Conference on Machine Learning, pp. 233–242. PMLR (2017)
2. Bioucas-Dias, J.M., Figueiredo, M.A.: A new twist: two-step iterative shrinkage/thresholding algorithms for image restoration. IEEE Trans. Image Process. **16**(12), 2992–3004 (2007)
3. Cheng, Z., et al.: Memory-efficient network for large-scale video compressive sensing. In: Proceedings of the IEEE/CVF Conference on Computer Vision and Pattern Recognition, pp. 16246–16255 (2021)
4. Choi, I., Jeon, D.S., Nam, G., Gutierrez, D., Kim, M.H.: High-quality hyperspectral reconstruction using a spectral prior. ACM Trans. Graph. (TOG) **36**(6), 1–13 (2017)
5. Gehm, M.E., John, R., Brady, D.J., Willett, R.M., Schulz, T.J.: Single-shot compressive spectral imaging with a dual-disperser architecture. Opt. Express **15**(21), 14013–14027 (2007)
6. Govender, M., Chetty, K., Bulcock, H.: A review of hyperspectral remote sensing and its application in vegetation and water resource studies. Water Sa **33**(2), 145–151 (2007)
7. Gregor, K., LeCun, Y.: Learning fast approximations of sparse coding. In: Proceedings of the 27th International Conference on International Conference on Machine Learning, pp. 399–406 (2010)
8. He, K., Zhang, X., Ren, S., Sun, J.: Delving deep into rectifiers: surpassing human-level performance on imagenet classification. In: Proceedings of the IEEE International Conference on Computer Vision, pp. 1026–1034 (2015)
9. Hu, J., Shen, L., Sun, G.: Squeeze-and-excitation networks. In: Proceedings of the IEEE Conference on Computer Vision and Pattern Recognition, pp. 7132–7141 (2018)
10. Huang, T., Dong, W., Yuan, X., Wu, J., Shi, G.: Deep gaussian scale mixture prior for spectral compressive imaging. In: Proceedings of the IEEE/CVF Conference on Computer Vision and Pattern Recognition, pp. 16216–16225 (2021)
11. Liu, Y., Yuan, X., Suo, J., Brady, D.J., Dai, Q.: Rank minimization for snapshot compressive imaging. IEEE Trans. Pattern Anal. Mach. Intell. **41**(12), 2990–3006 (2018)
12. Lu, B., Dao, P.D., Liu, J., He, Y., Shang, J.: Recent advances of hyperspectral imaging technology and applications in agriculture. Remote Sens. **12**(16), 2659 (2020)
13. Ma, J., Liu, X.Y., Shou, Z., Yuan, X.: Deep tensor ADMM-Net for snapshot compressive imaging. In: Proceedings of the IEEE/CVF International Conference on Computer Vision, pp. 10223–10232 (2019)
14. Ma, N., Zhang, X., Zheng, H.T., Sun, J.: ShuffleNet V2: practical guidelines for efficient CNN architecture design. In: Proceedings of the European Conference on Computer Vision (ECCV), pp. 116–131 (2018)
15. Magid, S.A., et al.: Dynamic high-pass filtering and multi-spectral attention for image super-resolution. In: Proceedings of the IEEE/CVF International Conference on Computer Vision, pp. 4288–4297 (2021)
16. Meng, Z., Ma, J., Yuan, X.: End-to-end low cost compressive spectral imaging with spatial-spectral self-attention. In: Vedaldi, A., Bischof, H., Brox, T., Frahm, J.-M. (eds.) ECCV 2020. LNCS, vol. 12368, pp. 187–204. Springer, Cham (2020). https://doi.org/10.1007/978-3-030-58592-1_12

17. Meng, Z., Yu, Z., Xu, K., Yuan, X.: Self-supervised neural networks for spectral snapshot compressive imaging. In: Proceedings of the IEEE/CVF International Conference on Computer Vision, pp. 2622–2631 (2021)

18. Miao, X., Yuan, X., Pu, Y., Athitsos, V.: l-Net: reconstruct hyperspectral images from a snapshot measurement. In: Proceedings of the IEEE/CVF International Conference on Computer Vision, pp. 4059–4069 (2019)

19. Park, J., Woo, S., Lee, J.Y., Kweon, I.S.: Bam: bottleneck attention module. arXiv preprint arXiv:1807.06514 (2018)

20. Qin, Z., Zhang, P., Wu, F., Li, X.: FcaNet: frequency channel attention networks. In: Proceedings of the IEEE/CVF International Conference on Computer Vision, pp. 783–792 (2021)

21. Su, K., Yu, D., Xu, Z., Geng, X., Wang, C.: Multi-person pose estimation with enhanced channel-wise and spatial information. In: Proceedings of the IEEE/CVF Conference on Computer Vision and Pattern Recognition, pp. 5674–5682 (2019)

22. Wagadarikar, A., John, R., Willett, R., Brady, D.: Single disperser design for coded aperture snapshot spectral imaging. Appl. Opt. **47**(10), B44–B51 (2008)

23. Wagadarikar, A.A., Pitsianis, N.P., Sun, X., Brady, D.J.: Video rate spectral imaging using a coded aperture snapshot spectral imager. Opt. Express **17**(8), 6368–6388 (2009)

24. Wang, H., Wu, X., Huang, Z., Xing, E.P.: High-frequency component helps explain the generalization of convolutional neural networks. In: Proceedings of the IEEE/CVF Conference on Computer Vision and Pattern Recognition, pp. 8684–8694 (2020)

25. Wang, L., Sun, C., Fu, Y., Kim, M.H., Huang, H.: Hyperspectral image reconstruction using a deep spatial-spectral prior. In: Proceedings of the IEEE/CVF Conference on Computer Vision and Pattern Recognition, pp. 8032–8041 (2019)

26. Wang, X., Kan, M., Shan, S., Chen, X.: Fully learnable group convolution for acceleration of deep neural networks. In: Proceedings of the IEEE/CVF Conference on Computer Vision and Pattern Recognition, pp. 9049–9058 (2019)

27. Woo, S., Park, J., Lee, J.Y., Kweon, I.S.: CBAM: convolutional block attention module. In: Proceedings of the European Conference on Computer Vision (ECCV), pp. 3–19 (2018)

28. Xiong, Z., Shi, Z., Li, H., Wang, L., Liu, D., Wu, F.: HSCNN: CNN-based hyperspectral image recovery from spectrally undersampled projections. In: Proceedings of the IEEE International Conference on Computer Vision Workshops, pp. 518–525 (2017)

29. Yang, J., et al.: Gaussian mixture model for video compressive sensing. In: 2013 IEEE International Conference on Image Processing, pp. 19–23. IEEE (2013)

30. Yang, Y., Sun, J., Li, H., Xu, Z.: Deep ADMM-Net for compressive sensing MRI. In: Proceedings of the 30th International Conference on Neural Information Processing Systems, pp. 10–18 (2016)

31. Yasuma, F., Mitsunaga, T., Iso, D., Nayar, S.K.: Generalized assorted pixel camera: postcapture control of resolution, dynamic range, and spectrum. IEEE Trans. Image Process. **19**(9), 2241–2253 (2010)

32. Yuan, X.: Generalized alternating projection based total variation minimization for compressive sensing. In: 2016 IEEE International Conference on Image Processing (ICIP), pp. 2539–2543. IEEE (2016)

33. Yuen, P.W., Richardson, M.: An introduction to hyperspectral imaging and its application for security, surveillance and target acquisition. Imaging Sci. J. **58**(5), 241–253 (2010)

34. Zhang, C., Bengio, S., Hardt, M., Recht, B., Vinyals, O.: Understanding deep learning (still) requires rethinking generalization. Commun. ACM **64**(3), 107–115 (2021)
35. Zhang, J., Zhao, H., Yao, A., Chen, Y., Zhang, L., Liao, H.: Efficient semantic scene completion network with spatial group convolution. In: Proceedings of the European Conference on Computer Vision (ECCV), pp. 733–749 (2018)
36. Zhang, J., Ghanem, B.: ISTA-Net: interpretable optimization-inspired deep network for image compressive sensing. In: Proceedings of the IEEE Conference on Computer Vision and Pattern Recognition, pp. 1828–1837 (2018)
37. Zhang, K., Gool, L.V., Timofte, R.: Deep unfolding network for image super-resolution. In: Proceedings of the IEEE/CVF Conference on Computer Vision and Pattern Recognition, pp. 3217–3226 (2020)
38. Zhang, Q.L., Yang, Y.B.: SA-Net: shuffle attention for deep convolutional neural networks. In: ICASSP 2021–2021 IEEE International Conference on Acoustics, Speech and Signal Processing (ICASSP), pp. 2235–2239. IEEE (2021)
39. Zhang, X., Zhou, X., Lin, M., Sun, J.: ShuffleNet: an extremely efficient convolutional neural network for mobile devices. In: Proceedings of the IEEE Conference on Computer Vision and Pattern Recognition, pp. 6848–6856 (2018)
40. Zhang, Y., Li, K., Li, K., Wang, L., Zhong, B., Fu, Y.: Image super-resolution using very deep residual channel attention networks. In: Proceedings of the European Conference on Computer Vision (ECCV), pp. 286–301 (2018)

Light Attenuation and Color Fluctuation for Underwater Image Restoration

Jingchun Zhou⬤, Dingshuo Liu⬤, Dehuan Zhang⬤, and Weishi Zhang$^{(\boxtimes)}$⬤

Dalian Maritime University, 1 Linghai Road, Dalian 116026, China
`teesiv@dlmu.edu.cn`

Abstract. Underwater images with low contrast and color distortion of different scenarios often pose a significant challenge in improving underwater image quality. Therefore, it is beneficial to restore the real restoration effect of the scene by estimating the degradation parameters related to their changes, and these parameters should be updated with the degradation scene to obtain the best visual effect. We propose a robust underwater image restoration method. Specifically, we adjust the color of the input image according to a background light (BL) estimation strategy guided by depth, chromatic aberration considering hue, and information entropy. At the same time, we adjust the depth map of the input image by computing color fluctuation and attenuation. According to qualitative and quantitative evaluation, the proposed method generates vivid results with a more natural appearance and more valuable information.

Keywords: Underwater image restoration · Background light · Depth map · Color fluctuation

1 Introduction

Underwater vision is critical for mining marine resources and conducting marine surveys. Due to light absorption and dispersion, underwater images acquired by optical cameras may suffer from color distortion and diminished contrast [1–6]. The degraded image and histogram are shown in Fig. 1. However, light is deflected before reaching the camera due to the excitation of particles present in the water, resulting in visual issues such as haze, and low contrast in the acquired images. The accuracy of vision tasks such as underwater object detection and segmentation suffers as a result of these image quality degradations. Hence, underwater image restoration is important for a variety of vision-based applications in underwater situations [7–11].

This work was supported in part by the National Natural Science Foundation of China (No. 61702074), the Liaoning Provincial Natural Science Foundation of China (No. 20170520196), and the Fundamental Research Funds for the Central Universities (Nos. 3132019205 and 3132019354).

© The Author(s), under exclusive license to Springer Nature Switzerland AG 2023
L. Wang et al. (Eds.): ACCV 2022, LNCS 13843, pp. 374–389, 2023.
https://doi.org/10.1007/978-3-031-26313-2_23

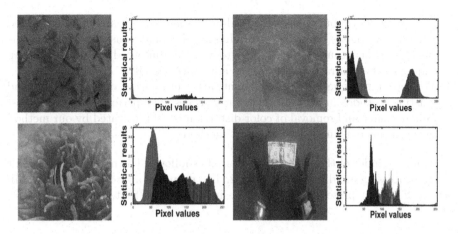

Fig. 1. The degraded images and histograms.

Other underwater applications, such as underwater item detection, object segmentation, and biological tracking, frequently use underwater image enhancement techniques as a pre-processing step. As a result, many approaches for restoring underwater pictures of diverse situations and degrees of degradation have been developed. The generality of previous approaches is frequently insufficient due to erroneous background light and transmission estimation. There is still a lot of work to be done on the details to solve the problem of color shift, decreased contrast, and details disappearance. As a result, based on background light estimation and transmission estimation, this research provides an underwater image restoration approach. Based on the degree of entropy, depth, and color difference, including hue, we develop a background light estimation model. We establish the depth map of the input image by computing color fluctuation and attenuation. Transmission maps (TM) obtained by accurate depth map calculations tend to retain more details, have higher contrast, and have better visual effects.

The technical contributions of this paper are summarized as follows:

1) In this work, we propose a novel estimate method for BL that consider bright and dark channel differences, color differences, and information entropy. Although the difference between bright and dark channels is an essential metric for depth, it is not the only clue for underwater. The blurred region [12] at infinity contains less information, and entropy is the key evaluation metric. When the difference between different color channels is large, the differential absorption of red light can be used. The BL of our method is more accurate, which effectively solves the wrong estimate of BL when there are white objects in the foreground by the DCP-based [13,14] method.

2) We calculate the color fluctuation and attenuation to estimate the scene depth. The deeper the scene depth, the larger the color attenuation. Previous work [12,15,16] suggested that the red channel attenuates strongly with

increasing depth, but this leads to failure in some specific scenes. Our method not only estimates depth by color channels but also considers light scattering. Using an accurate depth map to yield a computed transmission map improves the contrast and preserves more edge detail.

3) We report the qualitative and quantitative evaluation of our method and existing methods in natural underwater scenes. The performance of contrast enhancement and removal of color distortion is demonstrated by our method outperforms existing state-of-the-art methods.

The remainder of the paper is structured as follows. The methods for current image processing are discussed in Sect. 2. The proposed approach is described in Sect. 3. Section 4 presents experimental findings, while Sect. 5 presents conclusions.

2 Related Work

underwater image enhancement methods include the Model-free method, the Model-based method, and the Deep learning-based method.

2.1 Model-Free Method

Color correction and contrast improvement are typically possible using underwater image enhancement technologies based on the non-physical model by changing pixel values. The novel method to improve underwater image quality was proposed by Zhuang et al. [17]. Bayesian retinex underwater image enhancement is proposed to improve visual effect (BRUIE). To reduce the influence of noise, Huang et al. [18] created relative global histogram stretching. However, the color correction approach is frequently insufficient to repair it (RGHS). Fu et al. [19] developed a mean and mean square error-based enhancement (RBE) approach for histogram equalization. However, when restoring underwater images, techniques based on statistical methods often lead to over-enhancement or artifacts and noise. Underwater image enhancement methods based on non-physical models do not consider the scattering and attenuation of light, but directly adjust the pixels, usually resulting in excessive enhancement.

2.2 Model-Based Method

To remove fog in a single degraded image, Peng et al. [14] proposed the generalization of the dark channel prior (GDCP). In [16], the underwater light attenuation prior (ULAP) is used to estimate the scene's depth map and background light. Lee et al. [20] introduced an image-adaptive weighting factor to estimate the transmission map. Recently, a robust model for background light estimation and a new underwater dark channel prior was used to address the severe quality degradation and color distortion of underwater images [16]. Zhou et al. [21] suggested quadratic guided filtering into image restoration to obtain underwater images with the most realistic and natural appearance. Li et al. [3] proposed an underwater image restoration method based on blue-green channel dehazing and red channel correction (GBDRC). Due to the separate enhancement effect of the red channel, it usually leads to the over-saturation of red in the restoration results. This work presents an efficient program for underwater restoration. Our method effectively solves the underexposure of the restoration result caused by the large estimated value of the BL when the bright pixels are in the foreground [13, 22, 23]. Most restoration methods obtain transmission maps by using twice the minimum filter [13, 22, 23], which will cause the restoration result details to disappear. We establish the depth map of the input image by computing color fluctuation and attenuation. The previous methods [12, 15, 16] considered that the red value decreases with increasing depth. However, this prior approach fails in the special case. The proposed method considers the influence of light scattering. Transmission maps obtained by accurate depth maps tend to retain more details, have higher contrast, and have better visual effects.

2.3 Deep Learning-Based Method

With the development of science and technology, the application of deep learning in underwater image enhancement tasks is more and more common. The restored scene using the depth learning method of Water-net [24] is dark, and the contrast has not been significantly improved. Li et al. [25] designed a network structure supported by underwater scene priors that offer good adaptability for various underwater scenarios (UWCNN). Li et al. [26] trained a multi-color spatial embedding network driven by media transmission. The current depth learning method network model generalization ability is limited, and can not be applied to a variety of underwater scenes, so there are still shortcomings in enhancing the ability.

3 Proposed Method

This paper proposed a robust underwater image restoration method, the overall flow chart is displayed in Fig. 2. First, we design a background light estimation model that relies on prior features for depth, chromatic aberration, hue, and information entropy. Next, the depth map of the input image is roughly computed based on color fluctuation and attenuation. The transmission map obtained from the accurate depth map can retain more details of the image. The restored results improve the contrast while preserving the more valuable details. Ours qualitatively and quantitatively performs better than the existing methods, and the performance of contrast enhancement and color distortion removal is demonstrated by our method outperforming existing state-of-the-art methods.

3.1 Background Light Estimation

We usually use flat pixels away from the camera as background light estimates, hence estimating the background light (BL) involves considering depth information. In addition, the background light region is blurred [12] and usually has less

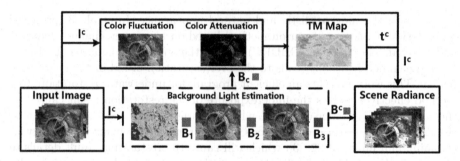

Fig. 2. Overview of the proposed method. We adjust the input color according to the background light through three background light candidates. At the same time, we estimate the depth map of the input image by calculating color fluctuations and attenuation. (Color figure online)

texture detail. The information entropy value is adopted to solve this problem, and the smaller value suggests that there is less information. In underwater conditions, red light has a longer wavelength, the blue and green light have shorter wavelengths. The red light is more attenuated than the blue and green light. The greater the chroma, the more depth in the field. In addition, we judge the dominant color of the degraded image and utilize the background light estimation to remove the influence of white objects or bright pixel areas in the foreground with higher robustness. First, the difference between light and dark channels can be used to estimate the depth. The greater the depth of the scene, the greater the difference in the intensity of light of different colors. If you make a difference between the light and dark channels, you can get the intensity difference of light of different colors. The farther the scene is from the camera, the greater the difference between light and dark channels. The bright channel I_{bright} and the dark channel I_{dark} are written as:

$$I_{bright}\left(\mathrm{x}\right) = \max_{y\in\Omega(x)}\left(\max_{c\in\{r,g,b\}} I_c\left(y\right)\right) \tag{1}$$

$$I_{bright}\left(\mathrm{x}\right) = \min_{y\in\Omega(x)}\left(\min_{c\in\{r,g,b\}} I_c\left(y\right)\right) \tag{2}$$

where $I_c\left(y\right)$ means the raw image and $\Omega\left(x\right)$ represent the local area of the input image where the pixel x is located. I_{bright} and I_{dark} are used in the estimation of the depth I_{depth}:

$$I_{depth}\left(\mathrm{x}\right) = I_{bright}\left(\mathrm{x}\right) - I_{dark}\left(\mathrm{x}\right) \tag{3}$$

In addition, using the histogram stretching method to increase the contrast of the image:

$$I_{depth_{hs}}\left(\mathrm{x}\right) = \frac{I_{depth}\left(\mathrm{x}\right) - \min\left(I_{depth}\left(\mathrm{x}\right)\right)}{\max\left(I_{depth}\left(\mathrm{x}\right)\right) - \min\left(I_{depth}\left(\mathrm{x}\right)\right)} \tag{4}$$

Calculated from the top 0.1% of the brightest pixels, the background light candidate value B_1 can be expressed as:

$$B_1 = \frac{1}{\left|P^{0.1\%}_{I_{\text{depth}_{\text{hs}}}}\right|} I^c \left(\underset{x \in P^{0.1\%}}{\arg\max} \sum_{c \in \{r,g,b\}} I_{\text{depth}_{\text{hs}}}(\mathbf{x}) \right) \tag{5}$$

where $P^{0.1\%}_{I_{\text{depth}_{\text{hs}}}}$ represents the top 0.1% of the brightest pixels. The second candidate for the background light is based on the hue considered the chromatic aberration, we define the dominant hue of the raw image:

$$I^B_{\text{mean}} > I^G_{\text{mean}} \; Bluish\,tone \tag{6}$$

$$I^B_{\text{mean}} \leq I^G_{\text{mean}} \; Greenish\,tone \tag{7}$$

where I^B_{mean} and I^G_{mean} are the average of the blue and green channel's intensity of the degraded images. The largest difference between blue/green and red channels is used as the second candidate value of the background light. I represents the original image.

$$B_2 = I \left[\max \left(I^B(x) - I^R(x) \right) \right] \; Bluish\,tone \tag{8}$$

$$B_2 = I \left[\max \left(I^G(x) - I^R(x) \right) \right] \; Greenish\,tone \tag{9}$$

The third candidate value of the background light has relied on information entropy. After the image has been divided into quadrants, it is estimated by calculating the local entropy in each image patch. Information entropy is described as follows:

$$E(i) = \sum_{i=0}^{N} P_y(i) \log_2 \left(P_y(i) \right) \tag{10}$$

where $P_y(i)$ represent the the ith pixel of the local patch. N is the maximum of the pixel values. The background light is selected from a smooth area at infinity, and the smooth area corresponds to lower information entropy. The lower information entropy area was obtained after looping once using the quadtree algorithm:

$$B_3 = \frac{1}{m \times n} \sum_{x \in \Omega(u)} C(x) \tag{11}$$

where $\Omega(u)$ represents the area with the minimum information entropy and $m \times n$ represents the total number of pixels in the area with the largest degree of smoothness.

$$B_{\max} = \max(B_1, B_2, B_3) \tag{12}$$

$$B_{\min} = \min(B_1, B_2, B_3) \tag{13}$$

where $B_{\max}$, $B_{\min}$ represent maximum and minimum value of B_1,B_2,B_3, respectively. We propose a background light estimation model:

$$a = \frac{|I > 0.5|}{I_{height} * I_{width}} \tag{14}$$

$$T(a, \xi) = \frac{1}{1 + e^{u(a-\xi)}} \tag{15}$$

$$\eta = T(a, \xi) \tag{16}$$

$$B = \eta * B_{\max} + (1 - \eta) * B_{\min} \tag{17}$$

where $I_{height} * I_{width}$ represents the total number of pixels in the input image, $|I > 0.5|$ means the number of bright pixels, a means the percentage of bright pixels in the input image. The value of ξ is 0.2, which is used to determine the brightness of the image. The empirical values of u are set to -32. Take the example of an image captured in a well-lit scene. When $a > \xi$, the degraded image was captured in a well-lit environment, and the obtained value of the background light is brighter, so a larger weight η is applied to $B_{\max}$. Figure 3 and Fig. 4 display the background light estimation, the restoration results, RGB color map of the proposed method based on B and each background light candidate B_1, B_2, B_3, we can observe that by adopting our method as the background light, the results obtained have the best visual effect and color distribution.

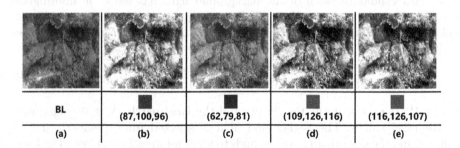

Fig. 3. Recovery results of different BL estimations. (a) The input image, (b)–(d) are the recovered images acquired by separately B_1, B_2, B_3, (e) our result.

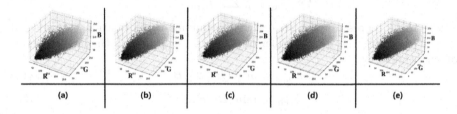

Fig. 4. The RGB space map of different BL estimations. (a) The input image, (b)–(d) are the RGB space maps acquired by separately B_1, B_2, B_3, (e) our result.

3.2 Depth Estimation

For depth map estimation, it is also characterized by smoothness and stability in large depth-of-field regions. The larger the depth of field, the more stable pixel in the sub-region. Brightness is brighter and saturation is susceptible to rapid decrease when there are many suspended particles. The difference between brightness and saturation (color degradation) is positively correlated with depth. First, we use color fluctuation to estimate the depth. The color fluctuation is written as follows:

$$S = k\sqrt{\frac{(r-m)^2 + (g-m)^2 + (b-m)^2}{3}}, m = \frac{r+g+b}{3} \qquad (18)$$

where m represents the average value of the three channels of a single pixel, and k is the scale coefficient, which is taken as 30 here. In areas with higher depth of field, more stable pixels and fewer color fluctuations. Our first depth map is estimated to be as follows:

$$H_s(T) = \frac{T - \min(T)}{\max(T) - \min(T)} \qquad (19)$$

$$d_{D_1} = 1 - H_s(S) \qquad (20)$$

where T is a vector. Our second depth map relies on the degree of color attenuation [27], the saturation of the image is gradually reduced by the haze, while the brightness will increase. The difference between saturation and brightness is positively related to the depth of the scene.

$$C(x) = I^v(x) - I^s(x) \qquad (21)$$

$$I^v(x) = \max_{c \in \{r,g,b\}} I^c(x) \qquad (22)$$

$$I^s(x) = \left(\max_{c \in \{r,g,b\}} I^c(x) - \min_{c \in \{r,g,b\}} I^c(x)\right) / \max_{c \in \{r,g,b\}} I^c(x) \qquad (23)$$

where $I^v(x)$ and $I^s(x)$ represent the brightness and saturation of the HSV space. where $C(x)$ used for the estimation of the depth map:

$$d_{D_2} = H_s(C) \qquad (24)$$

An estimation method for depth is proposed:

$$d(x) = \mu_2 * d_{D_2} + \mu_1 * d_{D_1} \qquad (25)$$

$$T(a, \xi) = \frac{1}{1 + e^{u(a-\xi)}} \qquad (26)$$

$$\mu_1 = T(\text{avg}(B^c), 0.5) \qquad (27)$$

$$\mu_2 = T(\text{avg}(I^r), 0.1) \qquad (28)$$

In Eq. 27 and 28, the two parameters μ_1, μ_2 measure the brightness of the image and the intensity of the red channel respectively. When the underwater image scene is dark, the color fluctuation is not obvious, so d_1 cannot represent the change of depth, and a small weight μ_1 is applied to d_1 at this time. When there is a certain red component in the underwater image since the background light occupies more of the observed intensity of the scene points farther from the camera, the far scene points may still have larger values in the red channel, so the depth map d_2 applies a larger weight μ_2. As can be seen from Fig. 5, the depth map obtained by our method most accurately expresses the depth information of underwater images and successfully separates the foreground and background.

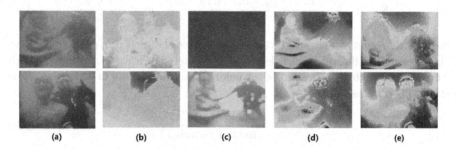

Fig. 5. Depth map comparison test. (a) Input image, (b)-(d) are the depth maps acquired by separately [14–16], (e) our result. (Color figure online)

The distance between the camera and the nearest scene point can be expressed as:

$$d_0 = 1 - \max_{x,c \in \{r,g,b\}} \frac{\max |B_c - I^c(x)|}{\max (B^k, 1 - B^k)} \tag{29}$$

The final depth map of the underwater image is as follows:

$$d_{f(x)} = D \times (d_0 + d(x)) \tag{30}$$

where the constant D is utilized to translate relative distances into real distances. The following is an estimated transmission map for the red channel:

$$t^r(x) = e^{-\beta^r d_{f(x)}} \tag{31}$$

where β^r is the red channel attenuation coefficient, $\beta^r \in \left[\frac{1}{8}, \frac{1}{5}\right]$ [28]. In [29], the connection between both the attenuation coefficients of various color channels is demonstrated using the special optical characteristics of water as follows:

$$\frac{\beta^k}{\beta^r} = \frac{B^r (m\lambda^k + i)}{B^k (m\lambda^r + i)}, k \in \{g, b\} \tag{32}$$

where m = −0.00113, i = 1.62517, and λ is the wavelength of the three color channels. The transmission map of the additional blue and green channels can be written as follows:

$$t^g\left(x\right) = t_f^r(x)^{\frac{\beta^g}{\beta^r}} \tag{33}$$

$$t^b\left(x\right) = t_f^r(x)^{\frac{\beta^b}{\beta^r}} \tag{34}$$

Figure 6 shows a comparative experiment of the transmission maps estimated by the four restoration models. The transmission map obtained by dark channel prior (DCP) [13] is difficult to distinguish foreground from background. The overall transmission of the restoration method is based on image blurriness and light absorption (IBLA) [12], and the proposed method is more accurate. The transmission map obtained by GDCP [14] is smaller due to the larger distance between the camera and objects in the foreground estimated by GDCP. Our method estimates the transmission map to correctly express scene depth while retaining more valuable details.

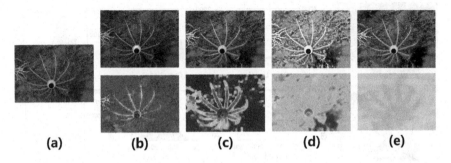

(a)   **(b)**   **(c)**   **(d)**   **(e)**

Fig. 6. Transformation maps comparison tests. (a) Input image, (b) DCP [13], (c) IBLA [12], (d) GDCP [14], (e) Our method.

The following is the final restoration equation:

$$J^c\left(x\right) = \frac{I^c\left(x\right) - B^c\left(x\right)}{\min\left(\max\left(t^c\left(x\right), 0.05\right), 0.95\right)} + B^c, c \in \{r, g, b\} \tag{35}$$

where the adjusted image is shown by $J^c\left(x\right)$. The white balance method is used in the suggested color correction and is based on the ideal gain factor [30].

4   Experiments and Results

The suggested method enhances the regional features of the image, for instance, the texture features of the sculptures and plates, in the red-marked area of Fig. 7. Figure 8 (a) displays the before-and-after comparison diagram. High-intensity pixels are corrected for the red and green channels (as shown in Fig. 8), while the green channel's pixel intensity values are decreased. As a result, the color sense of the recovered input images is substantially improved. On different underwater images from the UIEB dataset [24], we compare various underwater image processing methods and present the findings. These approaches consist of the following:These methods include UDCP [22], RBE [19], GBDRC [3], Water-net [24], ULAP [16], UWCNN [25].

Fig. 7. Local details comparison test. (a) Input image, (b) Our results. (Color figure online)

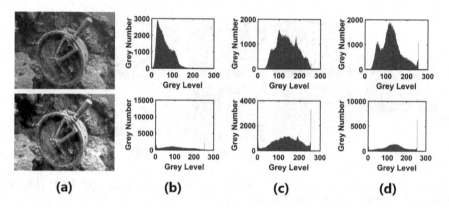

Fig. 8. (a) Original image and the restored image. Comparison of histograms of different channels restoration: (b) R channel, (c) G channel, (d) B channel. (Color figure online)

4.1 Qualitative Comparison

As displayed in Fig. 9(b), due to the overcompensation of red light, the restoration result of UDCP [22] is reddish. The restored images of RBE successfully reduces color cast and improves contrast, but it also generates a significant amount of black artifacts since it modifies the pixels without taking into account the causes of the deterioration. Low contrast can be seen in Fig. 9(e) and Fig. 9 (g) of the results produced by Water-net and UWCNN. Our method successfully raises the contrast of the image, as seen in Fig. 9(h). Figure 9(d) presents the underwater image restoration results of the GBDRC [3] method. The restored images of GBDRC [3] introduce a more severe color shift. Due to the limited enhancement effect of the red channel, it usually leads to over-saturation of red in the restoration results. ULAP method fails to remove color distortion in green-hued underwater scenes. It is not as good as the proposed method in terms of contrast and color saturation.

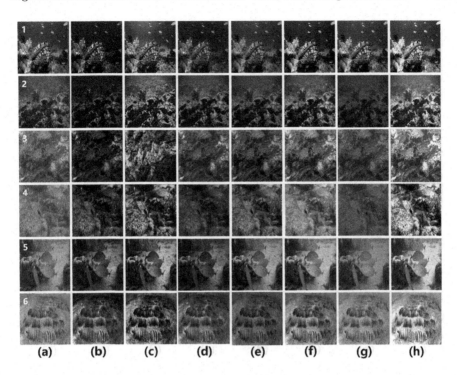

Fig. 9. Qualitative comparison of image enhancement between proposed and state-of-the-art methods. (a) Original image, (b) UDCP [22], (c) RBE [19], (d) GBDRC [3], (e) Water-net [24], (f) ULAP [16], (g) UWCNN [25], (h) Our method. (Color figure online)

Additionally, in order to more fairly assess the effectiveness and dependability of the method, we compare the underwater images of more scenes in the UIEB dataset based on UDCP [22], RBE [19], GBDRC [3], Water-net [24], ULAP [16], UWCNN [25] and the proposed method in Fig. 10. The methods vary in their ability to enhance the clarity and contrast of underwater photos, but the restoration results (Fig. 10(b) and Fig. 10(d)) of UDCP and GBDRC did not successfully eliminate the color deviation. Water-Net has a superior restoration impact and preserves more features, as demonstrated in Fig. 10(e), however, there is still some discrepancy with the restoration results of this paper. Compared to Water-Net, which creates underwater images with poor lighting, this algorithm's color and contrast are richer and more vivid. As shown in Fig. 10(c), RBE gives the recovery results of black artifacts. The clarity and color saturation of the results obtained by the ULAP method is not comparable to our method. In conclusion, it can be seen from the comparison in various environments that the restoration results of the algorithm in this paper not only have the highest contrast and color saturation but also successfully preserve edge details and alter the distortions of the initial image to get better visual performance.

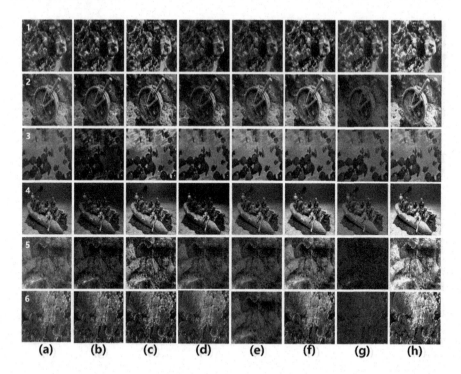

Fig. 10. Qualitative comparison of image enhancement between proposed and state-of-the-art methods. (a) Original image, (b) UDCP [22], (c) RBE [19], (d) GBDRC [3], (e) Water-net [24], (f) ULAP [16], (g) UWCNN [25], (h) Our method. (Color figure online)

4.2 Quantitative Evaluation

In this paper, we use the following metrics to evaluate the quality of underwater images: underwater image quality assessment metrics UCIQE [31], AG, EI, and UIQM [32]. Table 1 shows the evaluation metrics results obtained after the complete UIEB dataset [24] is processed by our method. Four metrics of our method rank in the top three among all methods, especially UCIQE, AG, and EI rank first. The images from the UIEB [24] dataset demonstrate our supremacy.

The findings show that the UCIQE [31], UIQM [32], AG, and EI of the method are more robust than the other approaches, indicating that our method can effectively improve the color saturation and texture details of images. RBE does not consider the degradation of underwater images, resulting in artifacts and noise in the restoration results. The image effect can be slightly reduced by using the objective measurements of GBDRC, but the color distortion still cannot be precisely corrected. Water-net, a deep learning-based solution, performs badly. The method suggested in this paper has superior contrast. The restoration results of UWCNN show that the method will lead to more serious color casts in underwater images, and the results of UDCP are over-saturated with blue and

Table 1. Comparison of the average metrics of UIEB images

	UDCP	RBE	GBDRC	Water-net	ULAP	UWCNN	Ours
UCIQE	0.5815	0.6023	0.5926	0.5839	0.6053	0.4765	**0.6215**
AG	5.1844	6.8699	4.6630	3.0843	6.0374	3.0843	**7.3144**
UIQM	**1.6459**	1.4073	1.4285	1.3647	1.4100	1.1047	1.4121
EI	51.066	70.765	45.963	57.864	59.414	30.308	**72.173**

green because only blue and green channels are considered in the restoration. Compared to previous methods, the restoration images produced by our solution often have greater visual quality and a better balance between the detail texture richness, color fidelity, and visual visibility of an image. The evaluation results on different metrics also provide convincing for the robustness and effectiveness of our method in recovering images with various scenes.

5 Conclusion

This research proposes an approach for underwater image restoration based on color floating and light attenuation. First, we provide a background light (BL) estimation model that takes into account hue, depth, entropy and chromatic aberration. Color casts in underwater images can be successfully removed by using accurate background lighting. Then, using the depth map to compute a new red channel transmission map (TM) estimationwe successfully increase image contrast while maintaining detailed information. In-depth analyses show the success of the background light estimating technique, the accuracy of the depth map method estimation, and the superiority of our method.

References

1. Li, C., Guo, J., Guo, C.: Emerging from water: underwater image color correction based on weakly supervised color transfer. IEEE Signal Process. Lett. **25**(3), 323–327 (2018)
2. Lin, Y., Zhou, J., Ren, W., Zhang, W.: Autonomous underwater robot for underwater image enhancement via multi-scale deformable convolution network with attention mechanism. Comput. Electron. Agric. **191**, 106497 (2021)
3. Li, C., Quo, J., Pang, Y., Chen, S., Jian, W.: Single underwater image restoration by blue-green channels dehazing and red channel correction. In: 2016 IEEE International Conference on Acoustics, Speech and Signal Processing (ICASSP) (2016)
4. Zhou, J., Yang, T., Ren, W., Zhang, D., Zhang, W.: Underwater image restoration via depth map and illumination estimation based on single image. Opt. Express. **29**(19), 29864–29886 (2021)
5. Zhou, J.C., Zhang, D.H., Zhang, W.S.: Classical and state-of-the-art approaches for underwater image defogging: a comprehensive survey. Front. Inform. Technol. Electr. Eng. **21**(12), 1745–1769 (2020)

6. Liu, R., Jiang, Z., Yang, S., Fan, X.: Twin adversarial contrastive learning for underwater image enhancement and beyond. IEEE Trans. Image Process. **31**, 4922–4936 (2022)

7. Zhou, J., Zhang, D., Ren, W., Zhang, W.: Auto color correction of underwater images utilizing depth information. IEEE Geosci. Remote Sens. Lett. **19**, 1–5 (2022)

8. Zhou, J., Yang, T., Chu, W., Zhang, W.: Underwater image restoration via backscatter pixel prior and color compensation. Eng. Appl. Artif. Intell. **111**, 104785 (2022)

9. Anwar, S., Li, C.: Diving deeper into underwater enhancement: a survey. Signal Process. Image Commun. **89**, 115978 (2019)

10. Zhuang, P., Wu, J., Porikli, F., Li, C.: Underwater image enhancement with hyper-Laplacian reflectance priors. IEEE Trans. Image Process. **31**, 5442–5455 (2022)

11. Jiang, Z., Li, Z., Yang, S., Fan, X., Liu, R.: Target oriented perceptual adversarial fusion network for underwater image enhancement. IEEE Trans. Circuits Syst. Video Technol. **32**, 6584-6589 (2022)

12. Peng, Y.T., Cosman, P.C.: Underwater image restoration based on image blurriness and light absorption. IEEE Trans. Image Process. **26**(4), 1579–1594 (2017)

13. He, K., Sun, J., Tang, X.: Single image haze removal using dark channel prior. IEEE Trans. Pattern Anal. Mach. Intell. **33**(12), 2341–2353 (2011)

14. Peng, Y., Cao, K., Cosman, P.C.: Generalization of the dark channel prior for single image restoration. IEEE Trans. Image Process. **27**(6), 2856–2868 (2018)

15. Nicholas, C.B., Anush, M., Eustice, R.M.: Initial results in underwater single image dehazing. In: Washington State Conference and Trade Center (WSCTC) (2010)

16. Song, W., Wang, Y., Huang, D., Tjondronegoro, D.: A rapid scene depth estimation model based on underwater light attenuation prior for underwater image restoration. In: Advances in Multimedia Information Processing (2018)

17. Zhuang, P., Li, C., Wu, J.: Bayesian Retinex underwater image enhancement. Eng. Appl. Artif. Intell. **101**(1), 104171 (2021)

18. Huang, D., Wang, Y., Song, W., Sequeira, J., Mavromatis, S.: Shallow-water image enhancement using relative global histogram stretching based on adaptive parameter acquisition. In: International Conference on Multimedia Modeling (2018)

19. Fu, X., Zhuang, P., Yue, H., Liao, Y., Zhang, X.P., Ding, X.: A Retinex-based enhancing approach for single underwater image. In: 2014 IEEE International Conference on Image Processing (ICIP) (2015)

20. Lee, H.S., Sang, W.M., Eom, I.K.: Underwater image enhancement using successive color correction and superpixel dark channel prior. Symmetry **12**(8), 1220 (2020)

21. Zhou, J., Liu, Z., Zhang, W., Zhang, D., Zhang, W.: Underwater image restoration based on secondary guided transmission map. Multim. Tools Appl. **80**(5), 7771–7788 (2021)

22. Drews, J.P., Nascimento, E., Moraes, F., Botelho, S., Campos, M.: Transmission estimation in underwater single images. In: IEEE International Conference on Computer Vision Workshops (2013)

23. Galdran, A., Pardo, D., Picón, A., Alvarez-Gila, A.: Automatic red-channel underwater image restoration. J. Vis. Commun. Image Represent. **26**, 132–145 (2015)

24. Li, C.: An underwater image enhancement benchmark dataset and beyond. IEEE Trans. Image Process. **29**, 4376–4389 (2020)

25. Li, C., Anwar, S.: Underwater scene prior inspired deep underwater image and video enhancement. Pattern Recogn. **98**(1), 107038 (2019)

26. Li, C., Anwar, S., Hou, J., Cong, R., Ren, W.: Underwater image enhancement via medium transmission-guided multi-color space embedding. IEEE Trans. Image Process. **30**, 4985–5000 (2021)

27. Zhu, Q., Mai, J., Shao, L.: A fast single image haze removal algorithm using color attenuation prior. IEEE Trans. Image Process. **24**(11), 3522–3533 (2015)

28. Chiang, J.Y., Chen, Y.C.: Underwater image enhancement by wavelength compensation and dehazing. In: IEEE Trans. Image Process.**21**(4), 1756–1769 (2012)

29. Zhao, X., Jin, T., Qu, S.: Deriving inherent optical properties from background color and underwater image enhancement. Ocean Eng. **94**, 163–172 (2015)

30. Song, W., Wang, Y., Huang, D., Liotta, A., Perra, C.: Enhancement of underwater images with statistical model of background light and optimization of transmission map. IEEE Trans. Broadcast. **66**(1), 153–169 (2020)

31. Miao, Y.: An underwater color image quality evaluation metric. IEEE Trans. Image Process. **24**(12), 6062–6071 (2015)

32. Panetta, K., Gao, C., Agaian, S.: Human-visual-system-inspired underwater image quality measures. IEEE J. Oceanic Eng. **41**(3), 541–551 (2016)

Learning to Predict Decomposed Dynamic Filters for Single Image Motion Deblurring

Zhiqiang Hu[1(✉)] and Tao Yu[2]

[1] Yokohama, Japan
zhiqianghu2021@gmail.com
[2] Tokyo Institute of Technology, Tokyo, Japan
yutao@mobile.ee.titech.ac.jp

Abstract. This paper tackles the large motion variation problem in the single image dynamic scene deblurring task. Although fully convolutional multi-scale-based designs have recently advanced the state-of-the-art in single image motion deblurring. However, these approaches usually utilize vanilla convolution filters, which are not adapted to each spatial position. Consequently, it is hard to handle large motion blur variations at the pixel level. In this work, we propose Decomposed Dynamic Filters (DDF), a highly effective plug-and-play adaptive operator, to fulfill the goal of handling large motion blur variations across different spatial locations. In contrast to conventional dynamic convolution-based methods, which only predict either weight or offsets of the filter from the local feature at run time, in our work, both the offsets and weight are adaptively predicted from multi-scale local regions. The proposed operator comprises two components: 1) the offsets estimation module and 2) the pixel-specific filter weight generator. We incorporate the DDF into a lightweight encoder-decoder-based deblurring architecture to verify the performance gain. Extensive experiments conducted on the GoPro, HIDE, Real Blur, SIDD, and DND datasets demonstrate that the proposed method offers significant improvements over the state-of-the-art in accuracy as well as generalization capability. Code is available at: https://github.com/ZHIQIANGHU2021/DecomposedDynamicFilters.

1 Introduction

Dynamic scene motion deblurring aims to rehabilitate an original sharp image from a blurry image caused by camera shakes, moving objects, or low shutter speeds. Blur artifacts significantly degrade the quality of captured images, which is harmful to many high-level vision applications, *e.g.*, face recognition systems, surveillance, and autonomous driving systems. Therefore, the accurate and efficient technique of eliminating blurring artifacts and recovering sharp images is

---

Z. Hu—Independent Researcher.

Supplementary Information The online version contains supplementary material available at https://doi.org/10.1007/978-3-031-26313-2_24.

L. Wang et al. (Eds.): ACCV 2022, LNCS 13843, pp. 390–408, 2023.
https://doi.org/10.1007/978-3-031-26313-2_24

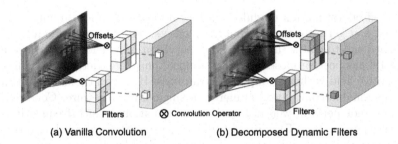

Fig. 1. The vanilla convolution and the proposed DDF. As for DDF, both the offsets and filter weight are adaptively predicted from multi-scale local regions. The red squares are the sampling positions and different colors of cubes indicate the spatially-varying filters of DDF. (Color figure online)

highly desired. To handle the blind motion deblurring problem, many conventional approaches attempt to estimate the blur kernel via some hand-crafted priors [1–7]. However, estimating a satisfactory blur kernel remains a challenging computer vision problem. Such hand-crafted priors can hardly generalize well to complex real-world examples, which results in degraded performance. To address these challenges, many deep learning-based approaches [8–16] try to utilize the neural network to deblur images in an end-to-end manner and significantly improve the performance. In particular, among the architectures, the coarse-to-fine scheme has been widely employed to restore the blurred image at either multiple scales (MSs) [8–10,12] or multiple patch (MPs) levels [11,13–16]. However, these methods usually employ a vanilla convolution filter as the base module, which suffers from two main issues in motion deburring tasks:

1) It is difficult to handle large variations in motion magnitude. More specifically, the identical geometric shape or receptive fields of vanilla convolution filters are applied to different pixels of an image. However, the magnitude of motion blur appears diversely in different regions (*e.g.,* moving vehicle pixels vs. sky). To tackle this problem, extremely deep networks and multi-scale architectures have been exploited to enhance the generalization ability to solve the large variance of motion problems. Consequently, this kind of approach suffers from ultra-heavy computational complexity and is hard to be deployed on lightweight devices, *e.g.,* smartphones and self-driving cars.
2) The weights of the vanilla convolution filters are also content-agnostic as shown in Fig. 1(a), regardless of the texture information of the local region. A spatially shared filter could be sub-optimal for the task of extracting feature across all pixels. In addition, once the network has been trained, the identical filters are utilized across different images, leading to ineffective feature extraction results.

To tackle the problems mentioned above, in this work, we focus on the design of efficient and adaptive filtering modules, dubbed as Decomposed Dynamic Filter (DDF), which is illustrated in Fig. 1(b). DDF decouples a conventional convolution filter into offsets and weights adaptive filters. The proposed DDF consists of two major components:

1) The offsets estimation module, which could learn from local multi-scale features, and generate the optimal filter offsets. The proposed module can be trained end-to-end without explicit supervision. The deformable convolution [17,18] has been proposed to adapt to local image geometry and enlarge the receptive field without sampling extra pixels. However, the offsets estimator of deformable convolution is merely a single-layer structure. Consequently, it does not perform well in large motion situations, which frequently occur in dynamic scenes. To address this issue, we propose a novel adaptive offsets estimation module, that can generate pixel-level representative offsets across the multi-scale spatial space. The proposed offsets estimator naturally solves the large motion problem by capturing long-range dependencies from multi-scale feature regions.

2) The pixel-specific filter weight generator. The weight of DDF is dynamically reconstructed by a linear combination of filter basis with assembling coefficients. Both the filter basis and the assembling coefficients are self-adaptively learned from multi-scale local regions by lightweight sub-networks. In contrast to the dynamic filter-based method [19,20], which explicitly predicts all pixel-specific filter weights from feature maps, our method achieves a better tradeoff between performance and memory usage. Finally, the learned weight and offsets are combined as a dynamic filter to extract the adaptive feature for the motion deblurring task. Deploying the proposed DDF for the motion deblurring network enables us to design a compact structure for the network, which a conventional network [9,11,13] cannot achieve without stacking a large number of subnet blocks. Overall, our contributions can be summarized as follows:

   - We proposed a novel adaptive operator module DDF, which is capable of learning the sampling positions and filter weights at the same time. Adaptively solve the motion variation problem. Moreover, the dynamic feature of DDF enables us to design an effective network structure without sacrificing accuracy.
   - We conducted extensive ablation evaluations on multiple benchmarks and confirmed that the spatial adaptability of DDF could empower various vanilla networks *e.g.,* U-Net [21], and achieve state-of-the-art performance.
   - To consolidate the generalization capability of DDF, and verify its effectiveness as a plug-and-play adaptive operator, we also plug it onto baseline networks for the real image noise removal task, which significantly improves the performance.

2   Related Works

2.1   Single-Scale Deep Image Deblurring

The **single-scale** approaches [22–24] aim to recover blurred images in an end-to-end manner. For instance, DeblurGAN [22], the adversarial learning algorithm, has been adopted with multiple residual blocks to restore the sharp image. DeblurGAN-v2 [23] advanced the DeblurGAN [22] by employing a much deeper architecture with an encoder-decoder architecture. However, the GAN-based methods often introduce unexpected artifacts into the image and make it hard to handle large motion situations. Yuan *et al.* [24] utilized optical flow information to guide deformable convolutions [18] offsets generation process. However, optical flow information is not always available for real-world applications.

2.2 Multi-scale, Multi-patch-Based Approaches

Multi-scale approaches have been verified to be an effective direction in image restoration scenarios. The pioneering work, Nah *et al.* [8] proposed a multi-scale deblurring network, which initiates from a coarse scale and then progressively deblurs the image at a finer scale. Tao *et al.* [9] proposed SRN, a scale-recurrent network responsible for aggregating features from different scales. The motion information from the previous coarser scale can be utilized for the following processing. Cho *et al.* [25] proposed MIMO-UNet, which employs a multi-scale U-Net structure to deblur the image in a coarse-to-fine strategy. The approach in [10] proposed a sharing method that takes a different level of blurs in each stage into consideration. Zhang *et al.* [11] introduced a multi-patch hierarchical scheme (DMPHN) to keep spatial resolution without any image down-sampling operation. The MPRNet [13] combines the **multi-patch** hierarchical structure with a global attention mechanism to further advance the state-of-the-art.

However, these methods usually adopt vanilla convolution kernels and consist of multiple large subnetworks, which lead to a long process time. Recently, **vision transformer (ViT)** with the ability of long-range dependency modeling, has shown promising performance in image restoration tasks [26–28]. However, as suggested in [29], the execution time of SwinIR [28] is approximately 1.99s on GoPro dataset, which is unacceptable for real-time applications. In contrast, we attempt to empower the lightweight network with pixel-adaptive ability, resulting in a lighter network for real-world applications.

2.3 Dynamic Filters

Image level dynamic filters predict filter weight based on input features at the image level. In particular, DyNet [30], DynamicConv [31], and CondConv [32] predict coefficients to combine several expert filters by employing attention mechanisms. However, the dynamic weights are generated at the image scale, making it hard to handle the motion deblur problem, which appears at pixel-level.

Pixel level dynamic filters [17–20,33–42] further extend the adaptiveness to the spatial dimension by using a per-pixel dynamic filter. The filter weights are dynamically predicted based on the input features. Deformable convolutions [17, 18] attempt to learn an offsets map at position level, to adapt to the geometric variations, while fixing the weight in kernels. Su *et al.* [19] proposed to adaptively generate pixel-specific [20] filters on an input image. CARAFE [33,34] proposed an adaptive operator for feature map upsampling, where an auxiliary branch is

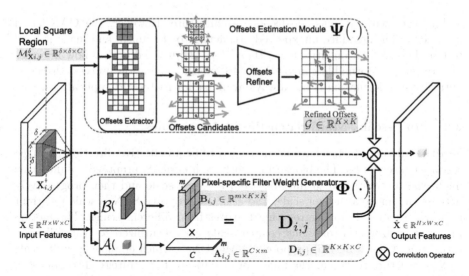

Fig. 2. The learning framework of DDF, which consists of two components: 1) The offsets estimator and 2) the pixel-specific filter weight generator.

utilized to predict a 2D filter at each pixel. However, these channel-wise shared filters are hard to capture cross-channel information leading to the sub-optimal result. Furthermore, various dynamic filter-based methods have been applied to facilitate computer vision tasks, such as video frame interpolation [35], video denoising [36], super-resolution [37,38], semantic segmentation [39,40], and point cloud segmentation [41,42].

However, the abovementioned methods directly predict all the parameters of dynamic filters, which require a large amount of memory for restoring the gradient in the backpropagation process. In contrast, our method learns to predict the dynamic pixel-adaptive convolution kernels in a memory-efficient manner and also inherits merits of pixel adaptive paradigm, detailed comparison results are in Sect. 3.4.

3   Our Approach

3.1   Overview

The success of Dynamic Convs [17–20,33,34] suggests that adaptively predicting the weight of filters at run-time improves the accuracy. However, it may lack the ability to dynamically adapt to the geometric variations and local image patch textures, at the same time. To this end, we propose DDF, such an operator enjoys benefits from modeling both geometric variations and local textures. The learning framework of DDF is shown in Fig. 2. In this section, we first revisit the general concept of dynamic convolutions, and then we introduce the architecture of the proposed DDF in detail.

3.2   Decomposed Dynamic Filters

We initiate from introducing the vanilla convolutions to make the definition of the proposed DDF. Let $\mathbf{X} \in \mathbb{R}^{H \times W \times C}$ denote the input feature map, where H, W, C represent its height, width, and channel numbers, respectively. $\mathbf{X}_{i,j} \in \mathbb{R}^C$ is the feature vector inside $\mathbf{X}$ at position i-th row and the j-th column. We also use $\mathcal{M}^{\delta}_{\mathbf{X}_{i,j}} \in \mathbb{R}^{\delta \times \delta \times C}$ represents the size-δ square region centered at i, j inside cube tensor $\mathbf{X}$. Hence, the conventional vanilla convolution can be expressed as

$$\mathbf{X}'_{i,j} = \mathcal{F}\left(\mathcal{M}^{\delta}_{\mathbf{X}_{i,j}}; \mathbf{\Theta}\right), \tag{1}$$

where we employ $\mathcal{F}$ to represent the convolution operation, $\mathbf{X}'$ is the output feature map, δ refers to the kernel size, and the convolution filter parameter $\mathbf{\Theta}$ remains the same across all the pixels over the image. In contrast, the proposed pixel-adaptive operator DDF is conditioned on the corresponding local region of feature map $\mathbf{X}$, which is formulated as

$$\hat{\mathbf{X}}_{i,j} = \mathcal{F}\left(\mathcal{M}^{\delta'}_{\mathbf{X}_{i,j}}; \mathbf{\Theta}_{DDF} \mid \mathcal{M}^{\delta'}_{\mathbf{X}_{i,j}}\right), \tag{2}$$

where $\hat{\mathbf{X}}$ is the output feature map generated by DDF, the parameter $\mathbf{\Theta}_{DDF}$ of DDF is composed of two independent part: 1) the pixel-specific filter weight $\mathbf{D}$, which consists of a list of spatially-varying filters $\{\mathbf{D}_{i,j}\} \in \mathbb{R}^{K^2 \times C}$, where $i \in \{1, 2, \ldots, H\}, j \in \{1, 2, \ldots, W\}$; 2) the adaptive offsets $\mathbf{S}$, $\{\mathbf{S}_{i,j}\} \in \mathbb{R}^{K^2 \times 2}$, where $i \in \{1, 2, \ldots, H\}, j \in \{1, 2, \ldots, W\}$, and K is the kernel size. To handle large motion variations for all the pixels and enable the DDF to see a larger region of the corresponding feature area. We utilize a set of $K \times K$ atrous convolution filters $\{\mathbf{W}^r\}_{r=1}^n$ with dilated rate r to extract features for the following filter predicting task. δ' refers to the maximum receptive filed of atrous convolution filters set $\{\mathbf{W}^r\}_{r=1}^n$, and calculated by $\delta' = K + (K-1)(r-1)$. More specifically, the proposed DDF is represented as

$$\hat{\mathbf{X}}_{i,j,k} = \sum_{(u,v) \in \Delta_K} \mathbf{D}_{i,j,u+\lfloor K/2 \rfloor, v+\lfloor K/2 \rfloor, k} \mathbf{X}_{i+u+\Delta x^{u+\lfloor K/2 \rfloor, v+\lfloor K/2 \rfloor}_{i,j}, j+v+\Delta y^{u+\lfloor K/2 \rfloor, v+\lfloor K/2 \rfloor}_{i,j}, k}, \tag{3}$$

where $\Delta_K \in \mathbb{Z}^2$ indicates the set of sampling positions for convolution operation, written as ($\times$ is Cartesian product) $\Delta_K = [-\lfloor K/2 \rfloor, \cdots, \lfloor K/2 \rfloor] \times [-\lfloor K/2 \rfloor, \cdots, \lfloor K/2 \rfloor]$, and $\{\Delta x_{i,j}, \Delta y_{i,j}\} \in \mathbf{S}_{i,j}$ are the learnable offsets at horizontal and vertical directions, respectively. k is the channel index, since we use depth-wise convolution each kernel in $\mathbf{D}$ has C channels, instead of $C_{\text{in}} \times C_{\text{out}}$. Our work aims to design a filtering operator with content-adaptive property. In contrast to vanilla content-agnostic convolution operator, the proposed dynamic filters leverage two meta branch modules to learn the parameter of $\mathbf{D}_{i,j}$ and $\mathbf{S}_{i,j}$ from the local feature region, which is formulated as follows:

$$\mathbf{D}_{i,j} = \mathbf{\Phi}\left(\mathcal{M}^{\delta'}_{\mathbf{X}_{i,j}}; \theta_D\right) \tag{4}$$

$$\mathbf{S}_{i,j} = \mathbf{\Psi}\left(\mathcal{M}^{\delta'}_{\mathbf{X}_{i,j}}; \theta_S\right), \tag{5}$$

where $\mathbf{\Phi}(\cdot)$ and $\mathbf{\Psi}(\cdot)$ are the meta generation networks parameterized by θ, which are responsible for the filter weight learning and offsets learning, respectively. We will give more detailed information in the following sections.

3.3 The Offsets Estimation Module

The deformable convolution [17,18] merely employs a one-layer vanilla convolution with an identical receptive field to estimate the offsets map, for the entire input feature. However, the same receptive field cannot handle large motion variation for all the pixels, leading to sub-optimal offsets estimation results. Furthermore, the meaningful context information is hard to be captured with the limited receptive field. To address this issue, we propose a multi-scale dynamic offsets estimator, which enables the DDF to see a larger region of the corresponding feature area and generate the optimal offsets. Our offsets estimator $\mathbf{\Psi}(\cdot)$ is composed of two parts: the offsets extractor and the offsets refiner arranged in sequence.

The Offsets Extractor
The atrous convolution has been verified to be a powerful operator for enlarging receptive field. To this end, our offset estimator $\mathbf{\Psi}(\cdot)$ first utilize a set of $K \times K$ atrous convolution filters $\{\mathbf{W}^r\}_{r=1}^n$ with dilated rate r to extract n set corresponding multi-scale offset $\hat{\mathbf{S}} = \left\{ \hat{\mathbf{S}}_{i,j}^0, \ldots, \hat{\mathbf{S}}_{i,j}^{n-1} \mid \hat{\mathbf{S}}_{ij} \in \mathbb{R}^{K \times K \times 2} \right\}$ along with the modulation scalar $\mathbf{\Delta}m = \left\{ \mathbf{\Delta}m_{i,j}^0, \ldots, \mathbf{\Delta}m_{i,j}^{n-1} \mid \mathbf{\Delta}m_{ij} \in \mathbb{R}^{K \times K} \right\}$. Because the modulation scalar $\mathbf{\Delta}m$, which was introduced in Deformable ConvNets v2, could evaluate the reliability of each $K \times K$ offsets, so we feed them into learnable guided refiner to decide the final offsets $\mathbf{S}_{ij}$ for the position i, j, from the multi-scale candidate offsets.

The Offsets Refiner
To adaptively select the offsets from generated N-set candidates, we also design a sub-module namely offsets refiner. Intuitively, the larger confidence value indicates a better offset estimation result. To this end, the learnable guided refiner decides the final offsets by selecting the one with the maximum confidence value from candidates. We use $\mathcal{G} \in \mathbb{R}^{K \times K}$ to denote the refined index, given the candidate modulation scalar set $\mathbf{\Delta}m \in \mathbb{R}^{K \times K \times n}$. For each position (u, v) in the spatial domain, we have

$$\mathcal{G}_{u,v} = \arg\max\left(\mathbf{\Delta}m_{u,v}^0, \mathbf{\Delta}m_{u,v}^1, \cdots, \mathbf{\Delta}m_{u,v}^{n-1}\right), \tag{6}$$

where $\arg\max(\cdot)$ generates the index for the maximum value. So values in the refined index range from 0 to $n-1$ and indicate the index of offsets, which should be chosen for the corresponding positions. However, the $\arg\max(\cdot)$ is not continuous, so the gradient cannot be achieved. To solve this problem, we employ the softmax with temperature to obtain the gradient for $\arg\max(\cdot)$ through backward propagation. As detailed in Eq. 7, ζ is the extra noise sampled from Gumbel $(0, 1)$ distribution, and τ is the temperature parameter which controls the distribution, and when the τ increases, the distribution becomes more uniform, as the τ approaches 0, the distribution becomes one-hot.

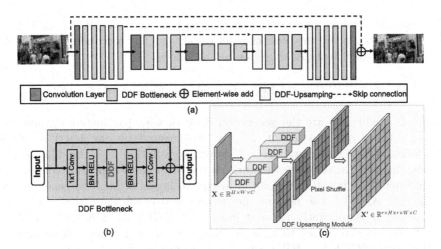

Fig. 3. The architecture of DDF-UNet (a) with DDF Bottleneck module (b), and DDF-Upsampling module (c). The DDF-UNet is a unified framework, suitable for various image restoration tasks, *e.g.,* real world image denoise.

$$\mathcal{G}_{u,v}^{j} = \frac{e^{(\mathcal{G}_{u,v}^{j}+\varsigma)/\tau}}{\sum_{m=0}^{n-1} e^{(\mathcal{G}_{u,v}^{m}+\varsigma)/\tau}} \quad j \in [0, n-1] \tag{7}$$

Therefore, the refiner index module can be trained by the loss function and yield the optimal offsets with respect to different scales for each pixel.

3.4 The Pixel-Specific Filter Weight Generator

The previous dynamic filter-based methods proposed to generate pixel-adaptive filter weight from the local feature. However, generating such a large number of filters ($C_{in} \times C_{out} \times K \times K$) cause extremely large memory usage, where C_{in} and C_{out} are the input channel number and output channel number, respectively. Since each gradient of pixel filter must be saved into memory when doing back-propagation (*e.g.,* input feature map with size $H \times W \times C_{in}$, the gradients size is $H \times W \times C_{in} \times C_{out} \times K \times K$). Thus, the image-level dynamic filters CondConv [32], DYconv [31] can hardly extend to pixel-level filters.

Motivated by the observation that the traditional convolution filter can be well represented by a linear combination of low-rank filter basis along with decomposition coefficients without losing performance [43], we propose the pixel-specific filter weight generator $\Phi(\cdot)$. The generated dynamic filter $\mathbf{D}_{i,j} \in \mathbb{R}^{K \times K \times C}$, which could decouple into pixel-adaptive basis $\mathbf{B}_{i,j} \in \mathbb{R}^{m \times K \times K}$ and dynamic coefficients $\mathbf{A}_{i,j} \in \mathbb{R}^{C \times m}$, formulated as $\mathbf{D}_{i,j} = \mathbf{B}_{i,j}\mathbf{A}_{i,j}$, m is a pre-defined small value, *e.g.,* $m = 4$.

The work in [43] leaves the coefficients $\mathbf{A}$ as the global parameter shared throughout the image, however, the globally shared filters are hard to capture cross-channel information. Hence, we propose to enable coefficients $\mathbf{A}$ to be a pixel-specific dynamic parameter and utilized two layers of MLP (MultiLayer Perceptron) to capture the cross-channel variations. The pixel-adaptive basis $\mathbf{B}$ and dynamic coefficients $\mathbf{A}$ are generated as follows:

$$\mathbf{B}_{i,j} \in \mathbb{R}^{m \times K \times K} = \mathcal{B}\left(\mathcal{M}^{\delta}_{\mathbf{X}_{i,j}}; \theta_B\right); \mathbf{A}_{i,j} \in \mathbb{R}^{C \times m} = \mathcal{A}\left(\mathbf{X}_{i,j}; \theta_A\right), \qquad (8)$$

where, $\mathcal{B}(\cdot)$ and $\mathcal{A}(\cdot)$ are the generation network with parameters θ_B and θ_A, respectively. In our experiment, $\mathcal{B}(\cdot)$ is implemented by one 1×1 convolution followed by a single layer $K \times K$ atrous convolution with the dilated rate $r = n$, the same as offsets estimator, for the purpose of capturing long-range dependencies. As for $\mathcal{A}(\cdot)$, we only utilized two layers of MLP to generate the coefficients $\mathbf{A}$. With the help of the decomposed coefficients, the number of parameters is significantly reduced from $(HWKKC)$ to $(CKKm + mHW)$. Specifically, m can be set to a small value, $e.g.$, $m = 1$, relatively yielding a $(HWKKC)/(HWKK + HW) \approx (C)$ times reduction of parameters.

4   Experiments

4.1   Datasets

To evaluate the proposed method, we conduct extensive experiments on three image deblurring benchmark datasets: 1) GoPro [8] which consisting of 3, 214 image pairs, in which 2,103 pairs are utilized for training our model and the rest 1111 pairs are for testing, 2) HIDE [44] contains 2,025 pairs of images, all of which are used for testing, and 3) RealBlur [45] dataset which consisting of 980 image pairs in RealBlur-R and RealBlur-J test sets, respectively. We train our models on 2,103 pairs of blurry and sharp images from the GoPro dataset, then test against all the test sets from three datasets. The average values of PSNR and SSIM [46] are utilized for performance comparison.

4.2   Implementation Details

Setting. We train our model for 2000 epochs by employing Adam optimizer [47] with default setting $\beta_1 = 0.9$, $\beta_2 = 0.999$ and $\epsilon = 10^{-8}$. The learning rate is set to be 2×10^{-4} and exponentially decays to 0 using power 0.3. All parameters are initialized using Xavier normalization. The batch size is set to 16. We randomly crop the images into 256×256 patches for training and also utilize horizontal flip and rotation for image augmentation. Experiments are conducted on the server with an intel E5-2690 CPU, and 4X NVIDIA Tesla v100 GPUs.

Network Architecture. The architecture of U-Net-based network [21] is illustrated in Fig. 3(a). We also propose an extension operator DDF-Bottleneck, which is shown in Fig. 3(b), and a DDF-Upsampling module, as shown in Fig. 3(c). According to the upsampling rate r the number of r^2 DDF is used. We utilized pixel-shuffle [48] to assemble the output features as an upsampling layer.

Fig. 4. The illustration of the learned offset (a) and filters (b). As shown in (a), for the slightly blurred regions, the estimated offsets are approximately uniformly distributed over the local area, while for the large motion regions, the sampling geometry of the filter is adjusted adaptively according to the motion blur patterns. The weights of the filter are also adaptively changed to each local region (b), which consolidates that our DDF has indeed learned spatial adaptability. (c) Visualization of the learned offsets of DCN v2 [18] and proposed offset estimator, compared to DCN v2, our offset estimator could capture a larger region of context information along the motion pattern. (d) Comparison results of original UNet, UNet equipped with DCN v2, and proposed DDF-UNet, respectively. Thanks to the spatial-adaptive capability of DDF, the large motion-blurred patch is better recovered than original-UNet and UNet-DCN v2.

4.3   Evaluation of DDF

Because our DDF module is a plug-and-play operator, to verify its effectiveness in improving motion deblurring accuracy, we plug it into various deblurring architectures, such as U-Net and MIMO-UNet [25]. For U-Net, we evaluate two variants of our model: 1) DDF-UNet which consists of 8 encoder blocks and 8 decoder blocks, respectively, and 2) DDF-UNet+ which consists of 20 blocks for each encoder and decoder, respectively. The ℓ_1 loss is used in our implementation, which is formulated as $L = \frac{1}{N} \sum_{n=1}^{N} \left\| \hat{\mathbf{Y}}^{(n)} - \mathbf{Y}^{(n)} \right\|_1$, where $\mathbf{Y}^{(n)}$ is the n-th corresponding sharp image, $\hat{\mathbf{Y}}^{(n)}$ is the network output, and N is the number of sample images in a mini-batch.

The detailed architecture is shown in Fig. 3(a). For MIMO-UNet and MIMO-UNet+ [25], we replace all the ResBlock in MIMO-UNet [25] with our DDF-Bottleneck module, and also replace the upsampling layer with our DDF-Upsampling module, dubbed as DDF-MIMO and DDF-MIMO+, correspondingly. We also use the same loss function: multi-scale frequency reconstruction (MSFR) loss, from the original work [25]. Embedding the DDF module con-

Table 1. Quantitative comparisons on GoPro [8], HIDE [44], and RealBlur [45] dataset. Our methods and the best results are **highlighted**.

Method	GoPro [8]		HIDE [44]		RealBlur-R [45]		RealBlur-J [45]		Param (M)	MACs (G)	Time (s)
	PSNR	SSIM	PSNR	SSIM	PSNR	SSIM	PSNR	SSIM			
DeblurGAN [22]	28.70	0.858	24.51	0.871	33.79	0.903	27.97	0.834	N/A	N/A	N/A
DeepDeblur [8]	29.08	0.914	25.73	0.874	32.51	0.841	27.87	0.827	11.72	4729	1.290
Zhang et al. [14]	29.19	0.931	–		35.48	0.947	27.80	0.847	N/A	N/A	N/A
DeblurGAN-v2 [23]	29.55	0.934	26.61	0.875	35.26	0.944	28.70	0.866	N/A	N/A	N/A
SRN [9]	30.26	0.934	28.36	0.915	35.66	0.947	28.56	0.867	8.06	20134	0.736
Shen et al. [44]	–		28.89	0.930	–		–		N/A	N/A	N/A
Gao et al. [10]	30.90	0.935	29.11	0.913	–		–		2.84	3255	0.316
DBGAN [49]	31.10	0.942	28.94	0.915	33.78	0.909	24.93	0.745	N/A	N/A	N/A
MT-RNN [12]	31.15	0.945	29.15	0.918	35.79	0.951	28.44	0.862	2.6	2315	0.323
DMPHN [11]	31.20	0.940	29.09	0.924	35.70	0.948	28.42	0.860	7.23	1100	0.137
SAPHN [16]	31.85	0.948	29.98	0.930	–		–		N/A	N/A	N/A
SPAIR [50]	32.06	0.953	30.29	0.931	–		28.81	0.875	N/A	N/A	N/A
HINet [15]	32.71	0.959	–		–		–		88.67	2401	0.247
MPRNet [13]	32.66	0.959	30.96	0.939	35.99	**0.952**	28.70	0.873	20.1	10927	1.023
Original-UNet	28.94	0.912	27.42	0.873	32.51	0.898	26.80	0.801	4.1	120	0.031
DDF-UNet (ours)	30.31	0.934	28.34	0.915	33.72	0.914	27.40	0.829	6.5	170	0.041
DDF-UNet+ (ours)	31.02	0.940	28.92	0.917	34.59	0.938	27.62	0.833	13.2	420	0.101
MIMO-UNet [25]	31.73	0.951	29.28	0.921	35.47	0.946	27.76	0.836	6.8	944	0.133
DDF-MIMO (ours)	32.68	0.958	29.72	0.928	35.62	0.948	27.98	0.849	9.2	1100	0.137
MIMO-UNet+ [25]	32.45	0.957	29.99	0.930	35.54	0.947	27.63	0.837	16.1	2171	0.290
DDF-MIMO+ (ours)	**32.89**	**0.961**	**30.99**	**0.931**	**36.10**	**0.952**	**28.76**	**0.874**	19.2	2370	0.320

tributes to remarkable performance gains for both architectures, as detailed in Table 1, *e.g.*, *w/*DDF in DDF-UNet lead to a 1.37 dB improvement in PSNR on the GoPro dataset, a toy example is shown in Fig. 4. For DDF-MIMO, a 0.95 dB gain in PSNR is verified by plugging the DDF onto MIMO-UNet [25] architecture. These results consolidate that, the spatial adaptability of DDF could empower the vanilla network, and achieve better performance.

4.4   Comparisons with State-of-the-Art Methods

We extensively compare our proposed method with state-of-the-art dynamic scene motion deblurring approaches, including DeepBlur [8], DeblurGAN v1, v2, [22,23], SRN [9], Gao *et al.* [10] and DMPHN [11], MPRNet [9] and so on. The quantitative results on the GoPro [8], HIDE [44], and RealBlur [45] test sets are listed in Table 1. The visual comparison results are illustrated in Fig. 5 and Fig. 6. As illustrated in the images, our method outperforms the other approaches in terms of deblurring quality, and handles large dynamic motion blur scenes quite well. It can be seen from the quantitative results that our DDF-MIMO+ outperforms the previous state-of-the-art MPRNet [13], in terms of PSNR, ours DDF-MIMO+ is ranked first, surpassing the best competitor [13]. In terms of inference-time, the proposed DDF-UNet can deblur one image at 41ms. In contrast, the stacked architectures, *e.g.*, SRN [9], DMPHN [11], and SAPHN [16] suffer from expensive computational costs because they need to stack more layers for achieving larger receptive fields. Our method is 17.9× and

Table 2. Ablation study based on GoPro [8] testing set for using different component combinations in DDF-UNet, where DCN v2 represents Deformable Convolution V2 [18]. DDF Offsets means the DDF offsets estimation module, while DDF Weight indicates the DDF pixel-specific filter weight generator. The best result is **highlighted**.

Version	Ori-UNet	DCN v2	DDF Offsets	DDF Weight	DDF-Upsampling	PSNR (dB)
Version 1	✓					28.94
Version 2	✓	✓				29.21
Version 3	✓		✓			29.67
Version 4	✓		✓	✓		30.10
Version 5	✓		✓	✓	✓	**30.31**

Table 3. Real Image Denoising results on the SIDD [51] and DND [52] datasets. Our methods and the best results are **highlighted**.

Method	SIDD [51]		DND [52]	
	PSNR ↑	SSIM ↑	PSNR ↑	SSIM ↑
DnCNN [53]	23.66	0.583	32.43	0.790
CBM3D [54]	25.65	0.685	34.51	0.851
CBDNet [55]	30.78	0.801	34.51	0.851
RIDNet [56]	38.71	0.914	38.06	0.942
DANet [57]	39.47	0.918	39.59	0.955
SADNet [58]	39.46	0.957	39.59	0.952
CycleISP [59]	39.52	0.957	39.56	**0.956**
MIRNet [60]	39.72	0.959	39.88	**0.956**
MPRNet [13]	39.71	0.958	39.80	0.954
NBNet [61]	39.75	**0.959**	39.89	0.955
Original UNet	37.02	0.895	37.80	0.947
DDF-UNet (ours)	39.62	0.957	39.81	0.954
DDF-UNet+ (ours)	**39.82**	**0.959**	**39.94**	**0.956**

31× faster than SRN [9] and DeepBlur [8], respectively. The experimental results demonstrate the optimal trade-off between the performance and computational complexity of the proposed method.

4.5 Ablation Studies

Analyses of the Spatial Adaptability. As illustrated in the Fig. 4, DDF handles large dynamic motion blur scenes quite well. We observe that the result of UNet suffers from artifacts and deficient deblurring results depicted in Fig. 4(d).

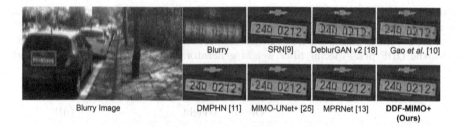

Fig. 5. Visual comparisons for the GoPro dataset [8].

Fig. 6. Visual comparisons for the HIDE [44] dataset.

In contrast, owing to the proposed DDF module, our model is capable of restoring sharper boundaries and richer details in the region containing large motion blur. In addition, according to the visualization of the offsets estimation result in Fig. 4(a), for the background region, the estimated offsets are approximately uniformly distributed in the area, while for the large motion regions, we can see that the sampling geometry of the filter is adjusted adaptively according to the motion blur patterns. Moreover, as shown in Fig. 4(b), the weights of filters are also adaptively changed for each local region, which demonstrates that our DDF has been empowered with spatial adaptability.

The Effectiveness of Offsets Estimator and Refiner. To demonstrate the effectiveness of each component in the proposed DDF including the adaptive offsets prediction module, and the kernel weight perdition module, we compare the results with several versions. The experimental results are listed in Table 2. **Version 1** is the original U-Net, as the baseline. **Version 2** is U-Net equipped with Deformable ConvNets V2 [18], **Version 3** is replaces deformable convolution with the adaptive offsets prediction module. It achieves an increase of 0.46 dB in PSNR, which means that the offsets adaptive adjustment ability is enhanced by the proposed adaptive offsets prediction module. Compared with deformable convolution, which could only capture a limited area of motion pattern as shown in Fig. 4(c), the proposed DDF demonstrates stronger fitting capabilities.

The Effectiveness of Pixel-Specific Filter Weight Generator. To further evaluate the effectiveness of the pixel-specific filter weight generator, we also

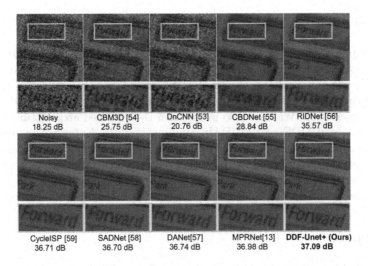

| Noisy | CBM3D [54] | DnCNN [53] | CBDNet [55] | RIDNet [56] |
| 18.25 dB | 25.75 dB | 20.76 dB | 28.84 dB | 35.57 dB |

| CycleISP [59] | SADNet [58] | DANet[57] | MPRNet[13] | DDF-Unet+ (Ours) |
| 36.71 dB | 36.70 dB | 36.74 dB | 36.98 dB | 37.09 dB |

Fig. 7. Visual comparisons for the SIDD [51] dataset.

propose **Version 4** test, which incrementally adds the filter weight generator to DDF. Thanks to the adaptive adjustment of weights, the PSNR has further increased by 0.43 dB.

The Effectiveness of the DDF-Upsampling Module. Finally, we further add the DDF-Upsampling module into the UNet as the **Version 5** test and get a 0.21 dB performance gain, which consolidates the effectiveness of the DDF-Upsampling module.

4.6 Generalization to Real Image Noise Removal Task

To demonstrate the generalization capability of DDF, we also applied the DDF-UNet+ to real-world image noise removal task. The real-world noise removal aims at restoring high-quality images from noisy inputs, which are spatially non-uniformly distributed. Thus, the spatially-adaptive operator is a natural method to solve such kinds of problems. The real-world noise removal dataset SIDD [51] and DND [52] are used for evaluation. We train our model by using 320 high-resolution images of the SIDD dataset and evaluate the test sets of SIDD [51] and DND [52]. The quantitative results are listed in Table 3. We compare DDF-UNet+ with state-of-the-art denoising methods, including the CBM3D [54], CBDNet [55], RIDNet [56], SADNet [58], DnCNN [53], CycleISP [59], NBNet [61], DANet [57], MIRNet [60], and MPRNet [13]. Our DDF-UNet+ achieves a 39.82 dB on PSNR for SIDD [51] dataset, and outperforms the best methods, in our experiments. The visualization results of the SIDD dataset are shown in Fig. 7. The results indicate that the DDF could handle the spatial-variance problem, and improve the performance.

5 Conclusion

In this paper, we proposed a new adaptive plug-and-play operator DDF for the challenging task of handling large motion blur variations across spatial locations. The weights and the offsets of DDF are adaptively generated from the local features by proposed meta networks, which are trained end-to-end without explicit supervision. We have also proposed a U-Net-based architecture powered by our proposed DDF and DDF-Upsampling module. Extensive experimental results demonstrated that the proposed DDF could empower the baseline to achieve better performance. Furthermore, the proposed DDF can be generalized to other computer vision tasks as a plug-and-play adaptive operator, *e.g.,* real image noise removal task, and also achieve state-of-the-art performance.

References

1. Gupta, A., Joshi, N., Lawrence Zitnick, C., Cohen, M., Curless, B.: Single image deblurring using motion density functions. In: Daniilidis, K., Maragos, P., Paragios, N. (eds.) ECCV 2010. LNCS, vol. 6311, pp. 171–184. Springer, Heidelberg (2010). https://doi.org/10.1007/978-3-642-15549-9_13
2. Liu, G., Chang, S., Ma, Y.: Blind image deblurring using spectral properties of convolution operators. IEEE Trans. Image Process. **23**, 5047–5056 (2014)
3. Tran, P., Tran, A.T., Phung, Q., Hoai, M.: Explore image deblurring via encoded blur kernel space. In: Proceedings of the IEEE/CVF Conference on Computer Vision and Pattern Recognition, pp. 11956–11965 (2021)
4. Ren, D., Zhang, K., Wang, Q., Hu, Q., Zuo, W.: Neural blind deconvolution using deep priors. In: Proceedings of the IEEE/CVF Conference on Computer Vision and Pattern Recognition, pp. 3341–3350 (2020)
5. Chakrabarti, A.: A neural approach to blind motion deblurring. In: Leibe, B., Matas, J., Sebe, N., Welling, M. (eds.) ECCV 2016. LNCS, vol. 9907, pp. 221–235. Springer, Cham (2016). https://doi.org/10.1007/978-3-319-46487-9_14
6. Sun, J., Cao, W., Xu, Z., Ponce, J.: Learning a convolutional neural network for non-uniform motion blur removal. In: Proceedings of the IEEE Conference on Computer Vision and Pattern Recognition, pp. 769–777 (2015)
7. Schuler, C.J., Hirsch, M., Harmeling, S., Schölkopf, B.: Learning to deblur. IEEE Trans. Pattern Anal. Mach. Intell. **38**, 1439–1451 (2015)
8. Nah, S., Hyun Kim, T., Mu Lee, K.: Deep multi-scale convolutional neural network for dynamic scene deblurring. In: Proceedings of the IEEE Conference on Computer Vision and Pattern Recognition, pp. 3883–3891 (2017)
9. Tao, X., Gao, H., Shen, X., Wang, J., Jia, J.: Scale-recurrent network for deep image deblurring. In: Proceedings of the IEEE Conference on Computer Vision and Pattern Recognition, pp. 8174–8182 (2018)
10. Gao, H., Tao, X., Shen, X., Jia, J.: Dynamic scene deblurring with parameter selective sharing and nested skip connections. In: Proceedings of the IEEE/CVF Conference on Computer Vision and Pattern Recognition, pp. 3848–3856 (2019)
11. Zhang, H., Dai, Y., Li, H., Koniusz, P.: Deep stacked hierarchical multi-patch network for image deblurring. In: Proceedings of the IEEE/CVF Conference on Computer Vision and Pattern Recognition, pp. 5978–5986 (2019)

12. Park, D., Kang, D.U., Kim, J., Chun, S.Y.: Multi-temporal recurrent neural networks for progressive non-uniform single image deblurring with incremental temporal training. In: Vedaldi, A., Bischof, H., Brox, T., Frahm, J.-M. (eds.) ECCV 2020. LNCS, vol. 12351, pp. 327–343. Springer, Cham (2020). https://doi.org/10.1007/978-3-030-58539-6_20

13. Zamir, S.W., et al.: Multi-stage progressive image restoration. In: Proceedings of the IEEE/CVF Conference on Computer Vision and Pattern Recognition, pp. 14821–14831 (2021)

14. Zhang, J., et al.: Dynamic scene deblurring using spatially variant recurrent neural networks. In: Proceedings of the IEEE Conference on Computer Vision and Pattern Recognition, pp. 2521–2529 (2018)

15. Chen, L., Lu, X., Zhang, J., Chu, X., Chen, C.: HINet: half instance normalization network for image restoration. In: Proceedings of the IEEE/CVF Conference on Computer Vision and Pattern Recognition, pp. 182–192 (2021)

16. Suin, M., Purohit, K., Rajagopalan, A.: Spatially-attentive patch-hierarchical network for adaptive motion deblurring. In: Proceedings of the IEEE/CVF Conference on Computer Vision and Pattern Recognition, pp. 3606–3615 (2020)

17. Dai, J., et al.: Deformable convolutional networks. In: Proceedings of the IEEE International Conference on Computer Vision, pp. 764–773 (2017)

18. Zhu, X., Hu, H., Lin, S., Dai, J.: Deformable ConvNets v2: more deformable, better results. In: Proceedings of the IEEE/CVF Conference on Computer Vision and Pattern Recognition, pp. 9308–9316 (2019)

19. Su, H., Jampani, V., Sun, D., Gallo, O., Learned-Miller, E., Kautz, J.: Pixel-adaptive convolutional neural networks. In: Proceedings of the IEEE/CVF Conference on Computer Vision and Pattern Recognition, pp. 11166–11175 (2019)

20. Zamora Esquivel, J., Cruz Vargas, A., Lopez Meyer, P., Tickoo, O.: Adaptive convolutional kernels. In: Proceedings of the IEEE/CVF International Conference on Computer Vision Workshops(2019)

21. Ronneberger, O., Fischer, P., Brox, T.: U-Net: convolutional networks for biomedical image segmentation. In: Navab, N., Hornegger, J., Wells, W.M., Frangi, A.F. (eds.) MICCAI 2015. LNCS, vol. 9351, pp. 234–241. Springer, Cham (2015). https://doi.org/10.1007/978-3-319-24574-4_28

22. Kupyn, O., Budzan, V., Mykhailych, M., Mishkin, D., Matas, J.: DeblurGAN: blind motion deblurring using conditional adversarial networks. In: Proceedings of the IEEE Conference on Computer Vision and Pattern Recognition, pp. 8183–8192 (2018)

23. Kupyn, O., Martyniuk, T., Wu, J., Wang, Z.: DeblurGAN-v2: deblurring (orders-of-magnitude) faster and better. In: Proceedings of the IEEE/CVF International Conference on Computer Vision, pp. 8878–8887 (2019)

24. Yuan, Y., Su, W., Ma, D.: Efficient dynamic scene deblurring using spatially variant deconvolution network with optical flow guided training. In: Proceedings of the IEEE/CVF Conference on Computer Vision and Pattern Recognition, pp. 3555–3564 (2020)

25. Cho, S.J., Ji, S.W., Hong, J.P., Jung, S.W., Ko, S.J.: Rethinking coarse-to-fine approach in single image deblurring. In: Proceedings of the IEEE/CVF International Conference on Computer Vision, pp. 4641–4650 (2021)

26. Wang, Z., Cun, X., Bao, J., Zhou, W., Liu, J., Li, H.: Uformer: a general U-shaped transformer for image restoration. In: Proceedings of the IEEE/CVF Conference on Computer Vision and Pattern Recognition, pp. 17683–17693 (2022)

27. Zamir, S.W., Arora, A., Khan, S., Hayat, M., Khan, F.S., Yang, M.H.: Restormer: efficient transformer for high-resolution image restoration. In: Proceedings of the IEEE/CVF Conference on Computer Vision and Pattern Recognition, pp. 5728–5739 (2022)
28. Liang, J., Cao, J., Sun, G., Zhang, K., Van Gool, L., Timofte, R.: SwinIR: image restoration using swin transformer. In: Proceedings of the IEEE/CVF International Conference on Computer Vision, pp. 1833–1844 (2021)
29. Mao, X., Liu, Y., Shen, W., Li, Q., Wang, Y.: Deep residual Fourier transformation for single image deblurring. arXiv preprint arXiv:2111.11745 (2021)
30. Zhang, Y., Zhang, J., Wang, Q., Zhong, Z.: DyNet: dynamic convolution for accelerating convolutional neural networks. arXiv preprint arXiv:2004.10694 (2020)
31. Chen, Y., Dai, X., Liu, M., Chen, D., Yuan, L., Liu, Z.: Dynamic convolution: attention over convolution kernels. In: Proceedings of the IEEE/CVF Conference on Computer Vision and Pattern Recognition, pp. 11030–11039 (2020)
32. Yang, B., Bender, G., Le, Q.V., Ngiam, J.: CondConv: conditionally parameterized convolutions for efficient inference. In: Advances in Neural Information Processing Systems, vol. 32 (2019)
33. Wang, J., Chen, K., Xu, R., Liu, Z., Loy, C.C., Lin, D.: CARAFE: content-aware reassembly of features. In: Proceedings of the IEEE/CVF International Conference on Computer Vision, pp. 3007–3016 (2019)
34. Wang, J., Chen, K., Xu, R., Liu, Z., Loy, C.C., Lin, D.: CARAFE++: unified content-aware reassembly of features. IEEE Trans. Pattern Anal. Mach. Intell. 44(9), 4674–4687 (2021)
35. Niklaus, S., Mai, L., Liu, F.: Video frame interpolation via adaptive convolution. In: Proceedings of the IEEE Conference on Computer Vision and Pattern Recognition, pp. 670–679 (2017)
36. Mildenhall, B., Barron, J.T., Chen, J., Sharlet, D., Ng, R., Carroll, R.: Burst denoising with kernel prediction networks. In: Proceedings of the IEEE Conference on Computer Vision and Pattern Recognition, pp. 2502–2510 (2018)
37. Xu, Y.S., Tseng, S.Y.R., Tseng, Y., Kuo, H.K., Tsai, Y.M.: Unified dynamic convolutional network for super-resolution with variational degradations. In: Proceedings of the IEEE/CVF Conference on Computer Vision and Pattern Recognition, pp. 12496–12505 (2020)
38. Magid, S.A., et al.: Dynamic high-pass filtering and multi-spectral attention for image super-resolution. In: Proceedings of the IEEE/CVF International Conference on Computer Vision, pp. 4288–4297 (2021)
39. Liu, J., He, J., Qiao, Yu., Ren, J.S., Li, H.: Learning to predict context-adaptive convolution for semantic segmentation. In: Vedaldi, A., Bischof, H., Brox, T., Frahm, J.-M. (eds.) ECCV 2020. LNCS, vol. 12370, pp. 769–786. Springer, Cham (2020). https://doi.org/10.1007/978-3-030-58595-2_46
40. He, J., Deng, Z., Qiao, Y.: Dynamic multi-scale filters for semantic segmentation. In: Proceedings of the IEEE/CVF International Conference on Computer Vision, pp. 3562–3572 (2019)
41. Xu, C., et al.: SqueezeSegV3: spatially-adaptive convolution for efficient point-cloud segmentation. In: Vedaldi, A., Bischof, H., Brox, T., Frahm, J.-M. (eds.) ECCV 2020. LNCS, vol. 12373, pp. 1–19. Springer, Cham (2020). https://doi.org/10.1007/978-3-030-58604-1_1
42. Xu, M., Ding, R., Zhao, H., Qi, X.: PAConv: position adaptive convolution with dynamic kernel assembling on point clouds. In: Proceedings of the IEEE/CVF Conference on Computer Vision and Pattern Recognition, pp. 3173–3182 (2021)

43. Wang, Z., Miao, Z., Hu, J., Qiu, Q.: Adaptive convolutions with per-pixel dynamic filter atom. In: Proceedings of the IEEE/CVF International Conference on Computer Vision, pp. 12302–12311 (2021)

44. Shen, Z., et al.: Human-aware motion deblurring. In: Proceedings of the IEEE/CVF International Conference on Computer Vision (ICCV) (2019)

45. Rim, J., Lee, H., Won, J., Cho, S.: Real-world blur dataset for learning and benchmarking deblurring algorithms. In: Vedaldi, A., Bischof, H., Brox, T., Frahm, J.-M. (eds.) ECCV 2020. LNCS, vol. 12370, pp. 184–201. Springer, Cham (2020). https://doi.org/10.1007/978-3-030-58595-2_12

46. Wang, Z., Bovik, A.C., Sheikh, H.R., Simoncelli, E.P.: Image quality assessment: from error visibility to structural similarity. IEEE Trans. Image Process. 13, 600–612 (2004)

47. Kingma, D.P., Ba, J.: Adam: a method for stochastic optimization. arXiv preprint arXiv:1412.6980 (2014)

48. Shi, W., et al.: Real-time single image and video super-resolution using an efficient sub-pixel convolutional neural network. In: Proceedings of the IEEE Conference on Computer Vision and Pattern Recognition, pp. 1874–1883 (2016)

49. Zhang, K., et al.: Deblurring by realistic blurring. In: Proceedings of the IEEE/CVF Conference on Computer Vision and Pattern Recognition, pp. 2737–2746 (2020)

50. Purohit, K., Suin, M., Rajagopalan, A., Boddeti, V.N.: Spatially-adaptive image restoration using distortion-guided networks. In: Proceedings of the IEEE/CVF International Conference on Computer Vision, pp. 2309–2319 (2021)

51. Abdelhamed, A., Lin, S., Brown, M.S.: A high-quality denoising dataset for smartphone cameras. In: Proceedings of the IEEE Conference on Computer Vision and Pattern Recognition, pp. 1692–1700 (2018)

52. Plotz, T., Roth, S.: Benchmarking denoising algorithms with real photographs. In: Proceedings of the IEEE Conference on Computer Vision and Pattern Recognition, pp. 1586–1595 (2017)

53. Zhang, K., Zuo, W., Chen, Y., Meng, D., Zhang, L.: Beyond a Gaussian denoiser: residual learning of deep CNN for image denoising. IEEE Trans. Image Process. 26, 3142–3155 (2017)

54. Dabov, K., Foi, A., Katkovnik, V., Egiazarian, K.: Image denoising by sparse 3-D transform-domain collaborative filtering. IEEE Trans. Image Process. 16, 2080–2095 (2007)

55. Guo, S., Yan, Z., Zhang, K., Zuo, W., Zhang, L.: Toward convolutional blind denoising of real photographs. In: Proceedings of the IEEE/CVF Conference on Computer Vision and Pattern Recognition, pp. 1712–1722 (2019)

56. Zhuo, S., Jin, Z., Zou, W., Li, X.: RIDNet: recursive information distillation network for color image denoising. In: Proceedings of the IEEE/CVF International Conference on Computer Vision Workshops (2019)

57. Yue, Z., Zhao, Q., Zhang, L., Meng, D.: Dual adversarial network: toward real-world noise removal and noise generation. In: Vedaldi, A., Bischof, H., Brox, T., Frahm, J.-M. (eds.) ECCV 2020. LNCS, vol. 12355, pp. 41–58. Springer, Cham (2020). https://doi.org/10.1007/978-3-030-58607-2_3

58. Chang, M., Li, Q., Feng, H., Xu, Z.: Spatial-adaptive network for single image denoising. In: Vedaldi, A., Bischof, H., Brox, T., Frahm, J.-M. (eds.) ECCV 2020. LNCS, vol. 12375, pp. 171–187. Springer, Cham (2020). https://doi.org/10.1007/978-3-030-58577-8_11

59. Zamir, S.W., et al.: CycleISP: real image restoration via improved data synthesis. In: Proceedings of the IEEE/CVF Conference on Computer Vision and Pattern Recognition, pp. 2696–2705 (2020)
60. Zamir, S.W., et al.: Learning enriched features for real image restoration and enhancement. In: Vedaldi, A., Bischof, H., Brox, T., Frahm, J.-M. (eds.) ECCV 2020. LNCS, vol. 12370, pp. 492–511. Springer, Cham (2020). https://doi.org/10.1007/978-3-030-58595-2_30
61. Cheng, S., Wang, Y., Huang, H., Liu, D., Fan, H., Liu, S.: NBNet: noise basis learning for image denoising with subspace projection. In: Proceedings of the IEEE/CVF Conference on Computer Vision and Pattern Recognition, pp. 4896–4906 (2021)

Efficient Hardware-Aware Neural Architecture Search for Image Super-Resolution on Mobile Devices

Xindong Zhang[1,2], Hui Zeng[2], and Lei Zhang[1,2(✉)]

[1] Department of Computing, The Hong Kong Polytechnic University, Hung Hom, China
{csxdzhang,cslzhang}@comp.polyu.edu.hk
[2] OPPO Research, Hung Hom, China

Abstract. With the ubiquitous use of mobile devices in our daily life, how to design a lightweight network for high-performance image super-resolution (SR) has become increasingly important. However, it is difficult and laborious to manually design and deploy different SR models on different mobile devices, while the existing network architecture search (NAS) techniques are expensive and unfriendly to find the desired SR networks for various hardware platforms. To mitigate these issues, we propose an efficient hardware-aware neural architecture search (EHANAS) method for SR on mobile devices. First, EHANAS supports searching in a large network architecture space, including the macro topology (e.g., number of blocks) and microstructure (e.g., kernel type, channel dimension, and activation type) of the network. By introducing a spatial and channel masking strategy and a re-parameterization technique, we are able to finish the whole searching procedure using one single GPU card within one day. Second, the hardware latency is taken as a direct constraint on the searching process, enabling hardware-adaptive optimization of the searched SR model. Experiments on two typical mobile devices demonstrate the effectiveness of the proposed EHANAS method, where the searched SR models obtain better performance than previously manually designed and automatically searched models. The source codes of EHANAS can be found at https://github.com/xindongzhang/EHANAS.

Keywords: NAS · Super-resolution · Mobile devices

1 Introduction

Image super-resolution (SR) aims at recovering high-resolution (HR) images from their degraded low-resolution (LR) counterparts. Benefiting from the rapid development of deep learning [22], convolutional neural networks (CNN) based SR models [6,7,19,27,50] have exhibited superior performance over traditional SR methods and shown promising practical values in improving image quality. However, many existing SR networks employ very complicated and cumbersome backbones in order to achieve high reconstruction accuracy, which is infeasible for many real-world applications running on resource-limited edge or mobile devices. Therefore, how to design and train

---

X. Zhang and H. Zeng—Equal contribution.
L. Zhang—This work is supported by the Hong Kong RGC RIF grant (R5001-18) and the PolyU-OPPO Joint Innovation Lab.

L. Wang et al. (Eds.): ACCV 2022, LNCS 13843, pp. 409–426, 2023.
https://doi.org/10.1007/978-3-031-26313-2_25

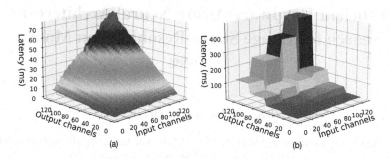

Fig. 1. Latency of applying a 3×3 convolution with different input and output channels to an image of 540×960 resolution using stride 1. The hardware platforms are (a) GPU of Dimensity 1000+ and (b) DSP of Snapdragon 865.

lightweight and efficient SR (LESR) models has been becoming increasingly important and attracting much attention.

One popular trend of LESR is to design convolution blocks with low-FLOPs (e.g., group-wise convolution, depth-wise convolution, and element-wise operator) and param-eter-free operators (e.g., splitting, shuffling, concatenation and attention) [1,8,16,17,29,36,40]. However, the FLOPs and number of parameters of an SR model cannot faithfully reflect its real hardware latency [34,46,49]. It still requires a large amount of human labor and resources to adapt and deploy such models on hardware devices. Network pruning is another direction to obtain LESR models by removing less important parameters or blocks from larger SR models [25,42]. However, the pruned model may be sub-optimal on both SR accuracy and inference latency.

The huge space of possible network architectures intertwined with the various hardware platforms makes it very challenging and cumbersome to manually design and deploy SR models on different hardware devices. On one hand, the network architecture varies from macro topology (e.g., number of blocks) to microstructure (e.g., kernel type, channel dimension, and activation type). On the other hand, different mobile or edge devices (e.g., CPU, GPU, DSP, and NPU) can have very different hardware resources such as computational capacity, memory access speed, and supporting operators. As shown in Fig. 1, even the same operator (e.g., a 3×3 convolution) can have very different hardware latency when evaluated on the same device using different input and output channels.

To alleviate the laborious work on network design and deployment, researchers have made several attempts to leverage the network architecture search (NAS) technique to autonomously search for LESR models [4,5,14,23,37,45]. However, most of these works conduct NAS based on computationally expensive reinforcement learning [14,23] or evolutionary algorithms [4,5,37,45], which take hundreds or even thousands of GPU hours to search a model. To speed up the searching process, one may compromise on the searching space (e.g., only searching a part of the microstructure) or searching step (e.g., using a large step), which may lead to sub-optimal models. In addition, most of the existing methods use the indirect proxy (e.g., FLOPs and number of parameters) to guide the searching process, without considering the hardware setting of target devices [4,5,14,23,37].

To solve the above-mentioned problems, we propose an efficient and hardware-aware NAS (EHANAS) method for SR on mobile devices. Our EHANAS is based on the differential NAS (DNAS) methods [41,43], which have recently proven their effectiveness and efficiency on image classification tasks compared to the NAS methods based on reinforcement learning or evolutionary algorithms [2,28,35,51,52]. However, with multiple convolution branches and intermediate feature maps, the DNAS methods still cost considerable computation and memory resources for searching each block. In this paper, we propose to search a set of spatial and channel masks, which can be used to re-parameterize one single convolution to achieve block search. In this way, our block search takes almost the same computation and memory cost as training one normal convolution block. Combined with a differential strategy for searching the number of blocks, our EHANAS model can be trained using one single GPU card and the whole process can be finished within one day. In addition, the hardware latency is taken as a direct constraint into the objective function using a pre-computed latency look-up table (LUT) from the target hardware device, making the searched model well optimized for the target device.

Our contributions are summarized as follows:

1) We present a highly efficient neural architecture search method for training and deploying SR models on mobile devices, using less than one GPU day.
2) We take the hardware latency as a direct constraint in the optimization process, which enables hardware-adaptive optimization of the searched model.
3) Experiments on two typical mobile devices validate the effectiveness of the proposed EHANAS method. The searched SR models achieve higher SR accuracy than previous ones with comparable or less hardware latency.

2   Related Work

LESR Network Design. Most of the manually designed LESR models mainly focus on reducing the number of FLOPs or network parameters. The pioneer LESR models, such as FSRCNN [8] and ESPCN [36], have validated the efficiency of a plain topology with several convolution blocks. Since then, a lot of more powerful modules have been proposed to improve SR performance while maintaining low FLOPs and small model sizes. For example, Ahn et al. [1] introduced a cascading residual network (CARN) with group convolution that has low FLOPs. Hui et al. [17] designed an information distillation network (IDN) to compress the number of filters per layer. IDN was then extended to the information multi-distillation network (IMDN) [16] which won the AIM 2019 constrained image SR challenge [47]. Liu et al. [29] further improved IMDN to residual feature distillation block (RFDB) and won the AIM 2020 [46] SR challenge. In NTIRE 2022 [26], more architectures and metrics are proposed and discussed for designing LESR. However, neither FLOPs nor parameters can faithfully reflect the real latency, especially on mobile devices [49]. Recently, Zhang et al. [49] carefully designed an edge-oriented convolution block for efficient SR on mobile devices. However, such a manual design consumes a huge amount of human labor and resources. In this work, we propose to automatically search a LESR model for the given target device and latency constraint in a very efficient way.

Network Pruning. Network pruning focuses on removing redundant or less important network parameters or blocks, which is a popular approach to compress large models to smaller ones [9,13,30,33]. For example, Li et al. [25] proposed a differentiable meta pruning method and applied it to SR models with a slight performance drop. Zhan et al. [45] utilized a hardware-aware filter pruning algorithm to design LESR models with latency constraints. Though network pruning is effective at reducing computational cost and accelerating inference speed, its upper bound is determined by the original model and it is very likely to generate a sub-optimal solution for the given hardware devices.

Neural Architecture Search. Neural architecture search (NAS) has emerged as a promising direction for automating the design of LESR models [4,5,14,24,37,38]. However, most of them use computationally intensive reinforcement learning or evolution methods to search models and employ indirect proxies (i.e., parameters and FLOPs) as optimization constraints. As a result, the searched models are usually unfriendly for mobile devices. Single-path NAS [38] provides a micro search space for coarse-grained hardware-aware search. However, it does not support searching the depth of the network which is vital for real-time models on mobile devices and likely to yield sub-optimality. Very recently, Zhan et al. [45] proposed a hardware-aware neural architecture and pruning search method, which takes hardware latency as a direct constraint. However, the proposed NAS method is based on a slow evolution algorithm and it contains three separate stages, including network search, pruning, and tuning. Different from it, we design a totally differentiable NAS pipeline where the searching and tuning are finished in one single stage in less than one GPU day.

3   Methodology

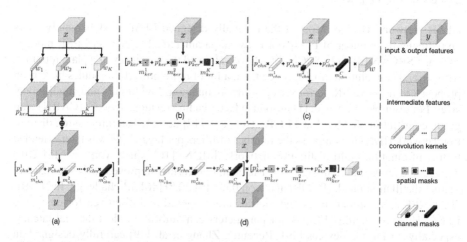

Fig. 2. Illustration of kernel type and channel dimension search. (a) The two-step search process of the DNAS method [41], contains multiple convolution branches and intermediate feature maps. (b) Kernel masking and (c) channel masking of the proposed method. (d) Re-parameterization of both kernel and channel masking for efficient search, where only one single convolution is required.

In this section, we discuss in detail the search for micro and macro network topology, hardware latency estimation, and latency-constrained optimization.

3.1 Block Search

The convolution block is the core module for feature extraction in SR models. A typical convolution block consists of three variables: kernel type, channel dimension, and activation type[1]. The kernel type and channel dimension search in the existing DNAS method [41] is shown in Fig. 2(a). As can be seen, in the kernel selection step, the input feature is passed into multiple convolution kernels, resulting in multiple intermediate features. The weighted summed feature is then fed into the channel selection step. Although the whole process is differentiable, the computation and memory cost increases linearly with the number of candidate kernels. To address this issue, we propose a kernel and channel masking strategy to conduct block searches at almost constant computation and memory costs.

Kernel Mask. Our kernel masking strategy is shown in Fig. 2(b). Given the input feature x, instead of employing multiple independent convolution kernels as candidates, we use a set of spatial masks $\{m_{ker}^k\}_{k=1}^K$ to dynamically adjust the spatial size of a shared convolution kernel w, where K is the number of kernel masks. In this way, the kernel search can be achieved by using one single convolution as:

$$y = (\sum_{k=1}^K p_{ker}^k \cdot m_{ker}^k \cdot w) * x + b \tag{1}$$

where y denotes the output feature, p_{ker}^k is the probability of choosing the k-th kernel mask and p_{ker}^k follows a Gumbel-Softmax distribution [10, 18, 31]:

$$p_{ker}^k = \frac{exp[(\theta_k + \epsilon_k)/\tau]}{\sum_{k=1}^K exp[(\theta_k + \epsilon_k)/\tau]} \tag{2}$$

where θ, ϵ, and τ represent the sampling parameter, Gumbel noise, and temperature, respectively.

With the consideration of mobile-friendly models, we set the spatial size of w to 5×5 and employ five kernel masks, including $1 \times 1, 1 \times 3, 3 \times 1, 3 \times 3$ and 5×5.

Channel Mask. Similarly, we can employ a set of channel masks to select the channel dimension as shown in Fig. 2(c). Denote by m_{chn}^c the c-th channel mask and by p_{chn}^c the corresponding probability (also following Gumbel-Softmax distribution), the channel selection process can be formulated as:

$$y = (\sum_{c=1}^C p_{chn}^c \cdot m_{chn}^c) \cdot (w * x + b) \tag{3}$$

where C is the total channel dimension of features.

---

[1] We do not consider those more complicated operators such as splitting, skip connection, and attention for block search since they are not friendly for resource-limited mobile devices [49].

Re-parameterization for Efficient Search. The kernel and channel selection method shown in Fig. 2(a) has two steps, which doubles the training latency. Benefiting from our kernel and channel masking strategy, Eq. 1 and Eq. 3 can be naturally merged into one single convolution:

$$y = w_{rep} * x + b_{rep} \tag{4}$$

where w_{rep} and b_{rep} are the weight and bias after re-parameterization:

$$\begin{cases} w_{rep} = (\sum_{c=1}^{C} p_{chn}^c \cdot m_{chn}^c) \cdot (\sum_{k=1}^{K} p_{ker}^k \cdot m_{ker}^k) \cdot w \\ b_{rep} = (\sum_{c=1}^{C} p_{chn}^c \cdot m_{chn}^c) \cdot b \end{cases} \tag{5}$$

The merged convolution is shown in Fig. 2(d).

Activation Search. The activation function is important for providing non-linear transformation capability to the SR model. However, most powerful activation functions are not supported by mobile devices. We thus incorporate two mobile-friendly activation functions, i.e., ReLU and identity mapping, as candidates for activation search. Denote by p_{act}^0 and p_{act}^1 the probabilities of selecting ReLU and identity mapping, respectively. The activation search can be formulated as follows:

$$\mathcal{A}(x) = p_{act}^0 \cdot ReLU(x) + p_{act}^1 \cdot x \tag{6}$$

where $\mathcal{A}$ denotes the weighted activation operation. Since both ReLU and identity mapping are linear functions, $\mathcal{A}$ could be further re-parameterized as follows:

$$\mathcal{A}(x) = \begin{cases} x, x \geq 0 \\ p_{act}^1 \cdot x, x < 0 \end{cases} \tag{7}$$

Compared to Eq. 6, Eq. 7 consumes less memory access and computation cost, which can further accelerate the searching speed.

The whole block search process, denoted by $\mathcal{C}$, can be formulated as follows:

$$\mathcal{C}(x) = \mathcal{A}(W_{rep} * x + b_{rep}) \tag{8}$$

3.2 Network Search

Based on the above block, we could search the overall network topology. Following prior arts on designing mobile-friendly SR models [49], we employ a plain network topology consisting of N blocks $\{C_n\}_{n=1}^N$, one skip connection, and one PixelShuffle operation $\mathcal{E}$, as shown in Fig. 3(a). The network search can be simplified to the search of the number of blocks, which is usually achieved by using discrete optimization in reinforce-learning or evolution-based NAS methods [4,5,14,37,45]. However, this is infeasible for DNAS. As shown in Fig. 3(b), we design a differential method to achieve this goal.

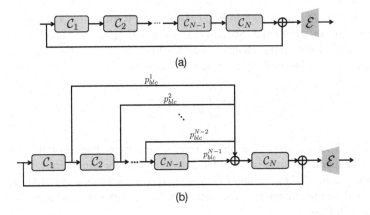

Fig. 3. Illustration of the network search. (a) A mobile-friendly plain topology for mobile SR consisting of N blocks $\{C_n\}_{n=1}^{N}$, one skip connection, and one PixelShuffle operation $\mathcal{E}$. (b) The differential search of the number of blocks.

Specifically, we assume the network has at least two blocks where the first block C_1 has a fixed number of input channels and the last block C_N has a fixed number of output channels, depending on the SR settings. For each block $C_n, n \leq N - 1$, we add a skip connection with probability p_{blc}^n to the input of the last block C_N. Denote by y_n the output of the n-th block and by $\circ$ the symbol of composition functions, we have:

$$y_n = \begin{cases} C_1(x), n = 1 \\ C_n \circ \ldots \circ C_1(x), 1 < n < N \end{cases} \tag{9}$$

Then the output of the network, denoted by $\mathcal{N}$, is a weighted summation of all paths as follows:

$$\mathcal{N}(x) = \mathcal{E} \circ [C_N \circ (\sum_{n=1}^{N-1} p_{blc}^n \cdot y_n) + x] \tag{10}$$

In this way, the search for block numbers is differentiable. As the probability of block paths $\{p_{blc}^n\}_{n=1}^{N-1}$ converges to a one-hot categorical vector, the depth of the searched network can be determined.

3.3 Hardware Latency Estimation

To search for a model that fits a target device, we take the hardware latency as a direct constraint in the optimization process. Following prior arts [41][2], we first calculate the hardware latency of each operator at different parameter sizes and record it using a

---

[2] The DL-based latency prediction model [12,48] can be also easily integrated into our framework, while we use pre-calculated LUT in this work for the purpose of straight latency comparison [49] and simplicity.

Lookup Table (LUT), as shown in Fig. 1. Under our formulation, the latency estimation is naturally differentiable. Specifically, using $LUT_k[c_i, c_o]$ to record the latency of the k-th kernel with input channel c_i and output channel c_o, the latency of the re-parameterized convolution (Eq. 4) can be calculated as:

$$T_{conv} = \sum_{c_o=1}^{C} p_{chn}^{c_o} \cdot (\sum_{c_i=1}^{C} p_{chn}^{c_i} \cdot (\sum_{k=1}^{K} p_{ker}^{k} \cdot LUT_k[c_i, c_o])) \tag{11}$$

Note that the input channel of the current layer is the output channel of the former layer. We do not annotate the layer index in the above formula for simplicity.

Similarly, using $LUT_R[c_o]$ and $LUT_I[c_o]$ to record the latency of ReLU and identity mapping with output channel c_o, the latency of the re-parameterized activation (Eq. 7) can be calculated as:

$$T_{act} = \sum_{c_o=1}^{C} p_{chn}^{c_o} \cdot (p_{act}^{0} \cdot LUT_R[c_o] + p_{act}^{1} \cdot LUT_I[c_o]) \tag{12}$$

Then the latency of the n-th convolution block can be easily obtained as follows:

$$T(\mathcal{C}_n) = T_{conv}^n + T_{act}^n \tag{13}$$

where T_{conv}^n and T_{act}^n are the latency of the n-th convolution and activation. The total latency of the network is the weighted summation of all blocks plus several additional operators:

$$T(\mathcal{N}) = \sum_{n=1}^{N-1} [p_{blc}^n \cdot T(\mathcal{C}_n)] + T_{add} \tag{14}$$

where T_{add} contains the latency of the last convolution, one skip connection and one PixelShuffle operation.

3.4 Latency Constrained Optimization

Previous works on LESR search usually contain several stages such as architecture search, network pruning, and tuning [4,5,14,24,37,45]. Benefiting from our totally differential pipeline, we can perform model architecture searching and tuning in just one single stage, which can greatly reduce the time for hardware adaptation. Denote by I_{LR} and I_{HR} a pair of LR and HR images, the latency constrained loss function for SR is defined as follows:

$$\mathcal{L}(\mathcal{N}) = ||\mathcal{N}(I_{LR}) - I_{HR}||_1 + \beta ||T(\mathcal{N}) - T_0||_1 \tag{15}$$

where $\mathcal{N}$ is the network parameters to be optimized, T_0 is the required latency on a target device, and β is a weighting parameter to balance the reconstruction loss and latency loss.

4 Experiments

In this section, we employ the proposed EHANAS method to search for LESR models on two typical hardware devices, including the DSP of snapdragon 865 and the GPU of Dimensity 1000+, under certain latency constraints and compare their performance with existing state-of-the-art LESR models on five SR benchmark datasets. We also conduct a comprehensive ablation study to analyze the influence of searching space on the performance of searched models.

4.1 Datasets and Implementation Details

We employ the DIV2K dataset [39], which consists of 800 training images, to search and train our EHANAS models. The DIV2K validation set and four benchmark SR datasets, i.e., Set5 [3], Set14 [44], BSD100 [32] and Urban [15], are used for model evaluation and comparison. PSNR and SSIM indexes calculated on the Y channel of YCbCr color space are used for performance evaluation.

We use bicubic interpolation to obtain LR images and randomly crop 32 patches of size 64×64 from the LR images as input for each training batch. Random rotations of $90°$, $180°$, and $270°$ are selected as the strategies for data augmentation. Since our EHANAS is a one-shot architecture, we use two ADAM optimizers for architecture search and weight tuning concurrently. Two typical hardware devices, i.e., the DSP of snapdragon 865 and the GPU of Dimensity 1000+, are employed to search hardware-aware LESR models. The latency look-up tables of different operators are pre-computed on both devices. We train the model for 500 epochs using a fixed learning rate at 5×10^{-4}. The parameter β for balancing the fidelity score and latency constraint in Eq. 15 is initialized as 1×10^{-4} for 10 epochs of warm-up, then increased to 3×10^{-2} linearly.

4.2 Quantitative Comparison

We first quantitatively compare the searched models by EHANAS against existing representative LESR models, including SRCNN [7], FSRCNN [8], ESPCN [36], ECBSR [49], VDSR [19], LapSRN [21], CARN-M [1], MoreMNAS-{B, C} [5], FALSR-{B, C} [4], TPSR-NoGAN [24], EDSR [27], IMDN [16], RLFN [20], FMEN [11] and EFDN [26]. In Table 1, we summarize the performance comparisons on the DSP of snapdragon 865 and GPU of dimensity 1000+. For the $\times 2$ up-scaling setting, which is more computationally intensive than the $\times 4$ setting, we search the EHANAS model on DSP of snapdragon 865 using three latency constraints, 30 ms for real-time speed, 80 ms for nearly real-time speed, and 600 ms for better accuracy to verify the scalability of the proposed method. For $\times 4$ up-scaling, we search a super real-time, a real-time, and a larger model using 15 ms, 30 ms, and 150 ms as latency constraints, respectively. As for the model settings on GPU of dimensity 1000+, we use {50 ms, 200 ms, 1200 ms} and {20 ms, 80 ms, 400 ms} for $\times 2$ and $\times 4$ upscaling tasks, respectively. In addition to the PSNR/SSIM indexes and latency, we also report some classical proxies such as the number of network parameters, FLOPs, activation, and convolution layers for reference.

Table 1. Performance comparison of different SR models on five benchmarks. PSNR/SSIM scores on Y channel are reported on each dataset. #Params, #FLOPs, #Acts, #Conv, and #Lat represent the total number of network parameters, floating-point operations, activation, convolution layers, and inference latency, respectively. The #FLOPs and #Acts are measured under the setting of generating an SR image of 1280×720 resolution on both scales. The #Lat is measured by generating an SR image of 1920×1080 resolution using the DSP of Snapdragon 865 and GPU of Dimensity 1000+. The best results of each group are highlighted in **bold**.

Scale	Model	#Params (K)	#FLOPs (G)	#Acts (M)	#Conv	#Lat (s) DSP	#Lat (s) GPU	Set5 [3]	Set14 [44]	B100 [32]	Urban100 [15]	DIV2K [39]
× 2	Bicubic	—	—	—	—	—	—	33.68/0.9307	30.24/0.8693	29.56/0.8439	26.88/0.8408	32.45/0.9043
	SRCNN [7]	24.00	52.70	89.39	3	1.591	0.890	36.66/0.9542	32.42/0.9063	31.36/0.8879	29.50/0.8946	34.61/0.9334
	ESPCN [36]	21.18	4.55	23.04	3	0.072	0.080	36.83/0.9544	32.40/0.9060	31.29/0.8870	29.48/0.8948	34.63/0.9335
	FSRCNN [8]	12.46	6.00	40.53	8	0.114	0.076	36.98/0.9556	32.62/0.9087	31.50/0.8904	29.85/0.9009	34.74/0.9340
	MOREMNAS-C [5]	25.00	5.50	269.11	49	—	—	37.06/0.9561	32.75/0.9094	31.50/0.8904	29.92/0.9023	34.87/0.9356
	ECBSR-M4C16 [49]	10.20	2.34	19.35	6	0.033	0.046	37.33/0.9580	32.81/0.9100	31.66/0.8931	30.31/0.9091	35.15/0.9380
	TPSR-NoGAN [24]	60.00	14.00	50.69	14	—	—	37.38/0.9583	33.00/0.9123	31.75/0.8942	30.61/0.9119	—
	EHANAS-GPU-50 ms	11.90	2.74	35.02	8	—	0.049	37.42/0.9585	32.95/0.9122	31.71/0.8940	30.36/0.9092	35.23/0.9383
	EHANAS-DSP-30 ms	35.40	8.13	44.97	7	0.029	—	**37.63/0.9593**	**33.15/0.9137**	**31.89/0.8960**	**30.98/0.9168**	**35.51/0.9408**
	IMDN-RTC [16]	19.70	4.57	65.20	28	1.101	1.076	37.51/0.9590	32.93/0.9122	31.79/0.8950	30.67/0.9120	35.34/0.9398
	LapSRN [21]	813.00	29.90	223.03	14	4.395	1.624	37.52/0.9590	33.08/0.9130	31.80/0.8950	30.41/0.9100	35.31/0.9400
	VDSR [19]	665.00	612.60	1121.59	20	8.946	3.379	37.53/0.9587	33.05/0.9127	31.90/0.8960	30.77/0.9141	35.43/0.9410
	CARN-M [1]	412.00	91.20	649.73	42	0.884	1.195	37.53/0.9583	33.26/0.9141	31.92/0.8960	31.23/0.9193	35.62/0.9420
	MOREMNAS-B [5]	1118.00	256.90	987.96	79	—	—	37.58/0.9584	33.22/0.9135	31.91/0.8959	31.14/0.9175	35.46/0.9402
	FALSR-B [4]	326.00	74.70	372.33	49	—	—	37.61/0.9585	33.29/0.9143	31.97/0.8967	31.28/0.9191	35.58/0.9408
	FALSR-C [4]	408.00	93.70	379.70	34	—	—	37.66/0.9586	33.26/0.9140	31.96/0.8965	31.24/0.9187	35.57/0.9407
	EDSR-R5C32 [27]	130.80	30.31	111.51	13	0.150	0.653	37.61/0.9590	33.06/0.9127	31.87/0.8959	30.90/0.9162	35.45/0.9407
	ECBSR-M10C32 [49]	94.70	21.81	82.02	12	0.062	0.203	37.76/0.9595	33.26/0.9136	32.04/0.8970	31.25/0.9190	35.68/0.9421
	EHANAS-GPU-200 ms	127.90	29.47	92.16	10	—	0.208	37.80/0.9597	33.31/0.9147	**32.05**/0.8972	31.32/0.9191	35.72/0.9425
	EHANAS-DSP-80 ms	99.40	22.89	89.40	10	0.077	—	**37.83/0.9596**	**33.33/0.9152**	32.04/**0.8974**	**31.36/0.9198**	**35.73/0.9426**
	ECBSR-M16C64 [49]	596.00	137.31	251.60	18	0.513	0.786	37.90/0.9600	33.34/0.9153	32.10/0.8982	31.71/0.9250	35.79/0.9430
	EDSR-R16C64 [27]	1334.90	307.89	546.51	37	1.447	2.372	37.99/0.9604	33.57/0.9175	32.16/0.8994	31.98/0.9272	35.85/0.9436
	IMDN [16]	660.30	152.04	406.43	34	10.610	12.792	37.99/0.9603	33.39/0.9156	32.14/0.8993	31.96/0.9267	35.87/0.9436
	EHANAS-GPU-1200 ms	1336.3	307.89	376.93	18	—	1.175	38.00/0.9605	33.53/0.9174	32.15/0.8995	32.00/0.9275	35.88/0.9435
	EHANAS-DSP-600 ms	1188.90	273.91	487.53	34	0.583	—	**38.05/0.9611**	**33.60/0.9180**	**32.18/0.8998**	**32.05/0.9280**	**35.89/0.9437**
× 4	Bicubic	—	—	—	—	—	—	28.43/0.8113	26.00/0.7025	25.96/0.6682	23.14/0.6577	28.10/0.7745
	SRCNN [7]	57.00	52.7	89.39	3	1.583	0.896	30.48/0.8628	27.49/0.7503	26.90/0.7101	24.52/0.7221	29.25/0.8090
	ESPCN [36]	24.90	1.44	6.45	3	0.026	0.032	30.52/0.8647	27.42/0.7516	26.87/0.7100	24.39/0.7211	29.32/0.8100
	FSRCNN [8]	12.00	5.00	10.81	8	0.032	0.028	30.70/0.8657	27.59/0.7535	26.96/0.7128	24.60/0.7258	29.36/0.8110
	ECBSR-M4C16 [49]	11.90	0.69	5.53	6	0.011	0.028	31.04/0.8785	27.78/0.7645	27.09/0.7200	24.79/0.7422	29.62/0.8187
	TPSR-NoGAN [24]	61.00	3.60	13.13	15	—	—	31.10/0.8779	27.95/0.7663	27.15/0.7214	24.97/0.7456	29.77/0.8200
	EHANAS-GPU-20 ms	21.00	1.21	9.22	10	—	0.022	31.25/0.8812	28.03/0.7680	27.20/0.7248	25.01/0.7480	29.80/0.8221
	EHANAS-DSP-15 ms	66.60	3.87	17.63	10	0.014	—	**31.57/0.8855**	**28.23/0.7725**	**27.31/0.7255**	**25.34/0.7595**	**29.94/0.8260**
	IMDN-RTC [16]	21.00	1.22	16.99	28	0.318	0.287	31.22/0.8810	27.92/0.7660	27.18/0.7217	24.98/0.7477	29.76/0.8200
	VDSR [19]	665.00	612.60	1121.59	20	9.036	3.365	31.35/0.8838	28.02/0.7678	27.29/0.7252	25.18/0.7525	29.82/0.8240
	LapSRN [21]	813.00	149.40	264.04	27	5.378	5.801	31.54/0.8850	28.19/0.7720	27.32/0.7280	25.21/0.7560	29.88/0.8250
	EDSR-R5C32 [27]	241.80	14.15	50.69	13	0.101	0.567	31.46/0.8845	28.07/0.7682	27.27/0.7250	25.21/0.7561	29.87/0.8251
	ECBSR-M10C32 [49]	98.10	5.65	21.20	12	0.017	0.063	31.66/0.8880	28.15/0.7705	27.34/0.7283	25.41/0.7650	29.98/0.8275
	EHANAS-GPU-80 ms	194.5	11.20	23.04	7	—	0.079	31.73/0.8885	28.33/**0.7759**	27.39/0.7300	25.43/0.7651	30.05/0.8281
	EHANAS-DSP-30 ms	177.70	10.45	47.89	26	0.027	—	**31.75/0.8887**	**28.34**/0.7758	**27.42/0.7302**	**25.45/0.7653**	**30.05/0.8283**
	CARN-M [1]	412.00	46.10	222.14	43	0.170	0.362	31.92/0.8903	28.42/0.7762	27.44/0.7304	25.62/0.7694	30.10/0.8311
	ECBSR-M16C64 [49]	602.90	34.73	63.59	18	0.071	0.209	31.92/0.8929	28.34/0.7756	27.48/0.7323	25.81/0.7780	30.15/0.8315
	EDSR-R16C64 [27]	1778.00	102.85	181.56	37	0.527	1.639	32.09/0.8938	28.58/0.7813	27.57/0.7357	26.04/0.7849	30.21/0.8336
	IMDN [16]	667.40	38.41	102.30	34	2.782	2.672	32.03/0.8929	28.42/0.7783	27.48/0.7320	25.96/0.7804	30.22/0.8336
	EHANAS-GPU-400 ms	1513.2	46.17	105.98	20	—	0.395	32.02/0.8930	28.50/0.7802	27.53/0.7334	26.00/0.7844	30.22/0.8336
	EHANAS-DSP-150 ms	1269.9	73.15	129.95	36	0.148	—	**32.11/0.8941**	**28.60/0.7814**	**27.58/0.7357**	**26.05/0.7850**	**30.25/0.8337**
	RLFN [20]	317.2	17.31	70.35	39	0.893	0.192	32.07/0.8927	28.59/0.7808	27.56/0.7349	26.09/0.7842	30.43/0.8367
	FMEN [11]	341.1	19.58	63.36	34	0.874	0.303	32.01/0.8925	28.56/0.7808	27.55/0.7346	26.00/0.7818	30.44/0.8367
	EFDN [26]	276.2	14.70	97.65	65	1.005	1.070	32.05/0.8920	28.57/0.7801	27.54/0.7342	25.99/0.7805	30.44/0.8365

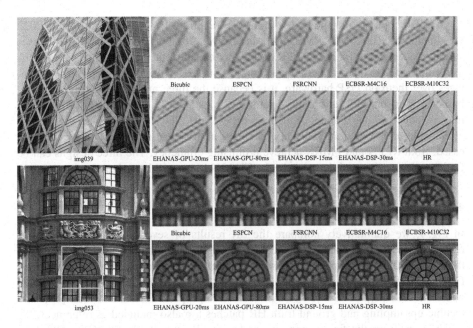

Fig. 4. Qualitative comparison of real-time and nearly real-time SR models on Urban100 for × 4 upscaling tasks. The searched EHANAS models can restore richer and sharper details than other competing models.

One can see that the searched models by EHANAS obtain clearly better performance than previous LESR models under most settings. Specifically, under the real-time setting of ×2 up-scaling, our EHANAS-DSP-30 ms model improves the PSNR by more than 0.3 dB on both the Set5 and DIV2K validation set compared to the second-best candidate ECBSR-M4C16. As for the nearly real-time setting of ×2 up-scaling, EHANAS-DSP-80 ms outperforms the second-best model ECBSR-M10C32 on all five datasets at comparable latency. One can see that our EHANAS-DSP-80 ms model can obtain close PSNR/SSIM indexes to IMDN and EDSR-baseline, but it is more than 18 and 137 times faster than them on the DSP hardware. Furthermore, our larger model, EHANAS-DSP-600 ms, achieves the best results among the five benchmarks, while it is around 2 and 18 times faster than EDSR-baseline and IMDN on DSP hardware, validating the scalability of our EHANAS method.

Similar observations can be made under the setting of ×4 up-scaling, where the EHANAS-DSP-15 ms, EHANAS-DSP-30 ms and EHANAS-DSP-150 ms models obtain higher PSNR and SSIM indexes on all datasets with less or comparable resources compared to their competitors. These results validate the effectiveness of using the proposed EHANAS method to search LESR models. Noted that the computational capacity of GPU of dimensity 1000+ is much lower than DSP of snapdragon 865, while our EHANAS method can also successfully search the desired models, achieving better PSNR/SSIM indexes than previous methods with lower computational cost and hardware resources.

We also compare our method with the top-ranking LESR designs in NTIRE 2022 [26], including RLFN [20], FMEN [11] and EFDN [26]. Our EHANAS-DSP-150 ms is slightly better except for the DIV2K, it may be that all of the three methods are specifically trained and tuned for this benchmark. Our EHANAS series have huge advantages over them on DSP hardware, it is because the three methods incorporate multi-branch design and DSP-unfriendly operations (e.g., PReLU, LReLU, and ESA) which may introduce a huge amount of memory access cost. Since the GPU hardware is programmable and computationally bounded, the above-mentioned drawbacks could be eased. Both RLFN and FMEN achieve promising efficiency. The three designs can be further enhanced on mobile scenarios by EHANAS, we will leave it as future research.

4.3   Qualitative Comparison

In Fig. 4, we qualitatively compare the SR results of several real-time and nearly real-time models under the ×4 up-scaling setting by using two example images from the Urban100 dataset. Specifically, we compare our searched EHANAS-DSP-30 ms, EHANAS-DSP-80 ms, EHANAS-GPU-50 ms, and EHANAS-GPU-200 ms models with FSRCNN [8], ESPCN [36], ECBSR-M4C16 [49] and ECBSRM10C32 [49]. The bicubic upsampling and ground truth HR patches are also included as references. As can be seen from the figure, previous real-time SR models like ESPCN, FSRCNN, and ECBSR-M4C16 tend to recover blurry and smooth texture around long edges in "img039", while our EHANAS-GPU-50 ms and EHANAS-DSP-30 ms can reproduce more details and well preserve the edge structure to some extent. On image "img053", our EHANAS-DSP-30 ms, EHANAS-DSP-80 ms, EHANAS-GPU-50 ms, and EHANAS-GPU-200 ms models successfully generate sharper and clearer edge details than other competing methods.

In Fig. 5, we provide the qualitative comparison of SR results among several representative and more complicated models, including CARN-M [1], EDSR-R16C64 [27] and IMDN [16]. On image "Barbara" from Set14, EHANAS-GPU-400 ms and EHANAS-DSP-150 ms well preserve the long edge structure, while other methods produce blurry or artificial details around edges. On image "img052", most of the compared methods yield either blurry or inaccurate edges and textures, while our EHANAS-DSP-150 ms can restore more accurate and sharper details.

Table 2. Ablation studies on the search space. The baseline results are from ECBSR-M4C16 [49]. By default, the kernel type, channel dimension, block number and activation are set to 3×3, 32, 8, ReLU, respectively, when they are not searched.

Method	Kernel	Channel	#Block	Act	#Lat(s)	Set5 [3]	Set14 [44]	B100 [32]	Urban100 [15]	DIV2K [39]
Baseline					0.033	37.33/0.9580	32.81/0.9100	31.66/0.8931	30.31/0.9091	35.15/0.9380
EHANAS	✓	✓			0.034	37.46/0.9586	32.98/0.9121	31.76/0.8944	30.56/0.9117	35.31/0.9393
EHANAS		✓	✓		0.035	37.51/0.9588	33.03/0.9130	31.80/0.8950	30.69/0.9131	35.37/0.9398
EHANAS	✓		✓		0.035	37.53/0.9588	33.03/0.9126	31.78/0.8949	30.65/0.9126	35.33/0.9395
EHANAS	✓	✓	✓		0.031	37.60/0.9592	33.12/0.9136	31.85/0.8958	30.91/0.9154	35.46/0.9401
EHANAS	✓	✓	✓	✓	**0.029**	**37.63/0.9593**	**33.15/0.9137**	**31.89/0.8960**	**30.98/0.9168**	**35.51/0.9408**

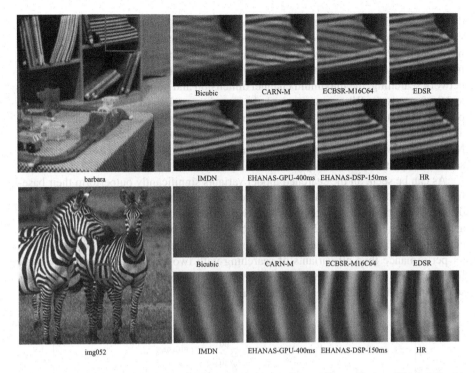

Fig. 5. Qualitative comparison of larger models for × 4 upscaling tasks on "Barbara" and "Img052" from B100 and Set14, respectively. The searched EHANAS models can restore clearer edges and structures than other competing models.

4.4 Search Cost Comparison

In this section, we compare the computation and memory cost by using the state-of-the-art DNAS method [41] and our proposed EHANAS to search SR models of different complexity. Specifically, we use the five kernel candidates as described in Sec. 3.1, set the maximum channel dimension to 64, and vary the number of blocks from 5 to 25 with step-length 5. The memory cost (measured in GB) and computing time of 100 training iterations (measured in seconds) of different settings are plotted in Fig. 6.

One can see that both the memory and computation cost of DNAS is about 3 times as much as our proposed EHANAS. This is because the DNAS method uses multiple independent convolution branches, while our EHANAS employs only one shared convolution. As the cost increases linearly with the number of network blocks, EHANAS can save a lot of computation and time, especially when the SR models are to be deployed on multiple hardware devices with different latency constraints.

4.5 Ablation Study

We conduct a series of ablation studies to investigate the influence of network search space on the searched model. Specifically, we conduct ablation experiments by using different combinations of the four variables, i.e., kernel type, channel dimension, activation type, and the number of blocks. Since one single variable can be directly determined for a certain latency, we search for at least two variables in each experiment. All models are searched under the ×2 up-scaling task with a 30 ms latency constraint. For network searching, the maximum channel dimension and number of blocks are set to 64 and 8, respectively. When not searched, the kernel type, channel dimension, block number, and activation are set to 3×3, 32, 8, and ReLU, respectively, following prior arts. The results of different model variants are reported in Table 2. The results of ECBSR-M4C16 [49], which is the state-of-the-art among manually design LESR models at the same latency level, are also reported for comparison.

As can be seen, all the searched model variants significantly outperform their baselines, which validates the advantage of the proposed EHANAS method over manual design. When performing searching with two variables, the combination of kernel type and block number (kernel+block for short) obtains the best performance, followed by channel+block. Searching with three variables, i.e., kernel+channel+block, obtains better performance than all variants of searching with two variables. Searching with all four variables further improves the performance. These results indicate that a larger search space can generally lead to a better model.

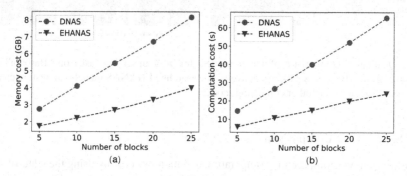

Fig. 6. Comparison of searching costs between the existing DNAS method [41] and our proposed EHANAS. (a) Memory cost (measured in GB) comparison of the entire model during the model searching process. (b) Computational cost (measured in second) comparison of training 100 iterations during the model searching process.

5   Conclusion and Discussions

In this paper, we proposed an efficient hardware-aware neural architecture search (EHA-NAS) method to automatically search light-weight and efficient SR models on mobile devices. EHANAS could finish the searching of both macro and micro-network topologies within one GPU day. Experiments on two typical hardware devices, GPU of Dimensity 1000+ and DSP of Snapdragon 865, validated the effectiveness of EHANAS in searching SR models under desired latency constraints. The searched SR models could work in real-time or nearly real-time while exhibiting much better accuracy than previously manually designed and automatically searched models.

While EHANAS is very efficient by benefiting from the proposed masking and re-parameterization strategy, the shared weights may slightly condense the searching space. In addition, an individual model has to be searched for each device under each latency constraint. In the future, we will study how to search for shared SR models that can be easily adapted to different hardware devices.

References

1. Ahn, N., Kang, B., Sohn, K.A.: Fast, accurate, and lightweight super-resolution with cascading residual network. In: Proceedings of the European Conference on Computer Vision (ECCV), pp. 252–268 (2018)
2. Baker, B., Gupta, O., Naik, N., Raskar, R.: Designing neural network architectures using reinforcement learning. arXiv preprint arXiv:1611.02167 (2016)
3. Bevilacqua, M., Roumy, A., Guillemot, C., Alberi-Morel, M.L.: Low-complexity single-image super-resolution based on nonnegative neighbor embedding (2012)
4. Chu, X., Zhang, B., Ma, H., Xu, R., Li, Q.: Fast, accurate and lightweight super-resolution with neural architecture search. In: 2020 25th International Conference on Pattern Recognition (ICPR), pp. 59–64. IEEE (2021)
5. Chu, X., Zhang, B., Xu, R.: Multi-objective reinforced evolution in mobile neural architecture search. In: Bartoli, A., Fusiello, A. (eds.) ECCV 2020. LNCS, vol. 12538, pp. 99–113. Springer, Cham (2020). https://doi.org/10.1007/978-3-030-66823-5_6
6. Dai, T., Cai, J., Zhang, Y., Xia, S.T., Zhang, L.: Second-order attention network for single image super-resolution. In: Proceedings of the IEEE/CVF Conference on Computer Vision and Pattern Recognition, pp. 11065–11074 (2019)
7. Dong, C., Loy, C.C., He, K., Tang, X.: Image super-resolution using deep convolutional networks. IEEE Trans. Pattern Anal. Mach. Intell. **38**(2), 295–307 (2015)
8. Dong, C., Loy, C.C., Tang, X.: Accelerating the super-resolution convolutional neural network. In: Leibe, B., Matas, J., Sebe, N., Welling, M. (eds.) ECCV 2016. LNCS, vol. 9906, pp. 391–407. Springer, Cham (2016). https://doi.org/10.1007/978-3-319-46475-6_25
9. Dong, P., et al.: RTMobile: beyond real-time mobile acceleration of RNNs for speech recognition. In: 2020 57th ACM/IEEE Design Automation Conference (DAC), pp. 1–6. IEEE (2020)
10. Dong, X., Yang, Y.: Searching for a robust neural architecture in four GPU hours. In: Proceedings of the IEEE/CVF Conference on Computer Vision and Pattern Recognition, pp. 1761–1770 (2019)
11. Du, Z., Liu, D., Liu, J., Tang, J., Wu, G., Fu, L.: Fast and memory-efficient network towards efficient image super-resolution. In: Proceedings of the IEEE/CVF Conference on Computer Vision and Pattern Recognition, pp. 853–862 (2022)
12. Gao, Y., Gu, X., Zhang, H., Lin, H., Yang, M.: Runtime performance prediction for deep learning models with graph neural network. Technical report, MSR-TR-2021-3. Microsoft (2021)
13. Gong, Y., et al.: A privacy-preserving-oriented DNN pruning and mobile acceleration framework. In: Proceedings of the 2020 on Great Lakes Symposium on VLSI, pp. 119–124 (2020)
14. Guo, Y., Luo, Y., He, Z., Huang, J., Chen, J.: Hierarchical neural architecture search for single image super-resolution. IEEE Signal Process. Lett. **27**, 1255–1259 (2020)
15. Huang, J.B., Singh, A., Ahuja, N.: Single image super-resolution from transformed self-exemplars. In: Proceedings of the IEEE Conference on Computer Vision and Pattern Recognition, pp. 5197–5206 (2015)

16. Hui, Z., Gao, X., Yang, Y., Wang, X.: Lightweight image super-resolution with information multi-distillation network. In: Proceedings of the 27th ACM International Conference on Multimedia, pp. 2024–2032 (2019)
17. Hui, Z., Wang, X., Gao, X.: Fast and accurate single image super-resolution via information distillation network. In: Proceedings of the IEEE Conference on Computer Vision and Pattern Recognition, pp. 723–731 (2018)
18. Jang, E., Gu, S., Poole, B.: Categorical reparameterization with gumbel-softmax. arXiv preprint arXiv:1611.01144 (2016)
19. Kim, J., Lee, J.K., Lee, K.M.: Accurate image super-resolution using very deep convolutional networks. In: Proceedings of the IEEE Conference on Computer Vision and Pattern Recognition, pp. 1646–1654 (2016)
20. Kong, F., et al.: Residual local feature network for efficient super-resolution. In: Proceedings of the IEEE/CVF Conference on Computer Vision and Pattern Recognition, pp. 766–776 (2022)
21. Lai, W.S., Huang, J.B., Ahuja, N., Yang, M.H.: Deep laplacian pyramid networks for fast and accurate super-resolution. In: Proceedings of the IEEE Conference on Computer Vision and Pattern Recognition, pp. 624–632 (2017)
22. LeCun, Y., Bengio, Y., Hinton, G.: Deep learning. Nature 521(7553), 436–444 (2015)
23. Lee, R., et al.: Journey towards tiny perceptual super-resolution. In: Vedaldi, A., Bischof, H., Brox, T., Frahm, J.-M. (eds.) ECCV 2020. LNCS, vol. 12371, pp. 85–102. Springer, Cham (2020). https://doi.org/10.1007/978-3-030-58574-7_6
24. Lee, R., et al.: Journey towards tiny perceptual super-resolution. In: Vedaldi, A., Bischof, H., Brox, T., Frahm, J.-M. (eds.) ECCV 2020. LNCS, vol. 12371, pp. 85–102. Springer, Cham (2020). https://doi.org/10.1007/978-3-030-58574-7_6
25. Li, Y., Gu, S., Zhang, K., Van Gool, L., Timofte, R.: DHP: differentiable meta pruning via hypernetworks. In: Vedaldi, A., Bischof, H., Brox, T., Frahm, J.-M. (eds.) ECCV 2020. LNCS, vol. 12353, pp. 608–624. Springer, Cham (2020). https://doi.org/10.1007/978-3-030-58598-3_36
26. Li, Y., et al.: Ntire 2022 challenge on efficient super-resolution: methods and results. In: Proceedings of the IEEE/CVF Conference on Computer Vision and Pattern Recognition, pp. 1062–1102 (2022)
27. Lim, B., Son, S., Kim, H., Nah, S., Mu Lee, K.: Enhanced deep residual networks for single image super-resolution. In: Proceedings of the IEEE Conference on Computer Vision and Pattern Recognition workshops, pp. 136–144 (2017)
28. Liu, H., Simonyan, K., Vinyals, O., Fernando, C., Kavukcuoglu, K.: Hierarchical representations for efficient architecture search. arXiv preprint arXiv:1711.00436 (2017)
29. Liu, J., Tang, J., Wu, G.: Residual feature distillation network for lightweight image super-resolution. In: Bartoli, A., Fusiello, A. (eds.) ECCV 2020. LNCS, vol. 12537, pp. 41–55. Springer, Cham (2020). https://doi.org/10.1007/978-3-030-67070-2_2
30. Ma, X., ET AL.: PCONV: the missing but desirable sparsity in DNN weight pruning for real-time execution on mobile devices. In: Proceedings of the AAAI Conference on Artificial Intelligence, vol. 34, pp. 5117–5124 (2020)
31. Maddison, C.J., Mnih, A., Teh, Y.W.: The concrete distribution: a continuous relaxation of discrete random variables. arXiv preprint arXiv:1611.00712 (2016)
32. Martin, D., Fowlkes, C., Tal, D., Malik, J.: A database of human segmented natural images and its application to evaluating segmentation algorithms and measuring ecological statistics. In: Proceedings Eighth IEEE International Conference on Computer Vision. ICCV 2001, vol. 2, pp. 416–423. IEEE (2001)
33. Niu, W., et al.: PatDNN: achieving real-time DNN execution on mobile devices with pattern-based weight pruning. In: Proceedings of the Twenty-Fifth International Conference on

Architectural Support for Programming Languages and Operating Systems, pp. 907–922 (2020)

34. Radosavovic, I., Kosaraju, R.P., Girshick, R., He, K., Dollár, P.: Designing network design spaces. In: Proceedings of the IEEE/CVF Conference on Computer Vision and Pattern Recognition, pp. 10428–10436 (2020)

35. Real, E., Aggarwal, A., Huang, Y., Le, Q.V.: Regularized evolution for image classifier architecture search. In: Proceedings of the AAAI Conference on Artificial Intelligence, vol. 33, pp. 4780–4789 (2019)

36. Shi, W., et al.: Real-time single image and video super-resolution using an efficient sub-pixel convolutional neural network. In: Proceedings of the IEEE Conference on Computer Vision and Pattern Recognition, pp. 1874–1883 (2016)

37. Song, D., Xu, C., Jia, X., Chen, Y., Xu, C., Wang, Y.: Efficient residual dense block search for image super-resolution. In: Proceedings of the AAAI Conference on Artificial Intelligence, vol. 34, pp. 12007–12014 (2020)

38. Stamoulis, D., et al.: Single-path nas: Device-aware efficient convnet design. arXiv preprint arXiv:1905.04159 (2019)

39. Timofte, R., Agustsson, E., Van Gool, L., Yang, M.H., Zhang, L.: NTIRE 2017 challenge on single image super-resolution: methods and results. In: Proceedings of the IEEE conference on computer vision and pattern recognition workshops, pp. 114–125 (2017)

40. Vu, T., Van Nguyen, C., Pham, T.X., Luu, T.M., Yoo, C.D.: Fast and efficient image quality enhancement via desubpixel convolutional neural networks. In: Proceedings of the European Conference on Computer Vision (ECCV) Workshops (2018)

41. Wan, A., et al.: Fbnetv2: differentiable neural architecture search for spatial and channel dimensions. In: Proceedings of the IEEE/CVF Conference on Computer Vision and Pattern Recognition, pp. 12965–12974 (2020)

42. Wang, L., et al.: Exploring sparsity in image super-resolution for efficient inference. In: Proceedings of the IEEE/CVF Conference on Computer Vision and Pattern Recognition, pp. 4917–4926 (2021)

43. Wu, B., et al.: FBNet: hardware-aware efficient convnet design via differentiable neural architecture search. In: Proceedings of the IEEE/CVF Conference on Computer Vision and Pattern Recognition, pp. 10734–10742 (2019)

44. Zeyde, R., Elad, M., Protter, M.: On single image scale-up using sparse-representations. In: Boissonnat, J.-D., et al. (eds.) Curves and Surfaces 2010. LNCS, vol. 6920, pp. 711–730. Springer, Heidelberg (2012). https://doi.org/10.1007/978-3-642-27413-8_47

45. Zhan, Z., et al.: Achieving on-mobile real-time super-resolution with neural architecture and pruning search. In: Proceedings of the IEEE/CVF International Conference on Computer Vision, pp. 4821–4831 (2021)

46. Zhang, K., et al.: AIM 2020 challenge on efficient super-resolution: methods and results. In: Bartoli, A., Fusiello, A. (eds.) ECCV 2020. LNCS, vol. 12537, pp. 5–40. Springer, Cham (2020). https://doi.org/10.1007/978-3-030-67070-2_1

47. Zhang, K., et al.: Aim 2019 challenge on constrained super-resolution: methods and results. In: 2019 IEEE/CVF International Conference on Computer Vision Workshop (ICCVW), pp. 3565–3574. IEEE (2019)

48. Zhang, L.L., et al.: Nn-meter: towards accurate latency prediction of deep-learning model inference on diverse edge devices. In: Proceedings of the 19th Annual International Conference on Mobile Systems, Applications, and Services, pp. 81–93 (2021)

49. Zhang, X., Zeng, H., Zhang, L.: Edge-oriented convolution block for real-time super resolution on mobile devices. In: Proceedings of the 29th ACM International Conference on Multimedia, pp. 4034–4043 (2021)

50. Zhang, Y., Li, K., Li, K., Wang, L., Zhong, B., Fu, Y.: Image super-resolution using very deep residual channel attention networks. In: Proceedings of the European Conference on Computer Vision (ECCV), pp. 286–301 (2018)
51. Zoph, B., Le, Q.V.: Neural architecture search with reinforcement learning. arXiv preprint arXiv:1611.01578 (2016)
52. Zoph, B., Vasudevan, V., Shlens, J., Le, Q.V.: Learning transferable architectures for scalable image recognition. In: Proceedings of the IEEE Conference on Computer Vision and Pattern Recognition, pp. 8697–8710 (2018)

Fine-Grained Image Style Transfer
with Visual Transformers

Jianbo Wang[1], Huan Yang[2(✉)], Jianlong Fu[2], Toshihiko Yamasaki[1],
and Baining Guo[2]

[1] The Univerisity of Tokyo, Tokyo, Japan
{jianbowang815,yamasaki}@cvm.t.u-tokyo.ac.jp
[2] Microsoft Research, Redmond, USA
{huayan,jianf,bainguo}@microsoft.com

Abstract. With the development of the convolutional neural network, image style transfer has drawn increasing attention. However, most existing approaches adopt a global feature transformation to transfer style patterns into content images (e.g., AdaIN and WCT). Such a design usually destroys the spatial information of the input images and fails to transfer fine-grained style patterns into style transfer results. To solve this problem, we propose a novel **ST**yle **TR**ansformer (**STTR**) network which breaks both content and style images into visual tokens to achieve a fine-grained style transformation. Specifically, two attention mechanisms are adopted in our STTR. We first propose to use self-attention to encode content and style tokens such that similar tokens can be grouped and learned together. We then adopt cross-attention between content and style tokens that encourages fine-grained style transformations. To compare STTR with existing approaches, we conduct user studies on Amazon Mechanical Turk (AMT), which are carried out with 50 human subjects with 1,000 votes in total. Extensive evaluations demonstrate the effectiveness and efficiency of the proposed STTR in generating visually pleasing style transfer results (Code is available at https://github.com/researchmm/STTR).

Keywords: Style transfer · Vision transformer

1 Introduction

Image style transfer has been receiving increasing attention in the creation of artistic images. Given one content and one style reference image, the model will produce an output image that retains the core elements of the content image but appears to be "painted" in the style of the reference image. It has many industrial applications, for example, clothes design [1], photo and video editing [2–5], material changing [6], fashion style transfer [7,8], virtual reality [9], and so on.

Supplementary Information The online version contains supplementary material available at https://doi.org/10.1007/978-3-031-26313-2_26.

In recent years, style transfer employs deep neural networks. Those methods could be divided into three categories: 1) optimization-based methods, 2) feed-forward approximation, and 3) zero-shot style transfer. Gatys et al. [10] propose to optimize the pixel values of a given content image by jointly minimizing the feature reconstruction loss and style loss. It could produce impressive results, but it requires optimizing the content image for many iterations for any content-style image pairs which are computationally expensive. To solve this problem, other researchers addressed this problem by building a feed-forward network [11–17], to explicitly learn the mapping from a photograph to a stylized image with a particular painting style. Thus it requires retraining a new model for any unseen new styles. Zero-shot style transfer is more effective since it could handle various styles and transfer images given even unseen styles. Huang et al. [18] propose an arbitrary style transfer method by matching the mean-variance statistics between content and style features, usually named adaptive instance normalization (AdaIN). AdaIN first normalizes the input content image, then scales and shifts it according to parameters calculated by different style images. A more recent work replaces the AdaIN layer with a pair of whitening and coloring transformations [19]. Many works follow the formulation of AdaIN and further improve it [20,21].

However, the common limitation of these methods is that simply adjusting the mean and variance of feature statistics makes it hard to synthesize complicated style patterns with rich details and local structures. As shown later in Fig. 2, Gatys et al.'s method [10], AdaIN [18], and WCT [19] always bring distorted style patterns in the transferred results, which makes it hard to recognize the original object from the style transferred image. In a more recent work [22], Deng et al. propose the StyTr^2 to learn semantic correlations between the content and style features by attention. Although StyTr^2 could produce visually pleasing results, there still exists structure distortion as shown later in Fig. 2. This is because StyTr^2 adopts a shallow feature extractor without pre-trained weights which limits its abilities to capture and transfer style patterns and makes foreground and background objects indistinguishable in the resulting image. Thus, how to learn a better representation to assemble the content and style patterns and transfer fine-grained style patterns while keeping content structure is still a challenging problem.

In this paper, we adopt a Transformer to tackle this problem. Recently, the breakthroughs of Transformer networks [23] in the natural language processing (NLP) domain has sparked great interest in the computer vision community to adapt these models for vision tasks. Inspired by those works which explicitly model long-range dependencies in language sequences and images, we develop a Transformer-based network to first break content and style images into visual tokens and then learn the global context between them. As similar content tokens lean to match with the same style tokens, fine-grained style transformation can be obtained. Specifically, the proposed STTR mainly consists of four parts: two backbones to extract and downsample features from the inputs (i.e., content and style images), two self-attention modules to summarize the style or content features, a cross-attention module to match style patterns into content patches adaptively, and a CNN-based decoder to upsample the output of cross-attention module to reconstruct the final result. We implement this by Transformer since its encoder consists of self-attention module while the decoder has cross-attention module to compute the correlations between content and style tokens.

Two backbones first extract compact feature representation from given content and style images and downsample them to a smaller spatial size. This could help to reduce the computation cost in the Transformer. Secondly, the self-attention modules encourage the style (or content) features with similar structures and semantic meanings to group together. Different from previous work, feeding content and style into the self-attention model before matching them could help to separate them into different distinctive semantic vectors (see Sect. 4.3 for more information). The cross-attention module in the decoder further incorporates style into content harmoniously without hurting the content structure. After that, a CNN-based decoder upsamples the output of the decoder to obtain the stylized results. The details of network architecture could be found in Sect. 3.

Our main contributions are as follows.

- We propose a fine-grained Transformer-based image style transfer method, capable of computing very local mapping between the content and style tokens.
- To better understand the effectiveness of STTR to model global context between style and content features, we provide a detailed ablation study to explore the contribution of the Transformer architecture and losses.
- We evaluated the performance of the proposed STTR with several state-of-the-art style transfer methods. Experimental results show that the STTR has a great capability of producing both perceptual quality and details in transferring style into a photograph. We also provide frame-wise video style transfer results which further demonstrate the effectiveness of our approach.

2   Related Work

2.1   Image Style Transfer

Image style transfer is a technique that aims to apply the style from one image to another content image. Typically, neural style transfer techniques could be divided into three aspects: 1) optimization-based methods, 2) feed-forward approximation, and 3) zero-shot style transfer.

Optimization-Based Methods. Gatys et al. [10] are the first to formulate style transfer as the matching of multi-level deep features extracted from a pre-trained deep neural network. The authors achieve style transfer by jointly minimizing the feature loss [24] and the style loss formulated as the difference of Gram matrices. Optimizing an image is computationally expensive and contains no learned representations for the artistic style, which is inefficient for real-time applications.

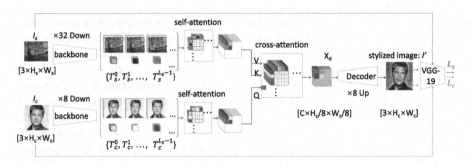

Fig. 1. An overview of our proposed Style Transformer (STTR). Our framework consists of four parts: two backbones which are used to extract features from the style and content image and break them into tokens, two self-attention modules to encourage the style (or content) tokens with similar structures and semantic meanings to group together, a cross-attention module observes the outputs and adaptively match the style code to the content features, and the CNN-based decoder upsamples the output of the Transformer decoder to reconstruct the final result. We use a fixed-weight VGG-19 network to compute the content and style loss as described in Sect. 3.2.

Feed-Forward Approximation. Fast feed-forward approaches [11–13] address this problem by building a feed-forward neural network, i.e., the style transfer network, to explicitly learn the transformation from a photograph to a particular painting style. They minimize the same feature reconstruction loss and style reconstruction loss as [25]. However, they have to train individual networks for every style, which is very inefficient.

Zero-Shot Style Transfer. Chen et al. [26] propose to match each content patch to the most similar style patch and swapped them. For fast arbitrary style transfer, Huang et al. [18] employ adaptive instance normalization (AdaIN) to normalize activation channels for stylization. Specifically, it follows an encoder-AdaIN-decoder formulation. The encoder uses the first few layers of a fixed VGG-19 network to encode the content and style images. The AdaIN layer is used to perform style transfer in the feature space. Then a decoder is trained to invert the AdaIN output to the image spaces. Unlike AdaIN, Whitening and Coloring Transform (WCT) [19] directly uses different layers of the VGG network as the encoders, transfers multi-level style patterns by recursively applying whitening and coloring transformation, and trains the decoders to invert the feature into an image. Many works follow the formulation of AdaIN and further improve it [20,21,27,28]. In SANET [29] and AdaAttN [30], the authors propose to learn semantic correlations between the content and style features by a learnable non-local module. However, those feature transformation methods always fail to maintain content structures since they simply transfer features across all spatial locations for each channel. Hong et al. [31] propose a unified architecture for both artistic and photo-realistic stylizations. In StyTr^2, the authors propose a transformer-based style transfer model and design the tokenizer with a single

---

Algorithm 1: The training process of the proposed STTR

Input: Content Image I_c, Style Image I_s
Output: Stylized image I'

1 $X_c \leftarrow$ extracted feature maps from I_c by content backbone.
2 $X_s \leftarrow$ extracted feature maps from I_s by style backbone.
3 Linear flat X_c into L_c visual tokens: $\{T_c^0, T_c^1, ..., T_c^{L_c-1}\}$. Linear flat X_s into L_s visual tokens: $\{T_s^0, T_s^1, ..., T_s^{L_s-1}\}$.
4 Compute style codes $\{C_s^0, C_s^1, ..., C_s^{L_s-1}\}$ with $\{T_s^0, T_s^1, ..., T_s^{L_s-1}\}$ by Transformer encoder.
5 Match $\{T_c^0, T_c^1, ..., T_c^{L_c-1}\}$ with semantic similar style codes $\{C_s^0, C_s^1, ..., C_s^{L_s-1}\}$ by Transformer decoder, generate decoded visual tokens: $\{T_d^0, T_d^1, ..., T_d^{L_c-1}\}$.
6 Reshape $\{T_d^0, T_d^1, ..., T_d^{L_c-1}\}$ with the same size of X_c, obtain X_d.
7 Reconstruct X_d by CNN-based decoder, obtain the final output I', it has the same size with I_c.
8 Compute the content and style loss defined in Sect. 3.2 by a fixed weight VGG-19 network.
9 Updates the weights by minimizing the loss value.

---

convolutional layer (an unfold operation followed by a convolutional filter). Due to the shallow feature extractor for the tokenizer, the learned correspondences between the content and style tokens are random.

2.2 Visual Transformer

Recently, there is impressive progress in the field of NLP, driven by the innovative architecture called Transformer [23]. In response, several attempts have been made to incorporate self-attention constructions into vision models. Those methods could be divided into two aspects: high-level vision and low-level vision.

High-Level Vision Transformer. Transformer can be applied to many high-level tasks like image classification. Dosovitskiy et al. propose a Vision Transformer (ViT) [32], dividing an image into patches and feeding these patches (i.e., tokens) into a standard Transformer. Recently, Transformers have also shown strong performance on other high-level tasks, including detection [33–37], segmentation [38–40], and pose estimation [41–44].

Low-Level Vision Transformer. Low-level vision tasks often take images as outputs (e.g., high-resolution or denoised images), which is more challenging than high-level vision tasks such as classification, segmentation, and detection, whose outputs are labels or boxes. iGPT [45] trains GPT v2 model [46] on flattened image sequences (1D pixel arrays) and shows that it can generate plausible image outputs without any external supervision. Zeng et al. [47] propose a Transformer-based Generation. Nowadays, researchers achieve good performance on Transformer networks for super-resolution and frame interpolation [48–51].

Image style transfer is also a sub-task of low-level vision tasks. Specifically, there exists a large appearance gap between input and output domains. This makes it difficult to produce a visually pleasing target output.

3   Approach

We show the pipeline of our proposed STTR in Fig. 1. Our method takes a content-style image pair as input and produces stylized results as output. In this section, we present the details of the network architecture and loss functions accordingly. The whole training process is illustrated in Algorithm 1.

3.1   Network Architecture

As shown in Fig. 1, our model contains four main components. We will describe the network architecture as below: two CNN-based backbones to extract compact feature representations, two self-attention modules to encode the style or content features, a cross-attention module to match style patterns into content patches adaptively, and a CNN decoder to transform the combined output features from Transformer to the final output I'.

Tokenizer. In our model, one image is divided into a set of visual tokens. Thus, we have to first convert the input image into a set of visual tokens. We assume that each of them represents a semantic concept in the image. We then feed these tokens to a Transformer. Let us denote the input feature map by $X \in \mathbb{R}^{H \times W \times C}$ (height H, width W, and channels C) and visual tokens by $T \in \mathbb{R}^{L \times C}$ where L indicates the number of tokens.

Filter-based tokenizer utilizes a deep CNN-based feature extractor to gradually downsample input images to obtain feature maps. After that, each position on the feature map represents a region in the input space (i.e., the receptive field). If the output size of feature maps is $H/32 \times W/32 \times C_2$ (height H, width W, and channels C_2), we then obtain $(H/32 \times W/32)$ patches (i.e., tokens). For each token, its dimension is C_2. As CNN densely slides the filter over the input image, it could produce much more smooth features. We further provide a detailed illustration of different tokenizers in the supplementary.

Backbone. To achieve fine-grained style transformation, inspired by the original Transformer [23], one image could be divided into a set of visual tokens as one sentence consisting of a few words. Thus, we have to first convert the input image into a set of visual tokens. We assume that each of them represents a semantic concept in the image. We then feed these tokens to a Transformer. Let us denote the input feature map by $X \in \mathbb{R}^{H \times W \times C}$ (height H, width W, and channels C) and visual tokens by $T \in \mathbb{R}^{L \times C}$ where L indicates the number of tokens.

We adopt ResNet-50 [52] as our backbone since it gradually downsamples the features from the input into a smaller spatial size. The original ResNet-50 [52] has four layers and downsamples features by 4, 8, 16, and 32 times. The output channel of each layer is 256, 512, 1024, and 2048, respectively. For extracting style features, we choose the output from the $4th$ layer while for content features we choose the $2nd$ layer. We would like to utilize the ability of the shallow network (the $2nd$ layer) to extract and retain detailed information of the spatial structure. For style features, higher-level semantic features are extracted by a deeper network (the $4th$ layer).

In summary, starting from the input content image $I_c \in \mathbb{R}^{H_c \times W_c \times 3}$ and style image $I_s \in \mathbb{R}^{H_s \times W_s \times 3}$, two backbones will extract features independently with the size of $H_c/8 \times W_c/8 \times 512$ and $H_s/32 \times W_s/32 \times 2048$ for content and style, respectively.

The extracted style and content features have a different number of channels as we described above. Thus we first use a 1×1 convolution to make them have the same channel number d. Specifically, we set $d = 256$. Next, we flatten the 3D features in spatial dimensions, resulting in 2D features, $(H_c/8 \cdot W_c/8) \times 256$ for content features while $(H_s/32 \cdot W_s/32) \times 256$ for style features.

Attention Layer. Our proposed STTR consists of an encoder module and a decoder module with several encoder or decoder layers of the same architecture. The encoder layer is composed of a self-attention layer and a feed-forward neural network while the decoder layer is composed of a self-attention layer, a feed-forward neural network and a cross-attention layer and the other feed-forward neural network.

In each attention layer, following the original Transformer [23], the input features X are first projected onto these weight matrices to get $Q = XW^Q$, $K = XW^K$ and $V = XW^V$, where the Q, K, and V denote the triplet of query, key, and value through one 1×1 convolution on each input features from an image (i.e. either content or style image). Then the output is given by:

$$Attention(Q, K, V) = softmax(\frac{QK^T}{\sqrt{d}})V, \tag{1}$$

where the Q, K, and V denote query, key and value as described above. All of the three inputs to the attention layer maintain the same dimension d.

The detailed network architecture of STTR's transformer could be found in the supplementary.

Transformer Encoder. The encoder is used to encode style features, it consists of six encoder layers. Each encoder layer has a standard architecture and consists of a self-attention module and a feed-forward network (FFN). Here, the number of the head is set to be eight. To supplement the image features with position information, fixed positional encodings are added to the flattened features before the features are fed into each attention layer.

Transformer Decoder. The decoder is used to reason relationships between content and style tokens while being able to model the global context among them. It consists of two multi-head attention layers and a feed-forward network (FFN). The first multi-head attention layer mainly learns the self-attention within content features while the second one learns the cross-attention between content and style features.

As shown in Fig. 1, the difference from that of the original Transformer is the input query of the decoder. We adopt content visual tokens as the query. Additionally, we also introduce a fixed positional encoding with the same size of style features.

CNN Decoder. The CNN decoder is used to predict the final stylized image. It upsamples the output of the Transformer (with the size of $H_c/8 \times W_c/8 \times 512$) into the original size the same with the input content image. To achieve this, the CNN decoder should upsample it three times. Each upsample module consists of three parts: one standard residual block defined in [52], one bilinear interpolation layer upsample by a factor of 2, and one 3×3 convolution.

Let $RBCk$ denotes a **R**esidual block-**B**ilinear interpolation-**C**onvolution layer where k indicates the channel number of the output features. The CNN decoder architecture consists of $RBC256 - RBC128 - RBC64 - RBC3$.

3.2   Objective Function

Following existing works [13,14,18,53], we use the pre-trained VGG-19 [54] to compute the loss function to train the STTR. The loss function $\mathcal{L}$ is defined as a combination of two loss terms, content loss $\mathcal{L}_c$ and the style loss $\mathcal{L}_s$:

$$\mathcal{L} = \mathcal{L}_c + \lambda \mathcal{L}_s, \tag{2}$$

where λ denote the weight of style loss. We empirically set $\lambda = 10$.

The content loss $\mathcal{L}_c$ is defined by the squared Euclidean distance between the feature representations of the content image I_c and the stylized image I'. Thus we define the content loss $\mathcal{L}_c$ as follows:

$$\mathcal{L}_c = \|f_4(I_c) - f_4(I')\|_2, \tag{3}$$

where we interpret $f_i(\cdot)$ as feature map extracted by a pre-trained VGG-19 network [54] at the layer i. Here, we adopt $relu1\_1$, $relu2\_1$, $relu3\_1$, and $relu4\_1$ as the layers for extracting features.

Similar to [18], the style loss is defined as follows:

$$\mathcal{L}_s = \sum_{i=1}^{4} (\|\mu(f_i(I_s)) - \mu(f_i(I'))\|_2 + \|\sigma(f_i(I_s)) - \sigma(f_i(I'))\|_2), \tag{4}$$

where $\mu(\cdot)$, $\sigma(\cdot)$ are the mean and standard deviation, computed across batch size and spatial dimensions independently for each feature channel.

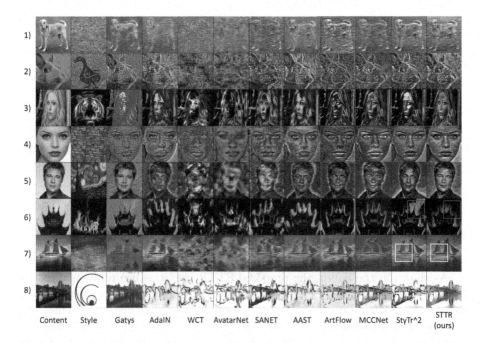

Content Style Gatys AdaIN WCT AvatarNet SANET AAST ArtFlow MCCNet StyTr^2 STTR (ours)

Fig. 2. Visual comparison. All content and style images are collected from websites and copyright-free. They are never observed during training. (Color figure online)

4   Experiments and Discussions

4.1   Training Details

We train our network by using images from MSCOCO [55] and WikiArt [56] as content and style data, respectively. Each dataset contains about 80,000 images. In each training batch, we randomly choose one pair of content and style images with the size of 512×512 as inputs. We implement our model with PyTorch and apply the Adam optimizer [57] with a learning rate of 10^{-5}.

4.2   Comparison Results

Qualitative Evaluations. There are many quantitative evaluation methods for image quality assessment [58,59]. However, as style transfer is a very subjective task and does not have a reference image, to evaluate our method, we first evaluate the quality of the results produced by our model. We visually compare our results to the state-of-the-art style transfer methods: the optimization-based method proposed by Gatys et al. [10], three feature transformation-based methods WCT [19], AdaIN [18], AAST [21], patch-based method Avatar-Net [60], attention-based methods (SANET [29] and StyTr [22]), ArtFlow [27], and MCC-Net [28]. Figure 2 shows the results.

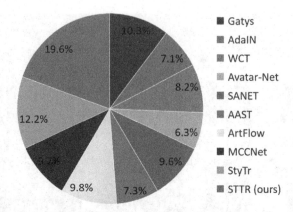

Fig. 3. User preference result of seven style transfer algorithms.

As shown in the figure, the proposed STTR performs favorably against the state-of-the-art methods. Both the content structure and style patterns appear well since we match the style tokens onto content tokens in a fine-grained manner. Although the optimization-based method [10] allows universal-style transfer, it is computationally expensive due to its iterative optimization process (see analysis about the speed in Sect. 4.2). Also, the results highly depend on many hyper-parameters, including the number of iterations, the trade-off loss weight, and the initial image. Thus, the results are not robust (e.g., see the 1st, 3rd, 6th, and 7th rows in Fig. 2). The AdaIN [18] method presents an efficient solution for arbitrary style transfer, but it generates sub-optimal results (e.g., see the 1st and 7th rows in Fig. 2) as it globally stylized the whole content image. The WCT [19] and Avatar-Net usually perform well, however, in some cases, they would bring strong distortions which makes it hard to recognize the original object from the style transferred image (e.g., see the 1st, 2nd, and 7th rows in Fig. 2). AAST [21] transfers color and texture in two independent paths but sometimes cannot produce well-colored results (see the 2nd and 4th rows in Fig. 2). In contrast, our method learns semantic relationships between content and style tokens and performs appealing results for arbitrary style, especially working very well on preserving content structure. SANET [29], ArtFlow [27], and MCCNet [28] also hard to generate appealing results especially when the content and style features could not be matched very well (e.g., see the 1st and 3rd rows in Fig. 2).

StyTr² [22] also adopt a transformer to build a style transfer model and it could produce visually pleasing results. However, it still cannot preserve the fine structures. The main difference is that our method learns correspondence on the semantic-level while StyTr² focuses on the region-level. This is because StyTr² adopts a shallow feature extractor to build the tokenizer. Thus the learned correspondences between the content and style tokens are random. For example, on the 6th row, StyTr² generates fires in the sky (marked in the red box) while in our method, the flame area is smoother and appears on the edge of the building.

It looks like StyTr^2 tends to copy-paste the texture in the style image onto the content image. The same thing happens on the $7th$ row. Our model understands the sail and the body of the boat are different objects so the result is clean. However, StyTr^2 produces results with large yellow areas across the sea and the sail (marked in the white box). It looks like StyTr^2 tends to copy-paste the texture in the style image onto the content image. Taking advantage of knowledge, our method could learn semantic-level correspondences between the content and style images and reduce distortion.

Perceptual Study. As the evaluation of style transfer is highly subjective, we conduct a user study to further evaluate the seven methods shown in Fig. 2. We use 10 content images and 20 style images. For each method, we use the released codes and default parameters to generate 200 results.

We hire 50 volunteers on Amazon Mechanical Turk (AMT) for our user study. Twenty of 200 content-style pairs are randomly selected for each user. For each style-content pair, we display the stylized results of seven methods on a web page in random order. Each user is asked to vote for the one that he/she likes the most. Finally, we collect 1000 votes from 50 users and calculate the percentage of votes that each method received.

The results are shown in Fig. 3, where our STTR obtains 19.6% of the total votes. It is much higher than that of AAST [21] whose stylization results are usually thought to be high-quality. Attention-based methods, StyTr^2 [22] and SANET [29] get sub-optimal results. This user study result is consistent with the visual comparisons in Fig. 2 and further demonstrates the superior performance of our proposed STTR.

Table 1. Execution time comparison (in seconds).

Method	Venue	Time (512 px)
Gatys et al. [10]	CVPR16	106.63
AdaIN [18]	CVPR17	0.13
WCT [19]	CVPR17	1.63
Avatar-Net [60]	CVPR18	0.49
SANET [29]	CVPR19	0.19
AAST [21]	ACMMM20	0.49
ArtFlow [27]	CVPR21	0.40
MCCNet [28]	AAAI21	0.15
StyTr^2 [22]	CVPR22	0.57
STTR (ours)	0.14	0.28

Efficiency. Table 1 shows the run time performance of the proposed method and other methods at 512 pixels image scales. All the methods are tested on a PC with an Intel(R) Xeon(R) Gold 6226R 2.90 GHz CPU and a Tesla V100 GPU.

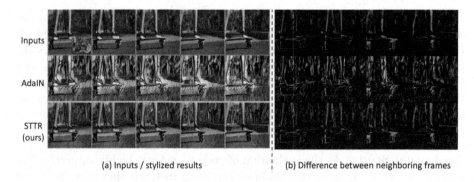

Inputs

AdaIN

STTR
(ours)

(a) Inputs / stylized results   (b) Difference between neighboring frames

Fig. 4. Visual comparison for video style transfer.

The optimization-based method [10] is impractically computationally expensive because of its iterative optimization process. WCT [19] is also relatively slower as it conducts multi-level coarse-to-fine stylization.

In contrast, our proposed STTR runs at 4 frames per second (fps) for 512×512 images. Therefore, our method could feasibly process style transfer in real time. Our model is much faster than Gatys et al. [10] and achieves better qualitative performance as shown in Fig. 2.

Memory Usage. Compared with two current SOTAs, our method has fewer parameters than StyTr^2 (ours: 45.643M v.s. StyTr^2: 48.339M) and takes less memory than AdaAttn (ours: 18391M v.s. AdaAttn: 25976M) on a 512 × 512 image. However, such memory costs could be further reduced by using fewer channel numbers.

Results for Video Style Transfer. Here we also provide results of video style transfer. As shown in Fig. 4, our model can perform video stylization on video sequence frame-by-frame. On the contrary, AdaIN [18] produces results with high motion blur. To show the stable results produced by our model, we further compute the difference between neighboring frames to show the smoothness between frames. It is clearly shown that the difference generated by our method is much more close to that from the input frames. It is because our method could well preserve the content structure and reduce the motion-blurred video frames.

4.3 Ablations

To verify the effect of each component in the STTR, we conduct an ablation study by visually comparing the generated results without each of them. All of the compared models are trained by the same 400,000 content-style pairs (i.e., trained for 5 epochs). More ablation experiments could be found in the supplementary.

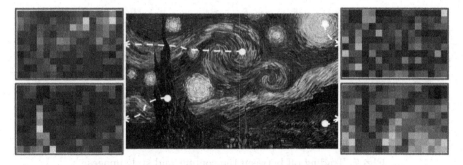

Fig. 5. Encoder attention maps for different sampling points on style image. The style image (e.g., Van Gogh's painting) is shown in the center. We further show four sampled points and their according attention maps with different colors. (Color figure online)

Fig. 6. Decoder attention maps for different sampling points on the output. The stylized image is shown in the center. We further show three sampled points and their according attention maps with different colors. On the upper left is the input style image. (Color figure online)

Learned Attention Maps. We can observe model with deeper encoder and decoder has stronger capability to preserve semantic similarity, so that similar style patterns (e.g., fire) can be transferred to similar content regions.

The encoder is used for encoding the style pattern while the decoder learns a matching between the content and style features.

In Fig. 5, we provide visualized attention maps to show that self-attention could encode style features and similar visual tokens can be grouped together. For the top right marked point (which locates the center of the sun), all of the regions related to other suns have a higher value (in yellow color) in their corresponding attention map. In Fig. 6, attention maps show the learned fine-grained relationships between content and style features. The lower left point in the content image has strong relationships (e.g., see its attention map) with the black tree in the style image. So the pixels around that point in the output are very dark (see the stylized results located around that point).

Inputs   λ=0   λ=10   λ=30   λ=50

Fig. 7. Trading off between the content and style images.

The Loss Weight λ. The degree of stylization can be modified by the hyper-parameter λ as described in Sect. 3.2. As shown in Fig. 7, changing λ in the training stage could control the magnitude of stylization.

5 Conclusion

Image style transfer mainly aims to transfer style patterns into the content images. Taking advantage of the breakthrough of vision Transformers, in this work, we propose a style Transformer for solving image style transfer tasks. Since STTR breaks content and style features into tokens and computes very local relationships between them, fine-grained style transformation could be obtained. Experiments demonstrate that the proposed model can produce visually pleasing results and preserve content structure very well without bringing a heavy timing cost. The proposed method also has the potential to be applied to video style transfer frameworks. There are still some limitations that call for continuing efforts. In the future, we would like to extend STTR to handle multiple style mixtures and work on light-weight Transformer architecture for style transfer.

References

1. Date, P., Ganesan, A., Oates, T.: Fashioning with networks: neural style transfer to design clothes. In: KDD ML4Fashion workshop, vol. 2 (2017)
2. Chen, D., Liao, J., Yuan, L., Yu, N., Hua, G.: Coherent online video style transfer. In: ICCV, pp. 1105–1114 (2017)
3. Zhang, W., Cao, C., Chen, S., Liu, J., Tang, X.: Style transfer via image component analysis. TMM **15**, 1594–1601 (2013)
4. Liu, J., Yang, W., Sun, X., Zeng, W.: Photo stylistic brush: robust style transfer via superpixel-based bipartite graph. TMM **20**, 1724–1737 (2017)
5. Virtusio, J.J., Ople, J.J.M., Tan, D.S., Tanveer, M., Kumar, N., Hua, K.L.: Neural style palette: a multimodal and interactive style transfer from a single style image. TMM **23**, 2245–2258 (2021)
6. Matsuo, S., Shimoda, W., Yanai, K.: Partial style transfer using weakly supervised semantic segmentation. In: ICME Workshops, pp. 267–272. IEEE (2017)

7. Kim, B.K., Kim, G., Lee, S.Y.: Style-controlled synthesis of clothing segments for fashion image manipulation. TMM **22**, 298–310 (2019)
8. Liu, Y., Chen, W., Liu, L., Lew, M.S.: SwapGAN: a multistage generative approach for person-to-person fashion style transfer. TMM **21**, 2209–2222 (2019)
9. Castillo, C., De, S., Han, X., Singh, B., Yadav, A.K., Goldstein, T.: Son of Zorn's lemma: targeted style transfer using instance-aware semantic segmentation. In: ICASSP, pp. 1348–1352. IEEE (2017)
10. Gatys, L.A., Ecker, A.S., Bethge, M.: Image style transfer using convolutional neural networks. In: CVPR, pp. 2414–2423 (2016)
11. Johnson, J., Alahi, A., Fei-Fei, L.: Perceptual losses for real-time style transfer and super-resolution. In: Leibe, B., Matas, J., Sebe, N., Welling, M. (eds.) ECCV 2016. LNCS, vol. 9906, pp. 694–711. Springer, Cham (2016). https://doi.org/10.1007/978-3-319-46475-6_43
12. Li, C., Wand, M.: Precomputed real-time texture synthesis with Markovian generative adversarial networks. In: Leibe, B., Matas, J., Sebe, N., Welling, M. (eds.) ECCV 2016. LNCS, vol. 9907, pp. 702–716. Springer, Cham (2016). https://doi.org/10.1007/978-3-319-46487-9_43
13. Ulyanov, D., Lebedev, V., Vedaldi, A., Lempitsky, V.S.: Texture networks: feed-forward synthesis of textures and stylized images. In: ICML, p. 4 (2016)
14. Dumoulin, V., Shlens, J., Kudlur, M.: A learned representation for artistic style. arXiv preprint arXiv:1610.07629 (2016)
15. Chen, D., Yuan, L., Liao, J., Yu, N., Hua, G.: Stylebank: an explicit representation for neural image style transfer. In: CVPR, pp. 1897–1906 (2017)
16. Li, Y., Fang, C., Yang, J., Wang, Z., Lu, X., Yang, M.H.: Diversified texture synthesis with feed-forward networks. In: CVPR, pp. 3920–3928 (2017)
17. Zhang, H., Dana, K.: Multi-style generative network for real-time transfer. In: Leal-Taixé, L., Roth, S. (eds.) ECCV 2018. LNCS, vol. 11132, pp. 349–365. Springer, Cham (2019). https://doi.org/10.1007/978-3-030-11018-5_32
18. Huang, X., Belongie, S.: Arbitrary style transfer in real-time with adaptive instance normalization. In: ICCV, pp. 1501–1510 (2017)
19. Li, Y., Fang, C., Yang, J., Wang, Z., Lu, X., Yang, M.H.: Universal style transfer via feature transforms. arXiv preprint arXiv:1705.08086 (2017)
20. Kitov, V., Kozlovtsev, K., Mishustina, M.: Depth-Aware Arbitrary style transfer using instance normalization. arXiv preprint arXiv:1906.01123 (2019)
21. Hu, Z., Jia, J., Liu, B., Bu, Y., Fu, J.: Aesthetic-aware image style transfer. In: ACM MM, pp. 3320–3329 (2020)
22. Deng, Y., Tang, F., Pan, X., Dong, W., Ma, C., Xu, C.: Stytr^2: unbiased image style transfer with transformers. In: CVPR (2021)
23. Vaswani, A., et al.: Attention is all you need. arXiv preprint arXiv:1706.03762 (2017)
24. Mahendran, A., Vedaldi, A.: Understanding deep image representations by inverting them. In: CVPR, pp. 5188–5196 (2015)
25. Gatys, L.A., Ecker, A.S., Bethge, M.: A neural algorithm of artistic style. arXiv preprint arXiv:1508.06576 (2015)
26. Chen, T.Q., Schmidt, M.: Fast patch-based style transfer of arbitrary style. arXiv preprint arXiv:1612.04337 (2016)
27. An, J., Huang, S., Song, Y., Dou, D., Liu, W., Luo, J.: Artflow: unbiased image style transfer via reversible neural flows. In: CVPR, pp. 862–871 (2021)
28. Deng, Y., Tang, F., Dong, W., Huang, H., Ma, C., Xu, C.: Arbitrary video style transfer via multi-channel correlation. In: AAA, vol. 1, pp. 1210–1217 (2021)

29. Park, D.Y., Lee, K.H.: Arbitrary style transfer with style-attentional networks. In: CVPR, pp. 5880–5888 (2019)
30. Liu, S., et al.: AdaAttN: revisit attention mechanism in arbitrary neural style transfer. In: ICCV, pp. 6649–6658 (2021)
31. Hong, K., Jeon, S., Yang, H., Fu, J., Byun, H.: Domain-aware universal style transfer. In: ICCV (2021)
32. Dosovitskiy, A., et al.: An Image is Worth 16x16 Words: Transformers for image recognition at scale. arXiv preprint arXiv:2010.11929 (2020)
33. Carion, N., Massa, F., Synnaeve, G., Usunier, N., Kirillov, A., Zagoruyko, S.: End-to-end object detection with transformers. In: Vedaldi, A., Bischof, H., Brox, T., Frahm, J.-M. (eds.) ECCV 2020. LNCS, vol. 12346, pp. 213–229. Springer, Cham (2020). https://doi.org/10.1007/978-3-030-58452-8_13
34. Beal, J., Kim, E., Tzeng, E., Park, D.H., Zhai, A., Kislyuk, D.: Toward transformer-based object detection. arXiv preprint arXiv:2012.09958 (2020)
35. Pan, X., Xia, Z., Song, S., Li, L.E., Huang, G.: 3D object detection with point-former. arXiv preprint arXiv:2012.11409 (2020)
36. Yuan, Z., Song, X., Bai, L., Zhou, W., Wang, Z., Ouyang, W.: Temporal-Channel Transformer for 3D Lidar-Based Video Object Detection in Autonomous Driving. arXiv preprint arXiv:2011.13628 (2020)
37. Zhu, X., Su, W., Lu, L., Li, B., Wang, X., Dai, J.: Deformable DETR: Deformable Transformers for End-to-End Object Detection. arXiv preprint arXiv:2010.04159 (2020)
38. Wang, H., Zhu, Y., Adam, H., Yuille, A., Chen, L.C.: MaX-DeepLab: End-to-End Panoptic Segmentation with Mask Transformers. arXiv preprint arXiv:2012.00759 (2020)
39. Wang, Y., et al.: End-to-End Video Instance Segmentation with Transformers. arXiv preprint arXiv:2011.14503 (2020)
40. Zheng, S., et al.: Rethinking semantic segmentation from a sequence-to-sequence perspective with transformers. arXiv preprint arXiv:2012.15840 (2020)
41. Huang, L., Tan, J., Liu, J., Yuan, J.: Hand-transformer: non-autoregressive structured modeling for 3D hand pose estimation. In: Vedaldi, A., Bischof, H., Brox, T., Frahm, J.-M. (eds.) ECCV 2020. LNCS, vol. 12370, pp. 17–33. Springer, Cham (2020). https://doi.org/10.1007/978-3-030-58595-2_2
42. Huang, L., Tan, J., Meng, J., Liu, J., Yuan, J.: HOT-net: non-autoregressive transformer for 3D hand-object pose estimation. In: ACM MM, pp. 3136–3145 (2020)
43. Lin, K., Wang, L., Liu, Z.: End-to-End Human Pose and Mesh Reconstruction with Transformer. arXiv preprint arXiv:2012.09760 (2020)
44. Yang, S., Quan, Z., Nie, M., Yang, W.: TransPose: Towards Explainable Human Pose Estimation by Transformer. arXiv preprint arXiv:2012.14214 (2020)
45. Chen, M., et al.: Generative pretraining from pixels. In: ICML, pp. 1691–1703. PMLR (2020)
46. Radford, A., Wu, J., Child, R., Luan, D., Amodei, D., Sutskever, I.: Language models are unsupervised multitask learners. OpenAI Blog 1, 9 (2019)
47. Zeng, Y., Yang, H., Chao, H., Wang, J., Fu, J.: Improving visual quality of image synthesis by a token-based generator with transformers. In: NeurIPS (2021)
48. Yang, F., Yang, H., Fu, J., Lu, H., Guo, B.: Learning texture transformer network for image super-resolution. In: CVPR, pp. 5791–5800 (2020)
49. Liu, C., Yang, H., Fu, J., Qian, X.: Learning trajectory-aware transformer for video super-resolution. In: CVPR (2022)
50. Qiu, Z., Yang, H., Fu, J., Fu, D.: Learning spatiotemporal frequency-transformer for compressed video super-resolution. arXiv preprint arXiv:2208.03012 (2022)

51. Liu, C., Yang, H., Fu, J., Qian, X.: TTVFI: Learning Trajectory-Aware Transformer for Video Frame Interpolation. arXiv preprint arXiv:2207.09048 (2022)
52. He, K., Zhang, X., Ren, S., Sun, J.: Deep residual learning for image recognition. In: CVPR, pp. 770–778 (2016)
53. Ulyanov, D., Vedaldi, A., Lempitsky, V.: Improved texture networks: maximizing quality and diversity in feed-forward stylization and texture synthesis. In: CVPR, pp. 6924–6932 (2017)
54. Simonyan, K., Zisserman, A.: Very deep convolutional networks for large-scale image recognition. arXiv preprint arXiv:1409.1556 (2014)
55. Lin, T.-Y., et al.: Microsoft COCO: common objects in context. In: Fleet, D., Pajdla, T., Schiele, B., Tuytelaars, T. (eds.) ECCV 2014. LNCS, vol. 8693, pp. 740–755. Springer, Cham (2014). https://doi.org/10.1007/978-3-319-10602-1_48
56. Nichol, K.: Painter by numbers, wikiart (2016)
57. Kingma, D.P., Ba, J.: Adam: A Method for Stochastic Optimization. arXiv preprint arXiv:1412.6980 (2014)
58. Zheng, H., Yang, H., Fu, J., Zha, Z.J., Luo, J.: Learning conditional knowledge distillation for degraded-reference image quality assessment. In: ICCV (2021)
59. Wang, Z., Bovik, A.C., Sheikh, H.R., Simoncelli, E.P.: Image quality assessment: from error visibility to structural similarity. TIP **13**, 600–612 (2004)
60. Sheng, L., Lin, Z., Shao, J., Wang, X.: Avatar-net: multi-scale zero-shot style transfer by feature decoration. In: CVPR, pp. 8242–8250 (2018)

MSF²DN: Multi Scale Feature Fusion Dehazing Network with Dense Connection

Guangfa Wang and Xiaokang Yu[✉]

College of Computer Science and Technology, Qingdao University, Qingdao, China
{2020020635,xyu}@qdu.edu.cn

Abstract. Single image dehazing is a challenging problem in computer vision. Previous work has mostly focused on designing new encoder and decoder in common network architectures, while neglecting the connection between the two. In this paper, we propose a multi scale feature fusion dehazing network based on dense connection, MSF²DN. The design principle of this network is to make full use of dense connection to achieve efficient reuse of features. On the one hand, we use a dense connection inside the base module of the encoder-decoder to fuse the features of different convolutional layers several times, and on the other hand, we design a simple multi-stream feature fusion module which fuses the features of different stages after uniform scaling and feeds them into the base module of the decoder for enhancement. Numerous experiments have demonstrated that our network outperforms the existing state-of-the-art networks.

Keywords: Image dehazing · Feature fusion · Dense connection

1 Introduction

In computer vision and computer graphics, high-quality images are the basis for advanced vision tasks, so obtaining clear image from hazy image has received a great deal of attention in the last two decades. Figure 1 shows an example of dehazing.

To describe the haze, an atmospheric scattering model [29, 30] was proposed, which has the following equation:

$$I(x) = t(x)J(x) + A(1 - t(x)) \tag{1}$$

where I is the hazy image received by the camera, J denotes a clear scene radiance, A represents the global atmospheric light, which is usually a constant, and t is a transmission map, which can be expressed as $t = e^{-\beta d(x)}$, d is the distance from the camera to the scene radiation, β is the atmospheric scattering coefficient, x describes the pixel position.

It is clear that this is an ill-posed problem, and in order to get a haze-free image, many statistical priors [5, 18, 19, 28, 37, 44] appear. These priors can solve

© The Author(s), under exclusive license to Springer Nature Switzerland AG 2023
L. Wang et al. (Eds.): ACCV 2022, LNCS 13843, pp. 444–459, 2023.
https://doi.org/10.1007/978-3-031-26313-2_27

this problem to some extent, but unfortunately, the robustness of these hand-designed priors is not strong and can't work in complex scenarios.

To avoid the limitations of prior methods, data-driven deep learning has been applied to dehazing with quite good result. Early researchers used convolutional neural networks(CNNs) [6,34,40,41] to estimate the exact transmission map and atmospheric value, however, obtaining the transmission map and atmospheric value from a single hazy image is not an easy task, and the atmospheric scattering model itself does not fully describe the cause of haze, so such a strategy has been gradually abandoned in recent years. Later researchers preferred to build a trainable end-to-end CNNs [7,10,11,16,24–27,33,39,43] to obtain haze-free image directly from hazy image, and such a strategy achieved better result. In continuous development, we found that simply stacking convolutional layers does not solve the dehazing problem well, so past work tends to develop a new network structure, such as Dilated Network [7], U-Net [10], Grid Network [25], and CycleGAN [35], or build a new enhancement module [10,31] to solve this problem, these algorithms do solve this problem well, but they all almost ignore the full use of features. MSBDN [10] is aware of this problem and uses the dense feature fusion module(DFF) to exploit features, but it is limited to the exploitation of features inside the encoder and decoder, ignoring the connection of features between the two.

In this work, we propose a multi scale feature fusion dehazing network based on dense connection, MSF^2DN. Our core principle is to make full use of the dense connection to achieve full utilization of the features in the U-shaped network architecture. In the base module of the encoder, we design a generic feature extraction module, MLFF, which incorporates shallow features into deep features to enhance feature delivery as well as reuse. In the base module of the decoder, in order to be able to apply dense connection to get fully enhanced features, we extend the base module of FFANet [31] and design a new enhancement module, DFFD. In each base module of the encoder and decoder, we add a pixel attention module and channel attention module [31] to enhance the performance of CNNs. At the network architecture level, the features at different scales are upsampled or downsampled to unify to the same scale, feeding into the multi stream feature fusion module(MSFF) we designed for simple processing and then feeding into the decoder base module for enhancement. We embed residual groups in the network to allow the model to learn to bypass unimportant information and focus the main performance on the dense haze region. Extensive experiments have shown that the performance of our method outperforms the state-of-the-art network. The contributions of this paper are summarized as follows:

- A base module, MLFF, based on dense connection and attention mechanisms, is designed for feature passing and reuse, ensuring a diversity of deep features.
- An effective feature enhancement module, DFFD, is extended to enable the network to adaptively assign more weights to important features using the channel attention module and the pixel attention module.
- A multi scale feature fusion network based on dense connection is designed to realize the effective utilization of features in the existing network architecture, and excellent experimental results are obtained.

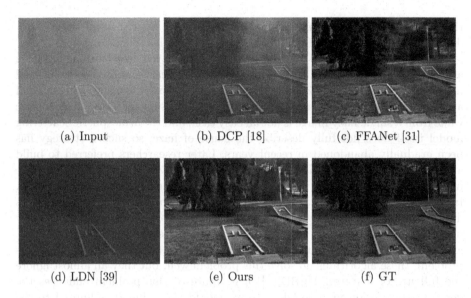

Fig. 1. Haze removal.

2   Related Work

2.1   Single Image Dehazing

Image dehazing is an important research topic in computer vision, aiming to obtain a haze-free image from a hazy image. Current dehazing methods can be divided into two categories: prior-based image dehazing [5,18,19,28,37,44] and learning-based image dehazing [6,7,10,11,16,24–27,33,34,39–41,43].

Prior-Based Image Dehazing. A priori-based dehazing methods rely on the atmospheric scattering model [29,30], which is an ill-posed problem, so researchers have solved this problem by mathematical statistics to obtain common features of hazy images or clear images, forming a prior or hypotheses. Tan [38] gets a clear image by maximizing local contrast, He *et al.* [18] design the dark channel prior by counting the clear image features, and obtaining the clear image based on this prior. Berman *et al.* [5] distribute the image pixels in the RGB color space and obtain the clustering relationship between clear image pixels and hazy image pixels to develop a non-local dehazing algorithm. Kim *et al.* [19] further develops dark channel prior [18] and use different functions to enhance image saturation to obtain clear images. Unfortunately, all these methods can only be used for a certain class of scenes, and they are all less robust in complex scenes, for example, dark channel prior [18] is ineffective in the sky.

Learning-Based Image Dehazing. With the rise of CNNs in the high-level vision task, such as object detection, recognition and related tasks [12,13,32], CNNs are also subsequently used in image dehazing. Early CNN-based dehazing networks [6,34,40,41] still adopt a multi-stage strategy, using CNNs to accurately estimate the transmission map and atmospheric value, and then substitute into an atmospheric scattering model to obtain the scene radiation. However, if the transmission map is not properly estimated, high-quality dehazing results will not be obtained. Therefore, the mainstream dehazing networks nowadays are end-to-end networks [7,10,11,16,24–27,33,39,43] that do not require the estimation of transmission maps and atmospheric value, these networks are directly from the hazy image to get a clear image. Such strategy often yields better results in synthetic atlases, but due to the lack of a theoretical basis, they can still be applied to reality with unnatural results, therefore, RefineNet [43] and PSDNet [8], which combine the prior and CNNs have emerged, but such methods still have much room for improvement as of now.

2.2 Dense Connection

As the network deepens, the network suffers from gradient vanishing/explosion problems as well as degradation problems. To solve this problem, many works, such as ResNet [15], Highway Network [36], FractalNets [21], have been proposed. All these works reveal the principle that creating a short path from lower to higher levels is beneficial to solving the degradation problem. Inspired by the above work, DenseNet [17] was proposed, which connects the network layers directly to ensure maximum information flow between the network layers. For each layer, the feature maps of all previous layers are its input, and its output feature maps are the input of all subsequent layers. Following such simple connection rules, DenseNet [17] naturally integrates the properties of identity mappings, deep supervision, and diversified depth, and it can be a good feature extractor.

2.3 Multi Scale Feature Fusion

Many CNNs used to solve vision tasks often use downsampling operations to reduce the number of parameters, but bring the problem of feature loss. In order to allow the network to get enough features, feature fusion(feature concatenation [42], dense connection [16,17]) is often adopted in the network design process. However, it is not enough to simply fuse the features to extract valid information. To exploit features between adjacent layers, Liu *et al.* [25] design grid-Net, but the portability of such a design is too weak. Dong *et al.* [10] design the DFF, which effectively fuses features from multiple scales, but this work only pays attention to the connection within the encoder and decoder.

3 Proposed Method

We propose a multi-scale feature fusion dehazing network with dense connection, MSF^2DN, which is extended from a U-shaped network and is end-to-end trainable. There are three major components: the multi-level feature fusion module(MLFF), the double feature fusion dehazing module(DFFD), and the multi-stream feature fusion module(MSFF). The specific network structure is shown in Fig. 2.

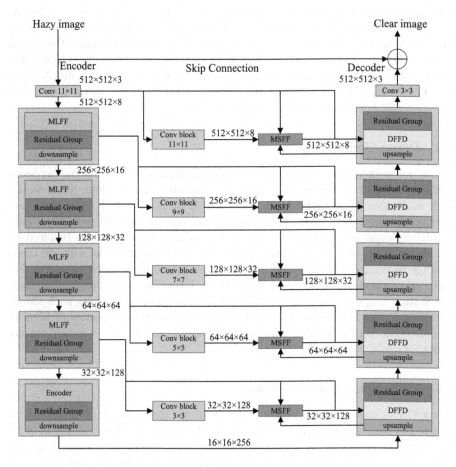

Fig. 2. Overall architecture of MSF^{2}DN.

3.1 Multi-level Feature Fusion Module

Previous work has usually used dense connections between base modules, but this approach still results in feature loss. In order to reduce the feature loss, we apply the dense connection inside the base module and thus design a multi-level feature fusion module(MLFF). As shown in Fig. 3, it consists of 4 convolutional layers, 2 attention modules, 1 activation function, and dense connections. Dense connections allow the network to skip unimportant information, such as thin haze or even clear areas, allowing most of the network's weights to be focused on the hard-to-solve dence haze areas. Our encoder consists of five MLFF modules, each stage of which downsamples features with a convolutional layer with a stride of 2.

Experiments have proven that adding dense connections within the base module of the encoder can indeed improve the performance of the network.

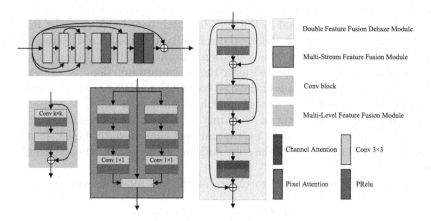

Fig. 3. Schematic diagram of the important module of MSF^{2}DN.

3.2 Double Feature Fusion Dehazing Module

FFANet's [31] base module has relatively powerful enhancements to features, but FFANet [31] does not make good use of the module, stacking too many base blocks. We extend a double feature fusion dehazing module(DFFD) in order to allow the combination of the base block and the dense connection, as shown in Fig. 3, which consists of 6 convolutional layers, 2 attention modules, 1 activation function, and the dense connection, which allows the network to focus on the important information while augmenting the features.

The decoder consists of five DFFD modules, each stage of which upsamples features with a deconvolutional layer with a stride of 2.

3.3 Multi-stream Feature Fusion Module

There is a very large amount of work in the field of image dehazing that involves skipping connection, but it is relatively simple to send features from the encoder base module to the corresponding decoder base module, ignoring the connection of features between the two stages. Referring to the connection of NBNet [9] architecture, we redesigned a simple multi-stream feature fusion module to process the features after upsampling and downsampling, aiming to obtain the features under different sense fields and fuse the features of the encoder base module and decoder base module. Our aim is to fuse the features of both phases and let the features obtained by the encoder base module guide the same-size decoder base module to reconstruct the image structure information. The specific detail is shown in Fig. 3.

3.4 Implementations Details

As shown in Fig. 2, in the encoder, each base block contains MLFF, Residual group, and downsample, and in the decoder, each base block contains Residual group, DFFD, and upsample, where the residual group contains 4 residual blocks [15] to deepen the network. The activation function is PRelu [14] and not every convolution function is connected after the activation function, as configured in Fig. 3. The convolution radius of the first convolutional layer of the network is set to 11. In addition, different sizes of convolutional kernels, 11, 9, 7, 5, and 3, are set at each stage of the network according to the feature map size of each layer in order to expect that a larger perceptual field can alleviate the localization of convolution, and the radius of the convolutional kernels of all other convolutional layers is 3.

We choose Mean Square Error(MSE) as the loss function, written as:

$$\mathcal{L}(G, x, y) = ||x - G(y)||_2 \tag{2}$$

where $G(\cdot)$, x, and y represent MSF^2DN, clear image, and hazy image, respectively.

The overall training process includes 100 epochs, and the batch size is 16. the optimizer is ADAM [20], β_1 is 0.9, β_2 is 0.999. The initial learning rate is set to 10^{-4}, and the learning rate is multiplied by 0.1 for every 25 epochs. All the experiments are conducted on one NVIDIA V100 GPU. **Our code and trained model is available at** https://github.com/Bruce-WangGF/MSFFDN.

4 Experimental Results

4.1 Datasets

We compare our method with state-of-the-art(SOTA) methods in two categories: synthetic [23] and real-world datasets [1–4].

Synthetic Datasets. RESIDE [23] was proposed by Li, B. *et al.* There are five subsets, where Indoor Training Set(ITS), Outdoor Training Set(OTS), Synthetic Objective Testing Set(SOTS) are synthetic sets, Real World task-driven Testing Set(RTTS) is the real-world dataset and Hybrid Subjective Testing Set(HSTS) includes both real-world and synthetic set. The datasets include a variety of indoor and outdoor scenes under daylight. In order to maintain the generalization ability of the model, we selected 22,000 images from ITS and OTS, of which 15,000 were randomly selected from ITS and 7,000 were randomly selected from OTS. The SOTS includes 500 indoor images and 500 outdoor hazy images and their corresponding clear images, which we choose as the testing set.

Real-World Datasets. To demonstrate the superiority of our method in the real world, we chose four real-world datasets: Dense HAZE [1], NH-HAZE [2], O-HAZE [3], I-HAZE [4]. They are from the NTIRE image dehazing challenge. Due to the small number of images, for each dataset, we choose 5 images as a validation set, 5 images as a testing set, and the rest of the images are expanded to 10,000 by cropping.

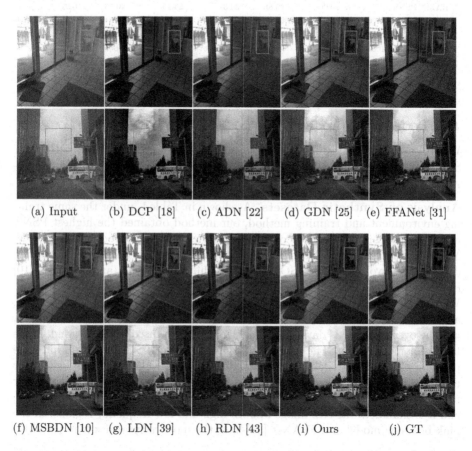

(a) Input   (b) DCP [18]   (c) ADN [22]   (d) GDN [25]   (e) FFANet [31]

(f) MSBDN [10]   (g) LDN [39]   (h) RDN [43]   (i) Ours   (j) GT

Fig. 4. Visual results comparison on SOTS [23] dataset. The green and pink window indicate the visible difference between each method.

4.2 Evaluation Metrics and Comparisons

In the field of image dehazing, Peak Signal to Noise Ratio(PSNR) and Structural Similarity index(SSIM) are often used as image quality evaluation metrics, we also adopt these two metrics.

Table 1. Quantitative evaluations on the benchmark dehazing datasets. Red texts and blue texts indicate the best and the second-best performance respectively.

	Matrix	DCP [18]	AodNet [22]	GDN [25]	FFANet [31]	MSBDN [10]	LDN [39]	RDN [43]	Ours
SOTS	PSNR	18.58	20.10	24.46	24.39	27.08	21.27	24.12	27.17
	SSIM	0.818	0.828	0.886	0.879	0.915	0.832	0.933	0.915
I-HAZE	PSNR	13.66	19.66	18.83	19.65	22.05	19.76	13.96	24.52
	SSIM	0.688	0.855	0.826	0.872	0.869	0.860	0.741	0.909
O-HAZE	PSNR	17.54	20.00	23.86	24.31	24.15	20.53	16.92	25.19
	SSIM	0.761	0.798	0.804	0.809	0.822	0.794	0.740	0.858
NH	PSNR	14.91	16.50	19.55	20.42	20.95	16.93	12.37	22.04
	SSIM	0.674	0.633	0.767	0.794	0.796	0.656	0.539	0.803
Dence	PSNR	14.15	15.50	15.82	18.46	18.27	15.67	12.15	18.37
	SSIM	0.552	0.498	0.576	0.629	0.603	0.506	0.426	0.622

4.3 Performance Analysis

We will analyze the advantages and disadvantages of our algorithm with other SOTA algorithms [10,18,22,25,31,39,43] on a synthetic dataset and four real-world datasets in both quantitative and qualitative aspects.

Analysis on Synthetic Datasets. As shown in Table 1, under the same training environment and training method, our method obtained the highest PSNR and the second-highest SSIM compared to other SOTA methods. Compared to MSBDN [10], our method has a 0.09 dB improvement in PSNR. Note that we downloaded two versions of SOTS from Github, our model and MSBDN [10] reach **34.21** dB PSNR and **34.00** dB PSNR respectively in the other version. We also give the qualitative analysis of our method and other SOTA methods, as shown in Fig. 4. We can observe that the DCP [18] performs relatively well, but the overall image is dark, and the RDN [43] with fused DCP [18] and CNNs has the same problem. The ADN [22], LDN [39], and MSBDN [10] all have the problem of incomplete dehazing at the green window. The GDN [25] has better results compared to the above methods, but the haze still appears in the lower right corner of the green window. Our method has a natural style for this image, and it is similar to the real image in both high and low-frequency regions. In the pink box, our model and FFANet [31] have the most natural result in the sky.

Analysis on Real-World Datasets. The advantage of our method over its performance on synthetic datasets is mainly in real-world datasets, where we divide four real datasets into two categories: thin datasets(O-HAZE [3], I-HAZE [4]) and thick datasets(NH-HAZE [2], Dence HAZE [1]). As shown in Table 1, our method obtains the best performance on O-HAZE [3] and I-HAZE [4].

We also present the dehazing results for both datasets in Fig. 5. We can observe that for the I-HAZE [4] example, the results of DCP [18], and RDN [43] are very dark and lose a lot of details. The performance of ADN [22], and LDN [39] is poor and the images appear gray. The results of GDN [25] have incongruent image tones and appear noisy. FFANet [31] has a halo effect at the green window. MSBDN [10] has a brighter image compared to GT as a whole, and the color saturation of the color palette is low as seen in the blue window. Our method is also brighter compared to GT, but better than MSBDN [10], and the overall style is more natural and similar to GT.

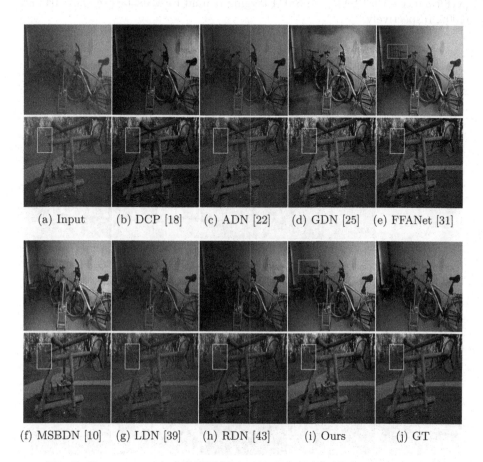

(a) Input   (b) DCP [18]   (c) ADN [22]   (d) GDN [25]   (e) FFANet [31]

(f) MSBDN [10]   (g) LDN [39]   (h) RDN [43]   (i) Ours   (j) GT

Fig. 5. Haze removal in I-HAZE [4] and O-HAZE [3]. (Color figure online)

In the case image of O-HAZE [3], all previous methods also present roughly the same problems as I-HAZE [4], and we give the main differences in the yellow window. As you can see, except for ADN [22], FFANet [31], LDN [39], and our method, none of the other methods can get the haze inside the window nowhere. FFANet [31] is also not as good as our method for the scenery at the yellow window.

How to dehaze dense hazy images in the real world has been a very tricky problem, and existing work does not yield a better performance due to the very small number of samples. Our method makes further progress on the dense hazy dataset. As shown in Table 1, our method obtains the best performance on NH-HAZE [2] with its PSNR and SSIM of 22.04 dB, 0.803, and the second-best MSBDN [10] with its PSNR and SSIM of 20.95 dB and 0.796, respectively. On the Dence HAZE [1] dataset, both of our methods obtain the second-best performance with PSNR and SSIM lagging behind FFANet [31] by 0.09 dB and 0.007, respectively.

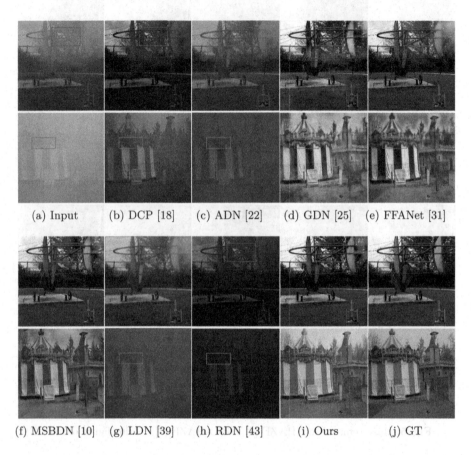

(a) Input   (b) DCP [18]   (c) ADN [22]   (d) GDN [25]   (e) FFANet [31]

(f) MSBDN [10]   (g) LDN [39]   (h) RDN [43]   (i) Ours   (j) GT

Fig. 6. Haze removal in NH-HAZE [2] and Dence HAZE [1]. (Color figure online)

Figure 6 shows the results of SOTA methods and our method in NH-HAZE [2] and Dence HAZE [1], and it can be seen that both the DCP [18] and the RDN [43] results combining DCP [18] and CNNs are very poor and show severe color bias. All methods show different degrees of dehazing incompleteness, especially ADN [22], LDN [39] is the most serious. We can observe that although FFANet [31] obtains a high matrix performance, it has a very poor visual effect. For the scenes in the red and orange window, the visual effect of the result obtained by our method completely surpasses that of the previous SOTA methods.

Although the four real-world datasets can simulate haze formation to a large extent, they are ultimately not obtained in a naturally occurring haze environment and therefore do not fully represent the formation of haze in the real world. We have taken several images of naturally occurring haze in the real world to compare our method with the SOTA methods. As you can see, our method still works, especially in the first image, where our method clearly surpasses the other SOTA methods in terms of sensory processing of the sky.

(a) Input   (b) DCP [18]   (c) ADN [22]   (d) GDN [25]   (e) FFANet [31]

(f) MSBDN [10]   (g) PSDNet [8]   (h) LDN [39]   (i) RDN [43]   (j) Ours

Fig. 7. Haze removal in real-world.

4.4 Model Complexity and Inference Time

We give the number of parameters of the model, the inference time for different image sizes, and the FLOPs of the model to measure the complexity of the model (input image size 512×512×3) in Table 2, using an RTX 3090 GPU. × in the table indicates that the model requires more than 24GB of video memory.

Compared to the suboptimal MSBDN [10], the number of parameters and FLOPs of our network are about $\frac{1}{4}$ and $\frac{1}{3}$ respectively, and the inference time is reduced accordingly. It can be seen that for 2048×2048 resolution image, our model can still inference normally, which indicates that our network uses less memory than MSBDN [10], FFANet [31], and GDN [25].

Table 2. Comparison of the number of parameters, FLOPs, and inference time.

	ADN [22]	GDN [25]	FFANet [31]	MSBDN [10]	LDN [39]	RDN [43]	Ours
Param(MB)	0.002	0.960	4.680	31.35	0.030	68.56	7.670
FLOPs(GB)	0.460	0.45	1.46	97.77	7.890	238.1	31.46
128×128(s)	0.004	0.073	0.267	0.304	0.006	−	0.110
256×256(s)	0.006	0.076	0.307	0.313	0.008	0.206	0.118
512×512(s)	0.014	0.100	0.486	0.333	0.019	0.216	0.140
1024×1024(s)	0.042	0.216	×	0.422	0.056	0.420	0.245
2048×2048(s)	0.204	×	×	×	0.245	1.236	0.736

4.5 Ablation Study

To demonstrate the effectiveness of our method, we perform ablation experiments to analyze each module, including MLFF, DFFD, MSFF, residual group, and dense connection.

As shown in Table 3, ✓ means that the module has been used, × means that the module has been removed directly, and − means that a simple module has been used instead of the module. In this section, we use the Conv block replacing MLFF and the FFA module [31] replacing DFFD.

The training configuration of the above network is consistent with Sect. 3.4, and the training and testing sets used for the ablation experiments are I-HAZE [4], the performance of the above model is shown in Table 3.

Effect of MLFF. MLFF is a general-purpose feature extractor that enables feature reuse and forwards pass without adding additional parameters, compared to simple stacked convolutional layers, using only dense connections. As can be seen in Table 3, our proposed MLFF improves the PSNR and SSIM from 23.92 dB, 0.904 to 24.52 dB, 0.909.

Effect of DFFD. The FFA module [31] has already achieved greater success in dehazing task, and we inherited this idea and further enhanced its capability by proposing the DFFD to make it a more effective dehazing module. As can be seen from Table 3, we have obtained an improvement of 1.13dB PSNR and 0.008 SSIM using the DFFD to replace the FFA module [31], which is sufficient proof that our proposed DFFD module is effective.

Effect of MSFF. As opposed to simply feeding features to the decoder, we propose a simple multi-stream processing module to fully fuse features from different sources and let the network select the important features, and our strategy is experimentally proven to be effective.

Effect of Residual Group. Previous experience tells us that sufficiently deep networks generally give better performance, so we add the residual group. Experiments have proven this to be effective. As shown in Table 3, the network obtains a PSNR, SSIM improvement of 1.03 dB and 0.045.

Effect of Dense Connection. As shown in Table 3, the PSNR and SSIM of the model without dense connection is only 21.31 dB and 0.853 respectively. After adding dense connections to each base module, PSNR and SSIM reach the best, which shows that dense connections do allow the network features to be passed on effectively and can make the encoder a good feature extractor.

Table 3. Ablation experiments on the effectiveness of each module.

MLFF	MSFF	DFFD	Dense connection	Residual group	PSNR	SSIM
−	✓	✓	✓	✓	23.92	0.904
✓	×	✓	✓	✓	23.86	0.905
✓	✓	−	✓	✓	23.39	0.901
✓	✓	✓	×	✓	21.31	0.853
✓	✓	✓	✓	×	23.49	0.864
✓	✓	✓	✓	✓	24.52	0.909

5 Conclusion

In this paper, we propose a novel MSF^{2}DN for single image dehazing, which consists of a multi level feature fusion module(MLFF), a double feature fusion dehazing module(DFFD), extended from an FFA block using a dense connection and attention mechanism, and a multi stream feature fusion module to deal with the features from different stages. Dense connections allow the network to skip relatively unimportant features such as thin haze or even clear areas, focusing the main performance of the network on dense haze areas. The ablation experiments prove that our proposed module is helpful for the improvement of network performance. We evaluate MSF^{2}DN on a synthetic dataset and real-world datasets and demonstrate that MSF^{2}DN outperforms existing SOTA methods.

References

1. Ancuti, C.O., Ancuti, C., Sbert, M., Timofte, R.: Dense haze: a benchmark for image dehazing with dense-haze and haze-free images. In: arXiv (2019)
2. Ancuti, C.O., Ancuti, C., Timofte, R.: NH-HAZE: an image dehazing benchmark with non-homogeneous hazy and haze-free images. In: 2020 IEEE/CVF Conference on Computer Vision and Pattern Recognition Workshops (CVPRW) (2020)
3. Ancuti, C.O., Ancuti, C., Timofte, R., Vleeschouwer, C.D.: O-HAZE: a dehazing benchmark with real hazy and haze-free outdoor images. In: 2018 IEEE/CVF Conference on Computer Vision and Pattern Recognition Workshops (CVPRW) (2018)
4. Ancuti, C.O., Ancuti, C., Timofte, R., Vleeschouwer, C.D.: I-HAZE: a dehazing benchmark with real hazy and haze-free indoor images (2018)
5. Berman, D., Treibitz, T., Avidan, S.: Non-local image dehazing. In: 2016 IEEE Conference on Computer Vision and Pattern Recognition (CVPR) (2016)

6. Cai, B., Xu, X., Jia, K., Qing, C., Tao, D.: DehazeNet: an end-to-end system for single image haze removal. IEEE Trans. Image Process. **25**(11), 5187–5198 (2016)
7. Chen, D., et al.: Gated context aggregation network for image dehazing and deraining. In: 2019 IEEE Winter Conference on Applications of Computer Vision (WACV), pp. 1375–1383. IEEE (2019)
8. Chen, Z., Wang, Y., Yang, Y., Liu, D.: PSD: principled synthetic-to-real dehazing guided by physical priors. In: Computer Vision and Pattern Recognition (2021)
9. Cheng, S., Wang, Y., Huang, H., Liu, D., Liu, S.: NBNet: noise basis learning for image denoising with subspace projection (2020)
10. Dong, H., et al.: Multi-scale boosted dehazing network with dense feature fusion. In: Proceedings of the IEEE/CVF Conference on Computer Vision and Pattern Recognition, pp. 2157–2167 (2020)
11. Engin, D., Gen, A., Ekenel, H.K.: Cycle-Dehaze: enhanced CycleGAN for single image dehazing. In: 2018 IEEE/CVF Conference on Computer Vision and Pattern Recognition Workshops (CVPRW) (2018)
12. Girshick, R.: Fast R-CNN. Computer Science (2015)
13. He, K., Gkioxari, G., Dollár, P., Girshick, R.: Mask R-CNN. In: IEEE Transactions on Pattern Analysis and Machine Intelligence (2017)
14. He, K., Zhang, X., Ren, S., Sun, J.: Delving deep into rectifiers: surpassing human-level performance on ImageNet classification. In: CVPR (2015)
15. He, K., Zhang, X., Ren, S., Sun, J.: Deep residual learning for image recognition. In: 2016 IEEE Conference on Computer Vision and Pattern Recognition (CVPR) (2016)
16. He, Z., Sindagi, V., Patel, V.M.: Multi-scale single image dehazing using perceptual pyramid deep network. In: 2018 IEEE/CVF Conference on Computer Vision and Pattern Recognition Workshops (CVPRW) (2018)
17. Huang, G., Liu, Z., Laurens, V., Weinberger, K.Q.: Densely connected convolutional networks. In: IEEE Computer Society (2016)
18. He, K., Sun, J., Tang, X.: Single image haze removal using dark channel prior. IEEE Trans. Pattern Anal. Mach. Intell. **33**, 2341–2353 (2011)
19. Kim, S.E., Park, T.H., Eom, I.K.: Fast single image dehazing using saturation based transmission map estimation. IEEE Trans. Image Process. **29**, 1985–1998 (2019)
20. Kingma, D., Ba, J.: Adam: a method for stochastic optimization. Comput. Sci. (2014)
21. Krizhevsky, A., Sutskever, I., Hinton, G.: ImageNet classification with deep convolutional neural networks. In: Advances in Neural Information Processing Systems, vol. 25(2) (2012)
22. Li, B., Peng, X., Wang, Z., Xu, J., Dan, F.: AOD-Net: all-in-one dehazing network. In: 2017 IEEE International Conference on Computer Vision (ICCV) (2017)
23. Li, B., Ren, W., Fu, D., Tao, D., Wang, Z.: Reside: a benchmark for single image dehazing (2017)
24. Li, R., Pan, J., Li, Z., Tang, J.: Single image dehazing via conditional generative adversarial network. In: 2018 IEEE/CVF Conference on Computer Vision and Pattern Recognition (CVPR) (2018)
25. Liu, X., Ma, Y., Shi, Z., Chen, J.: Griddehazenet: attention-based multi-scale network for image dehazing (2019)
26. Liu, X., Suganuma, M., Sun, Z., Okatani, T.: Dual residual networks leveraging the potential of paired operations for image restoration. In: 2019 IEEE/CVF Conference on Computer Vision and Pattern Recognition (CVPR) (2019)

27. Mei, K., Jiang, A., Li, J., Wang, M.: Progressive feature fusion network for realistic image dehazing. In: Jawahar, C.V., Li, H., Mori, G., Schindler, K. (eds.) ACCV 2018. LNCS, vol. 11361, pp. 203–215. Springer, Cham (2019). https://doi.org/10.1007/978-3-030-20887-5_13

28. Meng, G., Wang, Y., Duan, J., Xiang, S., Pan, C.: Efficient image dehazing with boundary constraint and contextual regularization. In: Proceedings of the 2013 IEEE International Conference on Computer Vision (2013)

29. Narasimhan, S.G., Nayar, S.K.: Chromatic framework for vision in bad weather. In: IEEE Computer Society Conference on Computer Vision and Pattern Recognition (2000)

30. Narasimhan, S.G., Nayar, S.K.: Vision and the atmosphere. Int. J. Comput. Vis. **48**(3), 233–254 (2002)

31. Qin, X., Wang, Z., Bai, Y., Xie, X., Jia, H.: FFA-Net: feature fusion attention network for single image dehazing. In: Proceedings of the AAAI Conference on Artificial Intelligence, vol. 34, pp. 11908–11915 (2020)

32. Ren, S., He, K., Girshick, R., Sun, J.: Faster R-CNN: towards real-time object detection with region proposal networks. IEEE Trans. Pattern Anal. Mach. Intell. **39**(6), 1137–1149 (2017)

33. Ren, W., et al.: Gated fusion network for single image dehazing. In: 2018 IEEE/CVF Conference on Computer Vision and Pattern Recognition (2018)

34. Ren, W., Liu, S., Zhang, H., Pan, J., Cao, X., Yang, M.-H.: Single image dehazing via multi-scale convolutional neural networks. In: Leibe, B., Matas, J., Sebe, N., Welling, M. (eds.) ECCV 2016. LNCS, vol. 9906, pp. 154–169. Springer, Cham (2016). https://doi.org/10.1007/978-3-319-46475-6_10

35. Shao, Y., Li, L., Ren, W., Gao, C., Sang, N.: Domain adaptation for image dehazing. In: Proceedings of the IEEE/CVF Conference on Computer Vision and Pattern Recognition, pp. 2808–2817 (2020)

36. Srivastava, R.K., Greff, K., Schmidhuber, J.: Training very deep networks. Comput. Sci. (2015)

37. Sulami, M., Glatzer, I., Fattal, R., Werman, M.: Automatic recovery of the atmospheric light in hazy images. In: IEEE International Conference on Computational Photography (2014)

38. Tan, R.T.: Visibility in bad weather from a single image. In: 2008 IEEE Computer Society Conference on Computer Vision and Pattern Recognition (CVPR 2008), 24–26 June 2008, Anchorage, Alaska, USA (2008)

39. Ullah, H., et al.: Light-DehazeNet: a novel lightweight CNN architecture for single image dehazing. IEEE Trans. Image Process. **30**, 8968–8982 (2021)

40. Yang, X., Xu, Z., Luo, J.: Towards perceptual image dehazing by physics-based disentanglement and adversarial training. In: Proceedings of the AAAI Conference on Artificial Intelligence, vol. 32 (2018)

41. Zhang, H., Patel, V.M.: Densely connected pyramid dehazing network. In: Proceedings of the IEEE Conference on Computer Vision and Pattern Recognition, pp. 3194–3203 (2018)

42. Zhang, Y., Tian, Y., Kong, Y., Zhong, B., Fu, Y.: Residual dense network for image super-resolution. In: 2018 IEEE/CVF Conference on Computer Vision and Pattern Recognition (2018)

43. Zhao, S., Zhang, L., Shen, Y., Zhou, Y.: RefineDNet: a weakly supervised refinement framework for single image dehazing. IEEE Trans. Image Process. **30**, 3391–3404 (2021)

44. Zhu, Q., Mai, J., Shao, L.: A fast single image haze removal algorithm using color attenuation prior. IEEE Trans. Image Process. **24**(11), 3522–3533 (2015)

MGRLN-Net: Mask-Guided Residual Learning Network for Joint Single-Image Shadow Detection and Removal

Leiping Jie[1,2] and Hui Zhang[2(✉)]

[1] Department of Computer Science, Hong Kong Baptist University, Hong Kong SAR, China
[2] Department of Computer Science and Technology, BNU-HKBU United International College, Zhuhai, China
amyzhang@uic.edu.cn

Abstract. Although significant progress has been made in single-image shadow detection or single-image shadow removal, only few works consider these two problems together. However, the two problems are complementary and can benefit from each other. In this work, we propose a Mask-Guided Residual Learning Network (MGRLN-Net) that jointly estimates shadow mask and shadow-free image. In particular, MGRLN-Net first generates a shadow mask, then utilizes a feature reassembling module to align the features from the shadow detection module to the shadow removal module. Finally, we leverage the learned shadow mask as guidance to generate a shadow-free image. We formulate shadow removal as a masked residual learning problem of the original shadow image. In this way, the learned shadow mask is used as guidance to produce better transitions in penumbra regions. Extensive experiments on ISTD, ISTD+, and SRD benchmark datasets demonstrate that our method outperforms current state-of-the-art approaches on both shadow detection and shadow removal tasks. Our code is available at https://github.com/LeipingJie/MGRLN-Net.

Keywords: Shadow detection and removal · Multi-task learning · Masked residual learning

1 Introduction

Shadows that help us better understand real-world scenes are cast by objects that block the propagation of light rays and are ubiquitous in our daily lives. However, they cause trouble to many tasks, *e.g.*, object detection, image segmentation, or scene analysis. Shadows can be cast into arbitrary shapes with different intensities at any position, making both shadow detection and removal challenging.

Due to their challenge and importance, shadow detection and removal are active research topics. Traditional methods [5,6,19,30] utilizing physical mod-

© The Author(s), under exclusive license to Springer Nature Switzerland AG 2023
L. Wang et al. (Eds.): ACCV 2022, LNCS 13843, pp. 460–476, 2023.
https://doi.org/10.1007/978-3-031-26313-2_28

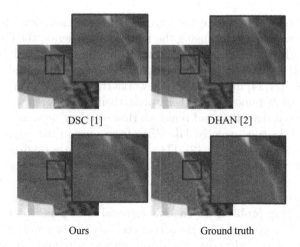

DSC [1]   DHAN [2]

Ours   Ground truth

Fig. 1. We compare our model with two state-of-the-art methods DSC [11] and DHAN [3]. As can be seen, our model produces better details.

els, handcrafted features, or prior knowledge, are not robust and lead to unsatisfactory performance. Leveraging large-scale annotated datasets and computational power, deep learning-based shadow detection and shadow removal approaches have shown their superiority. Modern shadow detection methods [13,15,22,33,35] formulate the shadow detection problem as a binary classification problem. They typically use different strategies to extract the global and local contexts from a single input image, including attention mechanisms [4,16], bidirectional fusion [35], and teacher-student learning [1]. Similarly, shadow removal approaches [12,29] primarily leverage Generative Adversarial Networks (GAN), where the generator attempts to produce faked shadow-free images while the discriminator tries to distinguish between the real shadow-free images and the generated fake shadow-free images. Despite superior performance, most approaches tackle these two problems individually. Intuitively, shadow detection and shadow removal are mutually beneficial. On the one hand, the shadow detection results provide strong guidance for shadow removal algorithms to adjust more on shadow pixels and less on non-shadow pixels. On the other hand, the shadow removal process expects more variation on shadowed pixels and less variation on non-shadowed pixels, which is also associated with identifying whether a pixel is a shadow pixel or not.

In this paper, we propose a unified network for joint shadow detection and removal. In practice, shadow detection and removal are formulated as classification and regression problems. For the shadow detection problem, the model only needs to predict whether a pixel is a shadow pixel or not. However, the model needs to answer how to transfer shadowed pixels to shadow-free pixels to solve the shadow removal problem, which is more challenging. Based on this, we design a compact and efficient shadow detection sub-network and a more complicated shadow removal sub-network. Specifically, we build our model in an encoder-decoder way, where the encoder extracts multi-level features while the decoder is responsible for fusing the features to generate the desired shadow masks and shadow-free images. We want to emphasize that although several papers [4,11,14] claimed for performing joint shadow detection and removal, they differ from ours. [11,14] introduced frameworks that could be trained for shadow detection or shadow removal. In other words, their frameworks were trained separately for shadow detection and removal. However, our network can be trained with the two tasks concurrently. [4] differs from ours in five aspects: (1) Their architecture is based on GAN. (2) They do not explicitly predict shadow mask images. (3) They use the recurrent unit to generate shadow attention, while we use it to remove shadows. (4) Our recurrent unit is shared while theirs is not. (5) Our model performs better on shadow detection and removal.

One challenging problem for shadow removal is to generate a natural transition effect in the penumbra regions (between the umbra and the shadow-free regions). Nevertheless, identifying and annotating penumbra regions is exceptionally time-consuming, expensive, or even impossible. To generate annotation for penumbra regions at low cost, previous methods [7] utilize morphological algorithms. Specifically, the penumbra region is defined as the area of the dilation mask minus the erosion mask. However, the kernels used for dilation and erosion are chosen empirically and thus are sometimes inappropriate. Thanks to our joint training pipeline, the shadow masks predicted by our network naturally contain penumbra regions. In other words, the shadow boundaries in the shadow mask do not transition hardly but softly. Consequently, we design a shadow mask-guided residual learning module to remove shadows. Specifically, the shadow-guided residual learning module consists of feature reassembling, feature refining, and prediction modules.

To verify the effectiveness of our proposed method, we conduct extensive experiments on three commonly used benchmark datasets: ISTD, ISTD+, and SRD. Comparisons are made with both state-of-the-art shadow detection and removal methods. Experimental results show that our network outperforms the state-of-the-art shadow detection and removal methods.

In summary, our main contributions are three-fold:

- We propose a novel network for joint shadow detection and shadow removal.
- We design an efficient shadow removal module that reassembles and refines the context features with the mask guidance to produce better transition effects in penumbra regions.
- We show that the proposed network outperforms the state-of-the-art shadow detection and removal methods on three widely used benchmark datasets ISTD [29], SRD [23] and ISTD+ [20].

2   Related Work

In this section, we review the shadow detection and the shadow removal approaches, respectively.

2.1 Shadow Detection

Before the era of deep learning, most shadow detection approaches relying on the physical properties [5,6] assumed color, illumination or statistical-based hand-craft features to be consistent [19,34]. Zhu et al. [34] combined mixed features, e.g., the intensity difference, the gradient, and the texture similarities, to train a boosted decision tree classifier. For better performance and robustness, Guo et al. [10] considered areas rather than individual pixels or edges to construct a graph of segments by classifying the pairwise segmented area, followed by the graph-cut algorithm. Later, Vicente et al. [28] distinguished the shadow area from the non-shadow region by training a kernel Least-Squares Support Vector Machine (LSSVM). Despite the improved performance, traditional approaches heavily rely on consistent color or illumination assumptions, which may not be suitable for real-world scenes. Therefore, the overall performance is not high and satisfactory. Like many other computer vision tasks, shadow detection is now dominated by deep learning approaches. Early solutions utilized the deep con-volutional neural network (CNN) as the feature extractor to replace handcraft designs. Khan et al. [18] proposed the first CNN-based approach for shadow detection. Unlike traditional methods, they used a 7-layer CNN to learn fea-tures along the object boundaries at a super-pixel level and then generated smooth shadow contours with a conditional random field model. Shen et al. [25] exploited the local structure of the shadow edge using the structured CNN and improved the local consistency of the estimated shadow map with the struc-tured labels. Later, due to the newly developed neural network architectures, such as U-Net [24], GAN [8], research on shadow detection tended to train neu-ral networks in an end-to-end manner, focusing more on using both global and local features at the same time. Hu et al. [13] demonstrated that the direction-aware context features could be learned by spatial recurrent neural network (RNN). Zhu et al. [35] presented a bidirectional feature pyramid network to explore and combine global and local context. Recently, Jie et al. [15,16] pro-posed a transformer-based network to capture attention along multi-level fea-tures. Unlike the common CNN architecture as the feature extractor, Nguyen et al. [22] added an additional parameter of sensitivity to the generator to optimize the based conditional GAN framework. More recently, Zheng et al. [33] proposed to explicitly learn and integrate the semantics of visual distraction areas with their differentiable Distraction-aware Shadow (DS) module. To alleviate the bur-den of annotation and boost performance, Chen et al. [1] introduced to explore the learning of multiple information of shadows using a multi-task mean teacher model with unlabeled data in a semi-supervised manner.

2.2 Shadow Removal

Similar to the shadow detection problem, shadow removal methods can also be divided into traditional and learning-based methods. Traditional approaches exploited physical properties, e.g., image illumination [31,32] and image gradi-ent [9]. Recently, shadow removal approaches using deep learning have become

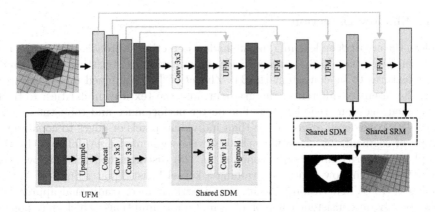

Fig. 2. Overview of our proposed network. Our network takes a single image as input and outputs the corresponding shadow mask and shadow-free image. The network is an encoder-decoder structure and is composed of a feature extractor (see Sect. 3.1), a shared shadow detection module (see Sect. 3.2) and a shared shadow removal module (see Fig. 3 and Fig. 4). The input image is fed into the feature extractor to obtain multi-level feature maps, which are fed into both the shadow detection and shadow removal module. The predicted shadow mask is also fed into the shadow removal module as weight guidance for the residual learning of the shadow-free images.

popular. Qu *et al.* [23] introduced a multi-context architecture to integrate high-level semantic context, mid-level appearance information, and local image details, which learns a mapping function between the shadow image and its shadow matte. Hu *et al.* [11] leverages the spatial context in different directions and attention mechanism for both shadow detection and removal. Chen *et al.* [2] proposed a two-stage context network to transfer contextual information from non-shadow patches to shadow patches. By formulating the shadow removal problem as an exposure fusion problem, Fu *et al.* [7] addressed shadow removal by fusing estimated over-exposure images and achieved state-of-the-art performance. Moreover, methods based on Generative Adversarial Network (GAN) show their potential. ST-CGAN [29] utilized two conditional GAN for both shadow detection and removal. MaskShadowGAN [12] proposed a cycle-GAN-based framework to identify the shadow-free to shadow image translation with learned guidance from shadow masks. Despite the boosting performance, only few works consider both shadow detection and shadow removal. We believe that the two complementary tasks can benefit from each other and should be considered together.

3   Methodology

In this section, we first introduce the overall architecture of our proposed method in Sect. 3.1. Next, we illustrate our shadow detection module in Sect. 3.2 and shadow removal module in Sect. 3.3, respectively. Finally, the loss functions will be presented in Sect. 3.4.

3.1 Network Architecture

As shown in Fig. 2, our method takes a single shadow image as input and outputs the corresponding shadow mask and shadow-free image. Specifically, we first utilize a pretrained EfficientNet [27] as our feature extractor, which obtains L different levels of encoder features $\{F_i\}_{i=1}^{L}$ ($L = 5$ here). These features are then fed into the following modules, including an Upsampling and Fusion Module (UFM), a Shadow Detection Module (SDM), and a Shadow Removal Module (SRM), to generate different levels of decoder features $\{D_i\}_{i=1}^{L}$ ($L = 5$ here), where F_i and D_i are of the same resolution. In UFM, it first upsamples the current decoder feature map $D_i (i \neq 0)$ to D_i' using a differentiable interpolation operator, and then concatenates D_i' with the corresponding encoder feature map F_{i-1}, followed by two consecutive 3×3 convolutional layers. We denote the output feature map of UFM as $\{U_i\}_{i=1}^{L}$ ($L = 4$ here).

3.2 Shadow Detection Module

Considering that our shadow detection module is used to help with shadow removal, we designed a compact and efficient subnetwork for shadow detection. Given any output feature map U_i from UFM, we stack a 3×3 and another 1×1 convolutional layer with the sigmoid function to generate the predicted shadow mask. In our model, the output feature map U_i from UFM is also fed into the shadow removal module, which implies that U_i contains the discriminative features for both shadow detection and removal when training is processed in a joint manner. Unlike previous methods that generate shadow masks from each decoder layer, we only generate two shadow masks from the last two decoder layers. Despite its simple structure, our shadow detection module predicts satisfactory shadow masks (more details are presented in Sect. 4.3).

3.3 Shadow Removal Module

As shown in Fig. 3, our proposed shadow removal module consists of three submodules: Feature Reassembling (FR), Recurrent Refinement (RR), and Residual Learning (RL).

Feature Reassembling. The feature reassembling submodule aims at reassembling the input feature U_i. Since our shadow detection module and shadow removal module share U_i, it is difficult to force U_i to be discriminative for both shadow detection and shadow removal. We argue that discriminative features for shadow detection and removal should be different but complementary, which means they can be transferred from one kind to the other. Based on this, we adopt an improved lightweight U-Net to accomplish this transformation. The UNet downsamples and upsamples three times, respectively, and keeps the input and output feature maps at the same resolution.

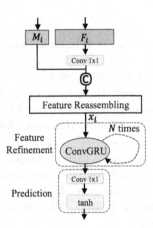

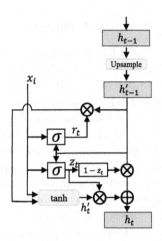

Fig. 3. Illustration of our proposed shadow removal module.

Fig. 4. Illustration of ConvGRU module.

Recurrent Refinement. Although the reassembled features are adapted for shadow removal, they still contain noises. Here we propose to remove them in a recurrent way. Specifically, the recurrent refinement submodule utilizes ConvGRU [26]. Given the input feature map x_i and the previous hidden state h_{t-1}, we first apply two 3×3 convolution layers on x_i and h_{t-1}, respectively, followed by a sigmoid function to get the update gate z_t. The same operation is performed to get the reset gate r_t. Then, r_t is used to generate candidate hidden state h'_t. Finally, the update gate z_t is used to adaptively select information from the previous hidden state h_{t-1} and the candidate hidden state h'_t to output h_t. The whole procedure can be formulated as follows:

$$
\begin{aligned}
z_t &= \sigma(Conv_z^x(x_i) + Conv_z^h(h_{t-1})), \\
r_t &= \sigma(Conv_r^x(x_i) + Conv_r^h(h_{t-1})), \\
h'_t &= tanh(Conv_h^x(x_i) + Conv_h^r(r_t \circ h_{t-1})), \\
h_t &= (1 - z_t) \circ h_{t-1} + z_t \circ h'_t,
\end{aligned}
\tag{1}
$$

where ©, Conv, σ, $\circ$ are concatenation operation, convolutional layer, sigmoid function and element-wise multiplication, respectively. It is worth mentioning that the recurrent refinement can be run N times. Empirically, we set $N = 2$ for speed-performance tradeoff.

Residual Learning. To get the final shadow-free image prediction, we use residual learning, which means we regress the residual image R_i based on the input RGB image instead of predicting the shadow-free image directly. This is quite effective in our experiment (see Sect. 4.5). More importantly, we impose the predicted shadow mask M_i on the residual output, which enables our network to generate desired transition effect between the shadow-free and penumbra regions.

We express this procedure as follows:

$$Free = M_i \circ R_i + RGB, \tag{2}$$

where $Free$, RGB, M_i, R_i represent the predicted shadow-free image, the input RGB shadow image, the predicted shadow mask, and the predicted residual image, respectively.

3.4 Objective Functions

For both predicted shadow mask and shadow-free images, we use $L1$ loss as follows:

$$L_{rgb} = \sum_{i=1}^{2} \|y_i - \hat{y}_i\|_1,$$
$$L_{mask} = \sum_{i=1}^{2} \|m_i - \hat{m}_i\|_1, \tag{3}$$

where m_i, $\hat{m}_i$, y_i, $\hat{y}_i$ are the predicted shadow mask, the ground truth shadow mask, the predicted shadow-free image, and the ground truth shadow-free image, respectively.

Furthermore, we also compute the feature loss using the pretrained $VGG\text{-}19$ network Ψ as follows:

$$L_{feature} = \sum_{l=1}^{\Omega} \|\Psi_l(y) - \Psi_l(\hat{y})\|_1, \tag{4}$$

where Ψ_l indicates the layer l, and Ω represents the $3th, 8th, 15th, 22th$ layers in the $VGG\text{-}19$ network.

Overall, our loss function is:

$$L = L_{mask} + \lambda_1 L_{rgb} + \lambda_2 L_{feature}, \tag{5}$$

where λ_1 and λ_2 are empirically set to 2.0 to balance between different losses.

4   Experimental Results

4.1   Datasets and Evaluation Metrics

Datasets. We train and evaluate our proposed method on three widely used benchmark datasets: ISTD [29], ISTD+ [20] and SRD [23]. ISTD consists of $1,300$ and 540 triplets of shadow, shadow mask, and shadow-free images for training and testing. ISTD+ is constructed based on the ISTD, where only the shadow-free images are adjusted for color consistency between shadow and shadow-free images, and thus has the same training and testing splits as ISTD. In contrast, SRD has $2,680$ and 408 shadow and shadow-free image pairs for training and testing, with no shadow masks provided. Since shadow masks are necessary for our pipeline, we follow MaskShadow-GAN [12] to generate shadow masks by using Otsu's algorithm with the difference between shadow and shadow-free images. The image resolution in ISTD and ISTD+ is 640 × 480, while SRD is 840 × 640.

Evaluation Metric. We employ the Balance Error Rate (BER) and Root Mean Square Error ($RMSE$) to quantitatively evaluate shadow detection and shadow removal performance. BER considers the performance of both shadow prediction and non-shadow prediction and can be formulated as follows:

$$BER = \left(1 - \frac{1}{2}\left(\frac{TP}{N_p} + \frac{TN}{N_n}\right)\right) \times 100, \qquad (6)$$

where TP, TN, N_p, and N_n are the number of true positive pixels, true negative pixels, shadow pixels, and non-shadow pixels, respectively. $RMSE$ is calculated in the LAB color space between the predicted shadow-free images and the ground truth shadow-free image. It is worth noting that the default evaluates code used by all methods (including ours) actually computes the mean absolute error (MAE), as mentioned in [17,20]. For both BER and $RMSE$, the smaller the value, the better the performance.

4.2 Implementation Details

Our proposed method is implemented in PyTorch and all the experiments are conducted on a NVIDIA single RTX 2080Ti GPU.

Training Settings. When training, we crop and resize the input images to 448×448 with batch size 8. The maximum learning rate max_{lr} is set to 0.000375 and decayed with 1-cycle policy. Specifically, the initial and the minimum learning rate are set to $max_{lr}/30$ and $max_{lr}/150$, while the percentage of the cycle spent increasing the learning rate is 0.1. We empirically train our network for 200 epochs using half-precision floating and AdamW optimizer, where the first momentum value, the second momentum value, and the weight decay are 0.9, 0.999, and 5^{-4}, respectively.

Testing Setting. When testing, we do not apply any data augmentations and post-processing operations, *e.g.*, conditional random filed (CRF) for shadow masks.

4.3 Comparison with State-of-the-Art Shadow Detection Methods

Since no ground truth shadow mask is provided for SRD, we only evaluate our shadow detection results on ISTD. As shown in Table 1, our model achieves the best performance against ST-CGAN [29], DSDNet [33], BDRAR [35] and DSC [11]. It is worth mentioning that DSDNet, BDRAR, and DSC are elaborately designed for the shadow detection task only. Nevertheless, we can still outperform DSDNet, DSC and BDRAR by 33.18%, 46.1% and 57.6%. More importantly, compared with the existing jointly training frameworks ST-CGAN and ARGAN for shadow detection and removal, our performance surpasses theirs significantly by 83.14% and 27.86%.

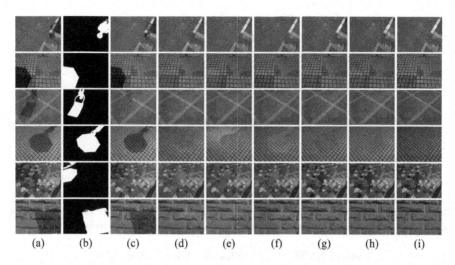

Fig. 5. Qualitative comparison on ISTD [29] dataset. From left to right: (a) input shadow image; (b) shadow mask; (c) Guo *et al.* [10]; (d) ST-CGAN [29]; (e) DSC [11]; (f) DHAN [3]; (g) Auto-Exposure [7]; (h) ours; (i) ground truth shadow-free image. Best viewed on screen.

4.4 Comparison with State-of-the-Art Shadow Removal Methods

We compare the performance of our network with different state-of-the-art methods since some only provide their performance on one or two benchmark datasets.

Comparison on ISTD Dataset. On the ISTD dataset, we compare with 8 other methods: Guo *et al.* [10], Zhang *et al.* [32], MaskShadow-GAN [12], ST-CGAN [29], DSC [11], DHAN [3], CANet [2], Auto-Exposure [7]. As can be seen from Table 2, our method achieves the best performance. In particular, our method outperforms Guo *et al.* [10], Zhang *et al.* [32], MaskShadow-GAN [12], ST-CGAN [29], DSC [11], DHAN [3], CANet [2], Auto-Exposure [7] by 45.91%, 41.03%, 32.12%, 32.66%, 24.59%, 21.04%, 18.21%, 15.03%, respectively. We also visualize our predicted shadow-free images in Fig. 5. Qualitatively our method generates satisfactory predictions on the ISTD benchmark dataset.

Comparison on the ISTD+ Dataset. On the ISTD+ dataset, we compare with 8 other methods: Guo *et al.* [10], Zhang *et al.* [32], ST-CGAN [29], DeshadowNet [23], MaskShadow-GAN [12], Param+M+D-Net [21], SP+M-Net [20], Auto-Exposure [7]. As presented in Table 3, our method achieves the best performance. Specifically, our model surpasses Guo *et al.* [10], ST-CGAN [29], DeshadowNet [23], MaskShadow-GAN [12], Param+M+D-Net [21], SP+M-Net [20], Auto-Exposure [7] by 48.36%, 63.8%, 58.55%, 40.57%, 21.25%, 19.23%, 25%, respectively.

Comparison on the SRD Dataset. On the SRD dataset, we compare with 6 other methods: Guo *et al.* [10], DeshadowNet [23], Auto-Exposure [7], DSC [11],

Table 1. Quantitative comparison of shadow detection performance on ISTD [29]. The best and the second best results are highlighted in bold and underlined, respectively.

Method	BER	Shadow	Non-Shadow
ST-CGAN [29]	8.60	7.69	9.23
DSDNet [33]	<u>2.17</u>	<u>1.36</u>	<u>2.98</u>
BDRAR [35]	2.69	**0.50**	4.87
DSC [11]	3.42	3.85	3.00
ARGAN [4]	2.01	–	–
Ours	**1.45**	1.65	**1.26**

Table 2. Quantitative comparison of shadow removal on ISTD [29]. The best and the second best results are highlighted in bold and underlined, respectively.

Method/RMSE	Shadow	Non-Shadow	All
Input Image	32.12	7.19	10.97
Guo et al. [10]	18.95	7.46	9.30
Zhang et al. [32]	14.98	7.29	8.53
MaskShadow-GAN [12]	12.67	6.68	7.41
ST-CGAN [29]	10.33	6.93	7.47
DSC [11]	9.76	6.14	6.67
DHAN [3]	8.14	6.04	6.37
CANet [2]	8.86	6.07	6.15
Auto-Exposure [7]	<u>7.77</u>	<u>5.56</u>	<u>5.92</u>
Ours	**7.65**	**4.52**	**5.03**

Table 3. Quantitative comparison of shadow removal on ISTD+ [20]. The best and the second best results are highlighted in bold and underlined, respectively.

Method/RMSE	Shadow	Non-Shadow	All
Input Image	40.2	2.6	8.5
Guo et al. [10]	22.0	3.1	6.1
Zhang et al. [32]	13.3	–	–
ST-CGAN [29]	13.4	7.7	8.7
DeshadowNet [23]	15.9	6.0	7.6
MaskShadow-GAN [12]	12.4	4.0	5.3
Param+M+D-Net [21]	9.7	<u>3.0</u>	4.0
SP+M-Net [20]	7.9	3.1	<u>3.9</u>
Auto-Exposure [7]	**6.5**	3.8	4.2
Ours	<u>6.69</u>	**2.46**	**3.15**

Table 4. Quantitative comparison of shadow removal on SRD [23]. The best and the second best results are highlighted in bold and underlined, respectively.

Method / RMSE	Shadow	Non-Shadow	All
Input Image	40.28	4.76	14.11
Guo *et al.* [10]	29.89	6.47	12.60
DeshadowNet [23]	11.78	4.84	6.64
Auto-Exposure [7]	8.56	5.75	6.51
DSC [11]	10.89	4.99	6.23
CANet [2]	**7.82**	5.88	5.98
DHAN [3]	8.94	<u>4.80</u>	<u>5.67</u>
Ours	<u>8.03</u>	**3.27**	**4.93**

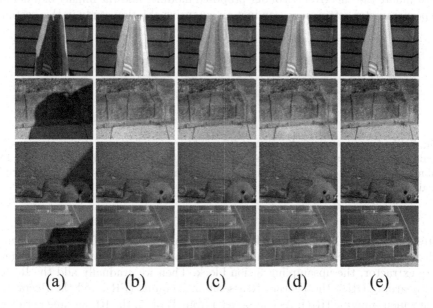

(a)   (b)   (c)   (d)   (e)

Fig. 6. Qualitative comparison on SRD [23] dataset. From left to right: (a) input shadow image; (b) DSC [11]; (c) DHAN [3]; (d) ours; (e) ground truth shadow-free image. Best viewed on screen.

CANet [2], DHAN [3]. As shown in Table 4, our method achieves the best performance. Quantitatively, our model outperforms Guo *et al.* [10], DeshadowNet [23], Auto-Exposure [7], DSC [11], CANet [2], DHAN [3] by 60.87%, 25.75%, 24.27%, 20.87%, 17.56%, 13.05%, respectively. Meanwhile, we also produce qualitatively satisfactory shadow-free predictions. As illustrated in Fig. 6, our method can predict a better consistent appearance as the ground truth shadow-free image.

Table 5. Ablation studies of modules in our model.

Baseline	RL	FR	RR	All
✓	×	×	×	7.95
✓	✓	×	×	6.43
✓	×	✓	×	5.93
✓	✓	✓	×	5.80
✓	✓	×	✓	5.32
✓	✓	✓	✓	**5.03**

Table 6. Ablation study on hyperparameter N in the recurrent refinement module.

N	Shadow	Non-Shadow	All
1	8.17	4.88	5.42
2	**7.65**	**4.52**	**5.03**
3	7.95	4.62	5.16
4	8.11	4.56	5.14

4.5 Ablation Studies

To evaluate the effectiveness of our proposed modules and the impact of different hyperparameter settings, we conduct an extensive ablation study in this section.

baseline   w/FR   w/RL   w/RR   GT

Fig. 7. Shadow removal results. From left to right are: prediction of the baseline model, prediction of the baseline with FR submodule, prediction of baseline with FR and RL submodules, prediction of the proposed model with all submodules, and ground truth shadow-free image.

Effectiveness of Our Network. To deeply analyze how different components affect performance, we first train a baseline model which only contains the feature extractor, the upsampling fusion block. Then we gradually add the Residual Learning (RL), the Feature Reassembling module (FR), and the Recurrent Refinement module (RR). As can be seen from Table 5, the RL module performs the best in terms of performance improvement. Every submodule in the shadow removal module is positive, and we achieve the best performance with all of them. It can be also seen from Fig. 7 that as FR, RR, and RL are gradually equipped with the baseline model, our predicted shadow-free images continue to improve.

Settings of Times N. Our recurrent refinement module contains a ConvGRU unit, which means we can run it recurrently without adding more training parameters. However, more running loops will lead to more time-consuming. We choose four different values $N = 1, 2, 3, 4$. As shown in Table 6, $N = 2$ achieves the best performance, but $N = 3$ and $N = 4$ show nearly the same performance.

input images   ground truths   our results

Fig. 8. Failure cases on shadow removal. (Color figure online)

4.6 Failure Cases

Despite the superior performance, our method fails with some hard cases. As shown in the second row of Fig. 8, when the handbag is completely shadowed, the original red color can not be fully recovered.

5 Conclusion

This paper proposes a mask-guided residual learning network for joint single-image shadow detection and removal. We design a compact and efficient shadow detection module to generate shadow masks and feed them into our shadow removal module. To transfer context features between shadow detection and shadow removal, we reassemble and refine the features to generate shadow removal context features, which are further used to learn residual RGB maps to compensate for the input shadow map. Meanwhile, the predicted shadow mask serves as the guidance weight for fusing the residual and original RGB map, which helps to generate better transition effects in the penumbra regions. Extensive experiments demonstrate that our proposed network achieves state-of-the-art shadow detection and removal performance on three widely used benchmark datasets ISTD, ISTD+, and SRD.

Acknowledgements. This work was supported by the National Natural Science Foundation of China (62076029), Guangdong Science and Technology Department (2017A030313362), Guangdong Key Lab of AI and Multi-modal Data Processing (2020KSYS007). and internal funds of the United International College (R202012, R201802, R5201904, UICR0400025-21).

References

1. Chen, Z., Zhu, L., Wan, L., Wang, S., Feng, W., Heng, P.A.: A multi-task mean teacher for semi-supervised shadow detection. In: Proceedings of the IEEE/CVF Conference on Computer Vision and Pattern Recognition (CVPR), pp. 5611–5620 (2020)
2. Chen, Z., Long, C., Zhang, L., Xiao, C.: CANet: a context-aware network for shadow removal. In: Proceedings of the IEEE/CVF International Conference on Computer Vision (ICCV), pp. 4743–4752 (2021)
3. Cun, X., Pun, C.M., Shi, C.: Towards ghost-free shadow removal via dual hierarchical aggregation network and shadow matting GAN. In: Proceedings of the AAAI Conference on Artificial Intelligence, pp. 10680–10687 (2020)
4. Ding, B., Long, C., Zhang, L., Xiao, C.: ARGAN: attentive recurrent generative adversarial network for shadow detection and removal. In: Proceedings of the IEEE/CVF International Conference on Computer Vision (ICCV) (2019)
5. Finlayson, G.D., Drew, M.S., Lu, C.: Entropy minimization for shadow removal. Int. J. Comput. Vision **85**(1), 35–57 (2009)
6. Finlayson, G.D., Hordley, S.D., Lu, C., Drew, M.S.: On the removal of shadows from images. IEEE Trans. Pattern Anal. Mach. Intell. **28**(1), 59–68 (2006). https://doi.org/10.1109/TPAMI.2006.18
7. Fu, L., et al.: Auto-exposure fusion for single-image shadow removal. In: Proceedings of the IEEE/CVF Conference on Computer Vision and Pattern Recognition (CVPR), pp. 10571–10580 (2021)
8. Goodfellow, I., et al.: Generative adversarial nets. In: Proceedings of International Conference on Neural Information Processing Systems (NeurIPS), pp. 2672–2680 (2014)
9. Gryka, M., Terry, M., Brostow, G.J.: Learning to remove soft shadows. ACM Trans. Graph. (TOG) **34**(5), 1–15 (2015)
10. Guo, R., Dai, Q., Hoiem, D.: Paired regions for shadow detection and removal. IEEE Trans. Pattern Anal. Mach. Intell. **35**(12), 2956–2967 (2012)
11. Hu, X., Fu, C.W., Zhu, L., Qin, J., Heng, P.A.: Direction-aware spatial context features for shadow detection and removal. IEEE Trans. Pattern Anal. Mach. Intell. **42**(11), 2795–2808 (2019)
12. Hu, X., Jiang, Y., Fu, C.W., Heng, P.A.: Mask-shadowGAN: learning to remove shadows from unpaired data. In: Proceedings of the IEEE/CVF International Conference on Computer Vision (ICCV), pp. 2472–2481 (2019)
13. Hu, X., Zhu, L., Fu, C.W., Qin, J., Heng, P.A.: Direction-aware spatial context features for shadow detection. In: Proceedings of the IEEE/CVF Conference on Computer Vision and Pattern Recognition (CVPR), pp. 7454–7462 (2018)
14. Inoue, N., Yamasaki, T.: Learning from synthetic shadows for shadow detection and removal. IEEE Trans. Circuits Syst. Video Technol. **31**(11), 4187–4197 (2021). https://doi.org/10.1109/TCSVT.2020.3047977
15. Jie, L., Zhang, H.: A fast and efficient network for single image shadow detection. In: ICASSP 2022–2022 IEEE International Conference on Acoustics, Speech and Signal Processing (ICASSP), pp. 2634–2638 (2022)
16. Jie, L., Zhang, H.: RMLANet: random multi-level attention network for shadow detection. In: 2022 IEEE International Conference on Multimedia and Expo (ICME), pp. 1–6 (2022)
17. Jin, Y., Sharma, A., Tan, R.T.: DC-ShadowNet: single-image hard and soft shadow removal using unsupervised domain-classifier guided network. In: Proceedings of

the IEEE/CVF International Conference on Computer Vision (ICCV), pp. 5027–5036 (2021)

18. Khan, S.H., Bennamoun, M., Sohel, F., Togneri, R.: Automatic feature learning for robust shadow detection. In: Proceedings of the IEEE/CVF Conference on Computer Vision and Pattern Recognition (CVPR), pp. 1939–1946 (2014)

19. Lalonde, J.-F., Efros, A.A., Narasimhan, S.G.: Detecting ground shadows in outdoor consumer photographs. In: Daniilidis, K., Maragos, P., Paragios, N. (eds.) ECCV 2010. LNCS, vol. 6312, pp. 322–335. Springer, Heidelberg (2010). https://doi.org/10.1007/978-3-642-15552-9_24

20. Le, H., Samaras, D.: Shadow removal via shadow image decomposition. In: Proceedings of the IEEE/CVF International Conference on Computer Vision (ICCV), pp. 8578–8587 (2019)

21. Le, H., Samaras, D.: From shadow segmentation to shadow removal. In: Vedaldi, A., Bischof, H., Brox, T., Frahm, J.-M. (eds.) ECCV 2020. LNCS, vol. 12356, pp. 264–281. Springer, Cham (2020). https://doi.org/10.1007/978-3-030-58621-8_16

22. Nguyen, V., Vicente, T.F.Y., Zhao, M., Hoai, M., Samaras, D.: Shadow detection with conditional generative adversarial networks. In: Proceedings of the IEEE/CVF International Conference on Computer Vision (ICCV), pp. 4510–4518 (2017)

23. Qu, L., Tian, J., He, S., Tang, Y., Lau, R.W.H.: DeshadowNet: a multi-context embedding deep network for shadow removal. In: Proceedings of the IEEE Conference on Computer Vision and Pattern Recognition (CVPR), pp. 4067–4075 (2017)

24. Ronneberger, O., Fischer, P., Brox, T.: U-Net: convolutional networks for biomedical image segmentation. In: Medical Image Computing and Computer-Assisted Intervention (MICCAI) (2015)

25. Shen, L., Chua, T.W., Leman, K.: Shadow optimization from structured deep edge detection. In: Proceedings of the IEEE/CVF Conference on Computer Vision and Pattern Recognition (CVPR), pp. 2067–2074 (2015)

26. Shi, X., Chen, Z., Wang, H., Yeung, D.Y., Wong, W.K., Woo, W.C.: Convolutional lstm network: a machine learning approach for precipitation nowcasting. In: Advances in Neural Information Processing Systems 28 (2015)

27. Tan, M., Le, Q.: EfficientNet: rethinking model scaling for convolutional neural networks. In: Proceedings of the 36th International Conference on Machine Learning (ICML), pp. 6105–6114 (2019)

28. Vicente, T.F.Y., Hoai, M., Samaras, D.: Leave-one-out kernel optimization for shadow detection and removal. IEEE Trans. Pattern Anal. Mach. Intell. **40**(3), 682–695 (2018)

29. Wang, J., Li, X., Yang, J.: Stacked conditional generative adversarial networks for jointly learning shadow detection and shadow removal. In: Proceedings of the IEEE Conference on Computer Vision and Pattern Recognition (CVPR), pp. 1788–1797 (2018)

30. Xiao, C., She, R., Xiao, D., Ma, K.L.: Fast shadow removal using adaptive multiscale illumination transfer. Comput. Graph. Forum **32**, 6105–6114 (2019)

31. Yang, Q., Tan, K.H., Ahuja, N.: Shadow removal using bilateral filtering. IEEE Trans. Image Process. **21**(10), 4361–4368 (2012)

32. Zhang, L., Zhang, Q., Xiao, C.: Shadow remover: image shadow removal based on illumination recovering optimization. IEEE Trans. Image Process. **24**(11), 4623–4636 (2015)

33. Zheng, Q., Qiao, X., Cao, Y., Lau, R.W.: Distraction-aware shadow detection. In: Proceedings of the IEEE/CVF Conference on Computer Vision and Pattern Recognition (CVPR), pp. 5167–5176 (2019)

34. Zhu, J., Samuel, K.G., Masood, S.Z., Tappen, M.F.: Learning to recognize shadows in monochromatic natural images. In: Proceedings of the IEEE/CVF Conference on Computer Vision and Pattern Recognition (CVPR), pp. 223–230 (2010)
35. Zhu, L., et al.: Bidirectional feature pyramid network with recurrent attention residual modules for shadow detection. In: Ferrari, V., Hebert, M., Sminchisescu, C., Weiss, Y. (eds.) ECCV 2018. LNCS, vol. 11210, pp. 122–137. Springer, Cham (2018). https://doi.org/10.1007/978-3-030-01231-1_8

Learnable Subspace Orthogonal Projection for Semi-supervised Image Classification

Lijian Li[1], Yunhe Zhang[1], and Aiping Huang[2(✉)]

[1] College of Computer and Data Science, Fuzhou University, Fuzhou 350116, China
[2] College of Physics and Information Engineering, Fuzhou University,
Fuzhou 350108, China
sxxhap@163.com

Abstract. In this paper, we propose a learnable subspace orthogonal projection (LSOP) network for semi-supervised image classification. Although projection theory is widely used in various machine learning methods, solving projection matrix is a highly complex process. We employ an auto-encoder to construct a scalable and learnable subspace orthogonal projection network, thus enjoying lower computational consumption of subspace acquisition and smooth cooperation with deep neural networks. With these techniques, a promising end-to-end classification network is formulated. Extensive experimental results on real-world datasets demonstrate that the proposed classification algorithm achieves comparable performance with fewer training data than other projection methods.

1 Introduction

Classification is widely used in various tasks [3,7,21] to associate data with one or more semantic labels. To boost predictive performance, many of them require to train classifier on a large-scale labeled data. Nevertheless, obtaining sufficient annotated data is time-consuming and laborious. With the impressive success in image classification using Convolutional Neural Networks (CNN), some deep semi-supervised learning methods [9,10,12,14,16,20] are developed. Among these methods, the pseudo label and the consistency regularization are two commonly used techniques. For example, [24] proposed an unsupervised data augmentation for semi-supervised learning by training with consistency regularization. Inspired by curriculum learning, [2] gradually increases the proportion of unmarked samples until all samples are used for model training. SimMatch [29] considers both semantic and instance similarities and enables semi-supervised learning through self-supervised technique. Some advanced methods are combinations of approaches involving pseudo label, self-supervision and data augmentation, such as MixMatch [1], FixMatch [19], Flexmatch [27], and SimMatch [29]. These methods focus on learning discriminative feature representations and decision boundaries to improve the quality of downstream tasks, creating potential room for improvement of classification network.

© The Author(s), under exclusive license to Springer Nature Switzerland AG 2023
L. Wang et al. (Eds.): ACCV 2022, LNCS 13843, pp. 477–490, 2023.
https://doi.org/10.1007/978-3-031-26313-2_29

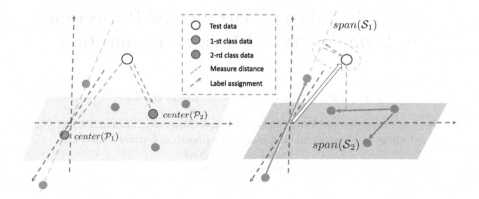

Fig. 1. Comparison of fitting data using a point and a latent subspace. The data are feature vectors in the vector space $\mathbb{R}^{3\times3}$.

Embedding projection theory into deep networks is one of the promising methods for performance improvement. Existing methods normally use a one-dimensional subspace as a center to infer category labels. However, it is possible that features of the same category are distributed in a latent multi-dimensional subspace rather than a point. Figure 1 shows possible label prediction results in two ways. The point-centered approach may ignore other potential associations among features. It makes more reasonable to assign the test data to the first category. The calculation of the distance to a subspace usually requires solving a projection matrix. However, in these methods the inverse process involved in solution of projection matrix leads to the high computational consumption of subspace acquisition. In addition, deep neural networks usually require multiple iterations, and the small batch processing of data will lead to repeated solution of the projection matrix of each subspace, resulting in further increase in overhead.

In this paper, we propose a learnable subspace orthogonal projection (LSOP) module to reduce the high computational consumption of subspace acquisition. Embedding the module into deep neural network, an effective end-to-end image semi-supervised classification model is subsequently formulated. The whole framework is outlined in Fig. 2. We assume that the similar samples can be distributed around the same latent high-dimensional subspace. This requires each latent subspace to preserve critical features and to be orthogonal to irrelevant features. To this end, a LSOP network is established to learn the corresponding orthogonal projection matrices for these latent subspaces. Followed by defining a classification loss, a deep network architecture for semi-supervised classification is constructed. With these techniques, we make projection theory benefiting from deep learning. Meanwhile, training on high-dimensional subspace reduces the need for label data, which alleviates the scarcity of labeled samples for semi-supervised classification. The main contributions of this paper are summarized as follows:

- The learnable subspace orthogonal projection (LSOP) network. We propose to learn orthogonal projections for high-dimensional subspaces, thus reducing the computational consumption of subspace acquisition and smooth cooperation with deep neural network.
- The extensibility of LSOP network. The proposed LSOP network is generalizable and could be a feasible solution to other orthogonal projection related deep learning, that is beyond the scope of this work.
- The end-to-end semi-supervised classification network. We employ the proposed LSOP network to construct an effective semi-supervised classifier. This facilitates training the classifier on high-dimensional subspaces to alleviate the scarcity of labeled samples.

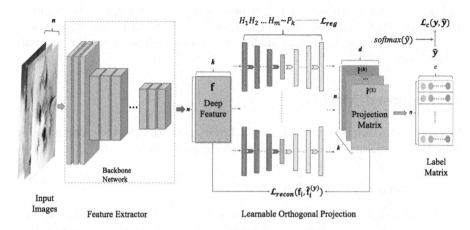

Fig. 2. An overview of the proposed classification method of learnable orthogonal projection. In the figure, we only use an input vector as an example. The parameters of each fully connected layer network are treated as a learnable orthogonal projection matrix of various subspaces. The orthogonal projection matrix is trained for each class of data subspaces by reconstruction loss. Then classification loss is used to keep these subspaces as far away from the other classes of data as possible.

2   Related Work

Projection theory has been widely used in many deep network models [4–6,13,15,17,18,22,25]. For example, [5] uses the orthogonal projection space spanned by a principal component analysis projection matrix to alleviate the discrimination difficulty. [25] proposes an auto-encoder framework based on an orthogonal projection constraint for anomaly detection. [4] employs orthogonal projection to design a subspace attention module for denoising. The orthogonal projection is more of an effective method with explicit interpretation for many tasks. Especially, it is a very practical approach to classification. [28] proposed a Capsule Projection Network (CapProNet) to classify deep features by one type of orthogonal projections. This article uses the closed-form solution of a projection matrix to obtain a projection. The parameters learned in the network is a weight matrix $W_l \in \mathbb{R}^{k \times d}$. The columns of the matrix form a basis of a subspace, i.e., $S_l = span(W_l)$ is spanned by the columns vectors of W_l. The orthogonal projection v_l of a vector x onto subspace S_l has following solution:

$$v_l = P_l x, \text{ and } P_l = W_l (W_l^T W_l)^{-1} W_l^T. \tag{1}$$

Then the length of projection $||v_l||_2$ is used to measure the affinity of a class. The operations of this procedure are differentiable, so the weight matrix W_l of each subspace can be updated. This paper computes matrix inverse with a hyper-power sequence to alleviate the computational consumption of matrix inverse. However, the consumption also increases significantly with the dimension d of subspace increases. To this end, [23] proposed a Matrix Capsule Convolution Projection (MCCP) module by replacing deep features with a feature matrices. This article reduces the dimensionality of vectors, making it easy to compute projections.

3   Proposed Method

In this section, we aim to construct a LSOP network and then formulate an end-to-end semi-supervised model for image classification.

3.1   Orthogonal Projection

A deep neural network $\mathcal{N}$ can be generally factorized into two phases: feature representation $\mathcal{N}_{fea}$ and data classification $\mathcal{N}_{cla}$. Given a set of data points $\mathcal{X} = \{\mathbf{x}_i, \mathbf{y}_i\}_{i=1}^n$ where $\mathbf{x}_i \in \mathbb{R}^m$ and its label vector $\mathbf{y}_i \in \{0, 1\}^c$, with m being the input dimension and c the number of classes. $\mathbf{f}_i = \mathcal{N}_{fea}(\mathbf{x}_i) \in \mathbb{R}^k$ is a k-dimensional deep feature vector, and $\widehat{\mathbf{y}}_i = \mathcal{N}_{cla}(\mathbf{f}_i) \in \mathbb{R}^c$ is an estimator of $\mathbf{y}_i$. For brevity, we assume that $\mathcal{N}_{cla}$ is a linear classifier, i.e., $\widehat{\mathbf{y}}_i = \mathbf{W}^T \mathbf{f}_i + \mathbf{b}$ for all $i = 1, \cdots, n$, where $\mathbf{W} \in \mathbb{R}^{k \times c}$ is a weight matrix and $\mathbf{b}$ is a bias of the last layer in $\mathcal{N}$. In this phase, we try to minimize $\sum_{i=1}^n loss(\mathbf{y}_i, \widehat{\mathbf{y}}_i) = \sum_{i=1}^n loss(\mathbf{y}_i, \mathbf{W}^T \mathbf{f}_i + \mathbf{b})$, where $loss(\cdot, \cdot)$ is a metric to evaluate the difference between two elements. Letting $\mathbf{W} = [\mathbf{w}_1, \cdots, \mathbf{w}_c]$ with $\mathbf{w}_i \in \mathbb{R}^k$, the classification module $\mathcal{N}_{cla}(\mathbf{f}_i)$ can be interpreted as computing a modified distance of $\mathbf{f}_i$ to c spaces spanned by $\mathbf{w}_i$. The above description is the simplest linear classifier used in various deep networks. We would like to construct a multi-dimensional subspace to obtain effectiveness. Intuitively, each class is represented using a k-dimensional feature vector $\mathbf{w}_i$, which motivates us to characterize a class more accurately by a spanned space of several vectors, instead of only one vector.

Letting $\mathcal{F} = \{\mathbf{f}_i\}_{i=1}^n$. For any $j \in \{1, \cdots, c\}$, we denote $\mathcal{S}_j = \{\mathbf{f}_i \in \mathcal{F} : \mathbf{x}_i$ belongs to the j-th class$\}$, and $\mathcal{S} \in \mathbb{R}^{k \times d_j}$ is a matrix containing all elements of $\mathcal{S}_j$ as columns with $d_j = Rank(\mathcal{S}_j)$. For any test data point $\mathbf{x}$, its low-dimensional feature vector $\mathbf{f} \in \mathbb{R}^k$ can be obtained by a feature representation $\mathcal{N}_{fea}$ with $\mathbf{f} = \mathcal{N}_{fea}(\mathbf{x})$. Naturally, for any test sample $\mathbf{x}$, we try to project its feature vector $\mathbf{f}$ onto the spanned subspaces by $\{\mathcal{S}_j\}_{j=1}^c$, i.e.,

$$span(\mathcal{S}_j) = \left\{ \sum_{i=1}^t \lambda_i \mathbf{v}_i : t \in \mathbb{N}, \mathbf{v} \in \mathcal{S}_j, \lambda_i \in \mathbb{R} \right\}. \tag{2}$$

Accordingly, the probability of the data point $\mathbf{x}$ belonging to the j-th class is defined as the distance of $\mathbf{f}$ to $span(\mathcal{S}_j)$. Actually, this distance is equal to the distance between $\mathbf{f}$ and its projection point onto $span(\mathcal{S}_j)$, denoted as $\mathcal{P}_{span(\mathcal{S}_j)}(\mathbf{f})$. By specifying Euclidean distance, it is expressed as $||\mathbf{f} - \mathcal{P}_{span(\mathcal{S}_j)}(\mathbf{f})||_2$.

The projection point $\mathcal{P}_{span(\mathcal{S}_j)}(\mathbf{f})$ can be regarded as the minimum distance of $\mathbf{f}$ onto the space $span(\mathcal{S}_j)$, i.e.,

$$\mathcal{P}_{span(\mathcal{S}_j)}(\mathbf{f}) = \arg \min_{\mathbf{g} \in span(\mathcal{S}_j)} ||\mathbf{f} - \mathbf{g}||_2. \tag{3}$$

Correspondingly, the projection point can be given by

$$\mathcal{P}_{span(\mathcal{S}_j)}(\mathbf{f}) = \mathbf{S}_j(\mathbf{S}_j^T \mathbf{S}_j)^{-1}\mathbf{S}_j^T \mathbf{f} = \mathbf{S}_j \mathbf{S}_j^\dagger \mathbf{f}, \tag{4}$$

where $\mathbf{S}_j^\dagger$ is the Moore-Penrose pseudo inverse, and $\mathcal{P}_{span(\mathcal{S}_j)} \doteq \mathbf{S}_j(\mathbf{S}_j^T \mathbf{S}_j)^{-1}\mathbf{S}_j^T \doteq \mathbf{S}_j \mathbf{S}_j^\dagger$ is the orthogonal projection matrix. It is observed that the sampled data points in the j-th class form a basis, though not necessarily orthonormal. Accordingly, this formulation comes with the following two merits. On the one hand, each class is approximated by a spanned subspace of some basis vectors, rather than a vector. On the other hand, the spanned subspace may exhibit a powerful representation ability, even if several data points are used, which is tailored for semi-supervised learning.

Nevertheless, the closed-form solution mentioned above requires the computational complexity of $\mathcal{O}(\sum_{j=1}^c d_j^3 + kd_j^2)$, which is evidently unaffordable when dealing with large-scale datasets. That motivates us to develop a learnable orthogonal projection method to optimize the projection computation in a deep learning network.

3.2 Learnable Orthogonal Projection

In this subsection, we attempt to solve an orthogonal projection matrix in a differentiable manner so that the proposed method serves as a module in deep neural networks. According to Eq. (3), when $\mathbf{f}_i$ belongs to $\mathcal{S}_j$, its projection onto subspace $span(\mathcal{S}_j)$ is exactly equal to itself. Accordingly, for each class, we can find the projection matrix of subspace $span(\mathcal{S}_j)$ by minimizing

$$J(\mathcal{P}_{span(\mathcal{S}_j)}) = \sum_{i=1}^n \left\| \mathbf{f}_i - \mathcal{P}_{span(\mathcal{S}_j)} \mathbf{f}_i \right\|_2^2, \tag{5}$$

where $\mathcal{P}_{span(S_j)}$ is a projection square matrix. We use a neural network to approximate this problem, and the whole network can be considered as a surrogate of the projection matrix. A single-layered neural network is insufficient, because it can be observed from this objective function that the optimal solution may fall into a trivial case, *i.e.*, $\mathcal{P}_{span(S_j)} = \mathbf{I}$. This is to say that the weights of the neural network tend to converge to the projection matrix of the original vector space. Actually, data points belonging to the same class are not necessarily distributed in only a low-dimensional vector space, thus S_j tends to expand to a large vector space. We expect to acquire a latent subspace that can contain data points of their associated class and is orthogonal to other subspaces produced by other points. Therefore, a multi-layered network is employed to learn hierarchical subspace structures.

We can use a network structure similar to the matrix structure $\mathbf{S}_j(\mathbf{S}_j^T\mathbf{S}_j)^{-1}\mathbf{S}_j^T$. We denote a subspace basis as $\mathcal{S} \in \mathbb{R}^{k \times d}$, where d is the subspace dimension and k is the full space dimension ($d < k$). Then we set the hiddle layer dimension to d and the input dimension to k. The network structure is like an undercomplete auto-encoder, which overcomes trivial solution. Consequently, it is formulated as the architecture for the projection matrix using m layers:

$$\mathcal{P}_{span(S_j)} \leftarrow H_1 H_2 \cdots H_m, \tag{6}$$

where H_i represents the weights of layers. For the j-th class, we denote the output of the network as $f_{\theta_j}(\cdot)$, and then train the network with the following loss:

$$\min_{\theta} \sum_{i=1}^{n} loss(f_\theta(\mathbf{f}_i), \mathbf{f}_i), \tag{7}$$

where $loss(\cdot, \cdot)$ is an alternative loss function, not limited to the mean square error. In this way, we construct a learnable orthogonal projection for each class, which maps all data points onto a subspace so that discriminative components are preserved. It is worth noting that the learnable orthogonal projection can be flexible to be embedded into multiple network structures. After the network is trained, any test data point is projected onto each subspace, and its projection residual represents the probability in the corresponding class.

The time complexity of the feedforward calculation of the network relies on matrix multiplication, and the process of network training avoids the matrix inverse operation of solving the projection matrix directly. Accordingly, the computational complexity of neural networks with back prorogation is $\mathcal{O}(\sum_{j=1}^{c} d_j^2 + kd_j^2)$. Therefore, this approach is more competitive in term of running time as the size of input data increases. In addition, this network can be solved by a mini-batch approach instead of putting all samples into the memory, which reduces the memory requirement.

3.3   Optimization Method

In this subsection, we elaborate how to build an end-to-end model for learnable orthogonal projection. Following Eq. (7), we construct projection matrices for each latent subspace. For simplicity, a projection reconstruction loss with ridge regression is given by:

$$\lambda \mathcal{L}_{recon} + \mu \mathcal{L}_{reg} \doteq \sum_{i=1}^{n} \left\| \mathbf{f}_i - f_{\theta_{(j=y_i)}}(\mathbf{f}_i) \right\|_2^2 + \lambda \left\| \theta \right\|_2^2. \tag{8}$$

Except the two losses above, we can add additional objective functions to exploit rich hierarchical semantic information from a given data. As an example, cross-entropy can be used to maximize intra-class information and minimize inter-class information in the subspace to be optimized. The predicted class $\widehat{\mathbf{y}}_i$ of the sample $\mathbf{x}_i$ is regarded as the probability distribution of the residual of the projection onto each class subspace. Simultaneously, we define the normalized predicted class probability as

$$\mathbf{p}_i = softmax(\widehat{\mathbf{y}}_i). \tag{9}$$

Accordingly, the classification loss specified as cross-entropy is given by

$$\mathcal{L}_c = -\frac{1}{n} \sum_{i=1}^{n} \mathbf{y}_i \log(\mathbf{p}_i). \tag{10}$$

Minimizing the cross-entropy loss makes the subspaces as orthogonal as possible. Otherwise, the probability matrix will be smoothed, then it can not close to the true label matrix (δ distribution). As mentioned above, the overall loss function is defined as

$$\mathcal{L} = \mathcal{L}_c + \lambda \mathcal{L}_{recon} + \mu \mathcal{L}_{reg}. \tag{11}$$

Gathering all above analyses, the procedures for solving the learnable orthogonal projection are summarized in Algorithm 1.

Unlabeled Data Training: For unlabeled data training in clustering method, we replace the clustering centers with our subspaces. The subspaces are first constructed with labeled samples. Then we compute the closest subspaces $\mathbf{S}_j$ of unlabeled samples, giving the unlabeled samples a pseudo-label j to update the network. The closest subspace is recalculated in next iteration. The subspace clustering is similar to k-means. The method enables the subspace classification boundaries to span a low-density region by minimizing the conditional entropy of the class probability of unlabeled data. These unlabeled samples can improve the ability of backbone network to extract features. It also allows the learnable parameters to fix better subspaces. We update the pseudo-labels for unlabeled samples at each iteration and then train at a smaller weight with labeled samples.

4   Experiment

In this section, we conduct comprehensive experiments on classification datasets compared with several state-of-the-art deep neural networks to validate the effectiveness of the proposed method.

Algorithm 1. Learnable Subspace Orthogonal Projection (LSOP)

Require: Mimi-batches of the input data $\mathcal{X} = \{\mathbf{x}_i, \mathbf{y}_i\}_{i=1}^n$, the number of classes c, regularization coefficient λ, balancing parameter μ and learning rate α, maximum epoch of training max_epoch.

Ensure: Neural network parameters θ.

 1: Initialize neural network parameters θ_j of c subspaces;
 2: **for** $t = 1$ **to** max_epoch **do**
 3:    **for** each minbatch **do**
 4:        Calculate projections onto each subspace by forward propagation;
 5:        Calculate reconstructed loss by Eq. (8);
 6:        Compute label matrix $\{\hat{\mathbf{y}}_i\}$ by Eq. (9);
 7:        Calculate classification loss by Eq. (10);
 8:        Accumulate overall loss $\mathcal{L}$ by Eq. (11);
 9:        Update network parameters θ by back propagation;
10:    **end for**
11: **end for**
12: **return** Neural network parameters θ.

4.1   Experiment Setting

Datasets. We use two benchmark datasets in experiments to evaluate the classification performance. The CIFAR dataset contains 60,000 colored natural images of 32×32 pixels. CIFAR10 and CIFAR 100 are divided into 10 and 100 classes, respectively. There are 50,000 images in training set, and 10,000 images in test set. For preprocessing, we normalize the data using the channel means and standard deviations. We use all 50,000 training images for the final run and report the final test error at the end of training. Following [8], we give rise to augmentations of CIFAR10 and CIFAR100, and denote augmentation datasets as CIFAR10+ and CIFAR100+, respectively. In semi-supervised classification, we randomly extract labeled images from each class, and the test error is reported.

Compared Methods. We test different classifiers in the network architectures such as ResNet [8], WideResNet [26] and DenseNet [11]. We use ResNet with 110 layers and WideResNet ($k = 8$) with 16 layers, as well as DenseNet-BC ($k = 12$) with 100 layers for CIFAR. The last layer of these networks generally serves as a function of classifying deep features. Our classifier can be trained in an end-to-end manner with the backbone network instead of trained independently. The CapProNet [28] and MCCP [23] can also serve as a classifier, and we apply it to these networks with their default setting. CapProNet [28] and MCCP [23] take advantage of an iterative algorithm to update the projection matrix. In contrast, we update weights using a neural network approach without additional matrix operations. We compare the effectiveness of different classifiers to evaluate the performance of the proposed method. In addition, Meta Pseudo Label [16] is an effective regularization strategy. We also apply LSOP to this approach to verify the effectiveness of our method.

Model Implementation and Training. We implement our code using PyTorch, and all experiments are run on a computer with a Tesla P100 GPU in Linux systems. We create c-way fully connected layers to replace the last layer of the original network. The 32×32 size images from CIFAR dataset are extracted by backbone networks, and the dimensions of the deep features are tuned as 64, 512 and 342, respectively. We initialize the input and output sizes of our fully connected layer with these values, and the hidden layer dimension is fixed as 8. The parameters of CapProNet are often d times larger than the original single-layered neural network, where d is a dimension of subspace. All parameters in compared deep neural networks are adopted as their default settings in their original papers, and the additional parameters of the final classifier are uniformly set to $c \times k \times d$. In order to provide a fair comparison with CapProNet, we also use a three-layered fully connected layer neural network to fit the projection matrix. Sometimes $S_j^T S_j$ may be irreversible. Therefore, we use a tiny bias on $S_j^\top S_j$ during the experiment to ensure its reversibility. A deep feature matrix $n \times k$ is fed to c-way fully connected layers, then we obtain a projection tensor of the size $n \times c \times k$. We use the defined projection probability distribution to generate a $n \times c$ label prediction matrix.

The mini-batch stochastic gradient descent is used to train all the networks. On CIFAR datasets, the networks are trained with 64 batches of 300 epochs. The initial learning rate is set to 0.1, and then it is divided by 10 at 150 and 250 training epochs. We use a weight decay λ of 10^{-4} and a momentum of 0.9 without dampening. The hyperparameter μ in loss is set to be 0.1. In semi-supervised learning experiments, the loss weight of unlabeled data is gradually incremented to 1.0 from epoch 30 to epoch 120. In a comparison of Meta Pseudo Label [16], we follow its original setup on WideResNet-28-8, training 50,000 iterations in the PyTorch version.

4.2   Experimental Result

Table 1. A comparison of error rates of backbone networks with CapProNet [28], MCCP [23] and LSOP on CIFAR10 and CIFAR100. Results of MCCP are reported by [23]. The datasets with "+" indicate standard data augmentation (*e.g.* horizontal flip or random crop).

Backbone network	Classifier	CIFAR10	CIFAR10+	CIFAR100	CIFAR100+
ResNet [8]	Baseline	13.63	6.41	44.74	27.22
	CapProNet	**13.25**	5.19	42.76	22.78
	MCCP	–	5.24	–	22.86
	LSOP	13.41	**5.12**	**42.22**	**21.73**
WideResNet $k = 8$ [26]	Baseline	11.33	4.81	34.83	22.07
	CapProNet	10.52	**4.04**	**33.10**	**20.12**
	LSOP	**10.35**	4.77	35.42	21.41
DenseNet-BC $k = 12$ [11]	Baseline	7.86	4.51	**26.40**	22.27
	CapProNet	7.93	**4.25**	28.58	**21.19**
	LSOP	**7.72**	4.86	27.34	21.45

Table 2. A comparison of error rates of backbone networks with CapProNet [28] and LSOP on CIFAR10 of training with 4,000 and 10,000 labels. The numbers with "+ PL" indicate training with pseudo labels and data augmentations.

Backbone network	Classifier	4,000	4,000 + PL	10,000	10,000 + PL
ResNet [8]	Baseline	49.20	23.60	38.03	15.21
	CapProNet	**47.48**	23.26	34.48	14.32
	LSOP	48.40	**22.84**	**32.83**	**14.15**
WideResNet $k = 8$ [26]	Baseline	36.85	19.88	**25.04**	12.85
	CapProNet	**35.21**	**19.42**	25.25	12.53
	LSOP	36.95	19.65	25.29	**12.29**
DenseNet-BC $k = 12$ [11]	Baseline	32.88	19.70	**21.06**	13.20
	CapProNet	32.01	**18.96**	21.82	**12.69**
	LSOP	**31.96**	19.33	21.24	12.88

In Table 1, we compare classification performance of different classifiers trained in an end-to-end manner at the same backbone network. In fully supervised experiments, our approach achieves encouraging performance on ResNet. On other backbone networks, the proposed method also comes with competitive performance. The hidden layer dimension of LSOP is uniformly set as 8 to facilitate comparison. The hidden layer dimension can be considered as a subspace dimension and then a single-layer linear classifier is considered as a linear subspace of $D = 1$. The proposed method achieves promising results on classifying deep features extracted from ResNet with $D = 64$, and comes with comparable performance on WideResnet with $D = 512$ and DenseNet with $D = 342$. Our method aims to design an efficient classifier that can be embedded in advanced methods.

To validate the performance of the proposed method in semi-supervised learning, we report the performance with a part of labeled data in CIFAR10. We use unlabeled data to train networks by pseudo labels and update the networks with lower weights. Table 2 shows that LSOP achieves better performance in semi-supervised learning. In addition, the proposed model is an efficient classifier that can be embedded in advanced methods. We replace the classifier of Meta Pseudo Labels [16] with our designed module and test the performance on CIFAR10 and CIFAR100 in Table 3. We can observe that LSOP achieves better classification accuracy. This shows that our method is a valid module that improves performance with limited labeled data.

4.3 Convergence and Time Complexity Analysis

Figure 3 shows the convergence curves of our method on CIFAR10 and CIFAR100. When the learning rate is set to 0.1, the loss converges about 60 epochs. At the 150-th epoch, the loss is further decreased due to the learning rate change.

We use a single-layer linear classifier as a baseline and consider the linear classifier as a single-dimensional subspace. CapProNet applies multi-dimensional

Table 3. A comparison of ACC of Meta Pseudo Labels [16] using a linear classifier and LSOP on CIFAR10 with 4,000 training labels and CIFAR100 of training with 10,000 training labels.

ACC	Meta Pseudo Labels	Meta Pseudo Labels with LSOP
CIFAR10/4k label	95.44	**95.68**
CIFAR100/10k label	77.86	**78.03**

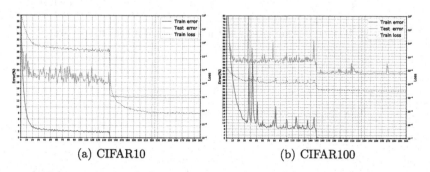

(a) CIFAR10   (b) CIFAR100

Fig. 3. Convergence curves of LSOP applied to ResNet110. Left is CIFAR10, and right is CIFAR100

subspace to classify, which brings additional cost. To address the problem, we propose a LSOP network. As shown in Sect. 3, the computational complexity of the closed-form solution in CapProNet is $\mathcal{O}(\sum_{j=1}^{c} d_j^3 + k d_j^2)$, while the computational complexity of LSOP is $\mathcal{O}(\sum_{j=1}^{c} d_j^2 + k d_j^2)$. Here, k is a deep feature dimension, d_j is the dimension of each latent subspace and c is the number of categories. Compared with the closed-form solution based approach CapProNet, LSOP reduces the computational consumption of subspace acquisition, which facilitates faster optimization for large-scale data.

We also present the time consumption comparison of CapProNet and LSOP to further demonstrate the efficiency of LSOP. Figures 4 and 5 show the evolution curves of time consumption with 50,000 samples and 10 categories. The experiments are performed on an AMD Ryzen 9 5900X 12-Core Processor without GPU. In addition, deep features are randomly generated and trained in minibatch to simulate the training of CIFAR dataset. From the figures, the time consumption of closed-form solution increases significantly with the increase of feature dimension k and subspace dimension d. In contrast, the LSOP method keeps the same level of time consumption as a baseline. This indicates that the proposed method can obtain performance gain by increasing subspace dimensions without computational cost.

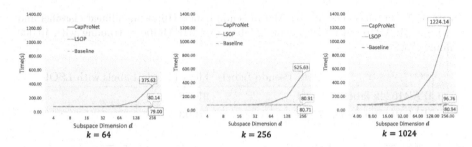

Fig. 4. Run-time comparison as the subspace dimension increases.

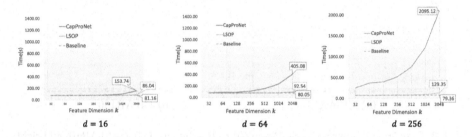

Fig. 5. Run-time comparison as the deep feature dimension increases.

5 Conclusion and Discussion

In this work, we propose a learnable orthogonal projection for deep neural networks that can be trained in an end-to-end fashion. We learn a high-dimensional subspace instead of a vector, bringing acceptable computational consumption. In the proposed method, a latent subspace is used to fit high-dimensional features to train a deep neural network with fewer samples. Although our method is effective in semi-supervised learning, several issues still need to be further explored. For example, the projection reconstruction loss can be constructed in other advanced ways to obtain better subspace projection matrices. Because this network structure is a transformed module, we can use more ways to construct this structure to adapt to various projection subspaces. We hope to propose adaptive network structures to find better projections from more discriminative latent subspaces in future work.

Acknowledgements. This work is in part supported by the National Natural Science Foundation of China under Grant U21A20472 and 62276065, and the National Key Research and Development Plan of China under Grant 2021YFB3600503.

References

1. Berthelot, D., Carlini, N., Goodfellow, I., Papernot, N., Oliver, A., Raffel, C.A.: MixMatch: a holistic approach to semi-supervised learning. In: Proceedings of the Neural Information Processing Systems, pp. 5049–5059 (2019)
2. Cascante-Bonilla, P., Tan, F., Qi, Y., Ordonez, V.: Curriculum labeling: revisiting pseudo-labeling for semi-supervised learning. In: Proceedings of the 33rd AAAI Conference on Artificial Intelligence, pp. 6912–6920 (2021)
3. Chen, E., Lee, C.: Towards fast and robust adversarial training for image classification. In: Proceedings of the 15th Asian Conference on Computer Vision, pp. 576–591 (2020)
4. Cheng, S., Wang, Y., Huang, H., Liu, D., Fan, H., Liu, S.: NBNet: noise basis learning for image denoising with subspace projection. In: Proceedings of the IEEE Conference on Computer Vision and Pattern Recognition, pp. 4896–4906 (2021)
5. Dou, H., Chen, C., Hu, X., Xuan, Z., Hu, Z., Peng, S.: PCA-SRGAN: incremental orthogonal projection discrimination for face super-resolution. In: Proceedings of the ACM Multimedia Conference, pp. 1891–1899 (2020)
6. Fu, Z., Zhao, Y., Chang, D., Zhang, X., Wang, Y.: Double low-rank representation with projection distance penalty for clustering. In: Proceedings of the IEEE Conference on Computer Vision and Pattern Recognition, pp. 5320–5329 (2021)
7. Hatakeyama, Y., Sakuma, H., Konishi, Y., Suenaga, K.: Visualizing color-wise saliency of black-box image classification models. In: Proceedings of the 15th Asian Conference on Computer Vision, pp. 189–205 (2020)
8. He, K., Zhang, X., Ren, S., Sun, J.: Deep residual learning for image recognition. In: Proceedings of the IEEE Conference on Computer Vision and Pattern Recognition, pp. 770–778 (2016)
9. He, R., Yang, J., Qi, X.: Re-distributing biased pseudo labels for semi-supervised semantic segmentation: a baseline investigation. In: Proceedings of the IEEE/CVF International Conference on Computer Vision, pp. 6910–6920 (2021)
10. Hu, Z., Yang, Z., Hu, X., Nevatia, R.: Simple: similar pseudo label exploitation for semi-supervised classification. In: Proceedings of the IEEE Conference on Computer Vision and Pattern Recognition, pp. 15099–15108 (2021)
11. Huang, G., Liu, Z., Van Der Maaten, L., Weinberger, K.Q.: Densely connected convolutional networks. In: Proceedings of the IEEE Conference on Computer Vision and Pattern Recognition, pp. 4700–4708 (2017)
12. Li, J., Xiong, C., Hoi, S.C.H.: CoMatch: semi-supervised learning with contrastive graph regularization. In: Proceedings of the IEEE/CVF International Conference on Computer Vision, pp. 9455–9464 (2021)
13. Li, X., Lin, C., Li, R., Wang, C., Guerin, F.: Latent space factorisation and manipulation via matrix subspace projection. In: Proceedings of the 37th International Conference on Machine Learning, pp. 5916–5926 (2020)
14. Sohn, K., et al.: FixMatch: simplifying semi-supervised learning with consistency and confidence. In: Proceedings of the Neural Information Processing Systems, pp. 1–13 (2020)
15. Mutny, M., Kirschner, J., Krause, A.: Experimental design for optimization of orthogonal projection pursuit models. In: Proceedings of the 34th AAAI Conference on Artificial Intelligence, pp. 10235–10242 (2020)
16. Pham, H., Dai, Z., Xie, Q., Le, Q.V.: Meta pseudo labels. In: IEEE Conference on Computer Vision and Pattern Recognition, pp. 11557–11568 (2021)

17. Ranasinghe, K., Naseer, M., Hayat, M., Khan, S., Khan, F.S.: Orthogonal projection loss. In: Proceedings of the IEEE/CVF International Conference on Computer Vision, pp. 12313–12323 (2021)
18. Saeed, M.S., Khan, M.H., Nawaz, S., Yousaf, M.H., Del Bue, A.: Fusion and orthogonal projection for improved face-voice association. In: Proceedings of the IEEE International Conference on Acoustics, Speech and Signal Processing, pp. 7057–7061 (2022)
19. Sohn, K., et al.: FixMatch: simplifying semi-supervised learning with consistency and confidence. In: Proceedings of the Neural Information Processing Systems, pp. 596–608 (2020)
20. Tang, Y., Chen, W., Luo, Y., Zhang, Y.: Humble teachers teach better students for semi-supervised object detection. In: Proceedings of the IEEE Conference on Computer Vision and Pattern Recognition, pp. 3132–3141 (2021)
21. Varamesh, A., Tuytelaars, T.: Mix'em: unsupervised image classification using a mixture of embeddings. In: Proceedings of the 15th Asian Conference on Computer Vision, pp. 38–55 (2020)
22. Wang, J., Feng, K., Wu, J.: SVM-based deep stacking networks. In: Proceedings of the 31st AAAI Conference on Artificial Intelligence, pp. 5273–5280 (2019)
23. Xiang, C., Wang, Z., Tian, S., Liao, J., Zou, W., Xu, C.: Matrix capsule convolutional projection for deep feature learning. IEEE Signal Process. Lett. **27**, 1899–1903 (2020). https://doi.org/10.1109/LSP.2020.3030550
24. Xie, Q., Dai, Z., Hovy, E.H., Luong, T., Le, Q.: Unsupervised data augmentation for consistency training. In: Proceedings of the Neural Information Processing Systems, pp. 6256–6268 (2020)
25. Yu, Q., Kavitha, M.S., Kurita, T.: Autoencoder framework based on orthogonal projection constraints improves anomalies detection. Neurocomputing **450**, 372–388 (2021)
26. Zagoruyko, S., Komodakis, N.: Wide residual networks. In: Proceedings of the British Machine Vision Conference, pp. 1–12 (2016)
27. Zhang, B., et al.: FlexMatch: boosting semi-supervised learning with curriculum pseudo labeling. In: Advances in Neural Information Processing Systems, pp. 18408–18419 (2021)
28. Zhang, L., Edraki, M., Qi, G.: CapProNet: deep feature learning via orthogonal projections onto capsule subspaces. In: Proceedings of the Neural Information Processing Systems, pp. 5819–5828 (2018)
29. Zheng, M., You, S., Huang, L., Wang, F., Qian, C., Xu, C.: SimMatch: semi-supervised learning with similarity matching. In: Proceedings of the IEEE/CVF Conference on Computer Vision and Pattern Recognition, pp. 14471–14481 (2022)

DENet: Detection-driven Enhancement Network for Object Detection Under Adverse Weather Conditions

Qingpao Qin[1], Kan Chang[1(✉)], Mengyuan Huang[1], and Guiqing Li[2]

[1] School of Computer and Electronic Information, Guangxi University,
Nanning, China
qqp@st.gxu.edu.cn, changkan0@gmail.com
[2] School of Computer Science and Engineering, South China University of
Technology, Guangzhou, China
ligq@scut.edu.cn

Abstract. Recently, the deep learning-based object detection methods have achieved a great success. However, the performance of such techniques deteriorates on the images captured under adverse weather conditions. To tackle this problem, a detection-driven enhancement network (DENet) which consists of three key modules for object detection is proposed. By using Laplacian pyramid, each input image is decomposed to a low-frequency (LF) component and several high-frequency (HF) components. For the LF component, a global enhancement module which consists of four parallel paths with different convolution kernel sizes is presented to well capture multi-scale features. For HF components, a cross-level guidance module is used to extract cross-level guidance information from the LF component, and affine transformation is applied in a detail enhancement module to incorporate the guidance information into the HF features. By cascading the proposed DENet and a common YOLO detector, we establish an elegant detection framework called DE-YOLO. Through experiments, we find that DENet avoids heavy computation and faithfully preserves the latent features which are beneficial to detection, and DE-YOLO is effective for images captured under both the normal condition and adverse weather conditions. The codes and pre-trained models are available at: https://github.com/NIvykk/DENet.

1 Introduction

Recently, the convolutional neural network (CNN)-based object detection methods, including the two-stage detectors [1–4] and the one-stage detectors [5–8], have achieved remarkable performance on benchmark datasets [9,10]. However, existing object detection models are usually trained on high-quality images. In real applications such as autonomous driving, images may be captured under adverse weather conditions, such as low-light and foggy conditions. Due to the large domain shift between the training and testing images, these object detection models may fail to provide reliable results under adverse weather conditions.

© The Author(s), under exclusive license to Springer Nature Switzerland AG 2023
L. Wang et al. (Eds.): ACCV 2022, LNCS 13843, pp. 491–507, 2023.
https://doi.org/10.1007/978-3-031-26313-2_30

To address this problem, one straightforward solution is to fine-tune the pre-trained object detection models on the target domain. However, it is expensive to collect a new dataset with handcrafted annotations on the target domain. Moreover, the fine-tuned models may suffer from a performance drop on the source domain. Therefore, such a solution is impracticable.

An alternative approach is to apply the unsupervised domain adaptation (UDA). The UDA-based methods [11–19] adopt the strategy of adversarial training, and attempt to learn robust domain-invariant features from both the labeled images on the source domain and the unlabeled low-quality images on the target domain. Such a strategy improves the performance on the target domain, while maintains a satisfactory detection results on the source domain. In addition, by using the UDA-based methods, there is no need to collect a large-scale annotated dataset for the new target domain. Despite the above advantages, if the gap between the two domains is too large, it is still hard for the UDA-based methods to align the features from the two different distributions.

As another potential solution, multi-task learning (MTL) is utilized by some methods [20,21]. Compared with the UDA-based methods, the MTL-based methods achieve a better performance on the target domain. However, the accuracy of this type of methods usually decreases on the source domain.

Intuitively, it is possible to improve the performance of detection under adverse weather conditions by utilizing the advanced image enhancement techniques [22–32] beforehand. However, in order to establish a sophisticated non-linear mapping from a low-quality image to the corresponding high-quality version, many enhancement models have a large model size. Applying such a complex model before the detector is harmful for real-time detection. Although there are some lightweight models which require short running time, they can only bring limited improvement to the performance of object detection as they are designed only for the human visual system. Another limitation lies in that many enhancement models are trained by using the enhancement loss, which measures the distance between the enhanced image and a clean ground-truth (GT). On one hand, a clean GT image may not be available in real applications. On the other hand, such a loss function treats each pixel equally and does not pay more attention to the structured features that are beneficial to object detection.

To tackle the limitations of the above methods, a detection-driven enhancement network (DENet) is proposed in this paper. Such a network is designed for the detection task, and is able to identify and pay special attention to those latent features that are important to object detection. In DENet, we use Laplacian pyramid [33] to decompose the input image into a low-frequency (LF) component and several high-frequency (HF) components. Usually, the weather-specific information, such as contrast and illumination, are more related to the LF component. Therefore, to alleviate the effects of adverse weather on detection, it is important to well capture and refine the multi-scale information in the LF component. To this end, a global enhancement module (GEM) which consists of four parallel paths with different convolution kernel sizes is designed for the LF component. Due to the reason that weather-specific information interacts with objects, we extract cross-level guidance information from the LF component, and then apply affine transformation to incorporate the guidance information into the features of each HF component, so that the HF information, such as edges and textures, can be well depicted. To avoid the disadvantages of the normal enhancement loss function, we assume that clean GT image is not available. DENet is combined with a normal YOLOv3 model and the detection loss is directly used for training. As there is no need to establish an accurate mapping to the clean GT image for each pixel, a lightweight design of DENet still leads to satisfactory detection results.

In summary, our contributions are threefold: 1) An extremely lightweight enhancement model (with only 45K parameters) called DENet is proposed. For effective and efficient enhancement, a Laplacian-pyramid-based structure is applied in DENet, where a GEM is designed for enhancing the LF component, and a detail enhancement module (DEM) is developed to refine the HF components adaptively. 2) By cascading DENet and a common detector such as YOLOv3 [7], an elegant end-to-end detection framework called DE-YOLO (cascaded detection-driven enhancement and YOLO) is obtained. When training DE-YOLO, we only use the normal detection loss, and does not require high-quality GT images. 3) Compared with different types of state-of-the-art (SOTA) methods, the proposed method is able to provide the most faithful detection results under both the normal condition and the adverse weather conditions, while requires very limited running time.

2   Related Work

2.1   UDA-Based and MTL-Based Methods

Recently, some researchers have proposed to apply the UDA-based methods to improve the performance of detection under adverse weather conditions. Chen et al. [11] introduced image-level and instance-level domain classifiers for the two-stage detector faster R-CNN [3]. Following this work, many two-stage-detector-based methods [12–15] have been proposed. For the one-stage detector, MS-DAYOLO [16] employed multi-scale image-level domain classifiers. Based on MS-DAYOLO, multi-scale instance-level domain adaptation and consistency regularization are introduced in DAYOLO [17], which result in a better performance. Sindagi et al. [18] proposed a domain adaptive object detection framework based on the prior knowledge of degradation models.

Some MTL-based methods have also been proposed. For example, Huang et al. [20] designed a framework which jointly learns three tasks, including visibility enhancement, object classification and localization. Cui et al. [21] explored the physical noise model under low-light condition, and trained a model to simultaneously predict the degradation parameters of images and detect objects, so that the intrinsic feature representation can be well extracted.

Note that except the basic detector, no extra parameters are needed in the testing phase of the UDA-based and MTL-based methods. Therefore, applying these two types of methods has no influence on the detection speed.

2.2 Image Enhancement Methods

Image enhancement methods can be used to improve the visual quality of the images taken under adverse weather conditions. For the low-light condition, many CNN-based low light image enhancement (LLIE) methods have been developed, including the retinex-based methods [22–24], the adversarial-learning-based methods [25], the mapping-based models [26], the unsupervised-learning-based methods [27,28], etc. For the foggy condition, the typical CNN-based defogging methods include the mapping-based methods [29,30] which directly predict the clean images, and the degeneration-based models [31,32] which attempt to estimate the transmission map of a hazy input.

2.3 Joint Enhancement and Detection Methods

Only a few joint enhancement and detection (JED) methods have been put forward. Liu et al. [34] proposed a joint low-light enhancement and face detection method, which establishes a reverse mapping to properly model the degradation of images, and a dual-path fusion architecture to fuse the features extracted from both the enhancement and face detection phases. However, this method requires both pair and unpair training data. Liu et al. [35] presented a JED framework called IA-YOLO, which uses a CNN-based predictor to learn the hyperparameters for the filters in a fully differentiable image processing (DIP) module. However, the filters in the DIP module are handcrafted and cascaded in a fixed order, which may limit the ability of DIP module. Different from IA-YOLO, our DENet decomposes the input image into LF and HF components and enhances each component adaptively. Such a structure can provide more flexibility to adaptively suppress the effects of weather-specific information and refine the latent features of objects.

3 Proposed Method

As shown in Fig. 1, our pipeline contains a DENet and a normal object detection model YOLOv3. DENet is responsible for adaptively enhancing the input low-light/foggy images, so that the weather-specific information can be well removed and the latent discriminative features can be well preserved. To reduce computational complexity and guarantee a reliable enhancement, a Laplacian-pyramid-based structure is applied in DENet (Sec. 3.1). Afterwards, the enhanced images are fed to YOLOv3 for detection. By training the cascaded DENet and YOLOv3 models in an end-to-end manner with the normal detection loss, a joint enhancement-detection framework DE-YOLO is obtained.

3.1 Laplacian-Pyramid-Based Enhancement

By using Laplacian pyramid decomposition [33], an input image $\mathbf{I}$ with a resolution of $h \times w$ can be decomposed into an LF component and several HF

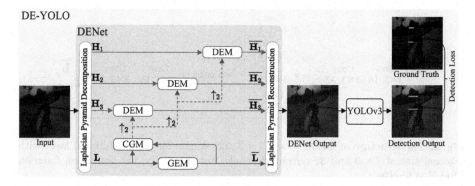

Fig. 1. Architecture of the proposed framework (in our setting, the number of decomposition levels in Laplacian pyramid is 4).

components. The LF component and the HF component at the ith decomposition level in Laplacian pyramid ($1 \le i < N$) are respectively calculated by

$$\mathbf{L} = G_N(\mathbf{I}) \tag{1}$$

$$\mathbf{H}_i = G_i(\mathbf{I}) - B(G_{i+1}(\mathbf{I}) \uparrow_2) \tag{2}$$

where N is the total number of decomposition levels; $B(.)$ denotes blurring the input by using a 2D Gausssian kernel with a size of 5×5; $\uparrow_2$ stands for upsampling an image by a factor of 2; $G_i(\mathbf{I}) \in \mathbb{R}^{\frac{h}{2^{i-1}} \times \frac{w}{2^{i-1}} \times 3}$ represents the ith level of image in Gaussian pyramid [36], which can be defined by

$$G_i(\mathbf{I}) = \begin{cases} \mathbf{I}, & i = 1 \\ B(G_{i-1}(\mathbf{I})) \downarrow_2, & 2 \le i \le N \end{cases} \tag{3}$$

where $\downarrow_2$ denotes down-sampling an image by a factor of 2. From Eqs. (1), (2) and (3), it is obvious that the decomposition is fully reversible.

As can be observed from Eq. (3), the image at the Nth level in Gaussian pyramid has been blurred $N - 1$ times and has the lowest resolution. Thus $\mathbf{L}$ in Laplacian pyramid is an LF component, which is likely to contain global illumination and large-scale structure. On the other hand, according to Eq. (2), $\mathbf{H}_i$ consists of HF residual details and has a larger resolution. From a high decomposition level to a low decomposition level, coarse to fine levels of image details are respectively stored in $\{\mathbf{H}_i\}$.

By taking advantage of Laplacian pyramid decomposition and reconstruction, a lightweight but very effective DENet is proposed. Since the LF component in Laplacian pyramid reveals global illumination, we design a GEM (Sect. 3.2) in DENet to improve the contrast and restore the visibility in the LF component. Note that the LF component in Laplacian pyramid has a small resolution, leading to a low computational burden in GEM. Thus using Laplacian pyramid decomposition and building GEM for the LF component is beneficial to the detection speed of DE-YOLO. When enhancing the global contrast/illumination, it is also

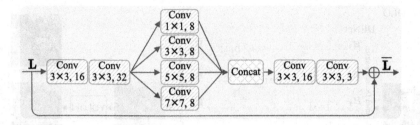

Fig. 2. The structure of GEM. "Conv 3×3, 32" stands for a convolutional layer with a kernel size of 3×3 and 32 output channels. For simplicity, the activation function LReLU is omitted.

necessary to enhance the local details accordingly. We notice that the HF components in Laplacian pyramid contain coarse-to-fine local details and those details are highly related to the LF component. Therefore, a DEM (Sect. 3.3) is deployed at each HF level to efficiently and effectively enhance the local details by incorporating the guidance information extracted from a cross-level guidance module (CGM) (Sect. 3.3). Finally, the enhanced LF and HF components are used to progressively reconstruct the enhanced image.

3.2 Global Enhancement Module for the LF Component

The structure of GEM is shown in Fig. 2. Unlike the common low-level vision tasks, the goal of our DENet is not to obtain an enhanced image which is close to the clean GT for human eyes. Thus there is no need to establish a sophisticated mapping from the low-quality image domain to the GT domain. This enables the structure of GEM to be simple enough.

In the front end of GEM, two convolutional layers are first used to extract features from the LF component with a dimension of $\frac{h}{2^{N-1}} \times \frac{w}{2^{N-1}} \times 3$. As GEM is built to enhance the global structure and contrast/illumination in images, it is reasonable to use different sizes of kernels to well capture multi-scale information, which is similar to the idea of the well-known Inception architecture [37]. Here we use four parallel convolutions with 1×1, 3×3, 5×5 and 7×7 filters, respectively. Since the resolution of the LF component is rather small, a kernel size of 7×7 is enough to cover a very large region in the original image. Therefore, environment-specific knowledge such as the lighting condition or the fog spreading over the whole image can be well depicted. To further reduce the computational complexity and the number of parameters, the output features of each parallel path are compressed to 8 channels. Through experiments we found that such a lightweight setting still leads to satisfactory detection results. Afterwards, the features from four parallel paths are concatenated and further fused by two 3×3 convolutional layers. To improve the performance of GEM, skip connection is applied, so that this structure can focus on learning the residual between the input LF component $\mathbf{L}$ and the corresponding enhanced output $\overline{\mathbf{L}}$.

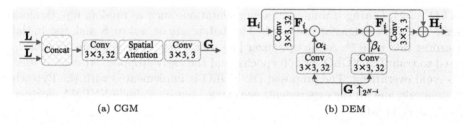

(a) CGM   (b) DEM

Fig. 3. The structures of CGM and DEM. The activation function LReLU is omitted.

3.3 Detail Enhancement Module for the HF Components

To enhance the HF components which contain coarse-to-fine local details in Laplacian pyramid, DEM and CGM are established, the structures of which are given in Fig. 3 (a) and (b), respectively.

CGM is used to extract the guidance information from the LF component. To embed the differences between the unprocessed component $\mathbf{L}$ and the enhanced component $\overline{\mathbf{L}}$, both $\mathbf{L}$ and $\overline{\mathbf{L}}$ are fed to CGM. In the front end of CGM, $\mathbf{L}$ and $\overline{\mathbf{L}}$ are concatenated. Then a 3×3 convolutional layer extracts 32 feature maps from the concatenated two components. Since the LF component is spatially correlated to the HF components, a spatial attention module [38] is utilized to localize the positions where LF and HF components are highly correlated. Finally, another 3×3 convolutional layer is used to further refine the 32 feature maps and generate the guidance $\mathbf{G}$ with a dimension of $\frac{h}{2^{N-1}} \times \frac{w}{2^{N-1}} \times 3$.

DEM is utilized to enhance the HF components under the guidance provided by CGM. Since the resolutions of the LF and each HF component are different, before entering DEM, the cross-level guidance information is upsampled by using bilinear interpolation. Note that the resolution of the HF component becomes larger as the decomposition level goes lower. As a result, building a sophisticated enhancement module for each HF component could induce intense computation, which significantly reduces detection speed. To efficiently and effectively enhance the HF components, we use a simple residual block, and apply affine transformation [39] to incorporate the guidance information into the extracted HF features. The affine transformation is defined as

$$\mathcal{M}(\mathbf{F}_i \mid \alpha_i, \beta_i) = \alpha_i \odot \mathbf{F}_i + \beta_i \tag{4}$$

where $\mathbf{F}_i$ stands for the extracted HF feature; $\odot$ denotes the element-wise multiplication; α_i and β_i are the scaling and shifting parameters at the ith decomposition level, respectively, which are learned by feeding the upsampled guidance information $\mathbf{G}$ to two different 3×3 convolutional layers.

4 Experiments and Analysis

4.1 Implementation Details

In our experiment, to facilitate a fair and comprehensive evaluation, the classical YOLOv3 [7] is applied as the detector. The image size for training and testing is 544×544. During training, data augmentations such as random filp, random scale and HSV augment are used. The batch size is set to 8 and the initial learning rate is 10^{-4}. Adam optimizer [40] with Cosine learning rate schedule is used to train DE-YOLO for 150 epochs, and the early stopping strategy is used to avoid overfitting. The proposed DE-YOLO is implemented with the Pytorch framework, and all the experiments are carried out on a single NVIDIA GeForce RTX 2080 Ti GPU.

4.2   Preparation of Datasets

The low-light and foggy weather conditions are evaluated, and the used datasets are summarized in Table 1. For low-light condition, exclusively dark (*ExDark*) [41] is used, which contains 7363 low-light images, where 12 object categories for detection are annotated. For foggy weather, the real-world task-driven testing set (*RTTS*) is chosen. It consists of 4322 images captured under real-world foggy condition, and 5 object categories are annotated. Besides, the unannotated realistic hazy images (*URHI*) dataset which contains 4807 unannotated natural hazy images is also used for training the UDA-based methods. Both *RTTS* and *URHI* are subsets in the *RESIDE* dataset [42].

Moreover, the well-known dataset *PASCAl VOC* [9] is used to generate synthetic low-light and foggy images. Note that although each synthetic degraded image has a corresponding GT high-quality version, the GT images are not used for training IA-YOLO and our DE-YOLO. To obtain synthetic low-light images, the original RGB images in *VOC* are degraded by gamma transformation:

$$g(\mathbf{I}) = \mathbf{I}^{\gamma} \tag{5}$$

For each image in *VOC*, γ is randomly selected from a range of $[1.5, 5]$. However, only 10 out of 20 categories in *VOC* dataset match with the 10 categories in *ExDark* dataset. Therefore, we first filter out the unmatched categories in *VOC*, and obtain two sub-sets called *VOC_train_I* and *VOC_test_I* for training and testing, respectively. Then all the images in *VOC_test_I* are degraded by Eq. (5), resulting in a synthetic low-light testing set *VOC_lowlight_test*. By randomly degrading 2/3 images in *VOC_train_I*, a hybrid training set *VOC_hybrid_train_I* is built.

Similarly, to generate synthetic foggy images, we build *VOC_train_II* and *VOC_test_II* by filtering out the *VOC* categories that do not match with *RTTS* dataset. Based on the atmospheric scattering model [43–45], the foggy datasets *VOC_hybrid_train_II* and *VOC_foggy_test* are obtained by:

$$\mathbf{J} = \mathbf{I}e^{-\lambda}\mathbf{d} + A(1 - e^{-\lambda}\mathbf{d}) \tag{6}$$

where $\mathbf{J}$ denotes the synthetic foggy image, A is the global atmospheric light and is set as 0.5 in our experiment, $\lambda = 0.05 + 0.01 * k$, k is a random integer number which ranges from 0 to 9. The scene depth of a pixel is computed by $d = -0.04 \times \rho + \sqrt{\max(h, w)}$, with ρ denoting the Euclidean distance from the current pixel to the central one, h and w being the height and width of the target image, respectively.

Table 1. Overview of the used datasets. NLI and LLI are short for normal-light and low-light images, respectively.

Dataset	Type	Images	Instances	Categories
VOC_train_I	NLI	12334	29135	10
VOC_test_I	NLI	3760	8939	10
VOC_hybrid_train_I	NLI + synthetic LLI	12334	29135	10
VOC_lowlight_test	synthetic LLI	3760	8939	10
ExDark (training)	realistic LLI	4800	–	–
ExDark (testing)	realistic LLI	2563	6450	10
VOC_train_II	fog-free	8111	19561	5
VOC_test_II	fog-free	2734	6604	5
VOC_hybrid_train_II	fog-free + synthetic foggy	8111	19561	5
VOC_foggy_test	synthetic foggy	2734	6604	5
URHI (training)	realistic foggy	4807	–	–
RTTS (testing)	realistic foggy	4322	29577	5

4.3 Object Detection on Low-Light Images

For the low-light condition, DSNet, IA-YOLO and proposed DE-YOLO is trained on *VOC_hybrid_train_I*. The *Baseline* methods YOLOv3(N) and YOLOv3(L) are obtained by training the normal YOLOv3 model [7] on *VOC_train_I* and *VOC_hybrid_train_I*, respectively. The LLIE methods, including MBLLEN [26], KinD [22], EnlightenGAN [25] and Zero-DCE [27], are used to preprocess the low-light images before applying YOLOv3(N) for detection. The pre-trained models of the four LLIE methods provided by their authors are directly applied. For the UDA-based methods, MS-DAYOLO [16] and DAYOLO [17] are re-trained on *VOC_train_I* on the source domain with labels and the training set of *ExDark* on the target domain without labels. Since a synthetic low-light dataset is proposed together with MAET in [21], MAET is trained on its own synthetic low-light dataset.

Table 2 shows comparisons among different methods on three testing datasets. The performance is evaluated by using the mean average precision (mAP) at an intersection over union (IoU) threshold of 0.5 (mAP50). From Table 2 we have the following observations: 1) Training YOLOv3(L) on the hybrid dataset achieves better performance than YOLOv3(N) on low-light testing datasets. However, when testing on normal-light dataset *VOC_test_I*, YOLOv3(L) is worse than YOLOv3(N), which suggests that YOLOv3(L) cannot be well generalized from one dataset to another. 2) Simply using the four LLIE methods (MBLLEN, KinD, EnlightenGAN, Zero-DCE) before YOLOv3 cannot significantly improve the performance of YOLOv3(N). 3) The two UDA-based methods MS-DAYOLO and DAYOLO bring limited improvements over YOLOv3(N) on two low-light testing datasets. As the UDA-based methods are trained on the target domain without labels, the performance is less satisfactory when the domain gap is large. 4) The two MTL-based methods achieve higher

Table 2. Performance comparisons on low-light images (mAP50 (%)).

Method		VOC_test_I	VOC_lowlight_test	ExDark
Baseline	YOLOv3(N) [7]	72.22	56.34	43.02
	YOLOv3(L) [7]	66.95	62.91	45.58
LLIE	MBLLEN [26]	–	58.36	43.49
	KinD [22]	–	52.57	39.22
	EnlightenGAN [25]	–	53.67	39.42
	Zero-DCE [27]	–	56.49	40.40
UDA	MS-DAYOLO [16]	72.01	58.20	44.25
	DAYOLO [17]	71.58	58.82	44.62
MTL	DSNet [20]	61.82	64.57	45.31
	MAET [21]	69.49	58.23	47.10
JED	IA-YOLO [35]	72.53	67.34	49.43
	DE-YOLO (ours)	**73.17**	**67.81**	**51.51**

mAP than UDA-based and LLIE-based approaches on the *ExDark* dataset, yet fall behind UDA-based approaches on the normal-light dataset *VOC_test_I*. 5) The two JED-based approaches are superior to other types of methods, and the proposed DE-YOLO yields the best performance among all the competing methods on all the three datasets. Particularly, on realistic low-light dataset *ExDark*, DE-YOLO surpasses YOLOv3(L) and the second best method IA-YOLO by 5.93% and 2.08%, respectively. Moreover, DE-YOLO achieves a even better performance than YOLOv3(N) on normal-light images, which well demonstrates the generalization ability of DE-YOLO.

The detection results obtained by different methods are visualized in Figs. 4 and 5. For the GT results, we just show the GT labels on the original low-light images. Although the LLIE methods and the JED method IA-YOLO are able to enhance the brightness of images, significant noises and artifacts can be observed from their results. On the contrary, DENet can suitably enhance the underexposed regions in images, while suppressing different kinds of artifacts and noises. Therefore, the detection results of DE-YOLO have fewer false-positive and false-negative results.

4.4 Object Detection on Foggy Images

Table 3 presents the detection results on foggy images. Similar to the settings on low-light images, YOLOv3(N) and YOLOv3(F) are the YOLOv3 [7] models trained on *VOC_train_II* and *VOC_hybrid_train_II*, respectively. Three representative defogging methods including GridDehazeNet [29], DCPDN [31] and MSBDN [30] are adopted to pre-process the foggy images before detection. The two UDA-based methods MS-DAYOLO [16] and DAYOLO [17] are re-trained on *VOC_train_II* on the source domain with labels and *URHI* on the target domain without labels. The MTL-based method DSNet [20] and the JED-based methods IA-YOLO [35] and DE-YOLO are re-trained on *VOC_hybrid_train_II*.

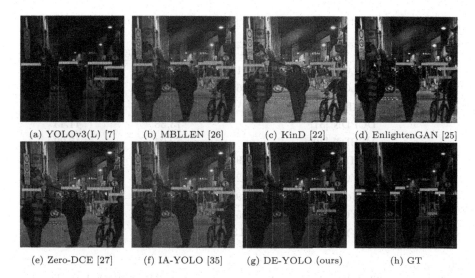

Fig. 4. Detection results obtained on image *2015_00402* from *ExDark*. MBLLEN, KinD, Zero-DCE, EnlightenGAN and IA-YOLO all generate significant noises. Although DE-YOLO is darker than the other methods, the image is clear and the contrast is suitable.

Fig. 5. Detection results obtained on image *2015_00542* from *ExDark*. Compared with other methods, DE-YOLO well suppresses artifacts and enhances the contrast of image. Besides, DE-YOLO is the only method that properly detects all the objects.

It can be seen from Table 3 that: 1) Although GridDehazeNet, DCPDN and MSBDN are worse than YOLOv3(F), applying the three defogging methods significantly improve the performance of YOLOv3(N). 2) Similar to the low-light

Table 3. Performance comparisons on foggy images (mAP50 (%)).

Method		VOC_test_II	VOC_foggy_test	RTTS
Baseline	YOLOv3(N) [7]	83.41	46.53	41.87
	YOLOv3(F) [7]	79.06	78.87	49.45
Defogging	GridDehazeNet [29]	–	72.09	46.03
	DCPDN [31]	–	73.38	44.43
	MSBDN [30]	–	72.04	45.90
UDA	MS-DAYOLO [16]	81.69	65.44	42.94
	DAYOLO [17]	80.12	66.53	44.15
MTL	DSNet [20]	71.49	81.71	49.86
JED	IA-YOLO [35]	84.05	83.22	52.36
	DE-YOLO (ours)	**84.13**	**83.56**	**53.70**

condition, the UDA-based methods are better than YOLOv3(N), but they are worse than YOLOv3(F) on the two foggy datasets. 3) Compared with the defogging and the UDA-based methods, DSNet achieves higher mAP values on the two foggy datasets. However, it suffers from a drop in mAP on the fog-free dataset *VOC_test_II*. 4) The proposed DE-YOLO achieves the best detection results on all the three testing sets. In particular, on the realistic foggy dataset *RTTS*, DE-YOLO provides mAP values 4.25% and 1.34% higher than YOLOv3(F) and IA-YOLO, respectively.

The qualitative comparisons among different methods on the image from *RTTS* are given in Fig. 6. For the GT result, the GT labels are directly showed on the original hazy image. We can find that DE-YOLO is able to deliver images with suitable contrast, which helps to increase the number of true-positive results and the confidences of the detected objects.

4.5   Ablation Study

Table 4 compares the contributions of GEM, DEM and CGM in DENet, and the results are reported on *ExDark*. Note that for the variant model which does not have CGM, the affine transformation in DEM is removed. Therefore, such a variant of DEM becomes a normal residual block. As can be seen, firstly, applying GEM leads to a mAP improvement of 2.79% over the normal YOLOv3(L). Secondly, additionally using DEM results in a even better performance. Finally, the best performance can be achieved by utilizing all the three modules, which demonstrates that these modules are complementary to each other.

In Table 5, the effects of the number of levels of Laplacian pyramid in DENet is evaluated. Note that when $N = 1$, Laplacian pyramid decomposition is not applied, and only GEM is used to enhance the input image. It is obvious that a larger number of decomposition levels results in more parameters and longer runtime. We find that the mAP50 increases monotonically with N when $N \leq 4$, and the performance decreases when $N > 4$.

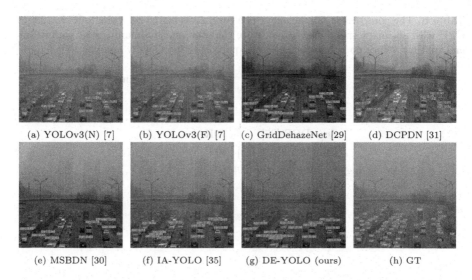

(a) YOLOv3(N) [7]   (b) YOLOv3(F) [7]   (c) GridDehazeNet [29]   (d) DCPDN [31]

(e) MSBDN [30]   (f) IA-YOLO [35]   (g) DE-YOLO (ours)   (h) GT

Fig. 6. Detection results obtained by different methods on image *BD_ Baidu_074* from *RTTS*. Our DE-YOLO detects more vehicles than the other methods.

Table 4. Ablation analysis on different modules of our method. Note that only the parameters of DENet are measured.

Method	GEM	DEM	CGM	Parameters (K)	mAP50 (%)
YOLOv3 (L)	–	–	–	–	45.58
DE-YOLO	✓	✗	✗	32	48.37
	✓	✓	✗	35	49.80
	✓	✓	✓	45	**51.51**

Table 5. The effects of the number of levels of Laplacian pyramid. The runtime is tested on a single RTX 2080Ti GPU with an image size of 544 × 544. Note that the reported numbers of parameters and runtime values are only measured on DENet.

N	Parameters (K)	Runtime (ms)	mAP50 (%)
1	32	3	46.28
2	38	4	50.09
3	42	5	51.27
4	45	6	**51.51**
5	49	7	51.16
6	51	8	51.01

4.6   Efficiency Analysis

Table 6 lists the number of parameters and runtime consumed by different enhancement-based methods. Note that during testing, the UDA-based and MTL-based methods do not require extra parameters and computation. There-

Table 6. The comparison of efficiency. The runtime is tested on a single RTX 2080Ti GPU with an image size of 544 × 544. Note that the reported numbers of parameters and runtime values do not include those required by the YOLOv3 model.

Method		Parameters	Runtime (ms)
LLIE	MBLLEN [26]	450K	72
	KinD [22]	8M	28
	Zero-DCE [27]	79K	7
	EnlightenGAN [25]	9M	15
Defogging	GridDehazeNet [29]	985K	49
	DCPDN [31]	67M	30
	MSBDN [30]	31M	51
JED	IA-YOLO [35]	165K	9
	DENet (ours)	**45K**	**6**

fore, they are excluded from Table 6 for comparison. Since both IA-YOLO and DE-YOLO include a normal YOLOv3 model, only the image enhancement sub-networks are compared. It can be found from Table 6 that the proposed DENet has a very small number of parameters and requires the shortest runtime. Such a lightweight and fast model is suitable for real-time applications.

5   Conclusion

To enable a faithful detection under adverse weather conditions, an adaptive image enhancement model DENet was presented. In DENet, the input image is decomposed by using Laplacian pyramid. After that, the LF component and HF components are respectively enhanced. To explore the correlation among different components, cross-level guidance information is extracted from the LF component and then incorporated into the features of the HF components. DENet is extremely lightweight, and thus is suitable for the applications that require real-time detection. By training DENet and a common YOLOv3 model in an end-to-end manner, a JED framework DE-YOLO was obtained. Experiments showed that DE-YOLO is able to achieve the highest mAP50 value among all the compared methods under the low-light and foggy conditions. Meanwhile, under the normal condition with clean input images, the performance of DE-YOLO is also better than the original YOLOv3, which suggests that the proposed method has a good generalization ability.

Acknowledgements. This work was supported in part by the National Natural Science Foundation of China (NSFC) (62171145, 61761005), and in part by Guangxi Key Laboratory of Multimedia Communications and Network Technology. Part of the experiments were carried out on the High-performance Computing Platform of Guangxi University.

References

1. Girshick, R.B., Donahue, J., Darrell, T., Malik, J.: Rich feature hierarchies for accurate object detection and semantic segmentation. In: Proceedings of the IEEE Conference on Computer Vision and Pattern Recognition (CVPR), pp. 580–587. Columbus, OH, USA (2014)
2. Girshick, R.B.: Fast R-CNN. In: Proceedings of the IEEE International Conference on Computer Vision (ICCV), pp. 1440–1448. Santiago, Chile (2015)
3. Ren, S., He, K., Girshick, R.B., Sun, J.: Faster R-CNN: towards real-time object detection with region proposal networks. In: Advances in neural information processing systems (NIPS), pp. 91–99. Montreal, Quebec, Canada (2015)
4. He, K., Gkioxari, G., Dollár, P., Girshick, R.B.: Mask R-CNN. In: Proceedings of the IEEE International Conference on Computer Vision (ICCV), pp. 2980–2988. Venice, Italy (2017)
5. Redmon, J., Divvala, S.K., Girshick, R.B., Farhadi, A.: You only look once: unified, real-time object detection. In: Proceedings of the IEEE Conference on Computer Vision and Pattern Recognition (CVPR), pp. 779–788. Las Vegas, NV, USA (2016)
6. Redmon, J., Farhadi, A.: YOLO9000: better, faster, stronger. In: Proceedings of the IEEE Conference on Computer Vision and Pattern Recognition (CVPR), pp. 6517–6525. Honolulu, HI, USA (2017)
7. Redmon, J., Farhadi, A.: YOLOv3: an incremental improvement. arXiv preprint arXiv:1804.02767 (2018)
8. Liu, W., et al.: SSD: single shot multibox detector. In: Leibe, B., Matas, J., Sebe, N., Welling, M. (eds.) ECCV 2016. LNCS, vol. 9905, pp. 21–37. Springer, Cham (2016). https://doi.org/10.1007/978-3-319-46448-0_2
9. Everingham, M., Gool, L.V., Williams, C.K.I., Winn, J.M., Zisserman, A.: The pascal visual object classes (VOC) challenge. Int. J. Comput. Vis. **88**(2), 303–338 (2010)
10. Lin, T.-Y., et al.: Microsoft COCO: common objects in context. In: Fleet, D., Pajdla, T., Schiele, B., Tuytelaars, T. (eds.) ECCV 2014. LNCS, vol. 8693, pp. 740–755. Springer, Cham (2014). https://doi.org/10.1007/978-3-319-10602-1_48
11. Chen, Y., Li, W., Sakaridis, C., Dai, D., Gool, L.V.: Domain adaptive faster R-CNN for object detection in the wild. In: Proceedings of the IEEE Conference on Computer Vision and Pattern Recognition (CVPR), pp. 3339–3348. Salt Lake City, UT, USA (2018)
12. Zhu, X., Pang, J., Yang, C., Shi, J., Lin, D.: Adapting object detectors via selective cross-domain alignment. In: Proceedings of the IEEE Conference on Computer Vision and Pattern Recognition (CVPR), pp. 687–696. Long Beach, CA, USA (2019)
13. Wang, T., Zhang, X., Yuan, L., Feng, J.: Few-shot adaptive faster R-CNN. In: Proceedings of the IEEE Conference on Computer Vision and Pattern Recognition (CVPR), pp. 7173–7182. Long Beach, CA, USA (2019)
14. Saito, K., Ushiku, Y., Harada, T., Saenko, K.: Strong-weak distribution alignment for adaptive object detection. In: Proceedings of the IEEE Conference on Computer Vision and Pattern Recognition (CVPR), pp. 6956–6965. Long Beach, CA, USA (2019)
15. He, Z., Zhang, L.: Multi-adversarial faster-rcnn for unrestricted object detection. In: Proceedings of the IEEE International Conference on Computer Vision (ICCV), pp. 6667–6676. Seoul, Korea (South) (2019)

16. Hnewa, M., Radha, H.: Multiscale domain adaptive yolo for cross-domain object detection. In: Proceedings of the IEEE International Conference on Image Processing (ICIP), pp. 3323–3327. Anchorage, AK, USA (2021)

17. Zhang, S., Tuo, H., Hu, J., Jing, Z.: Domain adaptive YOLO for one-stage cross-domain detection. In: Proceedings of the Asian Conference on Machine Learning (ACML), pp. 785–797. Virtual Event (2021)

18. Sindagi, V.A., Oza, P., Yasarla, R., Patel, V.M.: Prior-based domain adaptive object detection for hazy and rainy conditions. In: Vedaldi, A., Bischof, H., Brox, T., Frahm, J.-M. (eds.) ECCV 2020. LNCS, vol. 12359, pp. 763–780. Springer, Cham (2020). https://doi.org/10.1007/978-3-030-58568-6_45

19. Sasagawa, Y., Nagahara, H.: YOLO in the dark - domain adaptation method for merging multiple models. In: Vedaldi, A., Bischof, H., Brox, T., Frahm, J.-M. (eds.) ECCV 2020. LNCS, vol. 12366, pp. 345–359. Springer, Cham (2020). https://doi.org/10.1007/978-3-030-58589-1_21

20. Huang, S., Le, T., Jaw, D.: DSNet: joint semantic learning for object detection in inclement weather conditions. IEEE Trans. Pattern Anal. Mach. Intell. **43**(8), 2623–2633 (2021)

21. Cui, Z., Qi, G., Gu, L., You, S., Zhang, Z., Harada, T.: Multitask AET with orthogonal tangent regularity for dark object detection. In: Proceedings of the IEEE International Conference on Computer Vision (ICCV), pp. 2533–2542. Montreal, QC, Canada (2021)

22. Zhang, Y., Zhang, J., Guo, X.: Kindling the darkness: a practical low-light image enhancer. In: Proceedings of the ACM International Conference on Multimedia (MM), pp. 1632–1640. Nice, France (2019)

23. Wei, C., Wang, W., Yang, W., Liu, J.: Deep retinex decomposition for low-light enhancement. In: Proceedings of the British Machine Vision Conference (BMVC), p. 155. Newcastle, UK (2018)

24. Wu, W., Weng, J., Zhang, P., Wang, X., Yang, W., Jiang, J.: Uretinex-net: Retinex-based deep unfolding network for low-light image enhancement. In: Proceedings of the IEEE/CVF Conference on Computer Vision and Pattern Recognition, pp. 5901–5910. New Orleans, LA, USA (2022)

25. Jiang, Y., et al.: EnlightenGAN: deep light enhancement without paired supervision. IEEE Trans. Image Process. **30**, 2340–2349 (2021)

26. Lv, F., Lu, F., Wu, J., Lim, C.: MBLLEN: low-light image/video enhancement using CNNs. In: Proceedings of the British Machine Vision Conference (BMVC), p. 220. Newcastle, UK (2018)

27. Guo, C., et al.: Zero-reference deep curve estimation for low-light image enhancement. In: Proceedings of the IEEE Conference on Computer Vision and Pattern Recognition (CVPR), pp. 1777–1786. Seattle, WA, USA (2020)

28. Ma, L., Ma, T., Liu, R., Fan, X., Luo, Z.: Toward fast, flexible, and robust low-light image enhancement. In: Proceedings of the IEEE/CVF Conference on Computer Vision and Pattern Recognition, pp. 5637–5646. New Orleans, LA, USA (2022)

29. Liu, X., Ma, Y., Shi, Z., Chen, J.: GridDehazeNet: attention-based multi-scale network for image dehazing. In: Proceedings of the IEEE International Conference on Computer Vision (ICCV), pp. 7313–7322. Seoul, Korea (South) (2019)

30. Dong, H., Pan, J., Xiang, L., Hu, Z., Zhang, X., Wang, F., Yang, M.: Multi-scale boosted dehazing network with dense feature fusion. In: Proceedings of the IEEE Conference on Computer Vision and Pattern Recognition (CVPR), pp. 2154–2164. Seattle, WA, USA (2020)

31. Zhang, H., Patel, V.M.: Densely connected pyramid dehazing network. In: Proceedings of the IEEE Conference on Computer Vision and Pattern Recognition (CVPR), pp. 3194–3203. Salt Lake City, UT, USA (2018)

32. Yang, Y., Wang, C., Liu, R., Zhang, L., Guo, X., Tao, D.: Self-augmented unpaired image dehazing via density and depth decomposition. In: Proceedings of the IEEE/CVF Conference on Computer Vision and Pattern Recognition, pp. 2037–2046. New Orleans, LA, USA (2022)

33. Burt, P.J., Adelson, E.H.: The Laplacian pyramid as a compact image code. IEEE Trans. Commun. **31**(4), 532–540 (1983)

34. Liu, J., Xu, D., Yang, W., Fan, M., Huang, H.: Benchmarking low-light image enhancement and beyond. Int. J. Comput. Vision **129**(4), 1153–1184 (2021)

35. Liu, W., Ren, G., Yu, R., Guo, S., Zhu, J., Zhang, L.: Image-adaptive yolo for object detection in adverse weather conditions. In: Proceedings of the AAAI Conference on Artificial Intelligence (AAAI), vol. 36, pp. 1792–1800 (2022)

36. Adelson, E.H., Anderson, C.H., Bergen, J.R., Burt, P.J., Ogden, J.M.: Pyramid methods in image processing. RCA Eng. **29**(6), 33–41 (1984)

37. Szegedy, C., et al.: Going deeper with convolutions. In: Proceedings of the IEEE Conference on Computer Vision and Pattern Recognition (CVPR), pp. 1–9. Boston, MA, USA (2015)

38. Woo, S., Park, J., Lee, J.-Y., Kweon, I.S.: CBAM: convolutional block attention module. In: Ferrari, V., Hebert, M., Sminchisescu, C., Weiss, Y. (eds.) ECCV 2018. LNCS, vol. 11211, pp. 3–19. Springer, Cham (2018). https://doi.org/10.1007/978-3-030-01234-2_1

39. Wang, X., Yu, K., Dong, C., Change Loy, C.: Recovering realistic texture in image super-resolution by deep spatial feature transform. In: Proc. IEEE Conference on Computer Vision and Pattern Recognition (CVPR), pp. 606–615. Salt Lake City, UT, USA (2018)

40. Kingma, D.P., Ba, J.: Adam: a method for stochastic optimization. In: Proceedings of the International Conference on Learning Representations (ICLR), San Diego, CA, USA (2015)

41. Loh, Y.P., Chan, C.S.: Getting to know low-light images with the exclusively dark dataset. Comput. Vis. Image Underst. **178**, 30–42 (2019)

42. Li, B., et al.: Benchmarking single-image dehazing and beyond. IEEE Trans. Image Process. **28**(1), 492–505 (2019)

43. McCartney, E.J.: Optics of the atmosphere: scattering by molecules and particles. New York (1976)

44. Nayar, S.K., Narasimhan, S.G.: Vision in bad weather. In: Proceedings of the Seventh IEEE International Conference on Computer Vision, vol. 2, pp. 820–827. IEEE (1999)

45. Narasimhan, S.G., Nayar, S.K.: Contrast restoration of weather degraded images. IEEE Trans. Pattern Anal. Mach. Intell. **25**(6), 713–724 (2003)

RepF-Net: Distortion-Aware Re-projection Fusion Network for Object Detection in Panorama Image

Mengfan Li[1], Ming Meng[2(✉)], and Zhong Zhou[1]

[1] State Key Laboratory of Virtual Reality Technology and Systems,
Beihang University, Beijing, China
[2] School of Data Science and Media Intelligence,
Communication University of China, Beijing, China
mengming@buaa.edu.cn

Abstract. Panorama image has a large 360° field of view, providing rich contextual information for object detection, widely used in virtual reality, augmented reality, scene understanding, etc. However, existing methods for object detection on panorama image still have some problems. When 360° content is converted to the projection plane, the geometric distortion brought by the projection model makes the neural network can not extract features efficiently, the objects at the boundary of the projection image are also incomplete. To solve these problems, in this paper, we propose a novel two-stage detection network, RepF-Net, comprehensively utilizing multiple distortion-aware convolution modules to deal with geometric distortion while performing effective features extraction, and using the non-maximum fusion algorithm to fuse the content of the detected object in the post-processing stage. Our proposed unified distortion-aware convolution modules can be used to deal with distortions from geometric transforms and projection models, and be used to solve the geometric distortion caused by equirectangular projection and stereographic projection in our network. Our proposed non-maximum fusion algorithm fuses the content of detected objects to deal with incomplete object content separated by the projection boundary. Experimental results show that our RepF-Net outperforms previous state-of-the-art methods by 6% on mAP. Based on RepF-Net, we present an implementation of 3D object detection and scene layout reconstruction application.

1 Introduction

In recent years, panorama image has been widely used, and their 360° large field of view (FOV) provides rich contextual information for computer vision processing. As a fundamental task in computer vision, accurate object detection results enable subsequent applications such as virtual reality, augmented reality, and scene understanding to achieve better performance.

Supplementary Information The online version contains supplementary material available at https://doi.org/10.1007/978-3-031-26313-2_31.

Before deep learning, in order to handle the object detection task, traditional object detection methods are usually subdivided into three steps: information region selection, feature extraction, and classification [32]. In the information region selection stage, a multi-scale sliding window is used to scan the entire image. And then feature extraction algorithms such as histogram of oriented gradients [7] and haar-like [17] are used to generate semantic and robust image representations. Finally, classification algorithms such as support vector machine [10] are chosen as the classifier.

With the development of the convolutional neural network in computer vision, there are two types of network architectures for object detection. In the first type, the network has two stages: a regional proposal generation network to replace both information region selection and feature extraction stage and a classification network. On the other hand, the second network has only one stage, which integrates feature extraction and classification, and uses anchors for informative region selection.

Although the convolutional neural networks have better performance than traditional object detection methods, object detection in panorama image remains challenging due to the sphere-to-plane projections. First, the geometric deformation brought by sphere-to-plane projections makes it difficult to extract features effectively. Second, sphere-to-plane projections also divide the original complete context information and make the object information incomplete on the projection boundary.

In this paper, we propose a re-projection fusion object detection network architecture RepF-Net, and perform better accuracy on panorama image than previous state-of-the-art methods. We propose a unified distortion-aware convolution module in the convolutional layer of our network architecture, which can both deal with equirectangular projection deformation in the information region selection stage and stereographic projection deformation in the feature extraction stage. Moreover, we propose a non-maximum fusion algorithm in the post-processing stage of our network architecture, which can fuse the incomplete information caused by the sphere-to-plane projection boundary.

Our contributions can be summarized as follows:

- We propose a re-projection fusion object detection network architecture RepF-Net for panorama image, utilizing multiple distortion-aware modules to perform effective feature extraction, while using re-projection and non-maximum fusion in the post-processing stage to obtain better performance.
- We propose a unified distortion-aware convolution module to handle various geometric distortions caused by geometric transforms and projection models. It makes our network focus on the information areas to extract features more efficiently, resulting in faster convergence and better performance. We propose a non-maximum fusion algorithm to handle the object incomplete problem caused by the projection boundary to obtain better detection.

- We conduct numerous ablation experiments and comparison experiments to verify the effectiveness of our proposed methods. Meanwhile, our proposed RepF-Net outperforms the state-of-the-art by 6% on mAP. Furthermore, we present an implementation of 3D object detection and scene layout reconstruction application based on our methods.

2   Related Work

CNN and Object Detection: With the application of convolutional networks, there are two main network architectures for object detection: one-stage detection and two-stage detection. The two-stage detector adopts the R-CNN architecture, and followed by its variants FastR-CNN [13], FasterR-CNN [24] and MaskR-CNN [15]. The two-stage detector first gets candidate proposals through a region proposal network (RPN), and then refines the proposals through a classification network to obtain the final detection results. On the other hand, the one-stage detector based on global regression and classification, uses pre-defined anchors instead of RPN-generated region proposals, allowing bounding boxes with relevant classes to be extracted directly from the input image. Mainstream object detection methods based on this architecture include You Only Look Once (YOLO) [2, 21–23] and Single Shot Detection (SSD) [18]. There are also some object detection network architectures that do not rely on proposals or anchors, such as CornerNet [16] which directly detects the corners of the object, while CenterNet [9] directly detects the center of the object. These detectors are less accurate due to the lack of prior information on proposals and anchors.

CNN on Panorama Image: To make the convolution module extract features more efficiently on panorama image, deformable convolution (DeformConv) is proposed [6]. And Zhu et al. [34] further improved the deformable convolution to solve the problem of useless context regions interfering with feature extraction. While CNNs are able to learn invariance to common object transformations and intra-class variations, they require significantly more parameters, training samples, and training time to learn invariance to these distortions from the data. Meanwhile, Cohen et al. [5] proposed to use spherical CNN for classification and to encode rotational invariance into the network. However, overfitting combined with full rotation invariance reduces the discriminative power. In contrast, Benjamin et al. [4] encoded geometric distortions into convolutional neural networks, which are more compatible with existing CNN architectures and achieve better performance. And Clara et al. [12] directly improved deformable convolution and proposed equirectangular convolution (EquiConv), which is specially designed to eliminate geometric distortion under equirectangular projection. Similarly, orthographic convolution (OrthConv) [20] is designed to remove geometric distortions in orthographic projection.

Object Detection on Panorama Image: Deng et al. [8] first attempted to use existing object detection methods for object detection on panorama image. Due to the simplicity of converting a sphere into a Cartesian grid, equirectangular projection has been used as the primary sphere-to-plane projection method for projecting 360° content. However, the equirectangular projection applied to panorama image produces distortions leading to geometric deformation, which leads to different approaches to maintain performance. There are mainly two different approaches. The first approach proposes a multi-projection variant of the YOLO detector [28], which attempts to handle the geometric deformation problem with multiple stereographic projections. On this basis, Pengyu et al. [31] further optimized the parameters of multi-view projection and obtained better performance. On the other hand, the second approach optimizes the convolution layers by applying distortion-aware convolution modules, which handles the geometric deformation in the feature extraction stage [14].

Our method integrates these two main approaches, through a combination of multi-projection and distortion-aware convolution modules to deal with geometric distortions. In the stage of generating the candidate proposals of the projection area, we comprehensively use EquiConv and DeformConv for efficient feature extraction, and in the detection stage, we use a convolution module that can efficiently handle stereographic projection distortions. Moreover, in the post-processing stage, we fuse the re-projection detection results to handle the influence of the projection boundary to get the final results.

3   Method

Our goal is to design a network architecture for object detection from panorama image. Based on the trade-off of distortion reduction and efficiency improvement, we use the re-projection two-stage detector as our base network architecture. Before introducing our network, we first introduce our proposed unified distortion-aware convolution operator for general geometric distortions in Sect. 3.1. Then in Sect. 3.2, we introduce our proposed non-maximum fusion algorithm to fuse incomplete object content caused by the projection boundary. Subsequently, in Sect. 3.3, we describe the architecture of our proposed network, which combines multiple distortion-aware convolution modules in the feature extraction stage and the non-maximum fusion algorithm in the post-processing stage.

3.1   Unified Distortion-Aware Convolution

Zhu and Dai et al. [6,34] implement the convolution modules by adding additional parameters on the kernel offset, which can also be learned by the network. Therefore, the ability to learn object shape and deformation enables deformation convolution to extract features more efficiently. Although the offset parameters can be learned by training the network, they can also be calculated in advance for known geometric distortions [5,12,20]. Inspired by these works, we propose a unified distortion-aware convolution module, which can deal with all kinds of known geometric distortions.

The standard convolution sample a set of positions on the regular grid $R = \{(-1,-1),(-1,0)...,(0,1),(1,1)\}$ as the convolution kernel, for each position p_0, the operation result of the regular grid structure is assigned to the corresponding element of the output feature map f_{l+1} of the $l+1$th layer, where p_0+p_n indicates that the sampling position p_n enumerates the relative position of the pixels in the convolution region R, while the deformable convolution improves the feature extraction capability by adding an offset $\triangle p_n$ in the convolution region:

$$f_{l+1} = \sum_{p_n \in R} w(p_n) \cdot f_l(p_0 + p_n + \triangle p_n).$$ (1)

Because (θ, ϕ) is the coordinate in the spherical domain without distortion, and (x, y) is the projection plane coordinate with geometric distortion, so once we have the conversion formula between the two coordinates, which is the projection formula, we can get a deformable convolution module for the certain geometric distortion.

First, we need to calculate $(\triangle\theta, \triangle\phi)$ according to the size of the current convolutional feature layer s, and the conversion formula are represented as $xy2\theta\phi$ and $\theta\phi2xy$:

$$\triangle\theta, \triangle\phi = \frac{xy2\theta\phi(s, s) - xy2\theta\phi(0, 0)}{s}.$$ (2)

After that, we can calculate the offset of the current convolution kernel according to the position (x, y) of the convolution kernel in the feature layer:

$$\theta, \phi = xy2\theta\phi(x, y), \triangle x, \triangle y = \theta\phi2xy(\theta + \triangle\theta, \phi + \triangle\phi).$$ (3)

Finally, we can calculate the offset applied to deformable convolution, which is an offset relative to the original convolution kernel, not relative to the image domain itself, while s_f represents the size of the feature map:

$$R_{offset} = (\{(\triangle x, \triangle y)...\} - \{(x, y)...\}) * (s_f, s_f) - \{(-1, -1), ..., (1, 1)\}.$$ (4)

As shown in Fig. 1(a), we show the projection of a panorama image of the sphere onto the tangent plane. We assume that the radius of the sphere is $r = 1$, the viewpoint V is at $(1, 0, 0)$, the projection direction is towards the negative X-axis, and the center of the tangent plane is at $x = (-1, 0, 0)$. Now, the values of the point $PP(X, Y)$ on the projection tangent plane are projected from $P(\theta, \phi)$ on the sphere as:

$$\frac{d+1}{d+\cos\phi} = \frac{-X + s/2}{\sin\phi}, \frac{d+1}{d+\cos\theta} = \frac{-Y + s/2}{\sin\theta}.$$ (5)

While s represents the size of the projection plane, the original coordinates of the point $PP(X, Y)$ are $(-1, y, z)$. And Eq. 5 is the stereographic conversion formula.

We adopt the stereographic projection model which means d is constantly equal to 1. By substituting into the stereographic projection model, we can obtain stereographic convolution (SteConv), which removes the stereographic projection distortion. The comparison between the kernel sample region of Ste-Conv and standard convolution (StdConv) is shown in Fig. 1, (b) shows the sampling effect of the two convolution kernels, and (c) shows the comparison of the effects of the two kernels with different dilation and kernel size. Moreover, we substituted the equirectangular projection formula and implement a unified equirectangular convolution.

(a)   (b)   (c)

Fig. 1. Visualization of the stereographic projection model and stereographic convolution. Green - StdConv, red - SteConv. (Color figure online)

3.2 Non-maximum Fusion

In the state-of-the-art object detection pipelines, region proposals generated by convolutional neural networks replace traditional sliding windows, but multiple proposals often regress to the same region of interest. Hence, it is necessary to use non-maximum suppression (NMS) as a post-processing step to obtain the final detection as it significantly reduces the number of false positives. As an important part of the object detection pipeline, NMS first sorts all detection boxes according to their scores, and selects the detection box with the maximum score, while suppressing all other detection boxes whose overlapping score exceeds the predefined threshold. This process is recursively applied to all detection boxes.

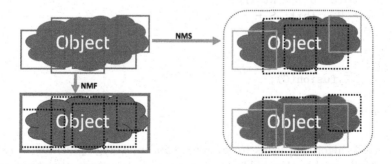

Fig. 2. Schematic illustration of NMS vs. NMF. Red - origin detect boxes, light green - NMS result, dark green - NMF result, black dotted line - boxes which be suppressed. (Color figure online)

514   M. Li et al.

The main problem of NMS is that it directly suppresses adjacent detection boxes. For the re-projection two-stage detection algorithm, there is no detection box located at the maximum value in re-projection detection boxes, while each detection box is a part of the detected object. Therefore, according to the design of the algorithm, after applying NMS to the re-projection detection box, the original complete object is detected as multiple continuous detection boxes or multiple incomplete components, which will lead to a decrease in average precision. This is because the NMS algorithm is designed to process the output value of the neural network, and only takes the local maximum value as the final detection output, and when processing the re-projection detection boxes, what we need is to associate a detection box cluster with an object. The multiple detection boxes in one cluster are fused, so as to fuse multiple incomplete parts of the object into the final detection box. While this problem can not be solved by NMS, even with some improvements to it [3,25]. We show an illustration of the problem in Fig. 2.

To this end, we propose a non-maximum fusion (NMF) algorithm, which improves the original NMS algorithm and fuses all detection boxes that have overlapping relationships with the maxima instead of direct suppression. The steps of the NNF algorithm are described as follows:

```
program non_max_fusion (B={b1, ... b_n}, S={S1, ... Sn}, Nt)
    {
        B is the list of initial detection boxes.
        S contains corresponding detection scores.
        Nt is the NMF threshold.
    };
begin:
    F ← {};
    while B is not empty do:
        m ← argmax S;
        C ← {bm};
        B ← B - C;
        for bi in B do:
            if iou(C, bi) > Nt then:
                B ← B - {bi}; S ← S - {si};
                C ← C U {bi};
            end
        end
        F ← F U fusion(C);
    end
    return F, S;
end.
```

The NNF algorithm leads to improvements in average precision measured over multiple overlap thresholds for re-projection two-stage object detectors. Since the NMF algorithm does not require any additional training and is simple to implement, it can be easily integrated into the object detection pipeline.

3.3   Re-projection Fusion Network Architecture

In the detection step, it is a common consensus that two-stage detectors can achieve higher accuracy. The first stage is the multi-view projection region proposal network (MVP-RPN), which can efficiently generate proposals on equirectangular projection images, and the second stage is the stereographic convolutional detector (SteNet), which can accurately refine proposals based on stereographic projection images. Projection region of interest align (PRoI-Align) is additionally introduced to bridge the multi-view projection region proposal network and the stereographic convolutional detector, by transforming proposals into projection field of view to obtain fixed-size stereographic projection images as input to SteNet. In the post-processing step. The detection boxes are first pre-processed using re-projection, and then non-maximum fusion is used to obtain the final detection. The overall architecture of RepF-Net is shown in Fig. 3.

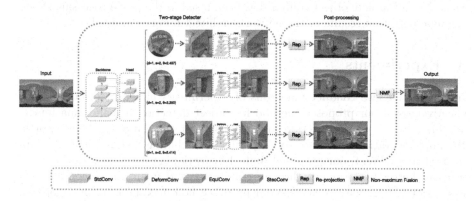

Fig. 3. This figure visualizes the two-stage network and post-processing architecture of RepF-Net.

MVP-RPN: Given a panorama image, MVP-RPN generates the objectness score for each candidate region proposal from its equirectangular projection representation. Different from ordinary RPN [24], in order to handle the geometric distortion brought by equirectangular projection, MVP-RPN comprehensively applies deformable convolution and equirectangular convolution in the backbone network to efficiently extract a distortion-aware feature map. Finally, MVP-RPN generates the position of the selected region proposal as the input for the next stage.

PRoI-Align: Given the region proposals generated by MVP-RPN, PRoI-Align converts the location information of region proposals into three-dimensional FOV parameters (d, s, θ), where d represents the distance of the projection plane from the sphere center, which is inversely proportional to region proposal size, s represents the size of the projection plane, which is directly proportional to region proposal size, θ represents the rotation angle of the projection plane relative to the sphere plane, which constitutes a one-to-one mapping relationship from the horizontal position of the region proposals. The three-dimensional FOV parameters can be substituted into the stereographic projection formula to obtain fixed-size stereographic projection images as the input of the next stage.

SteNet: Given the fixed-size stereographic projection images generated by PRoI-Align, SteNet applies another detection network to further localize region proposals. The same as MVP-RPN, SteNet comprehensively applies deformable convolution and stereographic convolution in the backbone network to efficiently extract a distortion-aware feature map, and offset the geometric distortion brought by stereographic projection. In the end, SteNet refines the detection box of the selected region proposal as the input for the next stage.

Post-processing: In the first step, the post-processing stage re-projects the detection box onto the equirectangular image as the input for the next stage. Non-maximum fusion is then applied to reduce the number of false positives. Since the incomplete object content has been fused in the post-processing stage, the final detection results of the network architecture are obtained.

4 Experiments

In this section, we conduct numerous of experiments aimed at evaluating the effectiveness of our proposed method for object detection in panorama image. We first describe our collection and extension of the datasets. Then explain the implementation details of the experiment, including training and development strategy. Next, our proposed unified distortion-aware convolution module achieves better performance through qualitative and quantitative comparative evaluation. After that, we verified our proposed non-maximum fusion algorithm through ablation experiments, which can achieve better performance in the post-processing stage. Finally, we compare our method with other state-of-the-art methods of object detection in panorama image and find that our method can outperform them.

4.1 Dataset

Collecting high-quality datasets with a sufficient number of images and the corresponding object detection groundtruth is critical for training complex models. However existing equirectangular projection image datasets, including Sun360 [27], PanoContext [30], SunCG [26], Stanford2D3D [1], and Structured3D [33], all lack standard object detection annotations. We define a dataset annotation protocol for object detection through protobuf, and according to the protocol converting equirectangular projection image annotation from the above datasets [1, 26, 27, 30, 33]. Simultaneously, we use the projection parameters $\{d = 1; s = 2, 3; \triangle\theta = 0, \frac{\pi}{24}, \frac{\pi}{12}, \ldots, 2\pi\}$ in the stereographic conversion formula to convert stereographic projection image annotation. We also made corrections for low-quality images in the original dataset, as well as wrong object annotations. Finally, the dataset we constructed contains 3423 equirectangular category annotations and 69760 stereographic category annotations. With the definition of the protocol, our dataset can be conveniently applied to various experiments and tasks. The split strategy of train/validation/test for the dataset is similar to [14], the dataset is divided into 85% for train and validation and 15% for test.

4.2 Implementation Details

Training Strategy: We implement our method using PyTorch and CUDA 11.6, and test it on two NVIDIA Titan X GPUs. All input RGB images are 640×640. Based on Yolov5 pre-training, we employ AdamW optimizer [19] to train the network for 500 epochs with a batch size of 8. Moreover, we use clustering of dataset annotation to generate anchors, while using Mosaic as data augmentation strategy [2].

Development Strategy: In order to reduce the time and memory requirement for the calculation of projection matrix and convolution offset matrix, we use the serialized MD5 value of the parameter as the cache key, and store the serialized calculated value in memory and file system. Moreover, we define protobuf for major APIs such as dataset processing, projection and detection, and communication between network architecture via gRPC.

4.3 Results of Unified Distortion-Aware Convolution

Performance Analysis of SteConv: A quantitative comparison of the object detection effect between our proposed SteConv, which is implemented through our proposed unified distortion-aware convolution module, and other convolutions modules is summarized in Table 1. DeformConv achieves better performance than StdConv because the added offset parameter can extract features more efficiently. On the other hand, the pre-defined offset parameters for geometric deformation in SteConv are more efficient than the parameters learned by the network, thus obtaining better performance than DeformConv.

Table 1. Comparison experiments of different kinds of convolution modules. The bold-face denotes the best performance in this experiment.

Model	mAP	Bed	Painting	TV	Sofa	Curtain	Table	Bedside
StdConv	78.7	88.1	87.5	86.8	79.3	77.6	71.0	74.7
DeformConv	78.9	86.0	87.0	**89.0**	**81.2**	**78.4**	70.4	74.7
SteConv	**79.8**	**90.0**	**88.8**	87.2	80.6	77.5	**72.0**	**76.8**

Ablation Study of SteConv: We experiment with the effect of the position and number of applying SteConv and DeformConv on detection accuracy. As shown in Fig. 4, layer1–5 represents the position of SteConv in backbone, and layer1–5+ represents the number of SteConv layers. Through the comparison experiment in (a), we can get that the main factors affecting the performance of SteConv are the size of the convolution layer and the richness of features. With the movement of the position, applying SteConv or DeformConv to the backbone layer closest to the detection head, accuracy reaches the best performance. We conclude that this is because more abstract convolution features can handle distortion better than larger feature layers, thus the final optimal effect is located in the last layer of the backbone. From the comparison experiments in (b), we can see that the accuracy continues to improve as we continue to replace layers with DeformConv. However, replacing more SteConv layers did not improve accuracy. We conclude this is because the SteConv pre-calculated from the geometric deformation formula is theoretically the upper limit of deformation that DeformConv can handle, while more SteConv stacking will bring anti-stereographic distortion.

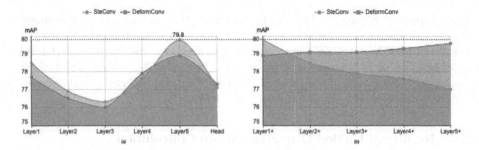

Fig. 4. The figure shows line charts of the position and number of SteConv and Deform-Conv layers and mAPs. In (a) layer1–5 means the layer position, in (b) layer1–5+ means the number of layers.

4.4   Results of Non-maximum Fusion

Quantitative Results: We conduct comparison experiments for the application of the non-maximum fusion algorithm in the post-processing stage of our proposed RepF-Net. From the analysis of our experimental results in Table 2, the non-maximum fusion algorithm fuse the detection boxes from multiple projection images, thus the addition of the non-maximum fusion algorithm further improves the detection accuracy especially when detecting large objects. Based on its effectiveness in handling detection box for both small and large objects, the non-maximum fusion algorithm achieves better performance than the non-maximum suppression algorithm.

Table 2. Quantitative results of RepF-Net, with or without NMF in post-processing stage. The boldface denotes the best performance in this experiment.

Model	mAP	TV	Painting	Bed	Curtain	Window	Bedside	Mirror
w/o. NMF	80.5	93.3	**93.1**	80.6	62.4	80.9	**80.4**	73.3
w. NMF	**84.2**	**95.5**	87.6	**87.0**	**79.2**	**81.0**	79.9	**79.2**

Qualitative Results: We show the qualitative results of the comparison between our proposed NMF and NMS in Fig. 5. NMS can achieve good results when detecting objects that can be completely detected in a single projection image, such as (a) in Fig. 5. However, when detecting objects that require the fusion of multiple projection images, it is inevitable that objects will be detected as multiple continuous detection boxes, such as (b) in Fig. 5, or only detect certain components of the object, such as (c) in Fig. 5. In contrast, our proposed NMF outperforms NMS in the above cases.

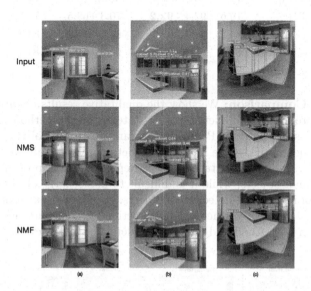

Fig. 5. Qualitative results of the comparison between the non-maximum suppression algorithm and the non-maximum fusion algorithm.

4.5 Comparison with the State-of-the-Art Methods

Comparison Experiment: We compare RepF-Net with baseline methods of object detection in panorama image and the results are given in Table 3. Rep-CNN as a two-stage detector achieves the best performance among the baseline methods due to the projection greatly reduced geometric distortion, and PanoBlitzNet as a one-stage detector also achieves good detection accuracy due to the introduction of the EquiConv. Finally, our RepF-Net combines the advantages of both methods and achieves better performance than the SoTA. Moreover, in RepF-Net+ we apply DeformConv in the backbone of our proposed RepF-Net to replace the convolution layout except for the SteConv layer. And it can be concluded that, on the basis of handling the geometric distortion by Ste-Conv, DeformConv can more efficiently extract features, therefore better generalize the geometric shape of the object and finally achieve the best performance.

Table 3. Performance comparison between baseline methods and RepF-Net. RepF-Net+ represents applying DeformConv on the basis of RepF-Net. The boldface denotes the best performance in this experiment.

Model	mAP	TV	Painting	Bed	Curtain	Window	Bedside
DPM [11]	29.4	31.0	56.0	35.2	29.5	21.8	–
Deng et al. [8]	68.7	70.0	68.0	76.3	69.5	62.6	–
Multi-Project Yolo [28]	69.4	87.5	80.7	17.2	73.4	76.9	78.2
PanoBlitzNet [14]	77.8	93.3	83.9	**95.3**	75.9	70.9	**91.4**
Rep-RCNN [31]	79.6	92.4	**92.2**	70.3	69.5	75.0	83.2
RepF-Net (w. NMF)	84.2	95.5	87.6	87.0	79.2	**81.0**	79.9
RepF-Net+	**86.0**	**95.5**	89.4	90.5	**79.4**	**81.0**	79.9

Qualitative Comparison: We show the qualitative results of the comparison between our proposed RepF-Net and other state-of-the-art methods. As shown in Fig. 6, the one-stage detector PanoBlitzNet can detect large objects and handle incomplete objects well, while has difficult detecting all small objects and has lower accuracy. And the two-stage detector Rep-CNN can improve the detection accuracy of small objects, while it is difficult to detect large objects, and there is a problem of incomplete detection of objects. In contrast, our proposed RepF-Net solves the problem of incomplete detection objects, and achieves better performance in both small and large object detection accuracy.

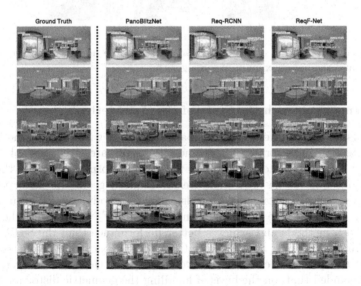

Fig. 6. Qualitative comparison of different object detection methods on panorama image.

5   Applications

On indoor scene understanding tasks, because of the richer contextual information encoded by the larger field of view, using panorama image can achieve
better performance than using perspective images. In the task of indoor scene
understanding, there are two main steps, object detection and layout recovery
[29]. While many methods achieve good performance in layout recovery [35],
there is still space for improvement in object detection. Based on our proposed
RepF-Net, we present an implementation of indoor scene understanding. And
the qualitative results of 3D object detection and scene layout reconstruction on
three datasets are shown in Fig. 7.

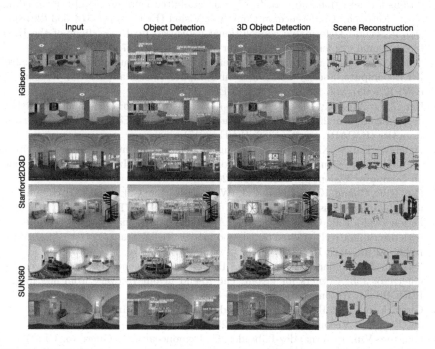

Fig. 7. Qualitative results of 3D object detection and scene layout reconstruction.

6   Conclusion

This paper presents a novel two-stage detection network, RepF-Net for object
detection in panorama image, while including a unified distortion-aware convolution module for geometric distortions, and a non-maximum fusion algorithm for
post-processing. Experiments validate the effectiveness of each module in our
method, and show that our network performs better performance than other
state-of-the-art object detectors. In addition, our network model has also been
applied to tasks of 3D object detection and scene reconstruction.

References

1. Armeni, I., Sax, S., Zamir, A.R., Savarese, S.: Joint 2D–3D-semantic data for indoor scene understanding. arXiv preprint arXiv:1702.01105 (2017)
2. Bochkovskiy, A., Wang, C.Y., Liao, H.Y.M.: Yolov4: optimal speed and accuracy of object detection. arXiv preprint arXiv:2004.10934 (2020)
3. Bodla, N., Singh, B., Chellappa, R., Davis, L.S.: Soft-NMS–improving object detection with one line of code. In: Proceedings of the IEEE International Conference on Computer Vision, pp. 5561–5569 (2017)
4. Cohen, T.S., Geiger, M., Köhler, J., Welling, M.: Spherical CNNs. arXiv preprint arXiv:1801.10130 (2018)
5. Coors, B., Condurache, A.P., Geiger, A.: SphereNet: learning spherical representations for detection and classification in omnidirectional images. In: Proceedings of the European Conference on Computer Vision (ECCV), pp. 518–533 (2018)
6. Dai, J., et al.: Deformable convolutional networks. In: Proceedings of the IEEE International Conference on Computer Vision, pp. 764–773 (2017)
7. Dalal, N., Triggs, B.: Histograms of oriented gradients for human detection. In: 2005 IEEE Computer Society Conference on Computer Vision and Pattern Recognition (CVPR 2005), vol. 1, pp. 886–893. IEEE (2005)
8. Deng, F., Zhu, X., Ren, J.: Object detection on panoramic images based on deep learning. In: 2017 3rd International Conference on Control, Automation and Robotics (ICCAR), pp. 375–380. IEEE (2017)
9. Duan, K., Bai, S., Xie, L., Qi, H., Huang, Q., Tian, Q.: CenterNet: keypoint triplets for object detection. In: Proceedings of the IEEE/CVF International Conference on Computer Vision, pp. 6569–6578 (2019)
10. Fan, R.E., Chang, K.W., Hsieh, C.J., Wang, X.R., Lin, C.J.: LIBLINEAR: a library for large linear classification. J. Mach. Learn. Res. **9**, 1871–1874 (2008)
11. Felzenszwalb, P.F., Girshick, R.B., McAllester, D., Ramanan, D.: Object detection with discriminatively trained part-based models. IEEE Trans. Pattern Anal. Mach. Intell. **32**(9), 1627–1645 (2010)
12. Fernandez-Labrador, C., Facil, J.M., Perez-Yus, A., Demonceaux, C., Civera, J., Guerrero, J.J.: Corners for layout: end-to-end layout recovery from 360 images. IEEE Robot. Autom. Lett. **5**(2), 1255–1262 (2020)
13. Girshick, R.: Fast R-CNN. In: Proceedings of the IEEE International Conference on Computer Vision, pp. 1440–1448 (2015)
14. Guerrero-Viu, J., Fernandez-Labrador, C., Demonceaux, C., Guerrero, J.J.: What's in my room? Object recognition on indoor panoramic images. In: 2020 IEEE International Conference on Robotics and Automation (ICRA), pp. 567–573. IEEE (2020)
15. He, K., Gkioxari, G., Dollár, P., Girshick, R.: Mask R-CNN. In: Proceedings of the IEEE International Conference on Computer Vision, pp. 2961–2969 (2017)
16. Law, H., Deng, J.: CornerNet: detecting objects as paired keypoints. In: Proceedings of the European Conference on Computer Vision (ECCV), pp. 734–750 (2018)
17. Lienhart, R., Maydt, J.: An extended set of Haar-like features for rapid object detection. In: Proceedings. International Conference on Image Processing, vol. 1, p. I. IEEE (2002)
18. Liu, W., et al.: SSD: single shot multibox detector. In: Leibe, B., Matas, J., Sebe, N., Welling, M. (eds.) ECCV 2016. LNCS, vol. 9905, pp. 21–37. Springer, Cham (2016). https://doi.org/10.1007/978-3-319-46448-0_2
19. Loshchilov, I., Hutter, F.: Fixing weight decay regularization in Adam (2018)

20. Meng, M., Xiao, L., Zhou, Y., Li, Z., Zhou, Z.: Distortion-aware room layout estimation from a single fisheye image. In: 2021 IEEE International Symposium on Mixed and Augmented Reality (ISMAR), pp. 441–449. IEEE (2021)
21. Redmon, J., Divvala, S., Girshick, R., Farhadi, A.: You only look once: unified, real-time object detection. In: Proceedings of the IEEE Conference on Computer Vision and Pattern Recognition, pp. 779–788 (2016)
22. Redmon, J., Farhadi, A.: Yolo9000: better, faster, stronger. In: Proceedings of the IEEE Conference on Computer Vision and Pattern Recognition, pp. 7263–7271 (2017)
23. Redmon, J., Farhadi, A.: Yolov3: an incremental improvement. arXiv preprint arXiv:1804.02767 (2018)
24. Ren, S., He, K., Girshick, R., Sun, J.: Faster R-CNN: towards real-time object detection with region proposal networks. Adv. Neural Inf. Process. Syst. **28** (2015)
25. Solovyev, R., Wang, W., Gabruseva, T.: Weighted boxes fusion: ensembling boxes from different object detection models. Image Vis. Comput. **107**, 104117 (2021)
26. Song, S., Yu, F., Zeng, A., Chang, A.X., Savva, M., Funkhouser, T.: Semantic scene completion from a single depth image. In: Proceedings of the IEEE Conference on Computer Vision and Pattern Recognition, pp. 1746–1754 (2017)
27. Xiao, J., Ehinger, K.A., Oliva, A., Torralba, A.: Recognizing scene viewpoint using panoramic place representation. In: 2012 IEEE Conference on Computer Vision and Pattern Recognition, pp. 2695–2702. IEEE (2012)
28. Yang, W., Qian, Y., Kämäräinen, J.K., Cricri, F., Fan, L.: Object detection in equirectangular panorama. In: 2018 24th International Conference on Pattern Recognition (ICPR), pp. 2190–2195. IEEE (2018)
29. Zhang, C., et al.: DeepPanoContext: panoramic 3D scene understanding with holistic scene context graph and relation-based optimization. In: Proceedings of the IEEE/CVF International Conference on Computer Vision, pp. 12632–12641 (2021)
30. Zhang, Y., Song, S., Tan, P., Xiao, J.: PanoContext: a whole-room 3D context model for panoramic scene understanding. In: Fleet, D., Pajdla, T., Schiele, B., Tuytelaars, T. (eds.) ECCV 2014. LNCS, vol. 8694, pp. 668–686. Springer, Cham (2014). https://doi.org/10.1007/978-3-319-10599-4_43
31. Zhao, P., You, A., Zhang, Y., Liu, J., Bian, K., Tong, Y.: Spherical criteria for fast and accurate 360 object detection. In: Proceedings of the AAAI Conference on Artificial Intelligence, vol. 34, pp. 12959–12966 (2020)
32. Zhao, Z.Q., Zheng, P., Xu, S.T., Wu, X.: Object detection with deep learning: a review. IEEE Trans. Neural Netw. Learn. Syst. **30**(11), 3212–3232 (2019)
33. Zheng, J., Zhang, J., Li, J., Tang, R., Gao, S., Zhou, Z.: Structured3D: a large photo-realistic dataset for structured 3D modeling. In: Vedaldi, A., Bischof, H., Brox, T., Frahm, J.-M. (eds.) ECCV 2020. LNCS, vol. 12354, pp. 519–535. Springer, Cham (2020). https://doi.org/10.1007/978-3-030-58545-7_30
34. Zhu, X., Hu, H., Lin, S., Dai, J.: Deformable ConvNets V2: more deformable, better results. In: Proceedings of the IEEE/CVF Conference on Computer Vision and Pattern Recognition, pp. 9308–9316 (2019)
35. Zou, C., et al.: Manhattan room layout reconstruction from a single 360° image: a comparative study of state-of-the-art methods. Int. J. Comput. Vis. **129**(5), 1410–1431 (2021). https://doi.org/10.1007/s11263-020-01426-8

Vision Transformer Compression and Architecture Exploration with Efficient Embedding Space Search

Daeho Kim[1] and Jaeil Kim[2]([✉])

[1] Department of Artificial Intelligence, Kyungpook National University,
Daegu, South Korea
[2] School of Computer Science and Engineering, Kyungpook National University,
Daegu, South Korea
threeyears@gmail.com

Abstract. This paper addresses theoretical and practical problems in the compression of vision transformers for resource-constrained environments. We found that *deep feature collapse* and *gradient collapse* can occur during the search process for the vision transformer compression. *Deep feature collapse* diminishes feature diversity rapidly as the layer depth deepens, and *gradient collapse* causes gradient explosion in training. Against these issues, we propose a novel framework, called VTCA, for accomplishing vision transformer compression and architecture exploration jointly with embedding space search using Bayesian optimization. In this framework, we formulate block-wise removal, shrinkage, cross-block skip augmentation to prevent *deep feature collapse*, and Res-Post layer normalization to prevent *gradient collapse* under a knowledge distillation loss. In the search phase, we adopt a training speed estimation for a large-scale dataset and propose a novel elastic reward function that can represent a generalized manifold of rewards. Experiments were conducted with DeiT-Tiny/Small/Base backbones on the ImageNet, and our approach achieved competitive accuracy to recent patch reduction and pruning methods. The code is available at https://github.com/kdaeho27/VTCA.

1 Introduction

Vision transformers have recently shown superior performance in learning long-range dependency property of sequential data and have attracted attention in various computer vision tasks. Modern architectures based on the transformer concept, such as ViT [10] and DeiT [28], are capable of learning significant visual representations from images and outperform traditional convolutional neural networks (CNNs) [13,16,17].

Despite the availability of vision transformers, such architectures have been demonstrated to be even more resource-intensive than CNNs and have deployment limitations in a resource-limited environment [35]. Due to the significant

---

Supplementary Information The online version contains supplementary material available at https://doi.org/10.1007/978-3-031-26313-2_32.

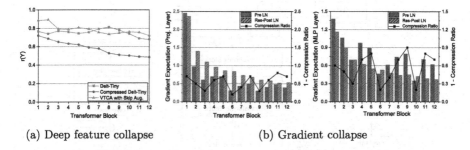

(a) Deep feature collapse   (b) Gradient collapse

Fig. 1. (a) Deep feature collapse and (b) gradient collapse occurred during search process for compression.

structural differences between CNNs and ViT, using successful CNN compression methods [14,15,18] for ViT is problematic. Previous studies for the transformer compression include pruning [7,35,36], neural architecture search (NAS) [6], and patch reduction [22,23,25]. Most studies compress the number of heads, the hidden dimensions of the multi-layer perceptron (MLP) layers, and dropping blocks.

However, we found that *deep feature collapse* and *gradient collapse* occur during the compression process, as shown in Fig. 1. *Deep feature collapse* denotes rapidly diminishing feature diversity as the transformer block deepens. This phenomenon occurs as the number of heads is compressed. As shown in Fig. 1a, the feature diversity $r(Y)$ decreases rapidly with compression of the number of heads of DeiT-Tiny. *Gradient collapse* refers to changes in the scale of the gradient as the compression rate changes. Figure 1b shows the gradient expectation of hidden dimensions in MLP and QKV dimensions in self-attention modules. With a Pre-LN transformer, the gradient scale changes according to the compression rate, which causes gradient exploding during training.

To prevent the collapse problems, this paper aims to establish compression and architectural search jointly. We call this <u>V</u>ision <u>T</u>ransformer <u>C</u>ompression and <u>A</u>rchitecture exploration (VTCA). Figure 2 illustrates the overall structure of VTCA: it compresses hidden dimensions in the MLP as well as the number of heads in the self-attention module, and searches the architecture to add cross-block skip augmentation and layer normalization under knowledge distillation. To search for the optimized architecture, we propose a novel search process based on Bayesian optimization (BO) for vision transformer compression, as shown in Fig. 3.

Our main contributions are as follows:

1. We formulate *deep feature collapse* and *gradient collapse* as problems occurring during the compression process for the vision transformer. To alleviate these problems, we propose a new framework based on BO, called VTCA, that integrates compression and architecture search.

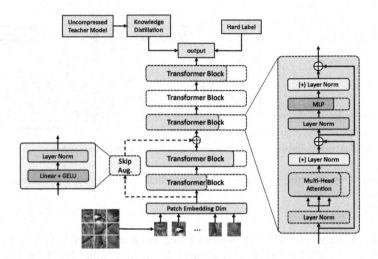

Fig. 2. The overall structure of VTCA, integrating compression and architecture exploration strategies: (1) **block-wise removal and shrinkage** — we compress self-attention head numbers, hidden dimension of MLP module, and blocks; (2) **cross-block skip augmentation**; (3) **addition of Res-Post layer normalization**; under knowledge distillation. For more details on the search space, see Sect. 3.3.

2. For efficient space search, we propose a normalized cross-entropy score (NCE score) with training speed estimation to define as a reward.
3. We propose an elastic reward function including compression rate and NCE score to evaluate compressed architectures. The reward function is represented as generalizing both naive and N2N (Network to Network) [1] reward functions, and it can control a trade-off between compression rate and accuracy.
4. Experiments are conducted with popular variants of ViT on ImageNet; our method performs better than or comparably with existing methods.

2   Preliminaries and Motivation

2.1   Vision Transformer

Follwing the success of transformer architectures in natural language processing (NLP) tasks [8,29], recent approaches such as ViT [10] and DeiT [28], have been introduced for computer vision tasks. The ViT block consists of a multi-head self-attention (MSA) and MLP modules with layer normalization [3] placed in front of each module. An input image is split into N patches and each patch is projected into a d-dimensional vector. Given the feature $Y_l \in \mathbb{R}^{N \times d}$ in l-th layer, the MSA module can be defined as:

$$\text{MSA}(Y_l) = \text{Concat}([A_{lh}Y_lW_{lh}^v]_{h=1}^{H_l})W_l^o \tag{1}$$

$$A_{lh} = \text{Softmax}\left(\frac{(Y_lW_{lh}^q)(Y_lW_{lh}^k)^T}{\sqrt{d_h}}\right) \tag{2}$$

where $A_{lh} \in \mathbb{R}^{N \times N}$ is self-attention map, $W_{lh}^v \in \mathbb{R}^{d \times (d/H)}$ is projection matrix in the h-th head, $W_l^o \in \mathbb{R}^{d \times d}$ is the output projection matrix. $W_{lh}^q \in \mathbb{R}^{d \times (d/H)}$ and $W_{lh}^k \in \mathbb{R}^{d \times (d/H)}$ are the query and value projection matrices, respectively.

The MLP module consists of two linear projections and extracts features from each patch independently. Given the MLP input feature $Z_l \in \mathbb{R}^{N \times d}$, the MLP can be defined:

$$\text{MLP}(Z_l) = \sigma(Z_lW^{1,l} + b^{1,l})W^{2,l} + b^{2,l} \tag{3}$$

where $W^{1,l} \in \mathbb{R}^{d \times d_m}$ and $W^{2,l} \in \mathbb{R}^{d_m \times d}$ are weights in the MLP module and σ is the non-linear activation function. The MLP and MSA modules are alternately stacked to construct a vision transformer model.

Most studies have focused on compressing or pruning the number of heads and the hidden dimension of MLP [6,33,35] at each block. We found that *deep feature collapse*, in which feature diversity diminish rapidly as the transformer block deepens, and *gradient collapse*, in which gradient expectation changes depending on the compression rate, occurred during compression.

2.2 Deep Feature Collapse

Feature collapse is defined as the occurrence of hard to distinguish features among patches in a layer as the block depth increases [9,26]. To distinguish from the *feature collapse* that occurs in vision transformers, we define *deep feature collapse* as occurring while compressing the number of heads H_l as the transformer block deepens.

Given an output feature Y_l in the l-th layer, feature diversity is measured as the difference between the features and the rank-1 matrix [9]:

$$r(Y_l) = \|Y_l - \mathbf{1}y_l^T\|, \text{ where } y_l^T = \text{argmin}_{y_l'}\|Y_l - \mathbf{1}y_l^T\| \tag{4}$$

where $\|\cdot\|$ is an ℓ_1, ℓ_∞-composite norm. The feature diversity $r(Y_l)$ of the architecture in which the number of heads is compressed decreases rapidly as the block deepens, as defined by the following theorem established in [9].

Theorem 1. *Given a transformer model in which the MSA and MLP modules are stacked, the feature diversity $r(Y_l)$ in the l-th layer is bound by that of input Y_0, i.e.,*

$$r(Y_l) \downarrow \leq \left(\frac{4H_l \downarrow \gamma\lambda'}{\sqrt{d}}\right)^{\frac{3^l-1}{2}} r(Y_0)^{3^l} \tag{5}$$

where H_l is the number of heads in the l-th layer, γ is a constant related to the weight norms, λ' is the Lipschitz constant of MLP and d is the feature dimension.

Because the $H_l \gamma \lambda' / \sqrt{d}$ are smaller than 1, feature diversity $r(Y_l)$ is decreasing as block depth l increases [9]. Furthermore, when the number of heads H_l in the l-th layer is compressed, the feature diversity is drastically reduced as shown in Fig. 1a. We call this *deep feature collapse*. To alleviate this problem, we propose a cross-block skip augmentation.

2.3   Gradient Collapse

The MSA and MLP modules contain linear layers, and projection dimensions such as QKV and MLP dimension are generally compressed. We found that the gradient scale became unstable with different compression rates for each transformer block, causing gradient explosion during training. We call this *gradient collapse*. The cause of this phenomenon is shown in the following theorem, established in [32].

Theorem 2. *Given a Pre-LN transformer with L layers assuming an output feature $\|Y_L\|_2^2$ are (ϵ, δ)-bounded and a hidden dimension d_m is same as a feature dimension d, the gradient of the weights of the last layer with probaility at least $0.99 - \delta - \frac{\epsilon}{0.9+\epsilon}$ is bounded by dimension d_m, i.e.,*

$$\|\frac{\partial \mathcal{L}}{\partial W^{2,L}}\|_F \leq O(d_m \sqrt{\frac{\ln d_m}{L}})$$

where L denotes number of blocks, and ϵ and $\delta = exp(-d\epsilon^2/8)$ are small numbers.

From Theorem 2, we can see that the scale of the Pre-LN transformer gradient is proportional to the dimension d_m being compressed. To alleviate this problem, we propose inserting additional layer normalization after the MSA and MLP layers. The approach, called Res-Post-LN, has been introduced [34] but has not been proven theoretically for effectiveness. Figure 1b shows that the gradient scale of Pre-LN becomes unstable with the compression rate. The instability of the gradient scale for each block causes gradient exploding. However, the gradient scale of Res-Post-LN is stable in each block. We demonstrate how Res-Post-LN prevents *gradient collapse* in Sect. 3.3.

3   Proposed Method

In this section, we introduce a search framework for exploring optimal architecture via the proposed BO process. The architecture domain is highly complex, and searching compression and architecture jointly is a high-dimensional problem that makes optimization procedures difficult to realize. To solve this issue, we

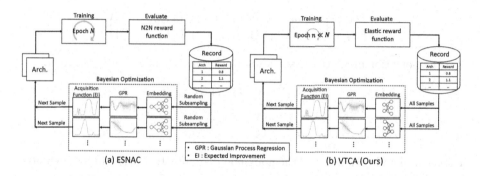

Fig. 3. Comparison of BO-based (a) ESNAC and (b) VTCA search process.

propose our VTCA to extend ESNAC [5] which achieves compression for CNN in the embedding space. ESNAC can only be used with CNN and is difficult to apply to a large-scale dataset because of its high search cost. We adopt training speed estimation for a large-scale dataset and propose a novel elastic reward function that can represent a generalized manifold of rewards including naive and N2N rewards [1]. We compare the loops of ESNAC and VTCA in Fig. 3.

3.1   Search Process with BO

The goal of the proposed method is to search a student transformer based on a given teacher network, maximizing the compression rate of weight parameters while still obtaining performance comparable to the teacher network. Formally, we aim to solve the following optimization problem:

$$x = \operatorname*{argmin}_{x \in \mathcal{X}} f(x), \tag{6}$$

where $\mathcal{X}$ denotes the domain of transformer architectures and the function $f(x) : \mathcal{X} \mapsto \mathbb{R}$ evaluates a reward for how well our criterion is satisfied. Instead of an N2N reward [1], we propose an elastic reward function that controls the compression rate-performance trade-off.

The problem becomes hard to tackle because there is no certain form of f, a consequence of the complex relationship between compressed architecture and the corresponding reward. We adopt a BO approach, which is promising for optimizing expensive black-box functions. During the BO process, we denote the sampled architecture in the t-th round as $x_{1:t}$. The evaluated architectures for times 1 through t are denoted as $x_{1:t}$. The samples can be modeled as Gaussian processes (GP) and can be defined as follows:

$$f(x_{1:t}) \sim \mathcal{N}(\mu(x_{1:t}), \mathcal{K}(x_{1:t}, x_{1:t})) \tag{7}$$

where μ is the mean function; and $\mathcal{K}(x_{1:t}, x_{1:t})$ is the variance matrix. Then, the joint distribution of the preceding evaluated architectures $f(x_{1:t})$ and the next compressed architecture $f(x_{t+1})$ can be represented by

$$\begin{bmatrix} f(x_{1:t}) \\ f(x_{t+1}) \end{bmatrix} \sim \left(\begin{matrix} \mu(x_{1:t}) \\ \mu(x_{t+1}), \end{matrix} \begin{bmatrix} \mathcal{K}(x_{1:t}, x_{1:t}), & \mathbf{k}(x_{1:t}, x_{t+1}) \\ \mathbf{k}(x_{t+1}, x_{1:t}), & k(x_{t+1}, x_{t+1}) \end{bmatrix} \right) \tag{8}$$

and the posterior predictive distibution of the next sample can be given by

$$f(x_{t+1}) \sim \mathcal{N}(\mu(x_{t+1}), \sigma(x_{t+1}))$$
$$\mu(x_{t+1}) = \mathbf{k}(x_{t+1}, x_{1:t})\mathcal{K}(x_{1:t}, x_{1:t})^{-1} f(x_{1:t}) \tag{9}$$
$$\sigma(x_{t+1}) = k(x_{t+1}, x_{t+1}) - \mathbf{k}(x_{t+1}, x_{1:t})\mathcal{K}(x_{1:t}, x_{1:t})\mathbf{k}(x_{1:t}, x_{t+1})$$

The mean μ and variance σ of the unexplored architecture x_{t+1} can be calculated via the historic architectures.

We obtain the next architecture x_{t+1} using the expected improvement (EI) acquisition function [4,21]. The EI recommends a next sample that is most likely to maximize the objective function over current evaluated architectures:

$$\text{EI}_t(x) = \mathbb{E}_t(\max(f(x) - f^*(x), 0)) \tag{10}$$

where $\mathbb{E}_t$ denotes the expectation over the posterior distribution at step t and $f^*(x)$ is the maximum value among evaluated architectures $f(x_t)$. The above algorithm is repeated up to a predefined step, and the architecture yielding the maximum value is returned.

3.2   Latent Embedding Space Search

The search space required to explore compression and architecture search jointly is very high-dimensional. High-dimensional BO suffers from drawbacks due to the curse of dimensionality. To address this issue, we adopt an architecture embedding function $h(\cdot; \theta)$ to map the compressed architecture to the embedding space according to the configuration parameters [5]. Here, θ represents the weight parameters for learning in the embedding function. We define the kernel function $k(x, x'; \theta)$ using an radial basis function (RBF) kernel:

$$k(x, x'; \theta) = \exp\left(-\frac{\|h(x; \theta) - h(x'; \theta)\|^2}{2\sigma^2} \right) \tag{11}$$

where σ is a hyperparameter and $h(\cdot, \theta)$ represents an embedding space for the high-dimensional architecture configuration. The functions $h(\cdot, \theta)$ and $k(x, x'; \theta)$ share the same weights θ. In what follows, we present the embedding function $h(\cdot, \theta)$ and describe how θ is learned during the search process.

The architecture embedding function $h(\cdot, \theta)$ needs to represent diverse compressed transformers adequately. In addition, it needs to be flexible enough to represent the inter- and intra-blocks relationships in the order of the transformer blocks. Therefore, we adopt a structured block correlation with two Bi-directional LSTMs motivated by [30]. One Bi-LSTM learns the relationships among the intra-block configuration information, the other Bi-LSTM among the inter-block configuration information. After passing the Bi-LSTMs, we concatenate all the hidden states, applying L2 normalization to these states to obtain the embedding vector.

During the search stage, the weights θ are determined. The weights are trained to minimize the negative log posterior probability:

$$\mathcal{L}(\theta) = -\frac{1}{|D|} \sum_{i:x_i \in D} \log p(f(x_i)|f(D\backslash x_i); \theta) \tag{12}$$

where $\backslash$ denotes relative complement; and $f(D\backslash x_i) = [f(x_1), \ldots, f(x_{i-1}), f(x_{i+1}), \ldots, f(x_t)]$. Based on $k(\cdot, \cdot; \theta)$, the mean and covariance matrix of $p(f(x_i)|f(D\backslash x_i); \theta)$, which is a Gaussian distribution, can be calculated analytically [5].

Multiple Kernel and Dimension Strategy. We adopt a multiple kernel strategy with diverse hidden dimensions per kernel. ESNAC trains a single model with different subsets of D instead of the entire evaluated architectures to avoid overfitting. The subset approach is helpful for small-scale datasets; however, a vision transformer that learns large-scale datasets is often unsuitable for evaluating architectures because of the large computation cost. Therefore, we determine the different dimensions of hidden states in the embedding function per kernel, allowing us to explore diverse architectures.

Training Speed Estimation. We employ training speed estimation (TSE) [24] because the full training of each architecture of the vision transformer is expensive. Some studies have shown a correlation between training speed and generalization performance [12,19,24]. TSE estimates generalization performance with far fewer epochs n than the full number of epochs N. However, we define a reward that considers the compression rate with the TSE for architecture compression. To define this reward, the TSE needs to be expressed as an upper bound score, such as a compression rate between 0 and 1, regardless of the loss function. Therefore, we propose a normalized cross-entropy score (NCE score) that extends NCE [20] during the search process:

$$NCE_{score} = K \cdot \frac{-\sum_{k=1}^{K} q(k|i) \log p(k|i)}{-\sum_{j=1}^{K} \sum_{k=1}^{K} q(y = j|i) \log p(k|i)} \tag{13}$$

where K is the number of classes, and i denotes input images. The numerator is the cross-entropy (CE) loss, and the denominator is the sum of the CEs for each class. Then, $NCE_{score} \in (0, 1)$ can be represented as upper-bounded scores to evaluate rewards.

Elastic Reward Function. We introduce an elastic reward function including compression rate and accuracy (NCE score) to evaluate compressed architectures. The N2N reward [1] was proposed as an alternative to a naïve reward to

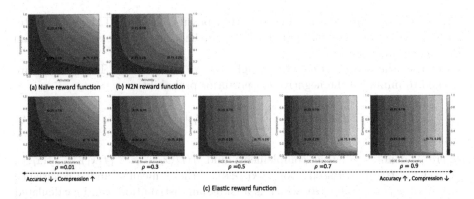

(a) Naïve reward function   (b) N2N reward function

p =0.01 p =0.3 p =0.5 p =0.7 p = 0.9

Accuracy ↓ , Compression ↑   Accuracy ↑ , Compression ↓

(c) Elastic reward function

Fig. 4. Manifold of reward functions : (a) naive reward, (b) N2N reward (c) elastic reward function.

maximize compression rate while preserving high accuracy. However, this reward cannot control the penalty between accuracy and compression rate. The elastic reward function is motivated by the sigmoid function and can be represented as a generalized function that incorporates naive and N2N reward functions [1] by adjusting the scale factor ρ. Figure 4 shows the manifold of the elastic reward functions. The scale factor ρ controls the trade-off between compression rate and accuracy. The larger the scale factor, the more the compression rate is penalized (↑ accuracy and ↓ compression). The smaller the scale factor, conversely, the more the accuracy is penalized (↓ accuracy and ↑ compression). The elastic reward function is defined as follows:

$$f(x) = \left(\frac{2}{1 + \exp(-10^{2\rho} \cdot C(x))} - 1 \right) \cdot A(x)$$

where $C(x)$ is the compression rate, $A(x)$ is the accuracy (NCE score), and ρ is the scale factor.

Training Loss. An architecture with optimal reward is trained with the following objective function [35]:

$$\min_{W,gt} \mathcal{L}(W, gt) = \ell(W, gt) + \lambda_l \ell_{distill}(W, W_t) \tag{14}$$

where $\ell(\cdot, \cdot)$ is cross-entropy loss and $\ell_{distill}(\cdot, \cdot)$ is knowledge distillation loss, namely KL-divergence between the compressed and teacher networks. W_t denotes weights for the uncompressed teacher network, and λ_l denotes the hyperparameter for scale of loss.

3.3 Search Space

We define the search space based on the teacher transformer. The search space is constructed from all the architectures that can be obtained by manipulating the teacher network with the following three operations: (1) block-wise removal and shrinkage, (2) cross-block skip augmentation and (3) addition of res-post layer normalization.

Block-Wise Removal and Shrinkage. Since we jointly compress and search the student architecture from the given teacher architecture, we only consider making architectures smaller than the given network. Block-wise removal refers to dropping the transformer block; block-wise shrinkage refers to compressing the number of heads H_l and the hidden dimension of MLP in the l-th layer.

Cross-Block Skip Augmentation. The addition of cross-block skip augmentation is employed to prevent *deep feature collapse* as described in Theorem 1. Cross-block skip augmentation connected from the k-th layer to the l-th layer can be formulated as:

$$\text{SkipAug}(Y_l) = Y_l + T_{lk}(Y_k; \Theta_{lk}) \tag{15}$$

where $T_{lk}(\cdot)$ is the augmentation operation from the k-th layer to the l-th layer and $\Theta_{lk} \in \mathbb{R}^{d \times d}$ denotes the weight matrix. The augmentation block consists of linear projection, an activation function (e.g., GELU), and layer normalization and can be defined as:

$$T_{lk}(Y_k; \Theta_{lk}) = \mathbb{I}(b_{lk})\text{LN}(\sigma(Y_k \Theta_{lk})), \text{ where } \mathbb{I}(b_{lk}) = \begin{cases} 1, & b_{lk} \in B \\ 0, & \text{otherwise.} \end{cases} \tag{16}$$

The $\mathbb{I}(b_{lk})$ is an indicator function for the cross-block skip augmentation set B, and the b_{lk} denotes skip augmentation blocks connected from the k-th layer to the l-th layer.

We analyze how cross-block skip augmentation prevents *deep feature collapse* in the following theorem.

Theorem 3. *Given a model with the cross-block skip augmentation, the diversity $r(Y_l)$ of features in the l-th layer can be bounded by that of the input data $r(Y_0)$:*

$$r(Y_l) \le \left(\frac{4H_l \gamma \lambda'}{\sqrt{d}}\right)^{\frac{3^l-1}{2}} r(Y_0)^{3^l} + \underbrace{\mathbb{I}(b_{lk})\alpha_{lk}r(Y_k)}_{\ge 0}$$

where $\alpha_{lk} = \lambda_{LN}\lambda_a \|\Theta_{lk}\|$. Here, Θ_{lk} is the weight matrix in the augmentation block from the k-th layer to the l-th layer, λ_{LN}, λ_a are the Lipschitz constants of layer normalization $LN(\cdot)$ and non-linear activation function $\sigma(\cdot)$ respectively, and $\mathbb{I}(b_{lk})$ is the indicator function defined in Eq. 16.

Comparing with Theorem 1, the cross-block skip augmentation introduces an additional term $\mathbb{I}(b_{lk})\alpha_{lk}r(Y_k)$, which is greater than or equal to zero and prevents the feature diversity from decreasing doubly exponentially. A detailed proof of Theorem 3 is given in Appendix A.1.

Adding Res-Post Layer Normalization. To prevent *gradient collapse*, we apply layer normalization at the end of each residual block as shown in Fig. 2. This is referred to as Res-Post-LN in this paper. Res-Post-LN has been proposed in [34], however its effectiveness has not been theoretically proven. We analyze how Res-Post-LN prevents *gradient collapse* in the subsequent theorem.

Theorem 4. *Given a Res-Post-LN transformer with L layers assuming the an output feature $\|Y_L\|_2^2$ are (ϵ, δ)-bounded and a hidden dimension d_m is same as a feature dimension d, the gradient of the weights of the last layer with probaility at least $0.99 - \delta - \frac{\epsilon}{0.9+\epsilon}$ is bounded by dimension d_m, i.e.,*

$$\|\frac{\partial \mathcal{L}}{\partial W^{2,L}}\|_F \leq O(\sqrt{\frac{d_m \ln d_m}{L}})$$

where L denotes number of blocks, and ϵ and $\delta = exp(-d\epsilon^2/8)$ are small numbers.

From Theorem 4, the scale of gradient for the Res-Post-LN transformer is less affected by the feature dimension d_m. As shown in Fig. 1b, the Pre-LN gradient expectation is fluctuates for each layer L according to the compression rate. However, the gradient expectation of Res-Post-LN is stable regardless of the compression rate. The stability of the gradient size for each block ensures stable learning. A detailed proof of Theorem 4 can be found in the supplementary material.

Representation for Block Configurations. The representation for each block configuration is defined by a vector of length $(2n + 3)$, where n is the maximum number of blocks in teacher network. The $2n$ dimensions encode a directed acyclic graph for cross-block skip augmentation. The first n-dimensions represent the input from another node, while the remaining n-dimensions represent the output from each node. The attribute of each block is denoted by three numbers: the number of heads, hidden dimensions of MLP, and drop block.

4   Experiments

We evaluate the VTCA method for image classifcation on the ImageNet challenge dataset [16]. We implement experiments for VTCA on DeiT-Tiny/Small/Base [28], comparing the automatically found compressed architectures to recent compression methods. We compare the compression rate and performance with varying scale factors ρ. We also perform an ablation study on how each architecture module affects the performance results.

4.1   Comparison Results

The experiment results are in Table 1. Here, the VTCA results are all obtained experimentally with a scale factor of 0.7. Our VTCA method achieves competitive accuracies compared with recent methods. We adopt several of the latest

Table 1. Comparison on ImageNet of vision transformer compressed by VTCA with other competitive methods.

Model	Method	Top-1 Acc (%)	FLOPs (G)	Design Type
DeiT-Tiny	Baseline [28]	72.2	1.3	–
	HVT [23]	69.64 (−2.56)	0.64	Patch Reduction
	SViTE [7]	70.12 (−2.08)	0.99	Pruning
	UVC [35]	71.8 (−0.4)	0.69	Pruning
	VTCA	71.63 (−0.57)	0.99	BO
DeiT-Small	Baseline [28]	79.8	4.6	–
	PatchSlimming [25]	79.4 (−0.4)	2.6	Patch Reduction
	IA-RED^2 [22]	79.1 (−0.7)	-	Patch Reduction
	PoWER [35]	78.3 (−1.5)	2.7	Patch Reduction
	HVT [23]	78.0 (−1.8)	2.4	Patch Reduction
	SViTE [7]	79.22 (−0.58)	3.14	Pruning
	SCOP [35]	77.5 (−2.3)	2.6	Pruning
	UVC [35]	79.44 (−0.36)	2.65	Pruning
	VTCA	79.45 (−0.35)	3.11	BO
DeiT-Base	Baseline [28]	81.8	17.6	–
	PatchSlimming [25]	81.5 (−0.3)	9.8	Patch Reduction
	IA-RED^2 [22]	80.9 (−0.9)	11.8	Patch Reduction
	VTP [36]	80.7 (−1.1)	10.0	Pruning
	UVC [35]	80.57 (−1.23)	8.0	Pruning
	VTCA	81.94 (+0.14)	11.9	BO

patch reductions, specifically PoWER [11], HVT [23], PatchiSlimming [25], and IA-RED^2 [22], as well as pruning methods, namely SCOP [27], VTP [36], SViTE [7], and UVC [35].

VTCA avoids accuracy losses compared to pruning and patch reduction methods. On DeiT-Tiny/Small it performs competitively on accuracy compared to UVC, the latest pruning method. In particular, VTCA on DeiT-Base achieves better accuracy than baseline while decreasing FLOPs. VTCA obtains 81.94% of Top-1 accuracy while FLOPs are comparable to IA-RED.^{2}. We observe that VTCA shows competitive accuracy, but FLOPs are higher than with the pruning method. This is due to slightly increased FLOPs with the addition of cross-block skip augmentation and layer normalization.

4.2 Effect of Scale Factor

We performed experiments on how the change of the scale factor ρ in our elastic reward function affects accuracy and compression rate, setting the scale factor ρ to 0.3, 0.5, 0.7, and 0.9; the results are shown in Table 2. Because accuracy becomes more important as the scale factor increases, we see an accuracy gain but with loss of FLOPs. Conversely, when the scale factor is decreased, we obtain a FLOPs gain; but performance losses.

4.3   Ablation Study

As VTCA foregrounds integrating compression and architecture search simultaneously, it is natural to question how each module contributes to the final result. We conducted an ablation study by removing each module; the results are shown in Table 3. The effectiveness of knowledge distillation has already been demonstrated in [35], but an ablation study on knowledge distillation was not performed.

Table 2. Changes in accuracy and FLOPs according to scale factor.

Model	Scale factor	Top-1 Acc. (%)	FLOPs (G)
DeiT-Tiny	$\rho = 0.9$	71.73	1.03
	$\rho = 0.7$	71.63	0.99
	$\rho = 0.5$	70.23	0.89
	$\rho = 0.3$	68.8	0.72

Table 3. Ablation study on the modules implemented on VTCA.

Method	Top-1 Acc. (%)	FLOPs (G)
Uncompressed baseline	72.2	1.3
Compression Only	69.78	0.84
Compression With Res-Post-LN Only	71.16	0.95
Compression With Skip Augmentation Only	70.89	0.91
VTCA-tiny	71.63	0.99

We first determined the result when we conduct only block-wise removal and shrink in our method, demonstrating that only performing compression will significantly impair accuracy on DeiT-Tiny by over 2.4%. That is expected, as simply compressing the model architecture makes it very unstable and prone to collapse.

We then conducted the experiment with Res-Post-LN only. This implies integrating only compression and Res-Post-LN with knowledge distillation. Better performance was achieved than with compression alone. Much better accuracy is obtained than with cross-block skip augmentation, owing to preventing *gradient collapse* and ensuring stable training.

When the experiment was performed with cross-block skip augmentation only, we observed that gradient exploding occurs in some architectures during the search process. This made it difficult to find an optimal architecture, resulting in performance loss; (e.g., approximately 1.4% drop on DeiT-Tiny). Overall, the results of our ablation studies support the effectiveness of optimizing compression and architecture search jointly.

5   Conclusion

In this paper, we propose a VTCA that jointly compresses and searches the architecture of a vision transformer. We consider *deep feature collapse*, in which the number of heads is compressed and the feature diversity rapidly decreases as the layer becomes deeper, and *gradient collapse*, in which the scale of the gradient changes rapidly for each layer as the weight dimensions compress. To alleviate this problem, we propose a cross-block skip augmentation to prevent *feature collapse* and Res-Post-LN architecture to prevent *gradient collapse*. Experiments demonstrate that VTCA achieves competitive performance compared to recent patch reduction and pruning methods. Our future work will extend VTCA to achieve as many FLOPs as pruning without accuracy loss.

Acknowledgements. This research was supported by Basic Science Research Program through the National Research Foundation of Korea (NRF) funded by the Ministry of Education (2020R1I1A3074639) and the Technology Innovation Program (20011875, Development of AI based diagnostic technology for medical imaging devices) funded By the Ministry of Trade, Industry & Energy (MOTIE, Korea).

A   Appendix

A.1   Proof of Theorem 3

Here, we prove Theorem 3 on how cross-block skip augmentation prevents feature collapse of vision transformers.

The feature diversity $r(T_{lk}(Y_l))$ outputted by the augmentation operation $T_{lk}(\cdot)$ can be bounded as:

$$r(T_{lk}(Y_k)) \leq \|T_{lk}(Y_k) - T_{lk}(1y_k^T)\| = \|\mathbb{I}(b_{lk})\text{LN}(\sigma(Y_k\Theta_{lk})) - \mathbb{I}(b_{lk})\text{LN}(\sigma(1y_k^T\Theta_{lk}))\|$$
$$= \|\mathbb{I}(b_{lk})[\text{LN}(\sigma(Y_k\Theta_{lk})) - \text{LN}(\sigma(1y_k^T\Theta_{lk}))]\|$$

where the inequality comes from Eq. 4 defining the feature diversity. The b_{lk} denotes skip augmentation blocks connected from the k-th layer to the l-th layer. The $\mathbb{I}(b_{lk})$ is an indicator function for the cross-block skip augmentation set B defined in Eq. 16.

Using Lipschitz continuity [2,31] of the linear projection, a non-linear activation function, and layer normalization, the bound can be further described as:

$$r(T_{lk}(Y_k)) \leq \mathbb{I}(b_{lk})\lambda_{LN}\lambda_a\|\Theta_{lk}\|\|Y_k - 1y_k^T\| = \mathbb{I}(b_{lk})\lambda_{LN}\lambda_a\|\Theta_{lk}\|r(Y_k)$$

where λ_{LN} and λ_a denotes the Lipschitz constant of layer normalization and the non-linear activation function respectively, and Θ_{lk} is the weight matrix. Combining with a multi-head attention module (Corollary 3.2 in [9]) and the cross-block skip augmentation, diversity after the SkipAug module is bounded as

$$r(Y_l) \leq \left(\frac{4H\gamma\lambda'}{\sqrt{d}}\right)^{\frac{3^l-1}{2}} r(Y_0)^{3^l} + \mathbb{I}(b_{lk})\lambda_{LN}\lambda_a\|\Theta_{lk}\|r(Y_k)$$

$$\leq \left(\frac{4H\gamma\lambda'}{\sqrt{d}}\right)^{\frac{3^l-1}{2}} r(Y_0)^{3^l} + \mathbb{I}(b_{lk})\alpha_{lk}r(Y_k)$$

where $\alpha_{lk} = \lambda_{LN}\lambda_a\|\Theta_{lk}\|$, γ is a constant related to the weight norms and λ' is the Lipschitz constant of MLP. The above inequality corresponds to Theorem 3.

References

1. Ashok, A., Rhinehart, N., Beainy, F., Kitani, K.M.: N2n learning: network to network compression via policy gradient reinforcement learning. arXiv preprint arXiv:1709.06030 (2017)
2. Aziznejad, S., Gupta, H., Campos, J., Unser, M.: Deep neural networks with trainable activations and controlled lipschitz constant. IEEE Trans. Signal Process. **68**, 4688–4699 (2020)
3. Ba, J.L., Kiros, J.R., Hinton, G.E.: Layer normalization. arXiv preprint arXiv:1607.06450 (2016)
4. Brochu, E., Cora, V.M., De Freitas, N.: A tutorial on bayesian optimization of expensive cost functions, with application to active user modeling and hierarchical reinforcement learning. arXiv preprint arXiv:1012.2599 (2010)
5. Cao, S., Wang, X., Kitani, K.M.: Learnable embedding space for efficient neural architecture compression. arXiv preprint arXiv:1902.00383 (2019)
6. Chen, M., Peng, H., Fu, J., Ling, H.: Autoformer: searching transformers for visual recognition. In: Proceedings of the IEEE/CVF International Conference on Computer Vision, pp. 12270–12280 (2021)
7. Chen, T., Cheng, Y., Gan, Z., Yuan, L., Zhang, L., Wang, Z.: Chasing sparsity in vision transformers: an end-to-end exploration. Adv. Neural. Inf. Process. Syst. **34**, 19974–19988 (2021)
8. Devlin, J., Chang, M.W., Lee, K., Toutanova, K.: Bert: pre-training of deep bidirectional transformers for language understanding. arXiv preprint arXiv:1810.04805 (2018)
9. Dong, Y., Cordonnier, J.B., Loukas, A.: Attention is not all you need: pure attention loses rank doubly exponentially with depth. In: International Conference on Machine Learning, pp. 2793–2803. PMLR (2021)
10. Dosovitskiy, A., et al.: An image is worth 16×16 words: transformers for image recognition at scale. arXiv preprint arXiv:2010.11929 (2020)
11. Goyal, S., Choudhury, A.R., Raje, S., Chakaravarthy, V., Sabharwal, Y., Verma, A.: Power-bert: accelerating bert inference via progressive word-vector elimination. In: International Conference on Machine Learning, pp. 3690–3699. PMLR (2020)
12. Hardt, M., Recht, B., Singer, Y.: Train faster, generalize better: stability of stochastic gradient descent. In: International Conference on Machine Learning, pp. 1225–1234. PMLR (2016)
13. He, K., Zhang, X., Ren, S., Sun, J.: Deep residual learning for image recognition. In: Proceedings of the IEEE Conference on Computer Vision and Pattern Recognition, pp. 770–778 (2016)
14. He, Y., Lin, J., Liu, Z., Wang, H., Li, L.J., Han, S.: Amc: automl for model compression and acceleration on mobile devices. In: Proceedings of the European Conference on Computer Vision (ECCV), pp. 784–800 (2018)

15. He, Y., Zhang, X., Sun, J.: Channel pruning for accelerating very deep neural networks. In: Proceedings of the IEEE International Conference on Computer Vision, pp. 1389–1397 (2017)
16. Krizhevsky, A., Sutskever, I., Hinton, G.E.: Imagenet classification with deep convolutional neural networks. In: Advances in Neural Information Processing Systems, vol. 25 (2012)
17. LeCun, Y., et al.: Backpropagation applied to handwritten zip code recognition. Neural Comput. $1(4)$, 541–551 (1989)
18. Liu, Z., Li, J., Shen, Z., Huang, G., Yan, S., Zhang, C.: Learning efficient convolutional networks through network slimming. In: Proceedings of the IEEE International Conference on Computer Vision, pp. 2736–2744 (2017)
19. Lyle, C., Schut, L., Ru, R., Gal, Y., van der Wilk, M.: A bayesian perspective on training speed and model selection. Adv. Neural. Inf. Process. Syst. **33**, 10396–10408 (2020)
20. Ma, X., Huang, H., Wang, Y., Romano, S., Erfani, S., Bailey, J.: Normalized loss functions for deep learning with noisy labels. In: International Conference on Machine Learning, pp. 6543–6553. PMLR (2020)
21. Mockus, J.B., Mockus, L.J.: Bayesian approach to global optimization and application to multiobjective and constrained problems. J. Optim. Theory Appl. **70**(1), 157–172 (1991)
22. Pan, B., Panda, R., Jiang, Y., Wang, Z., Feris, R., Oliva, A.: Ia-red^2?: interpretability-aware redundancy reduction for vision transformers. Adv. Neural. Inf. Process. Syst. **34**, 24898–24911 (2021)
23. Pan, Z., Zhuang, B., Liu, J., He, H., Cai, J.: Scalable vision transformers with hierarchical pooling. In: Proceedings of the IEEE/CVF International Conference on Computer Vision, pp. 377–386 (2021)
24. Ru, B., Lyle, C., Schut, L., Fil, M., van der Wilk, M., Gal, Y.: Speedy performance estimation for neural architecture search. arXiv preprint arXiv:2006.04492 (2020)
25. Tang, Y., Han, K., Wang, Y., Xu, C., Guo, J., Xu, C., Tao, D.: Patch slimming for efficient vision transformers. In: Proceedings of the IEEE/CVF Conference on Computer Vision and Pattern Recognition, pp. 12165–12174 (2022)
26. Tang, Y., et al.: Augmented shortcuts for vision transformers. In: Advances in Neural Information Processing Systems, vol. 34 (2021)
27. Tang, Y., et al.: Scop: scientific control for reliable neural network pruning. Adv. Neural. Inf. Process. Syst. **33**, 10936–10947 (2020)
28. Touvron, H., Cord, M., Douze, M., Massa, F., Sablayrolles, A., Jégou, H.: Training data-efficient image transformers & distillation through attention. In: International Conference on Machine Learning, pp. 10347–10357. PMLR (2021)
29. Vaswani, A., et al.: Attention is all you need. In: Advances in Neural Information Processing Systems, vol. 30 (2017)
30. Walch, F., Hazirbas, C., Leal-Taixe, L., Sattler, T., Hilsenbeck, S., Cremers, D.: Image-based localization using LSTMS for structured feature correlation. In: Proceedings of the IEEE International Conference on Computer Vision, pp. 627–637 (2017)
31. Wood, G., Zhang, B.: Estimation of the lipschitz constant of a function. J. Global Optim. **8**(1), 91–103 (1996)
32. Xiong, R., et al.: On layer normalization in the transformer architecture. In: International Conference on Machine Learning, pp. 10524–10533. PMLR (2020)
33. Yang, H., Yin, H., Molchanov, P., Li, H., Kautz, J.: Nvit: vision transformer compression and parameter redistribution. arXiv preprint arXiv:2110.04869 (2021)

34. Yao, Z., Cao, Y., Lin, Y., Liu, Z., Zhang, Z., Hu, H.: Leveraging batch normalization for vision transformers. In: Proceedings of the IEEE/CVF International Conference on Computer Vision, pp. 413–422 (2021)
35. Yu, S., et al.: Unified visual transformer compression. arXiv preprint arXiv:2203.08243 (2022)
36. Zhu, M., Tang, Y., Han, K.: Vision transformer pruning. arXiv preprint arXiv:2104.08500 (2021)

EPSANet: An Efficient Pyramid Squeeze Attention Block on Convolutional Neural Network

Hu Zhang[1,2], Keke Zu[1,2], Jian Lu[1,2(✉)], Yuru Zou[1,2], and Deyu Meng[3,4]

[1] Shenzhen Key Laboratory of Advanced Machine Learning and Applications, College of Mathematics and Statistics, Shenzhen University, Shenzhen, China
`{kekezu,jianlu,yuruzou}@szu.edu.cn`
[2] National Center for Applied Mathematics Shenzhen (NCAMS), Shenzhen, China
[3] Xi'an Jiaotong University, Xi'an, China
`dymeng@mail.xjtu.edu.cn`
[4] Macau University of Science and Technology, Macao, China

Abstract. Recently, it has been demonstrated that the performance of a deep convolutional neural network can be effectively improved by embedding an attention module into it. In this work, a novel lightweight and effective attention method named Pyramid Squeeze Attention (PSA) module is proposed. By replacing the 3×3 convolution with the PSA module in the bottleneck blocks of the ResNet, a novel representational block named Efficient Pyramid Squeeze Attention (EPSA) is obtained. The EPSA block can be easily added as a plug-and-play component into a well-established backbone network, and significant improvements on model performance can be achieved. Hence, a simple and efficient backbone architecture named EPSANet is developed in this work by stacking these ResNet-style EPSA blocks. Correspondingly, a stronger multi-scale representation ability can be offered by the proposed EPSANet for various computer vision tasks including but not limited to, image classification, object detection, instance segmentation, etc. Without bells and whistles, the performance of the proposed EPSANet outperforms most of the state-of-the-art channel attention methods. As compared to the SENet-50, the Top-1 accuracy is improved by 1.93% on ImageNet dataset, a larger margin of +2.7 box AP for object detection and an improvement of +1.7 mask AP for instance segmentation by using the Mask-RCNN on MS-COCO dataset are obtained.

Keywords: Computer vision · Attention module

1 Introduction

Attention mechanisms are widely used in many computer vision areas such as image classification [1,2], object detection [3], instance segmentation [4], semantic segmentation [5,6], scene parsing and action localization [7]. Specifically, there are two types of attention methods, which are channel attention and spatial attention.

L. Wang et al. (Eds.): ACCV 2022, LNCS 13843, pp. 541–557, 2023.
https://doi.org/10.1007/978-3-031-26313-2_33

Recently, it has been demonstrated that significant performance improvements can be achieved by employing the channel attention [8,9], spatial attention [10], or both of them [11]. The most commonly used method of channel attention is the Squeeze-and-Excitation (SE) module [12], which can significantly improve the performance with a considerably low cost. The drawback of the SENet is that it ignores the importance of spatial information. Therefore, the Bottleneck Attention Module (BAM) [10] and Convolutional Block Attention Module (CBAM) [11] are proposed to enrich the attention map by effectively combining the spatial and channel attention. However, there still exists two important and challenging problems. The first one is how to efficiently capture and exploit the spatial information of the feature map with different scales to enrich the feature space. The second one is that the channel or spatial attention can only effectively capture the local information but fail in establishing a long-range channel dependency. Correspondingly, many methods are proposed to address these two problems. The methods based on multi-scale feature representation and cross-channel information interaction, such as the PyConv [13], the Res2Net [14], and the HS-ResNet [15], are proposed. In the other hand, a long-range channel dependency can be established as shown in [6,16,17]. All the above mentioned methods, however, bring higher model complexity and thus the network suffers from heavy computational burden. Based on the above observations, in this work, a low-cost and high-performance novel module named Pyramid Squeeze Attention (PSA) is proposed. Firstly, the proposed PSA module uses the multi-scale pyramid convolution structure to process the input tensor at multiple scales. Secondly, the PSA module can effectively extract spatial information with different scales from each channel-wise feature map by squeezing the channel dimension of the input tensor. Third, a cross-dimension interaction can be built by extracting the channel-wise attention weight of the multi-scale feature maps. Finally, the softmax operation is employed to recalibrate the attention weight of the corresponding channels, and thus the interaction between the channels that are in different groups of the squeeze-concatenate module is established. Correspondingly, a novel block named Efficient Pyramid Squeeze Attention (EPSA) is obtained by replacing the 3×3 convolution with the PSA module in the bottleneck blocks of the ResNet. Furthermore, a novel backbone EPSANet is proposed by stacking these EPSA blocks as the ResNet style. The main contributions of this work are summarized as below:

- A novel Efficient Pyramid Squeeze Attention (EPSA) block is proposed, which can effectively extract multi-scale spatial information at a more granular level and develop a long-range channel dependency. The proposed EPSA block is very flexible and scalable and thus can be applied to a large variety of network architectures for numerous tasks of computer vision.
- A novel backbone architecture named EPSANet is proposed, which can learn richer multi-scale feature representation and adaptively re-calibrate the cross-dimension channel-wise attention weight.
- Extensive experiments demonstrated that promising results can be achieved by the proposed EPSANet across image classification, object detection and instance segmentation on both ImageNet and COCO datasets.

2   Related Work

Attention Mechanism. The attention mechanism is used to strength the allocation of the most informative feature expressions while suppressing the less useful ones, and thus makes the model attending to important regions within a context adaptively. The Squeeze-and-Excitation (SE) attention in [12] can capture channel correlations by selectively modulating the scale of channel. The CBAM in [11] can enrich the attention map by adding max pooled features for the channel attention with large-size kernels. Motivated by the CBAM, the GSoP in [18] proposed a second-order pooling method to extract richer feature aggregation. More recently, the Non-Local block [17] is proposed to build a dense spatial feature map and capture the long-range dependency via non-local operations. Based on the Non-Local block, the Double Attention Network (A^2Net) [19] introduces a novel relation function to embed the attention with spatial information into the feature map. Sequently, the SKNet in [20] introduces a dynamic selection attention mechanism that allows each neuron to adaptively adjust its receptive field size based on multiple scales of input feature map. The ResNeSt [21] proposes a similar Split-Attention block that enables attention across groups of the input feature map. The Fcanet [8] proposes a novel multi-spectral channel attention that realizes the pre-processing of channel attention mechanism in the frequency domain. The GCNet [1] introduces a simple spatial attention module and thus a long-range channel dependency is developed. The ECANet [9] employs the one-dimensional convolution layer to reduce the redundancy of fully connected layers. The DANet [16] adaptively integrates local features with their global dependencies by summing these two attention modules from different branches. The above mentioned methods either focus on the design of more sophisticated attention modules that inevitably bring a greater computational cost, or they cannot establish a long-range channel dependency. Thus, in order to further improve the efficiency and reduce the model complexity, a novel attention module named PSA is proposed, which aims at learning attention weight with low model complexity and to effectively integrate local and global attention for establishing the long-range channel dependency.

Multi-scale Feature Representations. The ability of the multi-scale feature representation is essential for various vision tasks such as, instance segmentation [4], face analysis [22], object detection [23], salient object detection [24], and semantic segmentation [5]. It is critically important to design a good operator that can extract multi-scale feature more efficiently for visual recognition tasks. By embedding a operator for multi-scale feature extraction into a convolution neural network (CNN), a more effective feature representation ability can be obtained. In the other hand, CNNs can naturally learn coarse-to-fine multi-scale features through a stack of convolutional operators. Thus, to design a better convolutional operator is the key for improving the multi-scale representations of CNNs.

3   Method

3.1   Revisting Channel Attention

Channel Attention. The channel attention mechanism allows the network to selectively weight the importance of each channel and thus generates more informative outputs. Let $X \in \mathbb{R}^{C \times H \times W}$ denotes the input feature map, where the quantity H, W, C represent its height, width, number of input channels respectively. A SE block consists of two parts: squeeze and excitation, which is respectively designed for encoding the global information and adaptively recalibrating the channel-wise relationship. Generally, the channel-wise statistics can be generated by using a global average pooling, which is used to embed the global spatial information into a channel descriptor. The global average pooling operator can be calculated by the following equation

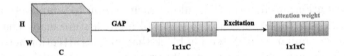

Fig. 1. SEWeight module.

$$g_c = \frac{1}{H \times W} \sum_{i=1}^{H} \sum_{j=1}^{W} x_c(i,j) \tag{1}$$

The attention weight of the c-th channel in the SE block can be written as

$$w_c = \sigma(W_1 \delta(W_0(g_c))) \tag{2}$$

where the symbol δ represents the Recitified Linear Unit (ReLU) operation as in [25], $W_0 \in \mathbb{R}^{C \times \frac{C}{r}}$ and $W_1 \in \mathbb{R}^{\frac{C}{r} \times C}$ represent the fully-connected (FC) layers. With two fully-connected layers, the linear information among channels can be combined more efficiently, and it is helpful for the interaction of the information of high and low channel dimensions. The symbol σ represents the excitation function, and a sigmoid function is usually used in practice. By using the excitation function, we can assign weights to channels after the channel interaction and thus the information can be extracted more efficiently. The above introduced process of generating channel attention weights is named SEWeight module in [12], the diagram of the SEWeight module is shown by Fig. 1.

3.2   PSA Module

The motivation of this work is to build a more efficient and effective channel attention mechanism. Therefore, a novel pyramid squeeze attention (PSA) module is proposed. As illustrated by Fig. 3, the PSA module is mainly implemented in four steps. First, the multi-scale feature map on channel-wise is obtained by implementing the proposed squeeze pyramid concat (SPC) module. Second, the channel-wise attention vector are obtained by using the SEWeight module to extract the attention of the feature map with different scales. Third, re-calibrated weight of multi-scale channel is obtained by using the Softmax to re-calibrate the channel-wise attention vector. Fourth, the operation of an element-wise product is applied to the re-calibrated weight and the corresponding feature map. Finally, a refined feature map which is richer in multi-scale feature information can be obtained as the output. As illustrated by Fig. 2, the essential operator for implementing the multi-scale feature extraction in the proposed PSA is the SPC, we extract the spatial information of the input feature map in a multi-branch way, the input channel dimension of each branch is C. By doing this, we can obtain more abundant positional information of the input tensor and process it at multiple scales in a parallel way. Thus a feature map that contains a single type of kernel can be obtained. Correspondingly, the different spatial resolutions and depths can be generated by using multi-scale convolutional kernels in a pyramid structure. And the spatial information with different scales on each channel-wise feature map can be effectively extracted by squeezing the channel dimension of the input tensor. Finally, each feature map with different scales F_i has the common channel dimension $C' = \frac{C}{S}$ and $i = 0, 1, \cdots, S-1$. Note that C should be divisible by S. For each branch, it learns the multi-scale spatial information independently and establish a cross-channel interaction in a local manner. However, a huge improvement in the amount of parameters will be resulted with the increase of kernel sizes. In order to process the input tensor at different kernel scales without increasing the computational cost, a method of group convolution is introduced and applied to the convolutional kernels. Further, we design a novel criterion for choosing the group size without increasing the number of parameters. The relationship between the multi-scale kernel size and the group size can be written as

$$G = \begin{cases} 2^{\frac{K-1}{2}} & K > 3 \\ 1 & K = 3 \end{cases} \tag{3}$$

where the quantity K is the kernel size, G is the group size. Finally, the multi-scale feature map generation function is given by

$$F_i = \text{Conv}(k_i \times k_i, G_i)(X) \quad i = 0, 1, 2 \cdots S - 1 \tag{4}$$

where the i-th kernel size $k_i = 2 \times (i + 1) + 1$, the i-th group size G_i and $F_i \in R^{C' \times H \times W}$ denotes the feature map with different scales. The whole multi-scale pre-processed feature map can be obtained by a concatenation way as

$$F = \text{Cat}([F_0, F_1, \cdots, F_{S-1}]) \tag{5}$$

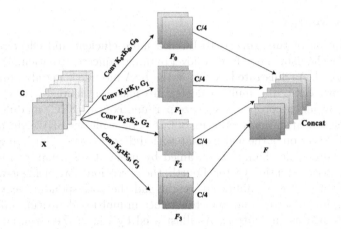

Fig. 2. A detailed illustration of the proposed Squeeze Pyramid Concat (SPC) module with $S = 4$, where 'Squeeze' means to equally squeeze in the channel dimension, K is the kernel size, G is the group size and 'Concat' means to concatenate features in the channel dimension.

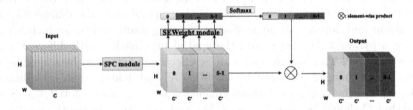

Fig. 3. The structure of the proposed Pyramid Squeeze Attention (PSA) module.

where $F \in R^{C \times H \times W}$ is the obtained multi-scale feature map. By extracting the channel attention weight information from the multi-scale pre-processed feature map, the attention weight vectors with different scales are obtained. Mathematically, the vector of attention weight can be represented as

$$Z_i = \text{SEWeight}(F_i), \quad i = 0, 1, 2 \cdots S - 1 \tag{6}$$

where $Z_i \in R^{C' \times 1 \times 1}$ is the attention weight. The SEWeight module is used to obtain the attention weight from the input feature map with different scales. By doing this, our PSA module can fuse context information in different scales and produce a better pixel-level attention for high-level feature maps. Further, in order to realize the interaction of attention information and fuse the cross-dimensions vector without destroying the original channel attention vector. And thus the whole multi-scale channel attention vector is obtained in a concatenation way as

$$Z = Z_0 \oplus Z_1 \oplus \cdots \oplus Z_{S-1} \tag{7}$$

where $\oplus$ is the concat operator, Z_i is the attention value from the F_i, Z is the multi-scale attention weight vector. A soft attention is used across channels to adaptively select different spatial scales, which is guided by the compact feature descriptor Z_i. A soft assignment weight is given by

$$att_i = \text{Softmax}(Z_i) = \frac{exp(Z_i)}{\sum_{i=0}^{S-1} exp(Z_i)} \tag{8}$$

where the Softmax is used to obtain the re-calibrated weight att_i of the multi-scale channel, which contains all the location information on the space and the attention weight in channel. By doing this, the interaction between local and global channel attention is realized. Next, the channel attention of feature re-calibration is fused and spliced in a concatenation way, and thus the whole channel attention vector can be obtained as

$$att = att_0 \oplus att_1 \oplus \cdots \oplus att_{S-1} \tag{9}$$

where att represents the multi-scale channel weight after attention interaction. Then, we multiply the re-calibrated weight of multi-scale channel attention att_i with the feature map of the corresponding scale F_i as

$$Y_i = F_i \odot att_i \quad i = 1, 2, 3, \cdots S - 1 \tag{10}$$

where $\odot$ represents the channel-wise multiplication, Y_i refers to the feature map that with the obtained multi-scale channel-wise attention weight. The concatenation operator is more effective than the summation due to it can integrally maintain the feature representation without destroying the information of the orginal feature map. In sum, the process to obtain the refined output can be written as

$$Out = \text{Cat}([Y_0, Y_1, \cdots, Y_{S-1}]) \tag{11}$$

As illustrated by the above analysis, our proposed PSA module can integrate the multi-scale spatial information and the cross-channel attention into the block for each feature group. Thus, a better information interaction between local and global channel attention can be obtained by our proposed PSA module.

3.3 Network Design

As shown by Fig. 4, a novel block named Efficient Pyramid Squeeze Attention (EPSA) block is further obtained by replacing the 3×3 convolution with the PSA module at corresponding positions in the bottelneck blocks of ResNet. The multi-scale spatial information and the cross-channel attention are integrated by our PSA module into the EPSA block. Thus, the EPSA block can extract multi-scale spatial information at a more granular level and develop a long-range channel dependency. Correspondingly, a novel efficient backbone network named EPSANet is developed by stacking the proposed EPSA blocks as

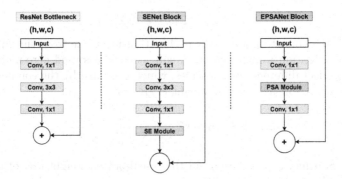

Fig. 4. Illustration and comparison of ResNet, SENet, and our proposed EPSANet blocks.

Table 1. Network design of the proposed EPSANet.

Output	ResNet-50	EPSANet(Small)-50	EPSANet(Large)-50
112×112	7×7, 64, stride 2		
56×56	3×3 max pool, stride 2		
56×56	$\begin{bmatrix} 1 \times 1, \ 64 \\ 3 \times 3, \ 64 \\ 1 \times 1, 256 \end{bmatrix} \times 3$	$\begin{bmatrix} 1 \times 1, \ 64 \\ PSA, \ 64 \\ 1 \times 1, 256 \end{bmatrix} \times 3$	$\begin{bmatrix} 1 \times 1, 128 \\ PSA, 128 \\ 1 \times 1, 256 \end{bmatrix} \times 3$
28×28	$\begin{bmatrix} 1 \times 1, 128 \\ 3 \times 3, 128 \\ 1 \times 1, 512 \end{bmatrix} \times 4$	$\begin{bmatrix} 1 \times 1, 128 \\ PSA, 128 \\ 1 \times 1, 512 \end{bmatrix} \times 4$	$\begin{bmatrix} 1 \times 1, 256 \\ PSA, 256 \\ 1 \times 1, 512 \end{bmatrix} \times 4$
14×14	$\begin{bmatrix} 1 \times 1, \ 256 \\ 3 \times 3, \ 256 \\ 1 \times 1, 1024 \end{bmatrix} \times 6$	$\begin{bmatrix} 1 \times 1, \ 256 \\ PSA, \ 256 \\ 1 \times 1, 1024 \end{bmatrix} \times 6$	$\begin{bmatrix} 1 \times 1, \ 512 \\ PSA, \ 512 \\ 1 \times 1, 1024 \end{bmatrix} \times 6$
7×7	$\begin{bmatrix} 1 \times 1, \ 512 \\ 3 \times 3, \ 512 \\ 1 \times 1, 2048 \end{bmatrix} \times 3$	$\begin{bmatrix} 1 \times 1, \ 512 \\ PSA, \ 512 \\ 1 \times 1, 2048 \end{bmatrix} \times 3$	$\begin{bmatrix} 1 \times 1, 1024 \\ PSA, 1024 \\ 1 \times 1, 2048 \end{bmatrix} \times 3$
1×1	7×7 global average pool,1000-d fc		

the ResNet style. The proposed EPSANet inherits the advantages of the EPSA block, and thus it has strong multi-scale representation capabilities and can adaptively re-calibrate the cross-dimension channel-wise weight. As shown by Table 1, two variations of the EPSANet, the EPSANet(Small) and EPSANet(Large) are proposed. For the proposed EPSANet(Small), the kernel and group size are respectively set as (3,5,7,9) and (1,4,8,16) in the SPC module. The proposed EPSANet(Large) has a higher group size and is set as (32,32,32,32) in the SPC module.

4   Experiments

4.1   Implementation Details

For image classification tasks, we employ the widely used ResNet [26] as the backbone model and perform experiments on the ImageNet [27] dataset. The training configuration is set as the reference in [12, 14, 26]. Accordingly, the standard data augmentation scheme is implemented and the size of the input tensor is cropped to 224 × 224 by randomly horizontal fliping and normalization. The optimisation is performed by using the stochastic gradient descent (SGD) with weight decay of 1e-4, momentum as 0.9 and a minibatch size of 256. The Label-smoothing regularization [?] is used with the coefficient value as 0.1 during training. The learning rate is initially set as 0.1 and is decreased by a factor of 10 after every 30 epochs for 100 epochs in total. For object detection tasks, the ResNet-50 along with FPN [29] is used as the backbone model, we use three representative detectors, Faster RCNN [23], Mask RCNN [4] and RetinaNet [30] on the MS-COCO [31] dataset. The default configuration setting is that the shorter side of the input image is resized to 800. The SGD is used with a weight decay of 1e-4, the momentum is 0.9, and the batch size is 2 per GPU within 12 epochs. The learning rate is set as 0.01 and is decreased by the factor of 10 at the 8th and 11th epochs, respectively. For instance segmentation tasks, we employ the main-stream detection system, Mask R-CNN [4] and also in companion with FPN. The settings of training configuration and dataset are similar to that of the object detection. Finally, all detectors are implemented by the MMDetection toolkit [32], and all models are trained on 8 Titan RTX GPUs.

Table 2. Comparison of various attention methods on ImageNet in terms of network parameters (in millions), floating point operations per second (FLOPs), Top-1 and Top-5 Validation Accuracy(%). For a fair comparison, the SKNet* is reduplicated to follow the same training configuration as the proposed EPSANet.

Network	Backbones	Parameters	FLOPs	Top-1 Acc (%)	Top-5 Acc (%)
ResNet [26]	ResNet-50	25.56M	4.12G	75.20	92.91
SENet [12]		28.07M	4.13G	76.71	93.70
CBAM [11]		28.07M	4.14G	77.34	93.66
A^2-Net [19]		33.00M	6.50G	77.00	93.50
SKNet* [20]		26.15M	4.19G	77.55	93.82
Res2Net+SE [14]		28.21M	4.29G	78.44	94.06
GCNet [1]		28.11M	4.13G	77.70	93.66
Triplet Attention [33]		25.56M	4.17G	77.48	93.68
FcaNet [8]		28.07M	4.13G	78.52	94.14
AANet [34]		25.80M	4.15G	77.70	93.80
ECANet [9]		25.56M	4.13G	77.48	93.68
EPSANet(Small)		**22.56M**	**3.62G**	77.49	93.54
EPSANet(Large)		27.90M	4.72G	**78.64**	**94.18**
ResNet [26]	ResNet-101	44.55M	7.85G	76.83	93.91
SENet [12]		49.33M	7.86G	77.62	94.10
CBAM [11]		49.33M	7.88G	78.49	94.06
AANet [34]		45.40M	8.05G	78.70	94.40
SKNet* [20]		45.68M	7.96G	78.84	94.29
Triplet Attention [33]		44.56M	7.95G	78.03	93.85
ECA-Net [9]		44.55M	7.86G	78.65	94.34
EPSANet(Small)		**38.90M**	**6.82G**	78.43	94.11
EPSANet(Large)		49.59M	8.97G	**79.38**	**94.58**

4.2   Image Classification on ImageNet

Table 2 shows the comparison results of our EPSANet with prior arts on ResNet with 50 and 101 layers. For the Top-1 accuracy, the proposed EPSANet(Small)-50 achieves a margin of 2.29% higher over the ResNet-50, and using 11.7% fewer parameters and requires 12.1% lower computational cost. Moreover, with almost the same Top-1 accuracy, the EPSANet(Small)-50 can save 54.2% parameter storage and 53.9% computation resources as compared to SENet-101. The EPSANet(Small)-101 outperforms the original ResNet-101 and SENet101 by 1.6% and 0.81% in Top-1 accuracy, and saves about 12.7% parameter and 21.1% computational resources. With the similar Top-1 accuracy on ResNet-101, the computational cost is reduced about 12.7% by our EPSANet(Small)-101 as compared to SRM, ECANet and AANet. What's more, our EPSANet(Large)-50 shows the best performance in accuracy, achieving a considerable improvement compared with all the other attention models. Specifically, the EPSANet(large)-50 outperforms the SENet, ECANet and FcaNet by about 1.93%,1.16% and 0.12% in terms of Top-1 accuracy respectively. With the same number of parameters, our EPSANet(Large)-101 achieves significant improvements by about 1.76% and 0.89% compared to the SENet-101 and CBAM, respectively. In sum, the above results demonstrate that our PSA module has gain a very competitive performance with a much lower computational cost.

4.3   Object Detection on MS COCO

As illustrated by Table 3, our proposed models can achieve the best performance for the object detection task. Similar to the classification task on ImageNet, the proposed EPSANet(Small)-50 outperforms the SENet-50 by a large margin with less parameters and lower computational cost. The EPSANet(Large)-50 can achieve the best performance compared with the other attention methods. From the perspective of complexity (in term of parameters and FLOPs), the EPSANet(Small)-50 offers a high competitive performance compared to the SENet50, i.e., by 1.5%, 1.3%, and 1.1%, higher in bounding box AP on the Faster-RCNN, Mask-RCNN, RetinaNet, respectively. What's more, as compared to the SENet50, the EPSANet(Small)-50 can further reducing the number of parameters to 87.5%, 88.3% and 86.4% on Faster RCNN, Mask RCNN and RetinaNet, respectively. The EPSANet(Large)-50 is able to boost the mean average precision by around 4% on the above three detectors as compared with the ResNet-50. It is worth noting that the most compelling performance improvement appears in the measurement of AP_L. With almost the same computational complexity, the AP performance can be improved by 1.9% and 1.1% by our proposed EPSANet(Large)-50 on both Faster-RCNN and Mask-RCNN detector, as compared to the FcaNet. The results demonstrate that the proposed EPSANet has good generalization ability and can be easily applied to other downstream tasks.

Table 3. Object detection results of different attention methods on COCO val2017.

Methods	Detectors	Parameters	FLOPs	AP	AP_{50}	AP_{75}	AP_S	AP_M	AP_L
ResNet-50 [26]	Faster R-CNN	41.53M	207.07G	36.4	58.4	39.1	21.5	40.0	46.6
SENet-50 [12]		44.02M	207.18G	37.7	60.1	40.9	22.9	41.9	48.2
ECANet-50 [9]		41.53M	207.18G	38.0	60.6	40.9	23.4	42.1	48.0
FcaNet-50 [8]		44.02M	215.63G	39.0	61.1	42.3	23.7	42.8	49.6
EPSANet(Small)-50		**38.56M**	**197.07G**	39.2	60.3	42.3	22.8	42.4	51.1
EPSANet(Large)-50		43.85M	219.64G	**40.9**	**62.1**	**44.6**	23.6	**44.5**	**54.0**
ResNet-50 [26]	Mask R-CNN	44.18M	275.58G	37.3	59.0	40.2	21.9	40.9	48.1
SENet [12]		46.66M	261.93G	38.7	60.9	42.1	23.4	42.7	50.0
GCNet-50 [1]		46.90M	279.60G	39.4	61.6	42.4	–	–	–
ECANet-50 [9]		44.18M	275.69G	39.0	61.3	42.1	24.2	42.8	49.9
FcaNet-50 [8]		46.66M	261.93G	40.3	62.0	44.1	25.2	43.9	52.0
EPSANet(Small)-50		**41.20M**	**248.53G**	40.0	60.9	43.3	22.3	43.2	52.8
EPSANet(Large)-50		46.50M	271.10G	**41.4**	**62.3**	**45.3**	23.6	**45.1**	**54.6**
ResNet-50 [26]	RetinaNet	37.74M	239.32G	35.6	55.5	38.3	20.0	39.6	46.8
SENet-50 [12]		40.25M	239.43G	37.1	57.2	39.9	21.2	40.7	49.3
EPSANet(Small)-50		**34.78M**	**229.32G**	38.2	58.1	40.6	**21.5**	41.5	51.2
EPSANet(Large)-50		40.07M	251.89G	**39.6**	**59.4**	**42.3**	21.2	**43.4**	**52.9**

Table 4. Instance segmentation results of different attention networks by using the Mask R-CNN on COCO val2017.

Network	AP	AP_{50}	AP_{75}	AP_S	AP_M	AP_L
ResNet-50 [26]	34.1	55.5	36.2	16.1	36.7	50.0
SENet-50 [12]	35.4	57.4	37.8	17.1	38.6	51.8
ResNet-50 + 1 NL-block [17]	34.7	56.7	36.6	–	–	–
GCNet [1]	35.7	58.4	37.6	–	–	–
FcaNet [8]	36.2	58.6	38.1	–	–	–
ECANet [9]	35.6	58.1	37.7	17.6	39.0	51.8
EPSANet(Small)-50	35.9	57.7	38.1	18.5	38.8	49.2
EPSANet(Large)-50	**37.1**	**59.0**	**39.5**	**19.6**	**40.4**	50.4

4.4   Instance Segmentation on MS COCO

For instance segmentation, our experiments are implemented by using the Mask R-CNN on MS COCO dataset. As illustrated by Table 4, our proposed PSA module outperforms the other channel attention methods by a considerably larger margin. Specifically, our EPSANet(Large)-50 surpass the FcaNet which can offer the best performance in existing methods, by about 0.9% , 0.4% and 1.4% on AP, AP_{50} and AP_{75} respectively. These results verified the effectiveness of our proposed PSA module.

5   Ablation Studies

In order to provide a comprehensive understanding about the efficiency of our proposed EPSANet. Here, we mainly conduct some ablation experiments to evaluate the performance of each part of the proposed block independently. Such as the effect of kernel size and group size, the benefit of the SPC and SE module, the lightweight performance, and the ability of multi-scale feature representation.

Table 5. Accuracy performance with the change of group size on the ImageNet [27] dataset.

Kernel size	Group size	Top-1 Acc(%)	Top-5 Acc(%)
(3,5,7,9)	(4,8,16,16)	77.25	93.40
(3,5,7,9)	(16,16,16,16)	77.24	93.47
(3,5,7,9)	(1,4,8,16)	**77.49**	**93.54**

Table 6. Accuracy performance with the change of kernel size on the CIFAR-100 [35].

Kernel Size	Group Size	Top-1 Acc(%)
(3,3,5,5)	(1,4,8,16)	79.27
(3,5,5,5)	(1,4,8,16)	79.06
(3,5,5,7)	(1,4,8,16)	79.67
(3,5,7,9)	(1,4,8,16)	**79.83**

5.1 Effect of the Kernel Size and Group Size

Firstly, we explore in detail the combinatorial relationship between the convolution kernel and the group size. The EPSANet(Small)-50 as our baseline model. As shown by Table 5, when the kernel size is fixed as (3,5,7,9), we adjust the group size of different sub-kernel properly. The results show that the best performance can be achieved when the group size is changed as (1,4,8,16). Correspondingly, when the group size is fixed as (1,4,8,16), we adjust the kernel size in different sub-group to explore the best combination relationship. As shown by Table 6, the best performance can be obtained by setting the kernel size as (3,5,7,9). All the above results also verified equation (3).

5.2 Effect of the SPC and SE Module

Secondly, we conduct an experiment to evulate the benefits coming from the SPC module and the SE module separately. As illustrated by Table 7, the 'SPC' is denote that remove the SE module and only replace the SPC module with the 3×3 convolution in the BottleNeck of the ResNet. The 'SE' is denote that the squeeze size of the SPC module is set as 1, which can be seem as remove the benefits come from the SPC module. The 'SPC+SE' is mean that equipped with the SPC and the SE module. As shown by Table 7, the SPC module and the SE module can bring a more about 0.90% and 0.95% improvement as compared to SENet-50 respectively. The results show that the benefits coming from the SPC module and the SE module are equally important. What's more, equipped with the SPC module and the SE module can achieves a large margin of 1.92% higher accuracy performance over SENet, while using 17.2% fewer parameters.

5.3   Effect of the Lightweight Performance

Third, as shown by Table 8, the proposed EPSANet can improve the Top-1 accuracy by about 1.76% and 0.98% over the MobileNetV2 and SENet respectively. Meanwhile, as compared to the most competitive model ECANet, the proposed EPSANet also achieves about 0.84% improvement in Top-1 accuracy. Thus, the efficiency and effectiveness of the proposed PSA module for lightweight CNN architectures has verified.

Table 7. The benefits coming from the SPC module and the SE module on the CIFAR-100 [35] dataset.

Model	Module	Parameters	Top-1 Acc(%)
SENet-50 [12]	SE	25.00M	77.91
EPSANet(Small)-50	SPC	20.70M	78.81
	SE	23.87M	78.86
	SPC+SE	20.71M	**79.83**

Table 8. Comparison of different lightweight attention methods on the ImageNet in terms of network parameters and Top-1 accuracy(%).

Network	Backbones	Parameters	Top-1 Acc (%)
MobileNetV2 [36]	MobileNetV2	3.50M	71.64
SENet [12]		3.89M	72.42
ECA-Net [9]		3.50M	72.56
EPSANet(ours)		3.75M	**73.40**

5.4   Effect of the Multi-scale Feature Representation

Finally, we mainly compare the proposed EPSANet with several classical multi-scale neural networks. These CNN models have more granular level, deeper and wider architectures, and their results all are copied from the original papers. As shown by Table 9, the proposed EPSANet(Large)-50 outperforms DenseNet-264 [37] and Inception-v3 in terms of Top-1 accuracy, respectively, by about 0.79%, 1.19%. The EPSANet(Large)-50 is very competitive to ResNeXt-101 [38], while the latter one employs more convolution filters and expensive group convolutions. In addition, The proposed EPSANet(Large)-50 is comparable to Res2Net-50 [14], PyConvResNet-50 [13]. All above results demonstrate that the proposed EPSANet has great potential to further improve the ability of multi-scale feature representation of the existing CNN models.

5.5   The Visualization Results

For an intuitive demonstration of the intrinsic multi-scale ability, as illustrated by Fig. 5, we visualize the class activation mapping (CAM) of the EPSANet(Small)-50 by using Grad-CAM. The visualization results demonstrated that the EPSANet is able to capture richer and more discriminative contextual information for a particular target class.

Table 9. Accuracy performance with several classical multi-scale neural networks on the ImageNet dataset.

Network	Top-1 Acc (%)	Top-5 Acc (%)
DenseNet-264(k = 32) [37]	77.85	93.78
InceptionV3 [28]	77.45	93.56
ResNeXt-101 [38]	78.80	94.40
Res2Net-50 [14]	77.99	93.85
Res2Net-50+SE [14]	78.44	94.06
PyConvResNet-50 [13]	77.88	93.80
EPSANet(Large)-50	78.64	94.18

Fig. 5. Visualization of GradCAM results. The results are obtained for six random samples from the ImageNet validation set and are compared for SENet50 and EPSANet(Small)-50.

6   Conclusion

In this paper, an effective and lightweight attention module named Pyramid Squeeze Attention (PSA) is proposed, which can fully extract the multi-scale spatial information and the important features across dimensions in the channel attention vectors. Correspondingly, the proposed Efficient Pyramid Squeeze Attention (EPSA) block inherits the advantage of the PSA module, which improves the multi-scale representation ability at a more granular level. Extensive qualitative and quantitative experiments demonstrated that the proposed EPSANet surpassed most conventional channel attention methods across a series of computer vision tasks.

Acknowledgements. This work was supported by the National Natural Science Foundation of China under grants U21A20455, 61972265, 11871348 and 61721002, by the Natural Science Foundation of Guangdong Province of China under grant 2020B1515310008, by the Macao Science and Technology Development Fund under Grant 061/2020/A2, by the Educational Commission of Guangdong Province of China under grant 2019KZDZX1007, the Pazhou Lab, Guangzhou, China.

References

1. Cao, Y., Xu, J., Lin, S., Wei, F., Hu, H.: GcNet: non-local networks meet squeeze-excitation networks and beyond. In: International Conference on Computer Vision Workshop (ICCVW), pp. 1971–1980 (2019)
2. Wang, F., et al.: Residual attention network for image classification. In: IEEE Conference on Computer Vision and Pattern Recognition (CVPR), pp. 3156–3164 (2017)
3. Tian, Z., Shen, C., Chen, H., He, T.: FCOS: fully convolutional one-stage object detection. In: IEEE International Conference on Computer Vision (ICCV), pp. 9626–9635 (2019)
4. He, K., Gkioxari, G., Doll'ar, P., Girshick, R.: Mask R-CNN. In: IEEE Transactions on Pattern Analysis and Machine Intelligence, vol. 42, no. 2, pp. 386–397 (2020)
5. Zhong, Z., et al.: Squeeze-and-attention networks for semantic segmentation. In: IEEE Conference on Computer Vision and Pattern Recognition (CVPR), pp. 13062–13071 (2020)
6. Chen, L.-C., Zhu, Y., Papandreou, G., Schroff, F., Adam, H.: Encoder-decoder with atrous separable convolution for semantic image segmentation. In: Ferrari, V., Hebert, M., Sminchisescu, C., Weiss, Y. (eds.) ECCV 2018. LNCS, vol. 11211, pp. 833–851. Springer, Cham (2018). https://doi.org/10.1007/978-3-030-01234-2_49
7. Zhao, H., Shi, J., Qi, X., Wang, X., Jia, J.: Pyramid scene parsing network. In: IEEE Conference on Computer Vision and Pattern Recognition (CVPR), pp. 6230–6239 (2017)
8. Qin, Z., Zhang, P., Wu, F., Li, X.: FcaNet: frequency channel attention networks. In: International Conference on Computer Vision (ICCV), pp. 763–772 (2021)
9. Wang, Q., Wu, B., Zhu, P., Li, P., Zuo, W., Hu, Q.: ECA-Net: efficient channel attention for deep convolutional neural networks. In: IEEE Conference on Computer Vision and Pattern Recognition (CVPR), pp. 11531–11539 (2020)
10. Park, J., Woo, S., Lee, J.Y., Kweon, I.S.: Bam: Bottleneck attention module. In: British Machine Vision Conference (BMVC) (2018)
11. Woo, S., Park, J., Lee, J.-Y., Kweon, I.S.: CBAM: convolutional block attention module. In: Ferrari, V., Hebert, M., Sminchisescu, C., Weiss, Y. (eds.) ECCV 2018. LNCS, vol. 11211, pp. 3–19. Springer, Cham (2018). https://doi.org/10.1007/978-3-030-01234-2_1
12. Hu, J., Shen, L., Sun, G.: Squeeze-and-excitation networks. In: IEEE Conference on Computer Vision and Pattern Recognition (CVPR), pp. 7132–7141 (2018)
13. Duta, I.C., Liu, L., Zhu, F., Shao, L.: Pyramidal convolution: rethinking convolutional neural networks for visual recognition (2020)
14. Gao, S.H., Cheng, M.M., Zhao, K., Zhang, X.Y., Yang, M.H., Torr, P.: Res2Net: a new multi-scale backbone architecture. In: IEEE Transactions on Pattern Analysis and Machine Intelligence, vol. 43, no. 2, pp. 652–662 (2021)
15. Yuan, P., et al.: HS-ResNet: hierarchical-split block on convolutional neural network (2020)

16. Fu, J., et al.: Dual attention network for scene segmentation. In: IEEE Conference on Computer Vision and Pattern Recognition (CVPR), pp. 3141–3149 (2019)
17. Wang, X., Girshick, R., Gupta, A., He, K.: Non-local neural networks. In: IEEE Conference on Computer Vision and Pattern Recognition (CVPR), pp. 7794–7803 (2018)
18. Gao, Z., Xie, J., Wang, Q., Li, P.: Global second-order pooling convolutional networks. In: IEEE Conference on Computer Vision and Pattern Recognition (CVPR), pp. 3019–3028 (2019)
19. Chen, Y., Kalantidis, Y., Li, J., Yan, S., Feng, J.: A2-Nets: double attention networks. In: Advances in Neural Information Processing Systems (NIPS), pp. 350–359 (2018)
20. Li, X., Wang, W., Hu, X., Yang, J.: Selective kernel networks. In: IEEE Conference on Computer Vision and Pattern Recognition (CVPR), pp. 510–519 (2019)
21. Zhang, H., et al..: ResNest: split-attention networks (2020)
22. Najibi, M., Samangouei, P., Chellappa, R., Davis, L.S.: SSH: single stage headless face detector. In: IEEE International Conference on Computer Vision (ICCV), pp. 4885–4894 (2017)
23. Ren, S., He, K., Girshick, R., Sun, J.: Faster R-CNN: towards real-time object detection with region proposal networks. In: IEEE Transactions on Pattern Analysis and Machine Intelligence, vol. 39, no. 6, pp. 1137–1149 (2017)
24. Zhao, J.X., Cao, Y., Fan, D.P., Cheng, M.M., Li, X.Y., Zhang, L.: Contrast prior and fluid pyramid integration for RGBD salient object detection. In: IEEE Conference on Computer Vision and Pattern Recognition (CVPR), pp. 3922–3931 (2019)
25. Nair, V., Hinton, G.E.: Rectified linear units improve restricted Boltzmann machines. In: International Conference on Machine Learning (ICML), pp. 807–814 (2010)
26. He, K., Zhang, X., Ren, S., Sun, J.: Deep residual learning for image recognition. In: IEEE Conference on Computer Vision and Pattern Recognition (CVPR), pp. 770–778 (2016)
27. Deng, J., Dong, W., Socher, R., Li, L.J., Li, K., Fei-Fei, L.: ImageNet: a largescale hierarchical image database. In: IEEE Conference on Computer Vision and Pattern Recognition (CVPR), pp. 248–255 (2009)
28. Szegedy, C., Vanhoucke, V., Ioffe, S., Shlens, J., Wojna, Z.: Rethinking the inception architecture for computer vision. In: IEEE Conference on Computer Vision and Pattern Recognition (CVPR), pp. 2818–2826 (2016)
29. Lin, T.Y., Doll'ar, P., Girshick, R., He, K., Hariharan, B., Belongie, S.: Feature pyramid networks for object detection. In: IEEE Conference on Computer Vision and Pattern Recognition, pp. 2117–2125 (2017)
30. Lin, T.Y., Goyal, P., Girshick, R., He, K., Doll'ar, P.: Focal loss for dense object detection. In: IEEE International Conference on Computer Vision (ICCV), pp. 2980–2988 (2017)
31. Lin, T.-Y., et al.: Microsoft COCO: common objects in context. In: Fleet, D., Pajdla, T., Schiele, B., Tuytelaars, T. (eds.) ECCV 2014. LNCS, vol. 8693, pp. 740–755. Springer, Cham (2014). https://doi.org/10.1007/978-3-319-10602-1_48
32. Chen, K., et al.: MMDetection: Open MMlab detection toolbox and benchmark (2019)
33. Misra, D., Nalamada, T., Arasanipalai, A.U., Hou, Q.: Rotate to attend: convolutional triplet attention module. In: IEEE Winter Conference on Applications of Computer Vision (WACV), pp. 3138–3147 (2021)

34. Bello, I., Zoph, B., Le, Q., Vaswani, A., Shlens, J.: Attention augmented convolutional networks. In: IEEE International Conference on Computer Vision (ICCV), pp. 3285–3294 (2019)
35. Krizhevsky, A., Hinton, G.: Learning multiple layers of features from tiny images. Handbook of Systemic Autoimmune Diseases (2009)
36. Mark, S., Andrew, G.H., Zhu, M., Andrey, Z., Chen, L.C.: MobileNetV2: inverted residuals and linear bottlenecks. In: IEEE Conference on Computer Vision and Pattern Recognition (CVPR), pp. 4510–4520 (2018)
37. Huang, G., Liu, Z., Van Der Maaten, L., Weinberger, K.Q.: Densely connected convolutional networks. In: IEEE Conference on Computer Vision and Pattern Recognition (CVPR), pp. 2261–2269 (2017)
38. Xie, S., Girshick, R., Doll'ar, P., Tu, Z., He, K.: Aggregated residual transformations for deep neural networks. In: IEEE Conference on Computer Vision and Pattern Recognition (CVPR), pp. 5987–5995 (2017)

Boosting Dense Long-Tailed Object Detection from Data-Centric View

Weichen Xu, Jian Cao[✉], Tianhao Fu, Hongyi Yao, and Yuan Wang

Peking University, Beijing, China
{xuweichen1999,tianhaofu1,yhy}@stu.pku.edu.cn, caojian@ss.pku.edu.cn

Abstract. Several re-sampling and re-weighting approaches have been proposed in recent literature to address long-tailed object detection. However, state-of-the-art approaches still struggle on the rare class. From data-centric view, this is due to few training data of the rare class and data imbalance. Some data augmentations which could generate more training data perform well in general object detection, while they are hardly leveraged in long-tailed object detection. We reveal that the real culprit lies in the fact that data imbalance has not been alleviated or even intensified. In this paper, we propose REDet: a rare data centric detection framework which could simultaneously generate training data of the rare class and deal with data imbalance. Our REDet contains data operations at two levels. At the instance-level, Copy-Move data augmentation could independently rebalance the number of instances of different classes according to their rarity. Specifically, we copy instances of the rare class in an image and then move them to other locations in the same image. At the anchor-level, to generate more supervision for the rare class within a reasonable range, we propose Long-Tailed Training Sample Selection (LTTSS) to dynamically determine the corresponding positive samples for each instance based on the rarity of the class. Comprehensive experiments performed on the challenging LVIS v1 dataset demonstrate the effectiveness of our proposed approach. We achieve an overall 30.2% AP and obtain significant performance improvements on the rare class.

1 Introduction

In real-world scenarios, training data generally exhibit a long-tailed class distribution, where a small number of classes have a large amount of data, but others have only a small amount of data [1]. Long-tailed object detection is receiving increasing attention because of the need for realistic scenarios.

Some existing approaches deal with this task by data re-sampling [2–5] or loss re-weighting [6–9]. Specifically, re-sampling approaches increase rare class instances by performing image-level resampling in the dataset, which is effective when a certain amount of image-level training data contains rare class instances. The re-weighting approaches increase the contribution of the rare class to the

---

Supplementary Information The online version contains supplementary material available at https://doi.org/10.1007/978-3-031-26313-2_34.

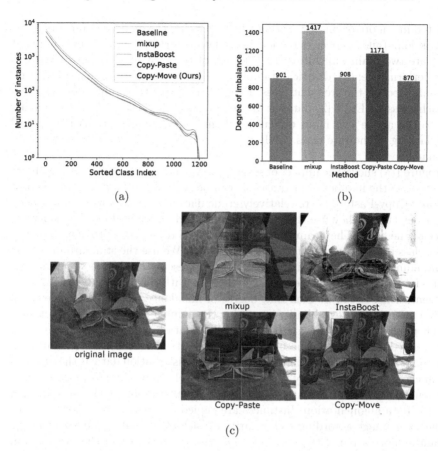

(a)

(b)

(c)

Fig. 1. (a) The number of instances of baseline and various data augmentations on LVIS v1 [2] train split. Classes' indices are sorted by instance counts of baseline. (b) The degree of imbalance between baseline and various data augmentations on LVIS v1 [2] train split. (c) Visualization of the original image and various data augmentations. For display, the image augmented by Copy-Paste is scaled to the same size as the other images.

gradient by modifying the loss function, which in turn increases the focus on the rare class. In addition, many remarkable efforts have focused on incremental learning [10], data augmentation [11], and decoupled learning [4,12,13].

However, state-of-the-art approaches still struggle on the rare class. In fact, the poor performance of current SOTA long-tailed detection methods is caused by the dataset quality itself. An intuitive example is that if we convert a dataset from the long-tailed dataset into a balanced dataset, there will be no such problem as long-tailed object detection. Thus, the benefits of improving the model or the loss function are far less obvious than improving the dataset directly. Recently, Data-Centric AI [14] has been a scorching research topic. The main idea is usually to do a series of operations on the data so that the gradient is updated in a more optimal direction when updating the model parameters. If we rethink long-tailed object detection from data-centric view, we could find that there are two main difficulties [1]: (1). lack of the rare class instances leads to poor performance; (2). drastic data imbalance makes the performance of the rare class affected by the frequent class. Figure 1(a) shows the number of instances of each class in LVIS [2] dataset. It can be seen that the task is challenging due to the above two main difficulties. Some data augmentations try to deal with lacking of the rare class, while these methods still cannot resolve the data imbalance.

Figure 1(a) shows the impact of several common data augmentations in object detection on the number of instances. It can be seen that mixup [15], InstaBoost [16], and Copy-Paste [11] are relatively crude data augmentations for long-tailed object detection. They use the same rules for all classes and do not consider the rarity of the class. They cannot solve the label co-occurrence problem. The frequent class is augmented at the same time. Here, We use the standard deviation of the number of instances in all classes to represent the degree of imbalance. Figure 1(b) illustrates the degree of imbalance with and without various data augmentations. It can be seen that degree of imbalance has not been alleviated or even intensified due to blindly increasing the number of instances in all classes.

Therefore, we can generate more rare class data by modifying the data in a more refined way. So we propose REDet: a rare data centric detection framework that could bridge the gap of handling long-tailed distribution data at the instance and anchor levels. Specifically, at the instance-level, we propose Copy-Move data augmentation, which introduces information about the long-tailed distribution into the data augmentation. Instances are copied and moved to other locations in the same image according to the rarity of each class. Without destroying the semantic information of the image, we increase the diversity of the rare class in the dataset to alleviate the lack of rare class instances and data imbalance. At the anchor-level, we propose Long-Tailed Training Sample Selection (LTTSS) to dynamically determine the corresponding positive samples for each instance based on the rarity of its class. Our approach has the lowest degree of imbalance compared to other data augmentations. It yields a new state-of-the-art and can be well applied to existing dense long-tailed object detection pipelines.

To sum up, our key contributions can be summarized as follows:

- We think about long-tailed object detection from data-centric view and propose degree of imbalance to evaluate several existing data augmentations.
- We propose REDet: a rare data centric detection framework in which Copy-Move and LTTSS work collaboratively to promote the instances balance and positive samples balance while increasing training data.
- Extensive experiments on the challenging LVIS dataset demonstrate the effectiveness of the proposed approach. Our approach achieves state-of-the-art results on LVIS by introducing long-tailed information in data augmentation and training sample selection.

2   Related Work

General Object Detection. Object detection approaches have achieved immense success in recent years, benefiting from the powerful classification ability of convolutional neural networks (CNN) [17–19]. Advanced object detectors can be categorized into two-stage and one-stage approaches. Two-stage approaches [20–22] first generate coarse proposals through region proposal network (RPN). Then, these proposals are further refined for accurate classification and bounding box regression. One-stage approaches [23–26] make predictions directly on the dense anchors or points without generating coarse proposals. In practice, one-stage detectors are more widely used in real-world scenarios. But the performance of the general object detectors degrades dramatically when it comes to the long-tailed distribution of data [6].

Long-Tailed Object Detection. Long-tailed object detection is more complex than general object detection due to the extreme data imbalance. It is receiving increasing attention [1]. One classic solution to this problem is loss re-weighting. The basic idea of the re-weighting method is to assign different weights to the training samples based on the rarity of the class. Tan et al. [6] proposed the equalization loss (EQL) that ignored the negative gradients from frequent samples. Seesaw loss [7] proposed compensation factor to avoid false positives of the rare class. EQLv2 [8] rethought the essential role of samples in the classification branch and adopted a gradient-guided mechanism to reweight the loss of each class. Li et al. [9] proposed the equalized focal loss (EFL) that rebalanced the loss contribution of positive and negative samples in one-stage detectors. Another useful solution is the re-sampling strategy. Repeat factor sampling (RFS) [2] over-sampled images containing rare classes to balance the data distribution at the image-level. At the instance-level, Forest R-CNN [3] set a higher non-maximum suppression (NMS) threshold for the rare class to get more proposals. Other works [4,5] used bi-level class balanced sampler or memory-augmented sampler to implement data resampling. However, both re-weighting and re-sampling approaches still struggle on the rare class due to the lack of consideration of the long-tailed distribution in dataset.

Data Augmentations. Data augmentations such as CutMix [27], InstaBoost [16], and Mosaic [28] can significantly boost object detection performance. However, as a simple technique, data augmentation is rarely discussed in long-tailed object detection. MiSLAS [29] proposed to use data mixup to enhance representation learning in long-tailed image classification. Ghiasi et al. [11] demonstrated that the simple mechanism of pasting objects randomly was good enough for the long-tailed instance segmentation task. Zhang et al. [30] addressed the data scarcity issue by augmenting the feature space, especially for the rare class. Simply using existing augmentation techniques for improving long-tailed object detection performance is unfavorable, which will lead to the problem of label co-occurrence. Specifically, frequent class labels frequently appear with rare class labels during data augmentation. Thus, the frequent class would be augmented more, which may bias the degree of imbalance. Instead, we dynamically increase the number of instances and positive samples according to the rarity of the class, which can solve the above problem well and have a higher data validity.

3   Method

The rare data centric detection framework we proposed is based on one-stage object detection network such as RetinaNet [23]. Figure 2 is an overview of the proposed REDet, which shows that our Copy-Move data augmentation is inserted before network, and LTTSS is used to select positive samples after network. For instances of the rare class, the copy times and the long-tailed scaling factor are calculated for Copy-Move and LTTSS, respectively.

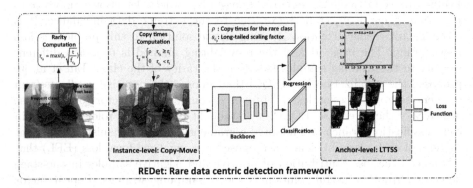

Fig. 2. Architecture overview of REDet. Our proposed method contains two main components: Copy-Move data augmentation at the instance-level and LTTSS at the anchor-level. In LTTSS, the red anchors represent original positive samples, and the green anchors represent the newly obtained positive samples after introducing the long-tailed information. (Color figure online)

3.1   Instance-Level: Copy-Move

The existing instance-level data augmentation approach [11] selected a random subset of instances from one image and pasted them onto another image. However, images generated in this way could look very different from authentic images in terms of co-occurrences of objects or scales of objects. For example, burgers, root beers, and buses could appear on the table simultaneously, and their scales would be vastly different from our normal perception. We believe there is a strong semantic correlation between foreground instances and backgrounds in the same image. Therefore, it is reasonable that an instance appears multiple times in the image. For example, root beers are more inclined to appear in the diet scene, and the increase of root beer instances does not destroy the semantic information in the original image. Accordingly, at the instance-level, we propose Copy-Move data augmentation to copy instances and then move them to other locations in the same image. In addition, we dynamically calculate copy times for each instance according to the rarity of the class to obtain better detection results for the rare class.

For each ground-truth instance g, we can get its class c_g. In general, a long-tailed object detection dataset, such as LVIS [2], will provide the number of images in which the class is annotated. This can implicitly reflect the rarity of each class. Thus, we can use the approach in RFS [2] to define the rarity of the class r_{c_g}:

$$r_{c_g} = \max(1, \sqrt{\frac{t}{f_{c_g}}}), \tag{1}$$

where f_{c_g} is the fraction of images in which the class is annotated, t is a hyper-parameter. Instances of the rare class will get a larger r_{c_g}. Then, the copy times t_g of the ground-truth instance g can be calculated as:

$$t_g = \begin{cases} \rho & r_{c_g} \geqq r_t \\ 0 & r_{c_g} < r_t \end{cases}, \tag{2}$$

where r_t is the threshold for determining whether the class is rare or not and ρ is the copy times of the rare class. we set $r_t = 3$ in LVIS. Thus, instances of the rare class will be copied more times.

For each image, we use Eq. (2) to calculate the copy times of each instance. If an instance belongs to the rare class and needs to be copied, we perform Copy-Move data augmentation cyclically. Specifically, a scaling factor is randomly selected from [0.8, 1.2] to perform scale jittering on the mask of the instance. Scale jittering randomly is essential to enhance the diversity of the instance. Then select a point from the image randomly as the upper left corner of the placement location, not restricting the scaled instance boundary to exceed the image boundary. Finally, the mask of the original instance is copied and moved to the target location. When all instances have been copied, we first deal with the occlusion between the copied instances. Our approach is that the instance copied first will be occluded by the instance copied later if there is overlap between the two instances. Therefore, we should not set too large copy times. Otherwise, excessive occlusion will destroy the semantic information of the image. Then, we handle the occlusion of the original instances by the copied instance. If the original instance is occluded and reduced by more than 10 pixels in width or height, we filter out the original instance. By Copy-Move data augmentation, the number of instances of the frequent class is maintained while the number of instances of the rare class is increased within a reasonable range, which facilitates long-tailed object detection.

While our main experimental results use the copy times t_g definition above, its precise rule is not crucial. In Appendix 1, we consider other instantiations of the copy times and demonstrate that these can be equally effective.

The previous data augmentations, such as mixup [15] and Copy-Paste [11], did not consider the rarity of the class and directly mixed instances from two images. However, instances of the rare class and instances of the frequent class often appear together, i.e., label co-occurrence. Blindly increasing instances of all classes do not alleviate the class imbalance, as shown in Fig. 1(b). Moreover, it is not efficient to blindly increase the number of instances of all classes. As we will introduce in Sect. 4.4, the data validity of the previous data augmentations is low. In contrast, our proposed Copy-Move approach introduces the long-tailed information in the dataset into the data augmentation and only increases the number of instances of the rare class. This can alleviate the class imbalance and increase the diversity of rare class instances while having higher data validity. In addition, our approach effectively enhances rare class instances and can be easily embedded in existing long-tailed object detection processing.

3.2   Anchor-Level: Long-Tailed Training Sample Selection

When training an object detector, all ground-truth instances must select their corresponding positive samples. These positive samples are further used for classification and box regression. Thus, positive samples are the ultimate supervision to guide neural network learning. After obtaining more instances of the rare class at the instance-level using the above Copy-Move data augmentation, we propose a Long-Tailed Training Sample Selection (LTTSS) to generate more suitable positive samples for the instances of the rare class. We introduce information about the long-tailed distribution into the training sample selection. Compared to generating positive samples using fixed rules for all classes, our LTTSS approach automatically divides positive samples according to the rarity of the class.

We use the rarity of the class r_{c_g} defined in Eq. (1). Then we can define the mapping between long-tailed scaling factor s_{c_g} and the rarity of the class r_{c_g} as:

$$s_{c_g} = 1 + \frac{\varepsilon}{1 + e^{-\gamma(r_{c_g} - \mu)}}, \tag{3}$$

where ε, γ and μ are hyperparameters and set $\varepsilon = 1$. In this way, the rare class will receive a larger s_{c_g} but no more than 2.

In training sample selection, we first obtain candidate positive samples for each ground-truth instance g. Specifically, for each pyramid level, we select the k_{c_g} anchors closest to the center of ground-truth instance box b_g according to the Euclidean distance. We define $k_{c_g} = \lfloor k \times s_{c_g} \rfloor$ where k is a hyperparameter with a default value of 9. Therefore, the rare class will get more candidate positive samples, at most $2k$. Assuming that there are n_l pyramid levels, a total of $n_l \times k_{c_g}$ candidate positive samples will be obtained for each ground-truth instance and we define it as C_g. Then we calculate intersection of union (IoU) between ground-truth instance box b_g and candidate positive samples C_g as $\mathcal{I}_g$. Mean m_g and standard deviation v_g of $\mathcal{I}_g$ are then calculated in order to filter. We define the long-tailed filtering threshold f_t as:

$$f_t = \frac{m_g + v_g}{s_{c_g}}. \tag{4}$$

Obviously, the threshold of the rare class is lowered as a way to retain more positive samples. Finally, we select positive candidate samples with IoU greater than or equal to the long-tailed filtering threshold f_t as the final positive samples. In particular, it is necessary to restrict the center of final positive samples inside the ground-truth instance box. The overall flow of LTTSS is shown in Algorithm 1. The bolded pseudo code indicates that information about the long-tailed distribution is used.

Compared with ATSS [31], our algorithm also automatically divides positive samples according to the statistical characteristics of instances. However, instead of using the same rule for all classes, we generate more positive samples for the rare class according to the rarity of the class. Particularly, the increase of positive samples is not blind. Due to the restriction that the center of the positive samples must be located in the center of the ground-truth instance box, we select as many training positive samples as possible for the rare class within a reasonable range.

Algorithm 1: Long-Tailed Training Sample Selection

Input:
    b_g: a ground-truth instance box;
    n_l: the number of pyramid levels;
    $\mathcal{A}_i$: the set of anchors in pyramid level i;
    $\mathcal{A}$: the set of anchors in all pyramid levels;
    r_{c_g}: the rarity of the class c_g;
    k: a hyperparameter with a default value of 9

Output:
    $\mathcal{P}_g$: the set of positive samples;
    $\mathcal{N}_g$: the set of negative samples;

compute the long-tailed scaling factor s_{c_g}: $s_{c_g} = 1 + \frac{1}{1+e^{-\gamma(r_{c_g}-\mu)}}$;

compute the number of candidate positive samples k_{c_g} selected in each pyramid level: $k_{c_g} = \lfloor k \times s_{c_g} \rfloor$;

for i in $[1, n_l]$ do
    $\mathcal{C}_g = \mathcal{C}_g \cup k_{c_g}$ anchors that closest to the center of b_g according to the
    Euclidean distance in $\mathcal{A}_i$

end

compute IoU $\mathcal{I}_g$ between b_g and $\mathcal{C}_g$; compute mean m_g and standard deviation v_g of $\mathcal{I}_g$;

compute the long-tailed filtering threshold f_t: $f_t = \frac{m_g + v_g}{s_{c_g}}$;

for each candidate c in $\mathcal{C}_g$ do
    if center of c in b_g and $\text{IoU}(c, b_g) > f_t$ then
        $\mathcal{P}_g = \mathcal{P}_g \cup c$
    end

end

$\mathcal{N}_g = \mathcal{A} - \mathcal{P}_g$;

return $\mathcal{P}_g, \mathcal{N}_g$

---

4   Experiments

4.1   Experimental Settings

Dataset. We perform experiments on the challenging LVIS v1 dataset [2]. LVIS is a large vocabulary benchmark for long-tailed object detection, which contains 1203 classes. It provides precise bounding box for various classes with long-tailed distribution. We train our models on the train set, which contains about 100k images. According to the number of images that each class appears in the train split, the classes are divided into three groups: rare (1–10 images), common (11–100 images) and frequent (>100 images). We report results on the val set of 20k images.

Evaluation Metric. We use the widely-used metric AP across IoU threshold from 0.5 to 0.95 to evaluate object detection results. In addition, we also report AP_r, AP_c, AP_f for rare, common and frequent classes to well characterize the long-tailed class performance. Unlike the COCO evaluation process, detection results of classes not listed in the image level labels will not be evaluated.

Implementation Details. We use the same training framework as EFL [9] as our baseline settings. Specifically, we adopt the ResNet-50 [18] initialized by ImageNet [32] pre-trained models as the backbone and feature pyramid network (FPN) [19] as the neck. Besides, we also perform experiments with ResNet-101, a larger backbone to validate the effectiveness of our method. Following the convention, we adopt multi-scale with horizontally flip augmentation during training. Specifically, we randomly resize the shorter edge of the image within $\{640, 672, 704, 736, 768, 800\}$ pixels and keep the longer edge smaller than 1333 pixels without changing the aspect ratio. During the inference phase, we resize the shorter edge of the input image to 800 pixels and keep the longer edge smaller than 1333 pixels without changing the aspect ratio. Our model is optimized by stochastic gradient descent (SGD) with momentum 0.9 and weight decay 0.0001 for 24 epochs. As mentioned in [23], in the one-stage detector, the prior bias of the last layer in the classification branch should be initialized to $-\log\frac{1-\pi}{\pi}$ with $\pi = 0.001$. To avoid abnormal gradients and stabilize the training process, we utilize the gradient clipping with a maximum normalized value of 35. Unlike the EFL settings, we use a total batch size of 8 on 8 GPUs (1 image per GPU) and set the initial learning rate to 0.01 with 1 epoch' warm up. The learning rate decays to 0.001, 0.0001 at the end of epoch 16 and 22, respectively. In addition, we keep the top 300 bounding boxes as prediction results and reduce the threshold of prediction score from 0.05 to 0.0 following [2]. We train all models with RFS [2].

For our proposed Copy-Move, the hyperparameter t used to calculate the rarity of the class is set to 0.001, and the threshold r_t used to determine whether Copy-Move should be used is set to 3. The copy times ρ of the rare class is set to 4, and more details about the impact of this hyperparameter are showcased in Sect. 4.3. In particular, we perform Copy-Move data augmentation with probability 0.5 and close it for the last 3 epochs, when the learning rate is decayed for the last time.

For our proposed LTTSS, we tile two anchors per location on the image with the anchor scale $\{6, 8\}$ with $k = 18$ to cover more potential candidates. In Eq. (3), hyperparameter γ and μ can adjust the slope and central region of the curve. They work together to control the influence range of long-tailed scaling factor s_{c_g}. We set $\gamma = 5.0$ and $\mu = 2.5$. More details about the impact of γ and μ are showcased in Sect. 4.3.

4.2   Benchmark Results

Table 1 demonstrates the effectiveness of our proposed REDet. We compare our approach with other works that report state-of-the-art performance and other augmentations that can significantly boost object detection performance. With ResNet-50 backbone, our proposed REDet achieves an overall 28.3% AP, which improves the baseline by 0.8% AP, and even achieves 1.4 points improvement on the rare class. It can be seen that Copy-Move and LTTSS work collaboratively to realize the instances equilibrium and positive samples equilibrium in long-tailed object detection and dramatically improve the performance of the rare class without sacrificing the frequent class. Compared with other state-of-the-art methods like EQL [6], EQLv2 [8], BAGS [13] and Seesaw Loss [7], our proposed method outperforms them by 3.2% AP, 2.8% AP, 2.3% AP and 1.9% AP, respectively. In addition, we also add data augmentations such as mixup [15], InstaBoost [16], Copy-Paste [11] to the baseline. In particular, Copy-Paste was trained in [11] in a decoupled strategy. Specifically, in the first stage, they trained the object detector for 180k steps using a 256 batch size. Then they fine-tuned the model with 36 epochs in the second stage. For a fair comparison, we train Copy-Paste with large scale jittering on the image size of 1024×1024 in an end-to-end strategy for 24 epochs. More training details can be found in Appendix 2. Compared to these methods, our proposed method outperforms them by 3.0% AP, 1.4% AP and 1.1% AP, respectively. This is mainly because the existing data augmentations do not consider the information of the long-tailed distribution in the dataset. Mixup and Copy-Paste simply mix or paste the instances from two images together. They do not consider the label co-occurrence problem, which exacerbates the imbalance and ultimately yields lower detection results. InstaBoost jitter the location of instances in all classes by calculating the location probability map, which hardly changes the number of instances in each class. It shows that blindly increasing the number of instances or jittering instances in long-tailed object detection is inefficient, requiring significant computational resources while failing to improve the final performance. Our proposed REDet introduces class rarity in data augmentation and positive sample sampling, which alleviates the imbalance in the dataset and leads to better performance in AP and AP_r.

We conduct experiments with larger ResNet-101 backbone. Our approach can still obtain consistent improvements in overall AP and AP_r by 1.0% and 1.4%, respectively. Compared to other data augmentations, our proposed approach still performs better in long-tailed object detection. It indicates that our REDet can alleviate the imbalance across different backbones. Our method achieves 30.2% AP and establishes a new state-of-the-art.

4.3 Ablation Study

We conduct a series of comprehensive ablation studies to verify the effectiveness of the proposed REDet. For all experiments, we use ResNet-50 as backbone for 24 epochs.

Table 1. Comparison with other state-of-the-art approaches and other augmentations on LVIS v1 val set. † indicates that the reported result is directly copied from referenced paper. + indicates that the augmentation is added to the baseline.

Backbone	Method	Strategy	AP	AP_r	AP_c	AP_f
ResNet-50	*Other methods*					
	EQL† [6]	End-to-end	25.1	15.7	24.4	30.1
	EQLv2† [8]	End-to-end	25.5	16.4	23.9	31.2
	BAGS† [13]	Decoupled	26.0	17.2	24.9	31.1
	Seesaw Loss† [7]	End-to-end	26.4	17.5	25.3	31.5
	EFL (Baseline)† [9]	end-to-end	27.5	20.2	26.1	32.4
	Augmentations					
	+ mixup [15]	End-to-end	25.3	18.5	23.3	30.5
	+ InstaBoost [16]	End-to-end	26.9	19.7	25.6	31.5
	+ Copy-Paste [11]	end-to-end	27.2	21.3	25.8	31.5
	REDet (Ours)	End-to-end	**28.3**	**21.6**	**26.8**	**32.9**
ResNet-101	*Other methods*					
	EQLv2† [8]	End-to-end	26.9	18.2	25.4	32.4
	BAGS† [13]	Decoupled	27.6	18.7	26.5	32.6
	Seesaw Loss† [7]	End-to-end	27.8	18.7	27.0	32.8
	EFL (Baseline)† [9]	end-to-end	29.2	23.5	27.4	33.8
	Augmentations					
	+ mixup [15]	End-to-end	28.8	21.4	27.1	33.8
	+ InstaBoost [16]	End-to-end	28.6	22.0	27.2	33.2
	+ Copy-Paste [11]	end-to-end	29.7	24.1	27.8	**34.4**
	REDet (Ours)	End-to-end	**30.2**	**24.9**	**28.5**	34.3

Influence of Components in Our Approach. There are two components in our REDet, Copy-Move and LTTSS. As shown in Table 2, both Copy-Move and LTTSS play significant roles in our approach. Copy-Move can achieve an improvement from 27.5% AP to 28.1% AP, and achieve 0.6 points improvement on the rare class without degrading the performance of the frequent class. Our approach calculates the copy times of an instance based on the rarity of the class, which alleviates the problem of the lack of rare class instances and makes the dataset more balanced. LTTSS generates more supervision for the rare class within a reasonable range at positive sample sampling and achieves an improvement from 27.5% AP to 27.8% AP. Combining the two components, our REDet takes the performance of the baseline from 27.5% to 28.3%. In particular, we can achieve a 1.4% improvement in the rare class. This is due to the fact that the instances and positive samples of the rare class grow within a reasonable range at the same time.

Table 2. Ablation study of each component in our approach. Copy-Move and LTTSS indicate Copy-Move augmentation, and long-tailed training sample selection, respectively.

Copy-Move	LTTSS	AP	AP_r	AP_c	AP_f
		27.5	20.2	26.1	32.4
✓		28.1	20.8	26.7	32.8
	✓	27.8	20.4	26.3	32.8
✓	✓	**28.3**	**21.6**	**26.8**	**32.9**

Influence of Number of Instances and Positive Samples. It can be seen that our proposed approaches, Copy-Move and LTTSS, increase the number of instances and positive samples of the rare class, respectively, according to the rarity of the class. In particular, the beneficial performance is brought by our specially designed rules that exploit the long-tailed information in the dataset rather than by brutally increasing the number of instances and positive samples. To prove this, we randomly and uniformly increase the number of instances and positive samples for all classes until they are close to the number of Copy-Move and LTTSS, respectively. Table 3 shows the experimental results. Compared to baseline, rand Copy-Move copies 3 instances for each class. This approach can not alleviate the degree of imbalance and can hardly have an impact on AP. The performance of the various classes was virtually unchanged. On the other hand, we reduce the threshold for all classes in positive sample sampling instead of calculating based on the rarity of the class. It can be seen that compared to baseline, the random LTTSS even reduces 0.1% AP and 1.0% AP_r due to blindly lowering the threshold for all classes.

Table 3. Ablation study of the number of instances and positive samples. Rand Copy-Move and rand LTTSS indicate randomly and uniformly increasing the number of instances and positive samples for all classes, respectively.

Method	Number	AP	AP_r	AP_c	AP_f
	Instances				
Baseline	429.8k	27.5	20.2	26.1	32.4
Rand Copy-Move	432.9k	27.5	20.2	25.9	32.5
Copy-Move	433.3k	**28.1**	**20.8**	**26.7**	**32.8**
	Positive samples				
Baseline	24.15M	27.5	20.2	26.1	32.4
Rand LTTSS	24.38M	27.4	19.2	26.0	32.6
LTTSS	24.38M	**27.8**	**20.4**	**26.3**	**32.8**

Influence of the Hyperparameter. We study the hyperparameters, i.e., ρ, γ, μ, adopted in different components of our REDet. In Table 4(a), we explore ρ in Copy-Move. ρ controls the times that the rare class instance is copied. When ρ is too small, the number of rare instances is still insufficient to alleviate the imbalance of the dataset. When ρ is too large, a more serious occlusion occurs between the copied and original instances during the movement. This corrupts the semantic information in the image and makes object detection more difficult. We find that $\rho = 4$ achieves the best performance. In Table 4(b), we explore γ, μ in LTTSS. γ and μ control the slope and central region of the curve and further control the influence range of the long-tailed scaling factor s_{c_g} as shown in Fig. 3. Results show that $\gamma = 5.0, \mu = 2.5$ achieves the best performance.

Table 4. Ablation study of the hyperparameter ρ, γ and μ, $\rho = 4, \gamma = 5.0, \mu = 2.5$ is adopted as the default setting in other experiments. (a) hyperparameter ρ. (b) hyperparameters γ and μ.

<table>
<tr><td colspan="5" align="center">(a)</td><td colspan="6" align="center">(b)</td></tr>
<tr><td>ρ</td><td>AP</td><td>AP_r</td><td>AP_c</td><td>AP_f</td><td>γ</td><td>μ</td><td>AP</td><td>AP_r</td><td>AP_c</td><td>AP_f</td></tr>
<tr><td>1</td><td>27.7</td><td>20.0</td><td>26.2</td><td>32.7</td><td>5.0</td><td>2.0</td><td>27.7</td><td>20.2</td><td>26.1</td><td>32.8</td></tr>
<tr><td>2</td><td>27.9</td><td>20.1</td><td>26.5</td><td>32.8</td><td>5.0</td><td>2.5</td><td>27.8</td><td>**20.4**</td><td>26.3</td><td>32.8</td></tr>
<tr><td>3</td><td>27.9</td><td>20.3</td><td>26.4</td><td>**32.9**</td><td>5.0</td><td>3.0</td><td>27.8</td><td>20.0</td><td>26.3</td><td>32.8</td></tr>
<tr><td>4</td><td>**28.1**</td><td>**20.8**</td><td>**26.7**</td><td>32.8</td><td>3.0</td><td>2.5</td><td>27.6</td><td>19.9</td><td>26.1</td><td>32.7</td></tr>
<tr><td>5</td><td>27.7</td><td>19.1</td><td>26.5</td><td>32.8</td><td>10.0</td><td>2.5</td><td>27.5</td><td>19.4</td><td>26.1</td><td>32.7</td></tr>
<tr><td>6</td><td>27.5</td><td>18.3</td><td>26.4</td><td>32.8</td><td>15.0</td><td>2.5</td><td>27.3</td><td>18.6</td><td>25.7</td><td>32.8</td></tr>
</table>

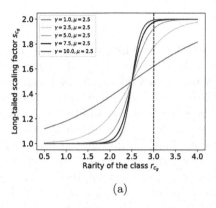
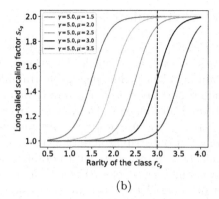

(a)   (b)

Fig. 3. Comparison of the long-tailed scaling factor s_{c_g} with different hyperparameters. The black vertical line represents the demarcation line between the rare and other classes. (a) Different γ with $\mu = 2.5$. (b) Different μ with $\gamma = 5.0$.

4.4 Data Validity Analysis

Performing data augmentation uniformly for all classes is inefficient. We propose a metric called data validity to measure this. We quantitatively demonstrated the data validity of several data augmentations and our proposed Copy-Move. In detail, We define data validity v_d as $v_d = \frac{\triangle AP}{\triangle n_i}$, where $\triangle n_i$ denotes increase in the number of instances and $\triangle AP$ denotes increase in AP. Specifically, we count the number of all instances augmented during 1 epoch while recording the final performance gain for each method. Table 5 shows the detailed results. Mixup and Copy-Paste blindly increase the number of instances by about 57%, 33%, respectively. However, increasing the number of instances of all classes does not alleviate the data imbalance and introduces severe occlusion. Their data validity is only $-8.9\text{e}{-}6$ and $-2.1\text{e}{-}6$, respectively. InstaBoost jitters instance's position through the probability map, which may lead to missing instances. Despite the positive data validity $6.5\text{e}{-}5$, it does not lead to performance gains. Our approach increases the instances of the rare class according to the rarity and maintains the frequent class instances unchanged, which ultimately yields greater data validity $1.7\text{e}{-}4$.

Table 5. Data validity v_d of several data augmentations and our proposed Copy-Move. $\triangle$ indicates the increase compared to baseline.

Method	n_i	$\triangle n_i$	AP	$\triangle AP$	v_d
Baseline [9]	429.8k	0.0k	27.5	0	
mixup [15]	676.8k	247.0k	25.3	-2.2	$-8.9\text{e}{-}6$
InstaBoost [16]	420.6k	-9.2k	26.9	-0.6	$6.5\text{e}{-}5$
Copy-Paste [11]	573.4k	143.6k	27.2	-0.3	$-2.1\text{e}{-}6$
Copy-Move (Ours)	433.3k	3.5k	28.1	$+0.6$	**$1.7\text{e}{-}4$**

5 Conclusion

In this paper, we boost dense long-tailed object detection from a new data-centric view. A rare data centric detection framework REDet is proposed to alleviate data imbalance while increasing training data. Novel Copy-Move data augmentation and Long-Tailed Training Sample Selection (LTTSS) work together to dynamically increase the number of instances and positive samples according to the rarity. Our proposed approach is the first to bridge the gap of handling long-tailed distribution data at the instance-level and anchor-level. It brings significant improvements with notably boosting on the rare class. Combining the two components, our REDet beats existing state-of-the-art approaches on the challenging LVIS v1 benchmark, which shows the superiority of our method. We hope that our REDet could be a standard procedure when training one-stage long-tailed object detection models.

Acknowledgments. This work was supported by the National Key Research and Development Program of China (Grant No. 2018YFE0203801).

References

1. Zhang, Y., Kang, B., Hooi, B., Yan, S., Feng, J.: Deep long-tailed learning: A survey. arXiv preprint arXiv:2110.04596 (2021)
2. Gupta, A., Dollar, P., Girshick, R.: Lvis: a dataset for large vocabulary instance segmentation. In: Proceedings of the IEEE/CVF Conference on Computer Vision and Pattern Recognition (CVPR) (2019)
3. Wu, J., Song, L., Wang, T., Zhang, Q., Yuan, J.: Forest R-CNN: large-vocabulary long-tailed object detection and instance segmentation. In: Proceedings of the 28th ACM International Conference on Multimedia, pp. 1570–1578. Association for Computing Machinery, New York (2020)
4. Wang, T., et al.: The devil is in classification: a simple framework for long-tail instance segmentation. In: Vedaldi, A., Bischof, H., Brox, T., Frahm, J.-M. (eds.) ECCV 2020. LNCS, vol. 12359, pp. 728–744. Springer, Cham (2020). https://doi.org/10.1007/978-3-030-58568-6_43
5. Feng, C., Zhong, Y., Huang, W.: Exploring classification equilibrium in long-tailed object detection. In: Proceedings of the IEEE/CVF International Conference on Computer Vision (ICCV), pp. 3417–3426 (2021)
6. Tan, J., et al.: Equalization loss for long-tailed object recognition. In: Proceedings of the IEEE/CVF Conference on Computer Vision and Pattern Recognition (CVPR) (2020)
7. Wang, J., et al.: Seesaw loss for long-tailed instance segmentation. In: Proceedings of the IEEE/CVF Conference on Computer Vision and Pattern Recognition (CVPR), pp. 9695–9704 (2021)
8. Tan, J., Lu, X., Zhang, G., Yin, C., Li, Q.: Equalization loss v2: a new gradient balance approach for long-tailed object detection. In: Proceedings of the IEEE/CVF Conference on Computer Vision and Pattern Recognition (CVPR), pp. 685–1694 (2021)
9. Li, B., et al.: Equalized focal loss for dense long-tailed object detection. In: Proceedings of the IEEE/CVF Conference on Computer Vision and Pattern Recognition (CVPR), pp. 6990–6999 (2022)

10. Hu, X., Jiang, Y., Tang, K., Chen, J., Miao, C., Zhang, H.: Learning to segment the tail. In: Proceedings of the IEEE/CVF Conference on Computer Vision and Pattern Recognition (CVPR) (2020)
11. Ghiasi, G., et al.: Simple copy-paste is a strong data augmentation method for instance segmentation. In: Proceedings of the IEEE/CVF Conference on Computer Vision and Pattern Recognition (CVPR), pp. 2918–2928 (2021)
12. Kang, B., et al.: Decoupling representation and classifier for long-tailed recognition. In: International Conference on Learning Representations (2020)
13. Li, Y., et al.: Overcoming classifier imbalance for long-tail object detection with balanced group softmax. In: Proceedings of the IEEE/CVF Conference on Computer Vision and Pattern Recognition (CVPR) (2020)
14. Rogers, A.: Changing the world by changing the data. In: ACL (2021)
15. Zhang, H., Cisse, M., Dauphin, Y.N., Lopez-Paz, D.: mixup: beyond empirical risk minimization. In: International Conference on Learning Representations (2018)
16. Fang, H.S., Sun, J., Wang, R., Gou, M., Li, Y.L., Lu, C.: Instaboost: boosting instance segmentation via probability map guided copy-pasting. In: Proceedings of the IEEE/CVF International Conference on Computer Vision (ICCV) (2019)
17. Krizhevsky, A., Sutskever, I., Hinton, G.E.: Imagenet classification with deep convolutional neural networks. In: Pereira, F., Burges, C., Bottou, L., Weinberger, K. (eds.) Advances in Neural Information Processing Systems, vol. 25. Curran Associates, Inc. (2012)
18. He, K., Zhang, X., Ren, S., Sun, J.: Deep residual learning for image recognition. In: Proceedings of the IEEE Conference on Computer Vision and Pattern Recognition (CVPR) (2016)
19. Lin, T.Y., Dollar, P., Girshick, R., He, K., Hariharan, B., Belongie, S.: Feature pyramid networks for object detection. In: Proceedings of the IEEE Conference on Computer Vision and Pattern Recognition (CVPR) (2017)
20. Girshick, R.: Fast r-cnn. In: Proceedings of the IEEE International Conference on Computer Vision (ICCV) (2015)
21. Ren, S., He, K., Girshick, R., Sun, J.: Faster r-cnn: towards real-time object detection with region proposal networks. In: Cortes, C., Lawrence, N., Lee, D., Sugiyama, M., Garnett, R. (eds.) Advances in Neural Information Processing Systems, vol. 28. Curran Associates, Inc. (2015)
22. Cai, Z., Vasconcelos, N.: Cascade r-cnn: delving into high quality object detection. In: Proceedings of the IEEE Conference on Computer Vision and Pattern Recognition (CVPR) (2018)
23. Lin, T.Y., Goyal, P., Girshick, R., He, K., Dollar, P.: Focal loss for dense object detection. In: Proceedings of the IEEE International Conference on Computer Vision (ICCV) (2017)
24. Liu, W., et al.: SSD: single shot multibox detector. In: Leibe, B., Matas, J., Sebe, N., Welling, M. (eds.) ECCV 2016. LNCS, vol. 9905, pp. 21–37. Springer, Cham (2016). https://doi.org/10.1007/978-3-319-46448-0_2
25. Redmon, J., Divvala, S., Girshick, R., Farhadi, A.: You only look once: unified, real-time object detection. In: Proceedings of the IEEE Conference on Computer Vision and Pattern Recognition (CVPR) (2016)
26. Duan, K., Bai, S., Xie, L., Qi, H., Huang, Q., Tian, Q.: Centernet: keypoint triplets for object detection. In: Proceedings of the IEEE/CVF International Conference on Computer Vision (ICCV) (2019)
27. Yun, S., Han, D., Oh, S.J., Chun, S., Choe, J., Yoo, Y.: Cutmix: regularization strategy to train strong classifiers with localizable features. In: Proceedings of the IEEE/CVF International Conference on Computer Vision (ICCV) (2019)

28. Alexey, B., Wang, C.Y., Liao, H.Y.M.: Yolov4: Optimal speed and accuracy of object detection. arXiv preprint arXiv:2004.10934 (2020)
29. Zhong, Z., Cui, J., Liu, S., Jia, J.: Improving calibration for long-tailed recognition. In: Proceedings of the IEEE/CVF Conference on Computer Vision and Pattern Recognition (CVPR), pp. 16489–16498 (2021)
30. Zang, Y., Huang, C., Loy, C.C.: FASA: feature augmentation and sampling adaptation for long-tailed instance segmentation. In: Proceedings of the IEEE/CVF International Conference on Computer Vision (ICCV), 3457–3466 (2021)
31. Zhang, S., Chi, C., Yao, Y., Lei, Z., Li, S.Z.: Bridging the gap between anchor-based and anchor-free detection via adaptive training sample selection. In: Proceedings of the IEEE/CVF Conference on Computer Vision and Pattern Recognition (CVPR) (2020)
32. Deng, J., Dong, W., Socher, R., Li, L.J., Li, K., Fei-Fei, L.: Imagenet: a large-scale hierarchical image database. In: 2009 IEEE Conference on Computer Vision and Pattern Recognition, pp. 248–255 (2009)

Multi-scale Residual Interaction for RGB-D Salient Object Detection

Mingjun Hu, Xiaoqin Zhang[✉], and Li Zhao

College of Computer Science and Artificial Intelligence, Wenzhou University,
Wenzhou, China
zhangxiaoqinnan@gmail.com, lizhao@wzu.edu.cn

Abstract. RGB-D salient object detection (SOD) is used to detect the most attractive object in the scene. There is a problem in front of the existing RGB-D SOD task: how to integrate the different context information between the RGB and depth map effectively. In this work, we propose the Siamese Residual Interactive Refinement Network (SiamRIR) equipped with the encoder and decoder to handle the above problem. Concretely, we adopt the Siamese Network shared parameters to encode two modalities and fuse them during decoding phase. Then, we design the Multi-scale Residual Interactive Refinement Block (RIRB) which contains Residual Interactive Module (RIM) and Residual Refinement Module (RRM). This block utilizes the multi-type cues to fuse and refine features, where RIM takes interaction between modalities to integrate the complementary regions with residual manner, and RRM refines features during fusion phase by incorporating spatial detail context with multi-scale manner. Extensive experiments on five benchmarks demonstrate that our method outperforms the state-of-the-art RGB-D SOD methods both quantitatively and qualitatively.

Keywords: RGB-D salient object detect · Multi-scale interactive · Siamese network

1 Introduction

Salient object detection (SOD) aims to segment the most attractive object from the scene [1–3]. As a pre-processing task, it plays an important role in computer vision tasks, such as semantic segmentation [4–6], object detection [7,8], person re-identification [9,10], and object tracking [11,12]. In the past years, various SOD methods have been proposed and achieved promising performances with only take RGB as the input [13–18], but may suffer from challenges when on the indistinguishable and complex scenarios. Alternatively, we can obtain some complementary informations from depth maps. In fact, owing to the popularity of depth sensing technologies and the importance of the depth information, RGB-D SOD has attracted the attention of researchers, and various RGB-D SOD methods have been designed to detect the salient object from the RGB image and corresponding depth maps [19–24]. Traditional RGB-D SOD methods

L. Wang et al. (Eds.): ACCV 2022, LNCS 13843, pp. 575–590, 2023.
https://doi.org/10.1007/978-3-031-26313-2_35

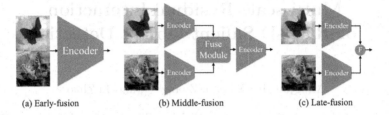

(a) Early-fusion   (b) Middle-fusion   (c) Late-fusion

Fig. 1. The architecture of three fusion manners. Early-fusion methods directly concatenate two modalities. Middle-fusion methods utilize two-stream architecture to fuse two modalities. Late-fusion methods fuse features as a post-processing step.

adopted the image priors with hand-crafted feature to detect the saliency object in scenes, including contrast [19], shape [25] and so on. However, the hand-crafted features cannot be represented well to the complex scenario, which limited the performance of these methods. Recently, benefiting from the progress of Convolutional Neural Networks (CNNs) and the representation ability of features, several CNN-based RGB-D SOD approaches were proposed [26,27]. Depending on merging the RGB and depth map features in different stages, these methods can be divided into three categories: early-fusion, middle-fusion and late-fusion, the architectures of these manners are shown in Fig. 1. Early-fusion schema merged the RGB and depth to a four-channels input and fed it into network directly [28,29]. While middle-fusion methods usually designed a two-branch architecture network to fused the features [23,27]. Late-fusion [30] methods extracted the features of RGB and depth map separately, and fuse these features as a post-processing step.

Though above middle-fusion methods have achieved promising performance, there is still a problem in front of them, which is how to integrate the different context information between the RGB and depth map effectively. To this end, we propose the Siamese Residual Interactive Refinement Network (SiamRIR) with residual manner to fuse two modalities and refine the features by incorporating the cues from encoder. Specifically, we adopt the Siamese Network as the encoder since it contains less parameters. Then, the Context Enhancement Module (CEM) is proposed to utilize the multi-scale features to improve the global context information. After that, we design a Residual Interactive Refinement Block (RIRB) to model the interactions during two modalities, which contains Residual Interactive Module (RIM) and Residual Refinement Module (RRM). The RIM takes interaction between the RGB and depth features to integrate the complementary regions, and RRM incorporates the spatial details which extracted by the encoder to refine the features.

In summary, the contributions of this paper are as follows:

- We propose a Siamese Residual Interactive Refinement Network (SiamRIR), which considers the different context cues. Our SiamRIR explores the complementary regions by taking interaction between modalities and refines the features by incorporating the spatial detail context.

- We design Multi-Scale Residual Interactive Refinement Block (RIRB) as decoder with residual manner to fuse the multi-type context. In this process, the complementary regions between two modalities are utilized by RIM, and the spatial details are explored by RRM with multi-scale manner, which can refine the features during the fusion phase, therefore the performance of SiamRIR is improved.
- We conduct extensive quantitative and qualitative evaluations on five RGB-D SOD benchmarks, which illustrates that SiamRIR outperforms previous state-of-the-art RGB-D SOD approaches.

2   Related Work

2.1   RGB-D Salient Object Detection

RGB-D salient object detection aims to detect the object in a scene that the human would be most interesting in. Peng [31] proposed a single-stream architecture to fuse the RGB and depth directly as inputs to predict the saliency maps. Song [22] adopted the multi-scale fusion to combine low-level, mid-level and high-level feature to calculate the saliency maps. Liu [32] fed the RGB-D four-channels into network to generate multiple level features. Then a depth recurrent network is applied to render salient object outline from deep to shallow hierarchically and progressively. The fusion strategy of these methods is called early-fusion, which merge the RGB and depth as single input of network. In contrast to early-fusion, middle-fusion can make full fusion of RGB and depth, thus there are many methods apply this strategy. Liu [33] proposed a two-stream network to fuse features from different level by directly adding the features. Zhang [34] designed a bilateral attention network with a complementary attention mechanism to better utilize salient informations in foreground and background. Huang [35] considered corresponding semantic information to distinguish the informative and non-informative regions in the input RGBD images. Chen [36] utilized RGB images to predict a hint map, then used hint map to enhance the depth map, this approach resolved the low-quality issue of depth maps. Wang [37] added an adaptive weights to depth maps to reduce the negative effects of unreliable depth maps.

Different from above approaches, our method considers the multi-type cues during fusion stage including the different context between two modalities, and spatial detail context from the features extracted by encoder.

2.2   Siamese Network

In order to reduce the number of parameter of the model, several works utilized Siamese network to extract the features of RGB and depth. Siamese network was proposed by Bromley [38] for hand-written signature verification. In their paper, two uniform networks were designed to deal with different signatures, where these two networks shared the same parameter. During the learning process,

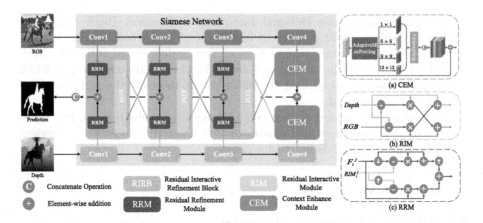

Fig. 2. The overall architecture of Siamese Residual Interactive Refinement Network (SiamRIR).

the features were constrained by the distance measure. Since it is suitable for calculating the distance from two similar inputs, Siamese network was further applied in sundry tasks where the inputs were similar, such as Chan [39] proposed a novel siamese implicit region proposal network with compound attention for visual tracking, and Fan [40] designed a multi-stage tracking framework, which consists of a sequence of RPNs cascaded from deep high-level to shallow low-level layers in a Siamese network. Recently, several works adopted Siamese network to salient object detection. For example, Zhao [41] proposed a lightweight and real-time model with a simple initialization strategy, which can make full use of the pre-trained model on ImageNet [42] to extract the discriminative features and utilized the depth to guide the fusion between RGB and depth.

Different from above RGB-D SOD methods, in this work, the Siamese network is applied to take advantage of the complementary regions between RGB and depth, rather than measuring distance. Specifically, we concatenate the RGB and depth along the batch dimension and fed it into the network [43], after that we fuse the features during decoding stage to achieve the interactive between RGB and depth in stead of measuring distance.

3   Approach

3.1   Architecture Overview

The architecture of the proposed framework is illustrated in Fig. 2. We utilize two backbones to extract the features from two modalities, where the parameters in these two backbones are shared (*i.e.*, Siamese Network). To be concise, we define the features of RGB branch in the encoder as $F_i^R (i \in \{1, 2, 3, 4\})$ and the features of depth map in the encoder as $F_i^D (i \in \{1, 2, 3, 4\})$. Then the features are fed into Context Enhance Module (CEM), to enhance the global context of

the features by different receptive fields. After that, we design a Residual Interactive Refinement Block (RIRB) to decode features from the CEM. Specifically,
the features are first input to Residual Interactive Module (RIM) to explore the
complementary regions by taking interactive between the RGB and depth map
with residual manner. Then, Residual Refinement Module (RRM) takes the features from RIM and encoder as inputs to refine the features with integrating the
spatial information from the encoder. Finally, in order to reduce the parameters
we adopt the element-wise addition to fuse the output of RRMs in the one RIRB
and the output of CEMs, then concatenate these features as the prediction. In
the following contents, we will describe the details of each components in the
architecture.

3.2 Context Enhance Module (CEM)

The global context is useful for SOD method to detect the object. Therefore
we design Context Enhance Module (CEM) to enhance the global context of
the features from the encoder. Specifically, we fed the output of Conv4 (*i.e.*,
F_4^R, F_4^D) into CEM, then we utilize four adaptive max pooling with different
sizes to acquire four feature maps with different receptive fields,

$$F_i = AdaptiveMaxPooling_i(F_4^j) \qquad (1)$$

where F_i denote the output of adaptive max pooling, $AdaptiveMaxPooling_i$ is
the adaptive max pooling with different size ($i = 1, 5, 9, 13$). F_4^j is the input of
CEM ($j \in \{R, D\}$). After that, we use convolution layer and ReLu to reduce the
numbers of channels for the features to one fourth of F_4^j and up-sample these
features to the size of F_4^j,

$$\overline{F}_i^j = \uparrow (ReLU(Conv(F_i^j))) \qquad (2)$$

where $ReLU(*)$ is the ReLU function, $Conv(*)$ is the convolution layer and $\uparrow$ is
the bilinear upsample operation. Finally, we concat these features and add the
input of CEM to it to generate the features which contain the global context,

$$CEM^j = Cat(\overline{F}_1^j, \overline{F}_5^j, \overline{F}_9^j, \overline{F}_{13}^j) + F_4^j \qquad (3)$$

where $Cat(*)$ denotes the concatenate operation. The details of this module are
shown in Fig. 2 (a).

3.3 Residual Interactive Refinement Block (RIRB)

As shown in Fig. 2, the Residual Interactive Refinement Block (RIRB) contains
two components, *e.g.*, Residual Interactive Module (RIM) and Residual Refinement Module (RRM). We embed RIRBs (*e.g.*, $RIRB_1, RIRB_2, RIRB_3$ represents the first RIRB from left to right) to decode the features, which can achieve
the interactions of two modalities. Specifically, we adopt RIM to calculate the
complementary regions between the features of two modalities with residual
manner. Then, RRM is applied to incorporate the spatial informations obtained
from the encoder to refine the features. In the following context, we will describe
the details of RIM and RRM.

Residual Interactive Module (RIM). In the training process, we utilize the same ground-truth to supervise the prediction of RGB and corresponding depth map, the predictions of these two modalities contains consistency. However, the informations contained in the RGB and the corresponding depth map are different (*e.g.*, RGB contains semantic informations, depth map contains spatial depth informations), this will lead the network to locate the different regions. In order to explore the complementary regions between the features of two modalities during decoding phase for adjusting the prediction, we design the Residual Interactive Module (RIM) with residual manner to interact with the features of two modalities. For the RIM_3, as is shown in Fig. 2 (b), the blue and green lines represent the feature extracted from RGB (*i.e.*, CEM^R), the feature extracted from depth map (*i.e.*, CEM^D), respectively. We firstly adopt the convolution layer to reduce the channels of features to 256, Sigmoid and BatchNormalization are used to map the value of features to the range of 0 to 1. Then we subtract the CEM^R from the CEM^D to obtain the complementary regions between these two features,

$$Com^R = ReLU(Bn(Conv(CEM^D))) \tag{4}$$
$$- ReLU(Bn(Conv(CEM^R))) \tag{5}$$
$$Com^D = ReLU(Bn(Conv(CEM^R))) \tag{6}$$
$$- ReLU(Bn(Conv(CEM^D))) \tag{7}$$

where $Bn(*)$ represents the BatchNormalize layer. Then we multiply the F^R and F^D by the corresponding $Com^j (j \in \{R, D\})$, the channels of Com^j also be reduced to 256 by convolution layer, which can assign the weights to the complementary regions between two modalities.

$$Weight^R = Com^R * Conv(CEM^D) \tag{8}$$
$$Weight^D = Com^D * Conv(CEM^R) \tag{9}$$

$$RIM^R = Weight^R + CEM^D \tag{10}$$
$$RIM^D = Weight^D + CEM^R \tag{11}$$

Finally, we add the $Weight^R$ and the F^R together, add the $Weight^D$ and the F^D together. The next RIMs (*e.g.*, RIM_2^j, RIM_1^j) takes the outputs of the previous RIRB as the inputs. Thus, the final prediction of the saliency map can be adjusted step by step.

Residual Refinement Module (RRM). Since, there are more semantic context than detailed context in the high-level features, the details in the the RIM^R and RIM^D are unsatisfactory. Hence, we design the Residual Refinement Module (RRM) to refine the features by incorporating the features from the encoding, which contains the spatial detail information. The RRM takes the output of the

RIM and features from the encoder as the inputs, which are extracted from different modalities. It is worth mentioning that, we adopt the multi-scale manner to explore the detail context contained in different scale features. The architecture of RRM is shown in Fig. 2 (c). Firstly, since the channels of F_i^j and RIM_i^j are different, we utilize the convolution layer to decrease the channels of F_i^j to 256. After that, we down-sample the F_i^j to the size of RIM_i^j and up-sample the RIM_i^j to the size of F_i^j, respectively.

$$\hat{F}_i^j = \downarrow Conv(F_i^j) \tag{12}$$

$$\hat{RIM}_i^j = \uparrow RIM_i^j \tag{13}$$

Then we subtract the $\hat{F}_i^j$ from the RIM_i^j and $\hat{RIM}_i^j$ from F_i^j respectively, to locate the redundant regions by incorporating the features from the encoding between these two modalities.

$$Redu_{i\ down}^R = \hat{F}_i^D - RIM_i^R \tag{14}$$

$$Redu_{i\ down}^D = \hat{F}_i^R - RIM_i^D \tag{15}$$

$$Redu_{i\ up}^D = F_i^D - \hat{RIM}_i^R \tag{16}$$

$$Redu_{i\ up}^R = F_i^R - \hat{RIM}_i^D \tag{17}$$

where $Redu_{i\ down}^j$ and $Redu_{i\ up}^j$ represent the redundant regions which subtract from different scales, then we multiply the $Redu_{i\ down}^j$ by $\hat{F}_i^j$ and add the $\hat{F}_i^j$. Meanwhile, multiply $Redu_{i\ up}^j$ by $\hat{F}_i^j$ and add the F_i^j.

$$RRM_i^R = \uparrow (Redu_{i\ down}^R * \hat{F}_i^D + \hat{F}_i^D) \tag{18}$$

$$+ Redu_{i\ up}^R * F_i^D + F_i^D \tag{19}$$

$$RRM_i^D = \uparrow (Redu_{i\ down}^D * \hat{F}_i^R + \hat{F}_i^R) \tag{20}$$

$$+ Redu_{i\ up}^D * F_i^R + F_i^R \tag{21}$$

At last, we add the features of these two different scales as the output of RRM_i^j.

3.4   Decoder Network

We integrate the outputs of CEM and RIRB as the prediction of the proposed method. Concretely, we sum the results of RRM in the same RIRB and sum the outputs of CEM, respectively. Then, we upsample the outputs of CEM and RIRBs to the size of ground-truth,

$$RIRB_i = \uparrow (RRM_i^R + RRM_i^D) \tag{22}$$

$$\overline{CEM} = \uparrow (CEM^R + CEM^D) \tag{23}$$

Notably, in the RIRBs and the features integration stage, we utilize the pixel-wise addition to integrate the features of two modalities, which can reduce the parameters of network and avoid the network modeling bias for a modalities. Inspired by [44] we concat $RIRB_i$ and $\overline{CEM}$ to retain the various levels of contexts, then convolution layer is adopted to reduce the channels of feature to 1 as the final prediction of out method. Besides, the $RIRB_i$ and $\overline{CEM}$ is also used to be the coarse maps,

$$S^f = Conv(Cat(RIRB_i, \overline{CEM})) \tag{24}$$
$$S_i^a = RIRB_i \tag{25}$$

where $Cat(*)$ represents the concatenate operation, S^f is the final prediction map of our method and S_i^a denotes the coarse maps to coarsely locate the objects. The S^f and S_i^a suffer from the same supervision operation to make sure these maps are consistent.

3.5   Implementation Details

Loss Function. In salient object detection fields, binary cross-entropy loss is the classical loss function to calculate the relation between the ground truth and the predicted saliency map, which is defined as:

$$\ell = -\frac{1}{H \times W} \sum_{i=1}^{H} \sum_{j=1}^{W} [G_{ij} \log (S_{ij})$$
$$+ (1 - G_{ij}) \log (1 - S_{ij})] \tag{26}$$

where H, W indicate the height and weight of the image respectively, G_{ij} denotes the ground truth of the pixel (i, j) and S_{ij} denotes the predicted saliency map of the pixel (i, j). In order to coarsely detect the results, we utilize the auxiliary loss ℓ_{aux}^i $(i = 1, 2, 3, 4)$ at decoder stages. Specifically, we apply 3×3 convolution layer to decrease the channel of the feature maps to 1. After that, these maps are fed into bilinear interpolation to up-sample the feature maps to ground truth size. The total loss function ℓ_{total} is formulated as:

$$\ell_{\text{total}} = \ell_f (S^f, G) + \sum_{i=1}^{4} \lambda_i \ell_{aux}^i (S_i^a, G) \tag{27}$$

where S^f is the final predicted result, λ_i indicates the weight of different loss we set λ_i as $\{1, 1, 1, 1\}$, S_i^a represents the coarse maps predicted.

Network Training. We apply Pytorch as our training platform. In the training process, we resize the input image to 384×384, then randomly crop a patch with the size of 240×240. Noticeably, we convert the depth map into three channel by simple gray color mapping. The module parameters are optimized by Adam optimization algorithm, with the batch size of 16, the momentum parameter 0.9 and the weight decay to $5e^{-4}$. We set the learning rate to $1e^{-4}$ and stop training after 48 epochs.

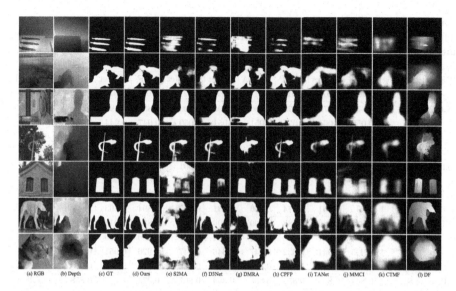

| (a) RGB | (b) Depth | (c) GT | (d) Ours | (e) S2MA | (f) D3Net | (g) DMRA | (h) CPFP | (i) TANet | (j) MMCI | (k) CTMF | (l) DF |

Fig. 3. Visual comparisons of the state-of-the-art RGB-D SOD methods and our method. As shown in this figure, the saliency maps generated by our method are closer to ground-truth than others, especially when the color of object is similar to background and complex background (*e.g.*, the chameleon in the second row, the street lights in the fourth row). (Color figure online)

4   Experiments

4.1   Datasets

NJU2000 [45] consists of 1985 RGB-D image pairs, which is collected from the internet, movies and photographs. NLPR [31] contains 1000 RGB-D image pairs respectively, with diverse scenarios collected by Kinect. Following [23], we select the 1500 image pairs from NJU2000 and 700 image pairs from NLPR as the training set. STERE [46] contains 1000 samples collected from internet and the depth maps are produced by sift flow algorithm [47]. SSD is a small-scale but high-resolution dataset with 80 image pairs picked up from movies. The last dataset is SIP [29], which contains 929 high-quality person images.

4.2   Evaluation Metrics

To quantitatively compare our method with other methods, we adopt five widely-used metrics, *i.e.*, S-measure (S_α), maximum F-measure (F_β^{max}), maximum E-measure (E_ϕ^{max}) and Mean Absolute Error (M).

Table 1. Quantitative results of the state-of-the-art method and the proposed method. The best and second scores are marked with red and blue, respectively. ↑ / ↓ for a metric means higher/lower value is better.

Dataset	Metrics		PCF (2018)	TANet (2019)	CPFP (2019)	DMRA (2019)	D3Net (2020)	MCINet (2021)	ASIF (2021)	FANet (2022)	FCMNet (2022)	SiamRIR (Ours)
NJU2K	S_α	↑	0.877	0.878	0.879	0.886	0.895	0.900	0.889	0.899	0.901	0.912
	M	↓	0.059	0.06	0.053	0.051	0.051	0.050	0.047	0.044	0.044	0.039
	E_ϕ^{max}	↑	0.924	0.925	0.926	0.927	0.932	0.920	0.921	0.914	0.929	0.948
	F_β^{max}	↑	0.872	0.874	0.877	0.886	0.889	0.873	0.900	0.892	0.907	0.911
STERE	S_α	↑	0.875	0.871	0.879	0.886	0.891	0.901	0.869	0.881	0.899	0.908
	M	↓	0.064	0.06	0.051	0.047	0.054	0.042	0.050	0.047	0.043	0.039
	E_ϕ^{max}	↑	0.925	0.923	0.925	0.938	0.93	0.929	0.926	0.908	0.939	0.943
	F_β^{max}	↑	0.86	0.861	0.874	0.886	0.881	0.872	0.894	0.863	0.904	0.899
NLPR	S_α	↑	0.874	0.886	0.888	0.899	0.906	0.917	0.884	0.913	0.916	0.926
	M	↓	0.044	0.041	0.036	0.031	0.034	0.027	0.050	0.026	0.024	0.023
	E_ϕ^{max}	↑	0.925	0.941	0.932	0.947	0.946	0.947	0.926	0.951	0.949	0.958
	F_β^{max}	↑	0.841	0.863	0.867	0.879	0.885	0.890	0.894	0.885	0.908	0.912
SIP	S_α	↑	0.842	0.835	0.85	0.806	0.864	0.867	0.373	–	0.858	0.873
	M	↓	0.071	0.075	0.064	0.085	0.063	0.056	0.269	–	0.062	0.054
	E_ϕ^{max}	↑	0.901	0.895	0.903	0.875	0.910	0.909	0.552	–	0.912	0.914
	F_β^{max}	↑	0.838	0.83	0.851	0.821	0.862	0.840	0.250	–	0.881	0.871
SSD	S_α	↑	0.841	0.84	0.807	0.857	0.858	0.860	0.849	–	0.855	0.877
	M	↓	0.062	0.063	0.082	0.058	0.059	0.052	0.059	–	0.055	0.043
	E_ϕ^{max}	↑	0.892	0.897	0.852	0.906	0.910	0.901	0.888	–	0.903	0.916
	F_β^{max}	↑	0.804	0.81	0.766	0.844	0.834	0.820	0.846	–	0.860	0.851

4.3 Comparisons with State-of-the-Art Methods

We compare our method with other state-of-the-art RGB-D SOD methods, including PCF [48], TANet [24], CPFP [23], DMRA [49], D3Net [29], MCINet [50], ASIF [51], FANet [52], FCMNet [53].

Quantitative Evaluation. Table 1 illustrates the quantitative evaluation result in terms of four metrics on five datasets. As shown in Table 1, on the NJU2K and NLPR dataset, our method achieves the best performance in terms of the four metrics, on the STERE, SIP and SSD dataset, our method achieves the best performance in terms of three metrics (*i.e.*, S_α, M and E_ϕ^{max}). In addition, our method achieves competitive results for the SIP dataset (*i.e.*, our approach ranks second in terms of the four metrics). This indicates the effectiveness of the proposed approach.

Qualitative Evaluation. In order to make the comparisons more intuitive, we further provide qualitative results. The visual results of our method and other state-of-the-art are shown in Fig. 3. From Fig. 3, we can find that the saliency maps generated by DF, CTMF and MMCI is not clear (*i.e.*, the edges of the salient object are slightly blurred). In addition, the results of DMRA and S2MA

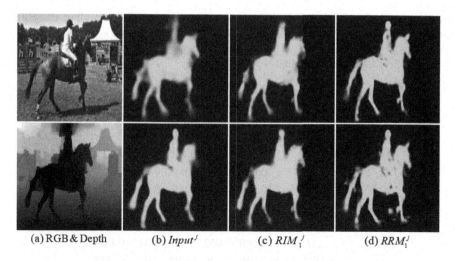

| (a) RGB & Depth | (b) $Input^j$ | (c) RIM_1^j | (d) RRM_1^j |

Fig. 4. The features of the RIRBs. From this figure we can observe that the complementary regions of the features are recovered by RIM and the details of the features are refined by RRM.

is not accurate (*e.g.*, in the fifth row, the saliency map of DMRA only detect one window and S2MA segment the wall as salient object). Moreover, the CPFP and D3MA are failure when the object is similar to background (*e.g.*, D3Net only detect one chameleon in the second, CPFP regard the background as a part of the dog since the color of background is similar to the head of the dog). In contrast to the above methods, the saliency maps predicted by our method are more accurate and clear, especially under the similar and complex background. Besides, when the quality of depth map is poor our method can also detect the object accurately (*e.g.*, the sword in the first row). Overall, the comparisons of quantitative and qualitative illustrate that our method achieve better performance than other state-of-the-art approaches and is less influenced by background and the quality of depth maps.

4.4 Ablation Study

To demonstrate the effectiveness of the components in our method, we perform ablation study on NJU2K, STERE and NLPR, as shown in Table 2. We first explore the validity of concat the features from different level decoder as the prediction. Then, we investigate the effect of RIRB on model performance, which contains the RIM and RRM. We will make detailed analysis of these factors in following parts.

Effectiveness of Multi-scale Features Fusion. In Table 2, baseline represents that we do not concat the features from various level decoder as the predictions, S_f represents we adopt the S_f as the predictions. By observing the

Table 2. Ablation studies with different components. '✓' means adding the corresponding component. ↑ / ↓ for a metric means higher/lower value is better.

Model			Baseline ✓	✓	✓	✓	✓
	l_f			✓	✓	✓	✓
	RRM				✓	✓	✓
	RIM					✓	✓
	CEM						✓
NJU2K	S_α	↑	0.881	0.892	0.896	0.908	**0.912**
	M	↓	0.057	0.050	0.048	0.041	**0.039**
	E_ϕ^{max}	↑	0.927	0.937	0.935	0.944	**0.948**
	F_β^{max}	↑	0.872	0.888	0.890	0.903	**0.911**
STERE	S_α	↑	0.876	0.887	0.892	0.906	**0.908**
	$M\downarrow$	↓	0.060	0.052	0.049	0.041	**0.039**
	E_ϕ^{max}	↑	0.919	0.926	0.931	0.941	**0.943**
	F_β^{max}	↑	0.853	0.873	0.877	0.897	**0.899**
NLPR	S_α	↑	0.897	0.908	0.916	0.920	**0.926**
	$M\downarrow$	↓	0.033	0.030	0.027	0.025	**0.023**
	E_ϕ^{max}	↑	0.941	0.944	0.952	0.954	**0.958**
	F_β^{max}	↑	0.867	0.886	0.894	0.905	**0.912**

first two rows of Table 2 we can find that the performance in terms of four metrics have declined, demonstrates that supervise the S_f is useful to improve the performance of network since S_f contains the multi-scale context informations.

Effectiveness of RIRB. In our method, the RIRB consists of two components which are RRM and RIM, the RRM can explore the complementary regions by interacting the features of two modalities with residual manner and we adopt the RIM to refine the features during decoding phase by incorporating the spatial detail context from the encoder. We can find from Table 2 that, after embed the RIM and RRM, the performance of our method is improved. Besides, the results of different variants to SiamRIR are listed in Table 3, where $R_i (i \in \{1,2,3\}$ represents there are different number of RIRB in the SiamRIR. From this table we can find that, as the number of RIRB increases the performance of SiamRIR gradually improves. This study demonstrates the effectiveness of the RIRB, which takes the features of two modalities and features from encoder interaction.

In order to illustrate the RIRB intuitively, we provide the visualization results of $RIRB_1$ which are shown in Fig. 4, where $Input^j$, RIM_1^j and RRM_1^j represent the input of the $RIRB_1$, the output of the RIM_1^j, the output of the RRM_1^j, respectively (e.g., $j = R$ where features in the first row, $j = D$ where features in the second row). By observing the first row in Fig. 4 (b) we can find that, after

Table 3. Ablation studies with RIRB. '✓' means adding the corresponding component. ↑ / ↓ for a metric means higher/lower value is better.

Model			NJU2K				STERE				NLPR			
R_1	R_2	R_3	$S_\alpha \uparrow$	$M \downarrow$	$E_\phi^{max} \uparrow$	$F_\beta^{max} \uparrow$	$S_\alpha \uparrow$	$M \downarrow$	$E_\phi^{max} \uparrow$	$F_\beta^{max} \uparrow$	$S_\alpha \uparrow$	$M \downarrow$	$E_\phi^{max} \uparrow$	$F_\beta^{max} \uparrow$
✓			0.891	0.048	0.933	0.887	0.893	0.048	0.93	0.878	0.909	0.029	0.946	0.888
	✓		0.904	0.043	0.938	0.902	0.903	0.041	0.937	0.892	0.925	0.025	0.954	0.911
		✓	**0.912**	**0.039**	**0.948**	**0.911**	**0.908**	**0.039**	**0.943**	**0.899**	**0.926**	**0.023**	**0.958**	**0.912**

the RIM_1^R the complementary regions of rider are located, then after the RRM_1^j the details of the rider and the head of horse are refined. The similar phenomenon can also be observed in the second row. Therefore, we can concluded that the features of two modalities can be adjusted (*i.e.*, the complementary regions are recovered and the spatial details are refined) by RIRBs with taking interaction of two modalities and spatial context, which can improve the performance of the proposed method.

Effectiveness of CEM. Since there are different size of objects in the scene, the global context informations are important for our method to detect the salient object. Therefor, we design the CEM to enhance the global context in the features from high-level encoder. From the Table 2 we can observe that, without the CEM, the performance of our method in three test datasets are decreased, which verifies the benefit of the CEM and also verifies the importance of global context cues to the SOD task.

5   Conclusion

In this work, we propose a novel RGB-D SOD method Siamese Residual Interactive Refinement Network (SiamRIR). In order to utilize the different context information during fusion stage effectively, we design a Multi-scale Residual Interactive Refinement Block (RIRB) with residual manner to interact the saliency maps of two modalities and the spatial detail information extracted by the encoder, which can explore the complementary regions and refine the features during decoding phase. And then, the Context Enhance Module (CEM) is proposed to improve the global context information. Extensive experiments illustrate that SiamRIR outperforms the state-of-the-art methods on RGB-D SOD task in terms of quantitative and qualitative.

Acknowledgements. This work was supported in part by the National Natural Science Foundation of China [grant nos. 61922064, U2033210, 62101387] and Zhejiang Xinmiao Talents Program [grant nos. 2022R429B046].

References

1. Wang, W., Lai, Q., Fu, H., Shen, J., Ling, H., Yang, R.: Salient object detection in the deep learning era: an in-depth survey. IEEE Trans. Pattern Anal. Mach. Intell. **44**(6), 3239–3259 (2021)
2. Cheng, M.M., Mitra, N.J., Huang, X., Torr, P.H., Hu, S.M.: Global contrast based salient region detection. IEEE Trans. Pattern Anal. Mach. Intell. **37**(3), 569–582 (2014)
3. Borji, A., Cheng, M.-M., Hou, Q., Jiang, H., Li, J.: Salient object detection: a survey. Comput. Vis. Media **5**(2), 117–150 (2019). https://doi.org/10.1007/s41095-019-0149-9
4. Wang, P., et al.: Understanding convolution for semantic segmentation, pp. 1451–1460 (2018)
5. Noh, H., Hong, S., Han, B.: Learning deconvolution network for semantic segmentation, pp. 1520–1528 (2015)
6. Long, J., Shelhamer, E., Darrell, T.: Fully convolutional networks for semantic segmentation, pp. 3431–3440 (2015)
7. Chen, Z.M., Jin, X., Zhao, B.R., Zhang, X., Guo, Y.: HCE: hierarchical context embedding for region-based object detection. IEEE Trans. Image Process. **30**, 6917–6929 (2021)
8. Hu, H., Gu, J., Zhang, Z., Dai, J., Wei, Y.: Relation networks for object detection, pp. 3588–3597 (2018)
9. Liu, W.: Pair-based uncertainty and diversity promoting early active learning for person re-identification. ACM Trans. Intell. Syst. Technol. (TIST) **11**(2), 1–15 (2020)
10. Zheng, Z., Zheng, L., Yang, Y.: A discriminatively learned CNN embedding for person reidentification. ACM Trans. Multimed. Comput. Commun. Appl. **14**(1), 1–20 (2017)
11. Mahadevan, V., Vasconcelos, N.: Biologically inspired object tracking using center-surround saliency mechanisms. IEEE Trans. Pattern Anal. Mach. Intell. **35**(3), 541–554 (2012)
12. Yilmaz, A., Javed, O., Shah, M.: Object tracking: a survey. ACM Comput. Surv. **38**(4), 13-es (2006)
13. Wang, W., Zhao, S., Shen, J., Hoi, S.C., Borji, A.: Salient object detection with pyramid attention and salient edges, pp. 1448–1457 (2019)
14. Hou, Q., Cheng, M.M., Hu, X., Borji, A., Tu, Z., Torr, P.H.: Deeply supervised salient object detection with short connections, pp. 3203–3212 (2017)
15. Chen, S., Tan, X., Wang, B., Hu, X.: Reverse attention for salient object detection, pp. 234–250 (2018)
16. Zhang, X., Wang, T., Qi, J., Lu, H., Wang, G.: Progressive attention guided recurrent network for salient object detection, pp. 714–722 (2018)
17. Jiang, H., Wang, J., Yuan, Z., Wu, Y., Zheng, N., Li, S.: Salient object detection: a discriminative regional feature integration approach, pp. 2083–2090 (2013)
18. Zhao, J.X., Liu, J.J., Fan, D.P., Cao, Y., Yang, J., Cheng, M.M.: EGNet: edge guidance network for salient object detection, pp. 8779–8788 (2019)
19. Cheng, Y., Fu, H., Wei, X., Xiao, J., Cao, X.: Depth enhanced saliency detection method, pp. 23–27 (2014)
20. Ren, J., Gong, X., Yu, L., Zhou, W., Ying Yang, M.: Exploiting global priors for RGB-D saliency detection, pp. 25–32 (2015)

21. Cong, R., Lei, J., Fu, H., Hou, J., Huang, Q., Kwong, S.: Going from RGB to RGBD saliency: a depth-guided transformation model. IEEE Trans. Cybern. **50**(8), 3627–3639 (2019)

22. Song, H., Liu, Z., Du, H., Sun, G., Le Meur, O., Ren, T.: Depth-aware salient object detection and segmentation via multiscale discriminative saliency fusion and bootstrap learning. IEEE Trans. Image Process. **26**(9), 4204–4216 (2017)

23. Zhao, J.X., Cao, Y., Fan, D.P., Cheng, M.M., Li, X.Y., Zhang, L.: Contrast prior and fluid pyramid integration for RGBD salient object detection, pp. 3927–3936 (2019)

24. Chen, H., Li, Y.: Three-stream attention-aware network for RGB-D salient object detection. IEEE Trans. Image Process. **28**(6), 2825–2835 (2019)

25. Ciptadi, A., Hermans, T., Rehg, J.M.: An in depth view of saliency (2013)

26. Zhao, S., Chen, M., Wang, P., Cao, Y., Zhang, P., Yang, X.: RGB-D salient object detection via deep fusion of semantics and details. Comput. Animation Virtual Worlds **31**(4–5), e1954 (2020)

27. Chen, H., Li, Y., Su, D.: Multi-modal fusion network with multi-scale multi-path and cross-modal interactions for RGB-D salient object detection. Pattern Recogn. **86**, 376–385 (2019)

28. Qu, L., He, S., Zhang, J., Tian, J., Tang, Y., Yang, Q.: RGBD salient object detection via deep fusion. IEEE Trans. Image Process. **26**(5), 2274–2285 (2017)

29. Fan, D.P., Lin, Z., Zhang, Z., Zhu, M., Cheng, M.M.: Rethinking RGB-D salient object detection: models, data sets, and large-scale benchmarks. IEEE Trans. Neural Netw. Learn. Syst. **32**(5), 2075–2089 (2020)

30. Chen, H., Deng, Y., Li, Y., Hung, T.Y., Lin, G.: RGBD salient object detection via disentangled cross-modal fusion. IEEE Trans. Image Process. **29**, 8407–8416 (2020)

31. Peng, H., Li, B., Xiong, W., Hu, W., Ji, R.: RGBD salient object detection: a benchmark and algorithms, pp. 92–109 (2014)

32. Liu, Z., Shi, S., Duan, Q., Zhang, W., Zhao, P.: Salient object detection for RGB-D image by single stream recurrent convolution neural network. Neurocomputing **363**, 46–57 (2019)

33. Liu, D., Hu, Y., Zhang, K., Chen, Z.: Two-stream refinement network for RGB-D saliency detection, pp. 3925–3929 (2019)

34. Zhang, Z., Lin, Z., Xu, J., Jin, W.D., Lu, S.P., Fan, D.P.: Bilateral attention network for RGB-D salient object detection. IEEE Trans. Image Process. **30**, 1949–1961 (2021)

35. Huang, N., Luo, Y., Zhang, Q., Han, J.: Discriminative unimodal feature selection and fusion for RGB-D salient object detection. Pattern Recogn. **122**, 108359 (2022)

36. Chen, Q., et al.: EF-Net: a novel enhancement and fusion network for RGB-D saliency detection. Pattern Recogn. **112**, 107740 (2021)

37. Wang, J., Chen, S., Lv, X., Xu, X., Hu, X.: Guided residual network for RGB-D salient object detection with efficient depth feature learning. Vis. Comput. **38**(5), 1803–1814 (2022)

38. Bromley, J., et al.: Signature verification using a "siamese" time delay neural network. Int. J. Pattern Recogn. Artif. Intell. **7**(04), 669–688 (1993)

39. Chan, S., Tao, J., Zhou, X., Bai, C., Zhang, X.: Siamese implicit region proposal network with compound attention for visual tracking. IEEE Trans. Image Process. **31**, 1882–1894 (2022)

40. Fan, H., Ling, H.: Siamese cascaded region proposal networks for real-time visual tracking, pp. 7952–7961 (2019)

41. Zhao, X., Zhang, L., Pang, Y., Lu, H., Zhang, L.: A single stream network for robust and real-time RGB-D salient object detection, pp. 646–662 (2020)
42. Deng, J., Dong, W., Socher, R., Li, L.J., Li, K., Fei-Fei, L.: Imagenet: a large-scale hierarchical image database, pp. 248–255 (2009)
43. Fu, K., Fan, D.P., Ji, G.P., Zhao, Q.: JL-DCF: joint learning and densely-cooperative fusion framework for RGB-D salient object detection, pp. 3052–3062 (2020)
44. Zhang, P., Liu, W., Zeng, Y., Lei, Y., Lu, H.: Looking for the detail and context devils: high-resolution salient object detection. IEEE Trans. Image Process. **30**, 3204–3216 (2021)
45. Ju, R., Ge, L., Geng, W., Ren, T., Wu, G.: Depth saliency based on anisotropic center-surround difference, pp. 1115–1119 (2014)
46. Niu, Y., Geng, Y., Li, X., Liu, F.: Leveraging stereopsis for saliency analysis, pp. 454–461 (2012)
47. Liu, C., Yuen, J., Torralba, A.: Sift flow: dense correspondence across scenes and its applications. IEEE Trans. Pattern Anal. Mach. Intell. **33**(5), 978–994 (2010)
48. Chen, H., Li, Y.: Progressively complementarity-aware fusion network for RGB-D salient object detection, pp. 3051–3060 (2018)
49. Piao, Y., Ji, W., Li, J., Zhang, M., Lu, H.: Depth-induced multi-scale recurrent attention network for saliency detection, pp. 7254–7263 (2019)
50. Huang, Z., Chen, H.X., Zhou, T., Yang, Y.Z., Liu, B.Y.: Multi-level cross-modal interaction network for RGB-D salient object detection. Neurocomputing **452**, 200–211 (2021)
51. Li, C., et al.: Asif-net: attention steered interweave fusion network for RGB-D salient object detection. IEEE Trans. Cybern. **51**(1), 88–100 (2020)
52. Zhou, X., Wen, H., Shi, R., Yin, H., Zhang, J., Yan, C.: FANet: feature aggregation network for RGBD saliency detection. Signal Process.: Image Commun. **102**, 116591 (2022)
53. Jin, X., Guo, C., He, Z., Xu, J., Wang, Y., Su, Y.: FCMNet: frequency-aware cross-modality attention networks for RGB-D salient object detection. Neurocomputing **491**, 414–425 (2022)

RGBD and Depth Image Processing

Multi-modal Characteristic Guided Depth Completion Network

Yongjin Lee, Seokjun Park, Beomgu Kang, and HyunWook Park[✉]

Korea Advanced Institute of Science and Technology, Daejeon, Republic of Korea
{dydwls462,diamondpark,almona,hwpark}@kaist.ac.kr

Abstract. Depth completion techniques fuse sparse depth map from LiDAR with color image to generate accurate dense depth map. Typically, multi-modal techniques utilize complementary characteristics of each modality, overcoming the limited information from a single modality. Especially in the depth completion, LiDAR data has relatively dense depth information for objects in the near distance but lacks the information of distant object and its boundary. On the other hand, color image has dense information for objects even in the far distance including the object boundary. Thus, the complementary characteristics of the two modalities are well suited for fusion, and many depth completion studies have proposed fusion networks to address the sparsity of LiDAR data. However, the previous fusion networks tend to simply concatenate the two-modality data and rely on deep neural network to extract useful features, not considering the inherited characteristics of each modality. To enable the effective modality-aware fusion, we propose a confidence guidance module (CGM) that estimates confidence maps which emphasizes salient region for each modality. In experiment, we showed that the confidence map for LiDAR data focused on near area and object surface, while those for color image focused on distant area and object boundary. Also, we propose a shallow feature fusion module (SFFM) to combine two types of input modality. Furthermore, a parallel refinement stage for each modality is proposed to reduce the computation time. Our results showed that the proposed model showed much faster computation time and competitive performance compared to the top-ranked models on the KITTI depth completion online leaderboard.

1 Introduction

Depth information is important in computer vision for various applications such as autonomous driving, and 3D reconstruction. For depth measurement, Light Detection and Ranging (LiDAR) sensors are commonly used, which measure accurate depth information. However, the LiDAR sensor provides the limited

---

Y. Lee and S. Park—These authors contributed equally.

Supplementary Information The online version contains supplementary material available at https://doi.org/10.1007/978-3-031-26313-2_36.

L. Wang et al. (Eds.): ACCV 2022, LNCS 13843, pp. 593–607, 2023.
https://doi.org/10.1007/978-3-031-26313-2_36

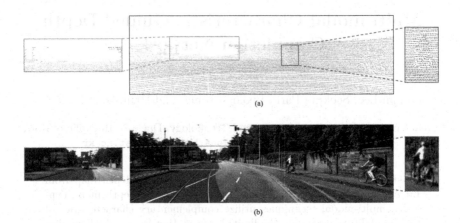

Fig. 1. Example of LiDAR data and color image showing their characteristic. The blue box, which represents distant area, shows that the LiDAR data has sparse depth information while the color image has dense color information. Also, the red box, which represents object, shows that the LiDAR data has depth information for object surface but hard to recognize object boundary. On the other hand, the object boundary can be easily recognized in color image. (Color figure online)

amount of valid depth points due to the hardware limitations. For example, the projected depth map of point cloud data measured by the Velodyne HDL-64E has a density of approximately 4% compared to the color image, which is insufficient for high-level applications such as autonomous driving [1].

To address the sparsity of depth data, which is a fundamental problem of the LiDAR sensor, color images can provide good complementary information. The two modalities, LiDAR data and color image, are completely complementary to each other. As shown in Fig. 1(a), the LiDAR data has depth information, but lacks the data points for distant area (blue) and object boundary (red), respectively. On the other hand, the color image counterpart part has dense color information. Therefore, the color image can complement the sparse part of LiDAR data to predict a dense depth map.

Recently, multi-modal depth completion networks have been proposed by developing architecture of neural network to extract effective fused features, such as feature extraction with the learned affinity among neighboring pixels [2–5], two-stage framework [6,7], a cross guidance module [8], and a content-dependent and spatially-variant kernel from color images [9]. These novel neural network architectures were specialized for extracting useful features related to each modality. However, the complementary characteristic of each modality was remained to be explored in the fusion step. To further improve the fusion process, attention and confidence-based approaches have been developed. The estimated attention and confidence maps were used to guide the extracted features [10–12]. Although these methods takes advantage of the complementary characteristic by using respective attention and confidence maps, the inherited characteristics of each modality was not fully considered.

Table 1. Characteristics of LiDAR data and color image.

	LiDAR data	Color image
Depth information	O	X
Distant area information	Sparse	Dense
Object information	Object surface	Object surface and boundary

The 2D depth map shares the property of extremely unbalanced distribution of structures in image space resulted from the perspective projection, because 3D point cloud data is projected on the 2D images. Close objects have a large area in the image plane with sufficient depth points, whereas distant objects have a small area with insufficient depth points. The data distribution of the depth map from LiDAR data was taken into consideration [13,14]. However, these modality characteristic based depth completion networks only considered the characteristic of LiDAR data.

In this study, we propose a multi-modal characteristic guided depth completion network that considers both characteristic of LiDAR data and color image, which are represented in Table 1. The proposed two-stage depth completion network predicts a dense coarse depth map in the first stage and refines it in the second stage. The confidence guidance module (CGM) is applied to the second stage to estimate confidence maps that represents salient region for each modality. To consider the multi-modal characteristic, the Sobel filter is utilized to detect the object boundary in the CGM and we show that the confidence maps are well predicted according to the properties of each modality. We also propose the shallow feature fusion module (SFFM) applied to combine two types of input modality with the sparsity invariant CNN (SI-Conv [1]). The color-refinement (CR) layer and depth refinement (DR) layer, each of which refines the depth maps in the second stage, are implemented in parallel to reduce the computation time. The final depth map is obtained by combining two depth maps from the refinement layers using the corresponding confidence maps.

To summarize, our contributions are as follows.

- We propose a multi-modal characteristic guided depth completion network to fully consider the both characteristic of LiDAR data and color image. The CGM plays an important role to estimate confidence map for each modality. The confidence map for LiDAR data focuses on the near area and object surface while those for color image focuses on the distant area and object boundary.
- We propose a simple and efficient combining module, SFFM, for sparse depth map by using sparsity invariant CNN. In the ablation study, the contribution of SFFM to performance improvement was shown.
- Our model showed much faster computation time and competitive performance compared to the top-ranked models on the KITTI depth completion online leaderboard by constructing the refinement layers and SFFM in parallel.

2   Related Work

We briefly review previous studies on depth completion grouped by three types: conventional neural network based, attention- and confidence-map based, and modality characteristic based approach.

2.1   Conventional Neural Network Based Approach

As with deep learning based models, most depth completion studies focus on developing the architecture of neural network to improve performance. Cheng et al. [2] and Cheng et al. [3] proposed a simple and efficient linear propagation model, convolutional spatial propagation network (CSPN), to address blur of the result depth map. CSPN learned the affinity among neighboring pixels to refine the initial estimated depth map. As CSPN was successfully applied to depth completion, Park et al. [4] and Cheng et al. [5] further improved CSPN by proposing non-local spatial propagation network and CSPN++, respectively. However, CSPN methods suffer from slow computation time.

Xu et al. [6] proposed a unified CNN framework that consisted of prediction and refinement network. The prediction network estimated coarse depth, surface normal and confidence map for LiDAR data, and then diffusion refinement module aggregated the predicted maps to obtain the final results. Similarly, Liu et al. [7] designed a two-stage residual learning framework consisting of sparse-to-coarse and coarse-to-fine. In the sparse-to-coarse stage, the coarse dense depth map was obtained and combined with the features from the color image by channel shuffle. The energy-based fusion was implemented in the coarse-to-fine stage.

In addition, Lee et al. [8] designed a cross guidance module for multi-modal feature fusion, propagating with intersection of the features from different modality. Zhao et al. [15] applied a graph structure to extract multi-modal representation. Ma et al. [16] proposed an autoencoder network with self-supervised training framework. Tang et al. [9] estimated content-dependent and spatially-variant kernels from color images, where the kernels weights were applied to sparse depth map.

Although these methods have the novel architectures to assemble the multi-modal information by concatenating the LiDAR data and color image, the complementary characteristic of each modalities was not directly used. Therefore, the methods lacks the rationale how the information of each modality is used.

2.2   Attention- and Confidence-Map Based Approach

Van et al. [10] designed a confidence map based depth completion model that extracted global and local information from LiDAR map and RGB image by estimating confidence maps for each global and local branch. Then the global and local features were weighted by their respective confidence map to predict dense depth map. Similarly, Qiu et al. [11] considered surface normal as intermediate representation and fused the color image and surface normal with learned attention maps. An additionally confidence map was predicted for LiDAR data to handle mixed LiDAR signals near foreground boundary. In addition, Hu *et al.* [12] proposed color-dominant and depth-dominant branches, and then combined the results of each branch with confidence map.

Like the above models, multi-branch networks adopting attention and confidence maps have shown high performance improvement. However, the extremely unbalanced distribution of structures resulted from the perspective projection in both modalities were not considered. Therefore, a more effective method for utilizing the property of modality is necessary.

2.3 Modality Characteristic Based Approach

LiDAR data and color image have their own characteristic because of the unique properties of sensors. Recent studies posed and addressed the problem of the extremely unbalanced distribution of structures. Li *et al.* [13] argued that most of the LiDAR data was distributed within a distance of 20 m, and the variance of depth for distant object farther than 30 m was quite large. Based on the claim, they proposed a multi-scale guided cascade hourglass network, considering the unbalanced data distribution for effective fusion of two different types of data. They extracted multi-scale features from color image and predicted multi-scale depth map to represent the different data distributions. Also, Lee *et al.* [14] changed the regression task to the classification task for depth completion by considering data distribution of the depth map. They separated the depth map and color image into multiple planes along the channel axis, and applied channel-wise guided image filtering to achieve accurate depth plane classification results. Although the modality characteristic based approaches showed the improved performance and properly addressed the unbalanced distribution problem, they did not consider the property of color image. Therefore, a more effective method that considers both properties of the LiDAR data and color image is necessary.

3   Methodology

3.1   Overall Network Architecture

The entire architecture of the proposed model is described in Fig. 2. Note that all encoder-decoder blocks, which are coarse prediction, color refinement, and depth refinement, have same network architecture containing residual blocks as shown in Fig. 3. Our model is a two-stage network. In the first stage, a coarse dense depth map called first depth map is predicted from a color image and a sparse depth map as follows:

$$D_c = CP(SFFM(I_c, I_s)) \tag{1}$$

where D_c denotes the coarse dense depth map from the first stage, I_c denotes the input color image, I_s denotes the input sparse depth map, the CP is the

Stage 1

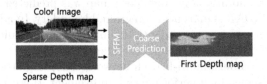

Stage 2

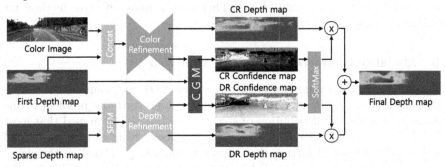

Fig. 2. Overall diagram of the proposed two-stage model. The coarse dense depth map is obtained in the first stage by coarse-prediction (CP) layer, and refined by color-refinement (CR) layer and depth-refinement (DR) layer in second stage. Shallow feature fusion module (SFFM) is applied to fuse the sparse depth map and dense data

coarse-prediction layer in Fig. 2, and the SFFM is the proposed feature fusion module.

In the second stage, the color-refinement (CR) and depth-refinement (DR) layers refine the coarse dense depth map with the color image and the sparse depth map respectively, and predict initial confidence maps at the same time, which can be written as:

$$(D_{cr},\ C_{ic}) = CR(D_c, I_c) \tag{2}$$

$$(D_{dr},\ C_{id}) = DR(SFFM(D_c, I_s)) \tag{3}$$

where D_{cr} denotes the dense depth map from the CR layer, C_{ic} denotes the initial confidence map from the CR layer, D_{dr} denotes the dense depth map from the DR layer, C_{id} denotes the initial confidence map from the DR layer.

The estimated initial confidence maps, C_{ic} and C_{id}, are refined to represent the characteristic of each modality through the confidence guidance module (CGM). The CGM receives two initial confidence maps and first depth map, and outputs CR confidence map and DR confidence map, which can be written as:

$$(C_{cr},\ C_{dr}) = CGM(D_c, C_{ic}, C_{id}) \tag{4}$$

where C_{cr} denotes the CR confidence map, and C_{dr} denotes the DR confidence map.

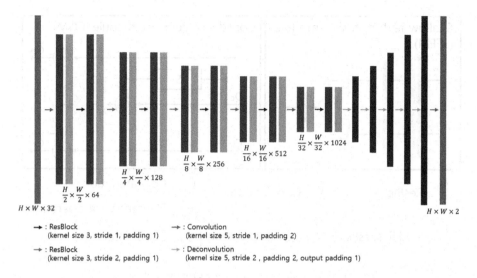

Fig. 3. Detailed architecture for coarse prediction, color refinement, and depth refinement layers

The CR and DR layers do not need to predict accurate depth maps for all regions. Each layer refines the exclusive region by using the confidence map that can effectively make use of the distinctive characteristics of different input data spaces. The two layers are complementary, and the final depth map is obtained through the fusion of the depth maps using the confidence map, which can be written as:

$$D_f(u,v) = \frac{e^{C_{cr}(u,v)} \cdot D_{cr}(u,v) + e^{C_{dr}(u,v)} \cdot D_{dr}(u,v)}{e^{C_{cr}(u,v)} + e^{C_{dr}(u,v)}} \tag{5}$$

where (u,v) denotes a pixel, and D_f denotes the final depth map.

3.2 Shallow Feature Fusion Module (SFFM)

The SFFM extracts the features, which is robust to the depth validity. The point cloud data is generated from the rotation of the LiDAR sensor, and the sparse depth map is generated by the projection of this point cloud data. Therefore, there is randomness in the validity of the sparse depth map even for the same scene. Also, since invalid pixels are encoded as zero values in the projected sparse depth map, when conventional convolution is used, it may be difficult to learn the kernel depending on the local density of valid pixels.

To solve this problem, we proposed the SFFM. The SFFM consists of parallel convolutional layers. For the sparse depth map, features invariant to the scale according to the validity of pixels are extracted using the sparsity invariant CNNs (SI-Conv [1]), and the color image is extracted by conventional convolution.

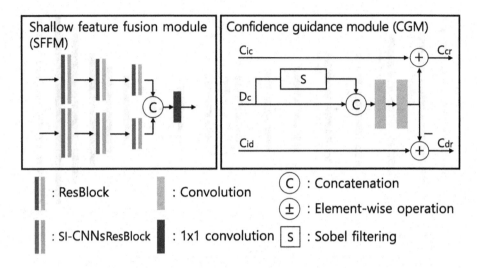

Fig. 4. Detailed architectures of SFFM and CGM.

Depending on the application of the SI-Conv, a high-density feature map can be extracted from the sparse depth map. To consider the remaining invalid pixels, the final feature map is extracted using 1×1 convolution on the concatenated features of dense color image and the high-density feature map. In this case, 1×1 convolution only needs to consider two cases, valid or invalid. SFFM makes it possible to effectively combine two data using only a small number of parameters.

3.3 Confidence Guidance Module (CGM)

A color image and a sparse depth map are the input signals of the CR layer and the DR layer, respectively, but there is no guarantee that each information will be used effectively. CGM is proposed to fully utilize the different characteristics of both data. The color image has dense data, so it has enough information about distant area and object boundaries. On the other hand, the sparse depth map is sparse but accurate, so it is useful to refine near area and object surface, which have many depth measurements. Therefore, the CR confidence map should have large values on distant area and object boundaries while the DR confidence map should have large values on near area and object surface. It makes that the two-modality data are fully utilized for depth completion.

CGM obtains the distance information of each pixel from the first depth map, and then obtains information about object boundaries from the first depth map by applying the Sobel filter [17], which are shown in Fig. 5. The sum of the two maps can adjust the confidence map. However, to reduce the scale difference, the final guidance map is obtained using concatenation and positive convolution. Finally, the guidance map has high values for object boundaries and distant pixels. This map is added to the CR initial confidence map and subtracted from the DR initial confidence map, to become two confidence maps.

3.4 Loss Function

The ground truth depth map is semi-dense and invalid pixels are represented as 0. Therefore, the loss is defined only for the valid pixels by calculating the mean squared error (MSE) between the final depth map and the ground truth map as follow:

$$L_{final} = \frac{1}{|V|} \sum_{(u,v) \in V} \left\| (D_{gt}(u,v) - D'_f(u,v)) \right\|^2 \tag{6}$$

where V denotes the set of valid pixels, $D'_f(u,v)$ denotes the final depth map at pixel (u,v) and $D_{gt}(u,v)$ denotes the ground truth depth map at pixel (u,v).

To train the network more stable, the loss for the first stage depth map was also computed in the early epochs as follows:

$$L_{first} = \frac{1}{|V|} \sum_{(u,v) \in V} \left\| (D_{gt}(u,v) - D_c(u,v)) \right\|^2 \tag{7}$$

where $D_c(u,v)$ denotes the coarse depth map called first depth map at pixel (u,v).

The overall loss can be written as:

$$L_{total} = C_{first} \times L_{first} + L_{final} \tag{8}$$

where C_{first} is a hyper-parameter of 0.3 at the first epoch and reduces to 0 at 5th epoch

4 Experiments

4.1 Experimental Setup

KITTI Depth Completion Dataset: The KITTI depth completion dataset is a large real-world street view dataset captured for autonomous driving research [1,18]. It provides sparse depth maps of 3D point cloud data and corresponding color images. The sparse depth maps have a valid pixel density of approximately 4% and the ground truth depth maps have a density of 16% compared to the color images ([1]). This dataset contains 86K training set, 1K validation set, and 1K test set without ground truth. KITTI receives the predicted depth maps of the test set and provides the evaluation results.

Implementation Details: We trained our network on two NVIDIA TITAN RTX GPUs with batch size of 8 for 25 epochs. We used the ADAM optimizer [19] with $\beta_1 = 0.9, \beta_2 = 0.99$ and the weight decay of 10^{-6}. The learning rate started at 0.001 and was halved for every 5 epochs. For data augmentation, color jittering and horizontal random flipping were adopted.

Evaluation Metrics: We adopt commonly used metrics for comparison study, including the inverse root mean squared error (iRMSE [1/km]), the inverse mean absolute error (iMAE [1/km]), the root mean squared error (RMSE [mm]), the mean absolute error (MAE [mm]) and the runtime ([s]).

4.2   Comparison with State-of-the-Art Methods

We evaluated the proposed model on the KITTI depth completion test set. Table 2 shows the comparison results with other top ranked methods. The proposed model shows the fastest runtime, and shows similar performance to SoTA model, PENet [12], and higher than other top-ranked methods on RMSE, which is the most important metric in depth completion. Moreover, our model shows higher performance than SoTA model in iRMSE and iMAE.

Table 2. Comparison with state-of-the-art methods on the KITTI Depth Completion test set.

Method	iRMSE	iMAE	RMSE	MAE	Runtime
CrossGuidance [8]	2.73	1.33	807.42	253.98	0.2 s
PwP [6]	2.42	1.13	777.05	235.17	0.1 s
DeepLiDAR [11]	2.56	1.15	758.38	226.50	0.07s
CSPN++ [5]	**2.07**	**0.90**	743.69	209.28	0.2 s
ACMNet [15]	2.08	0.90	744.91	**206.09**	0.08 s
GuideNet [9]	2.25	0.99	736.24	218.83	0.14 s
FCFR-Net [7]	2.20	0.98	735.81	217.15	0.13 s
PENet [12]	2.17	0.94	**730.08**	210.55	0.032s
Ours	2.11	0.92	733.69	211.15	**0.015 s**

Table 3. Ablation studies on the KITTI depth completion validation set. B: basic two-stage model, CR and DR: the second stage of B is replaced with the CR and DR layers.

Models	iRMSE	iMAE	RMSE	MAE
B	2.29	0.98	779.68	224.91
CR and DR	2.17	0.93	769.28	213.30
CR and DR + SFFM	2.17	0.91	764.93	212.71
CR and DR + SFFM + CGM	**2.17**	**0.91**	**759.90**	**209.25**

4.3   Ablation Studies

In this section, we conducted ablation studies on the KITTI validation dataset to verify the effectiveness of the proposed model. The experimental results are shown in Table 3. B is a basic two-stage model, which predicts a first depth map from the concatenated input of a color image and a sparse depth map in first stage, and predicts a final depth map from the concatenated input of a first depth map, a color image and a sparse depth map. The CR and DR replace the second stage of the basic two-stage model. Each encoder-decoder takes a first depth map concatenated with a color image or a sparse depth map. The results show the CR and DR layers archives significant improvement in all the metrics, and both of the SFFM and the CGM also gives a performance improvement.

Fig. 5. The middle results of CGM. (a) The reference color images, (b) first depth maps form stage 1, and (c) feature maps after applying the Sobel filter. (c) Sobel-filtered features have high intensity on the pixel of object boundary and distant area, meaning that the Sobel filter is an essential factor in CGM to represent the characteristics of each modality. (Color figure online)

4.4   Analysis for Predicted Confidence Map

We analyzed the predicted confidence map to verify that the proposed model properly utilized the characteristic of the two modality. In Fig. 5, the Sobel filter plays a important role to highlight the distant area and object boundary, where color image can complement LiDAR data by using the dense color information. With the first depth map through Sobel filter and the initial confidence maps from the CR and DR layers, the CGM outputs CR and DR confidence maps which are shown in Fig. 6. The CR confidence map highlights on the distant area and object boundary, where specialized for the dense color image, and the DR confidence map highlights on the near area and object surface, where specialize for the LiDAR data. It means that the proposed model properly utilizes the two modality inputs according to each characteristic.

Also, Fig. 7 shows that the results of multi-modal characteristic based depth completion network. The final depth map, Fig. 7(g), which is the weighted sum of CR depth map (Fig. 7(e)) and DR depth map (Fig. 7(f)), is similar to CR depth map for the distant area and object boundary, while it is similar to DR depth map for the near area and object surface.

CR confidence map

DR confidence map

Fig. 6. Qualitative result of the predicted CR and DR confidence maps. The CR confidence map focuses on the distant area and object boundary, while the DR confidence map focuses on the near area and object surface. It shows that the proposed model properly utilizes each modality input according to its characteristic.

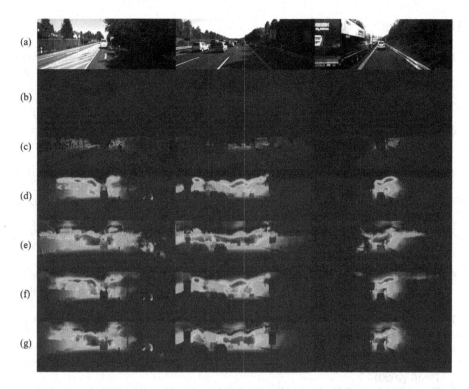

Fig. 7. Qualitative results on the KITTI depth completion validation dataset. (a) color images, (b) sparse depth maps, (c) ground truth depth maps, (d) first depth maps from CP layer, (e) CR depth maps from the CR layer, (f) DR depth maps from the DR layer, and (g) final depth maps.

5 Conclusion

The paper proposed a fast multi-modal characteristic guided depth completion network to estimate accurate dense depth maps. The proposed network has a two-stage structure including a shallow feature fusion module (SFFM), coasre-prediction (CP) layer, color-refinement (CR) and depth-refinement (DR) layers, and confidence guidance module (CGM). The first depth map from the CP layer is effectively refined in the CR and DR layers and consequently combined with the confidence map according to the multi-modal characteristic. Compared with the top-ranked models on the KITTI depth completion online leaderboard, the proposed model shows much faster computation time and competitive performance.

Acknowledgements. This work was conducted by Center for Applied Research in Artificial Intelligence(CARAI) grant funded by Defense Acquisition Program Administration(DAPA) and Agency for Defense Development(ADD) (UD190031RD).

References

1. Uhrig, J., Schneider, N., Schneider, L., Franke, U., Brox, T., Geiger, A.: Sparsity invariant CNNs. In: 2017 International Conference on 3D Vision (3DV), pp. 11–20. IEEE (2017)
2. Cheng, X., Wang, P., Yang, R.: Learning depth with convolutional spatial propagation network. IEEE Trans. Pattern Anal. Mach. Intell. **42**, 2361–2379 (2019)
3. Cheng, X., Wang, P., Yang, R.: Depth estimation via affinity learned with convolutional spatial propagation network. In: Proceedings of the European Conference on Computer Vision (ECCV), pp. 103–119 (2018)
4. Park, J., Joo, K., Hu, Z., Liu, C.-K., So Kweon, I.: Non-local spatial propagation network for depth completion. In: Vedaldi, A., Bischof, H., Brox, T., Frahm, J.-M. (eds.) ECCV 2020. LNCS, vol. 12358, pp. 120–136. Springer, Cham (2020). https://doi.org/10.1007/978-3-030-58601-0_8
5. Cheng, X., Wang, P., Guan, C., Yang, R.: CSPN++: learning context and resource aware convolutional spatial propagation networks for depth completion. Proc. AAAI Conf. Artif. Intell. **34**, 10615–10622 (2020)
6. Xu, Y., Zhu, X., Shi, J., Zhang, G., Bao, H., Li, H.: Depth completion from sparse lidar data with depth-normal constraints. In: Proceedings of the IEEE/CVF International Conference on Computer Vision, pp. 2811–2820 (2019)
7. Liu, L., et al.: FCFR-Net: feature fusion based coarse-to-fine residual learning for monocular depth completion. arXiv preprint arXiv:2012.08270 (2020)
8. Lee, S., Lee, J., Kim, D., Kim, J.: Deep architecture with cross guidance between single image and sparse lidar data for depth completion. IEEE Access **8**, 79801–79810 (2020)
9. Tang, J., Tian, F.P., Feng, W., Li, J., Tan, P.: Learning guided convolutional network for depth completion. IEEE Trans. Image Process. **30**, 1116–1129 (2020)
10. Van Gansbeke, W., Neven, D., De Brabandere, B., Van Gool, L.: Sparse and noisy lidar completion with RGB guidance and uncertainty. In: 2019 16th International Conference on Machine Vision Applications (MVA), pp. 1–6. IEEE (2019)
11. Qiu, J., et al.: Deeplidar: deep surface normal guided depth prediction for outdoor scene from sparse lidar data and single color image. In: Proceedings of the IEEE/CVF Conference on Computer Vision and Pattern Recognition, pp. 3313–3322 (2019)
12. Hu, M., Wang, S., Li, B., Ning, S., Fan, L., Gong, X.: PENet: towards precise and efficient image guided depth completion. In: 2021 International Conference on Robotics and Automation (ICRA), pp. 13656–13662. IEEE (2021)
13. Li, A., Yuan, Z., Ling, Y., Chi, W., Zhang, C., et al.: A multi-scale guided cascade hourglass network for depth completion. In: Proceedings of the IEEE/CVF Winter Conference on Applications of Computer Vision, pp. 32–40 (2020)
14. Lee, B.U., Lee, K., Kweon, I.S.: Depth completion using plane-residual representation. In: Proceedings of the IEEE/CVF Conference on Computer Vision and Pattern Recognition, pp. 13916–13925 (2021)
15. Zhao, S., Gong, M., Fu, H., Tao, D.: Adaptive context-aware multi-modal network for depth completion. IEEE Trans. Image Process. **30**, 5264–5276 (2021)
16. Ma, F., Cavalheiro, G.V., Karaman, S.: Self-supervised sparse-to-dense: self-supervised depth completion from lidar and monocular camera. In: 2019 International Conference on Robotics and Automation (ICRA), pp. 3288–3295. IEEE (2019)

17. Kanopoulos, N., Vasanthavada, N., Baker, R.L.: Design of an image edge detection filter using the Sobel operator. IEEE J. Solid-State Circuits **23**, 358–367 (1988)
18. Geiger, A., Lenz, P., Stiller, C., Urtasun, R.: Vision meets robotics: the KITTI dataset. Int. J. Robot. Res. **32**, 1231–1237 (2013)
19. Kingma, D.P., Ba, J.: Adam: a method for stochastic optimization. arXiv preprint arXiv:1412.6980 (2014)

Scale Adaptive Fusion Network for RGB-D Salient Object Detection

Yuqiu Kong[1], Yushuo Zheng[2], Cuili Yao[1(✉)], Yang Liu[1], and He Wang[3]

[1] School of Innovation and Entrepreneurship, Dalian University of Technology,
Dalian, China
`{yqkong,yaocuili1984,ly}@dlut.edu.cn`
[2] School of Mechanical Engineering, Dalian University of Technology, Dalian, China
`2256357628@mail.dlut.edu.cn`
[3] School of Computer Science and Technology, Dalian University of Technology,
Dalian, China
`mrs_wangher@mail.dlut.edu.cn`

Abstract. RGB-D Salient Object Detection (SOD) is a fundamental problem in the field of computer vision and relies heavily on multimodal interaction between the RGB and depth information. However, most existing approaches adopt the same fusion module to integrate RGB and depth features in multiple scales of the networks, without distinguishing the unique attributes of different layers, *e.g.*, the geometric information in the shallower scales, the structural features in the middle scales, and the semantic cues in the deeper scales. In this work, we propose a Scale Adaptive Fusion Network (SAFNet) for RGB-D SOD which employs scale adaptive modules to fuse the RGB-D features. Specifically, for the shallow scale, we conduct the early fusion strategy by mapping the 2D RGB-D images to a 3D point cloud and learning a unified representation of the geometric information in the 3D space. For the middle scale, we model the structural features from multi-modalities by exploring spatial contrast information from the depth space. For the deep scale, we design a depth-aware channel-wise attention module to enhance the semantic representation of the two modalities. Extensive experiments demonstrate the superiority of the scale adaptive fusion strategy adopted by our method. The proposed SAFNet achieves favourable performance against state-of-the-art algorithms on six large-scale benchmarks.

Keywords: RGB-D salient object detection · Multi-modal analysis and understanding · Multi-modal fusion strategy

1 Introduction

Salient object detection, aiming to locate and recognize the most attractive regions in the scene, has received wide research interest in recent years. As an effective pre-processing method, it has been applied to various computer vision tasks, such as scene classification [33], visual tracking [25], image editing [48], *etc.* Although RGB SOD methods [37–39] achieve satisfactory results in natural

L. Wang et al. (Eds.): ACCV 2022, LNCS 13843, pp. 608–625, 2023.
https://doi.org/10.1007/978-3-031-26313-2_37

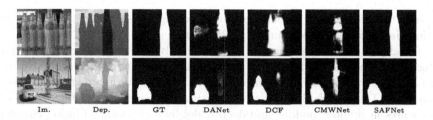

Fig. 1. Saliency prediction results from different fusion methods. From left to right: the input RGB and depth images, the ground truth images, saliency maps of the state-of-the-art detectors, DANet [45], DCF [14], CMWNet [20], and our proposed SAFNet. DANet and DCF employ the same fusion methods in multiple scales. CMWNet and SAFNet design adaptive fusion modules for different scales. Compared with them, the SAFNet can generate more accurate predictions by exploring complementary information from cross-modalities with effective fusion strategies.

scenes, their performances are limited when the scenes are complicated or the appearance of targets is not dominant in the RGB space. With the development of depth cameras, researchers can learn geometric and location information from the depth image which is complementary to the RGB image. It helps identify salient objects from distractors and leads to discriminative SOD models even in very cluttered environments (see Fig. 1).

Considering that there is a large gap between the distributions of RGB and depth data, existing RGB-D SOD algorithms usually focus on exploring effective fusion strategies to model the complementary information between the two modalities. These fusion strategies can be classified into early fusion [12,45], mid-level fusion [3,14,15,19,20,41,43], and late fusion [5,10]. Although these fusion strategies have improved the performance of saliency models, some issues still exist to be considered. First, the early fusion strategy assembles the RGB-D images (e.g., concatenation) and then feeds them into feature extractors. However, the RGB and depth images incorporate asynchronous information. The simple concatenation operation will eliminate distinctive features provided by the two modalities. In addition, feature extractors (e.g., VGG [34], ResNet [11]) are usually pre-trained on the RGB-based benchmarks, they are insufficient to learn both appearance and geometric features from the combined RGB-D data. Second, mid-level fusion strategies are the most important operations to integrate the cross-modal features from the RGB and depth images. However, most existing algorithms design and employ the same fusion operation in different scales of the network, e.g., the DANet [45] and DCF [14] in Fig. 1. They ignore unique attributes of features in multiple scales, such as the appearance and geometric information in the shallower scales, the structure cues in the middle scales, and the high-level semantic feature in the deeper scales. Despite CMWNet [20] considering the diversity of multi-scale features, it suffers from the inferior representation ability of fusion modules. Therefore, these methods demonstrate a limited capacity to explore discriminative cross-modal features from different levels of the network and lead to sub-optimal performance of the final prediction. Such as the visual examples in Fig. 1, DANet, DCF, and CMWNet fail to capture the true targets (the 1st row) and wrongly respond to the distractive regions in the image background (the 2nd row).

To address the above issues, a Scale Adaptive Fusion Network (SAFNet) is proposed for RGB-D SOD. We conduct in-depth studies of both early and mid-level fusion strategies and encourage the multi-scale interactions of cross-modalities. The SAFNet is a two-stream network and adaptively integrates RGB-D features in shallow, middle, and deep scales by a cross-modal fusion encoder. For the first issue, instead of early fusing the RGB-D images in the 2D space, we project them into the 3D space and represent them as the point cloud data. By learning the point cloud representation in the 3D space, we can explicitly model the pixel-wise affinity and explore the appearance and geometric information. For the second issue, we elaborate on the fusion module for each scale according to its characteristic to fully exploit the complementary information from the two modalities. Specifically, to combine cross-modal features from the shallower scale without eliminating the geometric information, we propose a Point Cloud based Fusion (PCF) method. It employs the PointNet++ [31] to learn point-wise representation in the 3D point cloud space, so that the network can explore detailed cues around the neighbourhood. For the middle scale features which abstract structure information from the shallower scale, we propose a Spatial Contrast Refinement (SCR) module to refine the integrated RGB-D features. By exploiting spatial contrastive information from the depth data, the network can learn more discriminative representations from the RGB-D features to better distinguish the targets from the background. To enhance the representation ability of the semantic feature on the deep scale, we design a Depth-aware Channelwise Attention (DCA) module to associate the synchronous feature from the cross-modalities.

The main contributions of our work are three folds: (1) (1) We propose a SAFNet for the RGB-D SOD. Effective early fusion and mid-level fusion strategies are studied in this work. We focus on designing scale adaptive fusion modules to sufficiently explore the complementary information from the cross-modalities. (2) To fuse the multi-modal features, in the shallow scale, a PCF module is proposed to integrate the appearance and geometric information in the 3D point cloud space; in the middle scale, an SCR module is designed to model the structural information in the scene; in the deep scale, a DCA module is adopted to enhance the representation ability of semantic cues. (3) Quantitative and qualitative on six large-scale datasets demonstrate the effectiveness of the proposed fusion strategies, and our method achieves favourable performance compared with the state-of-the-art algorithms.

2   Related Work

2.1   RGB-D SOD Methods

With the development of convolutional neural networks, the performances of RGB-D SOD methods have gained significant improvement compared to traditional hand-crafted based methods [4,18,32]. The recent RGB-D SOD models can be roughly categorized into single-stream methods [45,47] and two-stream methods [30,35,43,46]. The work [47] uses a small encoder to extract prior information from the depth image to enhance the robustness of the main RGB stream. Zhao et al. [45] design a lightweight single stream network that employs the depth map to guide the early and mid-level fusion between the RGB-D images. Although single stream networks can save computation costs and lead to real-time models, they are limited in representing geometric features of the depth image and integrating the multi-modal information. In contrast, two-stream networks separately extract features of RGB-D images and fuse them in different scales. For example, Zhang et al. [43] propose an asymmetric two-stream network, in which a flow ladder module is designed to explore the global and local cues of RGB image, and a depth attention module is designed to improve the discriminative ability of the fused RGB-D feature. The work [46] trains a specificity-preserving network to explore modality-specific attributes and shared information of RGB-D images. In addition, various learning strategies are exploited to enhance the interaction between the multi-modalities. In work [42], the mutual learning strategy is applied on each scale of the two-stream network to minimize the distance of the representations of RGB-D modalities. Ji et al. [14] first calibrate the depth data using a learning strategy and then fuse the RGB-D features with a cross reference module. The work [44] employs the self-supervised representation learning method to pre-train the network using only a few unlabelled RGB-D datasets, thereby learning good initialization parameters for the downstream saliency prediction task.

2.2 Cross-Modality Fusion Models for RGB-D SOD

The main concerns of RGB-D SOD methods are how to 1) integrate complementary information between the RGB-D modalities and 2) enhance the combination of the consistent semantic features from RGB-D images. To this end, recent RGB-D SOD methods design early fusion and mid-level fusion strategies to achieve the in-depth fusion between the two modalities. The early fusion based methods [24,45] usually concatenate the RGB-D images on the channel dimension. However, they ignore the distribution difference between the multi-modalities. Therefore, researchers make efforts to design effective mid-level fusion methods. In [43,45], attention based modules are proposed to select informative depth cues and provide guidance for the interaction of the two modalities. A cross reference module is proposed in [14] to fuse complementary features from RGB-D images. Zhou et al. [46] employ a cross-enhanced integration module to fuse RGB-D features in different scales of the encoder, and design a multi-modal feature aggregation module to gather modality-specific features in the decoder. Sun et al. [35] utilize a depth-sensitive attention module to achieve automatic multi-modal multi-scale integration for RGB-D SOD.

Although the above methods design effective modules or training strategies for the cross-modal fusion of two modalities, they usually apply the same fusion modules on different scales and thus ignore the distribution difference of features in multiple scales. In this work, we study the unique attribute of each scale and

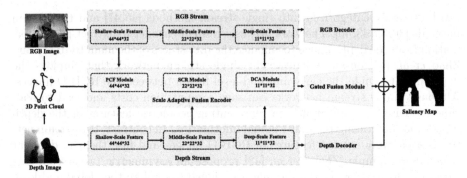

Fig. 2. Architecture of the proposed SAFNet.

design adaptive feature fusion methods for them, which leads to more satisfactory saliency detection results.

3   Algorithm

In this section, we first overview the architecture of the proposed SAFNet and then elaborate on each component of the network. The structure of the SAFNet is shown in Fig. 2.

3.1   Overview

Most existing methods for RGB-D SOD employ the same cross-modal fusion operation in different scales of the network, thus inevitably ignoring the distinctive attributes of multi-scale features. In this work, we propose a two-stream network, SAFNet, to adaptively integrate multi-modality features in different scales with customized fusion modules.

Given the paired RGB image I_c and depth image I_d, we adopt a two-stream network to extract the multi-scale features of the two modalities separately. Following the work [14], for each stream, we employ the architecture of work [37] as the backbone to generate hierarchical features. Its detailed structure is shown in Fig. 3. The three-level features before the second partial decoder are used as the shallow, middle, and deep scale features, respectively, which are denoted as $\{f_c^i\}_{i=1}^3$ for the RGB image, and $\{f_d^i\}_{i=1}^3$ for the depth image. It is followed by a scale adaptive fusion encoder which integrates the hierarchical features from cross-modalities according to their scale attributes. Specifically, for the shallow scale, we propose a Point Cloud Fusion (PCF) module which utilizes the PointNet++ method as the feature extractor $F_{shallow}(\cdot, \cdot)$ to learn the feature representation in the 3D point cloud space, $f_{shallow} = F_{shallow}(f_c^1, f_d^1)$. For the middle scale, we design a Spatial Contrast Refinement (SCR) module to refine the integrated multi-modal feature by exploring the spatial contrastive information. By this means, we can model the structural features in the scene. This process is denoted as $f_{middle} = F_{middle}(f_c^2, f_d^2)$. For the deep scale, a Depth-aware

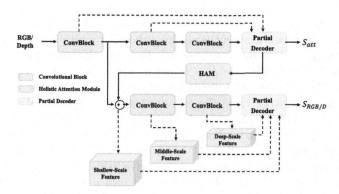

Fig. 3. Architecture of the RGB stream and depth stream. The implementations of the convolutional block, the holistic attention module, and the partial decoder follow the work [37].

Channel-wise Attention (DCA) module is adopted to enhance the representation ability of semantic cues from the RGB-D modalities, $f_{deep} = F_{deep}(f_c^3, f_d^3)$. The hierarchical integrated features, $f_{shallow}, f_{middle}$, and f_{deep} are then fed into the Gated Fusion Module (GFM) to generate a saliency map S_{fusion}. The final saliency map can be obtained by averaging S_{fusion} and the saliency predictions of the RGB and depth streams, S_{RGB} and S_D. The architecture of the fusion stream is illustrated in Fig. 4. Note that each partial decoder in the network generates a saliency map, which is supervised by the ground truth image.

3.2 Scale Adaptive Fusion Encoder

In this section, we present the architecture of the scale adaptive fusion encoder and elaborate on fusion modules at shallow, middle, and deep scales.

Point Cloud Fusion Module for Shallow Scale. Since features from RGB and depth modalities in the shallow scales, f_c^1 and $f_d^1 \in \mathcal{R}^{H_1 \times W_1 \times C_1}$, incorporate valuable cues of appearance and geometric information, it is more suitable to integrate them in the 3D space. We first project the input RGB-D images into the point cloud representation by transforming the 2D image coordinate (x, y) to the world coordinate system (x', y', z'),

$$
\begin{bmatrix} x' \\ y' \\ z' \end{bmatrix} = \frac{I_d(x, y)}{s} \begin{bmatrix} \frac{1}{f_x} & 0 & 0 \\ 0 & \frac{1}{f_y} & 0 \\ 0 & 0 & 1 \end{bmatrix} \begin{bmatrix} x \\ y \\ 1 \end{bmatrix}, \tag{1}
$$

where $I_d(x, y)$ is the depth value in position (x, y), f_x and f_y are the focal length parameters, and s is the scaling factor of the camera. The point-wise feature in the point cloud space can be initially represented by concatenating the shallow scale features of RGB and depth images along the channel dimension, $f_{pcd} = [f_c^1, f_d^1]$.

To learn the point-wise representation, we employ PointNet++ [31] to capture fine-grained details around the neighbourhood at multiple levels. The PointNet++ is an encoder-decoder architecture. Fed with the initial point cloud feature matrix f_{pcd} with the size $N \times (d + C)$, where $N(= H_1 \times W_1), d$, and C are the number of points, the dimension of coordinates, and the dimension of point-wise feature respectively, the encoder learn the representation hierarchically by a set of *set abstraction levels* (3 in our work), consisting of a sampling layer, a grouping layer, and a PointNet [9] layer. In each set abstraction level, the sampling layer chooses N' $(N' < N)$ points as centroids that best cover the entire point cloud with appropriate receptive fields. Then the grouping layer gathers the neighbour points of each centroid into a group with a ball query strategy. The output is a group of points with the size $N' \times K \times (d+C)$, where K is the upper limit number of points in the neighbourhood of the centroids. Finally, the PointNet layer encodes the feature of each group to learn the local pattern. The output feature matrix is of size $N' \times (d + C')$, where C' is the dimension of the feature. By sub-sampling the point cloud with the hierarchical set abstraction levels, the local context of the point cloud is captured at multiple scales. To learn the feature of each original point in the point cloud, the decoder adopts a set of *feature propagation levels*, skip links, and Multilayer Perceptrons (MLP) to propagate point features output by the encoder to all original points in a hierarchical manner. The output feature $\hat{f}_{shallow}$ has the size of $N \times C$ and then is reshaped to the size of $H_1 \times W_1 \times C$.

3D-2D Normalization. Since the fused feature in the shallow scale is in the 3D space, to seamlessly integrate it with subsequent features, we employ a normalization operation to project it to the 2D space to alleviate the difference in distributions.

$$f_{shallow} = InstanceNorm(RFB(\hat{f}_{shallow})),$$ (2)

where $InstanceNorm(\cdot)$ is the instance normalization layer [36], and $RFB(\cdot)$ is the Receptive Field Block (RFB) in work [37]. Note that if we replace the instance normalization layer with the batch normalization layer [13], the operation in Eq. 2 will degrade to a flat operation in the network. In Sect. 4.4, we experimentally verify the effectiveness of the instance normalization operation.

Spatial Contrast Refinement Module for Middle Scale. Mid-level layers of the RGB and depth streams encode the features of shallower scales and learn the structure information of the scene. To integrate middle-scale features of multiple modalities and explore the mild-level structure cues, we introduce a Graph Neural Network (GNN) that refines the fused multi-modal features according to the spatial contrastive relationship with other regions. We first wrap the middle-scale features of RGB-D images, f_c^2 and f_d^2, with a convolutional layer and then concatenate them in the channel dimension,

$$f_{mid} = Concat(Conv_{\theta_c}(f_c^2), Conv_{\theta_d})(f_d^2),$$ (3)

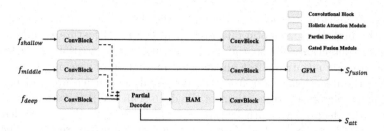

Fig. 4. Architecture of the fusion stream, which takes the multi-scale integrated features ($f_{shallow}$, f_{middle}, and f_{deep}) as input, and outputs a saliency map S_{fusion}.

where $Concat(\cdot, \cdot)$ is the concatenation operation, $Conv_{\theta_c}(f)$ and $Conv_{\theta_d}(f)$ are the convolution operations with parameters θ_c and θ_d, respectively. Then a fully-connected graph $G = (V, E)$ is constructed over the feature f_{mid}, where V is the node set and E is the edge set. Specifically, each pixel in f_{mid} is regarded as a node $n_i \in V(i = 1, 2, \cdots K)$, and K is the number of pixels in f_{mid}. The edge between node n_i and n_j is denoted as e_{ij}, and is weighted by the distance in the 3D space between the nodes,

$$w_{ij} = exp(-|(x_i, y_i, d_i) - (x_j, y_j, d_j)|), \qquad (4)$$

where (x, y) is the spatial coordinate of the node, d is the depth value. In addition, we depict the semantic affinity feature a_{ij} between each pair of nodes,

$$a_{ij} = MLP(Concat(f_{mid,i}, f_{mid,j}, f_g)), \qquad (5)$$

where $f_{mid,i}$, $f_{mid,j}$ are feature vectors of nodes n_i and n_j, MLP is the multilayer perceptron, and f_g is the global semantic feature by applying the Global Average Pooling (GAP) on f_{mid}. Based on graph G, we can update the feature of each node by a graph convolutional layer,

$$\hat{f}_{mid,i} = MLP(Concat(\sum_{j \in \mathcal{N}(n_i)} w_{ij}a_{ij}, f_{mid,i}, f_{mid,j}), \qquad (6)$$

where the set $\mathcal{N}(n_i)$ contains neighbours of the node n_i. We denote the output feature map of the GNN as $\hat{f}_{mid}$ by spatially arranging the feature $\{\hat{f}_{mid,i}\}_{i=i}^{K}$. The weight w_{ij} and the semantic feature a_{ij} indicate the spatial affinity and semantic correlation between the nodes n_i and n_j, respectively. Therefore, the GNN based refinement operation encourages closer regions, in both Euclidean and appearance space, to contribute more to the refined features. By this means, relevant pixels with the same saliency labels tend to be gathered together, leading to more accurate prediction results.

Depth-Aware Channel-Wise Attention Module for Deep Scale. We adopt a DCA module to make an effective alignment between the deep-scale features of multi-modalities. Compared to the deep-scale feature of the depth image, the high-level semantic information in the RGB feature is more crucial for saliency detection. The spatial-level integration (e.g., spatial-wise attention) may introduce a negative effect on the final prediction. Therefore, we learn the channel-wise attention vector from the deep-scale depth feature and use it to highlight the significant dimensions of the deep-scale RGB feature.

First, the deep-scale depth feature map $f_d^3 \in \mathcal{R}^{H_3 \times W_3 \times C_3}$ is encoded by a convolutional layer and is transformed into a 1-channel feature map. Then the feature map is reshaped into the size of $N_3 \times 1$, where $N_3 = H_3 \times W_3$, and a softmax layer is applied to it to generate a pixel-wise attention vector f_{d_att} which indicates the spatial significance of the depth feature. Second, the deep-scale RGB feature map f_c^3 is reshaped to the size of $N_3 \times C_3$, and is multiplied with the attention vector,

$$a_c = [R(f_c^3)]^T \times f_{d\_att}, \tag{7}$$

where $R(\cdot)$ is the reshape operation, and a_c is of the size $C_3 \times 1$. The above implementation learns the correlation between the depth and RGB modalities and adaptively integrates the appearance feature according to the spatial significance. We then utilize the channel-wise attention $a_c \in \mathcal{R}^{C_3 \times 1}$ to highlight the important dimension of the RGB feature map f_d^3,

$$f_{deep} = tile(a_c) \odot f_d^3, \tag{8}$$

in which the function $tile(\cdot)$ tiles the channel-wise attention vector to the size of f_d^3, and $\odot$ is the element-wise multiplication. As a result, the output feature map f_{deep} is equipped with a powerful representation ability of high-level semantic information.

3.3   Saliency Decoder

The decoders of the RGB and depth streams are based on the structure of the work [37], and output saliency maps S_{RGB} and S_D, respectively. In this section, we mainly elaborate on the saliency decoder of the fusion stream, which takes advantage of the multi-modal fusion features in different scales and generates a saliency map S_{fusion}.

First, the fusion features $f_{shallow}$, f_{mid}, and f_{deep} are wrapped by a Receptive Field Block (RFB) [23] to explore global context information, respectively. The output features are decoded as $\hat{f}_{shallow}$, $\hat{f}_{mid}$, and $\hat{f}_{deep}$. Then a Gated Fusion Module (GFM) is designed to integrate the multi-scale features successively,

$$\begin{cases} f_{sm} = Gate(Concat(\hat{f}_{shallow}, \hat{f}_{mid})) \odot \hat{f}_{shallow} + \hat{f}_{mid}, \\ f_{md} = Gate(Concat(\hat{f}_{mid}, \hat{f}_{deep})) \odot \hat{f}_{mid} + \hat{f}_{deep}, \\ f_{smd} = Gate(Concat(f_{sm}, f_{md})) \odot f_{sm} + f_{md}, \end{cases} \tag{9}$$

where $Gate(\cdot)$ is the gated function and formulated as a sequence of a 3×3 convolutional layer, a batch normalization layer, and a sigmoid layer. The gated function learns spatial-wise attention from features of multiple scales, which are then adaptively integrated by the guidance of attention. The output feature map f_{smd} incorporates effective information from different levels, and based on this, a prediction result S_{fusion} is generated using a 3×3 convolutional layer.

The final saliency map is obtained by averaging the saliency maps output by the three decoders, namely $S_{final} = (S_{RGB} + S_D + S_{fusion})/3$.

3.4 Loss Function

The proposed SAFNet is trained in an end-to-end manner. The total loss function $\mathcal{L}_{total}$ is a summation of the losses from the RGB stream, the depth stream, and the fusion stream, denoted as $\mathcal{L}_{RGB}, \mathcal{L}_D$, and $\mathcal{L}_{fusion}$, respectively,

$$\mathcal{L}_{total} = \mathcal{L}_{RGB} + \mathcal{L}_D + \mathcal{L}_{fusion}. \tag{10}$$

Each loss is defined as the binary cross-entropy loss between the predicted saliency map and the ground truth image,

$$\mathcal{L}_k(S_k, G) = G \log S_k + (1 - G) \log(1 - S_k), k \in \{RGB, D, fusion\} \tag{11}$$

where S_k is the saliency map and G is the ground truth image.

4 Experiments

4.1 Implementation Details

All experiments are implemented on the PyTorch platform with a single 2080Ti GPU. The backbone of each stream in the encoder is based on the ResNet-50 [11] and is initialized by the pre-trained parameters in ImageNet [17]. All input RGB and depth images are resized to 352×352. We employ the common-used data augmentation methods incorporating randomly horizontal flipping, cropping, and rotating. In the process of point cloud representation learning, both the focal lengths f_x and f_y are set as 44 (the same as the spatial size of the shallow-scale feature maps), and the scaling factor s is 255.0. The number of centroids in the 3 set abstraction levels is set as 2048, 1024, and 512, respectively. The number of channels of feature maps $(C, C', C^1, C^2$, and $C^3)$ is 32. In the training stage, the batch size is set as 8. We employ the Stochastic Gradient Descent (SGD) algorithm with momentum 0.9 to optimize the objective function. The learning rate is 0.0005. The network converges within 200 epochs.

4.2 Datasets and Metrics

Datasets. We evaluate the performance of the proposed SAFNet and the compared methods on six public RGB-D SOD benchmarks, including DUT-D [29] (1200 image pairs), NLPR [28] (1000 image pairs), NJUD [16] (1985 stereo image pairs), STERE [26] (1000 image pairs), SIP [8] (929 image pairs), and LFSD [21]

Table 1. The maximum F-measure, S-measure, E-measure, and MAE of the evaluated saliency models on six data sets. The top three scores of each method are marked as red, green, and blue, respectively.

Metric		S2MA CVPR20	UCNet CVPR20	HDFNet ECCV20	DANet ECCV20	PGAR ECCV20	CMWNet ECCV20	ATSA ECCV20	SPNet ICCV21	D3Net TNNLS21	DSA2F CVPR21	DCF CVPR21	HAINet TIP21	CDNet TIP21	CDINet ACMM21	SSP AAAI22	SAFNet Ours
DUT-D	F_{max}	0.909	–	0.926	0.911	0.938	0.905	0.936	–	–	0.938	0.941	0.932	0.944	0.934	0.947	0.950
	S_m	0.903	–	0.905	0.889	0.920	0.887	0.916	–	–	0.921	0.924	0.909	0.927	0.927	0.925	0.931
	E_m	0.921	–	0.938	0.929	0.950	0.922	0.954	–	–	0.956	0.957	0.939	0.957	0.956	0.954	0.962
	MAE	0.044	–	0.040	0.047	0.035	0.056	0.033	–	–	0.031	0.030	0.038	0.031	0.029	0.028	0.026
NLPR	F_{max}	0.910	0.917	0.917	0.908	0.922	0.913	0.905	0.925	0.907	0.916	0.917	0.917	0.924	0.916	0.923	0.934
	S_m	0.915	0.920	0.916	0.908	0.920	0.917	0.911	0.927	0.912	0.918	0.921	0.921	0.927	0.927	0.922	0.93
	e_m	0.942	0.955	0.948	0.945	0.954	0.941	0.947	0.959	0.945	0.952	0.956	0.952	0.955	0.950	0.959	0.965
	MAE	0.030	0.025	0.027	0.031	0.025	0.029	0.028	0.021	0.030	0.024	0.023	0.025	0.025	0.024	0.025	0.02
NJUD	F_{max}	0.899	0.908	0.924	0.905	0.918	0.913	0.904	0.935	0.910	0.917	0.917	0.920	0.919	0.921	0.923	0.925
	S_m	0.894	0.897	0.911	0.897	0.909	0.903	0.887	0.924	0.900	0.904	0.903	0.909	0.913	0.909	0.909	0.915
	E_m	0.917	0.934	0.934	0.926	0.935	0.923	0.926	0.953	0.916	0.937	0.941	0.931	0.940	0.936	0.939	0.947
	MAE	0.053	0.043	0.037	0.046	0.042	0.046	0.047	0.029	0.046	0.039	0.038	0.038	0.038	0.036	0.038	0.036
STERE	F_{max}	0.895	0.908	0.918	0.897	0.911	0.911	0.911	0.911	0.915	0.904	0.910	0.915	0.910	0.908	–	0.920
	S_m	0.890	0.903	0.906	0.892	0.907	0.905	0.896	0.907	0.899	0.897	0.905	0.909	0.909	0.903	–	0.907
	E_m	0.926	0.942	0.937	0.927	0.937	0.930	0.942	0.942	0.924	0.942	0.942	0.938	0.938	0.929	–	0.944
	MAE	0.051	0.039	0.039	0.048	0.041	0.043	0.038	0.037	0.046	0.039	0.042	0.038	0.041	–	0.047	0.036
SIP	F_{max}	0.891	0.896	0.904	0.901	0.893	0.890	0.885	0.916	0.881	0.891	0.900	0.916	0.888	0.884	0.895	0.914
	S_m	0.872	0.875	0.878	0.878	0.876	0.867	0.852	0.894	0.860	0.862	0.873	0.890	0.862	0.875	0.868	0.894
	E_m	0.913	0.918	0.921	0.917	0.912	0.909	0.899	0.930	0.902	0.911	0.921	0.925	0.905	0.915	0.910	0.922
	MAE	0.057	0.050	0.053	0.054	0.055	0.062	0.064	0.043	0.063	0.057	0.052	0.048	0.060	0.055	0.058	0.047
LFSD	F_{max}	0.862	0.878	0.882	0.871	0.834	0.900	0.883	0.881	0.840	0.903	0.867	0.880	0.898	0.890	0.870	0.901
	S_m	0.837	0.865	0.855	0.849	0.816	0.876	0.855	0.854	0.825	0.883	0.841	0.859	0.878	0.870	0.853	0.872
	E_m	0.863	0.906	0.879	0.881	0.870	0.908	0.897	0.897	0.863	0.923	0.883	0.895	0.912	0.913	0.891	0.914
	MAE	0.095	0.067	0.078	0.079	0.091	0.066	0.071	0.071	0.095	0.055	0.075	0.072	0.060	0.063	0.075	0.060

(100 image pairs). As the training settings of most methods, we select 800 samples from the DUT-D, 1485 samples from the NJUD, and 700 samples from the NLPR as the training set. The rest samples are treated as test sets.

Metrics. Four metrics are employed to evaluate the performance of saliency models, including the maximum F-measure [1] (F_{max}), S-measure [6] (S_m), E-measure [7] (E_m), and Mean Absolute Error (MAE) [2]. F-measure values comprehensively consider the precision and recall of saliency models. S-measure values measure the structural similarity between saliency maps and ground truth images. E-measure values capture pixel-level matching and image-level statistics information. MAE values depict errors in predicted saliency maps.

4.3   Comparison with State-of-the-Arts

We compare the proposed SAFNet with 15 state-of-the-art algorithms, including S2MA [22], UCNet [41], HDFNet [27], DANet [45], PGAR [3], CMWNet [20], ATSA [43], SPNet [46], D3Net [8], DSA2F [35], DCF [14], HAINet [19], CDNet [15], CDINet [40], and SSP [44]. For a fair comparison, the evaluated saliency maps are provided by their authors or generated by the public released codes.

Quantitative Evaluation. The quantitative performances of evaluated methods in terms of F-measure, S-measure, E-measure, and MAE are demonstrated in Table 1. It shows that the proposed SAFNet achieves satisfactory results and outperforms most state-of-the-art algorithms on six challenging datasets, indicating the generalization ability of our method.

Qualitative Evaluation. We illustrate the visual results of the evaluated methods in Fig. 5. It shows that our method can handle various challenging scenarios.

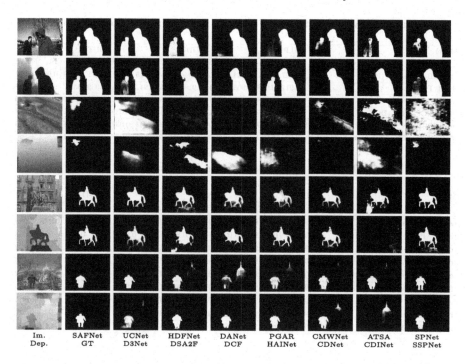

Fig. 5. Visual results of the proposed SAFNet and the compared methods.

For the first example which incorporates multiple objects with different appearances, our proposed SAFNet can capture all salient objects compared to many existing methods. In the second example, the target object is not salient in the color space and the size is small. The depth image provides valuable cues about the object and background. By properly integrating the complementary information of the RGB-D modalities, our method successfully distinguishes the salient object from the background. In contrast, most other methods fail to capture the target and wrongly respond to the background regions. In the third example, the appearance of the salient object is similar to the background. Many other methods present blurry predictions around the object boundary. Since the depth image shows obvious structural information, our method can segment the target accurately from the cluttered background. For the fourth example, many existing methods wrongly capture part of the building as saliency regions. In contrast, our method learns the contrast information in both color and depth space and recognizes accurate regions as saliency.

4.4 Ablation Studies

We conduct ablation studies to verify the effectiveness of the main components in the proposed SAFNet. We also compare the key modules of our method with

Table 2. Ablation studies on each main component of the SAFNet.

Model	NLPR				NJDU				DUT-D			
	F_{max}	S_m	E_m	MAE	F_{max}	S_m	E_m	MAE	F_{max}	S_m	E_m	MAE
(a) RGB-D Baseline (B)	0.897	0.891	0.934	0.036	0.894	0.896	0.915	0.051	0.911	0.895	0.932	0.044
(b) B+PCF	0.917	0.916	0.955	0.024	0.918	0.906	0.942	0.038	0.939	0.917	0.952	0.032
(c) B+PCF+SCR	0.921	0.918	0.955	0.024	0.919	0.908	0.094	0.036	0.941	0.919	0.955	0.030
(d) B+PCF+SCR+DCA	0.928	0.926	0.962	0.021	0.924	0.911	0.946	0.035	0.946	0.927	0.959	0.028
(e) B+PCF(BN norm)+SCR+DCA+GFM	0.930	0.929	0.965	0.020	0.926	0.913	0.944	0.034	0.948	0.928	0.960	0.026
(f) B+PCF+SCR+DCA+GFM (SAFNet)	0.934	0.930	0.965	0.020	0.929	0.915	0.947	0.033	0.950	0.931	0.962	0.026

Table 3. Ablation studies on fusion strategies.

Model	NLPR				NJDU				DUT-D			
	F_{max}	S_m	E_m	MAE	F_{max}	S_m	E_m	MAE	F_{max}	S_m	E_m	MAE
(a) RGB-D Baseline (B1)	0.903	0.904	0.942	0.029	0.902	0.896	0.927	0.043	0.924	0.904	0.940	0.039
(b) B1+PCF+PCF+PCF	0.917	0.916	0.954	0.026	0.914	0.899	0.931	0.042	0.941	0.917	0.950	0.032
(c) B1+SCR+SCR+SCR	0.918	0.916	0.951	0.026	0.913	0.904	0.940	0.037	0.939	0.918	0.951	0.032
(d) B1+DCA+DCA+DCA	0.920	0.914	0.951	0.027	0.912	0.896	0.932	0.043	0.931	0.909	0.946	0.036
(e) B1+DAM+DAM+DAM	0.919	0.916	0.954	0.025	0.919	0.905	0.938	0.039	0.936	0.916	0.950	0.032
(f) B1+CRM+CRM+CRM	0.917	0.915	0.953	0.026	0.912	0.899	0.936	0.040	0.931	0.912	0.945	0.035
(g) B1+CIM+CIM+CIM	0.917	0.913	0.953	0.026	0.910	0.896	0.934	0.041	0.935	0.911	0.945	0.035
(h) B1+RDE+DSE+DSE	0.919	0.916	0.953	0.025	0.921	0.905	0.938	0.039	0.937	0.916	0.948	0.032
(i) B1+PCF+SCR+DCA (SAFNet)	0.934	0.930	0.965	0.020	0.929	0.915	0.947	0.033	0.950	0.931	0.962	0.026

the advanced fusion methods of existing algorithms. The rationality of the scale adaptive fusion strategy is validated.

Effectiveness of Each Main Component in SAFNet. The experimental results of ablation studies on the effectiveness of the main components of our method are shown in Table 2. We design a set of baseline networks as comparisons. The RGB-D Baseline (B) in Table 2 (a) is the baseline network that takes both RGB and depth images as input. We employ a simple concatenation and convolution operation to integrate the RGB-D cross-modal features in the shallow, middle, and deep scales. The same simple fusion method is also used to replace the GFM in the saliency decoder to combine the features in different scales. Based on the baseline network, we successively replace the fusion strategies in different scales with the proposed PCF, SCR, and DCA. The quantitative performance is shown in Table 2 (b)–(d). In Table 2 (e) and (f), the GFM is adopted in the saliency decoder. Especially in Table 2 (e), the instance normalization operation in the PCF module is replaced by the batch normalization operation. Table 2 (f) shows the final performance of the proposed SAFNet.

Comparing the performances in Table 2 (a)–(d), we can observe that our proposed fusion strategies, PCF for the shallower scale, SCR for the middle scale, and DCA for the deep scale, can improve the performance of the baseline methods, which verifies the effectiveness of the proposed fusion methods. The improvement in Table 2 (f) over (d) indicates the validity of the GFM in the saliency decoder. We also validate the effectiveness of the 3D-2D Normalization module in the PCF module. Comparing Table 2 (e) and (f), we can see that the 3D-2D Normalization module slightly boosts the accuracy of the saliency modal. Theoretically, the 3D-2D Normalization operation projects the feature in 3D space to the 2D space. It ensures the distribution consistency of multi-scale features, which is necessary for the GFM in the saliency decoder.

Effectiveness of Fusion Strategies. In this section, we present a series of experiments to prove the superiority of the proposed fusion methods and the scale adaptive fusion strategy. For this purpose, we design the RGB-D Baseline (B1) by replacing the fusion modules, PCF, SCR, and DCA, in the proposed SAFNet with the simple concatenation and convolution operation (the GFM in the decoder remains). The performance is shown in Table 3 (a). In Table 3 (b)-(g), we employ the same fusion modules on different scales. In Table 3 (b)-(d), we adopt the proposed PCF, SCR, and DCA, respectively. The fusion module DAM in work [43] is utilized in Table 3 (e). Different from the DCA which is only based on the channel-wise attention module, the DAM consists of both channel-wise attention and spatial-wise attention. The CRM in Table 3 (f) is the multi-modal integration method proposed in work [14], and the CIM in Table 3 (g) is employed in work [46]. In Table 3 (h), we implement a similar idea in work [40], which uses the RDE in shallower layers and the DSE in deeper layers to enforce the information transmission between the RGB and depth streams. Table 3 (i) is the performance of the proposed SAFNet which utilizes the PCF, SCR, and DCA on different scales.

From the quantitative experiments in Table 3, we can see that all fusion methods achieve improvement over the baseline method (Table 3 (a)). The networks which employ scale adaptive fusion methods (Table 3 (h) and (i)) gain more promotion. Compared with the model in Table 3 (h), our method gives deep insight into the attributes of different scales in the network, and adopts early and mid-level fusion strategies to further enhance the interaction of multi-modal features. As a result, the proposed SAFNet achieves superior performance against the fusion strategies of existing methods.

5   Conclusion

In this work, we propose a Scale Adaptive Fusion Network (SAFNet) which takes account of different attributes of multi-scale features in the network for RGB-D SOD. For the shallow scale, we propose a Point Cloud Fusion (PCF) method to integrate the RGB and depth features in the 3D space. For the middle scale, a Spatial Contrast Refinement (SCR) module is designed to explore the structural information of the scene. For the deep scale, we adopt the Depth-aware Channel Attention (DCA) module to combine the semantic cues from the RGB-D features. In our work, both early and mid-level fusion strategies are adopted to enforce the in-depth fusion of the multi-modalities. Extensive experiments show that our proposed SAFNet achieves significant performance against the state-of-the-art algorithms and also verify the effectiveness of the scale adaptive fusion strategy exploited by our model.

Acknowledgements. This work is supported by the Ministry of Science and Technology of the People's Republic of China no. 2018AAA0102003, National Natural Science Foundation of China under Grant no. 62006037, and the Fundamental Research Funds for the Central Universities no. DUT22JC06.

References

1. Achanta, R., Hemami, S.S., Estrada, F.J., Süsstrunk, S.: Frequency-tuned salient region detection. In: IEEE Conference on Computer Vision and Pattern Recognition, pp. 1597–1604 (2009)
2. Borji, A., Sihite, D.N., Itti, L.: Salient object detection: a benchmark. In: Fitzgibbon, A., Lazebnik, S., Perona, P., Sato, Y., Schmid, C. (eds.) ECCV 2012. LNCS, vol. 7573, pp. 414–429. Springer, Heidelberg (2012). https://doi.org/10.1007/978-3-642-33709-3_30
3. Chen, S., Fu, Y.: Progressively guided alternate refinement network for RGB-D salient object detection. In: Vedaldi, A., Bischof, H., Brox, T., Frahm, J.-M. (eds.) ECCV 2020. LNCS, vol. 12353, pp. 520–538. Springer, Cham (2020). https://doi.org/10.1007/978-3-030-58598-3_31
4. Desingh, K., Krishna, K.M., Rajan, D., Jawahar, C.V.: Depth really matters: Improving visual salient region detection with depth. In: British Machine Vision Conference (2013)
5. Ding, Y., Liu, Z., Huang, M., Shi, R., Wang, X.: Depth-aware saliency detection using convolutional neural networks. J. Vis. Commun. Image Represent. **61**, 1–9 (2019)
6. Fan, D., Cheng, M., Liu, Y., Li, T., Borji, A.: Structure-measure: a new way to evaluate foreground maps. In: IEEE International Conference on Computer Vision, pp. 4558–4567 (2017)
7. Fan, D., Gong, C., Cao, Y., Ren, B., Cheng, M., Borji, A.: Enhanced-alignment measure for binary foreground map evaluation. In: International Joint Conference on Artificial Intelligence, pp. 698–704 (2018)
8. Fan, D., et al.: Rethinking RGB-D salient object detection: models, datasets, and large-scale benchmarks. IEEE Trans. Neural Netw. Learn. Syst. **32**(5), 2075–2089 (2020)
9. Garcia-Garcia, A., Gomez-Donoso, F., Rodríguez, J.G., Orts-Escolano, S., Cazorla, M., López, J.A.: Pointnet: a 3D convolutional neural network for real-time object class recognition. In: International Joint Conference on Neural Networks, pp. 1578–1584 (2016)
10. Han, J., Chen, H., Liu, N., Yan, C., Li, X.: CNNs-based RGB-D saliency detection via cross-view transfer and multiview fusion. IEEE Trans. Cybernatics **48**(11), 3171–3183 (2018)
11. He, K., Zhang, X., Ren, S., Sun, J.: Deep residual learning for image recognition. In: IEEE Conference on Computer Vision and Pattern Recognition, pp. 770–778 (2016)
12. Hou, Q., Cheng, M., Hu, X., Borji, A., Tu, Z., Torr, P.H.S.: Deeply supervised salient object detection with short connections. IEEE Trans. Pattern Anal. Mach. Intell. **41**(4), 815–828 (2019)
13. Ioffe, S., Szegedy, C.: Batch normalization: accelerating deep network training by reducing internal covariate shift. In: International Conference on Machine Learning, vol. 37, pp. 448–456 (2015)

14. Ji, W., et al.: Calibrated RGB-D salient object detection. In: IEEE Conference on Computer Vision and Pattern Recognition, pp. 9471–9481 (2021)
15. Jin, W., Xu, J., Han, Q., Zhang, Y., Cheng, M.: CDNet: Complementary depth network for RGB-D salient object detection. IEEE Trans. Image Process. **30**, 3376–3390 (2021)
16. Ju, R., Liu, Y., Ren, T., Ge, L., Wu, G.: Depth-aware salient object detection using anisotropic center-surround difference. Sig. Process. Image Commun. **38**, 115–126 (2015)
17. Krizhevsky, A., Sutskever, I., Hinton, G.E.: ImageNet classification with deep convolutional neural networks. In: Advances in Neural Information Processing Systems, pp. 1106–1114 (2012)
18. Lang, C., Nguyen, T.V., Katti, H., Yadati, K., Kankanhalli, M., Yan, S.: Depth matters: influence of depth cues on visual saliency. In: Fitzgibbon, A., Lazebnik, S., Perona, P., Sato, Y., Schmid, C. (eds.) ECCV 2012. LNCS, vol. 7573, pp. 101–115. Springer, Heidelberg (2012). https://doi.org/10.1007/978-3-642-33709-3_8
19. Li, G., Liu, Z., Chen, M., Bai, Z., Lin, W., Ling, H.: Hierarchical alternate interaction network for RGB-D salient object detection. IEEE Trans. Image Process. **30**, 3528–3542 (2021)
20. Li, G., Liu, Z., Ye, L., Wang, Y., Ling, H.: Cross-modal weighting network for RGB-D salient object detection. In: Vedaldi, A., Bischof, H., Brox, T., Frahm, J.-M. (eds.) ECCV 2020. LNCS, vol. 12362, pp. 665–681. Springer, Cham (2020). https://doi.org/10.1007/978-3-030-58520-4_39
21. Li, N., Ye, J., Ji, Y., Ling, H., Yu, J.: Saliency detection on light field. IEEE Trans. Pattern Anal. Mach. Intell. **39**(8), 1605–1616 (2017)
22. Liu, N., Zhang, N., Han, J.: Learning selective self-mutual attention for RGB-D saliency detection. In: IEEE Conference on Computer Vision and Pattern Recognition, pp. 13753–13762 (2020)
23. Liu, S., Huang, D., Wang, Y.: Receptive field block net for accurate and fast object detection. In: Ferrari, V., Hebert, M., Sminchisescu, C., Weiss, Y. (eds.) ECCV 2018. LNCS, vol. 11215, pp. 404–419. Springer, Cham (2018). https://doi.org/10.1007/978-3-030-01252-6_24
24. Liu, Z., Shi, S., Duan, Q., Zhang, W., Zhao, P.: Salient object detection for RGB-D image by single stream recurrent convolution neural network. Neurocomputing **363**, 46–57 (2019)
25. Mahadevan, V., Vasconcelos, N.: Saliency-based discriminant tracking. In: Computer Vision and Pattern Recognition, pp. 1007–1013 (2009)
26. Niu, Y., Geng, Y., Li, X., Liu, F.: Leveraging stereopsis for saliency analysis. In: IEEE Conference on Computer Vision and Pattern Recognition, pp. 454–461 (2012)
27. Pang, Y., Zhang, L., Zhao, X., Lu, H.: Hierarchical dynamic filtering network for RGB-D salient object detection. In: Vedaldi, A., Bischof, H., Brox, T., Frahm, J.-M. (eds.) ECCV 2020. LNCS, vol. 12370, pp. 235–252. Springer, Cham (2020). https://doi.org/10.1007/978-3-030-58595-2_15
28. Peng, H., Li, B., Xiong, W., Hu, W., Ji, R.: RGBD salient object detection: a benchmark and algorithms. In: Fleet, D., Pajdla, T., Schiele, B., Tuytelaars, T. (eds.) ECCV 2014. LNCS, vol. 8691, pp. 92–109. Springer, Cham (2014). https://doi.org/10.1007/978-3-319-10578-9_7
29. Piao, Y., Ji, W., Li, J., Zhang, M., Lu, H.: Depth-induced multi-scale recurrent attention network for saliency detection. In: IEEE International Conference on Computer Vision, pp. 7253–7262 (2019)

30. Piao, Y., Rong, Z., Zhang, M., Ren, W., Lu, H.: A2dele: adaptive and attentive depth distiller for efficient RGB-D salient object detection. In: IEEE Conference on Computer Vision and Pattern Recognition, pp. 9057–9066 (2020)
31. Qi, C.R., Yi, L., Su, H., Guibas, L.J.: Pointnet++: deep hierarchical feature learning on point sets in a metric space. In: Advances in Neural Information Processing Systems, pp. 5099–5108 (2017)
32. Quo, J., Ren, T., Bei, J.: Salient object detection for RGB-D image via saliency evolution. In: IEEE International Conference on Multimedia and Expo, pp. 1–6 (2016)
33. Ren, Z., Gao, S., Chia, L., Tsang, I.W.: Region-based saliency detection and its application in object recognition. IEEE Trans. Circuits Syst. Video Technol. **24**(5), 769–779 (2014)
34. Simonyan, K., Zisserman, A.: Very deep convolutional networks for large-scale image recognition. In: International Conference on Learning Representations (2015)
35. Sun, P., Zhang, W., Wang, H., Li, S., Li, X.: Deep RGB-D saliency detection with depth-sensitive attention and automatic multi-modal fusion. In: IEEE Conference on Computer Vision and Pattern Recognition, pp. 1407–1417 (2021)
36. Ulyanov, D., Vedaldi, A., Lempitsky, V.S.: Instance normalization: the missing ingredient for fast stylization. arXiv preprint arXiv:1607.08022 (2016)
37. Wu, Z., Su, L., Huang, Q.: Cascaded partial decoder for fast and accurate salient object detection. In: IEEE Conference on Computer Vision and Pattern Recognition, pp. 3907–3916 (2019)
38. Yan, S., Song, X., Yu, C.: SDCNet: size divide and conquer network for salient object detection. In: Asian Conference on Computer Vision, pp. 637–653 (2020)
39. Yang, S., Lin, W., Lin, G., Jiang, Q., Liu, Z.: Progressive self-guided loss for salient object detection. IEEE Trans. Image Process. **30**, 8426–8438 (2021)
40. Zhang, C., et al.: Cross-modality discrepant interaction network for RGB-D salient object detection. In: ACM Multimedia, pp. 2094–2102 (2021)
41. Zhang, J., et al.: UC-Net: uncertainty inspired RGB-D saliency detection via conditional variational autoencoders. In: IEEE Conference on Computer Vision and Pattern Recognition, pp. 8579–8588 (2020)
42. Zhang, J., et al.: RGB-D saliency detection via cascaded mutual information minimization. In: IEEE International Conference on Computer Vision, pp. 4318–4327 (2021)
43. Zhang, M., Fei, S.X., Liu, J., Xu, S., Piao, Y., Lu, H.: Asymmetric two-stream architecture for accurate RGB-D saliency detection. In: Vedaldi, A., Bischof, H., Brox, T., Frahm, J.-M. (eds.) ECCV 2020. LNCS, vol. 12373, pp. 374–390. Springer, Cham (2020). https://doi.org/10.1007/978-3-030-58604-1_23
44. Zhao, X., Pang, Y., Zhang, L., Lu, H., Ruan, X.: Self-supervised pretraining for RGB-D salient object detection. In: Association for the Advancement of Artificial Intelligence, pp. 3463–3471 (2022)
45. Zhao, X., Zhang, L., Pang, Y., Lu, H., Zhang, L.: A single stream network for robust and real-time RGB-D salient object detection. In: Vedaldi, A., Bischof, H., Brox, T., Frahm, J.-M. (eds.) ECCV 2020. LNCS, vol. 12367, pp. 646–662. Springer, Cham (2020). https://doi.org/10.1007/978-3-030-58542-6_39
46. Zhou, T., Fu, H., Chen, G., Zhou, Y., Fan, D., Shao, L.: Specificity-preserving RGB-D saliency detection. In: IEEE International Conference on Computer Vision, pp. 4661–4671 (2021)

47. Zhu, C., Cai, X., Huang, K., Li, T.H., Li, G.: PDNet: prior-model guided depth-enhanced network for salient object detection. In: IEEE International Conference on Multimedia and Expo, pp. 199–204 (2019)
48. Zhu, J., Wu, J., Xu, Y., Chang, E.I., Tu, Z.: Unsupervised object class discovery via saliency-guided multiple class learning. IEEE Trans. Pattern Anal. Mach. Intell. **37**(4), 862–875 (2015)

PBCStereo: A Compressed Stereo Network with Pure Binary Convolutional Operations

Jiaxuan Cai[ID], Zhi Qi[✉][ID], Keqi Fu[ID], Xulong Shi[ID], Zan Li[ID], Xuanyu Liu[ID], and Hao Liu

Southeast University, Nanjing, China
{jiaxuan_cai,101011256,220201602,long,lz21,liuxy17,nicky_lh}@seu.edu.cn

Abstract. Although end-to-end stereo matching networks achieve great performance for disparity estimation, most of them require far too many floating-point operations to deploying on resource-constrained devices. To solve this problem, we propose PBCStereo, the first lightweight stereo network using pure binarized convolutional operations. The degradation of feature diversity, which is aggravated by binary deconvolution, is alleviated via our novel upsampling module (IBC). Furthermore, we propose an effective coding method, named BIL, for the insufficient binarization of the input layer. Based on IBC modules and BIL coding, all convolutional operations become binary in our stereo matching pipeline. PBCStereo gets 39× saving in OPs while achieving comparable accuracy on SceneFlow and KITTI datasets.

Keywords: Stereo matching · Disparity estimation · Binary neural network

1 Introduction

Depth estimation plays an important role in complex computer vision tasks such as autonomous driving [10], augmented reality [1]and robot navigation [24]. Compared with the usage of expensive LiDARs, stereo matching algorithms that calculate the dense disparity from two input images provide a low-cost but equally accurate solution to depth estimation.

As the end-to-end CNNs are proposed for depth estimation, the accuracy of stereo matching has been greatly improved. At present, top 70 works on KITTI 2015 leaderboard have reached the overall three-pixel-error less than 2% [10]. While lots of effort has been carried out to improve the accuracy, the efficiency of stereo algorithms is still far from satisfactory. Because the large input image size and expensive convolutional operations consume such a large amount of floating point operations that the average FPS of those 70 works is only 1.2.

To cope with the challenge of heavy calculations in depth estimation, one strategy is adopting compact convolutional filters to replace standard convolution. For example, MABNet [32] and LWSN [30] have been proposed using

L. Wang et al. (Eds.): ACCV 2022, LNCS 13843, pp. 626–641, 2023.
https://doi.org/10.1007/978-3-031-26313-2_38

depthwise separable convolution to reduce FLOPs. LWANet [9] designed pseudo 3D convolution to replace regular 3D convolution for aggregating the cost volume with less computational cost. However, these approaches are difficult to optimize memory access in hardware deployment due to the change of convolution mode and still use expensive floating-point operations. Once targeting at the applications on resource-constrained edge devices, a highly efficient stereo matching algorithm becomes more urgent.

One effective approach to greatly reduce floating-point operations for resource-constrained devices is model binarization. Model binarization can achieve extreme compression ratio because both the weight and activation are represented by 1-bit [25] and floating point convolutions are replaced by XNOR and POPCOUNT operations [3]. Therefore, not only the cost of memory access, but also the amount of computation expense is greatly reduced. Binarization is also able to benefit stereo matching algorithms in terms of saving energy consumption for edge devices. StereoEngine [5] and StereoBit [6] made attempts to binarize the feature extraction module in stereo matching pipeline. Ignoring Stereobit's floating-point calculations in modules like aggregation and refinement, we find that its binary feature extraction module consumes 1.52G OPs, which is 2.7 times PBCStereo's total computational expense. There are two challenges for binarizing end-to-end stereo matching algorithms. Firstly, the degradation of feature diversity [16,31] is aggravated by binary deconvolution, which leads to the incomplete feature geometry as shown in Fig. 2. Secondly, the binarization of the input layer causes sharp decline of accuracy, resulting from the pixel distortion of binarized input images.

In this paper, we propose a stereo matching network, named PBCStereo, which replaces all floating point convolution with efficient binary operations. With 39× saving in OPs, the overall three-pixel-error of PBCStereo is 4.73% on KITTI 2015 benchmark. PBCStereo presents a reasonable balance between accuracy and energy-efficient computing, making depth estimation more suitable for deployment on embedded devices. The main contributions of this article are as follows:

- We design an embedded upsampling module to replace binary deconvolution, named IBC module, which uses interpolation and binary convolution to alleviate the phenomenon of feature homogenization.
- For the input layer, we propose a precision-preserving coding method named BIL to avoid the unary pixel distortion, so that all convolutional operations in our design become binarized without sacrificing performance.
- Based on the IBC module and BIL coding method, we design an efficient backbone PBCStereo. PBCStereo takes only 0.57G OPs with comparable accuracy for estimating the depth from a stereo pair at 512 × 256 resolution.

2 BNN Preliminaries

Quantization for neural networks can reduce the bit width of data, effectively decreasing the power consumption of computation. Among the existing quantization techniques, binarization extremely compresses both the weight and activation to only 1-bit. BNN [7] is a pioneering work that first verified the feasibility of binarization on small datasets such as MNIST and CIFAR-10. Subsequently, a series of works were proposed. XNOR-NET [27] proposed floating point scaling factors acting on the channel dimension to recover the information loss, enhancing the top-1 accuracy to 51.2% on ImageNet for the first time. Bi-RealNet [19] and BinaryDenseNet [2] respectively found that there were some specific structures that could effectively reduce the negative impact of information loss in the process of binarization. ReactNet [18] changed the traditional Sign and PRelu functions to enable explicit learning of the distribution reshape and shift at near-zero extra cost, mitigating the accuracy gap between the binarized model and its full-precision counterpart. However, these methods developed on ImageNet classification are not readily transferable to depth estimation directly.

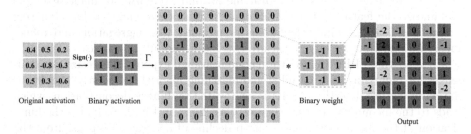

Fig. 1. The binary deconvolution process of a 3×3 input with stride $= 2$, padding $= 1$ and output padding $= 1$.

In BNNs, both weights and activations are restricted to -1 and 1. We define a binary convolutional layer as

$$O = X^b * W^b \tag{1}$$

O is the convolution output. X^b and W^b represent binary activations and binary weights. They are binarized through a sign function. Specifically,

$$x^b = sign(x^r) = \begin{cases} +1, & x^r \geq 0, \\ -1, & x^r < 0. \end{cases} \tag{2}$$

$$w^b = \frac{\|W^r\|_1}{n} sign(w^r) = \begin{cases} +\dfrac{\|W^r\|_1}{n}, & w^r \geq 0, \\ -\dfrac{\|W^r\|_1}{n}, & w^r < 0. \end{cases} \tag{3}$$

The superscripts b and r respectively refer to binary and real values. $\frac{\|W^r\|_1}{n}$ is a floating-point scaling factor proposed in XNOR-Net [27], meaning the average of absolute values of all weights.

Different from convolution, deconvolution adopts the expansion operator (Γ) of adding zero padding to both sizes of the input to improve the resolution, as shown in Fig. 1. Therefore, the binary deconvolutional layer can be rewritten as

$$X^{b'} = \Gamma(X^b) \tag{4}$$

$$O = X^{b'} * W^b \tag{5}$$

$X^{b'}$ is a new input after the expansion operation.

3   Method

In this section, we first analyze how binary deconvolution pollutes feature quality. Based on this analysis, we propose IBC module to effectively improve the quality of upsampling in Sect. 3.1. Then we put forward a precision-preserving BIL coding method for the input layer in Sect. 3.2. Finally, we introduce the overall network design of PBCstereo in Sect. 3.3.

(a)Input   (b)Ideal binary feature

(c) Binary feature obtained by binary deconvolution   (d) Binary feature obtained by IBC

Fig. 2. Comparison of the feature obtained by different upsampling methods. (a) Input image. (b) The ideal binary feature is obtained by real-valued deconvolution and sign function. (c) The feature recovered by binary deconvolution is incomplete. (d) The result of IBC module.

3.1   IBC Module

As shown in Fig. 2, the geometry obtained by binary deconvolution is incomplete, which indicates that there is a considerable information loss in the process of binary deconvolution. Given a binary activation and binary $k \times k \times C$ kernels, the output values could be an integer in the range of $-Ck^2$ to Ck^2. If there are p zeros in the $k \times k \times C$ convolution window, the range of output will be reduced to $p - Ck^2$ to $Ck^2 - p$. In other words, the operator (Γ) of adding zero padding dilutes the information in the feature map and makes features more difficult to be distinguished. So some effective structures are confused with the surrounding background and filtered out by *sign* function. Moreover, the smaller the number of channels, the more obvious this phenomenon is. For stereo matching algorithms, if the disparity map cannot maintain the same geometry as the original input, the final matching accuracy will be greatly affected.

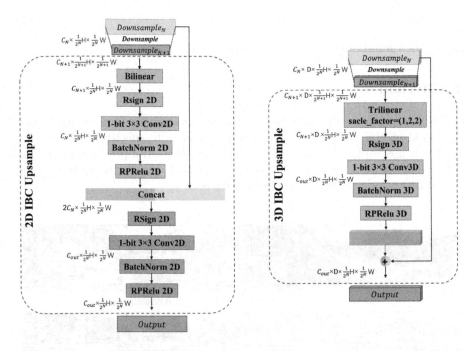

Fig. 3. The proposed IBC module, which respectively replaces 2D binary deconvolution and 3D binary deconvolution. The transformation of data dimension is marked.

For stereo matching algorithms, there are generally two forms of deconvolution, 2D and 3D. In order to improve the feature quality of upsampling and prevent the information from being diluted, we design 2D IBC and 3D IBC module respectively as shown in Fig. 3. Inspired by ReactNet [18], we choose *RSign* as the sign function and *RPrelu* as the activation function. We design the 2D IBC module in two stages. The first stage completes the expansion of the image size and the conversion of channel numbers. We first adopt bilinear interpolation to double the resolution of the input feature map $Downsample_{N+1}$, where the subscript $N + 1$ denotes the number of downsampling. Then, 1-bit convolutional layer changes the number of channels from C_{N+1} to C_N, the same as $Downsample_N$. In the second stage, we exploit context information to make up for the information loss due to binarization. To achieve this purpose, we concatenate $Downsample_N$ with the output in the first stage. Therefore, the shallow and deep features of the network will be effectively fused. Concatenating also makes use of more feature maps to alleviate the phenomenon of feature homogenization, increasing the output range to $-2C_N k^2$ to $2C_N k^2$. Meanwhile, all convolutional operations in IBC module are binarized, which is conducive to hardware acceleration. In addition to the 2D IBC module, we also implement an efficient 3D IBC module in a similar way, as shown in Fig. 3. The difference is that 3D deconvolution is generally applied to the part of cost aggregation. The resolution of cost aggregation is much smaller than that of feature extraction. 3D deconvolution also has one more dimension than 2D deconvolution, resulting in a larger range and more calculations after binarization. Therefore, instead of concatenating to build a larger feature map, we use the residual connection summation to make up for the information loss.

3.2 Binarizing Input Layer

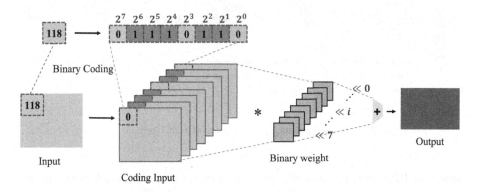

Fig. 4. The proposed BIL coding method. The binary vector after encoding denotes to the magnitude of the pixel.

In order to preserve the accuracy, most of binary neural networks use real-valued activations and weights in an input layer. Therefore, a floating point convolution engine is needed without reusing operations of XNOR and POPCOUNT [35]. There are two reasons for the sharp decline of accuracy after binarizing an input layer. The first reason is the lack of input channels. The input of CNNs contains generally RGB three channels, and some may even be a single channel grayscale image. Such a limited number of input channel is insufficient for binarization. The other reason is the information loss of binarized activations. For vision tasks, the value of the input image is between 0–255. Whether the input is normalized or not, directly turning an input image into a unary feature map results in a considerable loss of information. In this paper, we figure out a BIL coding method that binarizes the activations to a larger channel-wise size without much information loss. As shown in Fig. 4, we first encode the input activation to expand the number of channels. We encode a value between 0–255 by an eight-dimensional binary vector, e.g., translating 118 to 01110110. This increases the number of input channels from one dimension to 8 dimensions. Accordingly, we apply the weight factor 2^i to the corresponding i_{th} channel without retraining. On hardware, this process can be performed efficiently by shifting registers.

3.3 PBCStereo Overview

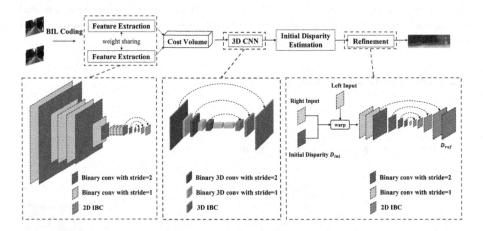

Fig. 5. Architecture overview of PBCStereo.

Based on IBC modules and BIL coding method, we propose a binary end-to-end stereo matching network PBCStereo, as shown in Fig. 5. At a light cost of calculations, PBCStereo receives a reasonable accuracy through increasing the discrimination between features. PBCStereo is the first lightweight stereo network that all convolutional operations are binarized. The pipeline of PBCStereo consists of four steps: feature extraction, cost volume aggregation, initial disparity computation and disparity refinement. We will introduce these modules in detail in the following. For ease of illustration, we define H and W as the height and weight of the input image, and D standing for the maximum disparity.

Feature Extraction. We adopt a Siamese network to extract the image features. The left and right input feature share the weights. For the first three layers, we set the convolution kernel size to 7×7, 5×5 and 3×3 respectively. The purpose of using larger convolution kernels is to build a larger receptive field and prevent the accuracy decline after BIL encoding. Then, the original input image will be quickly downsampled to $1/64$ resolution after a group of six convolutional layers with strides of 2. Next, features are restored to $1/8$ resolution through upsampling via three 2D IBC modules. Finally, we concatenate 384 feature maps at $1/8$ resolution together to generate a compact cost volume, which greatly saves computations for subsequent networks.

Cost Volume. After feature extraction, the left and right feature maps are both with the size of $384 \times \frac{H}{8} \times \frac{W}{8}$. Therefore, the corresponding maximum disparity should also be adjusted to $\frac{D}{8}$ here. Then, the cost volume is constructed by group-wise correlation [11]. 384 feature channels are divided into 48 groups, and the left feature group is cross-correlated with the corresponding right feature group over all disparity levels. At last, we get a 4D cost volume of $\frac{D}{8} \times \frac{H}{8} \times \frac{W}{8} \times 48$. For this 4D cost volume, we design a 3D binary convolution network via 3D IBC module to complete cost aggregation. Instead of stacking hourglass architectures in PSMNet [4], we only use a U-Net-like structure to obtain an initial guess of disparity D_{ini} at a smaller computational cost, and left the correction of it to the step of disparity refinement.

Disparity Refinement. In order to further make up for the information loss due to the binarization, we design the disparity refinement module as shown in the Fig. 5. Inspired by iResNet [15], the right image is fused with the initial disparity at 1/2 resolution to generate a new synthesized left image. Next, we calculate the difference between the left input image and the synthesized left image, and use this difference to estimate the residual disparity D_{ref} through disparity refinement sub-network. The summation of D_{ini} and D_{ref} is considered as the final disparity.

Disparity Regression. We use *softargmin* proposed in GCNet [13] for disparity regression as,

$$p_d = softmax(-c_d) \tag{6}$$

$$\hat{d} = \sum_{d=0}^{D} d \times p_d \tag{7}$$

p_d is the probability of each disparity d calculated from the softmax of cost volume c_d. $\hat{d}$ denotes the predicted disparity.

Loss Function. If the distributions of binary neural networks are more similar to that of real-valued networks, the performance will be improved [18]. Inspired by knowledge distillation [12], we take the real-valued network as the teacher network to guide the distribution of binary student network. However, we don't employ layer-wise distillation here, because the optimization of BNNs is challenging [17,25], and layer by layer distillation will further make the model difficult to converge. So we choose c_d and D_{ref} for distillation. The loss function of PBCStereo is defined as,

$$L(d, \hat{d}) = \alpha \cdot \frac{1}{N} \sum_{i=1}^{N} smooth_{L_1}(d_i - \hat{d}_i) + \frac{(1 - \alpha)}{2} \cdot (L_p + L_D) \tag{8}$$

in which

$$smooth_{L_1}(x) = \begin{cases} 0.5x^2, & |x| < 0.5, \\ |x| - 0.5, & |x| \geq 0.5. \end{cases} \tag{9}$$

$$L_p = \frac{1}{ND} \sum_{j=1}^{N} \sum_{d_i=0}^{D} \left| c_{d_i}^R - c_{d_i}^B \right| \qquad (10)$$

$$L_D = \frac{1}{N} \sum_{i=1}^{N} \left| D_{ref}^R - D_{ref}^B \right| \qquad (11)$$

N is the total number of labeled pixels. Superscript R and B denotes the real-valued network and binary network respectively.

4   Experiments

To evaluate the performance of PBCStereo, we conduct experiments on Scene-Flow, KITTI 2012 and KITTI 2015. The datasets and the experiment settings are introduced in Sect. 4.1. Furthermore, we perform ablation studies to validate the effectiveness of the proposed IBC module and binary encoding method for the input layer in Sect. 4.2. Finally, we compare PBCStereo with other published stereo matching algorithms in Sect. 4.3.

4.1   Experiment Details

Datasets. SceneFlow [22] is a large dataset rendered from various synthetic sequences, including FlyingThings3D, Driving and Monkaa. There are 39824 stereo pairs of size 960×540 with dense ground-truth disparity maps. We further divide the whole dataset into 35454 training images and 4370 testing images. The end-point error (EPE) is used as the evaluation metric.

Unlike SceneFlow, KITTI 2012 [10] and KITTI 2015 [23] are both real-world datasets with street views of size 1240×376, using LiDAR to collect ground-truth disparity maps. KITTI 2012 provides 194 stereo pairs for training and 195 stereo pairs for testing. End-point error in non-occluded areas (Noc) and in total (All) are used as the evaluation metric. For KITTI 2015, it consists of 200 training scenes and 200 testing scenes. The percentage of stereo disparity outliers (D1) is reported.

OPs Calculation. We count the binary operations (BOPs) following [19,27]. The floating point operations(FLOPs) caused by the BatchNorm are also listed. The total operations(OPs) is calculated as $OPs = \frac{BOPs}{64} + FLOPs$. In this paper, we take the input size of 512×256 as the standard for data analysis.

Implementation Details. Our PBCStereo is implemented using PyTorch on NVIDIA RTX 2080Ti GPU. We train our models by Adam optimizer with β_1=0.9 and β_2=0.999.

The maximum disparity D is set to 192 and the batch size is set to 12. The input is a grayscale image without normalization. During training, we randomly crop the input to size 512×256 for data augmentation. For SceneFlow, we adjust the learning rate with the cosine annealing [20], setting the maximum value of 0.001.

We train our network for 50 epochs in total on SceneFlow. For KITTI, we finetune our network for 400 epochs based on the model which is pretrained on SceneFlow. α is set to 0.8. Moreover, we repeat training for three times to submit the final model with the best performance.

4.2 Ablation Study

Ablation Study for IBC Module. To validate the effectiveness of IBC modules, we first replace it with ordinary binary deconvolution in our PBCStereo model. After the replacement, the end-point error decreases from 1.83 to 1.71 for SceneFlow. For KITTI 2015, the validation error decreases from 3.79 to 3.40. The evaluation results of our real-valued teacher network are also listed in Table 1. With the help of IBC modules, PBCstereo achieves 39× reduction in OPs with an acceptable cost in accuracy compared with the real-valued version. In Fig. 6, qualitative results on Middlebury 2014 and ETH3D show that our IBC module produces more distinct object boundaries than binary deconvolution.

| Image | BDeconv | IBC |

Fig. 6. Qualitative results on Middlebury 2014 and ETH3D. Note that the results are generated by our SceneFlow trained model without any fine-tuned training.

Table 1. Ablation study results on SceneFlow and KITTI 2015. The input layers are all real-valued here. We evaluate the EPE both on SceneFlow validation set and test set. We also compute error on KITTI 2015 validation set. The last column show the total amount of operations. BDeconv stands for the binary deconvolution.

Upsampling method	Network setting		SceneFlow		KITTI 2015	OPs
	Bit-width of input layer	Bit-width of other layers	EPE (val)	EPE (test)	Val Err (%)	
Deconv	32/32	32/32	1.13	1.13	2.62	22.31G
BDeconv	32/32	1/1	1.90	1.83	3.79	0.65G
IBC	32/32	1/1	1.76	1.71	3.40	0.66G

Further, we change the specific structure of the IBC module through experiments to analyze why our design can bring performance improvement. Each time we change just one of the following items of IBC module, *i.e.*, removal of skip-connection, 4× the resolution of feature map through interpolation, and joining the aggregated $Downsample_{N-1}$ with $Downsample_N$. Testing results of these modified models in Table 2 reveal that none of them has achieved the accuracy as good as the base module. Based on the observation, we conclude that skip-connection is the crucial structure in IBC module to enrich the feature map representation, because it not only expands the channel dimension, but also assembles context information from more layers. Although aggregating $Downsample_{N-1}$ with $Downsample_N$ achieves comparable accuracy with the proposed IBC module, this structure is at the cost of increasing model size and OPs.

Table 2. Evaluation of different structural settings of IBC module on SceneFlow, comparing to our base module shown in Fig. 3.

Settings	ΔModel Size	ΔOPs	ΔEPE
Without skip-connection	−97 KB	−28 M	−0.67
4× interpolation	−127 KB	+91 M	−0.10
$Downsample_{N-1}$	+40 KB	+80 M	−0.03

In addition, we also binarize two popular stereo networks of BGNET [33] and DeepPruner [8] through the method of ReactNet [18]. All convolutional layers except the input layer are binarized. For validation, we embed our IBC module to replace the binary deconvolution. As demonstrated by the quantitative results on SceneFlow in Table 3, the binary BGNET and DeepPruner with IBC modules present better performance than those with ordinary binary deconvolution.

Table 3. Ablation study results of IBC modules embedded into BGNET and Deep-Pruner on SceneFlow.

Method	Bit-width of input layer	Bit-width of other layers	Upsample	EPE
BGNET [33]	32/32	1/1	BDeconv	2.31
		1/1	IBC	2.23
DeepPrunerFast [8]	32/32	1/1	BDeconv	10.98
		1/1	IBC	10.30

Ablation Study for BIL. To validate the effectiveness of the proposed BIL coding method, we adopt four methods to binarize the input layer differently in PBCStereo. Dorefa-net [36], IRNet [26] and ReactNet [18] adjust the data distribution of the input layer in different ways, but the lack of input channels leads to accuracy drop. FracBNN [35] uses thermometer encoding to expand input dimension for the input layer. Although it has achieved good performance on CIFAR-10 dataset, thermometer encoding presents nonnegligible information loss in the tasks of pixel-level stereo matching. Compared with these methods, our BIL coding is quite efficient in this case, as shown in Table 4.

Table 4. Evaluation of different methods binarizing the input layer on SceneFlow. ΔEPE denotes the error caused by binarizing the input layer, comparing to our base model.

Method	Bit-width of input layer	EPE	ΔEPE
Base	32/32	1.71	–
Dorefa-net [36]	1/1	10.52	−8.81
IRNet [26]	1/1	7.82	−6.11
ReactNet [18]	1/1	6.22	−4.51
FracBNN(R = 8) [35]	1/1	2.58	−0.87
Ours	1/1	1.84	−0.13

Ablation Study for Loss Weight. We use the real-valued teacher model to guide the training of binary student model. The loss function consists of three parts, and the hyperparameter α controls the contribution of three parts to the final loss. As shown in Table 5, we conducted experiments with different values of α. We set $\alpha = 1$ as the baseline without distillation. When $\alpha = 0.8$, our model achieves the best performance with 3.43% error on KITTI 2015 validation set. We adopt the best model and submit the results to KITTI.

Table 5. Influence of the hyperparameter α on KITTI 2015 validation set.

Loss weight		KITTI 2015 Val error (%)
α	$(1-\alpha)/2$	
1	0	3.74
0.9	0.05	3.49
0.8	0.1	3.43
0.7	0.15	3.55
0.6	0.2	3.52
0	0.5	4.04

4.3   Evaluations on Benchmarks

We evaluate PBCStereo on SceneFlow and KITTI benchmark against competing
algorithms to prove the effectiveness of our model. As shown in Table 6 and
Table 7, PBCStereo exhibit a good balance between accuracy and computational
cost. Pure binary convolutional operations makes PBCStereo take only 0.57G
OPs for depth estimation. It even outperforms some real-valued networks such
as StereoNet [14] and LWANet [9]. The qualitative results of KITTI 2015 and
KITTI 2012 are shown in Fig. 7.

Table 6. Quantitative evaluation results on KITTI 2015 benchmark and SceneFlow
benchmark. For KITTI 2015, we report the percentage of pixels with end-point error
more than three pixels, including background regions(D1-bg), foreground regions(D1-
fg) and all regions(D1-all). Note that the model size is the number of bytes required
to store the parameters in the trained model.

Method	Kitti 2015			SceneFlow	Model size	OPs
	D1-bg	D1-fg	D1-all	EPE		
PSMNET [4]	1.86	5.62	2.32	1.09	20.4 MB	257.0 G
AANet [34]	1.99	5.39	2.55	0.87	15.6 MB	159.70 G
Content-CNN [21]	3.73	8.58	4.54	–	1.3 MB	157.30 G
MADnet [29]	3.75	9.20	4.66	–	14.5 MB	55.66 G
SGM-Net [28]	2.66	8.64	3.66	–	450 KB	28.0 G
DispNet [22]	4.32	4.41	4.34	1.68	168 M	17.83 G
StereoNet [14]	4.30	7.45	4.83	1.10	1.41 MB	14.08 G
BGNet [33]	2.07	4.74	2.51	1.17	11.5 MB	13.58 G
LWANet [9]	4.28	–	4.94	–	401 KB	7.03 G
MABNet_tiny [32]	3.04	8.07	3.88	1.66	188 KB	6.60 G
StereoBit [6]	3.50	–	4.57	–	–	–
Ours(1bit)	4.22	7.28	4.73	1.84	653 KB	**0.57 G**

KITTI 2015   (a) PBCStereo   (b)MADNET   KITTI 2012   (c) PBCStereo   (d) StereoBit

Fig. 7. Qualitative results on KITTI benchmark. On KITTI 2015, we compare our
evaluation results with MADNET [29]. On KITTI 2012, we compare our evaluation
results with StereoBit [6].

Table 7. Quantitative evaluation results on KITTI 2012. We report the percentage of pixels with end-point error more than two and three pixels, including non-occluded regions(-noc) and all regions(-all). The last column refers to the ratio of OPs of the corresponding algorithm to that of our method.

Method	Kitti 2012						OPs saving
	2-noc	2-all	3-noc	3-all	EPE(noc)	EPE(all)	
PSMNET [4]	2.44	3.01	1.49	1.89	0.5	0.6	451×
AANet [34]	2.90	3.60	1.91	2.42	0.5	0.6	280×
ContentCNN [21]	4.98	6.51	3.07	4.29	0.8	1.0	276×
SGM-Net [28]	3.60	5.15	2.29	3.50	0.7	0.9	49×
DispNet [22]	7.38	8.11	4.11	4.65	0.9	1.0	31×
StereoNet [14]	4.91	6.02	–	–	0.8	0.9	25×
BGNet [33]	3.13	3.69	1.77	2.15	0.6	0.6	24×
MABNet_tiny [32]	4.45	5.27	2.71	3.31	0.7	0.8	12×
StereoBit [6]	–	–	3.56	4.98	–	–	–
Ours(1bit)	7.32	8.16	3.85	4.46	0.9	1.0	–

5 Conclusion

In this paper, we propose the first compressed stereo network using pure binarized convolutional operations. Our PBCStereo gets 39× saving in OPs with comparable accuracy. To achieve the performance, we propose the IBC module to replace binary deconvolution, improving the upsampling quality for stereo matching. Moreover, we implement BIL encoding in the input layer to resist the usually severe information loss due to the binarization. We are looking forward to realizing PBCStereo in hardware-software co-design, deploying our algorithms on edge devices.

Acknowledgement. This work was supported by National Key R&D Program of China with Grant No. 2022YFB4400600, and the Fundamental Research Funds for the Central Universities with Grant No. 2242022k30052.

References

1. Abu Alhaija, H., Mustikovela, S.K., Mescheder, L., Geiger, A., Rother, C.: Augmented reality meets computer vision: efficient data generation for urban driving scenes. Int. J. Comput. Vis. **126**(9), 961–972 (2018). https://doi.org/10.1007/s11263-018-1070-x
2. Bethge, J., Yang, H., Bornstein, M., Meinel, C.: BinaryDenseNet: developing an architecture for binary neural networks. In: Proceedings of the IEEE/CVF International Conference on Computer Vision Workshops (2019)
3. Bulat, A., Tzimiropoulos, G.: XNOR-Net++: improved binary neural networks. arXiv preprint arXiv:1909.13863 (2019)

4. Chang, J.R., Chen, Y.S.: Pyramid stereo matching network. In: Proceedings of the IEEE Conference on Computer Vision and Pattern Recognition, pp. 5410–5418 (2018)
5. Chen, G., et al.: StereoEngine: an FPGA-based accelerator for real-time high-quality stereo estimation with binary neural network. IEEE Trans. Comput. Aided Des. Integr. Circuits Syst. **39**(11), 4179–4190 (2020)
6. Chen, G., Meng, H., Liang, Y., Huang, K.: GPU-accelerated real-time stereo estimation with binary neural network. IEEE Trans. Parallel Distrib. Syst. **31**(12), 2896–2907 (2020)
7. Courbariaux, M., Hubara, I., Soudry, D., El-Yaniv, R., Bengio, Y.: Binarized neural networks: training deep neural networks with weights and activations constrained to +1 or −1. arXiv preprint arXiv:1602.02830 (2016)
8. Duggal, S., Wang, S., Ma, W.C., Hu, R., Urtasun, R.: DeepPruner: learning efficient stereo matching via differentiable PatchMatch. In: Proceedings of the IEEE/CVF International Conference on Computer Vision, pp. 4384–4393 (2019)
9. Gan, W., Wong, P.K., Yu, G., Zhao, R., Vong, C.M.: Light-weight network for real-time adaptive stereo depth estimation. Neurocomputing **441**, 118–127 (2021)
10. Geiger, A., Lenz, P., Urtasun, R.: Are we ready for autonomous driving? The KITTI vision benchmark suite. In: 2012 IEEE Conference on Computer Vision and Pattern Recognition, pp. 3354–3361. IEEE (2012)
11. Guo, X., Yang, K., Yang, W., Wang, X., Li, H.: Group-wise correlation stereo network. In: Proceedings of the IEEE/CVF Conference on Computer Vision and Pattern Recognition, pp. 3273–3282 (2019)
12. Hinton, G., Vinyals, O., Dean, J., et al.: Distilling the knowledge in a neural network. arXiv preprint arXiv:1503.02531 (2015)
13. Kendall, A., et al.: End-to-end learning of geometry and context for deep stereo regression. In: Proceedings of the IEEE International Conference on Computer Vision, pp. 66–75 (2017)
14. Khamis, S., Fanello, S., Rhemann, C., Kowdle, A., Valentin, J., Izadi, S.: StereoNet: guided hierarchical refinement for real-time edge-aware depth prediction. In: Proceedings of the European Conference on Computer Vision (ECCV), pp. 573–590 (2018)
15. Liang, Z., et al.: Learning for disparity estimation through feature constancy. In: Proceedings of the IEEE Conference on Computer Vision and Pattern Recognition, pp. 2811–2820 (2018)
16. Liu, C., et al.: Circulant binary convolutional networks: enhancing the performance of 1-bit DCNNs with circulant back propagation. In: Proceedings of the IEEE/CVF Conference on Computer Vision and Pattern Recognition, pp. 2691–2699 (2019)
17. Liu, Z., Shen, Z., Li, S., Helwegen, K., Huang, D., Cheng, K.T.: How do Adam and training strategies help BNNs optimization. In: International Conference on Machine Learning, pp. 6936–6946. PMLR (2021)
18. Liu, Z., Shen, Z., Savvides, M., Cheng, K.-T.: ReActNet: towards precise binary neural network with generalized activation functions. In: Vedaldi, A., Bischof, H., Brox, T., Frahm, J.-M. (eds.) ECCV 2020. LNCS, vol. 12359, pp. 143–159. Springer, Cham (2020). https://doi.org/10.1007/978-3-030-58568-6_9
19. Liu, Z., Wu, B., Luo, W., Yang, X., Liu, W., Cheng, K.T.: Bi-Real Net: enhancing the performance of 1-bit CNNs with improved representational capability and advanced training algorithm. In: Proceedings of the European Conference on Computer Vision (ECCV), pp. 722–737 (2018)
20. Loshchilov, I., Hutter, F.: SGDR: stochastic gradient descent with warm restarts. arXiv preprint arXiv:1608.03983 (2016)

21. Luo, W., Schwing, A.G., Urtasun, R.: Efficient deep learning for stereo matching. In: Proceedings of the IEEE Conference on Computer Vision and Pattern Recognition, pp. 5695–5703 (2016)
22. Mayer, N., et al.: A large dataset to train convolutional networks for disparity, optical flow, and scene flow estimation. In: Proceedings of the IEEE Conference on Computer Vision and Pattern Recognition, pp. 4040–4048 (2016)
23. Menze, M., Heipke, C., Geiger, A.: Joint 3D estimation of vehicles and scene flow. ISPRS Ann. Photogramm. Remote Sens. Spat. Inf. Sci. **2**, 427 (2015)
24. Murray, D., Little, J.J.: Using real-time stereo vision for mobile robot navigation. Auton. Robots **8**(2), 161–171 (2000)
25. Qin, H., Gong, R., Liu, X., Bai, X., Song, J., Sebe, N.: Binary neural networks: a survey. Pattern Recogn. **105**, 107281 (2020)
26. Qin, H., et al.: Forward and backward information retention for accurate binary neural networks. In: Proceedings of the IEEE/CVF Conference on Computer Vision and Pattern Recognition, pp. 2250–2259 (2020)
27. Rastegari, M., Ordonez, V., Redmon, J., Farhadi, A.: XNOR-Net: ImageNet classification using binary convolutional neural networks. In: Leibe, B., Matas, J., Sebe, N., Welling, M. (eds.) ECCV 2016. LNCS, vol. 9908, pp. 525–542. Springer, Cham (2016). https://doi.org/10.1007/978-3-319-46493-0_32
28. Seki, A., Pollefeys, M.: SGM-Nets: semi-global matching with neural networks. In: Proceedings of the IEEE Conference on Computer Vision and Pattern Recognition, pp. 231–240 (2017)
29. Tonioni, A., Tosi, F., Poggi, M., Mattoccia, S., Stefano, L.D.: Real-time self-adaptive deep stereo. In: Proceedings of the IEEE/CVF Conference on Computer Vision and Pattern Recognition, pp. 195–204 (2019)
30. Wang, J., Duan, Z., Mei, K., Zhou, H., Tong, C.: A light-weight stereo matching network with color guidance refinement. In: Sun, F., Liu, H., Fang, B. (eds.) ICCSIP 2020. CCIS, vol. 1397, pp. 481–495. Springer, Singapore (2021). https://doi.org/10.1007/978-981-16-2336-3_46
31. Xie, B., Liang, Y., Song, L.: Diverse neural network learns true target functions. In: Artificial Intelligence and Statistics, pp. 1216–1224. PMLR (2017)
32. Xing, J., Qi, Z., Dong, J., Cai, J., Liu, H.: MABNet: a lightweight stereo network based on multibranch adjustable bottleneck module. In: Vedaldi, A., Bischof, H., Brox, T., Frahm, J.-M. (eds.) ECCV 2020. LNCS, vol. 12373, pp. 340–356. Springer, Cham (2020). https://doi.org/10.1007/978-3-030-58604-1_21
33. Xu, B., Xu, Y., Yang, X., Jia, W., Guo, Y.: Bilateral grid learning for stereo matching networks. In: Proceedings of the IEEE/CVF Conference on Computer Vision and Pattern Recognition, pp. 12497–12506 (2021)
34. Xu, H., Zhang, J.: AANet: adaptive aggregation network for efficient stereo matching. In: Proceedings of the IEEE/CVF Conference on Computer Vision and Pattern Recognition, pp. 1959–1968 (2020)
35. Zhang, Y., Pan, J., Liu, X., Chen, H., Chen, D., Zhang, Z.: FracBNN: accurate and FPGA-efficient binary neural networks with fractional activations. In: The 2021 ACM/SIGDA International Symposium on Field-Programmable Gate Arrays, pp. 171–182 (2021)
36. Zhou, S., Wu, Y., Ni, Z., Zhou, X., Wen, H., Zou, Y.: DoReFa-Net: training low bitwidth convolutional neural networks with low bitwidth gradients. arXiv preprint arXiv:1606.06160 (2016)

Author Index

L. Wang et al. (Eds.): ACCV 2022, LNCS 13843, pp. 643–645, 2023.
https://doi.org/10.1007/978-3-031-26313-2